MW00652033

Data Analytics for Accounting

SECOND EDITION

Vernon J. Richardson
University of Arkansas, Baruch College

Ryan A. Teeter
University of Pittsburgh

Katie L. Terrell
University of Arkansas

DATA ANALYTICS FOR ACCOUNTING, SECOND EDITION

Published by McGraw-Hill Education, 2 Penn Plaza, New York, NY 10121. Copyright © 2021 by McGraw-Hill Education. All rights reserved. Printed in the United States of America. Previous editions © 2019. No part of this publication may be reproduced or distributed in any form or by any means, or stored in a database or retrieval system, without the prior written consent of McGraw-Hill Education, including, but not limited to, in any network or other electronic storage or transmission, or broadcast for distance learning.

Some ancillaries, including electronic and print components, may not be available to customers outside the United States.

This book is printed on acid-free paper.

2 3 4 5 6 7 8 9 LKV 24 23 22 21

ISBN 978-1-260-83783-4 (bound edition)
MHID 1-260-83783-1 (bound edition)
ISBN 978-1-260-90431-4 (loose-leaf edition)
MHID 1-260-90431-8 (loose-leaf edition)

Portfolio Manager: *Steve Schuetz*
Product Developers: *Sarah Wood; Alexandra Kukla*
Marketing Manager: *Claire McLemore*
Content Project Managers: *Fran Simon; Angela Norris*
Buyer: *Susan K. Culbertson*
Design: *Egzon Shaquiri*
Content Licensing Specialists: *Lori Hancock*
Cover Image: *Rawpixel.com/Shutterstock*
Compositor: *SPi Global*

All credits appearing on page or at the end of the book are considered to be an extension of the copyright page.

Library of Congress Cataloging-in-Publication Data

Names: Richardson, Vernon J., author. | Teeter, Ryan, author. | Terrell,
  Katie, author.
Title: Data analytics for accounting / Vernon J. Richardson, University of
  Arkansas, Xi'an Jiaotong Liverpool University, Ryan A. Teeter,
  University of Pittsburgh, Katie L. Terrell, University of Arkansas.
Description: Second Edition. | New York : McGraw-Hill Education, 2020. |
  Revised edition of the authors' Data analytics for accounting, [2019]
Identifiers: LCCN 2019034761 | ISBN 9781260837834 (paperback)
Subjects: LCSH: Accounting–Data processing.
Classification: LCC HF5679 .R534 2020 | DDC 657.0285–dc23
LC record available at https://lccn.loc.gov/2019034761

The Internet addresses listed in the text were accurate at the time of publication. The inclusion of a website does not indicate an endorsement by the authors or McGraw-Hill Education, and McGraw-Hill Education does not guarantee the accuracy of the information presented at these sites.

mheducation.com/highered

Dedications

My wonderful daughter, Melissa,
for your constant love, encouragement and support.

—Vern Richardson

My wife, Erin, and children, Sylvia
and Theodore.

—Ryan Teeter

To my co-author, friend, and colleague, Vernon
Richardson. Thank you for inviting me to be on this
textbook journey. And thank you for your guidance and
patience—I'm thrilled to be a part of your team!

—Katie Terrell

Preface

Data Analytics is changing the business world—data simply surrounds us! So much data is available to businesses about each of us—how we shop, what we read, what we buy, what music we listen to, where we travel, whom we trust, where we invest our time and money, etc. Accountants can create value by addressing fundamental business and accounting questions using data analytics.

All accountants must develop data analytic skills to address the needs of the profession in the future. *Data Analytics for Accounting, 2e* recognizes that accountants don't need to become data scientists—they may never need to build a data repository or do the real hardcore Data Analytics or learn how to program a computer to do machine learning. However, there are seven skills that analytic-minded accountants must have to be prepared for a data-filled world, including:

1. An analytics mindset—recognize when and how Data Analytics can address accounting questions.
2. Data scrubbing and data preparation—comprehend the process needed to extract (query), clean and prepare the data before analysis.
3. Data quality—recognize what is meant by data quality, be it completeness, reliability, or validity.
4. Descriptive data analysis—perform basic analysis to understand the quality of the underlying data and their ability to address the business question.
5. Data analysis through data manipulation—demonstrate ability to sort, rearrange, merge, and reconfigure data in a manner that allows enhanced analysis.
6. Problem solving through statistical data analysis—identify and implement an approach that will use statistical data analysis to draw conclusions and make recommendations on a timely basis.
7. Data visualization and data reporting—report results of analysis in an accessible way to each varied decision maker and his or her specific needs.

Consistent with these skills, it's important to recognize that Data Analytics is a process. The process begins by identifying business questions that can be addressed with data, extracting and testing the data, refining our testing, and finally, communicating those findings to management. *Data Analytics for Accounting,* 2e describes this process by relying on an established data analytics model called the IMPACT cycle[1]

1. **I**dentify the question.
2. **M**aster the data.
3. **P**erform test plan.
4. **A**ddress and refine results.
5. **C**ommunicate insights.
6. **T**rack outcomes

[1] Jean Paul Isson and Jesse S. Harriott, *Win with Advanced Business Analytics: Creating Business Value from Your Data* (Hoboken, NJ: Wiley, 2013).

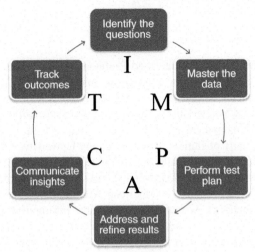

Adapted from *Win with Advanced Business Analytics: Creating Business Value from Your Data*, by Jean Paul Isson and Jesse S. Harriott.

The IMPACT cycle is described in the first four chapters and then the process is illustrated in audit, managerial accounting, financial accounting and tax in Chapters 5-9, adding an all-new tax chapter to *Data Analytics for Accounting*, 2e. In response to instructor feedback, *Data Analytics for Accounting*, 2e now also includes two new project chapters, giving students a chance to practice the full IMPACT model with multiple labs that build on each other.

Data Analytics for Accounting, 2e emphasizes hands-on practice. Students are provided with hands-on instruction (e.g., click-by-click instructions, screenshots, etc.) on datasets within the chapter; within the end-of-chapter materials; and in the labs at the end of each chapter. Throughout the text, students identify questions, extract and download data, perform testing, and then communicate the results of that testing.

The use of real-world data is highlighted by using data from **LendingClub**, **College Scorecard**, **Dillard's**, the **State of Oklahoma**, as well as other data from our labs. In particular, we emphasize the rich data from **Dillard's** sales transactions that we use in more than fifteen of the labs throughout the text (including Chapter 11).

Data Analytics for Accounting, 2e also emphasizes the various data analysis tools students will use throughout the rest of their career—Microsoft Excel, Microsoft Access (including SQL), Tableau (free student license), IDEA (free student license), and Weka (free student license). Using multiple tools allows students to learn which tool is best suited for the necessary data analysis, data visualization, and communication of the insights gained—for example, which tool is easiest for internal controls testing, which is best for analysis or querying (using SQL) big datasets, which is best for data visualizations, and so on.

About the Authors

Vernon J. Richardson

Vernon J. Richardson is a Distinguished Professor of Accounting and the G. William Glezen Chair in the Sam M. Walton College of Business at the University of Arkansas and a Visiting Professor at Baruch College. He received his BS, Master of Accountancy, and MBA from Brigham Young University and a PhD in accounting from the University of Illinois at Urbana-Champaign. He has taught students at the University of Arkansas, Baruch College, University of Illinois, Brigham Young University, Aarhus University, and University of Kansas and internationally at the China Europe International Business School (Shanghai), Xi'an Jiaotong Liverpool University, and the University of Technology Sydney.

Dr. Richardson is a member of the American Accounting Association. He has served as president of the American Accounting Association Information Systems section. He previously served as an editor of *The Accounting Review* and is currently an editor at *Accounting Horizons.* He has published articles in *The Accounting Review, Journal of Information Systems, Journal of Accounting and Economics, Contemporary Accounting Research, MIS Quarterly, International Journal of Accounting Information Systems, Journal of Management Information Systems, Journal of Operations Management,* and *Journal of Marketing.* Dr. Richardson is also the author of McGraw-Hill's *Accounting Information Systems* textbook.

Ryan A. Teeter

Ryan A. Teeter is a Clinical Assistant Professor of Accounting in the Katz Graduate School of Business at the University of Pittsburgh. He teaches accounting information systems, auditing, and accounting data analytics. Prior to receiving his PhD in accounting information systems from Rutgers University, he worked at Google in Mountain View, California. He has since worked with internal audit organizations at Siemens, Procter & Gamble, Alcoa/Arconic, and FedEx, helping to develop robotic process automation programs and data analytic solutions.

Dr. Teeter is a member of the American Accounting Association and has published articles in the *Journal of Strategic Technologies in Accounting* and *Issues in Accounting Education.* He has received grant funding for data analytics research from PwC.

Katie L. Terrell

Katie L. Terrell is an instructor in the Sam M. Walton College of Business at the University of Arkansas. She received her BA degrees in English literature and in the Spanish language from the University of Central Arkansas and her MBA from the University of Arkansas. She expects a doctoral degree by 2020. She has taught students at the University of Arkansas; Soochow University (Suzhou, China); the University College Dublin (Ireland); and Duoc UC, a branch of the Catholic University of Chile (Vina del Mar, Chile).

She is a member of the American Accounting Association and has published a *Statement on Management Accounting* for the Institute of Management Accountants on managing organizational change in operational change initiatives. Terrell was named the 2019 Business Professional of the Year (Education) by the national Beta Alpha Psi organization. She has recently been recognized for her innovative teaching by being the recipient of the Mark Chain/FSA Teaching Award for innovative graduate-level accounting teaching practices in 2016. She has worked with Tyson Foods, where she held various information system roles, focusing on business analysis, project management for ERP implementations and upgrades, and organizational change management.

Acknowledgments

Our sincere thanks to all who helped us on this project.

Our biggest thanks to the awesome team at McGraw-Hill Education, including Steve Schuetz, Tim Vertovec, Allie Kukla, Fran Simon, Kevin Moran, and Sarah Wood.

Our thanks also to each of the following:

The Walton College Enterprise Team (Paul Cronan, Ron Freeze, Michael Gibbs, Michael Martz, Tanya Russell) for their work helping us get access to the Dillard's data.

Shane Lunceford from LendingClub for helping gain access to LendingClub data.

Marcia Watson, University of North Carolina-Charlotte; Ryan Baxter, Boise State University; Antoinette Smith, Florida International University; and Lorrie Metzger, University at Buffalo for their accuracy check and review of the manuscript.

In addition, the following reviewers and classroom testers who provided ideas and insights for this edition. We appreciate their contributions.

Amelia Annette Baldwin
University of South Alabama
Dereck Barr-Pulliam
University of Wisconsin-Madison
Heather Carrasco
Texas Tech University
Elizabeth Felski
State University of New York at Geneseo
Chris C. Hsu
York College, City University of New York
Venkataraman Iyer
University of North Carolina at Greensboro
Andrea S. Kelton
Middle Tennessee State University
Brandon Lock
Baruch College, CUNY
Sharon M. Lightner
National University
Margarita Maria Lenk
Colorado State University
Partha Mohapatra
California State University, Sacramento
Uday Murthy
University of South Florida

Kalana Malimage
University of Wisconsin-Whitewater
Bonnie Morris
Duquesne University
Kathy Nesper
University at Buffalo
Ali Saeedi
University of Minnesota Crookston
Karen Schuele
John Carroll University
Drew Sellers
Kent State University
Joe Shangguan
Robert Morris University
Vincent J. Shea
St. John's University
Marcia Watson
University of North Carolina at Charlotte
Liu Yang
Southeast Missouri State University
Zhongxia Ye
University of Texas, San Antonio
Qiongyao (Yao) Zhang
Robert Morris University

Vernon Richardson
Ryan Teeter
Katie Terrell

Key Features

- **Emphasis on Skills:** Working through the IMPACT cycle framework, students will learn problem assessment, data preparation, data analysis, data visualization, control contesting, and more.
- **Emphasis on Hands-On Practice:** Students will be provided hands-on learning (click-by-click instructions with screenshots) on datasets within each chapter, within the end-of-chapter materials, and in the labs and comprehensive cases.
- **Emphasis on Datasets:** To illustrate data analysis techniques and skills, multiple practice datasets (audit, financial, and managerial data) will be used in every chapter. Students gain real-world experience working with data from **LendingClub, Dillard's, College Scorecard,** the **State of Oklahoma,** as well as financial statement data (via XBRL) from *Fortune* 100 companies.
- **Emphasis on Tools:** Students will learn how to conduct data analysis using Excel Access (including SQL), Tableau (free student license), IDEA (free student license), and Weka (free student license). Students will compare and contrast the different tools to determine which are best suited for basic data analysis and data visualization, which are easiest for internal controls testing, which are best for SQL queries, and so on.

Total Products Sold by State

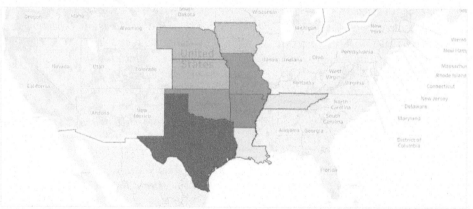

©Tableau Software, Inc. All rights reserved.

Main Text Features

Chapter Maps

These maps provide a guide of what we're going to cover in the chapter as well as a guide of what we've just learned and what's coming next.

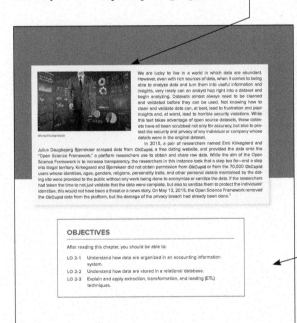

Chapter-Opening Vignettes

Because companies are facing the new and exciting opportunities with their use of Data Analytics to help with accounting and business decisions, we detail what they're doing and why in our chapter-opening vignettes.

Chapter 2

Mastering the Data

A Look at This Chapter

This chapter provides an overview of the types of data that are used in the accounting cycle and common data that are stored in a relational database. The second step of the IMPACT cycle is "mastering the data." We will describe how data are requested and *extracted* to answer business questions and how to *transform* data for use via data preparation, validation, and cleaning. We conclude with an explanation of how to *load* data into the appropriate tool in preparation for analyzing data to make decisions.

A Look Back

Chapter 1 defined Data Analytics and explained that the value of Data Analytics is in the insights it provides. We described the Data Analytics Process using the IMPACT cycle model and explained how this process is used to address both business and accounting questions. We specifically emphasized the importance of identifying appropriate questions that data analytics might be able to address.

A Look Ahead

Chapter 3 describes how to go from defining business problems to analyzing data, answering questions, and addressing business problems. We identify four types of data analytics and describe various approaches and techniques that are most relevant to analyzing accounting data.

We are lucky to live in a world in which data are abundant. However, even with rich sources of data, when it comes to being able to analyze data and turn them into useful information and insights, very rarely can an analyst hop right into a dataset and begin analyzing. Datasets almost always need to be cleaned and validated before they can be used. Not knowing how to clean and validate data can, at best, lead to frustration and poor insights and, at worst, lead to horrible security violations. While this text takes advantage of open source datasets, these datasets have all been scrubbed not only for accuracy, but also to protect the security and privacy of any individual or company whose details were in the original dataset.

In 2015, a pair of researchers named Emil Kirkegaard and Julius Daugbejerg Bjerrekær scraped data from OkCupid, a free dating website, and provided the data onto the "Open Science Framework," a platform researchers use to obtain and share raw data. While the aim of the Open Science Framework is to increase transparency, the researchers in this instance took that a step too far—and a step into illegal territory. Kirkegaard and Bjerrekær did not obtain permission from OkCupid or from the 70,000 OkCupid users whose identities, ages, genders, religions, personality traits, and other personal details maintained by the dating site were provided to the public without any work being done to anonymize or sanitize the data. If the researchers had taken the time to not just validate that the data were complete, but also to sanitize them to protect the individuals' identities, this would not have been a threat or a news story. On May 13, 2015, the Open Science Framework removed the OkCupid data from the platform, but the damage of the privacy breach had already been done.[1]

OBJECTIVES

After reading this chapter, you should be able to:

LO 2-1 Understand how data are organized in an accounting information system.
LO 2-2 Understand how data are stored in a relational database.
LO 2-3 Explain and apply extraction, transformation, and loading (ETL) techniques.

Learning Objectives

We feature learning objectives at the beginning of each chapter. Having these learning objectives provides students with an overview of the concepts to be taught in the chapter and the labs.

Progress Checks

Periodic progress check questions are posed to the students throughout each chapter. These checks provoke the student to stop and consider the concepts presented.

✓ **PROGRESS CHECK**

1. Referring to Exhibit 2-1, locate the relationship between the Supplier and Purchase Order tables. What is the unique identifier of each table? (The unique identifier attribute is called the primary key—more on how it's determined in the next learning objective.) Which table contains the attribute that creates the relationship? (This attribute is called the foreign key—more on how it's determined in the next learning objective.)

2. Referring to Exhibit 2-1, review the attributes in the Purchase Order table. There are two foreign keys listed in this table that do not relate to any of the tables in the diagram. Which tables do you think they are? What type of data would be

End-of-Chapter Materials

Answers to Progress Checks

Allow students to evaluate if they are on track with their understanding of the materials presented in the chapter.

 ANSWERS TO PROGRESS CHECKS

1. The unique identifier of the Supplier table is [Supplier ID], and the unique i Purchase Order table is [PO No.]. The Purchase Order table contains the f

2. The foreign key attributes in the Purchase Order table that do not relate in the view are EmployeeID and CashDisbursementID. These attributes to the Employee table (so that we can tell which employee was respor Purchase Order) and the Cash Disbursement table (so that we can tell i Orders have been paid for yet, and if so, on which check). The Employee a complete listing of each Employee, as well containing the details about e (for example, phone number, address, etc.). The Cash Disbursement tab listing of the payments the company has made.

Multiple Choice Questions

Quickly assess student's knowledge of chapter content.

Multiple Choice Questions

1. Mastering the data can also be described via the ETL process. Th stands for:
   a. extract, total, and load data.
   b. enter, transform, and load data.
   c. extract, transform, and load data.
   d. enter, total, and load data.

2. Which of the following describes part of the goal of the ETL process:
   a. identify which approach to data analytics should be used.
   b. load the data into a relational database for storage.
   c. communicate the results and insights found through the analysis.

Discussion Questions

Provide questions for group discussion.

Discussion Questions

1. The advantages of a relational database include limiting the amount of r that are stored in a database. Why is this an important advantage? Wha when redundant data are stored?

2. The advantages of a relational database include integrating business p is it preferable to integrate business processes in one information syste store different business process data in separate, isolated databases?

3. Even though it is preferable to store data in a relational database, stori separate tables can make data analysis cumbersome. Describe three rea the trouble to store data in a relational database.

4. Among the advantages of using a relational database is enforcing busine on your understanding of how the structure of a relational database help redundancy and other advantages, how does the primary key/foreign k

Problems

Challenge the student's ability to see relationships in the learning objectives by employing higher-level thinking and analytical skills.

Problems

The following problems correspond to the **College Scorecard** data. You sho answer each question by just looking at the data dictionary included in App you would like to use the raw data, feel free to do so (CollegeScorecard_Rav

1. Which attributes from the College Scorecard data would you need to c attendance across types of institutions (public, private nonprofit, or priva

2. Which attributes from the College Scorecard data would you need to scores across types of institutions (public, private nonprofit, or private fo

3. Which attributes from the College Scorecard data would you need to co diversity across types of institutions (public, private nonprofit, or private

4. If you were conducting a data analysis in order to compare the percenta who receive federal loans at universities above and below the median da across all institutions analysis would requi al steps

Labs

Give students hands-on experience working with different types of data and the tools used to analyze them. Students will conduct data analysis using Excel, Access (including SQL), Tableau, IDEA, XBRL, and Weka.

Lab 2-1   Create a Request for Data Extra

One of the biggest challenges you face with data a may have the best questions in the world, but if there hypothesis, you will have difficulty providing value. which the IT workers may be reluctant to share data data, the wrong data, or completely ignore your reque look for creative ways to find insight with an incompl

Company summary

Sláinte is a fictional brewery that has recently gone th ferent products. The brewery has only recently expand state to nine states, and now its business has begun sta

Comprehensive Cases

Use a real-life Big Data set based on **Dillard's** actual company data. This dataset allows students to build their skills and test their conclusions across concepts covered in each chapter. The Comprehensive Cases can be followed continuously from the first chapter or picked up at any later point in the book; enough information is provided to ensure students can get right to work.

Lab 2-8   Comprehensive Case: Dillard's S Connecting Excel to a SQL Data

Company summary

Dillard's is a department store with approximately 33(in Little Rock, Arkansas. You can learn more about Di (Ticker symbol = DDS) and the Wikipedia site for Di Dillard II is an accounting grad of the University of

Data Analytics for Accounting, 2e Content Updates

General Updates for the 2nd Edition

- Added additional End-of-Chapter Multiple Choice Questions and Problems throughout the text.
- Significantly revised many End-of-Chapter Problems for availability and auto-grading within Connect.
- Revised and added many new Discussion Questions in most chapters.

Chapter by Chapter Updates

Specific chapter changes for *Data Analytics for Accounting,* 2nd Edition, are as follows:

Chapter 1

- Updated the opening vignette and statistics on Alibaba sales and use of e-commerce.
- Updated the statistics and screenshots for Lending Club Analysis.
- Revised Connect questions for problems and labs.

Chapter 2

- Improved and clarified the discussion of relational databases, including updated figures.
- Expanded the discussion of different RDBMS (Access, SQLite, and SQL Server).
- Improved discussion of Excel and SQL. The brief introduction to how to use SQL now has its own place in a dedicated appendix at the end of the text, and it has been vastly expanded to teach beginners how to write queries.
- Expanded the discussion on data quality.
- Added a brief discussion of ETL v. ELT.
- Improved labs for clarity and a better learning experience, particularly Labs 2-1, 2-2, and 2-4.

Chapter 3

- Reorganized chapter structure to follow the descriptive, diagnostic, predictive, and prescriptive approaches to Data Analytics.
- New exhibits and examples to illustrate analytics approaches.
- Removed previous edition flowchart for model selection.
- Additional explanation and examples of each of the methods and approaches.
- Improved labs for clarity.

Chapter 4

- Updated the opening vignette.
- Improved the discussion on the differences between qualitative and quantitative data and the discussion of the normal distribution.
- Improved and clarified how to select a visualization based on the four chart types (qualitative vs. quantitative and declarative vs. exploratory).

- Updated the discussion on the Gartner Quadrant to take into account Gartner's January 2019 analysis of BI tools (focusing on Excel and Tableau).
- Extended the discussion on written and spoken communication.
- Added a lab to work with visualizing data and creating dashboards in Power BI to interactively compare the tool with Tableau.

Chapter 5

- Expanded discussion on the modern data environment.
- Included additional examples of the Audit Data Standard.
- Improved and clarified content to match the focus on descriptive, diagnostic, predictive, and prescriptive analytics.
- New labs (5-1 and 5-2) that have students transform data using a common data model.
- Improved existing labs.

Chapter 6

- Clarified chapter content to match the focus on descriptive, diagnostic, predictive, and prescriptive analytics.
- Improved labs.

Chapter 7

- Clarified chapter content and provided additional new exhibits and examples, such as variance analysis.
- Improved labs.

Chapter 8

- Reorganized chapter content to focus on financial statement analysis using descriptive, diagnostic, predictive, and prescriptive approaches.
- Added new content on common size and ratio analysis.
- Improved discussion of XBRL data.
- Improved XBRL dataset (in Lab 8-4), accessible via Microsoft Access and included options to do analysis in Excel.

Chapter 9

- All-new chapter on tax analytics, including examples of tax data, tax analysis, tax planning, and tax visualizations.

Chapter 10

- All-new basic project chapter that explores the order-to-cash and procure-to-pay cycles from different user perspectives.

Chapter 11

- All-new advanced project chapter, estimating sales returns at **Dillard's** with three question sets highlighting descriptive and exploratory analysis, hypothesis testing, and predictive analytics.

Appendixes

Several all-new appendixes have been added to ease the lab experience and introduce tools used or mentioned throughout the text:

- Appendix A: Basic Statistics Tutorial.
- Appendix B: Accessing the Excel Data Analysis Toolpak.
- Appendix C: Excel (Formatting, Sorting, Filtering, and PivotTables).
- Appendix D: SQL Part 1. This tutorial introduces the SQL language for extracting data and explains the following SQL syntax: SELECT, FROM, INNER JOIN, ON, WHERE, GROUP BY, HAVING, ORDER BY.
- Appendix E: SQLite. We have added SQLite files as an option for each lab that uses Microsoft Access. This lab explains how to download SQLite and how to use the tool.
- Appendix F: Power Query. This appendix contains a short tutorial on transforming data using Power Query. How to access data files on the University of Arkansas' remote desktop is also discussed.
- Appendix G: Tableau.
- Appendix H: SQL Part 2: On the heels of learning Tableau, students learn about more complex joins—LEFT and RIGHT.
- Appendix I: Power BI.
- Appendix J: Dillard's ER Diagram.
- Appendix K: Data Dictionaries.

Connect for Data Analytics for Accounting

With **Connect** for Data Analytics in Accounting, your students receive proven study tools and hands-on assignment materials as well as an adaptive eBook. All of the following assets are assignable in Connect.

SmartBook 2.0: A personalized and adaptive learning tool used to maximize the learning experience by helping students study more efficiently and effectively. Smartbook 2.0 highlights where in the chapter to focus, asks review questions on the materials covered and tracks the most challenging content for later review recharge. Smartbook 2.0 is available both online and offline.

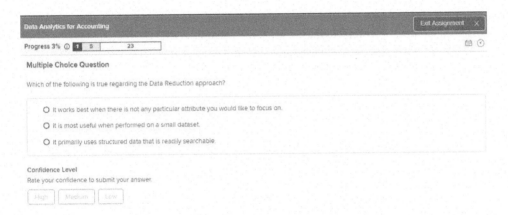

Orientation Videos: Video-based tutorial assignments are designed to train students via an overview video followed by a quiz for each of the assignment types they will find in Connect.

Multiple Choice Questions: The multiple choice questions from the end-of-chapter materials are assignable in Connect, providing students with instant feedback on their answers.

Problems: Select problems from the text are available for assignment in Connect to ensure students are building an analytical skill set.

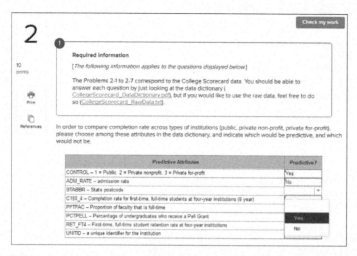

Labs: Select labs are assignable in Connect but will require students to work outside of Connect to complete the lab. Once completed, students go back into Connect to answer questions designed to ensure they completed the lab and understood the key skills and outcomes from their lab work.

Comprehensive Cases: Select comprehensive labs/cases are assignable in Connect but will require students to work outside of Connect to complete the lab using the **Dillard's** real-world Big Data set. Once students complete the comprehensive lab, they will go back into Connect to answer questions designed to ensure they completed the lab and understood the key skills and outcomes from their lab work.

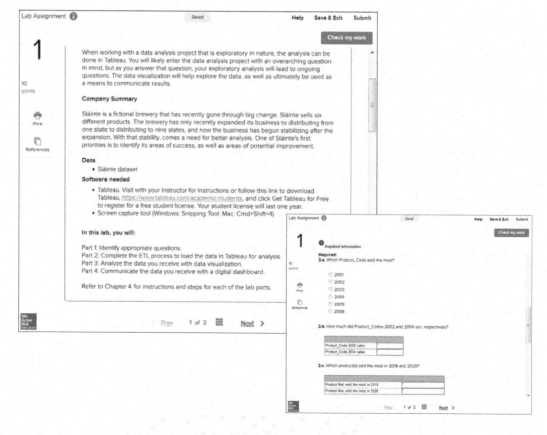

Lab Walkthrough Videos: Get the help you need, when you need it. These author-led videos will explain how to access and use the tools needed to complete processes essential to the labs.

Author Lecture Videos: Lecture Videos teach each chapter's core learning objectives and concepts through an author-developed, hands-on presentation, bringing the text content to life. The videos have the touch and feel of a live lecture, rather than a canned presentation, so you can learn at your own pace.

Test Bank: The test bank includes auto-graded multiple choice and true/false assessment questions. It is available in Connect and Test Builder.

You're in the driver's seat.

Want to build your own course? No problem. Prefer to use our turnkey, prebuilt course? Easy. Want to make changes throughout the semester? Sure. And you'll save time with Connect's auto-grading too.

65%
Less Time Grading

Laptop: McGraw-Hill; Woman/dog: George Doyle/Getty Images

They'll thank you for it.

Adaptive study resources like SmartBook® 2.0 help your students be better prepared in less time. You can transform your class time from dull definitions to dynamic debates. Find out more about the powerful personalized learning experience available in SmartBook 2.0 at **www.mheducation.com/highered/connect/ smartbook**

Make it simple, make it affordable.

Connect makes it easy with seamless integration using any of the major Learning Management Systems— Blackboard®, Canvas, and D2L, among others—to let you organize your course in one convenient location. Give your students access to digital materials at a discount with our inclusive access program. Ask your McGraw-Hill representative for more information.

Padlock: Jobalou/Getty Images

Solutions for your challenges.

A product isn't a solution. Real solutions are affordable, reliable, and come with training and ongoing support when you need it and how you want it. Our Customer Experience Group can also help you troubleshoot tech problems— although Connect's 99% uptime means you might not need to call them. See for yourself at **status. mheducation.com**

Checkmark: Jobalou/Getty Images

FOR STUDENTS

Effective, efficient studying.

Connect helps you be more productive with your study time and get better grades using tools like SmartBook 2.0, which highlights key concepts and creates a personalized study plan. Connect sets you up for success, so you walk into class with confidence and walk out with better grades.

Study anytime, anywhere.

Download the free ReadAnywhere app and access your online eBook or SmartBook 2.0 assignments when it's convenient, even if you're offline. And since the app automatically syncs with your eBook and SmartBook 2.0 assignments in Connect, all of your work is available every time you open it. Find out more at **www.mheducation.com/readanywhere**

"I really liked this app—it made it easy to study when you don't have your text-book in front of you."

- Jordan Cunningham, Eastern Washington University

Calendar: owattaphotos/Getty Images

No surprises.

The Connect Calendar and Reports tools keep you on track with the work you need to get done and your assignment scores. Life gets busy; Connect tools help you keep learning through it all.

Learning for everyone.

McGraw-Hill works directly with Accessibility Services Departments and faculty to meet the learning needs of all students. Please contact your Accessibility Services office and ask them to email accessibility@mheducation.com, or visit **www.mheducation.com/about/accessibility** for more information.

Top: Jenner Images/Getty Images, Left: Hero Images/Getty Images, Right: Hero Images/Getty Images

Brief Table of Contents

Preface iv

About the Authors vi

Acknowledgments vii

Key Features viii

Main Text Features ix

End-of-Chapter Materials x

Data Analytics for Accounting, 2e Content Updates xii

Connect for Data Analytics for Accounting xv

Chapter 1	Data Analytics for Accounting and Identifying the Questions	2
Chapter 2	Mastering the Data	38
Chapter 3	Performing the Test Plan and Analyzing the Results	92
Chapter 4	Communicating Results and Visualizations	138
Chapter 5	The Modern Accounting Environment	200
Chapter 6	Audit Data Analytics	224
Chapter 7	Managerial Analytics	268
Chapter 8	Financial Statement Analytics	326
Chapter 9	Tax Analytics	360
Chapter 10	Project Chapter (Basic)	390
Chapter 11	Project Chapter (Advanced): Analyzing Dillard's Data to Predict Sales Returns	408
Appendix A	Basic Statistics Tutorial	434
Appendix B	Accessing the Excel Data Analysis Toolpak	440
Appendix C	Excel (Formatting, Sorting, Filtering, and PivotTables)	442
Appendix D	SQL Part 1	453
Appendix E	SQLite	466
Appendix F	Power Query	470
Appendix G	Tableau	476
Appendix H	SQL Part 2	480
Appendix I	Power BI	483
Appendix J	Dillard's ER Diagram	491
Appendix K	Data Dictionaries	492

GLOSSARY 500

INDEX 504

Detailed TOC

Chapter 1
Data Analytics for Accounting and Identifying the
Questions 2

Data Analytics 4
How Data Analytics Affects Business 4
How Data Analytics Affects Accounting 5
  Auditing 5
  Financial Reporting 6
  Taxes 7
The Data Analytics Process
Using the Impact Cycle 8
  Step 1: Identify the Questions (Chapter 1) 8
  Step 2: Master the Data (Chapter 2) 8
  Step 3: Perform Test Plan (Chapter 3) 9
  Step 4: Address and Refine Results (Chapter 3) 11
  *Steps 5 and 6: Communicate Insights and Track
  Outcomes (Chapter 4 and each chapter thereafter)* 11
  Back to Step 1 12
Data Analytic Skills Needed by Analytic-Minded
Accountants 12
Hands-on Example of the Impact Model 13
  Identify the Questions 13
  Master the Data 13
  Perform Test Plan 15
  Address and Refine Results 17
  Communicate Insights 19
  Track Outcomes 19
Summary 20
Key Words 20
 Answers to Progress Checks 21
Multiple Choice Questions 23
Discussion Questions 24
Problems 24
Lab 1-0 How to Complete Labs in This Text 27
Lab 1-1 Data Analytics in Financial
        Accounting 28
Lab 1-2 Data Analytics in Managerial
        Accounting 31
Lab 1-3 Data Analytics in Auditing 33
Lab 1-4 Comprehensive Case: Dillard's Store
        Data 34

Chapter 2
Mastering the Data 38

How Data are Used and Stored in the Accounting
Cycle 40
Data and Relationships in a Relational Database 42
*Columns in a Table: Primary Keys, Foreign Keys, and
Descriptive Attributes* 42
Data Dictionaries 44
Extract, Transform, and Load (ETL) the Data 45
  Extract 46
  Transform 49
  Load 52
Summary 52
Key Words 53
Answers to Progress Checks 54
Multiple Choice Questions 55
Discussion Questions 56
Problems 57
Lab 2-1 Create a Request for Data Extraction 58
Lab 2-2 Use PivotTables to Denormalize and
        Analyze the Data 60
Lab 2-3 Resolve Common Data Problems in
        Excel and Access 67
Lab 2-4 Generate Summary Statistics in Excel 71
Lab 2-5 College Scorecard Extraction and Data
        Preparation 73
Lab 2-6 Comprehensive Case: Dillard's Store
        Data: How to Create an Entity-
        Relationship Diagram 75
Lab 2-7 Comprehensive Case: Dillard's Store
        Data: How to Preview Data from Tables
        in a Query 78
Lab 2-8 Comprehensive Case: Dillard's Store
        Data: Connecting Excel to a SQL
        Database 80
Lab 2-9 Comprehensive Case: Dillard's Store
        Data: Joining Tables 90

Chapter 3
Performing the Test Plan and Analyzing the Results 92

Performing the Test Plan 94
Descriptive Analytics 97
  *Example of Data Reduction in Internal
  and External Auditing* 98
  *Examples of Data Reduction in Other Accounting
  Areas* 99
Diagnostic Analytics 100
  Example of Profiling in Management Accounting 102
  Example of Profiling in an Internal Audit 103
  Example of Profiling in Auditing 103
  Example of the Clustering Approach in Auditing 105
Predictive Analytics 106

*Examples of the Regression Approach in
Managerial Accounting* 108
Examples of the Regression Approach in Auditing 108
Other Examples of the Regression in Accounting 108
Classification Terminology 109
Evaluating Classifiers 111
Overfitting 111
Prescriptive Analytics 112
Summary 114
Key Words 115
Answers to Progress Checks 116
Multiple Choice Questions 117
Discussion Questions 118
Problems 119
Lab 3-1   Data Reduction Using Fuzzy
Matching 121
Lab 3-2   Regression in Excel 125
Lab 3-3   Classification 127
Lab 3-4   Comprehensive Case: Dillard's Store
Data: Data Abstract (SQL) and
Regression (Part I) 130
Lab 3-5   Comprehensive Case: Dillard's Store
Data: Data Abstract (SQL) and
Regression (Part II) 135

Chapter 4
Communicating Results and Visualizations 138

Determine the Purpose of Your
Data Visualization 141
*Quadrants 1 and 3 versus Quadrants 2 and 4:
Qualitative versus Quantitative* 142
*A Special Case of Quantitative Data: The Normal
Distribution* 143
*Quadrants 1 and 2 versus Quadrants 3 and 4:
Declarative versus Exploratory* 144
Choosing the Right Chart 145
Charts Appropriate for Qualitative Data 145
Charts Appropriate for Quantitative Data 147
Tools to Help When Picking a Visual 149
*Learning to Create a Good Chart by (Bad)
Example* 151
Further Refining Your Chart to Communicate
Better 156
Data Scale and Increments 157
Color 157
Communication: More than Visuals—Using Words
to Provide Insights 158
Content and Organization 158
Audience and Tone 159
Revising 160

Summary 160
Key Words 161
Answers to Progress Checks 162
Multiple Choice Questions 163
Discussion Questions 164
Problems 164
Lab 4-1   Use PivotCharts to Visualize Declarative
Data 166
Lab 4-2   Use Tableau to Perform Exploratory
Analysis and Create Dashboards 168
Lab 4-3   Comprehensive Case: Dillard's
Store Data: Create Geographic Data
Visualizations in Tableau and in Power
BI 177
Lab 4-4   Comprehensive Case: Dillard's Store
Data: Visualizing Regression in
Tableau 196

Chapter 5
The Modern Accounting Environment 200

The Modern Data Environment 202
The Increasing Importance of the Internal Audit 203
Enterprise Data 203
Common Data Models 204
Automating Data Analytics 206
Continuous Monitoring Techniques 208
Alarms and Exceptions 208
Working Papers And Audit Workflow 209
Electronic Working Papers and Remote Audit Work 209
Summary 210
Key Words 210
Answers to Progress Checks 211
Multiple Choice Questions 212
Discussion Questions 213
Problems 213
Lab 5-1   Create a Common Data Model 215
Lab 5-2   Create a Dashboard Based on a Common
Data Model 217
Lab 5-3   Set Up a Cloud Folder 219
Lab 5-4   Review Changes to Working Papers 220
Lab 5-5   Identify Audit Data Requirements 221
Lab 5-6   Prepare Audit Plan 222

Chapter 6
Audit Data Analytics 224

When to Use Audit Data Analytics 226
Identify the Problem 226
Master the Data 226
Perform the Test Plan 228

Address and Refine Results 230
Communicate Insights 230
Track Outcomes 230
Descriptive Analytics 230
Age Analysis 231
Sorting 232
Summary Statistics 233
Sampling 233
Diagnostic Analytics and Benford's Law 235
Z-Score 235
Benford's Law 236
Drill-Down 239
Exact and Fuzzy Matching 239
Sequence Check 241
Stratification and Clustering 242
Creating Advanced Predictive and Prescriptive
Analytics 242
Regression 242
Classification 242
Probability 242
Sentiment Analysis 243
Applied Statistics 243
Artificial Intelligence 243
Additional Analyses 243
Summary 244
Key Words 244
Answers to Progress Checks 244
Multiple Choice Questions 245
Discussion Questions 246
Problems 247
Lab 6-1   Evaluate the Master Data for Interesting
Addresses 248
Lab 6-2   Perform Substantive Tests of Account
Balances 250
Lab 6-3   Finding Duplicate Payments 256
Lab 6-4   Comprehensive Case: Dillard's Store
Data: Hypothesis Testing (Part I) 257
Lab 6-5   Comprehensive Case: Dillard's Store
Data: Hypothesis Testing (Part II–Data
Visualization) 264

Chapter 7
Managerial Analytics 268

Identifying Management Accounting Questions 270
Relevant Costs 270
Key Performance Indicators and Variance Analysis 270
Cost Behavior 271
Balanced Scorecard and Key Performance
Indicators 272
Master the Data and Perform the Test Plan 276

Address and Refine Results 277
Summary 278
Key Words 279
Answers to Progress Checks 279
Multiple Choice Questions 280
Discussion Questions 281
Problems 282
Lab 7-1   Evaluate Management Requirements and
Identify Useful KPIs from a List 284
Lab 7-2   Create a Balanced Scorecard Dashboard
in Tableau 286
Lab 7-3   Comprehensive Case: Dillard's Store
Data: Creating KPIs in Excel (Part I) 295
Lab 7-4   Comprehensive Case: Dillard's Store Data:
Creating KPIs in Excel (Part II) 302
Lab 7-5   Comprehensive Case: Dillard's Store Data:
Creating KPIs in Excel (Part III) 309
Lab 7-6   Comprehensive Case: Dillard's Store
Data: Creating KPIs in Excel
(Part IV–Putting It All Together) 316
Lab 7-7   Comprehensive Case: Dillard's
Store Data: Advanced Models in
Tableau 321

Chapter 8
Financial Statement Analytics 326

Financial Statement Analysis 328
Descriptive Financial Analytics 328
Vertical and Horizontal Analysis 328
Other Classes of Ratios 329
Diagnostic Financial Analytics 331
Predictive Financial Analytics 331
Visualizing Financial Data 333
Showing Trends 333
Relative Size of Accounts 333
Text Mining and Sentiment Analysis 334
XBRL and Financial Data Quality 336
XBRL Data Quality 338
*XBRL, XBRL-GL, and Real-Time Financial
Reporting* 340
*Examples of Financial Statement Analytics Using
XBRL* 340
Summary 341
Key Words 341
Answers to Progress Checks 342
Multiple Choice Questions 343
Discussion Questions 344
Problems 344
Lab 8-1   Create a Horizontal and Vertical Analysis
Using XBRL Data 346

Lab 8-2   Create Dynamic Common Size
    Financial Statements 349
Lab 8-3   Analyze Financial Statement Ratios 352
Lab 8-4   Use PivotTables to Analyze Data from an
    XBRL Database 355

Chapter 9
Tax Analytics 360

Introduction to Tax Analytics 362
Mastering the Data through Tax
Data Management 363
Tax Data Analytics Visualizations 364
 Tax Data Analytics Visualizations and Tax
 Compliance 364
 Evaluating Sales Tax Liability 365
 Evaluating Income Tax Liability 365
Tax Data Analytics for Tax Planning 367
 What-If Scenarios 368
 What-If Scenarios for Potential Legislation, Deductions,
 and Credits 369
Summary 370
Key Words 370
Answers to Progress Checks 371
Multiple Choice Questions 371
Discussion Questions 373
Problems 373
Lab 9-1   State Sales Taxes and Create a Data
    Visualization 375
Lab 9-2   Comprehensive Case 1: Dillard's Store
    Data: Calculate Sales Tax for Dillard's
    States 379
Lab 9-3   Comprehensive Case 2: Dillard's Store
    Data: Calculate Sales Tax for Dillard's
    States Part 2—Compare Year over
    Year 381
Lab 9-4   Comprehensive Case 3: Dillard's Store
    Data: Calculate Sales Tax for Dillard's
    States Part 3—Calculate City Tax and
    Compare Tax Owed Year over Year 386
Lab 9-5   Comprehensive Case 4: Dillard's Store
    Data: Does a State's Tax Rate Affect
    Dillard's Decision to Open Stores
    There? 387

Chapter 10
Project Chapter (Basic) 390

Evaluating Business Processes 392
Question Set 1: Order-to-Cash 392
 Question 1.1: How Efficiently Are We Collecting Our
 Cash? 392

 Question 1.2: Is the Delivery Process Following the
 Expected Procedure? 396
 Question 1.3: What Is the Total Revenue and Balance in
 Accounts Receivable? 398
 Question 1.4: What Else Can You Determine about the
 O2C Process? 400
Question Set 2: Procure-to-Pay 400
 Question 2.1: How Long Are We Taking to Pay Our
 Invoices? 400
 Question 2.2: Are There Any Erroneous Payments? 404
 Question 2.3: Are We Missing Out on Discounts by
 Paying Late? 405
 Question 2.4: What Else Can You Determine about the
 P2P Process? 406

Chapter 11
Project Chapter (Advanced): Analyzing Dillard's Data
to Predict Sales Returns 408

Estimating Sales Returns 410
Question Set 1: Descriptive and Exploratory
Analysis 410
 Question 1.1: Which Attributes Could Help Predict
 Percentage of Returned Sales? 410
 Question 1.2: How Can We Explore the Product
 Hierarchy Through Data Visualization? 412
Question Set 2: Diagnostic Analytics—Hypothesis
Testing 422
 Question 2.1: Is the Percentage of Sales Returned
 Significantly Higher in January After the Holiday
 Season? 422
 Question 2.2: Is the Percentage of Sales Returned
 Significantly Different in Arkansas Than the Rest of the
 Country? 426
Question Set 3: Predictive Analytics 427
 Question 3.1: By Looking at Line Charts for 2014
 and 2015, Does the Average Percentage of Sales
 Returned in 2014 Seem to Be Predictive of Returns in
 2015? 427
 Question 3.2: Using Regression, What Can We Predict
 for Returns as a Percentage of Sales Based on
 Historical Transactions? 429

Appendix A
Basic Statistics Tutorial 434

Appendix B
Accessing the Excel Data Analysis Toolpak 440

Appendix C
Excel (Formatting, Sorting, Filtering, and
PivotTables) 442

Appendix D
SQL Part 1 453

Appendix E
SQLite 466

Appendix F
Power Query 470

Appendix G
Tableau 476

Appendix H
SQL Part 2 480

Appendix I
Power BI 483

Appendix J
Dillard's ER Diagram 491

Appendix K
Data Dictionaries 492

GLOSSARY 500

INDEX 504

Chapter 1

Data Analytics for Accounting and Identifying the Questions

A Look at This Chapter

Data Analytics is changing the business world. In this chapter, we define it and explain its impact on business and the accounting profession, noting that the value of Data Analytics is in the insights it provides. We also describe how to develop an analytics mindset. We describe the Data Analytics Process using the IMPACT cycle model and explain how this process is used to address both business and accounting questions. We specifically emphasize the importance of identifying appropriate questions that Data Analytics might be able to address.

A Look Ahead

Chapter 2 provides a description of how data are prepared and scrubbed to be ready for analysis to answer business questions. We explain how to extract, transform, and load data and then how to validate and normalize the data. In addition, we explain how data standards are used to facilitate the exchange of data between senders and receivers.

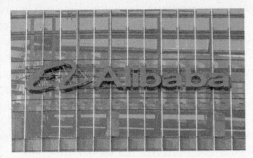
Shutterstock

The Chinese e-commerce company **Alibaba** is perhaps the biggest online commerce company in the world. Using its three main websites, Taobao.com, Tmall.com, and Alibaba.com, it hosts millions of businesses and hundreds of millions of users with $345 billion in 2018 sales last year (more than **eBay** and **Amazon** combined!). With so many transactions and so many users, Alibaba has worked to capture fraud signals directly from its extensive database of user behaviors and its network. It then analyzes them in real time using machine learning to accurately sort the potentially fraudulent users from the good ones. Alibaba has developed five stages of fraud detection for each user: (1) account check, (2) device check, (3) activity check, (4) risk strategy, and (5) manual review. These stages all combine to develop a risk score for each user. This fraud risk prevention score is so valuable to Alibaba and others that Alibaba shares and sells it to external customers. What will Data Analytics do next?

Sources: J. Chen, Y. Tao, H. Wang, and T. Chen, "Big Data Based Fraud Risk Management at Alibaba," *Journal of Finance and Data Science* 1, no. 1 (2015), pp. 1–10; and K. Pal, "How to Combat Financial Fraud by Using Big Data," 2016, http://www.kdnuggets.com/2016/03/combat-financial-fraud-using-big-data.html.

OBJECTIVES

After reading this chapter, you should be able to:

LO 1-1   Define Data Analytics.

LO 1-2   Understand why Data Analytics matters to business.

LO 1-3   Explain why Data Analytics matters to accountants.

LO 1-4   Describe the Data Analytics Process using the IMPACT cycle.

LO 1-5   Describe the skills needed by accountants.

LO 1-6   Explain how to translate common business questions into fields and values.

LO 1-1

Define Data
Analytics.

DATA ANALYTICS

Data surrounds us! By the year 2020, about 1.7 megabytes of new information will be created every second for every human being on the planet. In fact, more data have been created in the last 2 years than in the entire previous history of the human race.[1] With so much data available about each of us (i.e., how we shop, what we read, what we've bought, what music we listen to, where we travel, whom we trust, etc.), arguably, there is the potential for analyzing those data in a way that can answer fundamental business questions and create value.

We define **Data Analytics** as the process of evaluating data with the purpose of drawing conclusions to address business questions. Indeed, effective Data Analytics provides a way to search through large structured and unstructured data to discover unknown patterns or relationships.[2] In other words, Data Analytics often involves the technologies, systems, practices, methodologies, databases, statistics, and applications used to analyze diverse business data to give organizations the information they need to make sound and timely business decisions.[3] That is, the process of Data Analytics aims to transform raw data into knowledge to create value.

Big Data refers to datasets that are too large and complex for businesses' existing systems to handle utilizing their traditional capabilities to capture, store, manage, and analyze these datasets. Another way to describe Big Data is by use of 3 Vs: its volume (the sheer size of the dataset), velocity (the speed of data processing), and variety (the number of types of data). While sometimes *Data Analytics* and *Big Data* are terms used interchangeably, we will use the term *Data Analytics* throughout and focus on the ability to turn data into knowledge and knowledge into value.

 PROGRESS CHECK

1. How does having more data around us translate into value for a company?
2. Banks know a lot about us, but they have traditionally used externally generated credit scores to assess creditworthiness when deciding whether to extend a loan. How would you suggest a bank use Data Analytics to get a more complete view of its customers' creditworthiness? Assume the bank has access to a customer's loan history, credit card transactions, deposit history, and direct deposit registration. How could it assess whether a loan might be repaid?

LO 1-2

Understand why
Data Analytics
matters to
business.

HOW DATA ANALYTICS AFFECTS BUSINESS

There is little question that the impact of data analytics on business is overwhelming. In fact, in **PwC**'s 18th Annual Global CEO Survey, 86 percent of chief executive officers (CEOs) say they find it important to champion digital technologies and emphasize a clear vision of using technology for a competitive advantage, while 85 percent say they put a high value on Data Analytics. In fact, per **PwC**'s 6th Annual Digital IQ survey

---

[1]http://www.forbes.com/sites/bernardmarr/2015/09/30/big-data-20-mind-boggling-facts-everyone-must-read/#2a3289006c1d (accessed March 2019).
[2]Roger S. Debreceny and Glen L. Gray, "IT Governance and Process Maturity: A Multinational Field Study," *Journal of Information Systems* 27, no. 1 (Spring 2013), pp. 157–88.
[3]H. Chen, R. H. L. Chiang, and V. C. Storey, "Business Intelligence Research," *MIS Quarterly* 34, no. 1 (2010), pp. 201–3.

of more than 1,400 leaders from digital businesses, the area of investment that tops CEOs' list of priorities is business analytics.[4]

A recent study from McKinsey Global Institute estimates that Data Analytics could generate up to $3 trillion in value per year in just a subset of the total possible industries affected.[5] Data Analytics could very much transform the manner in which companies run their businesses in the near future because the real value of data comes from Data Analytics. With a wealth of data on their hands, companies use Data Analytics to discover the various buying patterns of their customers, investigate anomalies that were not anticipated, forecast future possibilities, and so on. For example, with insight provided through Data Analytics, companies could execute more directed marketing campaigns based on patterns observed in their data, giving them a competitive advantage over companies that do not use this information to improve their marketing strategies. Patterns discovered from past archives also enable businesses to identify opportunities and risks and better plan for the future. In addition to producing more value externally, studies show that Data Analytics affects internal processes, improving productivity, utilization, and growth.[6]

 PROGRESS CHECK

3. Let's assume a brand manager at **Samsung** identifies that an older demographic might be concerned with the use of a Samsung Galaxy smartphone and the radiation impact it might have on the brain. How might **Samsung** use Data Analytics to assess if this is a problem?

4. How might Data Analytics assess the higher cost of paying employees to work overtime? Consider how Data Analytics might be helpful in reducing a company's overtime direct labor costs in a manufacturing setting.

HOW DATA ANALYTICS AFFECTS ACCOUNTING

LO 1-3

Explain why Data Analytics matters to accountants.

Data Analytics is expected to have dramatic effects on auditing and financial reporting as well as tax and managerial accounting. We detail how we think this might happen in each of the following sections.

Auditing

Data Analytics plays an increasingly critical role in the future of audit. In a recent *Forbes Insights*/KPMG report, "Audit 2020: A Focus on Change," the vast majority of survey respondents believe both that:

1. Audit must better embrace technology.
2. Technology will enhance the quality, transparency, and accuracy of the audit.

Indeed, "As the business landscape for most organizations becomes increasingly complex and fast-paced, there is a movement toward leveraging advanced business analytic techniques to

[4]"Data Driven: What Students Need to Succeed in a Rapidly Changing Business World," PwC, https://www.pwc.com/us/en/faculty-resource/assets/pwc-data-driven-paper-feb2015.pdf, February 2015 (accessed March 20, 2019).

[5]"Open Data: Unlocking Innovation and Performance with Liquid Information," McKinsey Global Institute, http://www.mckinsey.com/insights/business_technology/open_data_unlocking_innovation_and_performance_with_liquid_information, October 2013 (accessed September 7, 2015).

[6]Joseph Kennedy, "Big Data's Economic Impact," https://www.ced.org/blog/entry/big-datas-economic-impact, December 3, 2014 (accessed January 9, 2016).

refine the focus on risk and derive deeper insights into an organization."[7] Many auditors believe that auditor data analytics will, in fact, lead to deeper insights that will enhance audit quality. This sentiment of the impact of Data Analytics on the audit has been growing for several years now and has given many public accounting firms incentives to invest in technology and personnel to capture, organize, and analyze financial statement data to provide enhanced audits, expanded services, and added value to their clients. As a result, Data Analytics is expected to be the next innovation in the evolution of the audit and professional accounting industry.

Given the fact that operational data abound and are easier to collect and manage, combined with CEOs' desires to utilize these data, the accounting firms may now approach their engagements with a different mindset. No longer will they be simply checking for errors, material misstatements, fraud, and risk in financial statements or merely be reporting their findings at the end of the engagement. Instead, audit professionals will now be collecting and analyzing the company's data similar to the way a business analyst would to help management make better business decisions. This means that, in many cases, external auditors will stay engaged with clients beyond the audit. This is a significant paradigm shift. The audit process will be changed from a traditional process toward a more automated one, which will allow audit professionals to focus more on the logic and rationale behind data queries and less on the gathering of the actual data.[8] As a result, audits will not only yield important findings from a financial perspective, but also information that can help companies refine processes, improve efficiency, and anticipate future problems.

> "It's a massive leap to go from traditional audit approaches to one that fully integrates big data and analytics in a seamless manner."[9]

Data Analytics also expands auditors' capabilities in services like testing for fraudulent transactions and automating compliance-monitoring activities (like filing financial reports to the SEC or to the IRS). This is possible because Data Analytics enables auditors to analyze the complete dataset, rather than the sampling of the financial data done in a traditional audit. Data Analytics enables auditors to improve its risk assessment in both its substantive and detailed testing.

Financial Reporting

Data Analytics also potentially has an impact on financial reporting. With the use of so many estimates and valuations in financial accounting, some believe that employing Data Analytics may substantially improve the quality of the estimates and valuations. Data from within an enterprise system and external to the company and system might be used to address many of the questions that face financial reporting. Many financial statement accounts are just estimates and so accountants often ask themselves questions like this to evaluate those estimates:

1. How much of the accounts receivable balance will ultimately be collected? What should the allowance for loan losses look like?
2. Is any of our inventory obsolete? Should our inventory be valued at market or cost (applying the lower-of-cost-or-market rule)? When will it be out of date? Do we need to offer a discount on it now to get it sold?

[7]Deloitte, "Adding Insight to Audit: Transforming Internal Audit Through Data Analytics." Accessed January 10, 2016. http://www2.deloitte.com/content/dam/Deloitte/ca/Documents/audit/ca-en-audit-adding-insight-to-audit.pdf.
[8]PwC, "Data Driven: What Students Need to Succeed in a Rapidly Changing Business World," http://www.pwc.com/us/en/faculty-resource/assets/PwC-Data-driven-paper-Feb2015.pdf, February 2015 (accessed January 9, 2016).
[9]EY, "How Big Data and Analytics Are Transforming the Audit." Accessed January 27, 2016. https://eyo-iis-pd.ey.com/ARC/documents/EY-reporting-ssue-9.pdf,posted April 2015.

3. Has our goodwill been impaired due to the reduction in profitability from a recent merger? Will it regain value in the near future?
4. How should we value contingent liabilities like warranty claims or litigation? Do we have the right amount?

Data Analytics may also allow an accountant or auditor to assess the probability of a goodwill write-down, warranty claims or the collectability of bad debts based on what customers, investors, and other stakeholders are saying about the company in blogs and in social media (like Facebook and Twitter). This information might help the firm determine both its optimal response to the situation and appropriate adjustment to its financial reporting.

It may be possible to use Data Analytics to scan the environment—that is, scan Google searches and social media (such as Instagram and Facebook) to identify potential risks and opportunities to the firm. For example, in a data analytics sense, it may allow a firm to monitor its competitors and its customers to better understand opportunities and threats around it. For example, are its competitors, customers, or suppliers facing financial difficulty, etc., that might affect the company's interactions with them and/or open up new opportunities that otherwise it wouldn't have considered?

Tax

Traditionally, tax work dealt with compliance issues based on data from transactions that have already taken place. Now, however, tax executives must develop sophisticated tax planning capabilities that assist the company with minimizing its taxes in such a way to avoid or prepare for a potential audit. This shift in focus makes tax data analytics valuable for its ability to help tax staffs to predict what will happen rather than reacting to what just did happen. Arguably, one of the things that Data Analytics does best is predictive analytics—predicting the future! An example of how tax data analytics might be used is the capability to predict the potential tax consequences of a potential international transaction, R&D investment, or proposed merger or acquisition.

One of the issues of performing predictive Data Analytics is the efficient organization and use of data stored across multiple systems on varying platforms that were not originally designed for the tax department. Organizing tax data into a data warehouse to be able to consistently model and query the data is an important step toward developing the capability to perform tax data analytics. This issue is exemplified by the 29 percent of tax departments that find the biggest challenge in executing an analytics strategy is integration with the IT department and available technology tools.[10]

⊘ PROGRESS CHECK

5. How could the use of internal audit data analytics find the pattern that one accountant enters the majority of the journal entries each quarter? How might this data be used to check if segregation of duties was appropriately maintained? Why might this be an issue that would need addressing?
6. How specifically will Data Analytics change the way a tax staff does its taxes?

[10]Deloitte, "The Power of Tax Data Analytics," http://www2.deloitte.com/us/en/pages/tax/articles/top-ten-things-about-tax-data-analytics.html (accessed October 12, 2016).

LO 1-4

Describe the Data Analytics Process using the IMPACT cycle.

THE DATA ANALYTICS PROCESS USING THE IMPACT CYCLE

Data Analytics is a process to identify business questions and problems that can be addressed with data. We start to describe our Data Analytics Process by using an established Data Analytics model called the IMPACT cycle by Isson and Harriott (as shown in Exhibit 1-1).

We explain the full IMPACT cycle briefly here, but in more detail in later in Chapters 2, 3, and 4. We use its approach throughout this textbook.

EXHIBIT 1-1
The IMPACT Cycle

Source: Isson, J. P., and J. S. Harriott. *Win with Advanced Business Analytics: Creating Business Value from Your Data.* Hoboken, NJ: Wiley, 2013.

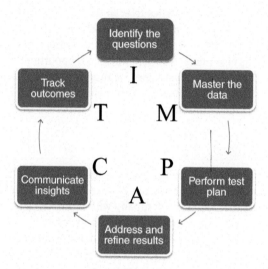

Step 1: Identify the Questions (Chapter 1)

It all begins with understanding a business problem that needs addressing. Questions can arise from many sources, including how to better attract customers, how to price a product, or how to find errors or fraud. Having a concrete, specific question that is potentially answerable by Data Analytics is an important first step.

Accountants and auditors might be interested in questions like the following:

- Are employees circumventing internal controls over payments?
- Are there any suspicious travel and entertainment expenses?
- How can we increase the amount of add-on sales of additional goods to our customers?
- Are our customers paying us in a timely manner?
- How can we predict the allowance for loan losses for our bank loans?
- How can we find transactions that are risky in terms of accounting issues?
- Who authorizes checks above $100,000?
- How can errors be identified?

Step 2: Master the Data (Chapter 2)

Mastering the data requires one to know what data are available and whether those data might be able to help address the business problem. We need to know everything about the data, including how to access, availability, reliability (if there are errors), and what time periods are covered to make sure the data coincide with the timing of our business problem, etc.

In addition, to give us some idea of the data questions, we may want to consider the following:

- Review data availability in a firm's internal systems (including those in the financial reporting system or enterprise systems that might occur in its accounting processes—financial, procure-to-pay, production, order-to-cash, human resources).
- Review data availability in a firm's external network, including those that might already be housed in an existing data warehouse.
- Data dictionaries and other contextual data—to provide details about the data.
- Extraction, transformation, and loading.
- Data validation and completeness—to provide a sense of the reliability of the data.
- Data normalization—to reduce data redundancy and improve data integrity.
- Data preparation and scrubbing—Data Analytics professionals estimate that they spend between 50 and 90 percent of their time cleaning data so the data can be analyzed.[11]

Step 3: Perform Test Plan (Chapter 3)

After mastering the data and after the data are ready (in step 2), we are prepared for analysis. With the data ready for analysis, we need to think of the right approach to the data to be able to answer the question.

In Data Analytics, we work to extract knowledge from the data to address questions and problems. Using all available data, we see if we can identify a relationship between the **response or dependent variables** and those items that affect the response (also called **predictor**, **explanatory**, or **independent variables**). To do so, we'll generally make a model, or a simplified representation of reality, to address this purpose.

An example might be helpful here. Let's say we are trying to predict each of your classmates' performance on their next intermediate accounting exam. The response or dependent variable will be the score on the next exam. What helps predict the performance of each exam will be our predictor, explanatory, or independent variables. Variables such as study time, score on last exam, IQ, and standardized test scores (ACT, SAT, etc.), as well as student enjoyment of accounting, might all be considered. Perhaps given your experience you can name other predictor variables to include in our model predicting exam performance.

The research question, the model, the data availability, and the expected statistical inference may all suggest the use of different data approaches. Provost and Fawcett[12] detail eight different approaches to data analytics depending on the question. We will discuss the most applicable ones to accounting more formally in Chapter 3 and highlight accounting questions that they might address. The eight different approaches include the following:

- **Classification**—An attempt to assign each unit (or individual) in a population into a few categories. An example classification might be, of all the loans this bank has offered, which are most likely to default? Or which loan applications are expected to be approved? Or which transactions would a credit card company flag as potentially being fraudulent and deny payment?
- **Regression**—A data approach used to predict a specific dependent variable value based on independent variable inputs using a statistical model. An example regression analysis might be, given a balance of total accounts receivable held by a firm, what is the appropriate level of allowance for doubtful accounts for bad debts?

---

[11]"One-Third of BI Pros Spend Up to 90% of Time Cleaning Data," http://www.eweek.com/database/one-third-of-bi-pros-spend-up-to-90-of-time-cleaning-data.html, posted June 2015 (accessed March 15, 2016).

[12]Foster Provost and Tom Fawcett, *Data Science for Business: What You Need to Know about Data Mining and Data-Analytic Thinking* (Sebastopol, CA: O'Reilly Media, 2013).

- **Similarity matching**—An attempt to identify similar individuals based on data known about them. The opening vignette mentioned Alibaba and its attempt to identify seller and customer fraud based on various characteristics known about them to see if they were similar to known fraud cases.
- **Clustering**—An attempt to divide individuals (like customers) into groups (or clusters) in a useful or meaningful way. In other words, identifying groups of similar data elements and the underlying drivers of those groups. For example, clustering might be used to segment a customer into a small number of groups for additional analysis and marketing activities.
- **Co-occurrence grouping**—An attempt to discover associations between individuals based on transactions involving them. Amazon might use this to sell another item to you by knowing what items are "frequently bought together" or "Customers who bought this item also bought . . ." as shown in Exhibit 1-2.

EXHIBIT 1-2

Example of Co-occurrence Grouping on Amazon .com

Source: Amazon Inc.

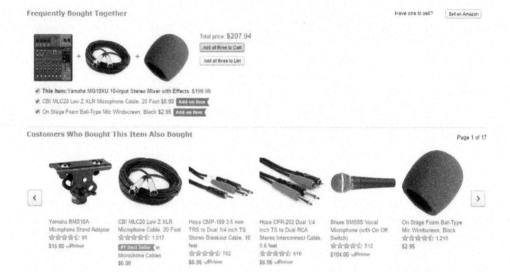

- **Profiling**—An attempt to characterize the "typical" behavior of an individual, group, or population by generating summary statistics about the data (including mean, standard deviations, etc.). By understanding the typical behavior, we'll be able to more easily identify abnormal behavior. When behavior departs from that typical behavior—which we'll call an anomaly—then further investigation is warranted. Profiling might be used in accounting to identify fraud or just those transactions that might warrant some additional investigation (e.g., travel expenses that are three standard deviations above the norm).
- **Link prediction**—An attempt to predict a relationship between two data items. This might be used in social media. For example, because an individual might have 22 mutual Facebook friends with me and we both attended Brigham Young University, is there a chance we would like to be Facebook friends as well? Exhibit 1-3 provides an example of this used in Facebook. Link prediction in an accounting setting might work to use social media to look for relationships between related parties that are not otherwise disclosed.
- **Data reduction**—A data approach that attempts to reduce the amount of information that needs to be considered to focus on the most critical items (i.e., highest cost,

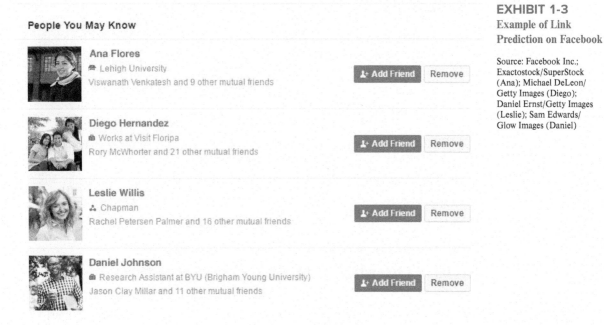

EXHIBIT 1-3
Example of Link
Prediction on Facebook

Source: Facebook Inc.;
Exactostock/SuperStock
(Ana); Michael DeLeon/
Getty Images (Diego);
Daniel Ernst/Getty Images
(Leslie); Sam Edwards/
Glow Images (Daniel)

highest risk, largest impact, etc.). It does this by taking a large set of data (perhaps the population) and reducing it with a smaller set that has the vast majority of the critical information of the larger set. An example might include the potential to use these techniques in auditing. While auditing has employed various random and stratified sampling over the years, Data Analytics suggests new ways to highlight which transactions do not need the same level of vetting as other transactions.

Step 4: Address and Refine Results (Chapter 3)

After the data have been analyzed (in step 3 of the IMPACT cycle), the fourth step is to address and refine results. Data analysis is iterative. We slice and dice the data, find correlations, ask ourselves further questions, ask colleagues what they think, and revise and rerun the analysis. But once that is complete, we have the results ready to communicate to interested stakeholders.

Steps 5 and 6: Communicate Insights and Track Outcomes (Chapter 4 and each chapter thereafter)

Once the results have been determined (in step 4 of the IMPACT cycle), insights are formed by decision makers and are communicated (the "C" in the IMPACT cycle) and some outcomes will be continuously tracked (the "T" in the IMPACT cycle).

Chapter 4 discusses ways to communicate results, including the use of static reports, digital dashboards, and data visualizations. Data Analytics is especially interested in reporting results that help decision makers see the data in an all-new way to develop insights that help answer business questions. Digital dashboards and data visualizations are particularly helpful in communicating results.

Back to Step 1

Of course, the IMPACT cycle is iterative, so once insights are gained and outcomes are tracked, new questions emerge and the IMPACT cycle begins anew.

 PROGRESS CHECK

7. Let's say we are trying to predict how much money college students spend on fast food each week. What would be the response, or dependent, variable? What would be examples of independent variables?

8. How might a data reduction approach be used in auditing to spend time and effort on the most important items?

<table>
<tr><td>

LO 1-5

Describe the skills needed by accountants.

</td></tr>
</table>

DATA ANALYTIC SKILLS NEEDED BY ANALYTIC-MINDED ACCOUNTANTS

While we don't believe that accountants need to become data scientists—they may never need to build a data repository or do the real, hardcore Data Analytics—they must know how to do the following:

- Clearly articulate the business problem the company is facing.
- Communicate with the data scientists about specific data needs and understand the underlying quality of the data.
- Draw appropriate conclusions to the business problem based on the data and make recommendations on a timely basis.
- Present their results to individual members of management (CEOs, audit managers, etc.) in an accessible manner to each member.

Consistent with that, in this text, we emphasize seven skills that analytic-minded accountants should have:

1. Develop an analytics mindset—recognize when and how data analytics can address business questions.
2. Data scrubbing and data preparation—comprehend the process needed to clean and prepare the data before analysis.
3. Data quality—recognize what is meant by data quality, be it completeness, reliability, or validity.
4. Descriptive data analysis—perform basic analysis to understand the quality of the underlying data and its ability to address the business question.
5. Data analysis through data manipulation—demonstrate ability to sort, rearrange, merge and reconfigure data in a manner that allows enhanced analysis.
6. Define and address problems through statistical data analysis—identify and implement an approach that will use statistical data analysis to draw conclusions and make recommendations on a timely basis.
7. Data visualization and data reporting—report results of analysis in an accessible way to each varied decision maker and his or her specific needs.

We address these seven skills throughout the first four chapters in the text in hopes that the analytic-minded accountant will develop and practice these skills to be ready to address business questions. We then demonstrate these skills in the labs and hands-on analysis throughout the rest of the book.

HANDS-ON EXAMPLE OF THE IMPACT MODEL

Here we provide a complete, hands-on example of the IMPACT model to show how it could be implemented for a specific situation.

Let's suppose I am trying to get a loan to pay off some credit card debt and my friend has told me about a new source of funds that doesn't involve a bank. In recent years, facilitated by the Internet, peer-to-peer lenders allow individuals to both borrow and lend money to each other. While there are other peer-to-peer lenders, in this case, we will specifically consider the LendingClub.

My question is whether I will be able to get a loan, given my prior loan history (poor), credit score, and the like. According to our approaches mentioned above, this would be an example of a classification approach because we are attempting to predict whether a person applying for a loan will be approved and funded or whether she will be denied a loan.

> **LO 1-6**
>
> Explain how to translate common business questions into fields and values.

Identify the Questions

Stated specifically, our question is, "Given my borrower profile, can I expect the LendingClub to extend a loan to me?"

Master the Data

LendingClub is a U.S.-based, peer-to-peer lending company, headquartered in San Francisco, California. LendingClub facilitates both borrowing and lending by providing a platform for unsecured personal loans between $1,000 and $35,000. The loan period is for either 3 or 5 years. There is information available that allows potential investors to search and browse the loan listings on the LendingClub website and select loans in which they would like to invest. The available information includes information supplied about the borrower, amount of the loan, loan grade (and related loan interest rate), and loan purpose. Investors invest in the loans and make money from interest. LendingClub makes money by charging borrowers an origination fee and investors a service fee. Since 2007, hundreds of thousands of borrowers have obtained more than $44 billion in loans via LendingClub.[13]

Some basic lending statistics are included on the LendingClub Statistics website (Exhibit 1-4). Each bar represents the volume of loans each quarter during its respective year.

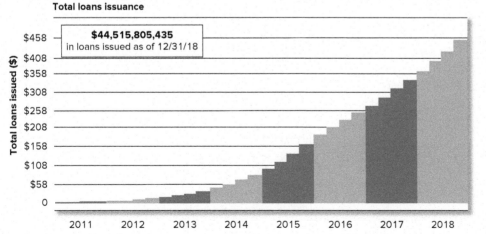

EXHIBIT 1-4
LendingClub Statistics

Source: Accessed March, 2019. https://www.lending-club.com/info/statistics.action.

[13]https://www.lendingclub.com/ (accessed September 29, 2016).

Borrowers borrow money for a variety of reasons, including refinancing other debt and paying off credit cards, as well as borrowing for other purposes (Exhibit 1-5).

EXHIBIT 1-5

LendingClub Statistics by Reported Loan Purpose

68.18% of LendingClub borrowers report using their loans to refinance existing loans or pay off their credit cards as of 12/31/18.

Source: Accessed March, 2019. https://www.lending-club.com/info/statistics.action.

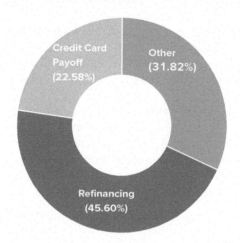

LendingClub actually provides datasets: data on the loans they approved and funded as well as data for the loans that were declined. In this chapter, we will emphasize the rejected loans and the reasons why they were rejected.

The datasets and the data dictionary are available at https://www.lendingclub.com/info/download-data.action.

As we learn about the data, it is important to know what is available to us. To that end, there is a **data dictionary** that provides descriptions for all of the data attributes of the dataset. A cut-out of the data dictionary for the rejected stats file (i.e., the statistics about those loans rejected) is shown in Exhibit 1-6.

EXHIBIT 1-6

2007–2012 LendingClub Data Dictionary for Declined Loan Data

Source: Accessed March, 2019. Available at https://www.lendingclub.com/info/download-data.action.

RejectStats File	Description
Amount Requested	Total requested loan amount
Application Date	Date of borrower application
Loan Title	Loan title
Risk_Score	Borrower risk (FICO) score
Dept-To-Income Ratio	Ratio of borrower total monthly debt payments divided by monthly income.
Zip Code	The first 3 numbers of the borrower zip code provided from loan application.
State	Two digit State Abbreviation provided from loan application.
Employment Length	Employment length in years, where 0 is less than 1 and 10 is greater than 10.
Policy Code	policy_code=1 if publicly available. policy_code=2 if not publicly available

We could also take a look at the data files available for the funded loan data. However, for our analysis in the rest of this chapter, we use the Excel file "RejectStatsA Ready," which has rejected loan statistics from 2007 to 2012. It is a cleaned-up, transformed file ready for analysis. We'll learn more about data scrubbing in Chapter 2.

Exhibit 1-7 provides a cut-out of the 2007–2012 "Approved Loan" dataset provided.

Amount Requested	Application Date	Loan Title	Risk_Score
2175	12/19/2012	major_purchase	850
35000	8/13/2012	other	850
10000	9/19/2012	major_purchase	850
10000	11/9/2012	car	850
3000	11/27/2012	vacation	850
5000	5/20/2012	Lower Rate	850
20000	9/8/2012	Home loan	850
8000	10/22/2012	Loan is for new kitch	850
18500	7/19/2012	bussiness loan	850
10000	7/11/2012	car	850
25000	10/6/2010	debt_consolidation	849
1000	9/9/2012	Hospital expenses	849
35000	5/26/2012	small_business	849
6800	7/13/2012	Be my Own Boss	849
25000	8/10/2012	home_improvement	849
35000	12/2/2012	debt_consolidation	848
1500	11/13/2012	other	848

EXHIBIT 1-7
2007–2012 Declined Loan Applications (RejectStatsA) Dataset

Source: Microsoft Excel, 2016.

Perform Test Plan

Considering our question, "Will I receive a loan from LendingClub?" and the available data, we will do three analyses to predict whether we will receive a loan, including:

1. The debt-to-income ratios and number of rejected loans.
2. The length of employment and number of rejected loans.
3. The credit (or risk) score and number of rejected loans.

Because LendingClub collects this information, we believe it will give LendingClub an idea if the borrower will be able to pay back the loan and give us an idea if our loan will be approved or rejected.

The first analysis we perform considers the *debt-to-income ratio*. That is, how big is the debt compared to the size of the annual income earned?

To consider the debt-to-income ratio in our analysis, three buckets (labeled DTI bucket) are constructed for each grouping of the debt-to-income ratio. These three buckets include the following:

1. High (debt is greater than 20 percent of income).
2. Medium ("mid") (debt is between 10 and 20 percent of income).
3. Low (debt is less than 10 percent of income).

Once those buckets are constructed, we are ready to analyze the breakdown of rejected loan applications by the debt-to-income ratio.

The Excel PivotTable is an easy way to make comparisons between the different levels of DTI. When we run a PivotTable analysis, we highlight the loans, which count the number of loans applied for and rejected, and the DTI bucket (see Exhibit 1-8). The PivotTable counts the number of loan applications in each of the three DTI buckets: high, medium (mid), and low. This suggests that because the high DTI bucket has the highest number of

EXHIBIT 1-8

LendingClub Declined Loan Applications by DTI (Debt-to-Income) DTI bucket includes high (debt > 20 percent of income), medium ("mid") (debt between 10 and 20 percent of income), and low (debt < 10 percent of income). (PivotTable shown here required manually sorting rows to get in proper order.)

Source: Microsoft Excel, 2016.

Row Labels ▾	Count of Rejected Loans
High	312,986
Low	171,228
Mid	161,200
Grand Total	**645,414**

PivotTable Fields

Choose fields to add to report:

- ☑ **Rejected Loans**
- ☐ Amount Requested
- ☐ Application Date
- ☐ Loan Title
- ☐ Risk_Score
- ☐ Risk Score Bucket
- ☐ Debt-To-Income Ratio
- ☑ **DTI Bucket**
- ☐ Zip Code
- ☐ State
- ☐ Employment Length
- ☐ EmploymentNum

loan applications, perhaps the applicant asked for a loan that was too big given his or her income. LendingClub might have seen that as too big of a risk and chosen to not extend the loan to the borrower using the debt-to-income ratio as an indicator.

The second analysis was on the length of employment and its relationship with rejected loans (see Exhibit 1-9). Arguably, the longer the employment, the more stable of a job and income stream you will have to ultimately repay the loan. LendingClub reports the number of years for each of the rejected applications. The PivotTable analysis lists the number of loans by the length of employment. Almost 77 percent (495,109 out of 645,414) out of the total rejected loans had worked at a job for less than 1 year, suggesting potentially an important reason for rejecting the requested loan. Perhaps some had worked a week, or just a month, and still want a big loan?

EXHIBIT 1-9

LendingClub Declined Loan Applications by Employment Length (Years of Experience) DTI bucket includes high (debt > 20 percent of income), medium ("mid") (debt between 10 and 20 percent of income), and low (debt < 10 percent of income). (PivotTable shown here required manually sorting rows to get in proper order.)

Source: Microsoft Excel, 2016.

Row Labels ▾	Count of Rejected Loans
<1 year	495,109
1 year	20,732
2 years	21,987
3 years	17,487
4 years	13,848
5 years	12,865
6 years	9,829
7 years	7,221
8 years	6,652
9 years	5,083
10+ years	34,601
Grand Total	**645,414**

PivotTable Fields

Choose fields to add to report:

- ☑ **Rejected Loans**
- ☐ Amount Requested
- ☐ Application Date
- ☐ Loan Title
- ☐ Risk_Score
- ☐ Risk Score Bucket
- ☐ Debt-To-Income Ratio
- ☐ DTI Bucket
- ☐ Zip Code
- ☐ State
- ☑ **Employment Length**
- ☐ EmploymentNum

The third analysis we perform is to consider the credit or risk score of the applicant. As noted in Exhibit 1-10, risk scores are typically classified in this way with those in the excellent and very good category receiving the lowest possible interest rates and best terms with a credit score above 750. On the other end of the spectrum are those with very bad credit (with a credit score less than 600).

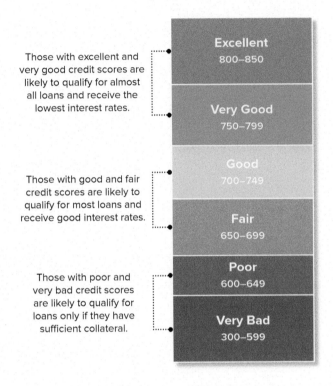

Those with excellent and very good credit scores are likely to qualify for almost all loans and receive the lowest interest rates.

Those with good and fair credit scores are likely to qualify for most loans and receive good interest rates.

Those with poor and very bad credit scores are likely to qualify for loans only if they have sufficient collateral.

Excellent
800–850

Very Good
750–799

Good
700–749

Fair
650–699

Poor
600–649

Very Bad
300–599

EXHIBIT 1-10
Breakdown of Customer Credit Scores (or Risk Scores)

Source: Cafecredit.com.

Another predictor of loan repayment is the credit score that the borrower has. We classify the sample according to this breakdown into excellent, very good, good, fair, poor, and very bad credit according to their credit score noted in Exhibit 1-10.

Address and Refine Results

After performing a PivotTable analysis (as seen in Exhibit 1-11), we count the number of rejected loan applications by credit (risk) score. We'll note in the rejected loans that nearly 82 percent [(167,379 + 151,716 + 207,234)/645,414] of the applicants have either very bad, poor, or fair credit ratings, suggesting this might be a good reason for a loan rejection. We also note that only 0.3 percent (2,494/645,414) of those rejected loan applications had excellent credit.

So, if these are the applications that were all rejected, the question is how many of these that might apply for a loan not only had excellent credit, but also had worked more than 10 years and had asked for a loan that was less than 10 percent of their income (in the low DTI bucket)? Use of a PivotTable (as shown in Exhibit 1-12) allows us to consider this three-way interaction and provides an answer of 365 out of 645,414 (0.057 percent of the total). This might suggest that the use of these three metrics is reasonable at predicting loan rejection because the number who have excellent credit, worked more than 10 years, and requested a loan that was less than 10 percent of their income was such a small percentage of the total.

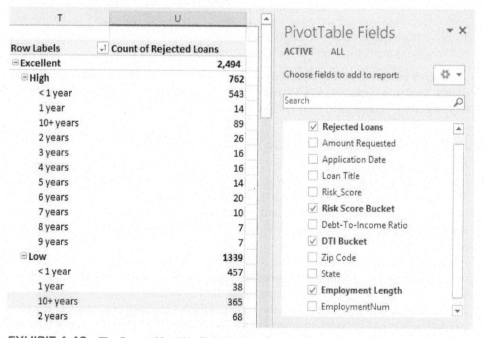

Row Labels ▾	Count of Rejected Loans
Excellent	2,494
Very Good	20,036
Good	96,555
Fair	207,234
Poor	151,716
Very Bad	167,379
Grand Total	**645,414**

PivotTable Fields

Choose fields to add to report:

- ☑ **Rejected Loans**
- ☐ Amount Requested
- ☐ Application Date
- ☐ Loan Title
- ☐ Risk_Score
- ☑ **Risk Score Bucket**
- ☐ Debt-To-Income Ratio
- ☐ DTI Bucket
- ☐ Zip Code
- ☐ State
- ☐ Employment Length
- ☐ EmploymentNum

MORE TABLES...

EXHIBIT 1-11 The Count of LendingClub Rejected Loan Applications by Credit or Risk Score Classification Using PivotTable Analysis (PivotTable shown here required manually sorting rows to get in proper order.)

Source: Microsoft Excel, 2016.

Row Labels ▾	Count of Rejected Loans
⊟ **Excellent**	2,494
⊟ High	762
< 1 year	543
1 year	14
10+ years	89
2 years	26
3 years	16
4 years	16
5 years	14
6 years	20
7 years	10
8 years	7
9 years	7
⊟ Low	1339
< 1 year	457
1 year	38
10+ years	365
2 years	68

PivotTable Fields ▾ ✕

ACTIVE   ALL

Choose fields to add to report: ⚙ ▾

Search 🔍

- ☑ **Rejected Loans**
- ☐ Amount Requested
- ☐ Application Date
- ☐ Loan Title
- ☐ Risk_Score
- ☑ **Risk Score Bucket**
- ☐ Debt-To-Income Ratio
- ☑ **DTI Bucket**
- ☐ Zip Code
- ☐ State
- ☑ **Employment Length**
- ☐ EmploymentNum

EXHIBIT 1-12 The Count of LendingClub Declined Loan Applications by Credit Score, Debt-to-Income, and Employment Length Using PivotTable Analysis (highlighting added)

Source: Microsoft Excel, 2016.

Perhaps those with excellent credit just asked for too big of a loan given their existing debt and that is why they were rejected. Exhibit 1-13 shows the PivotTable analysis. The analysis shows those with excellent credit asked for a larger loan (16.2 percent of income) given the debt they already had as compared to any of the others, suggesting a reason even those potential borrowers with excellent credit were rejected.

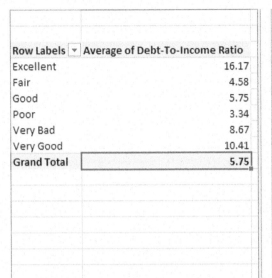

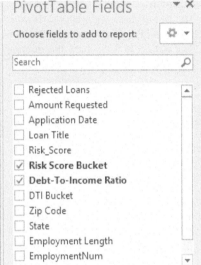

EXHIBIT 1-13

The Average Debt-to-Income Ratio (shown as a percentage) by Credit (Risk) Score for LendingClub Declined Loan Applications Using PivotTable Analysis

Source: Microsoft Excel, 2016.

Communicate Insights

Certainly further and more sophisticated analysis could be performed, but at this point we have a pretty good idea of what LendingClub uses to decide whether to extend a loan. We can communicate these insights either by showing the PivotTables or stating what three of the determinants are.

Track Outcomes

There are a wide variety of outcomes that could be tracked. But in this case, it might be best to see if we could predict future outcomes. For example, the data we analyzed was from 2007–2012. We could make our predictions for subsequent years based on what we had found in the past and then test and see how accurate we are with those predictions. We could also change our prediction model when we learn new insights and additional data become available.

In this chapter, we discussed how businesses and accountants derive value from Data Analytics. We gave some specific examples of how Data Analytics is used in business, auditing, managerial accounting, financial accounting, and tax accounting.

We introduced the IMPACT model and explained how it is used. And then we talked specifically about the importance of identifying the question. We walked through the first few steps of the IMPACT model and introduced eight data approaches. We also discussed the data analytic skills needed by analytic-minded accountants.

We followed this up by looking at the case of why LendingClub rejected loans for a set of its customers using the IMPACT model. We performed this analysis using various filtering and PivotTable tasks.

PROGRESS CHECK

9. Doing your own analysis, download the rejected loans dataset titled "RejectStatsA Ready" and perform an Excel PivotTable analysis by state and figure out the number of rejected applications for the state of California. That is, count the loans by state and see what percentage of the rejected loans came from California. How close is that to the relative proportion of the population of California as compared to that of the United States?

10. Doing your own analysis, download the rejected loans dataset titled "RejectStatsA Ready" and run an Excel PivotTable by risk (or credit) score classification and DTI bucket to determine the number of rejected loans requested by those rated as having an excellent credit score.

Summary

- With data all around us, businesses and accountants are looking at Data Analytics to extract the value that the data might possess.
- Data Analytics is changing the audit and the way that accountants look for risk. Now, auditors can consider 100 percent of the transactions in their audit testing. It is also helpful in finding anomalous or unusual transactions. Data Analytics is also changing the way financial accounting, managerial accounting, and taxes are done at a company.
- The IMPACT cycle is a means of doing Data Analytics that goes all the way from identifying the question, to mastering the data, to performing data analyses and communicating results. It is recursive in nature, suggesting that as questions are addressed, new important questions may emerge that can be addressed in a similar way.
- Eight data approaches address different ways of testing the data: classification, regression, similarity matching, clustering, co-occurrence grouping, profiling, link prediction, and data reduction. These are explained in more detail in Chapter 3.
- Data analytic skills needed by analytic-minded accountants are specified and are consistent with the IMPACT cycle, including the following:
  - Develop an analytics mindset.
  - Data scrubbing and data preparation.
  - Data quality.
  - Descriptive data analysis.
  - Data analysis through data manipulation.
  - Define and address problems through statistical data analysis.
  - Data visualization and data reporting.

Key Words

Big Data (*4*)   Datasets that are too large and complex for businesses' existing systems to handle utilizing their traditional capabilities to capture, store, manage, and analyze these datasets.

classification (*9*)   A data approach that attempts to assign each unit in a population into a few categories potentially to help with predictions.

clustering (*10*)   A data approach that attempts to divide individuals (like customers) into groups (or clusters) in a useful or meaningful way.

co-occurrence grouping (10) A data approach that attempts to discover associations between individuals based on transactions involving them.

Data Analytics (4) The process of evaluating data with the purpose of drawing conclusions to address business questions. Indeed, effective Data Analytics provides a way to search through large structured and unstructured data to identify unknown patterns or relationships.

data dictionary (14) Centralized repository of descriptions for all of the data attributes of the dataset.

data reduction (10) A data approach that attempts to reduce the amount of information that needs to be considered to focus on the most critical items (i.e., highest cost, highest risk, largest impact, etc.)

link prediction (10) A data approach that attempts to predict a relationship between two data items.

profiling (10) A data approach that attempts to characterize the "typical" behavior of an individual, group or population by generating summary statistics about the data (including mean, standard deviations, etc.).

predictor (or independent or explanatory) variable (9) A variable that predicts or explains another variable.

response (or dependent) variable (9) A variable that responds to, or is dependent, on another.

regression (9) A data approach used to predict a specific dependent variable value based on independent variable inputs using a statistical model.

similarity matching (10) A data approach that attempts to identify similar individuals based on data known about them.

 # ANSWERS TO PROGRESS CHECKS

1. The plethora of data alone does not necessarily translate into value. However, if we carefully use the data to help address critical business problems and questions, the data may create value.

2. Banks could certainly use credit scores from companies like **Experian, TransUnion**, and **Equifax**, but if they have access to all of the banking information of their clients, arguably they could make more informed decisions. Banks would know how much money they have and how they spend it. Banks would know if they had prior loans and if they were paid in a timely manner. Banks would know where they work and their monthly income via the direct deposits. All of these combined, in addition to a credit score, might be used to assess creditworthiness to gain a better evaluation of customers' creditworthiness when they would like a loan. It might also give us needed information for a marketing campaign to target potential creditworthy customers.

3. The brand manager at **Samsung** might use Data Analytics to see what is being said about **Samsung's** phones on social media websites (e.g., **Snapchat, Instagram**, and **Facebook**), particularly those that attract an older demographic. This will help the manager assess if there is a problem with the perceptions of its phones.

4. Data Analytics might be used to collect information on the amount of overtime. Who worked overtime? What were they working on? Do we actually need more full-time employees to reduce the level of overtime (and its related costs to the company and to the employees)? All of these questions could be addressed by looking at recent records explaining the use of overtime records.

5. Data Analytics could tabulate the number of journal entries by an accountant to see who entered the most journal entries. This might be an issue if there was a perception of a problem in risk, such as segregation of duties in having one person enter so many journal entries or just how the accounting workload is distributed across accounting staff.

6. The tax staff would become much more adept at efficiently organizing data from multiple systems across an organization and performing Data Analytics to help with tax planning to structure transactions in a way that might minimize taxes.

7. The dependent variable could be the amount of money spent on fast food. Independent variables could be proximity of the fast food, ability to cook own food, discretionary income, socioeconomic status, etc.

8. The data reduction approach might help auditors spend more time and effort on the riskiest transactions or on those that might be anomalous in nature. This will help them more efficiently spend their time on items that may well be of highest importance.

9. An analysis of the rejected loans suggests that 85,793 of the total 645,414 rejected loans were from the state of California. That represents 13.29 percent of the total rejected loans. This is greater than the relative population of California to the United States as of the 2010 census, of 12.1 percent (37,253,956/308,745,538).

Row Labels ▾	Count of Rejected Loans
AK	1,608
AL	10,959
AR	7,868
AZ	13,830
CA	85,793
CO	11,697
CT	10,589
DC	1,524
DE	2,287
FL	49,620
GA	23,774
HI	3,715

PivotTable Fields

Choose fields to add to report:

☑ **Rejected Loans**
☐ Amount Requested
☐ Application Date
☐ Loan Title
☐ Risk_Score
☐ Risk Score Bucket
☐ Debt-To-Income Ratio
☐ DTI Bucket
☐ Zip Code
☑ **State**

Source: Microsoft Excel, 2016.

10. A PivotTable analysis of the rejected loans suggests that more than 30.6 percent (762/2,494) of those in the excellent risk/credit score range asked for a loan with a debt-to-income ratio of more than 20 percent.

Row Labels ▾	Count of Rejected Loans
⊟ **Excellent**	**2,494**
High	762
Mid	393
Low	1,339
⊟ **Very Good**	**20,036**
High	9,593
Mid	4,022
Low	6,421
⊟ **Good**	**96,555**
High	59,241
Mid	18,291
Low	19,023

PivotTable Fields

Choose fields to add to report:

☑ **Rejected Loans**
☐ Amount Requested
☐ Application Date
☐ Loan Title
☐ Risk_Score
☑ **Risk Score Bucket**
☐ Debt-To-Income Ratio
☑ **DTI Bucket**
☐ Zip Code
☐ State

Source: Microsoft Excel, 2016.

Multiple Choice Questions

1. Big Data is often described by the three Vs, or
   a. volume, velocity, and variability.
   b. volume, velocity, and variety.
   c. volume, volatility, and variability.
   d. variability, velocity, and variety.

2. Which approach to Data Analytics attempts to assign each unit in a population into a small set of classes (or groups) where the unit best fits?
   a. Regression
   b. Similarity matching
   c. Co-occurrence grouping
   d. Classification

3. Which approach to Data Analytics attempts to identify similar individuals based on data known about them?
   a. Classification
   b. Regression
   c. Similarity matching
   d. Data reduction

4. Which approach to Data Analytics attempts to predict relationship between two data items?
   a. Profiling
   b. Classification
   c. Link prediction
   d. Regression

5. Which of these terms is defined as being a central repository of descriptions for all of the data attributes of the dataset?
   a. Big Data
   b. Data warehouse
   c. Data dictionary
   d. Data Analytics

6. Which skills were *not* emphasized that analytic-minded accountants should have?
   a. Develop an analytics mindset
   b. Data scrubbing and data preparation
   c. Classification of test approaches
   d. Define and address problems through statistical data analysis

7. Which skills were *not* emphasized that analytic-minded accountants should have?
   a. Data quality
   b. Descriptive data analysis
   c. Data visualization
   d. Data and systems analysis and design

8. The IMPACT cycle includes all *except* the following process:
   a. perform test plan.
   b. visualize the data.
   c. master the data.
   d. track outcomes.

9. The IMPACT cycle includes all *except* the following process:
   a. data preparation.
   b. communicate insights.
   c. address and refine results.
   d. perform test plan.

10. By the year 2020, about 1.7 megabytes of new information will be created every:
    a. week.
    b. second.
    c. minute.
    d. day.

Discussion Questions

1. Define Data Analytics and explain how a university might use its techniques to recruit and attract potential students.

2. Give an example of how Data Analytics creates value for businesses.

3. Give an example of how Data Analytics creates value for accounting.

4. How might Data Analytics be used in financial reporting? And how might it be used in doing tax planning?

5. Describe the IMPACT cycle. Why does its order of the processes and its recursive nature make sense?

6. Why is identifying the question such a critical first step in the IMPACT process cycle?

7. What is included in mastering the data as part of the IMPACT cycle described in the chapter?

8. In the chapter, we mentioned eight different data approaches. Which data approach was used by **Alibaba,** as mentioned in the chapter-opening vignette?

9. What data approach mentioned in the chapter might be used by Facebook to find friends?

10. Auditors will frequently use the data reduction approach when considering potentially risky transactions. Provide an example of why focusing on a portion of the total number of transactions might be important for auditors to assess risk.

11. Which data approach might be used to assess the appropriate level of the allowance for doubtful accounts?

12. Why might the debt-to-income attribute included in the declined loans dataset considered in the chapter be a predictor of declined loans? How about the credit (risk) score?

13. To address the question "Will I receive a loan from **LendingClub**?" we had available data to assess the relationship among (1) the debt-to-income ratios and number of rejected loans, (2) the length of employment and number of rejected loans, and (3) the credit (or risk) score and number of rejected loans. What additional data would you recommend to further assess whether a loan would be offered? Why would it be helpful?

Problems

1. Navigate to the Additional Student Resources page on Connect. Under Chapter 1 Data Files, download and consider the **LendingClub** data dictionary file "LCDataDictionary" specifically the LoanStats tab. This represents the data dictionary for the loans that were funded. Choosing some of the data attributes listed there, which attributes do you think might predict which loans will go delinquent and which will ultimately be fully repaid? How could we test that?

2. Download and consider the rejected loans dataset of **LendingClub** data titled "RejectStatsA Ready." Given the analysis performed in the chapter, what three items do you believe would be most useful in predicting loan acceptance or rejection? What additional data do you think could be solicited either internally or externally that would help you predict loan acceptance or rejection?

3. Download the rejected loans dataset of **LendingClub** data titled "RejectStatsA Ready" from the Connect website and do an Excel PivotTable by state; then figure out the number of rejected applications for the state of Arkansas. That is, count the loans by state and compute the percentage of the total rejected loans in the USA that came from Arkansas. How close is that to the relative proportion of the population of Arkansas as compared to the overall U.S. population (per 2010 census)?

4. Download the rejected loans dataset of **LendingClub** data titled "RejectStatsA Ready" from the Connect website and do an Excel PivotTable by state; then figure out the number of rejected applications for each state. Reorder these and make a graph ordering the states and the number of rejected loans from highest to lowest. Is there a lot of variability among states?

   For Problems 5, 6, and 7, we will be cleaning a data file in preparation for subsequent analysis.

   The analysis performed on **LendingClub** data in the chapter was for the years 2007–2012. For this and subsequent problems, please download the declined loans table for 2013–2014 from the Connect website.

5. Consider the 2013 declined loan data from **LendingClub** titled "RejectStatsB2013" from the Connect website. Similar to the analysis done in the chapter, let's scrub the risk score data. First, because our analysis requires risk scores, debt-to-income data, and employment length, we need to make sure each of them has valid data.

   a. Open the file in Excel.

   b. Sort the file based on risk score and remove those observations (the complete row or record) that have a missing score or a score of zero, if needed.

   c. Assign each risk score to a risk score bucket similar to the chapter. That is, classify the sample according to this breakdown into excellent, very good, good, fair, poor, and very bad credit according to their credit score noted in Exhibit 1-10. Classify those with a score greater than 850 as "Excellent." Consider using nested if–then statements to complete this. Or sort by risk score and manually input into appropriate risk score buckets.

   d. Run a PivotTable analysis that shows the number of loans in each risk score bucket. Which group had the most rejected loans (biggest count)? Which group had the least rejected loans (smallest count)? This is the deliverable. Is it similar to Exhibit 1-11 performed on years 2007–2012?

6. Consider the 2013 declined loan data from **LendingClub** titled "RejectStatsB2013." Similar to the analysis done in the chapter, let's scrub the debt-to-income data. Because our analysis requires risk scores, debt-to-income data, and employment length, we need to make sure each of them has valid data.

   a. Sort the file based on debt-to-income and remove those observations (the complete row or record) that have a missing score, a score of zero, or a negative score.

   b. Assign each valid debt-to-income ratio into three buckets (labeled DTI bucket) by classifying each debt-to-income ratio into high (>20.0 percent), medium (10.0–20.0 percent), and low (<10.0 percent) buckets. Consider using nested if-then statements to complete this. Or sort the row and manually input.

   c. Run a PivotTable analysis that shows the number of loans in each DTI bucket. Any interpretation of why these loans were declined based on debt-to-income ratios?

7. Consider the 2013 declined loan data from **LendingClub** titled "RejectStatsB2013." Similar to the analysis done in the chapter, let's scrub the employment length. Because our analysis requires risk scores, debt-to-income data, and employment length, we need to make sure each of them has valid data.

a. Sort the file based on employment length and remove those observations (the complete row or record) that have a missing score ("NA"). Note that we are including the employment lengths of zero, different than the analysis in the chapter text.

b. Sort the file based on debt-to-income and remove those observations (the complete row or record) that have a missing score, a score of zero, or a negative score, similar to that done in Problem 1-6.

c. Sort the file based on risk score and remove those observations (the complete row or record) that have a missing score or a score of zero, similar to that done in Problem 1-5.

d. There should now be 669,993 observations. Any thoughts on what biases are imposed when we remove observations? Is there another way to do this?

e. Run a PivotTable analysis to show the number of Excellent Risk Scores but High DTI Bucket loans in each Employment year bucket. Any interpretation of why these loans were declined?

Lab 1-0 How to Complete Labs in This Text

The labs in this book will provide valuable hands-on experience in generating and analyzing accounting problems. Each lab will provide a company summary with relevant facts, techniques that you will use to complete your analysis, software that you'll need, and an overview of the lab steps.

When you've completed your lab, you will submit a lab report showing your thought process with written responses and validating that you've completed specific checkpoints by taking screenshots along the way. This lab will demonstrate how to use basic lab tools.

In this lab, you will:

Part 1: Create a Word document on OneDrive.

Part 2: Take a screenshot of your document.

Part 3: Add another screenshot and submit your document.

Submit two screenshots.

Part 1: Create a New Word Document on OneDrive

On Office.com

1. Open your web browser and go to www.office.com.
2. Click All Microsoft and then click OneDrive and log in using your university or personal email address and password.
3. Click **+ New > OneDrive Word document.** A new window will open with a new blank document.
4. Type "Lab 1-0 Data Analytics Lab Overview [Your name] [Your university email address]" in the first line (e.g., *Lab 1-0 Data Analytics Lab Overview Ryan Teeter rteeter@pitt.edu*).
5. Click **File> Save As > Save As** and name the document "*Lab 1-0 Data Analytics Lab Overview Ryan Teeter rteeter@pitt.edu.*" (You can also click the document name in the title bar (e.g., Document2) and change it there.
6. Because your document is in the cloud, changes are saved automatically and you won't lose your document when you log out of a lab computer.
7. Keep your document open and go to the next part of the lab.

Part 2: Take a Screenshot of Your Document

In Windows

1. Click the **Start** button and Search for "Snipping Tool."
2. Click **New** (**Rectangular Snip**) and draw a rectangle across your screen that includes your entire window.
3. A preview window with your screenshot will appear.
4. Press **Ctrl + C** to copy your screenshot.
5. Go to your Word document and press **Ctrl + V** to paste the screenshot into your document.
6. Keep your document open and go the next part of the lab.

On a Mac

1. Press **Cmd + Shift + 4** and draw a rectangle across your screen that includes your entire window.
2. Your screenshot will be saved in your Desktop folder.
3. Drag the screenshot file into your Word document.
4. Keep your document open and go the next part of the lab.

Part 3: Add Another Screenshot and Submit Your Document

1. Open a new web browser window and go to mhhm.com.
2. Take a screenshot of your results (label it 1-0A) of the page and paste it into your lab document.
3. Save your document and submit it to your instructor. To download your document for OneDrive, click **File > Save As > Download a Copy.**

End of Lab

Lab 1-1   Data Analytics in Financial Accounting

Let's see how we might perform some simple Data Analytics. The purpose of this lab is to help you identify relevant questions that may be answered using Data Analytics.

Company summary

You were just hired as an analyst for a credit rating agency that evaluates publicly listed companies in the United States. The company already has some Data Analytics tools that it uses to evaluate financial statements and determine which companies have higher risk and which companies are growing quickly. The company uses these analytics to provide ratings that will allow lenders to set interest rates and determine whether to lend money in the first place. As a new analyst, you're determined to make a good first impression.

Technique

- Some experience with spreadsheets and basic formulas is helpful here.

Software needed

- Word processor
- Web browser
- Screen capture tool (Windows: Snipping Tool; Mac: Cmd + Shift + 4)

In this lab, you will:

Part 1: Identify appropriate questions, and develop a hypothesis for each question.
Part 2: Master the data.
Part 3: Perform a simple analysis.

Part 1: Identify the Questions

Think about ways that you might analyze data from a financial statement. You could use a horizontal analysis to view trends over time, a vertical analysis to show account proportions, or ratios to analyze relationships.

1. Create a new word processing document and name the file "**Lab 1-1 Data Analytics in Financial Accounting Lab—[Your name] [Your email address].**"
2. Use what you know about financial statement analysis (or search the web if you need a refresher) to generate three different metrics for evaluating financial performance.

For example, if you wanted to evaluate a company's profit margin from one year to the next your question might be, "Has [Company X's] gross margin increased in the last three years?" **Type your three questions in your document.**

3. Next to each question **generate a hypothetical answer to the question** to help you identify what your expected output would be. You may use some insight or intuition or search for industry averages to inform your hypothesis. For example: "Hypothesis: Apple Inc's gross margin has increased slightly in the past 3 years."

4. Save your document.

Part 2: Master the Data

To answer your questions, you'll need to evaluate specific account values or financial statement paragraphs. As an analyst, you have access to the Security and Exchange Commission's (SEC's) EDGAR database of XBRL financial statements as well as a list of XBRL tags from the Financial Accounting Standards Board (FASB). XBRL stands for eXtensible Business Reporting Language and is used to make the data in financial statements machine-readable. Public companies have been preparing XBRL reports since 2008. While there are some issues with XBRL data, such data have become a useful means for comparing and analyzing financial statements. Every value, date, and paragraph is "tagged" with a label that identifies what each specific value represents, similar to assigning attributes in a database. Because companies tag their financial statements with XBRL tags, you can use those tags to identify specific data that you need to answer your questions from Part 1.

Analyze your questions:

5. **Evaluate each question from Part 1.** There are specific data attributes that will help you find the answer you're looking for. For example, if your question was "Has [Company X's] gross margin increased in the last 3 years?" and the expected answer is "Apple Inc's gross margin has increased slightly in the past 3 years," this tells you what attributes (or fields) to look for: *company name, gross margin (sales revenues – cost of goods sold), year.*

6. For each of your questions, **identify the account or data attribute you need** to answer your question. Then use FASB's XBRL taxonomy (see next section for instructions) to identify the specific XBRL tags that represent those accounts. For example:

> *Company name* = EntitySectorIndustryClassificationPrimary
>
> *Gross margin* = GrossProfit
>
> *Sales revenues* = SalesRevenueNet
>
> *Cost of goods sold* = CostOfGoodsAndServicessold
>
> *Year* = DocumentPeriodEndDate

7. Save your document.

Identify XBRL tags from the FASB's taxonomy:

8. Open a web browser, and go to xbrlview.fasb.org.

9. Click the + next to US GAAP (2019-01-31).

10. Click the **ALL (Main/Entire)** option, and then click **Open** to load the taxonomy.

11. Navigate through the financial statements to determine which accounts you need to answer your questions from Part 1. The name of the XBRL tag is found in the properties pane next to "Name." For example, the tag for Total Assets can be found by clicking + Statement of Financial Position [Abstract], + Statement [Table], + Statement [Line Items], + Assets [Abstract], + Assets, Total, as shown in Lab Exhibit 1-1A. You may also use the search function.

Note: Be careful when you use the search function. The tag you see in the results may appear in the wrong statement. Double-click the tag to expand the tree and show where the account appears.

LAB EXHIBIT 1-1A

Browse the XBRL Taxonomy for Financial Fact Tags Needed for Your Analysis

Source: Google.

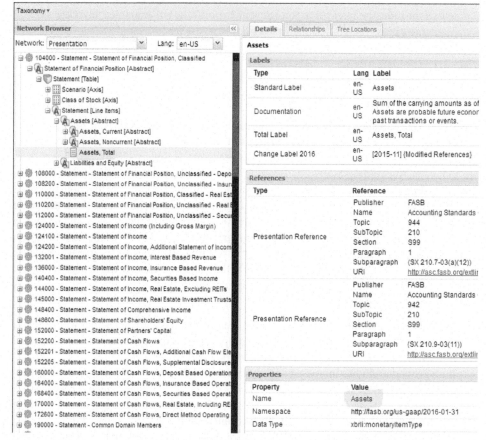

Part 3: Perform the Analysis

Now that you've identified your questions and the data sources, you can build your model and perform your analysis. Because XBRL data are dynamic, we'll use a tool that pulls live data based on your inputs.

12. In your web browser, click on the eBook via Connect to locate the table of contents where you will find **Additional Student Resources > Financial Statement Analysis**.
13. Log into your Google Account.
14. Click **File > Make a Copy. . .**
15. In your new document, **add your tags** from Part 2 under the Financial Facts header, similar to Exhibit 1-1B.

Financial Statement Analysis

LAB EXHIBIT 1-1B

Add Your Tags to
Perform a Simple
Analysis Using XBRL
Data

Source: Google.

Company 1 Ticker	AAPL	(e.g. MSFT)	EntitySectorIndustryClassificationPrimary
Most Recent Year	2017	(e.g. 2014)	DocumentPeriodEndDate
Period	FY	(e.g. FY or Q2)	
Round to	100,000	(e.g. 100,000)	

Apple Inc

Financial Facts	2014	2015	2016	2017
SalesRevenueNet	$ 1,827,950	$ 2,337,150	$ 2,156,390	$ 2,292,340
CostofGoodsAndServicesSold	$ 1,122,580	$ 1,400,890	$ 1,313,760	$ 1,410,480
GrossProfit	$ 705,370	$ 936,260	$ 842,630	$ 881,860
[Add XBRL Tag Here]	#ERROR!	#ERROR!	#ERROR!	#ERROR!
[Add XBRL Tag Here]	#ERROR!	#ERROR!	#ERROR!	#ERROR!

Analysis				
Return on Asset		74.20%	62.08%	64.74%
Profit Margin		40.06%	39.08%	38.47%
Asset Turnover		1.85	1.59	1.68

16. Under the Analysis header, **use formulas to create your analysis** from Part 1. You may enhance your output by using conditional formatting or other visualizations that will be covered in Chapter 4.
17. Take a screenshot (label it 1-1A) of your analysis and paste it into your lab document.
18. Save your document and submit it to your instructor.

End of Lab

Lab 1-2 Data Analytics in Managerial Accounting

Let's see how we might use customer data to understand some simple data analytics. The purpose of this lab is to help you identify relevant questions that may be answered using data analytics.

Company summary

LendingClub is a U.S.-based, peer-to-peer lending company, headquartered in San Francisco, California. LendingClub facilitates both borrowing and lending by providing a platform for unsecured personal loans between $1,000 and $35,000. The loan period is for either 3 or 5 years. You have been brought in to help managers improve their loan application process.

Technique
- Some critical and creative thinking is helpful here.

Software needed
- Word processor

In this lab, you will:

Part 1: Identify appropriate questions and develop a hypothesis for each question.
Part 2: Identify fields and values in a database that are relevant to your questions.

Part 1: Identify the Questions

LendingClub currently assigns a risk score to all loan applicants. This risk score is used to determine (1) whether a loan is accepted and (2) what interest rate approved loans will receive. The risk score has been used for the past 5 years, but LendingClub thinks there may be better ways to evaluate this given that the number of defaulted loans has increased in the past 2 years. It would like you to propose a model that would help it potentially assign a risk score to loan applicants.

1. Create a new word processing document and name the file "**Lab 1-2 Data Analytics in Managerial Accounting Lab – [Your name] [Your email address]**."
2. Use what you know about loan risk (or search the web if you need a refresher) to identify three different questions that might influence risk. For example, if you suspect risky customers live in a certain location, your question might be "Where do the customers live?" **Type your three questions in your document.**
3. Next to each question, **generate a hypothetical answer to each question** to help you identify what your expected output would be. You may use some insight or intuition or search the Internet for ideas on how to inform your hypothesis. For example: "Hypothesis: Risky customers likely live in coastal towns."
4. Finally, identify the data that you would need to answer each of your questions. For example, to determine customer location, you might need the city, state, and zip code. Additionally, if you hypothesize a specific region, you'd need to know which cities, state, and/or zip codes belong to that region. **Add your required data sources to each question in your document.**
5. **Save** your document.

Part 2: Master the Data

To answer your questions, you'll need to evaluate specific data that LendingClub collects. It has provided a listing of fields that it collects in Table 1-2A.

LAB TABLE 1-2A

Names and Descriptions of Selected Data Attributes Collected by LendingClub

Attribute	Description
id	Loan identification number
member_id	Membership id
loan_amnt	Requested loan amount
emp_length	Employment length
issue_d	Date of loan issue
loan_status	Fully paid or charged off
pymnt_plan	Payment plan: yes or no
purpose	Loan purpose: e.g., wedding, medical, debt_consolidation, car
zip_code	Zip code
addr_state	State
dti	Debt-to-income ratio
delinq_2y	Late payments within the past two years
earliest_cr_line	Oldest credit account
inq_last_6mnths	Credit inquiries in the past 6 months
open_acc	Number of open credit accounts
revol_bal	Total balance of all credit accounts
revol_util	Percentage of available credit in use
total_acc	Total number of credit accounts
application_type	Individual or joint application

6. Evaluate each question from Part 1. Do the data you identified in your questions exist in the table provided? **Write the applicable fields next to each question in your document.**

7. Are there data values you identified that don't exist in the table? **Write where else you might look to collect the missing data or how you might suggest collecting those it.**

8. Save your document and submit to your instructor.

End of Lab

Lab 1-3   Data Analytics in Auditing

The purpose of this lab is to help you identify relevant questions that may be answered using data analytics in auditing. Let's evaluate how we might use master and transaction data from an enterprise resource planning system to perform some simple data analytics to assist the financial statement audit.

Company summary

ABC Company is a large retailer that collects its order-to-cash data in a large ERP system that was recently updated to comply with the AICPA's audit data standards. ABC Company currently collects all relevant data in the ERP system and digitizes any contracts, orders, or receipts that are completed on paper. The credit department reviews customers who request credit. Sales orders are approved by managers before being sent to the warehouse for preparation and shipment. Cash receipts are collected by a cashier and applied to a customer's outstanding balance by an accounts receivable clerk.

You have been assigned to the audit team that will perform the internal controls audit of ABC Company.

Technique

- Familiarity with database structure and primary-foreign key relationships may be helpful.

Software needed

- Word processor
- Web browser
- Screen capture tool (Windows: Snipping Tool; Mac: Cmd + Shift + 4)

In this lab, you will:

Part 1: Identify appropriate questions and develop a hypothesis for each question.

Part 2: Translate questions into target fields and value in a database and perform a simple analysis.

Part 1: Identify the Questions

Your audit team has been tasked with identifying potential internal control weaknesses within the order-to-cash process.

1. Create a new word processing document and name the file "**Lab 1-3 Data Analytics in Auditing Lab – [Your name] [Your email address].**"
2. Use what you know about internal controls over the order-to-cash process (or search the web if you need a refresher) to identify three different questions that might indicate internal control weakness. For example, if you suspect that a manager may be delaying approval of shipments sent to customers, your question might be "Are any shipping managers approving shipments more than 2 days after they are received?" **Type your three questions in your document.**
3. Next to each question **generate a hypothetical answer to each question** to help you identify what your expected output would be. You may use some insight or intuition or search the Internet for ideas on how to inform your hypothesis. For example: "Hypothesis: Only 1 or 2 shipping managers are approving shipments more than 2 days after they are received."
4. Finally, identify the data that you would need to answer each of your questions. For example, to determine the timing of approval and who is involved, you might need the approver id, the order date, and the approval date. **Add your required data sources to each question in your document.**
5. **Save** your document.

Part 2: Master the Data

To answer your questions, you'll need to evaluate the data that are available in the audit data standards.

6. Open your web browser and search for "Audit data standards order to cash." Follow the link to the "Audit Data Standards Library–AICPA," then look for the "Audit Data Standard–Order to Cash Subledger Standard" PDF document.
7. Quickly scan through the document for fields that relate to each question you identified in Part 1. For example, if you're looking for the shipment timing and approval data, you would need the *Shipments_Made_YYYYMMDD_YYYYMMDD* table and *Approved_By, Entered_Date,* and *Approved_Date* fields. **List the tables and fields from the audit data standard in your document needed for each question.**
8. Identify any data that don't appear in the audit data standard that might also be relevant to your questions.
9. Save your document and submit it to your instructor.

End of Lab

Lab 1-4 Comprehensive Case: Dillard's Store Data

The purpose of this lab is to help you identify relevant questions for Dillard's Inc. based on its data.

Company summary

Dillard's is a department store with approximately 330 stores in 29 states. Its headquarters is in Little Rock, Arkansas. You can learn more about Dillard's by looking at finance.yahoo. com (ticker symbol = DDS) and the Wikipedia site for DDS. You'll quickly note that William T. Dillard II is an accounting grad of the University of Arkansas and the Walton College of Business, which may be why he shared transaction data with us to make available for this lab and labs throughout this text.

Technique

The data for this lab and all other Dillard's labs must be accessed through the University of Arkansas Remote Desktop. Directions for accessing the Remote Desktop can be found at www.mhhe.com/richardsondaa2e. See your instructor for login credentials. From the Walton College website, we note the following:

The Dillard's Department Store Database contains retail sales information gathered from store sales transactions. The sale process begins when a customer brings items intended for purchase (clothing, jewelry, home décor, etc.) to any store register. A Dillard's sales associate scans the individual items to be purchased with a barcode reader. This populates the transaction table (TRANSACT), which will later be used to generate a sales receipt listing the item, department, and cost information (related price, sale price, etc.) for the customer. When the customer provides payment for the items, payment details are recorded in the transaction table, the receipt is printed, and the transaction is complete. Other tables are used to store information about stores, products, and departments.

Source: Accessed July 15, 2019. http://walton.uark.edu/enterprise/dillardshome.php.

This retail sales information, UA_DILLARDS, was provided to the Walton College of Business by Dillard's Stores Inc. The information consists of five tables with more than 128 million rows already populated and ready for use.

This is a gifted dataset that is based on real operational data. Like any real database, integrity problems may be noted. This can provide a unique opportunity not only to expose students to real data, but also to illustrate the effects of data integrity problems.

Software needed

- Word processor
- Web browser
- Screen capture tool (Windows: Snipping Tool; Mac: Cmd + Shift + 4)
- Access to the dataset is available at http://walton.uark.edu/enterprise/dillardshome.php. If you plan on doing additional labs on Dillard's data, you must receive permission from the Walton College to access the data before use. Additional access instructions are available from your instructor or on the Connect website.

In this lab, you will:

Part 1: Identify appropriate questions for a retailer.
Part 2: Translate questions into target tables, fields, and values in the Dillard's database.

Part 1: Identify the Questions

1. Create a new word processing document and name the file "**Lab 1-4 Comprehensive Case – Dillard's Data [Your name] [Your email address].**"
2. Assume that Dillard's wants to improve profitability. Name three questions that could be asked to assess current profitability levels for each product and how profitability could be improved in the near future.

3. Assume that **Dillard's** wishes to improve its online sales and profitability on those sales. What three questions could be asked to see where **Dillard's** stands on its online sales?
4. Save your document.

LAB EXHIBIT 1-4A

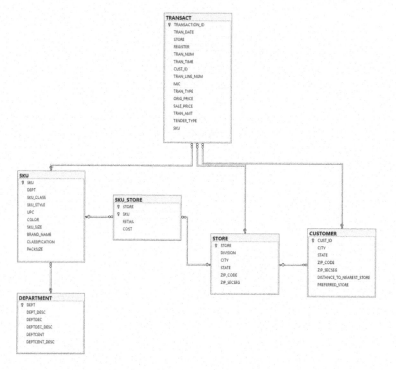

Part 2: Master the Data

To answer your questions and related questions, access the Data Dictionary and Entity Relationship Diagram for the Dillard's Entity Relationship data at http://walton.uark.edu/enterprise/dillardshome.phpor consider the information in Exhibits 1-4A and 1-4B.

5. You're trying to learn about where **Dillard's** stores are located to identify locations for the next additional store. Consider the STORE table. What questions could be asked about store location given data availability?
6. What questions would you have regarding data fields in the SKU table that could be used to help address the cost of shipping? What additional information would be helpful to address this question?
7. What table and fields could address the question of the profit margin (sales price less cost) on each product (SKU) available for sale?

Metadata

Source: Accessed September 25, 2017. http://walton.uark. edu/enterprise/dillardshome. php.

Attribute	Description	Values
AMT	Total amount of the transaction charge to the customer	26.25, 44.00, . . .
BRAND	The brand name of the stock item	TOMMY HI, MARK ECK, . . .
CITY	City where the store is located	ST. LOUIS, TAMPA, . . .
CLASSID	Stock Item Classification	5305, 4505, 8306, . . .
COLOR	The color of the stock item	BLACK, KHAKI, . . .
COST	The cost of the stock item	9.00, 15.00, . . .
DEPT	Department where the stock item belong	800, 801, 1100, . . .
DEPTDESC	Description of the department	CLINIQUE, LESLIE, . . .
INTERID	Internal ID	265005802, 671901998, . . .
MIC	Master Item Code	862, 689, . . .
ORGPRICE	Original price of the item stock	75.00, 44.00, . . .
PACKSIZE	The quantity of item per pack	1, 3, . . .
QUANTITY	Item quantity of the transaction	1, 2, 3, . . .
REGISTER	Register Number of the current transaction	580, 30, 460, . . .
RETAIL	The retail price of the stock item	19.75, 34.00, . . .
SALEDATE	Sale price of the item stock	2005-01-20, 2005-06-02, . . .
SEQ	Sequence number	298100028, 213500030, . . .
SIZE	The size of the stock item	L, 070N, 22, . . .
SKU	Stock Keeping Unit number of the stock item	4757355, 2128748, . . .
SPRICE	Sale price of the item stock	26.25, 65.00, . . .
STATE	State where the store is located	FL, MO, AR, . . .
STORE	Store Number	2, 3, 4, 100, . . .
STYLE	The specific style of the stock item	51 MERU08, 9 126NAO, . . .
STYPE	Type of the transaction (Return or Purchase)	P, R
TRANNUM	Transaction Code	09700, 01800, . . .
UPC	Universal Product Code for the stock item	000400004087945, . . .
VENDOR	The vendor number of the stock item	5511283, 2726341, . . .
ZIP	ZIP Code	33710, 63126, . . .

8. If you're interested in learning which product is sold most often at each store, what tables and fields would you consider?
9. Save your document and submit it to your instructor.

End of Lab

Chapter 2

Mastering the Data

A Look at This Chapter

This chapter provides an overview of the types of data that are used in the accounting cycle and common data that are stored in a relational database. The second step of the IMPACT cycle is "mastering the data." We will describe how data are requested and *extracted* to answer business questions and how to *transform* data for use via data preparation, validation, and cleaning. We conclude with an explanation of how to *load* data into the appropriate tool in preparation for analyzing data to make decisions.

A Look Back

Chapter 1 defined Data Analytics and explained that the value of Data Analytics is in the insights it provides. We described the Data Analytics Process using the IMPACT cycle model and explained how this process is used to address both business and accounting questions. We specifically emphasized the importance of identifying appropriate questions that data analytics might be able to address.

A Look Ahead

Chapter 3 describes how to go from defining business problems to analyzing data, answering questions, and addressing business problems. We identify four types of data analytics and describe various approaches and techniques that are most relevant to analyzing accounting data.

Wichy/Shutterstock

We are lucky to live in a world in which data are abundant. However, even with rich sources of data, when it comes to being able to analyze data and turn them into useful information and insights, very rarely can an analyst hop right into a dataset and begin analyzing. Datasets almost always need to be cleaned and validated before they can be used. Not knowing how to clean and validate data can, at best, lead to frustration and poor insights and, at worst, lead to horrible security violations. While this text takes advantage of open source datasets, these datasets have all been scrubbed not only for accuracy, but also to protect the security and privacy of any individual or company whose details were in the original dataset.

In 2015, a pair of researchers named Emil Kirkegaard and Julius Daugbejerg Bjerrekaer scraped data from **OkCupid**, a free dating website, and provided the data onto the "Open Science Framework," a platform researchers use to obtain and share raw data. While the aim of the Open Science Framework is to increase transparency, the researchers in this instance took that a step too far—and a step into illegal territory. Kirkegaard and Bjerrekaer did not obtain permission from **OkCupid** or from the 70,000 **OkCupid** users whose identities, ages, genders, religions, personality traits, and other personal details maintained by the dating site were provided to the public without any work being done to anonymize or sanitize the data. If the researchers had taken the time to not just validate that the data were complete, but also to sanitize them to protect the individuals' identities, this would not have been a threat or a news story. On May 13, 2015, the Open Science Framework removed the **OkCupid** data from the platform, but the damage of the privacy breach had already been done.[1]

OBJECTIVES

After reading this chapter, you should be able to:

LO 2-1   Understand how data are organized in an accounting information system.

LO 2-2   Understand how data are stored in a relational database.

LO 2-3   Explain and apply extraction, transformation, and loading (ETL) techniques.

---

[1]B. Resnick, "Researchers Just Released Profile Data on 70,000 OkCupid Users without Permission," 2016, http://www.vox.com/2016/5/12/11666116/70000-okcupid-users-data-release (accessed October 31, 2016).

As you learned in Chapter 1, Data Analytics is a process, and we follow an established data analytics model called the IMPACT cycle as introduced in Chapter 1.[2] The IMPACT cycle begins with identifying business questions and problems that can be, at least partially, addressed with data (the "I" in the IMPACT model). Once the opportunity or problem has been identified, the next step is **mastering the data** (the "M" in the IMPACT model), which requires you to identify and obtain the data needed for solving the problem. Mastering the data requires a firm understanding of what data are available to you and where they are stored, as well as being skilled in the process of extracting, transforming, and loading (ETL) the data in preparation for data analysis. While the extraction piece of the ETL process may often be completed by the information systems team or the database administrator, it is also possible that you will have access to raw data that you will need to extract out of the source database. Both methods of requesting data for extraction and of extracting data yourself are covered in this chapter. The mastering the data step can be described via the ETL process. The ETL process is made up of the following five steps:

Step 1   Determine the purpose and scope of the data request (extract).
Step 2   Obtain the data (extract).
Step 3   Validate the data for completeness and integrity (transform).
Step 4   Sanitize the data (transform).
Step 5   Load the data in preparation for data analysis (load).

This chapter will provide details for each of these five steps.

HOW DATA ARE USED AND STORED IN THE ACCOUNTING CYCLE

LO 2-1

Understand how data are organized in an accounting information system.

Before you can identify and obtain the data, you must have a comfortable grasp on what data are available to you and where such data are stored. A basic understanding of accounting processes and its associated data, how those data are organized, and why the data was captured, can help you request the right data and facilitate that request so that you know exactly where each piece of data is held.

Accounting data can be presented in many formats. When you think of accounting data, you might think of financial statements, budgets, and managerial reports regarding point-of-sale, cost, supply chain, or customer relationship management data. All of these reports are the result of compiling data into a structured format that is ready for consumption. Financial statements get placed online or mailed out to investors, budgets get approved and managed, and managerial reports are sent to decision-makers to monitor progress. However, each of these documents originated with data in its rawest form. Sometimes you will be required to make decisions or perform analysis based on these formalized documents, but when you are performing data analysis, it is always preferable to receive data in its rawest form (not aggregated or organized with subheadings) so that you have more flexibility with your analysis and so there is no question about what the data represents. Because of that preference, in this chapter, we will focus on how raw data is stored so that you can learn how to access that data for your data analysis projects.

Even with the focus on raw data and where it is stored, there is variety in how data can be stored. Most commonly, data is stored in either flat files or a database. For many of our examples and hands-on activities in this text, we will transform our data that is stored in a database into a flat file. The most common example of a flat file that you are

---

[2]J. P. Isson and J. S. Harriott, *Win with Advanced Business Analytics: Creating Business Value from Your Data* (Hoboken, NJ: Wiley, 2013).

likely used to is a range of data in an Excel spreadsheet. Put simply, a flat file is a means of maintaining all of the data you need in one place. We can do a lot of incredible data analysis and number crunching in flat files in Excel, but as far as storing our data, it is generally inefficient to store all of the data that you need for a given business process all in one place. Instead, a relational database is frequently used for data storage because it is more capable of ensuring data integrity and maintaining "one version of the truth" across multiple processes. There are a variety of applications that support relational databases (these are referred to as Relational Database Management Systems or RDBMS). We cover three different RDBMS in this textbook: Microsoft Access, SQLite, and Microsoft SQL Server.

- **Microsoft Access:** for any user of Microsoft products (Word, Excel, PowerPoint, etc.) the navigation of Microsoft Access is familiar, so it is a relatively easy entry point for working with relational databases. It is a great entry tool to learn how tables are related via primary and foreign keys because entire databases can be built via a graphical user interface instead of having to use SQL statements to create tables and relationships. The usage of Microsoft Access throughout the textbook is meant to provide an entry-level view into data management and the structure of a relational database, as well as a good starting point for writing SQL queries to extract data.
- **SQLite:** SQLite is an open-source solution to data management. For a user that is at least somewhat familiar with relational database management, it is a friendly tool, and presents an intuitive interface for writing SQL statements. The usage of SQLite throughout the textbook is meant to provide an open-source alternative to Microsoft Access. It also provides a good starting point for writing SQL queries to extract data.
- **Microsoft SQL Server:** Microsoft SQL Server can support enterprise-level data in ways that smaller RDBMS programs, such as Access and SQLite, cannot. While both Microsoft Access and SQLite can be (and are) used in professional settings, the usage of SQL Server throughout the textbook is meant to provide experience that replicates working with much larger and more complex datasets that you will likely experience in the professional world.

There are many other examples of relational database management systems, including Teradata, MySql, Oracle RDBMS, IBM DB2, Amazon RDS, and PostGreSQL.

Regardless of the DBMS, relational databases have principles that guide how they are modeled.

Exhibit 2-1, a simplified version of a Unified Modeling Language (UML) class diagram, is an illustration or a drawing of the tables and their relationships to each other (i.e., a database schema). Relational databases are discussed in greater depth in Learning Objective 2-2.

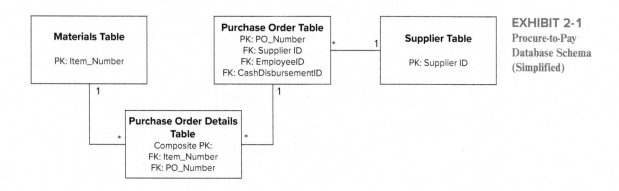

EXHIBIT 2-1
Procure-to-Pay
Database Schema
(Simplified)

LO 2-2

Understand how data are stored in a relational database.

DATA AND RELATIONSHIPS IN A RELATIONAL DATABASE

In this text, we will work with data in a variety of forms, but regardless of the tool we use to analyze data, structured data should be stored in a normalized **relational database**. There are occasions for working with data directly in the relational database, but many times when we work with data analysis, we'll prefer to export the data from the relational database and view it in a more user-friendly form. The benefit of storing data in a normalized database outweighs the downside of having to export, validate, and sanitize the data every time you need to analyze the information.

Storing data in a normalized, relational database instead of a **flat file** ensures that data are complete, not redundant, and that business rules and internal controls are enforced; it also aids communication and integration across business processes. Each one of these benefits is detailed here:

- *Completeness.* Ensures that all data required for a business process are included in the dataset.
- *No redundancy.* Storing redundant data is to be avoided for several reasons: It takes up unnecessary space (which is expensive), it takes up unnecessary processing to run reports to ensure that there aren't multiple versions of the truth, and it increases the risk of data-entry errors. Storing data in flat files yields a great deal of redundancy, but normalized relational databases require there to be one version of the truth and for each element of data to be stored in only one place.
- *Business rules are enforced.* As will become increasingly evident as we progress through the material in this text, relational databases can be designed to aid in the placement and enforcement of internal controls and business rules in ways that flat files cannot.
- *Communication and integration of business processes.* Relational databases should be designed to support business processes across the organization, which results in improved communication across functional areas and more integrated business processes.[3]

It is valuable to spend some time basking in the benefits of storing data in a relational database because it is not necessarily easier to do so when it comes to building the data model or understanding the structure. It is arguably more complex to normalize your data than it is to throw redundant data without business rules or internal controls into a spreadsheet.

Columns in a Table: Primary Keys, Foreign Keys, and Descriptive Attributes

When requesting data, it is critical to understand how the tables in a relational database are related. This is a brief overview of the different types of attributes in a table and how these attributes support the relationships between tables. It is certainly not a comprehensive take on relational data modeling, but it should be adequate in preparing you for creating data requests.

Every column in a table must be both unique and relevant to the purpose of the table. There are three types of columns: primary keys, foreign keys, and descriptive attributes.

Each table must have a **primary key**. The primary key is typically made up of one column. The purpose of the primary key is to ensure that each row in the table is unique, so it is often referred to as a "unique identifier." It is rarely truly descriptive; instead, a collection of letters or simply sequential numbers are often used. As a student, you are probably

[3]G. C. Simsion and G. C. Witt, *Data Modeling Essentials* (Amsterdam: Morgan Kaufmann, 2005).

already very familiar with your unique identifier—your student ID number at the university is the way you as a student are stored as a unique record in the university's data model! Other examples of unique identifiers that you are familiar with would be check numbers and driver's license numbers.

One of the biggest differences between a flat file and a relational database is simply how many tables there are—when you request your data into a flat file, you'll receive one big table with a lot of redundancy. While this is often ideal for analyzing data, when the data are stored in the database, each group of information is stored in a separate table. Then, the tables that are related to one another are identified (e.g., Supplier and Purchase Order are related; it's important to know which Supplier the Purchase Order is from). The relationship is created by placing a **foreign key** in one of the two tables that are related. The foreign key is another type of attribute, and its function is to create the relationship between two tables. Whenever two tables are related, one of those tables must contain a foreign key to create the relationship.

The other columns in a table are **descriptive attributes**. For example, Supplier Name is a critical piece of data when it comes to understanding the business process, but it is not necessary to build the data model. Primary and foreign keys facilitate the structure of a relational database, and the descriptive attributes provide actual business information.

Refer to Exhibit 2-1, the database schema for a typical procure-to-pay process. Each table has an attribute with the letters "PK" next to them—these are the primary keys for each table. The primary key for the Materials Table is "Item_No.," the primary key for the Purchase Order Table is "PO_Number.," and so on. Several of the tables also have attributes with the letters "FK" next to them—these are the foreign keys that create the relationship between pairs of tables. For example, look at the relationship between the Supplier Table and the Purchase Order Table. The primary key in the Supplier Table is "SupplierID." The line between the two tables links the primary key to a foreign key in the Purchase Order Table, also named "SupplierID."

The Line Items Table in Table 2-1 has so much detail in it that it requires two attributes to combine as a primary key. This is a special case of a primary key often referred to as a **composite primary key**, in which the two foreign keys from the tables that it is linking combine to make up a unique identifier. The theory and details that support the necessity of this linking table are beyond the scope of this text—if you can identify the primary and foreign keys, you'll be able to identify the data that you need to request. Table 2-2 shows a subset of the data that are represented by the Purchase Order table. You can see that each of the attributes listed in the class diagram appears as a column, and the data for each purchase order are accounted for in the rows.

Purchase Order Detail		
PO_Number	Item_Number	Quantity Purchased
1787	10	50
1787	25	50
1789	5	30
1790	5	100

TABLE 2-1
Line Items Table: Purchase Order Detail Table

Purchase Order Table						
PO_Number	Date	Created By	Approved By	Supplier ID	Employee ID	CashDisbursement ID
1787	11/1/2020	1001	1010	1	52	2001
1788	11/1/2020	1005	1010	2	52	2003
1789	11/8/2020	1002	1010	1	52	2004
1790	11/15/2020	1005	1010	1	52	2004

TABLE 2-2
Purchase Order Table

⊘ **PROGRESS CHECK**

1. Referring to Exhibit 2-1, locate the relationship between the Supplier and Purchase Order tables. What is the unique identifier of each table? (The unique identifier attribute is called the primary key—more on how it's determined in the next learning objective.) Which table contains the attribute that creates the relationship? (This attribute is called the foreign key—more on how it's determined in the next learning objective.)

2. Referring to Exhibit 2-1, review the attributes in the Purchase Order table. There are two foreign keys listed in this table that do not relate to any of the tables in the diagram. Which tables do you think they are? What type of data would be stored in those two tables?

3. Refer to the two tables that you identified in Progress Check 2 above that would relate to the Purchase Order table, but are not pictured in this diagram. Draw a sketch of what the UML Class Diagram would look like if those tables were included. Draw the two classes to represent the two tables (i.e., rectangles), the relationships that should exist, and identify the Primary Keys for the two new tables.

DATA DICTIONARIES

In the previous section, you learned about how data are stored by focusing on the procure-to-pay database schema. Viewing schemas and processes in isolation clarifies each individual process, but it can also distort reality—these schemas typically do not represent their own separate databases. Rather, each process-specific database schema is a piece of a greater whole, all combining to form one integrated database.

As you can imagine, once these processes come together to be supported in one database, the amount of data can be massive. Understanding the processes and the basics of how data are stored is critical, but even with a sound foundation, it would be nearly impossible for an individual to remember where each piece of data is stored, or what each piece of data represents.

Creating and using a **data dictionary** is paramount in helping database administrators maintain databases and analysts identify the data they need to use. In Chapter 1, you were introduced to the data dictionary for the LendingClub. The same cut-out of the LendingClub data dictionary is provided in Exhibit 2-2 as a reminder.

Because the LendingClub data are provided in a flat file, the only two attributes necessary to describe the data are the attribute name (e.g., Amount Requested) and a description of that attribute. The description ensures that the data in each attribute are used and analyzed in the appropriate way—it's always important to remember that technology will do exactly what you tell it to, so you must be smarter than the computer! If you run analysis on an attribute thinking it means one thing, when it actually means another, you could make some big mistakes and bad decisions even when you're working with great data. It's critical to get to know the data through database schemas and data dictionaries thoroughly before attempting to do any data analysis.

When you are working with data stored in a relational database, you will have more attributes to keep track of in the data dictionary. Table 2-3 provides an example of a data dictionary for a generic Supplier table:

RejectStats File	Description
Amount Requested	Total requested loan amount
Application Date	Date of borrower application
Loan Title	Loan title
Risk_Score	Borrower risk (FICO) score
Dept-To-Income Ratio	Ratio of borrower total monthly debt payments divided by monthly income.
Zip Code	The first 3 numbers of the borrower zip code provided from loan application.
State	Two digit State Abbreviation provided from loan application.
Employment Length	Employment length in years, where 0 is less than 1 and 10 is greater than 10.
Policy Code	policy_code=1 if publicly available. policy_code=2 if not publicly available

EXHIBIT 2-2
2007–2012 LendingClub Data Dictionary for Declined Load Data

Source: Accessed March, 2019. Available at https://www.lendingclub.com/info/download-data.action

Primary or Foreign Key?	Required	Attribute Name	Description	Data Type	Default Value	Field Size	Notes
PK	Y	Supplier ID	Unique Identifier for Each Supplier	Number	n/a	10	
	N	Supplier Name	Official Name of Supplier	Short Text	n/a	30	
FK	N	Supplier Type	Type Code for Different Supplier Categories	Number	Null	10	1: Vendor 2: Misc

TABLE 2-3 Supplier Data Dictionary

PROGRESS CHECK

4. What is the purpose of the primary key? A foreign key? A nonkey (descriptive) attribute?
5. How do data dictionaries help you understand the data from a database or flat file?

EXTRACT, TRANSFORM, AND LOAD (ETL) THE DATA

LO 2-3

Explain and apply extraction, transformation, and loading (ETL) techniques.

Once you have familiarized yourself with the data via data dictionaries and schemas, you are prepared to request the data from the database manager or extract the data yourself. The ETL process begins with identifying which data you need and is complete when the clean data are loaded in the appropriate format into the tool to be used for analysis.

This process involves:

1. Determining the purpose and scope of the data request.
2. Obtaining the data.

3. Validating the data for completeness and integrity.
4. Cleaning the data.
5. Loading the data for analysis.

Extract

Determine exactly what data you need in order to answer your business questions. Requesting data is often an iterative practice, but the more prepared you are when requesting data, the more time you will save for yourself and the database team in the long run.

Requesting the data involves the first two steps of the ETL extraction process. Each step has questions associated with it that you should try to answer.

Step 1: Determine the Purpose and Scope of the Data Request

- What is the purpose of the data request? What do you need the data to solve? What business problem will they address?
- What risk exists in data integrity (e.g., reliability, usefulness)? What is the mitigation plan?
- What other information will impact the nature, timing, and extent of the data analysis?

Once the purpose of the data request is determined and scoped, as well as any risks and assumptions documented, the next step is to determine whom to ask and specifically what is needed, what format is needed (Excel, PDF, database), and by what deadline.

Step 2: Obtain the Data

- How will data be requested and/or obtained? Do you have access to the data yourself, or do you need to request a database administrator or the information systems department to provide the data for you?
- If you need to request the data, is there a standard data request form that you should use? From whom do you request the data?
- Where are the data located in the financial or other related systems?
- What specific data are needed (tables and fields)?
- What tools will be used to perform data analytic tests or procedures and why?

Obtaining the Data via a Data Request

Determining not only what data are needed, but also which tool will be used to test and process the data will aid the database administrator in providing the data to you in the most accessible format.

It is also necessary to specify the format in which you would like to receive the data; it is often preferred to receive data in a flat file (i.e., if the data you requested reside in multiple tables or different databases, they should be combined into one file without any hierarchy or relationships built in), with the first row containing column headings (names of the fields requested), and each subsequent row containing data that correspond with the column headings. Subtotals, breaks, and subheadings complicate data cleaning and should not be included.[4] When you receive the data, make sure that you understand the data in each column; the data dictionary should prove extremely helpful for this. If a data dictionary is unavailable, then you should plan to meet with database users to get a clear understanding of the data in each column.

[4]T. Singleton, "What Every IT Auditor Should Know about Data Analytics," n.d., from http://www.isaca.org/Journal/archives/2013/Volume-6/Pages/What-Every-IT-Auditor-Should-Know-About-Data-Analytics.aspx#2.

In a later chapter, you will be provided a deep dive into the Audit Data Standards (ADS) developed by the American Institute of Certified Public Accountants (AICPA).[5] The aim of the ADS is to alleviate some of the headaches associated with requesting data for audits by providing a guide to standardize audit data requests and the format in which the data are provided from the company being audited to the auditor. These include the following:

1. Order-to-Cash subledger standards
2. Procure-to-Pay subledger standards
3. Inventory subledger standards
4. General Ledger standards

While the ADSs provide an opportunity for standardization, they are voluntary. Regardless of whether your request for data will conform to the standards, a **data request form** template can make communication easier between data requester and provider.

Example Standard Data Request Form:

Requester Name:	
Requester Contact Number:	
Requester Email Address:	
Please provide a description of the information needed (indicate which tables and which fields you require):	
What will the information be used for?	
Frequency (circle one)	One-Off Annually Termly Other:_____
Format you wish the data to be delivered in (circle one):	Spreadsheet Text File Word Document Other: _____
Request Date:	
Required Date:	
Intended Audience:	
Customer (if not requester):	

Once the data are received, you can move on to the transformation phase of the ETL process. The next step is to ensure that the data that have been extracted are complete and correct.

[5]For a description of the audit data standards, please see this website: https://www.aicpa.org/interestareas/frc/assuranceadvisoryservices/pages/assuranceandadvisory.aspx.

Obtaining the Data Yourself

At times, you will have direct access to a database or information system that holds all or some of the data you need. In this case, you may not need to go through a formal data request process, and you can simply extract the data yourself.

After identifying the goal of the data analysis project in the first step of the IMPACT cycle, you can follow a similar process to how you would request the data if you are going to extract it yourself:

1. Identify the tables that contain the information you need. You can do this by looking through the data dictionary or the relationship model.
2. Identify which attributes, specifically, hold the information you need in each table.
3. Identify how those tables are related to each other.

Once you have identified the data you need, you can start gathering the information. There are a variety of methods that you could take to retrieve the data. Two will be explained briefly here—SQL and Excel—and there is a deep dive into SQL in appendices D and H, as well as a deep dive into Excel's VLookup in appendix C.

SQL: "Structured Query Language" (SQL, often pronounced sequel) is a computer language that can be used to create, update, and delete records and tables in relational databases, but in Data Analysis, the focus is on extracting data—that is, to select the precise attributes and records that fit the criteria of our data analysis goal. Using SQL, we can combine data from one or more tables and organize the data in a way that is more intuitive and useful for data analysis than the way the data is stored in the relational database. A firm understanding of the data—the tables, how they are related, and their respective primary and foreign keys—is integral to extracting the data.

Typically, data should be stored in the database and analyzed in another tool such as Excel, IDEA, or Tableau. However, you can choose to extract only the portion of the data that you wish to analyze via SQL instead of extracting full tables and transforming the data in Excel, IDEA, or Tableau. This is especially preferable when the raw data stored in the database is large enough to overwhelm Excel. Excel 2016 can only hold 1,048,576 rows on one spreadsheet. When you attempt to bring in full tables that exceed that amount, even when you use Excel's powerful Power BI tools, it will slow down your analysis if the full table isn't necessary.

There is more description about writing queries and a chance to practice creating joins in Appendix H.

Excel: When your data are not stored in a relational database, if you want to do exploratory analysis (more on this in a later chapter) or if the tables you wish to extract aren't too large for Excel, the tables that contain the data you need can be extracted in whole into Excel and worked with directly in a spreadsheet. The advantage of this is that further analysis will almost certainly be done in Excel, so it could be beneficial to have all the data readily available for further questions to drill down into once the initial question is answered. Understanding the primary key and foreign key relationships is also integral to working with the data directly in Excel.

When your data are stored directly in Excel, you can also use Excel functions and formulas to combine data from multiple Excel tables into one table, similar to how you can join data with SQL in Access or another relational database. One of Excel's most useful tools for looking up data from two separate tables and matching them based on a matching primary key/foreign key relationship is the VLookup function. There are a variety of ways that the VLookup function can be used, but for extracting and transforming data it is best used to add a column to a table.

More information about creating VLookup functions in Excel is provided in Appendix C.

The question of whether to use SQL or Excel's tools (such as VLookup) is primarily answered by where the data are stored. Since data are most frequently stored in a relational database (as discussed earlier in this chapter, due to the efficiency and data integrity benefits relational databases provide), SQL will often be the best option for retrieving data, after which that data can be loaded into Excel or another tool for further analysis. Another benefit of SQL queries is that they can be saved and reproduced at will or at regular intervals. Having a saved SQL query can make it much easier and more efficient to re-create data requests. However, if the data is already stored in a flat file in Excel, there is little reason to use SQL. Sometimes when you are performing exploratory analysis, even if the data are stored in a relational database, it can be beneficial to load entire tables into Excel and bypass the SQL step - this should be considered carefully before doing so, though, because relational databases handle large amounts of data much better than Excel can. Writing SQL queries can also make it easier to load only the data you need to analyze into Excel so that you do not overwhelm Excel's resources

Transform

Step 3: Validating the Data for Completeness and Integrity

Any time data is moved from one location to another, it is possible that some of the data could have been lost during the extraction. It is critical to ensure that the extracted data are complete (that the data you wish to analyze were extracted fully) and that the integrity of the data remains (that none of the data have been manipulated or tampered with during the extraction). Being able to validate the data successfully requires you to not only have the technical skills to perform the task, but also to know your data well. If you know what to reasonably expect from the data in the extraction (How many records should have been extracted? What are some checksums you can rely on to ensure the data is complete and hasn't been tampered with?), then you have a higher likelihood of identifying errors or issues from the extraction. The following four steps should be completed to validate the data after extraction:

1. *Compare the number of records* that were extracted to the number of records in the source database. This will give you a quick snapshot into whether any data were skipped or didn't extract properly due to an error or datatype mismatch. This is a critical first step, but it will not provide information about the data themselves other than ensuring that the record counts match.
2. *Compare descriptive statistics for numeric fields:* Calculating the minimums, maximums, averages, and medians will help ensure that the numeric data were extracted completely.
3. *Validate Date/Time fields* in the same way as numeric fields by converting the datatype to numeric and running descriptive statistic comparisons.
4. *Compare string limits for text fields:* Text fields are unlikely to cause an issue if you extracted your data into Excel because Excel allows a generous maximum character number (for example, Excel 2016 allows 32,767 characters per cell). However, if you extracted your data into a tool that does limit the number of characters in a string, you will want to compare these limits to the source database's limits per field to ensure that you haven't cut off any characters.

If an error is found, depending on the size of the dataset, you may be able to easily find the missing or erroneous data by scanning the information with your eyes. However, if the dataset is large, or if the error is difficult to find, it may be easiest to go back to the extraction and examine how the data were extracted, fix any errors in the SQL code, and re-run the extraction.

Step 4: Cleaning the Data

After validating the data, you should pay close attention to the state of the data and clean it as necessary to improve the quality of the data and subsequent analysis. The following four items are some of the more common ways that data will need to be cleaned after extraction and validation:

1. *Remove headings or subtotals:* Depending on the extraction technique used and the file type of the extraction, it is possible that your data could contain headings or subtotals that are not useful for analysis. Of course, these issues could be overcome in the extraction steps of the ETL process if you are careful to request the data in the correct format or to only extract exactly the data you need.
2. *Clean leading zeroes and nonprintable characters:* Sometimes data will contain leading zeroes or "phantom" (nonprintable) characters. This will happen particularly when numbers or dates were stored as text in the source database but need to be analyzed as numbers. Nonprintable characters can be white spaces, page breaks, line breaks, tabs, etc., and can be summarized as characters that our human eyes can't see, but that the computer interprets as a part of the string. These can cause trouble when joining data because, while two strings may look identical to our eyes, the computer will read the nonprintable characters and will not find a match.
3. *Format negative numbers:* If there are negative numbers in your dataset, ensure that the formatting will work for your analysis. For example, if your data contain negative numbers formatted in parentheses and you would prefer this formatting to be as a negative sign, this needs to be corrected and consistent.
4. *Correct inconsistencies across data, in general:* If the source database did not enforce certain rules around data entry, it is possible that there are inconsistencies across the data—for example, if there is a state field, Arkansas could be formatted as "AR," "Ark," "Ar.," etc. These will need to be replaced with a common value before you begin your analysis if you are interested in grouping data geographically.

A Note about Data Quality

As you prepare your data for analysis, you should pay close attention to the quality of the data. Incorrect or invalid data can skew your results and lead to inaccurate conclusions. Low-quality data contain numerous errors, obsolete or incorrect data, or invalid data.

Here are five main data quality issues to pay attention to when you analyze a dataset for the first time:

1. *Dates:* The most common problems revolve around the date format because there are so many different ways a date can be presented. For example, look at the different ways you can show July 6, 2022: 6-Jul-2022; 6.7.2022; 44018 (in Excel); 07/06/2022 (in the United States); 06/07/2022 (in Europe); and the list goes on. You need to format the date to match the acceptable format for your tool. The ISO 8601 standard indicates you should format dates in the year-month-day format or 2022-07-06 and most professional query tools accept this format. If you use Excel to transform dates to this format, highlight your dates and go to Home > Number > Format Cells and choose Custom. Then type in YYYY-MM-DD and click OK.
2. *Numbers:* Numbers can be misinterpreted, particularly if they are manually entered. For example, 1 or I; 0 or O; 3 or E; 7 or seven. Watch for invalid number formats when

Format Cells Window in Excel

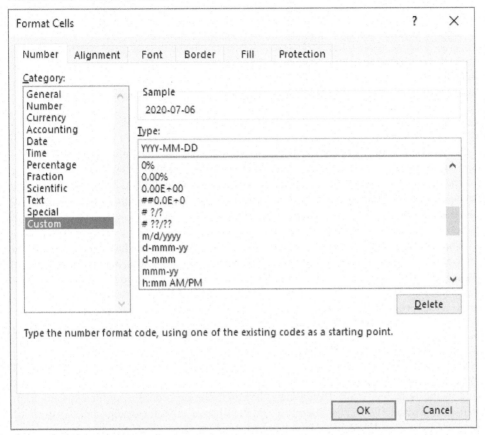

Source: Microsoft Excel, 2016.

you start sorting and analyzing your date then go back and correct them. Additionally, accounting artifacts such as dollar signs, commas, parenthesis are pervasive in spreadsheet data (e.g. $12,345.22 or (1,422.53)). As you clean the data remove any extra accounting characters so numbers appear in their raw form (e.g. 12345.22 or -1422.53).

3. *International characters and encoding:* When you work with data that spans multiple countries it is likely that you will come across accent marks or special characters, such as accent marks (á or À), umlats (Ü), invisible computer characters (TAB, RETURN, linebreak, null), or special characters that are used in query and scripting languages (*, #, ", '). In many cases, these can be corrected with a find and replace or contained in quote marks so they are ignored by the query language. Additionally, while most modern computer programs use UNICODE as the text encoding language, older databases will generate data in the ASCII format. If your tool fails to populate your dataset accurately, having international characters and symbols is likely to be a cause.

4. *Languages and measures:* Similar to international characters, data elements may contain a variety of words or measures that have the same meaning. For example, cheese or fromage; ketchup or catsup; pounds or lbs; $ or €; Arkansas or AR. In order to properly analyze the comparable data, you'll need to translate them into a common format by choosing one word as the standard and replacing the equivalent words. Also make sure the measure doesn't change the meaning. The total value in U.S. dollars is not the same thing as the total value in euros. Make sure you're comparing apples to apples or euros to euros.

5. *Human error:* Whenever there is manual input into the data, there is a high probability that data will be bad simply because it was mistyped or entered into the wrong place. There's no hard and fast rule for dealing with input errors other than being vigilant and making corrections (e.g., find and replace) when they occur.

Load

Step 5: Loading the Data for Data Analysis

If the extraction and transformation steps have been done well by the time you reach this step, the loading part of the ETL process should be the simplest step. It is so simple, in fact, that if your goal is to do your analysis in Excel and you have already transformed and cleaned your data in Excel, you are finished. There should be no additional loading necessary.

However, it is possible that Excel is not the last step for analysis. The data analysis technique you plan to implement, the subject matter of the business questions you intend to answer, and the way in which you wish to communicate results will all drive the choice of which tool you use to perform your analysis.

Throughout the text, you will be introduced to a variety of different tools to use for analyzing data beyond Access and Excel. These will include Tableau, Weka, and IDEA. As these tools are introduced to you, you will learn how to load data into them.

ETL or ELT?

If loading the data into Excel is indeed the last step, are you actually "extracting, transforming, and loading," or is it "extracting, loading, and transforming?"

The term *ETL* has been in popular use since the 1970s, and even though methods for extracting and transforming data have gotten easier to use, more accessible, as well as more robust, the term has stuck. Increasingly, however, the procedure is shifting toward ELT. Particularly with tools such as Microsoft's Power BI suite, all of the loading and transforming can be done within Excel, with data directly loaded into Excel from the database, and then transformed (also within Excel). The most common method for mastering the data that we use throughout this textbook is more in line with ELT than ETL; however, even when the order changes from ETL to ELT, it is still more common to refer to the procedure as ETL.

 PROGRESS CHECK

6. Describe two different methods for obtaining data for analysis.
7. What are five common data quality issues that must be fixed before analysis can take place?

Summary

- The first step in the IMPACT cycle is to identify the questions that you intend to answer through your data analysis project. Once a data analysis problem or question has been identified, the next step in the IMPACT cycle is mastering the data, which can be broken down to mean obtaining the data needed and preparing it for analysis.

- In order to obtain the right data, it is important to have a firm grasp of what data are available to you and how that information is stored.
  - Data are often stored in a relational database, which helps to ensure that an organization's data are complete and to avoid redundancy. Relational databases are made up of tables with uniquely identified records (this is done through primary keys) and are related through the usage of foreign keys.
- To obtain the data, you will either have access to extract the data yourself or you will need to request the data from a database administrator or the information systems team. If the latter is the case, you will complete a data request form, indicating exactly which data you need and why.
- Once you have the data, they will need to be validated for completeness and integrity—that is, you will need to ensure that all of the data you need were extracted and that all data are correct. Sometimes when data are extracted, some formatting or sometimes even entire records will get lost, resulting in inaccuracies. Correcting the errors and cleaning the data is an integral step in mastering the data.
- Finally, after the data have been cleaned, there may be one last step of mastering the data, which is to load them into the tool that will be used for analysis. Often, the cleaning and correcting of data occur in Excel and the analysis will also be done in Excel. In this case, there is no need to load the data elsewhere. However, if you intend to do more rigorous statistical analysis than Excel provides, or if you intend to do more robust data visualization than can be done in Excel, it may be necessary to load the data into another tool following the transformation process.

Key Words

composite primary key (*43*)   A special case of a primary key that exists in linking tables. The composite primary key is made up of the two primary keys in the table that it is linking.

data dictionary (*44*)   Centralized repository of descriptions for all of the data attributes of a dataset.

data request form (*47*)   A method for obtaining data if you do not have access to obtain the data directly yourself.

descriptive attributes (*43*)   Attributes that exist in relational databases that are neither primary nor foreign keys. These attributes provide business information, but are not required to build a database. An example would be "Company Name" or "Employee Address."

ETL (*45*)   The extract, transform, and load process that is integral to mastering the data.

flat file (*41*)   A means of storing data in one place, such as in an Excel spreadsheet, as opposed to storing the data in multiple tables, such as in a relational database.

foreign key (*43*)   An attribute that exists in relational databases in order to carry out the relationship between two tables. This does not serve as the "unique identifier" for each record in a table. These must be identified when mastering the data from a relational database in order to extract the data correctly from more than one table.

mastering the data (*40*)   The second step in the IMPACT cycle; it involves identifying and obtaining the data needed for solving the data analysis problem, as well as cleaning and preparing the data for analysis.

primary key (*42*)   An attribute that is required to exist in each table of a relational database and serves as the "unique identifier" for each record in a table.

relational database (*41*)   A means of storing data in order to ensure that the data are complete, not redundant, and to help enforce business rules. Relational databases also aid in communication and integration of business processes across an organization.

✓ ANSWERS TO PROGRESS CHECKS

1. The unique identifier of the Supplier table is [Supplier ID], and the unique identifier of the Purchase Order table is [PO No.]. The Purchase Order table contains the foreign key.

2. The foreign key attributes in the Purchase Order table that do not relate to any tables in the view are EmployeeID and CashDisbursementID. These attributes probably relate to the Employee table (so that we can tell which employee was responsible for each Purchase Order) and the Cash Disbursement table (so that we can tell if the Purchase Orders have been paid for yet, and if so, on which check). The Employee table would be a complete listing of each Employee, as well containing the details about each employee (for example, phone number, address, etc.). The Cash Disbursement table would be a listing of the payments the company has made.

3.

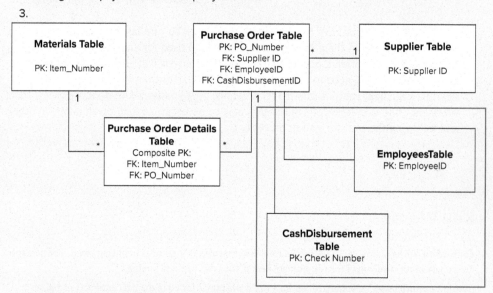

4. The purpose of the primary key is to uniquely identify each record in a table. The purpose of a foreign key is to create a relationship between two tables. The purpose of a descriptive attribute is to provide meaningful information about each record in a table. Descriptive attributes aren't required for a database to run, but they are necessary for people to gain business information about the data stored in their databases.

5. Data dictionaries provide descriptions of the function (e.g., Primary Key or Foreign Key when applicable), datatype, and field names associated with each column (attribute) of a database. Data dictionaries are especially important when databases contain several different tables and many different attributes in order to help analysts identify the information they need to perform their analysis.

6. Depending on the level of security afforded to a business analyst, she can either obtain data directly from the database herself or she can request the data. When obtaining data herself, the analyst must have access to the raw data in the database and a firm knowledge of SQL and data extraction techniques. When requesting the data, the analyst doesn't need the same level of extraction skills, but she still needs to be familiar with the data enough in order to identify which tables and attributes contain the information she requires.

7. Four common issues that must be fixed are removing headings or subtotals, cleaning leading zeroes or nonprintable characters, formatting negative numbers, and correcting inconsistencies across the data.

Multiple Choice Questions

1. Mastering the data can also be described via the ETL process. The ETL process stands for:
   a. extract, total, and load data.
   b. enter, transform, and load data.
   c. extract, transform, and load data.
   d. enter, total, and load data.

2. Which of the following describes part of the goal of the ETL process:
   a. identify which approach to data analytics should be used.
   b. load the data into a relational database for storage.
   c. communicate the results and insights found through the analysis.
   d. identify and obtain the data needed for solving the problem.

3. The advantages of storing data in a relational database include which of the following?
   a. Help in enforcing business rules
   b. Increased information redundancy
   c. Integrating business processes
   d. All of the above
   e. Only A and B
   f. Only B and C
   g. Only A and C

4. The purpose of transforming data is:
   a. to validate the data for completeness and integrity.
   b. to load the data into the appropriate tool for analysis.
   c. to obtain the data from the appropriate source.
   d. to identify which data are necessary to complete the analysis.

5. Which attribute is required to exist in each table of a relational database and serves as the "unique identifier" for each record in a table?
   a. Foreign key
   b. Unique identifier
   c. Primary key
   d. Key attribute

6. The metadata that describes each attribute in a database is which of the following?
   a. Composite primary key
   b. Data dictionary
   c. Descriptive attributes
   d. Flat file

7. As mentioned in the chapter, which of the following is *not* a common way that data will need to be cleaned after extraction and validation?
   a. Remove headings and subtotals.
   b. Format negative numbers.
   c. Clean up trailing zeroes.
   d. Correct inconsistencies across data.

8. Why is Supplier ID considered to be a primary key for a Supplier table?

   a. It contains a unique identifier for each supplier.

   b. It is a 10-digit number.

   c. It can either be for a vendor or miscellaneous provider.

   d. It is used to identify different supplier categories.

9. What are attributes that exist in a relational database that are neither primary nor foreign keys?

   a. Nondescript attributes

   b. Descriptive attributes

   c. Composite key

   d. Relational table attributes

10. Which of these is *not* included in the five steps of the ETL process?

    a. Determine the purpose and scope of the data request.

    b. Obtain the data.

    c. Validate the data for completeness and integrity.

    d. Scrub the data.

Discussion Questions

1. The advantages of a relational database include limiting the amount of redundant data that are stored in a database. Why is this an important advantage? What can go wrong when redundant data are stored?

2. The advantages of a relational database include integrating business processes. Why is it preferable to integrate business processes in one information system, rather than store different business process data in separate, isolated databases?

3. Even though it is preferable to store data in a relational database, storing data across separate tables can make data analysis cumbersome. Describe three reasons it is worth the trouble to store data in a relational database.

4. Among the advantages of using a relational database is enforcing business rules. Based on your understanding of how the structure of a relational database helps prevent data redundancy and other advantages, how does the primary key/foreign key relationship structure help enforce a business rule that indicates that a company shouldn't process any purchase orders from suppliers who don't exist in the database?

5. What is the purpose of a data dictionary? Identify four different attributes that could be stored in a data dictionary, and describe the purpose of each.

6. In the ETL process, the first step is extracting the data. When you are obtaining the data yourself, what are the steps to identifying the data that you need to extract?

7. In the ETL process, if the analyst does not have the security permissions to access the data directly, then he or she will need to fill out a data request form. While this doesn't necessarily require the analyst to know extraction techniques, why does the analyst still need to understand the raw data very well in order to complete the data request?

8. In the ETL process, when an analyst is completing the data request form, there are a number of fields that the analyst is required to complete. Why do you think it is important

for the analyst to indicate the frequency of the report? How do you think that would affect what the database administrator does in the extraction?

9. Regarding the data request form, why do you think it is important to the database administrator to know the purpose of the request? What would be the importance of the "To be used in" and "intended audience" fields?

10. In the ETL process, one important step to process when transforming the data is to work with NULL, N/A, and zero values in the dataset. If you have a field of quantitative data (e.g., number of years each individual in the table has held a full-time job), what would be the effect of the following?

    a. Transforming NULL and N/A values into blanks

    b. Transforming NULL and N/A values into zeroes

    c. Deleting records that have NULL and N/A values from your dataset

    (*Hint:* Think about the impact on different aggregate functions, such as COUNT and AVERAGE.)

Problems

The following problems correspond to the **College Scorecard** data. You should be able to answer each question by just looking at the data dictionary included in Appendix K, but if you would like to use the raw data, feel free to do so (CollegeScorecard_RawData.txt).

1. Which attributes from the College Scorecard data would you need to compare cost of attendance across types of institutions (public, private nonprofit, or private for-profit)?

2. Which attributes from the College Scorecard data would you need to compare SAT scores across types of institutions (public, private nonprofit, or private for-profit)?

3. Which attributes from the College Scorecard data would you need to compare levels of diversity across types of institutions (public, private nonprofit, or private for-profit)?

4. If you were conducting a data analysis in order to compare the percentage of students who receive federal loans at universities above and below the median cost of attendance across all institutions, your analysis would require several steps. One of the steps is to know what question needs to be answered first in order to complete the analysis. Come up with a set of questions that need to be answered.

5. If you were analyzing the levels of diversity across public and private institutions using the College Scorecard data, how would you define diversity in terms of the data provided? Would it be beneficial to combine attributes?

6. Which attributes from the College Scorecard data would you need to compare completion rate across types of institutions (public, private nonprofit, or private for-profit)?

7. Which attributes from the College Scorecard data would you need to compare the percentage of students who receive federal loans at universities above and below the median cost of attendance across all institutions (public, private nonprofit, or private for-profit)?

8. Which attributes from the College Scorecard data would you need to determine if different regions of the country have significantly different costs of attendance?

9. Use the College Scorecard data to determine if different regions of the country have significantly different costs of attendance (same as Problem 6) and fill out a data request form in order to extract the appropriate data. Use the template from the chapter as a guide.

One of the biggest challenges you face with data analysis is getting the right data. You may have the best questions in the world, but if there are no data available to support your hypothesis, you will have difficulty providing value. Additionally, there are instances in which the IT workers may be reluctant to share data with you. They may send incomplete data, the wrong data, or completely ignore your request. Be persistent, and you may have to look for creative ways to find insight with an incomplete picture.

Company summary

Sláinte is a fictional brewery that has recently gone through big changes. Sláinte sells six different products. The brewery has only recently expanded its business to distributing from one state to nine states, and now its business has begun stabilizing after the expansion. With that stability comes a need for better analysis. You have been hired by Sláinte to help management better understand the company's sales data and provide input for its strategic decisions.

Data

- Data request form

Technique

- No technical experience is necessary for this lab.

Software needed

- Word processor

In this lab, you will:

Part 1: Identify appropriate questions and develop a hypothesis for each question.
Part 2: Generate a request for data.
Part 3: Assess the data you receive.

Part 1: Identify the Questions

One of Sláinte's first priorities is to identify its areas of success as well as areas of potential improvement. Your manager has asked you to focus specifically on sales data at this point. This includes data related to sales orders, products, and customers.

Q1. Given that you are new and trying to get a grasp on Sláinte's operations, **list three questions related to sales** that would help you begin your analysis. For example, *how many products were sold in each state?*

Q2. Now **hypothesize the answers** to each of the questions. Remember, your answers don't have to be correct at this point. They will help you understand what type of data you are looking for. For example: *500 in Missouri, 6,000 in Pennsylvania, 4,000 in New York, etc.*

Q3. Finally, for each question, **identify the specific tables and attributes** that are needed to answer your questions. Use **Lab Exhibit 2-1A** for guidance on what tables and attributes are available. For example, to answer the question about state sales, you would need the [Customer_St] attribute that is located in the [Customer] master table as well as the [Sales_Order_Quantity_Sold] attribute in the [Sales] table. If you had access to store or distribution center location data, you may also look for a [State] field there, as well.

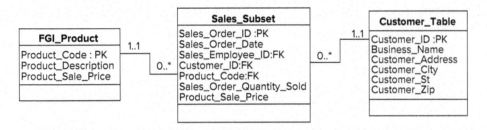

Part 2: Generate a Request for Data

Now that you've identified the data you need for your analysis, complete a data request form.

1. Open the **Data Request Form.**
2. Enter your **contact information.**
3. In the **description field,** identify the tables that you'd like to analyze, along with the time periods (e.g., past month, past year, etc.).
4. Select a **frequency.** In this case, this is a "One-off request."
5. Enter a **request date** (today) and a **required date** (one week from today).
6. Choose a **format** (spreadsheet).
7. Indicate **what the information will be used for** in the appropriate box (internal analysis).
8. Take a screenshot (label it 2-1A) **of your completed form.**

Part 3: Perform an Analysis of the Data

After a few days, Rachel, an IT worker, responds to your request. She gives you the following tables and attributes:

Sales_Subset Table	
Attribute	**Description of Attribute**
Sales_Order_ID (PK)	Unique identifier for each sales order
Sales_Order_Date	The date of the sales order, regardless of the date the order is entered
Sales_Employee_ID (FK)	Unique identifier (from Employee_Listing table) for person who created the record
Sales_Order_Quantity_Sold	Sales order line quantity
Product_Sale_Price	Sales order line price per unit

FGI_Product Table	
Attribute	**Description of Attribute**
Product_Code (PK)	Unique identifier for each product
Product_Description	Product description (plain English) to indicate the name or other identifying characteristics of the product
Product_Sale_Price	Price per unit of the associated product

You may notice that while there are a few attributes that may be useful in your sales analysis, the list may be incomplete and be missing several values. This is normal with data requests.

Q4. Take a moment and **identify any attributes that you are missing** from your original request that would be necessary to answer the question "How many products were sold in each state?"

Q5.   **Evaluate your original questions and responses.** Can you still answer the original questions that you identified in step 1?

Q6.   Is there another question you could answer from the data Rachel provided?

End of Lab

Lab 2-2 Use PivotTables to Denormalize and Analyze the Data

Efficient relational databases contain normalized data. That is, each table contains only data that are relevant to the object, and tables' relationships are defined with primary key/ foreign key pairs. For example, each record in a customer table is assigned a unique ID (e.g., customer 152883), and the remaining attributes (e.g., customer address) describe that customer. In a sales order table, the only customer data you find is a foreign key pointing to the customer (e.g., customer 152883) we are selling merchandise to. The foreign key value connects the sales order record to the customer record and allows any or all of the linked attributes to appear on the sales order form or report.

With Data Analytics, efficient databases are not as helpful. Rather, we would like to "denormalize" the data or combine all of the related data into one large file that can be easily evaluated for summary statistics or be used to create meaningful PivotTables. Excel calls this the Internal Data Model. In Access (or other relational databases, such as SQLite or SQL Server), we create a query. This lab will take you through this process. This lab will help you learn how to create relationships between related spreadsheets in Excel using Excel's Internal Data Model. The Internal Data Model is available in Excel for PC versions from 2013 onward, but the screenshots are all taken from Excel 2016. If you are using a different version of Excel, you may experience slightly different screens.

This lab will also help prepare you for using the Internal Data Model (alternative 2) in future labs to transform data, as well as to aid in understanding of primary and foreign key relationships.

Company summary

Sláinte is a fictional brewery that has recently gone through big changes. Sláinte sells six different products. The brewery has only recently expanded its business to distributing from one state to nine states, and now its business has begun stabilizing after the expansion. With that stability comes a need for better analysis. One of Sláinte's first priorities is to identify its areas of success, as well as areas of potential improvement.

Data

- Sláinte dataset

Technique

- Some experience with relational databases, spreadsheets, and PivotTables is useful for this lab. Relying on Appendix C about PivotTables might be helpful.
- Some experience with SQL is useful for this lab. Relying on Appendix D on SQL might be helpful.

Software needed

- Excel
- Access or SQLite
- Screen capture tool (Windows: Snipping Tool; Mac: Cmd + Shift + 4)

In this lab, you will:

Part 1: Identify appropriate questions and develop a hypothesis for each question.

Part 2: Master your data and prepare it for analysis in Excel.

- You will be presented with four different alternatives, the first of which is "to do nothing" to master the data. The following three alternatives present three different methods of ETL to create the same results.
- **Work through each ETL alternatives (2 through 4) to learn different methods of ETL and assess when you would prefer to use each.**
- **Alternatives 1 through 3 assume that the data is already stored in Excel.**
- **Alternative 4 assumes that the data is stored in a relational database. You can opt to use the Access database file or the SQLite file for this alternative.**

Part 3: Perform an analysis using PivotTables.

Part 4: Address and refine your results.

Part 5: Communicate your findings.

Part 1: Identify the Questions

Sláinte has brought you in to help determine potential areas for sales growth in the next year. Additionally, management has noticed that the company's margins aren't as high as they had budgeted and would like you to help identify some areas where they could improve their pricing, marketing, or strategy.

Specifically, they would like to know how many of each product were sold, the product's actual name (not just the product code), and the months in which different products were sold.

Q1. Given Sláinte's request, **identify the data attributes and tables** needed to answer the question. You can rely on Lab Exhibit 2-2A to help answer this question.

Part 2: Master the Data: Prepare Data for Analysis in Excel

The requested Sláinte data are available in the Slainte_Subset.xlsx file and include the following tables and fields, presented in a UML diagram:

LAB EXHIBIT 2-2A

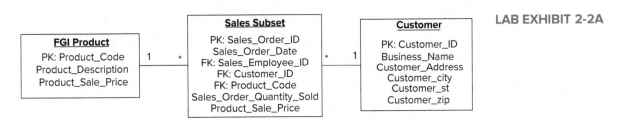

Depending on your desired analysis, there are a few alternative approaches for ETL that you could use to prepare the data for analysis:

1. Do nothing.
2. Use the Excel Internal Data Model.
3. Merge the data into a single table using Excel Query Editor.

We will work through each alternative throughout this lab to expose you to different methods of ETL.

Alternative 1 (data stored in Excel): Do nothing

If you are simply trying to calculate statistics or make comparisons using attributes within a *single table,* there is no need to transform the tables. Simply load the table, make sure the data are clean, and proceed to analysis.

For example, to find the total number of each item sold, you would need only the [Sales_Subset] table and its attributes [Product_Code] and [Sales_Order_Quantity_Sold].

> Q2. List two other questions that could be answered using only a single table from the Slainte dataset.

Alternative 2 (data stored in Excel): Use the Excel Internal Data Model

For analyses that require *two or more tables,* you need to define the relationships between the tables before you can proceed with your analysis.

With the Excel's Internal Data Model, you can create these relationships directly within Excel.

For example, if you want to find the total number of each item sold and show the product name instead of just the code, you would need [Sales_Order_Quantity_Sold] from the [Sales_Subset] table and [Product_Description] from the [FGI_Product] table. These two tables are joined together on the [Product_Code] primary/foreign key.

1. Open the **Slainte_Subset.xlsx** file.
2. Click the **Data** tab on the ribbon.
3. Click the **Relationships** button in the **Data Tools** section.
4. In the **Manage Relationships** window, click **New. . .**
5. Create a relationship between [Sales_Subset] and [FGI_Product] as shown in Exhibit 2-2B. Start with the table that contains the foreign key, then choose the related table that contains the primary key. In this case:
   a. Table: [Sales_Subset]
   b. Related Table: [FGI_Product]
   c. Column (Foreign): [Product_Code]
   d. Related Column (Primary): [Product_Code]

LAB EXHIBIT 2-2B
Define the Primary
Key/Foreign Key
Relationships in Excel

Source: Microsoft Excel,
2016.

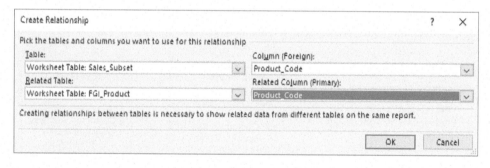

6. Click **OK** to save the relationship. The window will close, and you will return to the **Manage Relationships** window. Click **New. . .**
7. Now create a relationship between [Sales_Subset] and [Customer]. In this case:
   a. **Table:** [Sales_Subset]
   b. **Related Table:** [Customer]
   c. **Column (Foreign):** [Customer_ID]
   d. **Related Column (Primary):** [Customer_ID]
8. Click **OK** to save the relationship.
9. Take a screenshot (label it 2-2A) of the **Manage Relationships** window with both relationships created.

10. Click **Close** in the **Manage Relationships** window to return to the spreadsheets. While the spreadsheets do not appear to have changed with the new relationships, we have created a powerful engine for analyzing our data. We will have access to any of the records and related fields in any of the tables without additional work, such as Find and Replace or VLookup.
11. Save your workbook as **Slainte_Relationships.xlsx.**

This spreadsheet is now ready for analysis. But before we analyze the data, work through Alternative 3 to learn a different method of ETL.

Q3. How comfortable are you with identifying primary key/foreign key relationships?

Alternative 3 (data stored in Excel): Merge the data into a single table using Excel Query Editor

While relationships are incredibly useful when dealing with multiple tables, there are times when it is useful to combine all of the data together in one table. Both queries and PivotTables can be more straightforward when you don't have to continually define the relationships. The downside to working with a single table is that you must work with a larger file size and there are a lot of redundant data.

1. Create a **new blank spreadsheet** in Excel.
2. Click the **Data** tab on the ribbon.
3. Click the **New Query** button in the **Get & Transform Data** section.
   - This button is named **Get Data** in Excel 365.
4. Choose **From File > From Workbook.**
5. Locate the **Slainte_Subset.xlsx** file on your computer, and click **Import.**
6. In the **Navigator,** check **Select multiple items,** then check the three tables to import, shown in Exhibit 2-2C:
   a. [Customer]
   b. [FGI_Product]
   c. [Sales_Subset]

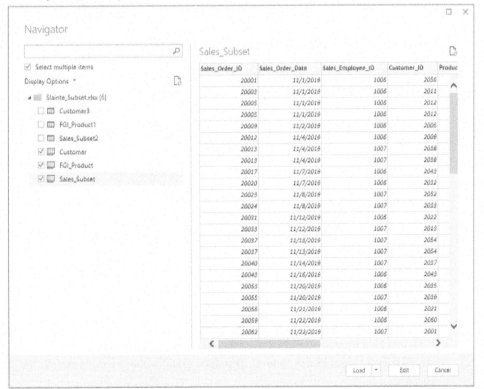

LAB EXHIBIT 2-2C
Select Multiple Tables to Join

Source: Microsoft Excel, 2016.

7. Click **Edit**. The Power Query Editor will appear.
   • This button is named **Transform Data** in Excel 365.
8. In the queries menu (which can be found on your far left within the Power Query Editor), you will find the three tables you just imported. Click **Sales_Subset** to see a preview of the Sales_Subset data.

We now want to merge all three of these tables together, using Sales_Subset as our base. We'll start with merging the Sales_Subset and Customer tables.

9. With Sales_Subset as the active table, click the **Home** tab, then choose **Merge Queries** from the **Combine** section. From the dropdown menu, again select **Merge Queries**. A new **Merge** window will appear.
10. In the **Merge** window, the **[Sales_Subset]** query will appear at the top.

LAB EXHIBIT 2-2D

Select the Primary and Foreign Keys in the Merge Window to Create a Large Table in Excel's Query Editor

Source: Microsoft Excel, 2016.

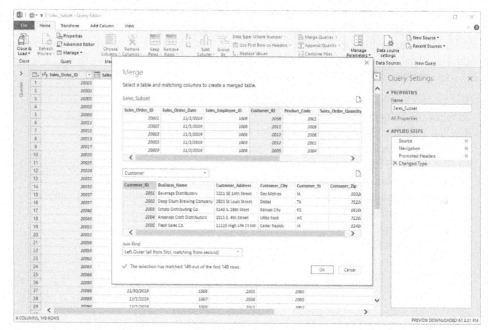

11. To join the **[Sales_Subset]** and **[Customer]** queries, do the following:
    a. Select the **[Customer]** query from the middle drop-down list.
    b. Click the **[Customer_ID]** column in both the **[Sales_Subset]** and **[Customer]** queries.
    c. From the **Join Kind** drop-down list, choose **Left Outer (all from first, matching from second)**. This means **[Sales_Subset]. [Customer_ID]** will be identified as the foreign key.
    d. Click **OK** to return to the **Query Editor.**
    e. If your new column isn't already namedCustomer, double-click the newly added attribute title and rename it **[Customer]**.
    f. Finally, click the **opposing arrows icon** next to the **[Customer]** column title. Select **Expand** and click **OK**. The customer attributes have now been added to the **[Sales_Subset]** query.
12. To join the **[Sales_Subset]** and **[FGI_Product]** queries, do the following:
    a. Click **Merge Queries** again from the **Home** tab (ensure that Sales_Subset is still the active table).
    b. Select **[FGI_Product]** from the middle drop-down list.
    c. Click the **[Product_Code]** column in both the **[Sales_Subset]** and **[FGI_Product]** queries.
    d. From the **Join Kind** drop-down list, choose **Left Outer (all from first, matching from second)**. This means **[Sales_Subset]. [Product_Code]** will be identified as the foreign key.

e. Click **OK** to return to the **Query Editor.**

f. Double-click the newly added **[NewColumn]** attribute title and rename it **[Product].**

g. Finally, click the **opposing arrows icon** next to the **[Product]** column title. Select **Expand** and click **OK.** The product attributes have now been added to the **[Sales_Subset]** query.

13. Maximize the **Query Editor** window, and take a screenshot (label it 2-2B).

14. Click **Close & Load** twice (top left corner of the Power Query Editor) to return to Excel.

15. In the Workbook Queries pane on the right (named **Queries & Connections** in Excel 365), select **Sales_Subset** to view the data. (If the data has not automatically imported into a table, right-click **[Sales_Subset]** and choose **Load To. . .**).

16. Rename the active sheet with the full set of data **[Sales_Order_Merge].**

Note: You can also directly load your merged table into a PivotTable if that is the analysis you're going to perform.

17. Save your workbook as **Slainte_Merge.xlsx.**

Q4. Have you used the Query Editor in Excel before? Double-click the [Sales_Subset] query and click through the tabs on the ribbon. Which options do you think will be useful in the future?

Alternative 4 (data stored in a relational database): Use SQL queries to retrieve the data.

Extracting data with SQL queries can not only be very efficient, but sometimes necessary. There are instances where datasets will be too large for Excel, and Access or another query tool (such as SQLite) will be the only way to analyze the data effectively.

1. Open the **Slainte_Subset.accdb** file.

2. Open the SQL editor by navigating to the **Create** tab on the ribbon.

3. Click the **Query Design** button in the Queries section to open the SQL Designer. Here you should see three tables.

4. Click **Close** on the Show Table window.

5. In the top left corner, click **SQL** icon and then select **SQL View** to open the SQL Editor.

6. In the SQL Editor, type the following lines of code:

```
SELECT Sales_Subset.*, FGI_Product.*, Customer.*
FROM Customer
INNER JOIN
(FGI_Product INNER JOIN Sales_Subset
ON FGI_Product.Product_Code = Sales_Subset.Product_Code)
ON Customer.Customer_ID = Sales_Subset.Customer_ID;
```

7. Click **Run** from the **Design** tab on the Ribbon to view your combined query output.

8. Take a screenshot of your query output (label it 2-2C).

9. Right-click the Query and click **Save** to save your query as **Slainte_Merge.**

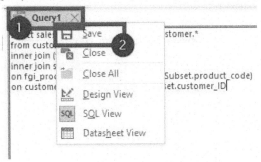

10. From here you can either click **External Data** menu to export your data or you can close your file without exporting. For practice, export to Excel. Then, open Excel and choose **Data > Get Data > From Database > From Microsoft Access Database**, then navigate to your database and import the query.

Part 3: Perform an Analysis Using PivotTables and Queries

Now that the data have been organized, you're ready for some basic analysis. Given the sales data, management has asked you to prepare a report showing the total number of each item sold each month between January and April 2020. This means that we should create a PivotTable with a column for each month, a row for each product, and the sum of the quantity sold where the two intersect.

1. **Open** any of the files you created in Part 2 in Excel, and click the **Insert** tab on the ribbon.
2. Click **PivotTable** in the **Tables** section.
3. In the **Create PivotTable** window click **Add this data to the Data Model.** *Note:* If you have only one table, choose **Select a table or range** and choose your sheet.
4. Click **OK** to create the PivotTable. A **PivotTable Fields** pane appears on the right.
   - *Note:* If at any point while working with your PivotTable, your PivotTable Fields list disappears, you can make it reappear by ensuring that your active cell is within the PivotTable itself. If the Field List still doesn't reappear, navigate to the Analyze tab in the Ribbon, and select Field List.
5. Click the **arrow toggle** next to each table to show the available fields. If you don't see your three tables, click the **All** option directly below the **PivotTable Fields** pane title.
6. Take a screenshot of your PivotTable field list (label it 2-2D).
7. Because you defined relationships or merged the tables in Part 2, you can drag any of the attributes from your list of fields to their respective Filters, Columns, Rows, or Values. Do that now:
   a. **Columns: [Sales_Order_Date] (Month)** from **[Sales_Subset].** *Note:* When you add a date, Excel will automatically try to group the data by Year, Quarter, etc. For now, remove the other options.
   b. **Rows: [Product_Description]** from **[FGI_Products].**
      - *Note: If you imported the data from the Access database query, it will be named Product.Product_Description*

8. a. **Values: [Sales_Order_Quantity_Sold]** from **[Sales_Subset].**
   b. **Filters: None.**
9. Finally, to show only the four months from January to April, click the drop-down arrow next to **Column Labels** in the PivotTable (not in the Field list) and uncheck **Nov** and **Dec.**
10. *Optional step:* Clean up your PivotTable. Rename labels and the title of the report to something more useful.
11. Take a screenshot of your PivotTable (label it 2-2E).
12. Save a copy of your workbook as **Slainte_Pivot.xlsx.**

To perform a similar, but less flexible analysis in Access, do the following:

1. Open your **Slainte_Subset.accdb** file from Part 2.
2. Click **Create > Query Design.** Close the window that appears.
3. Click **SQL View** in the top-left corner.

4. Enter the following query:

```
SELECT Product_Description, Sum(Sales_Order_Quantity_Sold) AS Total_Sales
FROM Slainte_Merge
WHERE Sales_Order_Date Between #1/1/2020# And #4/30/2020#
GROUP BY Product_Description;
```

5. Click **Run** to show the results.
6. Take a screenshot (label it 2-2F).
7. Save your query as **Total_Sales_By_Product** and close your database.

Part 4: Address and Refine Your Results

Now that you've completed a basic analysis to answer management's question, take a moment to think about how you could improve the report and anticipate questions your manager might have.

Q5. If the owner of Sláinte wishes to identify which product sold the most, how would you make this report more useful?

Q6. If you wanted to provide more detail, what other attributes would be useful to add as additional rows or columns to your report, or what other reports would you create?

Part 5: Communicate Your Findings

Let's make this easy for others to understand using visualization and explanations.

Q7. Write a brief paragraph about how you would interpret the results of your analysis in plain English. For example, which data points stand out?

Q8. In Chapter 4, we'll discuss some visualization techniques. Describe a way you could present these data as a chart or graph.

End of Lab

Lab 2-3 Resolve Common Data Problems in Excel and Access

There are several issues with this dataset that we'll need to resolve before we can process the data. This will require some cleaning, reformatting, and other techniques.

Company summary

LendingClub is a peer-to-peer marketplace where borrowers and investors are matched together. The goal of LendingClub is to reduce the costs associated with these banking transactions and make borrowing less expensive and investment more engaging. LendingClub provides data on loans that have been approved and rejected since 2007, including the assigned interest rate and type of loan. This provides several opportunities for data analysis.

Data

- Download the LendingClub datasets: ApproveStats from the Connect website

Technique

- Some experience with Excel is useful for this lab.

Software needed

- Excel
- Screen capture tool (Windows: Snipping Tool; Mac: Cmd + Shift + 4)

In this lab, you will:

- Understand and clean the data to enable analysis for various problems.

Part 1: Identify the Questions

You've already identified some analysis questions for **LendingClub** in Chapter 1. Here, you'll focus on data quality. Think about some of the common issues with data you receive from other people. For example, is the date field in the proper format? Do number fields contain text or vice versa?

> Q1. What do you expect will be major data quality issues with **LendingClub**'s data?

Part 2: Master the Data

The **LendingClub** collects different sets of data, including LoanStats for approved loans and RejectStats for rejected loans. There are significantly more data available for LoanStats.

For this lab, we will analyze approved loans using the Lab_2-3_ApproveStats.xlsx file.

There are 145 different attributes. To save some time, we've identified 19 of the most interesting in Lab Exhibit 2-3A.

LAB EXHIBIT 2-3A

Attribute	Description
id	Loan identification number
member_id	Membership ID
loan_amnt	Requested loan amount
emp_length	Employment length
issue_d	Date of loan issue
loan_status	Fully paid or charged off
pymnt_plan	Payment plan: yes or no
purpose	Loan purpose: e.g., wedding, medical, debt_consolidation, car
zip_code	The first three digits of the applicant's zip code
addr_state	State
dti	Debt-to-income ratio
delinq_2y	Late payments within the past 2 years
earliest_cr_line	Oldest credit account
inq_last_6mnths	Credit inquiries in the past 6 months
open_acc	Number of open credit accounts
revol_bal	Total balance of all credit accounts
revol_util	Percentage of available credit in use
total_acc	Total number of credit accounts
application_type	Individual or joint application

Source: LoanStatsXXXX.csv

> Q2. Given this list of attributes, what types of questions do you think you could answer regarding approved loans? (If you worked through Lab 1-2, what

concerns do you have with the data's ability to predict answers to the questions you identified in Chapter 1)?

1. Take a moment and explore the data.

   Q3. Is there anything in the data that you think will make analysis difficult? For example, are there any special symbols, nonstandard data, or numbers that look out of place?

   Q4. What would you do to clean the data in this file?

Let's identify some issues with the data.

- There are many attributes without any data, and that may not be necessary.
- The **[int_rate]** values are written in ##.##%, but analysis will require #.####.
- The **[term]** values include the word "months," which should be removed for numerical analysis.
- The **[emp_length]** values include "n/a", "<", "+", "year", and "years"–all of which should be removed for numerical analysis.
- Dates, including **[issue_d]**, can be more useful if we expand them to show the day, month, and year as separate attributes. Dates cause issues in general because different systems use different date formats (e.g., 1/9/2009, Jan-2009, 9/1/2009 for European dates, etc.), so typically some conversion is necessary.

First, remove the unwanted data:

2. **Save** your file as "**Loans2007-2011.xlsx**" to take advantage of some of Excel's features.
3. **Delete** the first row that says "Notes offered by prospectus. . .".
4. **Delete** the last two rows that include "Total amount funded. . .".
5. **Delete** columns that have no values, including [id], [member_id], and [url].
6. **Repeat** for any other blank columns or unwanted attributes.

Next, fix your numbers:

7. Select the **[int_rate]** column.
8. In the **Home** tab, go to the **Number** section and change the number type from **Percentage** to **General** using the drop-down menu.
9. **Repeat** for any other attributes with percentages.
10. Take a screenshot (label it 2-3A) of your partially cleaned data file.

Then, remove any words from numerical values:

11. Select the **[term]** column.
12. Use **Find & Replace** (**Ctrl+H** or **Home > Editing > Find & Select > Replace**) to find the words "months" and "month" and replace them with a null/blank value. *Important:* Be sure to include the space before the words and go from the longest variation of the word to the shortest. In this case, if you replaced "month" first, you would end up with a lot of values that still had the letter "s" from "months."
13. Now select the **[emp_length]** column and find and replace the following values:

Original Value	New Value
na or n/a	0
< 1 year	0
1 year	1
2 years	2
3 years	3
4 years	4
5 years	5

Original Value	New Value
6 years	6
7 years	7
8 years	8
9 years	9
10+ years	10
, (comma)	(blank)

14. Take a screenshot (label it 2-3B) of your partially cleaned data file, showing the [term] column.

Analytics Tool: Python

Note: *Finding and replacing 13 values by hand may be tedious, but it is efficient for a one-off analysis and a small file. If you plan to re-perform this analysis multiple times or find and replace dozens of items or you have a file that is larger than Excel can handle, you're better off using a scripting language, such as Python. You can download Python free from python.org, and a quick search on Google will help you find tutorials to start with the basics.*

Here's what the script would look like for the find and replace function where you would list the original value as item *and the replacement value as* replacement:

```
import csv

ifile = open('file', 'rb')
reader = csv.reader(ifile,delimiter='\t')
ofile = open('file', 'wb')
writer = csv.writer(ofile, delimiter='\t')

s = ifile.read()
for item, replacement in zip(findlist, replacelist):
s = s.replace(item, replacement)
s = s.replace(item, replacement)
ofile.write(s)

ifile.close()
ofile.close()
```

Finally, transform those dates:

15. Right-click the column to the right or the **[issue_d]** column, and choose **Insert** to add a blank column.
16. Name the new column **[issue_month]**.
17. Use the =MONTH([column address for issue_d]) formula to extract the month from the date in your new column and copy your formula to the bottom of the sheet. You should see a month number value in each cell. If it still has a date format, change the number format to **General** in the **Home** tab.
18. Now convert the formulas to data values. Select the new **[issue_month]** column that contains your formula.

19. **First, copy all of the values in the [issue_month] column (you can use the keyboard shortcut Copy [Ctrl+C])** and then replace the existing data in the same column with the values by using the following keyboard shortcut: **Paste Special [Ctrl+Alt+V].** Choose **Values [V],** then click **OK.**
20. Save your file.
21. Add another blank column and name it **[issue_year].**
22. Use the =YEAR([column address for issue_d]) formula to extract the year from the date in your new column and copy your formula to the bottom of the sheet. You should see a year number value in each cell. If it still has a date format, change the number format to **General** in the **Home** tab.
23. Now, convert the formula to data values like you did with the Issue_month column (Select the new **[issue_year]** column that contains your formula, then **Copy [Ctrl+C]** and **Paste Special [Ctrl+Alt+V].** Choose **Values [V].** Click **OK**).
24. Save your file.
25. Take a screenshot (label it 2-3C) of your cleaned data file, showing the new date columns.

   Q5. Why do you think it is useful to reformat and extract parts of the dates before you conduct your analysis? What do you think would happen if you didn't?

   Q6. Did you run into any major issues when you attempted to clean the data? How did you resolve those?

End of Lab

Lab 2-4   Generate Summary Statistics in Excel

When you're working with a new or unknown set of data, validating the data is very important. When you make a data request, the IT manager who fills the request should also provide some summary statistics that include the total number of records and mathematical sums to ensure nothing has been lost in the transmission. This lab will help you calculate summary statistics in Excel.

Company summary

LendingClub is a peer-to-peer marketplace where borrowers and investors are matched together. The goal of LendingClub is to reduce the costs associated with these banking transactions and make borrowing less expensive and investment more engaging. LendingClub provides data on loans that have been approved and rejected since 2007, including the assigned interest rate and type of loan. This provides several opportunities for data analysis.

Data
- Download the LendingClub dataset: Lab_2-4_ApproveStats.xlsx from the Connect website

Technique
- Some experience with Excel is useful for this lab.

Software needed
- Excel
- Screen capture tool (Windows: Snipping Tool; Mac: Cmd + Shift + 4)

In this lab, you will:
- Calculate summary statistics using Excel.

Quickly View Summary Statistics in Excel

For basic validation, we'll use Excel. Remember, there is a limitation on the number of records that Excel can handle, so this is best for smaller- to medium-sized files. Excel's toolbar at the bottom of the window provides quick access to a summary of any selected values.

1. Open **Lab_2-4_ApproveStats.xlsx.**
2. Select the **[loan_amnt]** column. At the bottom right of the window, you will see the **Average, Count,** and **Sum** calculations, shown in Lab Exhibit 2-4A. Compare those to the validation given by **LendingClub**:
3. *Funded loans: $3,503,840,175*
   Number of approved loans: 235,629

LAB EXHIBIT 2-4A
Summary Statistics Provided by the Excel Toolbar at the Bottom Showing Average, Count, and Sum

Source: Microsoft Excel, 2016.

	A	B	C	D	E	F	G	H	I	J	K
1	Notes offered by Prospectus (https://www.lendingclub.com/info/prospectus.action)										
2	id	member_	loan_amn	funded_a	funded_a	term	int_rate	installmer	grade	sub_grade	emp_title e
3			10400	10400	10400	36	0.0699	321.08	A	A3	Truck Driv 8
4			15000	15000	15000	60	0.1239	336.64	C	C1	MANAGEN 1
5			9600	9600	9600	36	0.1366	326.53	C	C3	Admin Spι 1
6			7650	7650	7650	36	0.1366	260.2	C	C3	Technical <
7			12800	12800	12800	60	0.1714	319.08	D	D4	Senior Sal 1
8			21425	21425	21425	60	0.1559	516.36	D	D1	Programm 6
9			23325	23325	23325	36	0.1431	800.71	C	C4	Teacher 1
10			17000	17000	17000	36	0.1366	578.22	C	C3	Deputy sh 1
11			2500	2500	2500	36	0.1199	83.03	B	B5	Manufactι <
12			12975	12975	12975	36	0.1786	468.17	D	D5	Sales 1
13			5250	5250	5250	36	0.1144	172.98	B	B4	Store Mar 2
14			16000	16000	16000	60	0.1144	351.4	B	B4	Foreign Sε 6
15			10000	10000	10000	36	0.1199	332.1	B	B5	Investmeι 8
16			21075	21075	21075	60	0.2199	581.95	E	E5	Paralegal 1

LoanStats3c

Ready   Average: 14870.15679   Count: 235630   Sum: 3503840175   100%

Q1. Do your numbers match the numbers provided by **LendingClub**? What explains the discrepancy, if any?

4. Right-click on the **summary** toolbar and choose **Numerical Count** from the list. You should now see four values in the bar.

Q2. Does the Numerical Count provide a more useful/accurate value for validating your data? Why or why not do you think that is the case?

Q3. What other summary values might be useful for validating your data?

5. Take a screenshot (label it 2-4A) showing your expanded summary toolbar with four (or more) values.

View More Detailed Summary Statistics in Excel

If we want to view more summary statistics than just the ones provided in the summary toolbar, or even if we would prefer to retrieve an output of summary statistics instead of having to select the data to view it, we can run the "Descriptive Statistics" tool using the Data Analysis ToolPak.

6. Ensure that the Data Analysis ToolPak is added in to your Excel (for instructions on doing so are provided in Appendix B at the end of the textbook).
7. Click the **Data** tab on the ribbon and select **Data Analysis** to open the Data Analysis ToolPak options.

8. Select Descriptive Statistics and click **OK**.

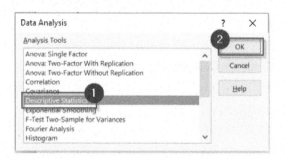

9. For the input range, select the column of data associated with loan_amnt.
10. If you selected the First Row (the label that says "Loan Amnt"), place a checkmark next to Labels in First Row.
11. Place a check mark next to Summary Statistics.
12. Click **OK**.

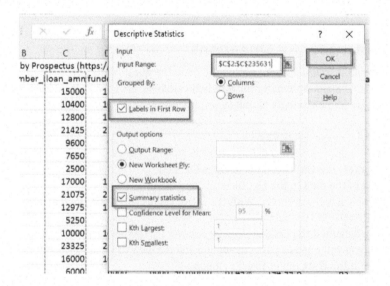

14. The output with the summary statistics will be provided on a new spreadsheet.
15. Take a screenshot (label it 2-4B) showing your Summary Statistics output.

End of Lab

Lab 2-5   College Scorecard Extraction and Data Preparation

This lab will help you learn how to extract data from a text file in preparation for analysis in Excel. This lab is in preparation for future labs in Chapter 3 that will analyze college scorecard data.

Data summary

The data used are a subset of the College Scorecard dataset that is provided by the U.S. Department of Education. These data provide federal financial aid and earnings information, insights into the performance of schools eligible to receive federal financial aid, and the outcomes of students at those schools. You can learn more about how the data are used and view the raw data yourself at https://collegescorecard.ed.gov/data/. However, for this lab, you should use the text file provided to you.

Data

- CollegeScorecard Datasets: CollegeScorecard_RawData

Technique

- Some experience with Excel is useful for this lab.

Software needed

- Text Editor (Windows: Notepad; Mac: TextEdit)
- Excel
- Screen capture tool (Windows: Snipping Tool; Mac: Cmd + Shift + 4)

In this lab, you will:

- Extract data into a text editor and transform it into structured, ready-to-analyze data in Excel.

Part 1: Identify the Questions

Because this lab is focused on mastering the data, the question has been identified for you. We will begin with a simple question with two variables, SAT average and completion rate for first-time, full-time students at four-year institutions.

Part 2: Master the Data

1. Open the text file CollegeScoreCardRawData.txt.
2. Select all of the data in the text file and copy them.
3. Open a new Excel workbook. With the active cell as A1, paste the text data.
4. Take a screenshot (label it 2-5A).
5. The data defaulted to pasting into only column A. To view each attribute in its own column, you will need to parse the data using the Text to Columns feature in Excel. Navigate to the **Data** tab in Excel's ribbon.
6. Make sure that the all of the data in column A are selected (not just the first row of data), then click the **Text to Columns** button to open up a wizard to guide your data transformation.
7. The wizard provides two options: delimited and fixed width. Delimited means separated, and in Excel (and other applications), it references a character that separates (or delimits) data.

   Q1. By looking through the data in the text file, what do you think the delimiter is?

8. Leaving **delimited** checked (as is the default), click **Next** in the wizard, and select the appropriate delimiter. Make sure to un-check the **default** option, Tab.
9. Click **Finish** in the wizard.
10. Take a screenshot (label it 2-5B).

11. To ensure that you captured all of the data through the extraction from the txt file, we need to validate it. Validate the following checksums:
    - You should have 7,704 records (rows).
    - Compare the attribute names (column headers) to the attributes listed in the data dictionary (found in Appendix K of this chapter). Are you missing any, or do you have any extras?
    - The average SAT score should be 1,059.07 (this is leaving NULL values as NULL).

    Q2. In the checksums, you validated that the average SAT score for all of the records is 1,059.07. When we work with the data more rigorously, several tests will require us to transform NULL values. If you were to transform the NULL SAT values into 0, what would happen to the average (would it stay the same, decrease, or increase)? How would that change to the average affect the way you would interpret the data? Do you think it's a good idea to replace NULL values with 0s in this case?

12. Now that the data have been validated, you can clean the data. How you clean the data is determined by the question you intend to answer. In this case, we're preparing our data to run a regression test using the two attributes SAT_AVG and C150_4. As you'll learn in Chapter 3, a regression test won't run with non-numeric values (i.e., we can't leave the NULL values in, and we can't transform them to blanks). Earlier you discussed the cons of replacing NULL values with 0s.

    To avoid the issues with NULL, blanks, and 0s, we will remove all of the records that contain NULL values in either SAT_AVG or C150_4. Do so.

13. Perform a =COUNT() to verify the number of records that remain after removing all records associated with NULL values in SAT_AVG or C150_4. 1,271 records should remain.

14. Take a screenshot that includes the data and the result of the =COUNT() function. (label it 2-5C).

Your data is now ready for the test plan. This lab will continue in Chapter 3.

Lab 2-6 Comprehensive Case: Dillard's Store Data: How to Create an Entity-Relationship Diagram

Company summary

Dillard's is a department store with approximately 330 stores in 29 states. Its headquarters is in Little Rock, Arkansas. You can learn more about Dillard's by looking at finance.yahoo.com (Ticker symbol = DDS) and the Wikipedia site for DDS. You'll quickly note that William T. Dillard II is an accounting grad of the University of Arkansas and the Walton College of Business, which may be why he shared transaction data with us to make available for this lab and labs throughout this text.

Data

The data for this lab and all other Dillard's labs must be accessed through the University of Arkansas Remote Desktop. Directions for accessing the Remote Desktop can be found at www.mhhe.com/richardsondaa2e. See your instructor for login credentials.

Software needed

- Microsoft SQL Server Management Studio (available on the Remote Desktop at the University of Arkansas)

In this lab, you will:

- Create an ERD (entity-relationship diagram), which provides some quick information on the data that's provided in the database. In one diagram, you can view all tables to see the entire database, or you can pick just the two you're working with to focus on those attributes.

Part 1: Identify the Questions

Dillard's is trying to figure out when its customers spend more on individual transactions. We ask questions regarding how Dillard's sells its products.

> Q1. How would a view of the entire database or certain tables out of that database allow us to get a feel for the data?
>
> Q2. What types of data would you guess that Dillard's, a retail store, gathers that might be useful? How could Dillard's suppliers use these data to predict future purchases?

Part 2: Master the Data and Part 3: Perform an Analysis of the Data

For this lab, we will create an ERD (entity-relationship diagram) to view the structure of the database.

1. Log on to **Remote Desktop** at the University of Arkansas.
2. Press the Windows key to open the Start menu. **Microsoft SQL Server Management Studio** will be on the right of the menu that appears. Open SQL Server to access the **WCOB_DILLARDS** data.
3. Input the **Server Name** in the **Connect to Server** window that your instructor provided you.

Source: Microsoft Excel, 2016.

4. Leave the default for authentication to Windows Authentication, and click **Connect.**
5. Expand the **Databases** folder in the **Object Explorer** window.

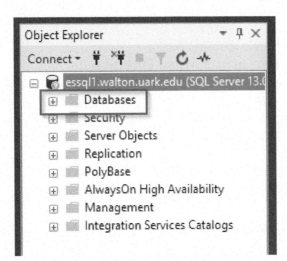

Source: Microsoft Excel, 2016.

6. Scroll down to the **WCOB_DILLARDS** database and expand it.
7. Right-click **Database Diagrams** to reveal the below window.

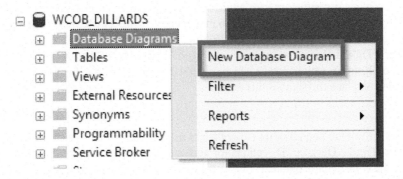

Source: Microsoft SQL Server Management Studio.

8. Select **New Database Diagram.**
9. A window indicating that you cannot create tables will appear, click **OK.** Because we do not need to create or edit any tables, viewing them is sufficient.

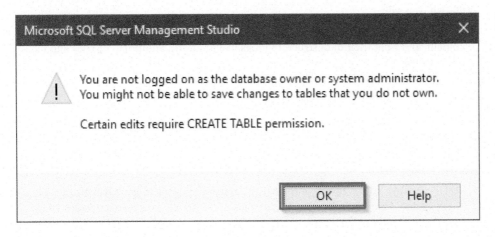

Source: Microsoft SQL Server Management Studio

10. Select the tables you would like to view. For this lab, highlight all of the tables and select **Add**.

11. Take a screenshot (label it 2-6A). To ensure you can see all of the tables in your screenshot, you can select **View < Zoom** and select **To Fit**.

Part 4: Address and Refine Results

Q3. What is the primary key for the TRANSACT table? What is the primary key for the SKU table?

Q4. How do we connect the SKU database to the TRANSACT table? How do we join tables from two different related tables?

End of Lab

Lab 2-7 Comprehensive Case: Dillard's Store Data: How to Preview Data from Tables in a Query

Company summary

Dillard's is a department store with approximately 330 stores in 29 states. Its headquarters is in Little Rock, Arkansas. You can learn more about Dillard's by looking at finance.yahoo. com (Ticker symbol = DDS) and the Wikipedia site for DDS. You'll quickly note that William T. Dillard II is an accounting grad of the University of Arkansas and the Walton College of Business, which may be why he shared transaction data with us to make available for this lab and labs throughout this text.

Data

The data for this lab and all other Dillard's labs must be accessed through the University of Arkansas Remote Desktop. Directions for accessing the Remote Desktop can be found at www.mhhe.com/richardsondaa2e. See your instructor for login credentials.

Software needed

- Microsoft SQL Server Management Studio (available on the Remote Desktop at the University of Arkansas)

In this lab, you will:

- Learn how to get a snippet of the data to better understand the data fields, what they contain, and what their data structure looks like to inform additional queries and database analysis.

Part 1: Identify the Questions

Data Analytics requires a lot of give and take. Often, you will learn a bit, modify the search, modify the analysis, and try again, especially while you are getting to know the data. All the while, you are asking yourself questions, trying to make your search efficient and effective. Questions like these:

Q1. How would a diagram of the entire database allow us to get a feel for the data? How does looking at examples of the actual data stored in some of the tables help you understand the data?

Q2. What types of data would you guess that **Dillard's**, a retail store, gathers that might be useful? How could **Dillard's** suppliers use these data to predict future purchases?

Part 2: Master the Data and Part 3: Perform an Analysis of the Data

1. Log on to **Remote Desktop** at the University of Arkansas.
2. Open **Microsoft SQL Server Management Studio** to access the **WCOB_DILLARDS** data.
3. Input the **Server Name** in the **Connect to Server** window that you were provided through the Walton.uark.edu/enterprise website.

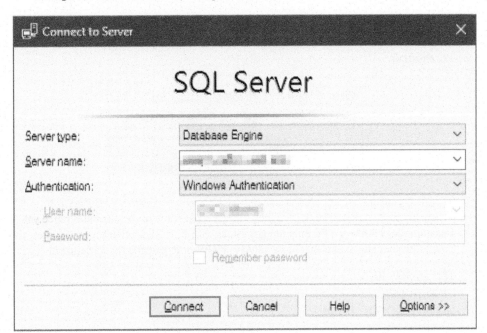

Source: Microsoft SQL Server Management Studio.

4. Leave the default for authentication to **Windows Authentication** and click **Connect.**
5. Select **New Query** from the menu at the top of the SQL Server application.

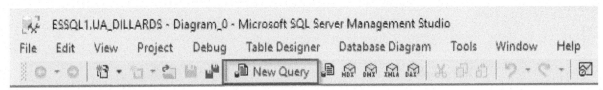

Source: Microsoft SQL Server Management Studio.

6. If the drop-down indicating which database you are intending to query doesn't say "WCOB_DILLARDS" (e.g., it frequently defaults to "Master"), select the drop-down window and scroll down to WCOB_DILLARDS, then click **Enter.** You could also type WCOB_DILLARDS instead of waiting to scroll to it.

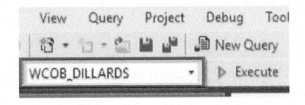

Source: Microsoft SQL Server Management Studio.

7. Because this dataset is massive, it can take a very long time for the system to return the complete set of data for some of the bigger tables (such as TRANSACT). If you would like to view just the top few rows of a dataset to get the feel for what type of data is in the table, you can do so with a query.

    In the SELECT line, you can type TOP # before the columns you would like to see. Any type of filtering, aggregating, and ordering will still work through the rest of the query, but selecting the top few will help the query run faster by returning a subset of the result.

8. To view the top 10 rows in the TRANSACT table, type the following query into the query window:

```
SELECT TOP 10 *
FROM TRANSACT
```

9. To see the result of the query, click **Execute. F5** also works to run queries as a PC shortcut.

Source: Microsoft SQL Server Management Studio.

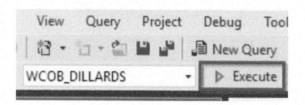

10. Take a screenshot of your results (label it 2-7A).
11. When you look at these results, you may wonder what some of the attributes represent. For example, TRAN_TYPE only returns values with P. To view other types of values, you could filter out any record that has a TRAN_TYPE of P. Execute the following query:

```
SELECT TOP 10 *
FROM TRANSACT
WHERE TRAN_TYPE <> 'P'
```

Part 4: Address and Refine Results

Q3. What do you think 'P' and 'R' represent in the TRAN_TYPE table? How might transactions differ if they are represented by 'P' or 'R'?

Q4. What benefit can you gain from selecting only the top few rows of your data, particularly from a large dataset?

End of Lab

Lab 2-8   Comprehensive Case: Dillard's Store Data: Connecting Excel to a SQL Database

Company summary

Dillard's is a department store with approximately 330 stores in 29 states. Its headquarters is in Little Rock, Arkansas. You can learn more about **Dillard's** by looking at finance.yahoo.com (Ticker symbol = DDS) and the Wikipedia site for DDS. You'll quickly note that William T. Dillard II is an accounting grad of the University of Arkansas and the Walton College of

Business, which may be why he shared transaction data with us to make available for this lab and labs throughout this text.

Data

The data for this lab and all other **Dillard's** labs must be accessed through the University of Arkansas Remote Desktop. Directions for accessing the Remote Desktop can be found at www.mhhe.com/richardsondaa2e. See your instructor for login credentials.

Software needed

- Microsoft SQL Server Management Studio (available on the Remote Desktop at the University of Arkansas)
- Excel 2016 (available on the Remote Desktop at the University of Arkansas)

In this lab, you will:

- Learn how to access databases, run queries, and perform analyses in Excel.

Part 1: Identify the Questions

Because, as accountants, we are most familiar with Microsoft Excel, we'd like to learn how to access the data and run queries in Excel. But the question is still why use Excel?

Q1. What can you do in Excel that is much more difficult to do in other data management programs?

Q2. Because most accountants are familiar with Excel, name three data management functions you can do easier in Excel than any other program. How does that familiarity help you with your analysis?

Part 2: Master the Data and Part 3: Perform an Analysis of the Data

1. Log on to **Remote Desktop** at the University of Arkansas.

Connecting Excel to a SQL Server Database

While executing queries in SQL Server is a great method for viewing data, if you want to eventually load data into Excel for additional analysis or visualization, it is easiest to write the queries directly in Excel. This puts the entire ETL (or ELT) process in one tool, Excel.

2. From the Remote Desktop, click the windows key to access the Start Menu and open a new Excel workbook.
3. From the **Data** tab, click **New Query > From Database > From SQL Server Database.**

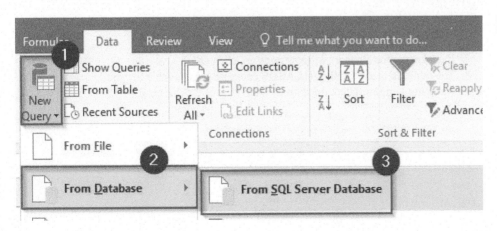

Source: Microsoft Excel, 2016.

4. In the Microsoft SQL database pop-up window, input the server name that you were provided through the Walton.uark.edu/enterprise website. The database name is WCOB_DILLARDS.

Source: Microsoft SQL Server Management Studio.

5. Click **OK.**
6. If presented an option to change credentials, keep the default to use your current credentials, and then click **Connect.**

Source: Microsoft SQL Server Management Studio.

7. If an **Encryption Support** window pops up, click **OK.**
8. The tables in the **WCOB_DILLARDS** database are available for you to select in the **Navigator** window. Click once on **STORE** to preview the data.

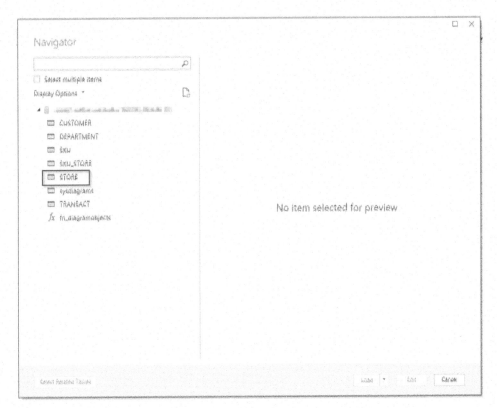

Source: Microsoft SQL Server
Management Studio.

9. The data will preview on the right side of the **Navigator** window. Click **Load** to load the data into a table in Excel.

   As long as the dataset that you have loaded is under the Excel row limit of 1,048,576, the entire table will be available for you to work with in Excel. You can analyze the data using Excel's formulas, functions, and statistical tools, as well as create PivotTables and charts.

10. Create a PivotTable for this set of data by selecting all of the data from the Store table and then clicking **PivotTable** on the **Insert** tab of the Excel ribbon.

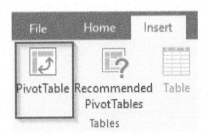

Source: Microsoft Excel,
2016.

11. We can quickly view a count of how many stores are in each state. Drag and drop STATE into the **ROWS** section of the **PivotTable Fields** window and **STORE** into the **VALUES** section.

Source: Microsoft Excel, 2016.

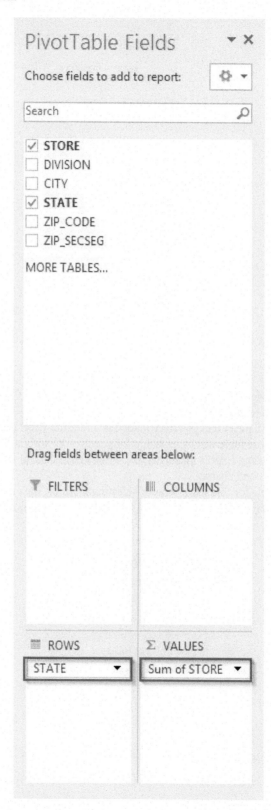

12. It is likely that the PivotTable assumed you wanted to SUM the Store ID, which provides nonsense data. We need to change that aggregate to a COUNT instead.

Click the drop-down next to Sum of STORE in the **VALUES** section of the **PivotTable Fields** window and select **Value Field Settings.**

Source: Microsoft Excel, 2016.

13. Select **Count** to change the way the data for number of stores per state are summarized, and then click **OK**.
14. You have now created a summarized view of the data that shows the number of stores in each state. To make this even easier to interpret, you can sort the data so that you see the states that have the highest number of stores first. To do so, have your active cell anywhere in the Count of Store column, right-click the cell, select **Sort,** then select **Sort Largest to Smallest.**

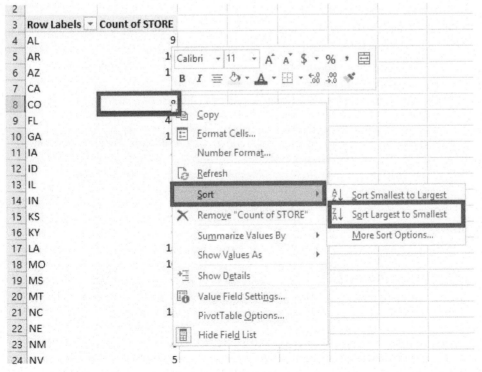

Source: Microsoft Excel, 2016.

Source: Microsoft Excel, 2016.

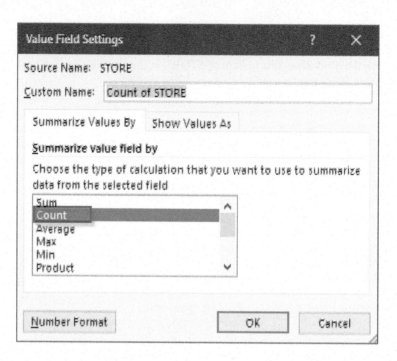

15. Take a screenshot (label it 2-8A) of the PivotTable.

Q3. Reference your PivotTable and find which state has the highest number of **Dillard's** stores. Which states have the fewest? How many stores are there across the country?

Q4. Counting the number of stores per state is one example of how the data that have been loaded from SQL Server into Excel can become useful information through a PivotTable. What are other ways that you could organize the STORE data in a PivotTable to come up with meaningful information?

Writing Queries Directly in Excel

While executing queries in SQL Server is a great method for viewing data, if you want to eventually load data from a query result into Excel for analysis or visualization, it is easiest to write the queries directly in Excel. This puts the entire ETL process in one tool, Excel.

1. Open a new Excel workbook.
2. From the **Data** tab, click **New Query > From Database > From SQL Server Database.**

Source: Microsoft Excel, 2016.

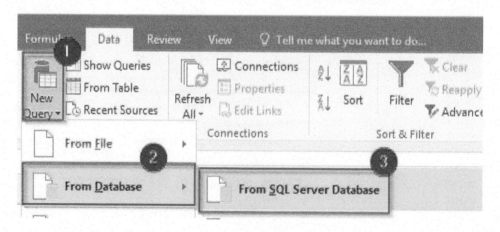

3. In the **Microsoft SQL database** pop-up window, input the server information that you received when accessing the WCOB_DILLARDS data. The Database name is WCOB_DILLARDS.

Important Note: If you just worked through the first part of this lab (connecting to data), this step is where the process begins to be different. Instead of clicking **OK,** you will click **SQL statement (optional).**

Source: Microsoft SQL Server Management Studio.

4. For this query, we will pull in enough data to answer a variety of questions about transaction line items in each state. We'll select all of the columns from the TRANSACT table and the STATE column from the STORE table. In order to do that, we'll join the two tables together in our query.

   Q5.   Joins are made based on their primary key/foreign key relationship. Looking at the ERD or the dataset, which two columns form the relationship between the TRANSACT and STORE tables?

5. Type this query into the **SQL statement** box:

```
SELECT TRANSACT.*, STATE
FROM TRANSACT
INNER JOIN STORE
ON TRANSACT.STORE = STORE.STORE
WHERE TRAN_DATE BETWEEN '20160901' AND '20160905'
```

Source: Microsoft SQL Server Management Studio.

6. Click **OK** to continue.
7. If presented with a box questing your credentials, click **Connect** using your current credentials in the next window.

Source: Microsoft Excel, 2016.

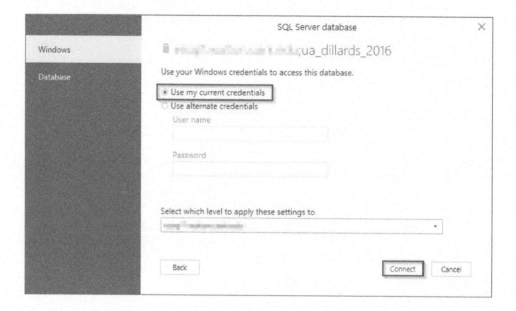

8. If presented with a window about encryption support, click **OK** on the **Encryption Support** window.
9. Excel will provide you a preview of your data before loading it. If the query loads successfully (i.e., if you see the preview, instead of an error), click **Load** to load the data into an Excel table.
10. It may take a few minutes to load. Even though the query we ran was only for 15 days of transactions, there are still more than 1 million transactions (or rows) to return.

Part 4: Calculate Summary Statistics

Calculating summary statistics such as mean, median, and mode for quantitative data can be helpful to get a quick feeling for the components of a large dataset.

11. While you can calculate these statistics by hand, you can also have Excel calculate them automatically through the **Data Analysis ToolPak.** If you haven't added this component into Excel yet, follow this menu path: **File > Options > Add-ins.** From this window, select the **Go. . .** button, and then place a check mark in the box next to **Analysis ToolPak.** Once you click **OK,** you will be able to access the ToolPak from the **Data** tab on the Excel ribbon.
12. We will calculate descriptive statistics for the attributes ORIG_PRICE, SALE_PRICE, TRAN_AMT.

    Q6. Looking at the first several rows of data, compare the amounts in ORIG_PRICE, SALE_PRICE, TRAN_AMT. What do you think TRANS_AMT represents?

13. Click the **Data Analysis** button from the **Data** tab on the Excel ribbon and select **Descriptive Statistics.**

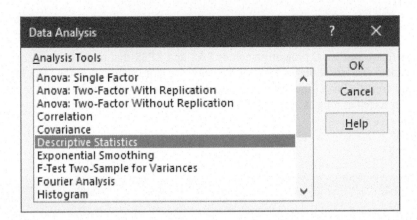

Source: Microsoft Excel, 2016.

14. For the **Input Range,** select the three columns associated with the three attributes that we are measuring. Leave the default to columns, and place a check-mark in **Labels in First Row.**

15. Place a check mark next to **Summary Statistics,** then press **OK.**

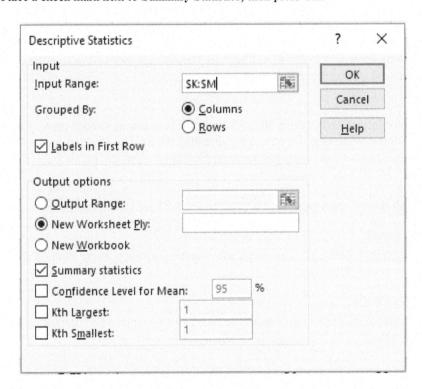

Source: Microsoft Excel, 2016.

It may take awhile for the statistics to run because you're working with so many rows.

Q7. What are the means for each of the attributes (ORIG_PRICE, SALE_PRICE, TRAN_AMT)?

Q8. The mean from TRAN_AMT is lower than the means for both ORIG_PRICE and SALE_PRICE, why do you think that is? (*Hint:* It is not an error).

Part 5: Address and Refine Results

Q9. How does doing a query within Excel allow quicker and more efficient access and analysis of the data?

Q10. Is 5 days of data sufficient to capture the statistical relationship among and between different variables? What will Excel do if you have more than 1 million rows?

Note: There are statistical programs such as SAS and SPSS that allow for transformation and statistical analysis of bigger datasets. You can also store your data in the Data Model in Excel and create a PivotTable from the data model. This will allow you to analyze massive datasets in Excel, as long as your PivotTable doesn't exceed the row limit.

End of Lab

Lab 2-9   Comprehensive Case: Dillard's Store Data: Joining Tables

Company summary

Dillard's is a department store with approximately 330 stores in 29 states. Its headquarters is in Little Rock, Arkansas. You can learn more about Dillard's by looking at finance.yahoo. com (Ticker symbol = DDS) and the Wikipedia site for DDS. You'll quickly note that William T. Dillard II is an accounting grad of the University of Arkansas and the Walton College of Business, which may be why he shared transaction data with us to make available for this lab and labs throughout this text.

Data

The data for this lab and all other Dillard's labs must be accessed through the University of Arkansas Remote Desktop. Directions for accessing the Remote Desktop can be found at www.mhhe.com/richardsondaa2e. See your instructor for login credentials.

Technique

- This lab is most easily performed if Labs 2-6 and 2-7 have already been completed.

Software needed

- Microsoft SQL Server Management Studio (available on the Remote Desktop at the University of Arkansas)

In this lab, you will:

- Learn how to do a table join, joining two tables all on your own and running an analysis of the data.

Part 1: Identify the Questions

1. Consult the entity-relationship diagram to view the variables available in the TRANSACT table and the CUSTOMER table. Consult Lab 2-6 for instructions to access the ERD.

    Q1.   If we wanted to join the TRANSACT and the CUSTOMER tables, what fields (or variables) would we use to join them?

Part 2: Master the Data and Part 3: Perform an Analysis of the Data

2. Log on to **Remote Desktop** at the University of Arkansas.
3. Open **Microsoft SQL Server Management Studio** to access the **WCOB_Dillards** data.
4. Input the **Server Name** in the **Connect to Server** window that you were provided through the Walton.uark.edu/enterprise website.

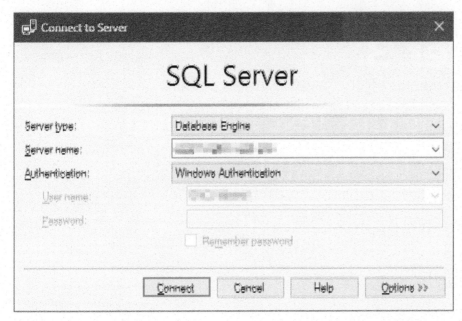

Source: Microsoft SQL Server
Management Studio.

5. Leave the default for authentication to **Windows Authentication,** and click **Connect.**
6. Select **New Query** from the menu at the top of the **SQL Server** application.

Source: Microsoft SQL Server Management Studio.

7. If the drop-down indicating which database you are intending to query doesn't say
   "WCOB_DILLARDS" (e.g., it frequently defaults to "Master"), select the drop-down
   window and scroll down to WCOB_DILLARDS, then click **Enter.** You could also type
   WCOB_DILLARDS instead of waiting to scroll to it.

Source: Microsoft SQL Server
Management Studio.

8. Given the description in the text and in Labs 2-6 and 2-7, you have the tools you need
   to join two tables, TRANSACT and CUSTOMER and run a query on customer state
   that will count the number of sales made to customers by state. Run the query for the
   entire dataset; do not filter based on a limited set of days.
9. This query may take a few minutes to run. Once the results have returned, you can
   check your results by looking at how many transactions at Dillard's have originated
   Customers from Arkansas (AR): 2673089.

   Q2. How many different states are listed?

   Q3. Why are there so many more states listed than 50?

   Q4. What do you assume the blank values represent? If you were to analyze these
        data to learn more about the number of customers from different places have
        shopped at **Dillard's**, what would you do with these data: group them, leave
        them out, leave them alone? Why?

End of Lab

Chapter 3

Performing the Test Plan and Analyzing the Results

A Look at This Chapter

Data Analytics involves various models and techniques used to understand the environment, make comparisons, and predict the future. In this chapter, we evaluate several different approaches and models and identify when to use them and how to interpret the results. We also provide specific accounting-related examples of when each of these specific data approaches and models is appropriate to address our particular question.

A Look Back

Chapter 2 provided a description of how data are prepared and scrubbed to be ready to use to answer business questions. We explained how to extract, transform, and load data and then how to validate and normalize the data. In addition, we explained how data standards are used to facilitate the exchange of data between both senders and receivers.

A Look Ahead

Chapter 4 will demonstrate various techniques that can be used to effectively communicate the results of your analyses. Additionally, we discuss how to refine your results and translate your findings into useful information for decision makers.

jaruek/123RF

Liang Zhao Zhang, a San Francisco–based janitor, made more than $275,000 in 2015. The average janitor in the area earns just $26,180 a year. Zhang, a **Bay Area Rapid Transit (BART)** janitor, has a base pay of $57,945 and $162,050 in overtime pay. With benefits, the total was $276,121. While some call his compensation "outrageous and irresponsible," Zhang signed up for every available overtime slot that became available. To be sure, Zhang worked more than 4,000 hours last year and received overtime pay. Can BART predict who might take advantage of overtime pay? Should it set a policy restricting overtime pay? Would it be better for BART to hire more regular, full-time employees instead of offering so much overtime? Can Data Analytics help with these questions?

Using a profiling data analytics approach detailed in this chapter, BART could generate summary statistics of its workers and their overtime pay to see the extent that overtime is required and taken advantage of.

Using regression and classification approaches to Data Analytics would help to classify which employees are most likely to exceed normal bounds and why. BART, for example, has a policy of offering overtime by seniority. So do the most senior employees sign up first and leave little overtime to others? Will a senior employee get paid more for overtime than more junior-level employees? If so, is that the best policy for the company and its employees?

Source: http://www.cnbc.com/2016/11/04/how-one-bay-area-janitor-made-276000-last-year.html.

OBJECTIVES

After reading this chapter, you should be able to:

LO 3-1 Understand four categories of Data Analytics.

LO 3-2 Describe some descriptive analytics approaches, including summary statistics and data reduction.

LO 3-3 Explain the diagnostic approach to Data Analytics, including profiling and clustering.

LO 3-4 Understand predictive analytics, including regression and classification.

LO 3-5 Describe the use of prescriptive analytics, including machine learning and artificial intelligence.

LO 3-1

Understand four categories of data analytics.

PERFORMING THE TEST PLAN

The third step of the IMPACT cycle model, or the "P," is "performing test plan." In this step, different Data Analytics approaches help us understand what happened, why it happened, what we can expect to happen in the future, and what we should do. These Data Analytics approaches or techniques help to address our business questions and provide information to support accounting and management decisions.

Data Analytics approaches rely on a series of tasks and models that are used to understand data and gain insight into the underlying cause and effect of business decisions. Many accounting courses introduce students to basic models that describe the results of periodic transactions (e.g. ratios, trends, and variance analysis). These simple calculations help accountants fulfill their traditional role as historians summarizing the results from the past to inform stakeholders of the status of the business.

While these simple techniques provide important information, their value is limited to providing information in hindsight. The contributing value of Data Analytics increases as the focus shifts from hindsight to foresight and from summarizing information to optimizing business outcomes as we go from descriptive analytics to prescriptive analytics (as illustrated in Exhibit 3-1). For example, lean accounting relies more heavily on data analysis to accurately predict changes in budgets and forecasts to minimize disruption to the business. These models that more accurately predict the future and prescribe a course of action come at a cost of increasing complexity in terms of manipulating and calculating appropriate data, and the implications of the results.

There are four main categories of data analytics, shown in Exhibit 3-1:

- **Descriptive analytics** are procedures that summarize existing data to determine what has happened in the past. Some examples of descriptive analytics include summary statistics (e.g. Count, Min, Max, Average, Median), distributions, and proportions.
- **Diagnostic analytics** are procedures that explore the current data to determine why something has happened the way it has, typically comparing the data to a benchmark. As an example, diagnostic analytics allow users to drill-down in the data and see how it compares to a budget, a competitor, or trend.
- **Predictive analytics** are procedures used to generate a model that can be used to determine what is likely to happen in the future. Examples of predictive analytics include regression analysis, forecasting, classification, and other predictive modeling.

EXHIBIT 3-1
Four Main Categories of Data Analytics

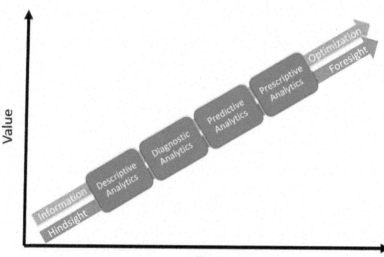

- **Prescriptive analytics** are procedures that model data to enable recommendations for what should be done in the future. These typically include developing more advanced machine learning and artificial intelligence models to recommend a course of action based on a current problem.

The choice of Data Analytics model depends largely on the type of question that you're trying to answer and your access to the data needed to answer the question. Descriptive and diagnostic analytics are typically paired when you would want to describe the past data and then compare it to a benchmark to determine why the results are the way they are, similar to the accounting concepts of planning and controlling. Likewise, predictive and prescriptive analytics make good partners when you would want to predict an outcome and then make a recommendation on how to follow up, similar to an auditor flagging a transaction as high risk and then following a decision flowchart to determine whether to request additional evidence or include it in audit findings.

As you move from one Data Analytics approach to the next, you trade hindsight and information, which are traditionally accounting domain areas for foresight and optimization.

Ultimately, the model you use comes down to the questions you are trying to answer. We highlighted the Data Analytics approaches in Chapter 1. Here we categorize them into the four main analytics categories, summarized in Table 3-1:

1. Descriptive analytics:
   - *Summary statistics* describe a set of data in terms of their location (mean, median), range (standard deviation, minimum, maximum), shape (quartile), and size (count).
   - *Data reduction or filtering* is used to reduce the amount of observations to focus on relevant items (i.e., highest cost, highest risk, largest impact, etc.). It does this by taking a large set of data (perhaps the population) and reducing it to a smaller set that has the vast majority of the

Type of analytic	Example in accounting
Descriptive analytics	*Understand what happened.*
Summary statistics	Calculate the average and medium income, age range, and highest and lowest purchases of customers during the 4th quarter.
Data reduction or filtering	Filter data to only include transactions within the current reporting period.
Diagnostic analytics	*Understand why it happened.*
Profiling	Identify outlier transactions to determine exposure and risk. Compare individual segments to a benchmark.
Clustering	Identify groups of store locations that are outperforming the rest.
Similarity matching	Understand the underlying behavior of high-performing divisions.
Co-occurrence grouping	Identify related party and intracompany transactions based on the individuals involved in a the transaction.
Predictive analytics	*Estimate a future value or category.*
Regression	Calculate the fixed and variable costs in a mixed cost equation or determine the number of days a shipment is likely to take.
Classification	Determine whether or not certain demongraphics, such as age, zip code, income level or gender are likely to engage in fraudulent transactions.
Link prediction	Predict participation of individuals based on their underlying common attributes, such as an incentive.
Prescriptive analytics	*Make recommendations for a course of action.*
Decision support systems	Tax software takes input from a preparer and recommends whether to take a standard deduction or an itemized deduction.
Artificial intelligence	Audit analysis monitors changing transactions and suggests follow up when new abnormal patterns appear.

TABLE 3-1
Summary of Data
Analytics Approaches

critical information of the larger set. For example, auditing may use data reduction to narrow transactions based on relevance or size. While auditing has employed various random and stratified sampling over the years, Data Analytics suggests new ways to highlight which transactions do not need the same level of vetting as other transactions.

2. Diagnostic analytics:
   - *Profiling* identifies the "typical" behavior of an individual, group, or population by compiling summary statistics about the data (including mean, standard deviations, etc.) and comparing individuals to the population. By understanding the typical behavior, we'll be able to identify abnormal behavior more easily. Profiling might be used in accounting to identify transactions that might warrant some additional investigation (e.g., outlier travel expenses or potential fraud).
   - *Clustering* helps identify groups (or clusters) of individuals (such as customers) that share common underlying characteristics—in other words, identifying groups of similar data elements and the underlying drivers of those groups. For example, clustering might be used to segment a customer into a small number of groups for additional analysis and risk assessment. Likewise, transactions might also be put into clusters to understand underlying relationships.
   - *Similarity matching* is a grouping technique used to identify similar individuals based on data known about them. The opening vignette in Chapter 1 mentioned Alibaba and its attempt to identify seller and customer fraud based on various characteristics known about them to see if they were similar to known fraud cases.
   - *Co-occurrence grouping* discovers associations between individuals based on common events, such as transactions they are involved in. Amazon might use this to sell another item to you by knowing what items are "frequently bought together" or "Customers who bought this item also bought . . ." as shown in Chapter 1.

3. Predictive analytics:
   - *Regression* estimates or predicts the numerical value of a dependent variable based on the slope and intersect of a line and the value of an independent variable. An R^2 value indicates how closely the line fits to the data used to calculate the regression. An example of regression analysis might be, given a balance of total accounts receivable held by a firm, what is the appropriate level of allowance for doubtful accounts for bad debts?
   - *Classification* predicts a class or category for a new observation based on the manual identification of classes from previous observations. Membership of a class may be binary in the case of decision trees or indicate the distance from a decision boundary. Some examples of classification include predicting which loans are likely to default, credit applications that are expected to be approved, the classification of an operating or financing lease, or identification of suspicious transactions. In each of these cases, prior data must be manually identified as belonging to each class to build the predictive model.
   - *Link prediction* predicts a relationship between two data items, such as members of a social media platform. For example, if two individuals have mutual friends on social media and both attended the same university, it is likely that they know each other and the site may make a recommendation for them to connect. Chapter 1 provides an example of this used in Facebook. Link prediction in an accounting setting might work to use social media to look for relationships between related parties that are not otherwise disclosed to identify related party transactions.

4. Prescriptive analytics:
   - *Decision support systems* are rule-based systems that gather data and recommend actions based on the input. Tax preparation software, investment advice tools, and auditing tools recommend courses of actions based on data that are input as part of an interview or interrogation process.
   - *Machine learning and artificial intelligence* are learning models or intelligent agents that adapt to new external data to recommend a course of action. For example, an artificial intelligence model may observe opinions given by an audit partner and adjust the model to reflect changing levels of risk appetite and regulation.

While these are all important and applicable data approaches, in the rest of the chapter we limit our discussion to the more common models, including summary statistics, data reduction, profiling, clustering, regression, classification, and artificial intelligence. You'll find that these data approaches are not mutually exclusive and that actual analysis may involve parts of several approaches to arrive at the intended test of the data and result.

 PROGRESS CHECK

1. Using Table 3-1, identify the appropriate approach for the following questions:
   a. Will a customer purchase item X if given incentive A?
   b. Should we offer a customer a line of credit?
   c. How many items will the customer purchase?
2. What is the main difference between descriptive and diagnostic methods?

DESCRIPTIVE ANALYTICS

LO 3-2

Describe some descriptive analytics approaches, including summary statistics and data reduction.

Descriptive analytics help summarize what has happened in the past. For example, a financial accountant would sum all of the sales transactions within a period to calculate the value for Sales Revenue that appears on the income statement. An analyst would count the number of records in a data extract to ensure the data are complete before running a more complex analysis. An auditor would filter data to limit the scope to transactions that represent the highest risk. In all these cases, basic analysis provides an understanding of what has happened in the past to help decision makers achieve good results and correct poor results.

Here we look at two main approaches that are used by accountants today: summary statistics and data reduction.

Summary Statistics

Summary statistics describe the location, spread, shape, and dependence of a set of observations. These commonly include the count, sum, minimum, maximum, mean or average, standard deviation, median, quartiles, correlation covariance, and frequency that describe a specific measurable value, shown in Table 3-2.

Statistic	Excel formula	Description
Sum	SUM()	The total value of all numerical values
Mean	=AVERAGE()	The center value; sum of all observations divided by the number of observations
Median	=MEDIAN()	The middle value that divides the top half of the data from the bottom half
Minimum	=MIN()	The smallest value
Maximum	=MAX()	The largest value
Count	=COUNT()	The number of observations
Frequency	=FREQUENCY()	The number of observations in each of a series of numerical or categorical buckets
Standard deviation	=STDEV()	The variability or spread of the data from the mean; a larger standard deviation means a wider spread away from the mean
Quartile	=QUARTILE()	The value that divides a quarter of the data from the rest; indicates skewness of the data
Correlation coefficient	=CORREL()	How closely two datasets are correlated or predictive of one another

TABLE 3-2
Description of
Summary Statistics

The use of summary statistics helps the user understand what the data look like. For example, the sum function can be used to determine account balances. The mean and median can be used to aggregate transactions by employee, location, or division. The standard deviation and frequency help to identify normal behavior and trends in the data.

Data Reduction

As you recall, the **data reduction** approach attempts to reduce the amount of detailed information considered to focus on the most critical, interesting, or abnormal items (i.e., highest cost, highest risk, largest impact, etc.). It does this by filtering through a large set of data (perhaps the total population) and reducing it to a smaller set that has the vast majority of the critical information of the larger set. The data reduction approach is done primarily using *structured data*—that is, data that are stored in a database or spreadsheet and are readily searchable.

Data reduction involves the following steps (using an example of an employee creating a fictitious vendor and submitting fake invoices):

1. *Identify the attribute you would like to reduce or focus on.* For example, an employee may commit fraud by creating a fictitious vendor and submitting fake invoices. Rather than evaluate every employee, an auditor may be interested only in employee records that have addresses that match vendor addresses.
2. *Filter the results.* This could be as simple as using filters in Excel, or using the WHERE phrase in a SQL query. It may also involve a more complicated calculation. For example, employees who create fictitious vendors will often use addresses that are similar, but not exactly the same, as their own address to foil basic SQL queries. Here the auditor should use a tool that allows fuzzy matching, which uses probability to identify likely similar addresses.
3. *Interpret the results.* Once you have eliminated irrelevant data, take a moment to see if the results make sense. Calculate the summary statistics. Have you eliminated any obvious entries? Looking at the list of matching employees, the auditor might tweak the probability in the fuzzy match to be more or less precise to narrow or broaden the number of employees who appear.
4. *Follow up on results.* At this point, you will continue to build a model or use the results as a targeted sample for follow-up. The auditor should review company policy and follow up with each employee who appears in the reduced list as it represents risk.

Example of Data Reduction in Internal and External Auditing

While auditing has employed various random and stratified sampling over the years, Data Analytics suggests new ways to highlight transactions that do not need the same level of vetting or further analysis as other transactions. One example might be to filter the travel and entertainment (T&E) transactions to find specific values, including whole-dollar amounts of T&E expenses. Whole-dollar amounts have a greater likelihood of being made up or fraudulent (as illustrated in Exhibit 3-2).

Auditors may filter data to consider only those transactions being paid to specific vendors, such as mobile payment processors. Because anyone can create a payment account using processors such as Square Payments, there is a higher potential for the existence of a fictitious or employee-created vendor. The data reduction approach allows us to focus more time and effort on those vendors and transactions that might require additional analysis to make sure they are legitimate.

Vendor	Amount
A	$ 4.35
B	$ 10.00
C	$ 17.00
A	$ 5.32
D	$ 54.23
B	$ 32.33
C	$ 33.00
Total	$ 156.23

Vendor	Amount
B	$ 10.00
C	$ 17.00
B	$ 32.33
C	$ 33.00
Total	$ 92.33

EXHIBIT 3-2
Use filters to reduce data

Another example of the data reduction approach is gap detection, where we look for missing numbers in a sequence, such as payments made by check. Finding out why certain check numbers were skipped and not recorded requires additional analysis and consideration.

Data reduction may also be used to filter all the transactions between known related party transactions. Focusing specifically on related party transactions allows the auditor to focus on those transactions that might potentially be sensitive and/or risky.

Finally, data reduction might be used to compare the addresses of vendors and employees to ensure that employees are not siphoning funds to themselves. Use of fuzzy match looks for correspondences between portions, or segments, of the text of each potential match, shown in Exhibit 3-3. Once potential matches between vendors and employees are found, additional analysis must be conducted to figure out if funds have been, or potentially could be, siphoned.

Examples of Data Reduction in Other Accounting Areas

Data reduction approaches are also used in operational audit settings. For example, filtering the data to find cases where there are duplicate invoice payments might be an efficient way to find errors or fraud. Once duplicate invoice payments are found, additional work can be done to identify the reasons this has occurred. It may also be a way to reduce costs when duplicate payments are found and procedures are set in place to mitigate duplicate payments from occurring in the future.

Data reduction approaches may also be useful in a financial statement analysis setting, perhaps performed by financial analysts, pension funds, or individual investors. Among other uses, **XBRL (eXtensible Business Reporting Language)** is used to facilitate the exchange of financial reporting information between the company and the Securities and Exchange Commission (SEC). The SEC then makes it available to all interested parties, including suppliers, competitors, investors, and financial analysts. XBRL requires that the data be tagged according to the XBRL taxonomy. Using these tagged data in common size

Employee	Street Address
K Mercer	375 Bohemia St.
S Compton	9203 Poplar Ave.
N Macdonald	365 Smith Court
M Roy	743 Oak Meadow Drive
F Jefferson	148 Richardson St
K Galvan	64 Marconi Ave.
C Osborne	8552 Race Ave.
J Oneill	83 High Ridge Rd.
F Mcdonald	932 Summit St.

Vendor	Street Address
Zaphex	9887 Henry Smith Rd.
Treefax	7341 West Durham Ave.
Betatech	30 Ketch Harbour Ave.
Medianix	58 Pine St.
Iceron	148 Richardson Street
Tripplecore	646 Church St.
Canla	355 Beacon Street
Opeit	645 Windsor Dr.
Bigfase	8347 Garfield St.

EXHIBIT 3-3
A fuzzy matching shows a likely match of an employees and vendor

financial statements, financial analysts, loan officers, auditors, accountants, information system specialists, and investors develop models to access all the relevant financial or nonfinancial data to help interpret the financial data to predict future earnings, forecast solvency or liquidity, and analyze profitability. The use of XBRL and the modeling by financial data takes all the details of the financial statements, footnotes, and other financial and nonfinancial data and summarizes them in models of future earnings, solvency, liquidity, and profitability. We'll explore XBRL further in Chapter 8.

 PROGRESS CHECK

3. Describe how the data reduction approach could be used to evaluate employee travel and entertainment expenses.

4. Explain how XBRL might be used by lenders to focus on specific areas of interest.

LO 3-3

Explain the diagnostic approach to Data Analytics, including profiling and clustering

DIAGNOSTIC ANALYTICS

Diagnostic analytics provide insight into why things happened or how individual data values relate to the general population. Once you summarize data using descriptive techniques, you can drill-down and discover the numbers that are driving an outcome. Benchmarks give context to the data by giving analysts a reference point (or line) to compare the data to. For example, the arithmetic mean of a data set gives you context for a specific value. These benchmarks may be based on past activity, a comparison with a major competitor or an entire industry.

Two primary methods of diagnostic analytics include profiling and cluster analysis. In both of these cases the analysis provides insight into where a specific value lies relative to the rest of the sample or population. The farther the distance from the rest of the observations, the more interesting the individual value becomes. These outliers could represent risk or opportunities to learn more about the business process or partnerships driving the behavior.

Profiling

As you recall, **profiling** involves gaining an understanding of a typical behavior of an individual, group, or population (or sample). Profiling is done primarily using **structured data**—data that are stored in a database or spreadsheet and are readily searchable. Using these data, analysts can use common summary statistics to describe the individual, group, or population, including knowing its mean, standard deviation, sum, etc. Profiling is generally performed on data that are readily available, so the data have already been gathered and are ready for further analysis.

Profiling is used to discover patterns of behavior. In Exhibit 3-4, for example, the higher the Z-score (farther away from the mean), the more likely a customer will have a delayed shipment (blue circle). As shown in the Exhibit, a Z-score of three represents three standard deviations away from the mean. We use profiling to explore the attributes of that vendor that we may want to avoid in the future.

Data profiling can be as simple as calculating summary statistics on transactional data, such as the average number of days to ship a product, the typical amount we pay for a product, or the number of hours an employee is expected to work. On the other hand, profiling can be used to develop complex models to predict potential fraud. For example, you might create a profile for each employee in a company that may include a combination of salary, hours worked, and travel and entertainment purchasing behavior. Sudden deviations from an employee's past behavior may represent risk and warrant follow-up by the internal auditors.

Similar to evaluating behavior, data profiling is typically used to assess data quality and internal controls. For example, data profiling may identify customers with incomplete or erroneous master data or mistyped transactions.

Average Days to Ship

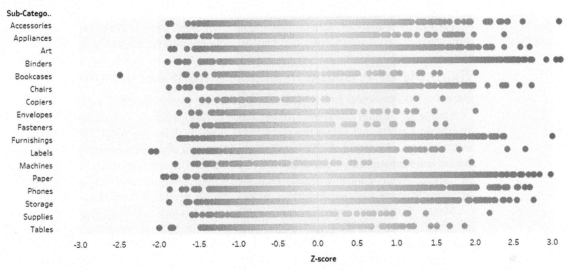

EXHIBIT 3-4 **Z-Scores Provide an Example of Profiling That Helps Identify Outliers (in this case, customers with unusually high average days to ship)**

Data profiling typically involves the following steps:

1. *Identify the objects or activity you want to profile.* What data do you want to evaluate? Sales transactions? Customer data? Credit limits? Imagine a manager wants to track sales volume for each store in a retail chain. She might evaluate total sales dollars, asset turnover, use of promotions and discounts, and/or employee incentives.
2. *Determine the types of profiling you want to perform.* What is your goal? Do you want to set a benchmark for minimum activity, such as monthly sales? Have you set a budget that you wish to follow? Are you trying to reduce fraud risk? In the retail store scenario, the manager would likely want to compare each store to the others to identify which ones are underperforming or overperforming.
3. *Set boundaries or thresholds for the activity.* This is a benchmark that may be manually set, such as a budgeted value, or automatically set, such as a statistical mean, quartile, or percentile. The retail chain manager may define underperforming stores as those whose sales activity falls below the 20th percentile of the group and overperforming stores as those whose sales activity is above the 80th percentile. These thresholds are automatically calculated based on the total activity of the stores, so the benchmark is dynamic.
4. *Interpret the results and monitor the activity and/or generate a list of exceptions.* Here is where dashboards come into play. Management can use **dashboards** to quickly see multiple sets of profiled data and make decisions that would affect behavior. As you evaluate the results, try to understand what a deviation from the defined boundary represents. Is it a risk? Is it fraud? Is it just something to keep an eye on? To evaluate her stores, the retail chain manager may review a summary of the sales indicators and quickly identify under- and overperforming stores. She is likely to be more concerned with underperforming stores because they represent major challenges for the chain. Overperforming stores may provide insight into marketing efforts or customer base.
5. *Follow up on exceptions.* Once a deviation has been identified, management should have a plan to take a course of action to validate, correct, or identify the causes of the abnormal behavior. When the retail chain manager notices a store that is underperforming

compared to its peers, she may follow up with the individual store manager to understand his concerns or offer a local promotion to stimulate sales.

As with most analyses, data profiles should be updated periodically to reflect changes in firm activity and identify activity that may be more relevant to decision making.

Example of Profiling in Management Accounting

Advanced Environmental Recycling Technologies (ticker symbol AERT) makes wood-plastic composite for decking that doesn't rot and keeps its form, color, and shape indefinitely. It has developed a recipe and knows the standards of how much wood, plastic, and coloring goes into each foot of decking. AERT has developed standard costs and constantly calculates the means and standard deviations of the use of wood, plastic, coloring, and labor for each foot of decking. As the company profiles each production batch, it knows that when significant variances from the standard cost occur, those variances need to be investigated further.

Management accounting relies heavily on diagnostic analytics in the planning and controlling process. By comparing the actual results of activity to the budgeted expectation, management determines the processes and procedures that resulted in favorable and unfavorable activity. For example, in a manufacturing company like AERT, variance analysis compares the actual cost, price, and volume of various activities with standard equivalents, shown in Exhibit 3-5. The unfavorable variances appear in orange as the actual cost exceeds the budgeted cost or are to the left of the budget reference line. Favorable variances appear to the right of the budget reference line in blue. Sales exceed the budgeted sales. As sales volume increases, the costs (negative values) also increase, leading to an unfavorable variance in orange.

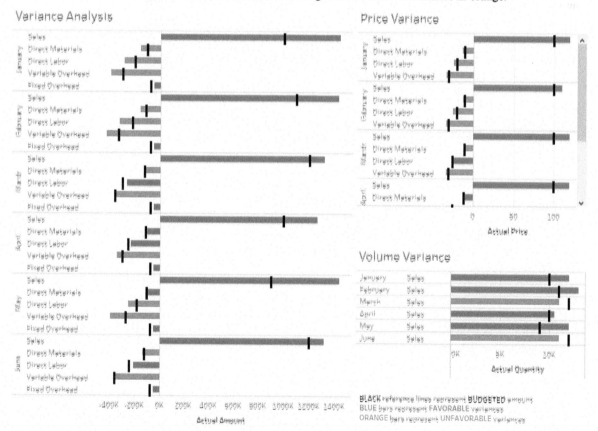

EXHIBIT 3-5   Variance Analysis Is an Example of Data Profiling

Example of Profiling in an Internal Audit

Profiling might also be used by internal auditors to evaluate travel and entertainment (T&E) expenses. In some organizations, total annual T&E expenses are second only to payroll and so represent a major expense for the organization. By profiling the T&E expenses, we can understand the average amount and range of expenditures and then compare and contrast with prior period's mean and range to help identify changing trends and potential risk areas for audit and potentially for tax purposes. This will help indicate areas where there is lack of controls, changes in procedures, or individuals more willing to spend excessively in potential types of T&E expenses, etc., which might be associated with higher risk.

The use of profiling in internal audits might unearth when employees misuse company funds, like in the case of Tom Coughlin, an executive at Walmart, who misused "company funds to pay for CDs, beer, an all-terrain vehicle, a customized dog kennel, even a computer as his son's graduation gift—all the while describing the purchases as routine business expenses."[1]

Example of Profiling in Auditing

Profiling is also useful in continuous auditing. If we consider the dollar amount of each transaction, we can develop a Z-score by knowing the mean and standard deviation. Using our statistics knowledge and assuming a normal distribution, any transaction that has a Z-score of 3 or above would represent abnormal transactions that might be associated with higher risk. We can investigate further seeing if those transactions had appropriate approvals and authorization.

An analysis of **Benford's law** could also be used to assess a set of transactions. Benford's law is an observation about the frequency of leading digits in many real-life sets of numerical data. The law states that in many naturally occurring collections of numbers, the significant leading digit is likely to be small. If the distribution of transactions for an account like "sales revenue" is substantially different than Benford's law would predict, then we would investigate the sales revenue account further and see if we can explain why there are differences from Benford's law. Exhibit 3-6 shows an illustration of Benford's law using the first digit of employee transactions. An abnormal frequency of transaction beginning with the number four may indicate that employees are attempting to circumvent internal controls, such as an approval limit. While the number one also exceeds the expected value, we would expect a larger volume of smaller numbers. We will discuss additional applications of Benford's law in Chapter 6.

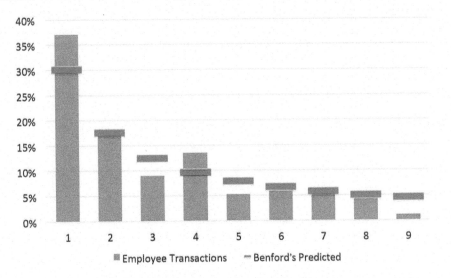

EXHIBIT 3-6
Benford's Law Applied to Large Numerical Data Sets (including employee transactions)

■ Employee Transactions   ▬ Benford's Predicted

[1] http://www.washingtonpost.com/wp-dyn/content/article/2005/07/14/AR2005071402055.html (accessed August 2, 2017).

Cluster Analysis

The **clustering** data approach works to identify groups of similar data elements and the underlying relationships of those groups. More specifically, clustering techniques are used to group data/observations into a specific number of clusters or groups so that all the data within any cluster are similar, while data across clusters are different. Cluster analysis works by calculating the minimum distance between each observation and the center of each cluster, shown in Exhibit 3-7.

EXHIBIT 3-7

Clustering Is Used to Find Three Natural Groupings of Vendors Based on Purchase Activity

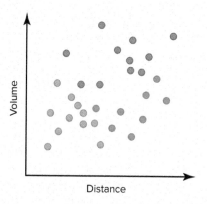

When you are exploring the data for these patterns and don't have a specific question, you would use an **unsupervised approach**. For example, consider the question: *"Do our vendors form natural groups based on similar attributes?"* In this case, there isn't a specific target because you don't yet know what similarities our vendors have. You may use *clustering* to evaluate the vendor attributes and see which ones are closely related. You could also use **co-occurrence grouping** to match vendors by geographic region; *data reduction* to simplify vendors into obvious categories, such as wholesale or retail or based on overall volume of orders; or *profiling* to evaluate vendors with similar on-time delivery behavior, shown in Exhibit 3-4. In any of these cases, the data drive the analysis, and you evaluate the output to see if it matches our intuition. These exploratory exercises may help to define better questions, but are generally less useful for making decisions.

As an example, Walmart may want to understand the types of customers who shop at its stores. Because Walmart has good reason to believe there are different market segments of people, it may consider changing the design of the store or the types of products to accommodate the different types of customers, emphasizing the ones that are most profitable to Walmart. To learn about the different types of customers, managers may ask whether customers agree with the following statements using a scale of 1–7 (on a Likert scale):

- Enjoy: I enjoy shopping.
- Budget: I try to avoid shopping because it is bad for the budget.
- Eating: I like to combine my shopping with eating out.
- Coupons: I use coupons when I shop.
- Quality: I care more about the quality of the products than I do about the price.
- Apathy: I don't care about shopping.
- Comparing: You can save a lot of money by comparing prices between various stores.

Additionally, they would ask about numerical customer behavior:

- Income: The household income of the respondent (in dollars).
- Shopping at Walmart: How many times a month do you visit Walmart?

Accountants may analyze the data and plot the responses to see if there are correlations within the data on a scatterplot. The visual plot of the relationship between responses to the various questions may help cluster the various customers into different clusters and help Walmart cater to specific customer clusters better through superior insights.

Example of the Clustering Approach in Auditing

The clustering data approach may also be used in an auditing setting. Imagine a group insurance setting where fraudulent claims associated with payment were previously found by internal auditors through happenstance and/or through hotline tips. Based on current internal audit tests, payments are the major concern of the business unit. Specifically, the types of related risks identified are duplicate payments, fictitious names, improper/incorrect information entered into the systems, and suspicious payment amounts.

Clustering is useful for anomaly detection in payments to insurance beneficiaries, suppliers, etc. By identifying transactions with similar characteristics, transactions are grouped together into clusters. Those clusters that consist of few transactions or small populations are then flagged for investigation by the auditors as they represent groups of outliers. Examples of these flagged clusters include transactions with large payment amounts and/or a long delay in processing the payment.

The dimensions used in clustering may be simple correlations between variables, such as payment amount and time to pay, or more complex combinations of variables, such as ratios or weighted equations. As they explore the data, auditors develop attributes that they think will be relevant through intuition or data exploration. Exhibit 3-8 illustrates clustering of insurance payments based on the following attributes:

1. Payment amount: The value of the transaction payment.
2. Days to Pay: The number of days from the original recorded transaction to the payment date.

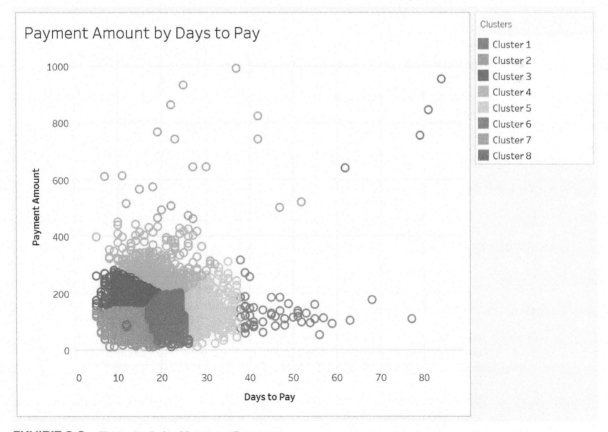

EXHIBIT 3-8   Cluster Analysis of Insurance Payments

The data are normalized to reduce the distortion of the data and other outliers are removed. They are then plotted with the number of days to pay on the *y* axis and the payment amount on the x-axis. Of the eight clusters identified, three clusters highlight potential anomalies that may require further investigation as part of an internal or external audit.

- Cluster 6 payments (purple) have a long duration between the processing to payment dates.
- Cluster 7 payments (pink) have high payment amounts.
- Cluster 8 payments (brown) have high payment amounts and a long duration between the processing date and the payment date.

With this insight auditors may assess the risk associated with these payments and understand transaction behavior relative to acceptable behavior defined in internal controls.

 PROGRESS CHECK

5. Profiling is also used in law enforcement, such as offender or criminal profiling. Offender profiling is a tool used by law enforcement to identify likely suspects, analyze data patterns to help predict future offenses by criminals, and identify potential victims. Compare and contrast this type of profiling with the profiling data approach used in accounting (mentioned earlier in this section).

6. Identify a reason the sales amount of any single product may or may not follow Benford's law.

7. Name three clusters of customers who might shop at Walmart.

8. In Exhibit 3-8, Cluster 1 of the group insurance highlighted claims have a long period from death to payment dates. Why would that cluster be of interest to internal auditors?

PREDICTIVE ANALYTICS

LO 3-4

Understand predictive analytics, including regression and classification.

Before we discuss predictive analytics, we need to bring you up to speed on some data-specific terms:

- A *target* is an expected attribute or value that we want to evaluate. For example, if we are trying to predict whether a transaction is fraudulent, the target might be a specific "fraud score." If we're trying to predict an interest rate, the target would be "interest rate."
- A *class* is a manually assigned category applied to a record based on an event. For example, if the credit department has rejected a credit line for a customer, the credit department assigns the class "Rejected" to the customer's master record. Likewise, if the internal auditors have confirmed that fraud has occurred, they would assign the class "fraud" to that transaction.

On the other hand, we may ask questions with specific outcomes, such as: "Will a new vendor ship a large order on time?" When you are performing analysis that uses historical data to predict a future outcome, you will use a **supervised approach**. You might use **regression** to predict a *specific value* to answer a question such as, "How many days do we predict it will take a new vendor to ship an order?" Again, the prediction is based on the activity we have observed from other vendors, shown in Exhibit 3-9. We use historical data to create the new model. Using a **classification** model, you can predict *whether* a new vendor belongs to one class or another based on the behavior of the others, shown in Exhibit 3-10. **Causal modeling, similarity matching**, and **link prediction** are additional supervised approaches where you attempt to identify causation (which can be expensive), identify a series of characteristics that predict a model, or attempt to identify other relationships, respectively.

Regression

Regressions allow the accountant to develop models to predict expected outcomes. These expected outcomes might be to predict the number of days to ship products relative to the volume of orders placed by the customer, shown in Exhibit 3-9.

Regression is a supervised method used to predict specific values. In this case, the number of days to ship is dependent on the number of items in the order. Therefore, we can use regression to predict the number of days it takes Vendor A to ship based on the volume in the order. (Vendor A is represented by the gold star in Exhibits 3-9 and 3-10).

Regression analysis involves the following process:

1. *Identify the variables that might predict an outcome.* The inputs are called independent variables, where the output is a dependent variable.
2. *Determine the functional form of the relationship.* Is it a linear relationship where each input plots to another? Are you trying to divide the records into different groups or classes?
3. *Identify the parameters of the model.* What are the relative weights of each variable or the thresholds of each branch in a classification?
4. *Evaluate the goodness of fit.* Calculate the correlation coefficient or R^2 value to determine whether the data are close to the line or not. In general, the better the fit (e.g., $R^2 > 0.8$), the more accurate the prediction will be.

The following discussion primarily identifies the structure of the model—that is, the relationship between the dependent variable and the plausible independent variables—in this way:

$$\text{Dependent variable} = f(\text{Independent variables})$$

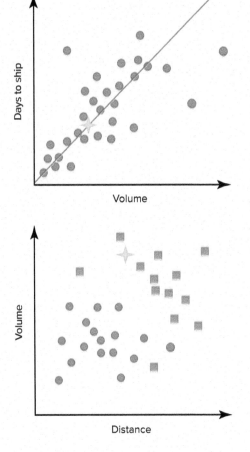

EXHIBIT 3-9
Regression

EXHIBIT 3-10
Classification

The dependent variable might be the amount that should be considered in an allowance for doubtful accounts; the independent variables that might predict the level needed to reserve it may be current aged loans, loan type, customer loan history, and collections success. Dependent variables could be continuous (e.g., salary or loan history) or categorical (e.g., home ownership or customer type). Continuous variables may provide more interesting results than a one or two class categorical variable.

Examples of the Regression Approach in Managerial Accounting

Accounting firms experience a great amount of employee turnover each year (between 15 and 25 percent each year).[2] Understanding and predicting employee turnover is a particularly important determination for accounting firms. Each year, they must predict how many new employees might be needed to accommodate growth, to supply needed areas of expertise, and to replace employees who have left. Accounting firms might predict employee turnover by predicting the following regression model in this way:

Employee turnover $= f$ (Current professional salaries, Health of the economy [GDP], Salaries offered by other accounting firms or by corporate accounting, etc.)

Using such a model, accounting firms could then begin to collect the necessary data to test their model and predict the level of employee turnover.

Examples of the Regression Approach in Auditing

One of the key tasks of auditors of a bank is to consider the amount of the allowance for loan losses or for non-banks to consider the allowance for doubtful accounts (i.e., those receivables that may never be collected). These allowances are often subject to manipulation to help manage earnings.[3] The Financial Accounting Standards Board (FASB) recently issued Accounting Standards Update 2016-13, which requires that banks provide an estimate of expected credit losses (ECLs) by considering historical collection rates, current information, and reasonable and supportable forecasts, including estimates of prepayments.[4] Using these historical and industry data, auditors may work to test a model to establish a loan loss reserve in this way:

Allowance for loan loses amount $= f$ (Current aged loans, Loan type, Customer loan history, Collections success)

Other Examples of the Regression in Accounting

For example, in Chapter 1, we worked to understand why LendingClub rejected certain loan applications. As we considered all of the possible explanations, we found that there were at least three possible indicators that a loan might be rejected, including the debt-to-income ratios, length of employment, and credit (risk) scores, suggesting a model that:

Loan rejection $= f$ (Debt-to-income ratio, Length of employment, Credit [risk] score)

[2] http://www.cpafma.org/articles/inside-public-accounting-releases-2015-national-benchmarking-report/ (accessed November 9, 2016).
[3] A. S. Ahmed, C. Takeda, and S. Thomas, "Bank Loan Loss Provisions: A Reexamination of Capital Management, Earnings Management and Signaling Effects," *Journal of Accounting and Economics* 28, no. 1 (1999), pp. 1–25.
[4] http://www.pwc.com/us/en/cfodirect/publications/in-brief/fasb-new-impairment-guidance-financial-instruments.html (accessed November 9, 2016).

Another example of the regression approach might be the approval of individual credit card transactions. Assume you go on a trip; in the morning you are in Pittsburgh and by the very next day, you are in Shanghai. Will your credit card transaction in Shanghai automatically be rejected? Credit card companies establish models to predict fraud and decide whether to accept or reject a proposed credit card transaction. A potential model may be the following:

$$\text{Transaction approval} = f(\text{Location of current transaction, Location of last transaction, Amount of current transaction, Prior history of travel of credit card holder, etc.})$$

Classification

The goal of classification is to predict whether an individual we know very little about will belong to one class or another. For example, will a customer have his or her balance written off? The key here is that we are predicting *whether* the write-off will occur or not (in other words, there are two classes: "Write-Off" and "Good").

Classification is a supervised method that can be used to predict the class of a new observation. In this case, blue circles represent "on-time" vendors. Green squares represent "delayed" vendors. The gold star represents a new vendor with no history.

Classification is a little more involved as we are now dealing with machine learning and complex probabilistic models. Here are the general steps:

1. *Identify the classes you wish to predict.*
2. *Manually classify an existing set of records.*
3. *Select a set of classification models.*
4. *Divide your data into training and testing sets.*
5. *Generate your model.*
6. *Interpret the results and select the "best" model.*

Classification Terminology

First, a bit of terminology to prepare us for our discussion.

Training data are existing data that have been manually evaluated and assigned a class. We know that some customer accounts have been written off, so those accounts are assigned the class "Write-Off." We will train our model to learn what it is that those customers have in common so we can predict whether a new customer will default or not.

Test data are existing data used to evaluate the model. The classification algorithm will try to predict the class of the test data and then compare its prediction to the previously assigned class. This comparison is used to evaluate the accuracy of the model or the probability that the model will assign the correct class.

Decision trees are used to divide data into smaller groups, and **decision boundaries** mark the split between one class and another.

Exhibit 3-11 provides an illustration of both decision trees and decision boundaries. Decision trees split the data at each branch into two or more groups. In this example, the first branch divides the vendor data by geographic distance and inserts a decision boundary through the middle of the data. Branches 2 and 3 split each of the two new groups by vendor volume. Note that the decision boundaries in the graph on the right are different for each grouping.

Pruning removes branches from a decision tree to avoid overfitting the model. In other words, pruning reduces the number of times we split the groups of data into smaller groups, as shown in Exhibit 3-11. *Pre-pruning* occurs during the model generation. The model stops creating new branches when the information usefulness of an additional branch is low. *Post-pruning* evaluates the complete model and discards branches after the fact. Exhibit 3-12 provides an illustration of how pruning might work in a decision tree.

EXHIBIT 3-11
Example of Decision
Trees and Decision
Boundaries

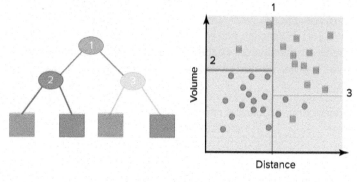

EXHIBIT 3-12
Illustration of Pruning
a Decision Tree

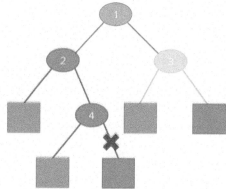

Linear classifiers are useful for ranking items rather than simply predicting class probability. These classifiers are used to identify a decision boundary. Exhibit 3-13 shows an illustration of linear classifiers segregating the two classes.

A linear discriminant uses an algebraic line to separates the two classes. In the example noted here, the classification is a function of both volume and distance:

$$\text{Class}(x) = \bigcirc \quad \text{if } 1.0 \times \text{Volume} - 1.5 \times \text{Distance} + 50 > 0$$

$$\text{Class}(x) = \blacksquare \quad \text{if } 1.0 \times \text{Volume} - 1.5 \times \text{Distance} + 50 \leq 0$$

We don't expect linear classifiers to perfectly segregate classes. For example, the green square that appears below the line in Exhibit 3-13 would be incorrectly classified as a circle and considered an error.

Support vector machine is a discriminating classifier that is defined by a separating hyperplane that works first to find the widest margin (or biggest pipe) and then works to find the

EXHIBIT 3-13
Illustration of Linear
Classifiers

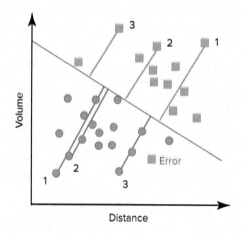

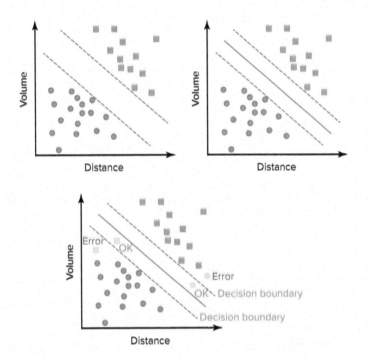

EXHIBIT 3-14
Support Vector Machines
With support vector
machines, first find the
widest margin (biggest
pipe); then find the
middle line.

EXHIBIT 3-15
Support Vector
Machine Decision
Boundaries
SVMs have two decision
boundaries at the edges
of the pipes.

middle line. Exhibits 3-14 and 3-15 provide an illustration of support vector machines and how they work to find the best decision boundary.

Evaluating Classifiers

When classifiers wrongly classify an observation, they are penalized. The larger the penalty (error), the less accurate the model is at predicting a future value, or classification.

Overfitting

Rarely will datasets be so clean that you have a clear decision boundary. You should always be wary of classifiers that are too accurate. Exhibit 3-16 provides an illustration of overfitting and underfitting. You want a good amount of accuracy without being too perfect. Notice how the error rate declines from 6 to 3 to 0. You want to be able to generalize your results, and complete accuracy creates a complex model with little predictive value.

Exhibit 3-17 provides a good illustration of the trade-offs between the complexity of the model and the accuracy of the classification. While you may be able to come up with a very complex model with the training data, chances are it will not improve the accuracy of

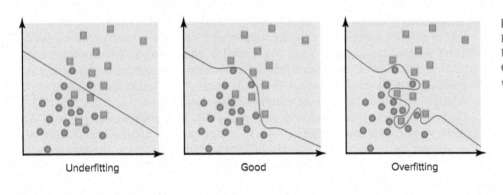

EXHIBIT 3-16
Illustration of
Underfitting and
Overfitting the Data
with a Predictive Model

EXHIBIT 3-17
Illustration of the
Trade-Off between
the Complexity of
the Model and the
Accuracy of the
Classification

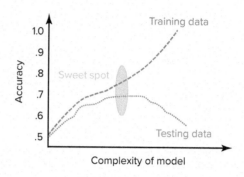

correctly classifying the test data. There is, in some sense, a sweet spot, where the model is most accurate without being so complex to thus allow classification of both the training as well as the test data.

> ### ✅ PROGRESS CHECK
>
> 9. If we are trying to predict the extent of employee turnover, do you believe the health of the economy, as measured using GDP, will be positively or negatively associated with employee turnover?
>
> 10. If we are trying to predict whether a loan will be rejected, would you expect credit score to be positively or negatively associated with loan rejection by a bank such as **LendingClub**?

LO 3-5

Describe the use of prescriptive analytics, including decision support systems, machine learning and artificial intelligence.

PRESCRIPTIVE ANALYTICS

Prescriptive analytics answer the question *"What do we do next?"* We have collected the data; analyzed and profiled the data; and in some cases, developed predictive models to estimate the proper class or target value. Once those analyses have been performed, the decision process can be aided by rules-based decision support systems, machine learning models, or added to an existing artificial intelligence model to improve future predictions.

These analytics are the most complex and expensive because they rely on multiple variable and inputs, structured and unstructured data, and in some cases the ability to understand and interpret natural language command into data-driven queries.

Decision Support Systems

Decision support systems are information systems that support decision-making activity within a business by combining data and expertise to solve problems and perform calculations. They are designed to be interactive and adapt to the information collected by the user. In the accounting domain, they are typically built around a series of rules or If . . . then . . . branching statements that guide the user through the process to the result.

One of the best examples of decision support systems is the calculation of income tax using off the shelf tax software. Tools like TurboTax guide a non-technical user through a series of interview questions and have them enter a numerical income value or answer a yes/no question. The answers to those questions determine what calculations to include, which schedules to complete, and what the value of the tax return will be.

Decision support systems can help with application of accounting rules as well. For example, when a company classifies a lease as a financing or operating lease, it must consider whether the lease meets a number of criteria. Using a decision support system, a controller could evaluate a new lease and answer five questions to determine the proper classification, shown in Exhibit 3-18.

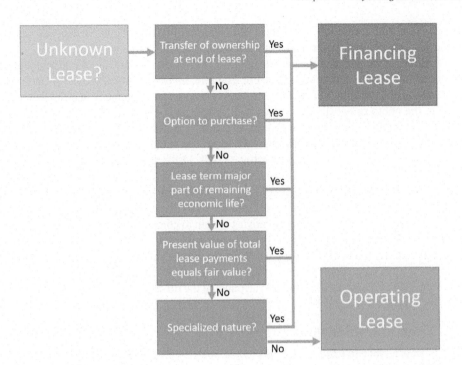

EXHIBIT 3-18
Lease Classification
Flowchart

Under a previous version of the FAB lease standard, there would have been bright lines to indicate hard rules to determine the lease (for example, "The lease term is greater than or equal to 75 percent of the estimated economic life of the leased asset."). Decision support systems are easier to use when you have clear rules. Under the newer standard, more judgment is needed to reach the most appropriate conclusion for the business. More on this later.

Auditors use decision support systems as part of their audit procedures. For example, they indicate a series of parameters such as tolerable and expected error rates. A tool like IDEA will calculate the appropriate sample size for evaluating source documents. Once the procedure has been performed, i.e., source documents are evaluated, the auditor will then input the number or extent of exceptional items and the decision support system might classify the audit risk as low, medium, or high for that area.

Machine Learning and Artificial Intelligence

We have discussed some machine learning techniques, including classification and cluster analysis in the previous sections. What these all have in common is the use of algorithms and statistical models to generate a previously unknown model that relies on patterns and inferences. Both unsupervised exploratory analysis and supervised model generation provide insight and predictive foresight into the business and decisions made by the accountants and auditors. They can also model judgment and decision making to recommend a class or action based on new, unknown data.

Take lease classification, for instance. With the recent accounting standard, the language has moved from bright lines ("75 percent of the useful life") to judgment ("major part"). While it may be tempting to rely on the accountant to manually make this decision for each new lease, machine learning will do it more quickly and more accurately than the manual classification. A company with a sufficiently large portfolio of previously classified leases may use those leases as a training set for a machine learning model. Using the data attributes from these leases (e.g., useful life, total payments, fair value, originating firm) and the prior manual classification (e.g., financing, operating) of the company's leases, the model can evaluate a new lease and assign the appropriate classification. Post-classification verification and correction in the case of an inappropriate outcome is then fed into the model to improve the performance of the model.

Artificial intelligence models work similarly in that they learn from the inputs and corrections to improve decision making. For example, image classification allows auditors to take aerial photography of inventory or fixed assets and automatically identify the objects within the photo rather than having an auditor manually check each object. Classification of closed-circuit footage enables automatic counting of foot traffic in a retail location for managers. Modeling of past judgment decisions by audit partners makes it possible to determine whether an allowance or estimate falls within a normal range for a client and is acceptable or should be qualified. Artificial intelligence models that track sentiment in social media and popular press posts to predict positive stock market returns for analysts.

For most application of artificial intelligence models, the computational power is such that most companies will outsource the underlying system to companies like Microsoft, Amazon, or Google rather than develop it themselves. These companies provide the datasets to train and build the model, and the platforms provide the algorithms and code. When public accounting firms outsource data clients may be hesitant to allow their financial data to be used in these platforms without additional assurance surrounding the privacy and security of their data.

 PROGRESS CHECK

11. How might you expect managers to use decision support systems when evaluating employee bonuses?
12. How do machine learning and artificial intelligence models improve their recommendations over time?

Summary

- In this chapter, we addressed the third step of the IMPACT cycle model: the "P" for "performing test plan." That is, how are we going to test or analyze the data to address a problem we are facing?
- We identified descriptive analytics that help describe what happened with the data, including summary statistics, and data reduction and filtering.
- We provided examples of diagnostic analytics that help users identify relationships in the data that uncover why certain events happen through profiling, clustering, similarity matching, and co-occurrence grouping.
- We explained examples of predictive analytics and introduced some data mining concepts related to regression, classification, and link prediction that can help predict future events or values.
- We discussed predictive analytics, including decision support systems and artificial intelligence and provided some example of how these systems can make recommendations for future actions.
- We introduced some specific models and terminology related to these tools, including Benford's law, test and training data, decision trees and boundaries, linear classifiers, and support vector machines. We identified cases where creating models that overfit existing data are not very accurate at predicting the future.
- We presented some classification terminology—including test and training data, decision trees and boundaries, linear classifiers, and support vector machines—and talked about the perils of under- and overfitting the training data and their consequences in predictions using the test data.

Key Words

Benford's law (*103*)   An observation about the frequency of leading digits in many real-life sets of numerical data. The law states that in many naturally occurring collections of numbers, the significant leading digit is likely to be small.

causal modeling (*106*)   A data approach similar to regression, but used when the relationship between independent and dependent variables where it is hypothesized that the independent variables cause or are associated with the dependent variable.

classification (*106*)   A data approach used to assign each unit in a population into a few categories potentially to help with predictions.

clustering (*103*)   A data approach used to divide individuals (like customers) into groups (or clusters) in a useful or meaningful way.

co-occurrence grouping (*103*)   A data approach used to discover associations between individuals based on transactions involving them.

data reduction (*98*)   A data approach used to reduce the amount of information that needs to be considered to focus on the most critical items (i.e., highest cost, highest risk, largest impact, etc.).

decision boundaries (*109*)   Technique used to mark the split between one class and another.

decision support system (*112*)   An information system that supports decision-making activity within a business by combining data and expertise to solve problems and perform calculations.

decision tree (*109*)   Tool used to divide data into smaller groups.

descriptive analytics (*94*)   Procedures that summarize existing data to determine what has happened in the past. Some examples include summary statistics (e.g. Count, Min, Max, Average, Median), distributions, and proportions.

diagnostic analytics (*94*)   Procedures that explore the current data to determine why something has happened the way it has, typically comparing the data to a benchmark. As an example, these allow users to drill-down in the data and see how it compares to a budget, a competitor, or trend.

fuzzy match (*124*)   A computer-assisted technique of finding matches that are less than 100 percent perfect by finding correspondencies between portions of the text of each potential match.

link prediction (*106*)   A data approach used to predict a relationship between two data items.

predictive analytics (*94*)   Procedures used to generate a model that can be used to determine what is likely to happen in the future. Examples include regression analysis, forecasting, classification, and other predictive modeling.

prescriptive analytics (*95*)   Procedures that model data to enable recommendations for what should be done in the future. These typically include developing more advanced machine learning and artificial intelligence models to recommend a course of action based on a current problem.

profiling (*100*)   A data approach used to characterize the "typical" behavior of an individual, group, or population by generating summary statistics about the data (including mean, standard deviations, etc.).

regression (*106*)   A data approach used to estimate or predict, for each unit, the numerical value of some variable using some type of statistical model.

similarity matching (*106*)   A data approach used to identify similar individuals based on data known about them.

structured data (*100*)   Data that are organized and reside in a fixed field with a record or a file. Such data are generally contained in a relational database or spreadsheet and are readily searchable by search algorithms.

summary statistics (*97*)   Describe the location, spread, shape, and dependence of a set of observations. These commonly include the count, sum, minimum, maximum, mean or average, standard deviation, median, quartiles, correlation covariance, and frequency that describe a specific measurable value.

supervised approach/method (*103*)   Approach used to learn more about the basic relationships between independent and dependent variables that are hypothesized to exist.

support vector machine (*110*)   A discriminating classifier that is defined by a separating hyperplane that works first to find the widest margin (or biggest pipe).

training data (*109*) Existing data that have been manually evaluated and assigned a class, which assists in classifying the test data.

test data (*109*) A set of data used to assess the degree and strength of a predicted relationship established by the analysis of training data.

unsupervised approach/method (*103*) Approach used for data exploration looking for potential patterns of interest.

XBRL (*99*) (eXtensible Business Reporting Language) A global standard for exchanging financial reporting information that uses XML.

 # ANSWERS TO PROGRESS CHECKS

1. a. Link prediction
    b. Classification
    c. Regression

2. While descriptive analytics focuses on what happened, diagnostic analytics focuses on why it happened. Descriptive and diagnostic analytics are typically paired because you would want to describe the past data and then compare it to a benchmark to determine why the results are the way they are, similar to the accounting concepts of planning and controlling.

3. Data reduction may be used to filter out ordinary travel and entertainment expenses so an auditor can focus on those that are potentially erroneous or fraudulent.

4. The XBRL tagging allows an analyst or decision maker to focus on one or a category of expenses of most interest to a lender. For example, lenders might be most interested in monitoring the amount of long-term debt, interest payments, and dividends paid to assess if the borrower will be able to repay the loan. Using the capabilities of XBRL, lenders could focus on just those individual accounts for further analysis.

5. In some sense, profiling techniques to find criminals and accounting anomalies are very similar. Profiling to find criminals often looks to the physical characteristics (race, sex, mental state, etc.) to predict whether the person has or is likely to commit a crime (and is illegal to use in some jurisdictions). Accounting looks to other, nonphysical characteristics such as the amounts, totals, and types of expenditures to identify potential anomalies.

6. A dollar store might sell everything for exactly $1.00. In that case, the use of Benford's law for any single product or even for every product would not follow Benford's law!

7. Three clusters of customers who might consider Walmart could include thrifty shoppers (looking for the lowest price), shoppers looking to shop for all of their household needs (both grocery and non-grocery items) in one place, and those customers who live close to the store (good location).

8. The longer time between the death and payment dates begs one to ask why it has taken so long for payment to occur and if the interest required to be paid is likely large. Because of these issues, there might be a possibility that the claim is fraudulent or at least deserves a more thorough review to explain why there was such a long delay.

9. We certainly could let the data speak and address this question directly. In general, when the health of the economy is stronger, there are fewer layoffs and fewer people out looking for a job, which means less turnover. Additional analysis could determine whether the turnover is voluntary or involuntary.

10. Chapter 1 illustrated that Lending Club collects the credit score data, and the initial analysis there suggested the higher the credit score, the less likely to be rejected. Given this evidence, we would predict a negative relationship between credit score and loans that are rejected.

11. Decision support systems follow rules to determine the appropriate amount of a bonus. Following a set of rules, the system may evaluate management goals, such as a sales target or number of new accounts, to calculate and recommend the appropriate bonus compensation.

12. Machine learning and artificial intelligence models learn by incorporating new data and through manual correction of data. For example, when a misclassified lease is corrected, the accuracy of the recommended classification of future leases improves.

Mc Graw Hill **connect**®

Multiple Choice Questions

1. _____ is a set of data used to assess the degree and strength of a predicted relationship.
   a. Training data
   b. Unstructured data
   c. Structured data
   d. Test data

2. Data that are organized and reside in a fixed field with a record or a file. Such data are generally contained in a relational database or spreadsheet and are readily searchable by search algorithms. The term matching this definition is:
   a. training data.
   b. unstructured data.
   c. structured data.
   d. test data.

3. An observation about the frequency of leading digits in many real-life sets of numerical data is called:
   a. leading digits hypothesis.
   b. Moore's law.
   c. Benford's law.
   d. clustering.

4. Which approach to data analytics attempts to predict a relationship between two data items?
   a. Similarity matching
   b. Classification
   c. Link prediction
   d. Co-occurrence grouping

5. In general, the more complex the model, the greater the chance of:
   a. overfitting the data.
   b. underfitting the data.
   c. pruning the data.
   d. a more accurate prediction of the data.

6. In general, the simpler the model, the greater the chance of:
   a. overfitting the data.
   b. underfitting the data.
   c. pruning the data.
   d. the need to reduce the amount of data considered.

7. _____ is a discriminating classifier that is defined by a separating hyperplane that works first to find the widest margin (or biggest pipe) and then works to find the middle line.

a. Linear classifier

b. Support vector machine

c. Decision tree

d. Multiple regression

8. _____ mark the split between one class and another.

a. Decision trees

b. Identified questions

c. Decision boundaries

d. Linear classifiers

9. Models associated with regression and classification data approaches have all *except* this important part:

a. identifying which variables (we'll call these independent variables) might help predict an outcome (we'll call this the dependent variable).

b. the functional form of the relationship (linear, nonlinear, etc.).

c. the numeric parameters of the model (detailing the relative weights of each of the variables associated with the prediction).

d. test data.

10. Which approach to data analytics attempts to assign each unit in a population into a small set of classes where the unit belongs?

a. Classification

b. Regression

c. Similarity matching

d. Co-occurrence grouping

Discussion Questions

1. What is the difference between a target and a class?

2. What is the difference between a supervised and an unsupervised approach?

3. What is the difference between training datasets and test (or testing) datasets?

4. Using **TABLE 3-1** as a guide, what are three data approaches associated with the descriptive approach?

5. Using **TABLE 3-1** as a guide, what are three data approaches associated with the diagnostic approach?

6. How might the data reduction approach be used in auditing?

7. How might classification be used in approving or denying a potential fraudulent credit card transaction?

8. How is similarity matching different from clustering?

9. How does fuzzy match work? Give an accounting situation where it might be most useful.

10. Compare and contrast the profiling data approach and the development of standard cost for a unit of production at a manufacturing company. Are they substantially the same, or do they have differences?

11. Exhibits 3-9, 3-10, and 3-13 suggest that volume and distance are the best predictors of "days to ship" for a wholesale company. Any other variables that would also be useful in predicting the number of "days to ship"?

Problems

1. How could the fuzzy match be used to find undisclosed related party transactions?

2. An auditor is trying to figure out if the inventory at an electronics store chain is obsolete. What characteristics (e.g., data elements about the store, customers, employees, and inventory) might be used to help establish a model predicting inventory obsolescence?

3. An auditor is trying to figure out if the goodwill its client recognized when it purchased a factory has become impaired. What characteristics might be used to help establish a model predicting goodwill impairment?

4. How might clustering be used to describe customers who owe money (accounts receivable)?

5. Why would the use of data reduction be useful to highlight related party transactions (e.g., CEO has her own separate company that the main company does business with)?

6. How could an investor use XBRL to do an analysis of the industry's inventory turnover?

7. Name three accounts that would be appropriate and interesting to apply Benford's law in auditing those accounts. Why would an auditor choose those three accounts? When would a departure from Benford's law encourage the auditor to investigate further?

Appendix: Setting Up A Classification Analysis

To answer the question "Will a new vendor ship a large order on time?" using classification, you should clearly identify your variables, define the scope of your data, and assign classes. This is related to "master the data" in the IMPACT model.

Identify Your Variables

Because this question is related to vendors and order shipments, take a moment to think about attributes that might be predictive. What attributes would you need to address the following questions: Would the total number of order items potentially cause a delay? Are certain types of items shipped more timely than others? How about the overall shipping weight. . .does that impact the timeliness of shipments? Does the vendor's physical distance from a company's warehouse matter? How about the age of vendor relationship or number of vendor employees? What else?

Define the Scope

Because you are looking at vendor shipments, you would need—at the basic level—data related to the original purchase order (order date, number of items), shipping data (shipping date, weight), and vendor master data (location, age, size). This will help you narrow down your data request and make it more likely that you'll get the data you request by an established deadline. As you're preparing your data, you'll want to join these tables so that each record represents an order. You'll also want to calculate any figures of merit, such as the number of days (Ship date – Order date), volume (total number of items on the order or physical size) or distance (**Vendor address – Warehouse address**) (see Table 3-A1).

PO#	Total Items: Sum (Qty)	Order Date	Ship Date	Days to Ship: (Ship Date – Order Date	Vendor	Distance (mi): (V Coordinates – WH Coordinates)*	Weight (lb)
123456	15	7/30/2020	8/2/2020	3	ABC Company	45	160

TABLE 3-A1
Vendor Shipments

Distance Formula

You can use a distance formula in Excel to calculate the distance in miles or kilometers between the warehouse and the vendor. First, you determine the latitude and longitude based on the address, then use the following formula. Note: Use first number 3959 for miles or 6371 for kilometers.

```
3959 * ACOS(SIN(RADIANS([Lat])) * SIN(RADIANS([Lat2])) +
COS(RADIANS([Lat])) * COS(RADIANS([Lat2])) * COS(RADIANS
([Long2]) - RADIANS([Long])))
```

Assign Classes

Take a moment to define your classes. You are trying to predict whether a given order shipment will either be "On-time" or "Delayed" based on the number of days it takes from the order date to the shipping date. What does "on-time" mean? Let's define "on-time" as an order that ships in 5 days or less and a "delayed" order as one that ships later than 5 days. You'll use this rule to add the class as a new attribute to each of your historical records (see Table 3-A2).

On-time = (Days to ship ≤ 5)

Delayed = (Days to ship > 5)

TABLE 3-A2
Shipment Class

PO#	Total Items: Sum (Qty)	Order Date	Ship Date	Days to ship: (Ship Date – Order Date)	Vendor	Distance (mi): (V Coordinates – WH Coordinates)*	Weight (lb)	Class
123456	15	7/30/2020	8/2/2020	3	ABC Company	45	160	On-time
123457	20	7/30/2020	8/5/2020	6	XYZ Company	120	800	Delayed

Lab 3-1   Data Reduction Using Fuzzy Matching

Auditors use data reduction to focus their efforts on testing internal controls and limiting their scope. For example, they may want to look only at transactions for a given year. In this lab, you will learn to use filters in Excel and perform some fuzzy matches on vendor and employee records, a common auditor analysis.

Company summary

These data are for a generic manufacturing company. You have been asked to see if there are any potentially fictitious vendors or employees who may have created fake companies in an effort to commit fraud.

Data

- Fuzzy.xlsx—contains employee and vendor data

Technique

- Some Excel experience is handy here. You will use tables, filters, and the Fuzzy Lookup add-in.

Software needed

- Excel
- Fuzzy Lookup add-in: https://www.microsoft.com/en-us/download/details. aspx?id=15011 Note: this add-in requires the Windows version of Excel. For Excel 2019 or later, see Software Instructions on Connect.

In this lab, you will:

Part 1: Identify a problem that will require data reduction techniques.

Part 2: Master the data and prepare for analysis.

Part 3: Perform data reduction.

Part 1: Identify the Problem

Fictitious vendors represent risk to a company. One way employees can embezzle funds from a company is to create a fictitious vendor (a.k.a., shell vendor) and then submit an invoice for services that were never performed. Where there are poor internal controls, the employee receives the payment and deposits the check.

Q1.   What data do you think might exist to show that a vendor is related to an employee? Which attributes would you focus on?

Q2.   How might you attempt to detect these connections between vendors and employees?

Q3.   If you were the employee committing fraud, what would you try to do with the data to evade detection?

Part 2: Master the Data and Prepare for Analysis

You have requested the employee and vendor master data tables to aid in your analysis. The IT supervisor has sent you an Excel sheet with the following tables and attributes:

Employees

EmployeeID

EmployeeFirstName

EmployeeLastName

EmployeeGender

EmployeeHireDate

EmployeeStreetAddress

EmployeeCity

EmployeeState

EmployeeZip

EmployeePhone

Vendors

VendorID

VendorName

VendorType

VendorSince

VendorContact

VendorBillingAddress

VendorBillingCity

VendorBillingState

VendorBillingZip

VendorBillingPhone

Your first step is to understand the data and prepare it in Excel to perform some matching.

1. Open **Fuzzy.xlsx** in Excel.
2. Quickly browse through the worksheets to ensure that they are complete.
3. Go to the **Employees** tab and click any data element.
4. Select the entire data table (**Ctrl + A**).
5. Go to the **Home** tab, **Styles** section, and click **Format as Table**. Any style will do.
6. In the **Format as Table** box that appears, make sure the **My table has headers** box is checked, and click **OK**.
7. In the **Table Tools > Design** tab, under **Properties**, change the table name from **Table1** to **Employees**.
8. Now go to the **Vendors** tab and click any data element. Repeat steps 4–7 and name the new table **Vendors**.
9. Take a screenshot of either table (label it 3-1A).
10. Save your file as **Fuzzy-Tables.xlsx**.

Part 3: Perform Data Reduction

Now you're ready to find those fictitious vendors. There are many different approaches for working with the data to narrow your focus. These can be used with other data sources as well.

Tool: Filtering

Excel Filters allow you to quickly find data with common attributes and help to limit the scope of your analysis. Assume that the auditors have analyzed all vendors prior to 2019 and have resolved any outstanding issues. By analyzing only the vendors from 2019, you avoid unnecessary analysis and reduce the time it will take for the computer to run the analysis.

11. Open **Fuzzy-Tables.xlsx** and click the **Vendors** worksheet.
12. Click the drop-down arrow next to **VendorSince** to show filtering options, shown below.

13. To select only 2019 records, uncheck **Select All** and then check the box next to **2019** and click **OK**.

Source: Microsoft Excel 2016.

14. Select the table and headers (**Ctrl + A** twice) and copy the values (**Ctrl + C**).
15. Create a new worksheet tab called **Vendors2019** and paste the filtered values there (**Ctrl + V**).
16. Select your new table and format it as a table called "**Vendors2019**."
17. Take a screenshot (label it 3-1B).
18. Save your file as **Fuzzy-Tables-2019.xlsx**.

Tool: Fuzzy Match

SQL queries and PivotTables require exact matches between two data points to identify related data. Foreign keys must match primary keys exactly in databases or else a relationship doesn't exist. Names and addresses, as well as other manually entered text values are more prone to errors and manipulation. Think about your questions from Part 1 of this lab. Wouldn't one way to avoid detection be to change something subtle in the address—for example "Street" to "St." or "Center Ave" to "Center"? A human could understand that these are the same thing, but a computer cannot without some help.

Fuzzy Lookup is a plugin for Excel that enables these mostly similar matches and finds things that might otherwise evade detection by a computer system.

19. Download and enable **Fuzzy Lookup for Excel** if you haven't already.
20. Open Fuzzy-Tables-2019.xlsx if you haven't already.

21. In the ribbon, click **Fuzzy Lookup > Fuzzy Lookup**. A panel will appear on the right showing the tables you defined in Part 2 of this lab.
22. For the **Left Table**, choose **Vendors2019**, and for the **Right Table**, choose **Employees**.
23. In the **Left Columns** list, click **VendorBillingAddress**, and from the **Right Columns** list, click **EmployeeStreetAddress**.
24. Click the **Join** icon button in between the two lists. A new relationship will appear in the **Match Columns** list.
25. In the **Output Columns** list, uncheck everything except:
    a. Vendors2019.VendorName
    b. Vendors2019.VendorContact
    c. Vendors2019.VendorBillingAddress
    d. Vendors2019.VendorBillingZip
    e. Vendors2019.EmployeeFirstName
    f. Vendors2019.EmployeeLastName
    g. Vendors2019.EmployeeStreetAddress
    h. Vendors2019.EmployeeZip
    i. Vendors2019.FuzzyLookup.Similarity
26. **Number of Matches** should be 1, suggesting the need for an exact match.
27. The **Similarity Threshold** slider represents the percentage similarity. You can slide it left if you want less similar matches or slide it right for more similar. 1.0 is an exact match.

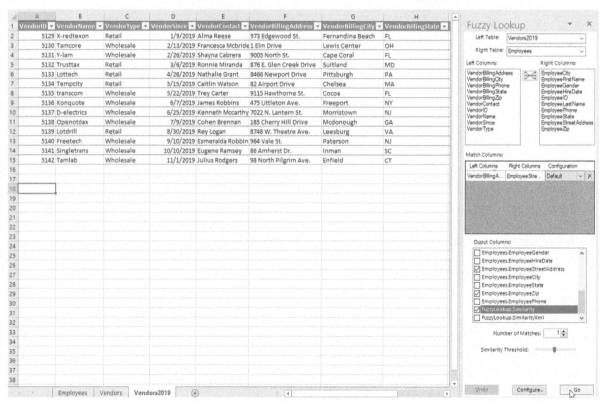

Source: Microsoft Excel 2016.

28. Create a new worksheet tab called **FuzzyMatch**.
29. Click cell **A1**, then click **Go** in the **Fuzzy Lookup** panel. A list will appear with all of the vendors and any potential fuzzy match.

30. Format the output as a table named **FuzzyMatch,** then filter out any records with 0.0000 Similarity.

    Q4.   How many vendors have similar addresses to employees?

    Q5.   What do you notice about the street vendor and employee street addresses?

    Q6.   Are there any false positives (fuzzy matches that aren't really matches)?

31. Take a screenshot (label it 3-1C).

End of Lab

Lab 3-2   Regression in Excel

Company summary

The data used are a subset of the **College Scorecard** dataset that is provided by the U.S. Department of Education. These data provide federal financial aid and earnings information, insights into the performance of schools eligible to receive federal financial aid, and the outcomes of students at those schools. You can learn more about how the data are used and view the raw data yourself at https://collegescorecard.ed.gov/data/. However, for this lab, you should use the text file provided to you.

Data

- CollegeScorecard Datasets: CollegeScorecard_CleanedData from Lab 2-5

Technique

- Some experience with Excel is useful for this lab.

Software needed

- Excel
- Screen capture tool (Windows: Snipping Tool; Mac: Cmd + Shift + 4)

In this lab, you will:

    Part 1: Identify the questions.
    Part 2: Load the data.
    Part 3: Perform a regression analysis in Excel.

Part 1: Identify the Questions

This lab relies upon the steps completed in Lab 2-5 in which the data were prepared.

We will begin with a simple regression with two variables, SAT average and completion rate for first-time, full-time students at four-year institutions.

    Q1.   Would you expect SAT average and completion rate to be correlated? If so, would you expect the correlation to be positive or negative?

    Q2.   When determining relationships between variables, one of the criteria for a potential causal relationship is that the cause must happen before the effect. Regarding SAT average and completion rate, which would you determine to be the potential cause? Which would be the effect?

    Q3.   Identifying the cause and effect as you did in Q2 can help you determine the explanatory and response variables. Which variable, SAT average or completion rate, is the explanatory variable?

Part 2: Master the Data

These steps were performed in Lab 2-5. You can either use the already prepared data in the file Lab 3-3, College Scorecard Data (Cleaned post-Lab 2-5).xlsx, or you can use the file that you saved after completing Lab 2-5. (See Appendix K for the data dictionary for this dataset.)

Part 3: Perform an Analysis of the Data

1. To perform a regression test in Excel, you need to first download the **Data Analysis ToolPak**. To do so, Follow this menu path: **File > Options > Add-ins**. From this window, select the **Go . . .** button, and then place a checkmark in the box next to **Analysis ToolPak**. Once you click **OK**, you will be able to access the **ToolPak** from the **Data** tab on the Excel ribbon.
2. Click the **Data Analysis** button from the **Data** tab on the Excel ribbon and select **Regression**.
3. A regression window will pop up for you to input the **Y range** and the **X range**.

LAB EXHIBIT 3-2A

Source: Microsoft Excel 2016.

4. Select the entire column of data that is associated with the response variable for the Y range, then select the entire column of data that is associated with the explanatory variable for the X range. For a description of the variables, refer to the data dictionary in Appendix K.
5. If you selected the labels in your ranges, place a checkmark in the box next to **Labels**.
6. Click **OK**. This will run the regression test and place the output on a new spreadsheet in your Excel workbook.
7. Take a screenshot of your regression output (label it 3-2A).

End of Lab

Company summary

LendingClub is a peer-to-peer marketplace where borrowers and investors are matched together. The goal of LendingClub is to reduce the costs associated with these banking transactions and make borrowing less expensive and investment more engaging. LendingClub provides data on loans that have been approved and rejected since 2007, including the assigned interest rate and type of loan. This provides several opportunities for data analysis.

Data

- Download the LendingClub datasets: LoanStats3a.csv, RejectStatsA.csv, LCClass.csv from the Connect website

Software needed

- Excel
- Weka—available at www.cs.waikato.ac.nz/ml/weka
- Screen capture tool (Windows: Snipping Tool; Mac: Cmd + Shift + 4)

In this lab, you will:

- Analyze the data using various classification models.

Part 1: Identify the Questions

Thinking about LendingClub's function as a marketplace for investors and borrowers, what might stakeholders want to know? Has LendingClub's model changed over the years? If we understood what affected an interest rate decision, could we game the system to our advantage? Take a moment and come up with some general questions that could be answered through data analysis.

Q1. Thinking about loan applicants in general, how would you expect them to fall into different groups?

Q2. When evaluating previous loan data, what would you expect your target variable to be?

Q3. What factors do you think would affect whether a loan will be accepted or rejected?

Q4. Identify the data you would need to answer your questions and validate your hypothesis.

Part 2: Master the Data

For this lab, you should download the LendingClub data and prepare it for some more advanced analysis in Chapter 3.

Note: You have the choice to manually clean and combine the data here from LoanStats3a.csv and RejectStatsA.csv or use the cleaned data in LCClass.csv file. If you run into any issues cleaning the data, skip to the completed file and continue to Part 3.

The LendingClub data contains two different file types including LoanStats3a for approved loans and RejectStatsA for rejected loans. There are significantly more data available for LoanStats3a. There are 107 different attributes. To save some time, we've identified 19 of the most interesting in Lab Tables 3-3A and 3-3B.

Q5. Given this list of attributes, what concerns do you have with the data's ability to predict answers to the questions you identified before?

Between the two groups of data files, we notice that there are some attributes in common, though not very many (see Lab Table 3-3C).

Attribute	Description
id	Loan identification number
member_id	Membership id
loan_amount	Requested loan amount
emp_length	Employment length
issue_d	Date of loan issue
loan_status	Fully paid or charged off
pymnt_plan	Payment plan: yes or no
purpose	Loan purpose: e.g., wedding, medical, debt_consolidation, car
zip_code	The first three digits of the applicant's zip code
addr_state	State
dti	Ratio of monthly debt payments to monthly income
delinq_2y	Late payments within the past two years
earliest_cr_line	Oldest credit account
inq_last_6mnths	Credit inquiries in the past 6 months
open_acc	Number of open credit accounts
revol_bal	Total balance of all credit accounts
revol_util	Percentage of available credit in use
total_acc	Total number of credit accounts
application_type	Individual or joint application

Attribute	Description
Amount Requested	Requested loan amount
Application Date	Date of loan application
Loan Title	Brief description of loan purpose
Risk_Score	**LendingClub**'s calculated value
Debt-To-Income Ratio	Ratio of monthly debt payments to monthly income
Zip Code	The first three digits of the applicant's zip code
State	State
Employment Length	Employment length
Policy Code	Internal number

Common	RejectStatsA.csv	LoanStats3a.csv
Amount	Amount Requested	loan_amnt
Month	=MONTH("Application Date")	=MONTH("issue_d")
Purpose	Loan Title	purpose
DebtToIncome	Debt-to-Income	dti
State	State	addr_state
YearsOfEmployment	Employment	emp_length
Class	REJECT	ACCEPT

Q6.   What does the lack of attributes in the RejectStatsA files tell us about the data that **LendingClub** retains on rejected loans?

Q7.   How will that affect a classification analysis?

We will need to convert the data into a useful format before we can perform any analysis. We need to generate two sets of data, one for classification and one for regression and clustering.

Cleaning the Data for Classification

Goal: Combine approved and rejected data for a given year, assign a class to each record.

Issues

- Approved and rejected loans contain different data attributes.
- Date data values are recorded in different formats (1/9/2011 vs. Jan-2011).
- Years of employment contain text values and should be numbers.

In Excel

1. Create a new spreadsheet.
2. Type the common attributes from Table 3-3C into the first row.
3. Open the LoanStats3a.csv and RejectStatsA.csv files in Excel.
4. Delete all columns that don't match those listed in Table 3-3C and remove the summary data at the bottom of the file and the link reference in the first row of the file.
5. Use the =MONTH formula to extract the month from the date.
6. Copy the Month column and **Paste Special > Values** into the **Month** column.
7. Use find and replace to remove any % signs from the DebtToIncome values.
8. Add a new Class column and enter **REJECT** to the rejected loans and **APPROVE** to the approved loans.
9. Copy and paste the values from each .csv file into your new spreadsheet. Note: The order of the columns may be different in the source files, so make sure you could either reorganize the columns in the source files or copy and paste each column at a time into the correct column in the new sheet.
10. Find and replace the employment values using Lab Table 3-3D.

LAB TABLE 3-3D

Original Value	New Value
na or n/a	0
< 1 year	0
1 year	1
2 years	2
3 years	3
4 years	4
5 years	5
6 years	6
7 years	7
8 years	8
9 years	9
10+ years	10
, (comma)	(blank)

11. Save your file as **LCClass.csv**. Be sure to choose .csv as the file type.
12. Take a screenshot (label it 3-3A).

Part 3: Perform an Analysis of the Data

We will try multiple classification models and compare their results using Weka. Download Weka at www.cs.waikato.ac.nz/ml/weka.

13. Open **Weka** and click the **Explorer** button.
14. Click **Open file . . .** Change the Files of Type to CSV data files (*.csv) and then locate your **LCClass.csv** file. Then click **Open**.
15. Click **Visualize All** found just above and right of the graph.
16. Take a screenshot (label it 3-3B).

17. Click the **Classify** tab.
18. Run each of the following classification models. For each tool, click on **Choose . . .** and then **Start** to run the analysis. Note: watch the status bar at the bottom to know when a model is finished running. The results will appear on the screen showing the classification matrix and resulting model. As you complete these models, make a note of the accuracy percentage for each. This shows what percent of the loans was correctly classified.
    a. **Weka > Classifiers > Trees > Random Forest**.
    b. **Weka > Classifiers > Meta > AdaBoostM1**.
    c. **Weka > Classifiers > Functions > Logistic**.
    d. **Weka > Classifiers > Bayes > BayesNet**.

    Q8. Which model has the highest accuracy? How do you know?

Part 4: Address and Refine Results

Review the accuracy rates of each of the models. As a rule of thumb, a good model has an accuracy rate of 70% or higher, though 100% may indicate overfitting. Accuracy of 50%–70% is okay, but not great. Less than that and you're better off flipping a coin to choose a class.

    Q9. How useful is your classification model in predicting which applicants will be approved or rejected? How do you know?

Review the details of models, including the accuracy percentage and the decision boundaries of each of the variables in Weka.

    Q10. How would you interpret the results of your analysis in plain English?

End of Lab

Lab 3-4   Comprehensive Case: Dillard's Store Data: Data Abstract (SQL) and Regression (Part I)

Company summary

Dillard's is a department store with approximately 330 stores in 29 states. Its headquarters is in Little Rock, Arkansas. You can learn more about Dillard's by looking at finance.yahoo.com (Ticker symbol = DDS) and the Wikipedia site for DDS. You'll quickly note that William T. Dillard II is an accounting grad of the University of Arkansas and the Walton College of Business, which may be why he shared transaction data with us to make available for this lab and labs throughout this text.

Data

The data for this lab and all other Dillard's labs must be accessed through the University of Arkansas Remote Desktop. Directions for accessing the Remote Desktop can be found at www.mhhe.com/richardsondaa2e. See your instructor for login credentials.

Software needed

- Microsoft SQL Server Management Studio (available on the Remote Desktop at the University of Arkansas)
- Excel 2016 (available on the Remote Desktop at the University of Arkansas)

In this lab, you will:

- Conduct analysis on three important questions that help us understand when customers spend more on individual transactions.

Part 1: Identify the Questions

Dillard's is trying to figure out when its customers spend more on individual transactions. We ask questions regarding how Dillard's sells its products.

Q1. Customers in which states had the highest transaction balances over the entire sample period?

Q2. Do customers in the state with the highest transaction balances have a significantly higher transaction balance from September 1, 2016, to September 15, 2016, than all other states?

Q3. Are online transaction amounts statistically greater than or lesser than non-online transactions during the time period September 1, 2016, to September 15, 2016?

Part 2: Master the Data

For this lab, you should access the TRANSACT and the STORE tables from the Dillard's WCOB_DILLARDS dataset from the University of Arkansas. You may have learned how to do so from past labs, or feel free to ask your instructor for access. You can also learn how to do so in Appendix F.

1. Run the following SQL query in Microsoft SQL Server Management Studio to address the first question to identify which state had the highest customer transaction balance. (Recall that transaction is defined for each individual item purchased.)

    Refer to Appendix J of the textbook to view an ER Diagram for the Dillard's data.

```
SELECT STATE, AVG(TRAN_AMT) AS Average
FROM TRANSACT
INNER JOIN STORE
ON TRANSACT.STORE = STORE.STORE
WHERE TRAN_DATE BETWEEN '20160901' AND '20160915'
GROUP BY STATE
ORDER BY AVG(TRAN_AMT) DESC
```

The output should return the following:

AR 28.455765

SC 20.544199

LA 20.530411

TX 20.482441

. . .

Take a screenshot of your results in SQL Server(label it 3-4A).

Part 3: Perform an Analysis of the Data

2. Noting that Arkansas (State ='AR') has the highest transaction balance, let's address our second question: "Do customers in the state with the highest transaction balances have a significantly higher transaction balance from September 1, 2016, to September 15, 2016, than all other states?"

3. To address Q2, you will need to connect to SQL Server data through Excel using Data > Get & Transform and the Analysis ToolPak. If you need a refresher on how to use that tool, refer to the textbook's Appendix B.

    Once you connect to the SQL Server dataset in Excel and expand the options to input a query, input the following SQL query to extract the data needed for our analysis.

```
SELECT TRANSACT.*, STORE.STATE
FROM TRANSACT
INNER JOIN STORE
ON TRANSACT.STORE = STORE.STORE
WHERE TRAN_DATE BETWEEN '20160901' AND '20160909'
ORDER BY TRAN_DATE
```

4. Once the query runs, there is no need to transform the data in Power Query for this lab. Immediately load the data into Excel.

5. Once the data are in Excel, you'll need to transform the State data to perform regression analysis on the state of Arkansas to address Q2. To do so, make a new column just right of the existing dataset and label it **Arkansas-dummy** in column Q. Type the formula =IF([@STATE]="AR",1,0) in each row. It will assign a value of 1 to transactions at stores in Arkansas and a value of 0 for transactions at stores outside of the Arkansas. Copy this formula all the way down to cover each row.

M	N	O	P	Q	R
TRAN_AMT ▾	TENDER_TYPE ▾	SKU ▾	STATE ▾	Arkansas-dummy ▾	
-2.31	BANK	9999999950	TX	=IF([@STATE]="AR",1,0)	

Source: Microsoft Excel 2016.

6. Perform a regression analysis by performing the following steps.

   a. Click on **Data Analysis** button in the **Data** tab in the ribbon. If you do not have the Data Analysis ToolPak added in, see the Appendix B, to learn how to add it to Excel.

   b. Click **Regression** (as shown below), and then click **OK**.

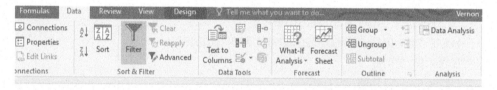

Source: Microsoft Excel 2016.

   c. Reference the cells that contain the **Tran_AMT** in the **Input Y Range** and **Arkansas-dummy** in the **Input X Range** and then click **OK**.

Source: Microsoft Excel 2016.

d. Your output should look like the screenshot below. The **t Stat** greater than 2.0 suggests that the transaction amount (Tran_Amt) is statistically greater in Arkansas than in all other states.

SUMMARY OUTPUT

Regression Statistics	
Multiple R	0.064904
R Square	0.00421253
Adjusted R Square	0.00421151
Standard Error	43.5169749
Observations	978659

ANOVA

	df	SS	MS	F	Significance F
Regression	1	7840145.656	7840145.66	4140.06097	0
Residual	978657	1853309284	1893.7271		
Total	978658	1861149430			

	Coefficients	Standard Error	t Stat	P-value	Lower 95%	Upper 95%	Lower 95.0%	Upper 95.0%
Intercept	18.2918975	0.046362863	394.5377	0	18.2010278	18.3827672	18.2010278	18.3827672
Arkansas-dummy	9.44360093	0.146768974	64.3433055	0	9.15593867	9.73126319	9.15593867	9.73126319

Source: Microsoft Excel 2016.

7. Take a screenshot of your results (label it 3-4B).

We are now ready to address our third question: Are online transaction amounts statistically greater than or lesser than non-online transactions during the time period September 1, 2016, to September 15, 2016? Because we found that transactions in Arkansas are statistically higher than all other states, we will include that finding in our analysis as well, making this a multivariate regression.

8. To address this question, we need to transform the **Store** variable into an online-dummy variable. **Dillard's** handles all of their online sales through a fulfillment center in Maumelle, Arkansas. This location has the store number 698. We will use an IF statement to transform all transactions in store number 698 into a 1 to indicate they are online sales, and all other transactions will be indicated as a 0. The IF statement

is the following (we have hidden a few columns in the middle of the table to make the screenshot easier to read):

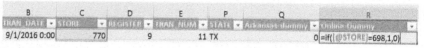

B	C	D	E	P	Q	R
TRAN_DATE	STORE	REGISTER	TRAN_NUM	STATE	Arkansas-dummy	Online-Dummy
9/1/2016 0:00	770	9	11 TX		0	=if([@STORE]=698,1,0)

Source: Microsoft Excel 2016.

Once this is complete, copy the calculation for all cells in the column.

We're now ready for regression analysis. Reference the cells that contain the **Tran_AMT** in the **Input Y Range** and reference **Arkansas-dummy** and **Online-dummy** in the **Input X Range** and click **OK**.

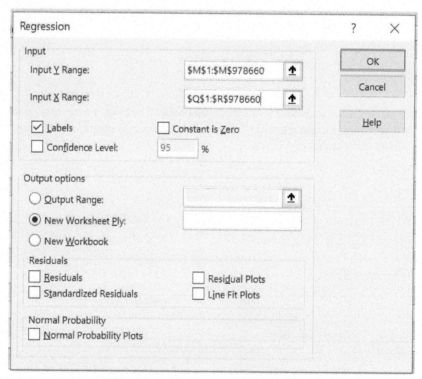

Source: Microsoft Excel 2016.

The results of the regression analysis suggesting that both Transactions in Arkansas and Transactions done online are associated with greater transaction amounts are below.

Regression Statistics	
Multiple R	0.07725471
R Square	0.00596829
Adjusted R Square	0.00596626
Standard Error	43.4786158
Observations	978659

ANOVA

	df	SS	MS	F	Significance F
Regression	2	11107880.71	5553940.36	2937.98648	0
Residual	978656	1850041549	1890.39003		
Total	978658	1861149430			

	Coefficients	Standard Error	t Stat	P-value	Lower 95%	Upper 95%	Lower 95.0%	Upper 95.0%
Intercept	18.2918975	0.046321996	394.885782	0	18.2011079	18.3826871	18.2011079	18.3826871
Arkansas-dummy	1.25838288	0.24548219	5.12616771	2.9576E-07	0.77724603	1.73951972	0.77724603	1.73951972
Online-Dummy	12.2732399	0.29519671	41.5764792	0	11.6946642	12.8518155	11.6946642	12.8518155

Source: Microsoft Excel 2016.

9. Take a screenshot of your results (label it 3-4C).

Part 4: Address and Refine Results

Q4. How would you interpret the results of your analysis of Q1 in plain English? Why do you think the state of Arkansas had the highest transaction volume?

Q5. The analysis of Q2 addressed whether Arkansas had a statistically higher transaction volume than other states. How did the regression tests show or not show a statistical difference? Does this have any implications for the marketing for **Dillard's**? Do you think it is because Arkansas is the home base for **Dillard 's**?

Q6. The regression analysis suggests that online sales are associated with greater transactions amounts. Why do you think that is so?

End of Lab

Lab 3-5 Comprehensive Case: Dillard's Store Data: Data Abstract (SQL) and Regression (Part II)

Company summary

Dillard's is a department store with approximately 330 stores in 29 states. Its headquarters is in Little Rock, Arkansas. You can learn more about **Dillard's** by looking at finance.yahoo. com (Ticker symbol = DDS) and the Wikipedia site for DDS. You'll quickly note that William T. Dillard II is an accounting grad of the University of Arkansas and the Walton College of Business, which may be why he shared transaction data with us to make available for this lab and labs throughout this text.

Data

The data for this lab and all other **Dillard's** labs must be accessed through the University of Arkansas Remote Desktop. Directions for accessing the Remote Desktop can be found at www.mhhe.com/richardsondaa2e. See your instructor for login credentials.

Software needed

- Microsoft SQL Server Management Studio (available on the Remote Desktop at the University of Arkansas)
- Excel 2016 (available on the Remote Desktop at the University of Arkansas)

In this lab, you will:

- Conduct analysis on one important question that helps us understand when customers spend more on individual transactions.

Part 1: Identify the Questions

Dillard's is trying to figure out when its customers spend more on individual transactions. We ask questions regarding how **Dillard's** sells its products.

Q1. Did customers who charged their purchases to a **Dillard's** credit card spend more on each transaction during the time period September 1, 2016, to September 15, 2016?

Part 2: Master the Data

1. See Lab 3-4 to see how to access the dataset.

Part 3: Perform an Analysis of the Data

2. To get the necessary data to address Q1, you will need to run the same query as Lab 3-4 and get the data into Excel ready for analysis.
3. For those who use the **Dillard's** credit card, it is noted as "DLRD" in the TENDER_ TYPE field. We need to compare those who use the Dillard's credit card to all other transactions. To prepare for this analysis, we need to make a DLRD-dummy variable (labeled as "DLRD-dummy") that carries the value of 1 if a **Dillard's** credit card was used and a value of 0 otherwise. Please make the transformation in this way and copy down for every row as in Lab Exhibit 3-5A.

M	N	O	P	Q	R	S	T	U
TRAN_AMT	TENDER_TYPE	SKU	STATE	Arkansas-dummy	Online-Dummy	DLRD-dummy		
-2.31	BANK	9999999950	TX	0		0	=IF([@[TENDER_TYPE]]="DLRD",1,0)	
2.55	BANK	9999999950	LA	0		0		

LAB EXHIBIT 3-5A

Source: Microsoft Excel 2016.

4. Once this is complete, we are ready for statistical analysis. Given the results of Lab 3-4 that transaction amount is positively associated with the state of Arkansas and online

sales, we will include them in our multivariate analysis. Click the **Data Analysis** button and select **Regression** as pictured below.

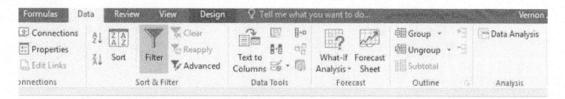

LAB EXHIBIT 3-5B

Source: Microsoft Excel 2016.

5. Click **Regression** and include **Tran_Amt** as the Y variable and **Arkansas-dummy**, **Online-dummy**, and **DLRD-dummy** as the X variables and run the regression.
6. Take a screenshot (label it 3-5A) of your results.

Part 4: Address and Refine Results

Q2. How would you interpret the results of your analysis of Q1 in plain English? Was the relationship statistically significant (Was the *t*-statistic greater than 2)? Why do you think the use of the **Dillard's** card increased the amount spent on each transaction?

Q3. Why did we also include Arkansas state sales and online sales as other explanatory variables (*X*- or independent variables) in this regression analysis? Are these results still significant after the inclusion of the use of the **Dillard's** credit card?

Q4. Are there any other data from the TRANSACT table that might help us predict the transaction amount?

Q5. If we had any other data to predict transaction amount, what would you use? Brainstorm freely to come up with what could explain these different levels of transaction amounts!

End of Lab

Chapter 4

Communicating Results and Visualizations

A Look at This Chapter

This chapter wraps up the introduction to the IMPACT model by explaining how to communicate your results through data visualization and through written reports. Creating a chart takes more skill and practice than simply adding in a bar chart through the Excel chart wizard, and this chapter will help you identify the purpose for your data visualization so that you can choose the best chart for your dataset. We will also help you learn how to refine your chart so that it communicates as efficiently and effectively as possible. The chapter concludes by describing how to provide a written report tailored to specific audiences who will be interested in the results of your data analysis.

A Look Back

In Chapter 3, we considered various models and techniques used for data analytics and discussed when to use them and how to interpret the results. We also provided specific accounting-related examples of when each of these specific data approaches and models is appropriate to address our particular question.

A Look Ahead

The next chapter looks at one application of DA in accounting—auditing. Chapter 5 considers how both internal and external auditors are using technology in general—and audit analytics specifically—to evaluate firm data and generate support for management assertions. We emphasize audit working papers, audit planning, continuous monitoring, and continuous data assurance.

One of the first uses of a heat map as a form of data visualization is also one of history's most impactful. In the mid-1800s, there was a worldwide cholera pandemic. Scientists were desperate to determine the cause to put a stop to the pandemic, and one of those scientists, John Snow, studied a particular London neighborhood that was suffering from a large number of cholera cases in 1854. Snow created a map of the outbreak that included small bar charts on the streets indicating the number of people affected by the disease across different locations in the neighborhood. He suspected that the outbreak was linked to water, so he also drew small crosses on the map to indicate water sources. Through this visualization, Snow was able to identify that the people who were dying nearly all had one thing in common—they were drinking out of the same water source. This led to the discovery of cholera being conveyed through contaminated water. Exhibit 4-1A shows Snow's 1854 cholera map.

Software and methods for creating heat maps to visualize epidemics has improved since 1854, but the purpose still exists. Using a heat map to visualize clusters of people impacted by epidemics helps researchers, health professionals, and policy makers identify patterns and ultimately inform decisions about how to resolve epidemics. For example, in Exhibit 4-1B this map can help readers quickly come to insight about where the overdose epidemic is most prevalent.

Without Snow's hypothesis, methods for testing it, and ultimately communicating the results through data visualization, the 1854 cholera outbreak would have continued with scientists still being uncertain of the cause of cholera.

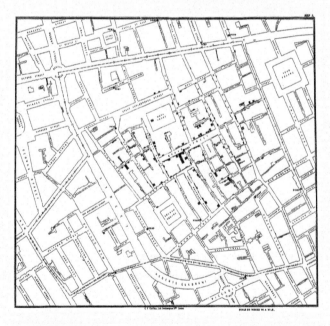

EXHIBIT 4-1A

Source: John Snow. *On the Mode of Communication of Cholera*. 2nd ed. London: John Churchill, 1855.

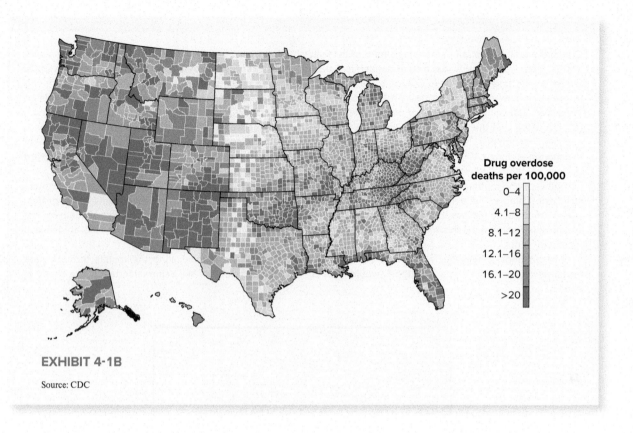

Drug overdose
deaths per 100,000

0–4
4.1–8
8.1–12
12.1–16
16.1–20
>20

EXHIBIT 4-1B

Source: CDC

OBJECTIVES

After reading this chapter, you should be able to:

LO 4-1   Determine the purpose of your data visualization.

LO 4-2   Choose the best chart for your dataset.

LO 4-3   Refine your chart to communicate efficiently and effectively.

LO 4-4   Communicate your results in a written report.

Data are important, and data analytics are effective, but they are only as important and effective as we can communicate and make the data understandable. One of the authors often asks her students what they would do if they were interns and their boss asked them to supply information regarding in which states all of the customers their organization served were located. Would they simply point their boss to the Customers table in the sales database? Would they go a step further and isolate the attributes to the Company Name and the State? Perhaps they could go a step further and run a quick query or PivotTable to perform a count on the number of customers in each different state that the company serves? If they were to give their boss what she actually wanted, however, they should provide a short written summary of the answer to the research question, as well as an organized chart to visualize the results. Data visualization isn't just for people who are "visual" learners. When the results of data analysis are visualized appropriately, the results are made easier and quicker to interpret for everybody. Whether the data you are analyzing are "small" data or "big" data, they still merit synthesis and visualization to help your stakeholders interpret the results with ease and efficiency.

Think back to some of the first data visualizations and categorizations you were exposed to (the food guide pyramid/food plate, the animal kingdom, the periodic table) and, more modernly, how frequently infographics are applied to break down a series of complicated information on social media. These charts and infographics make it easier for people to understand difficult concepts by breaking them down into categories and visual components.

DETERMINE THE PURPOSE OF YOUR DATA VISUALIZATION

As with selecting and refining your analytical model, communicating results is more art than science. Once you are familiar with the tools that are available, your goal should always be to share critical information with stakeholders in a clear, concise manner. This could involve a chart or graph, a callout box, or a few key statistics. Visualizations have become very popular over the past three decades. Managers use dashboards to quickly evaluate key performance indicators (KPIs) and quickly adjust operational tasks; analysts use graphs to plot stock price and financial performance over time to select portfolios that meet expected performance goals.

In any project that will result in a visual representation of data, the first charge is ensuring that the data are reliable and that the content necessitates a visual. In our case, however, ensuring that the data are reliable and useful has already been done through the first three steps of the IMPACT model.

At this stage in the IMPACT model, determining the method for communicating your results requires the answers to two questions:

1. Are you explaining the results of previously done analysis, or are you exploring the data through the visualization? (Is your purpose declarative or exploratory?)
2. What type of data is being visualized (conceptual, qualitative data or data-driven, quantitative data)?

Scott Berinato, senior editor at **Harvard Business Review**, summarizes the possible answers to these questions[1] in a chart shown in Exhibit 4-2. The majority of the work that we will do with the results of data analysis projects will reside in quadrant 2 of Exhibit 4-2, the declarative, data-driven quadrant. We will also do a bit of work in Exhibit 4-2's quadrant 4, the data-driven, exploratory quadrant. There isn't as much qualitative work to be done, although we will work with categorical qualitative data occasionally. When we do work

> LO 4-1
>
> Determine the purpose of your data visualization.

[1]S. Berinato, *Good Charts: The HBR Guide to Making Smarter, More Persuasive Data Visualizations* (Boston: Harvard Business Review Press, 2016).

with qualitative data, it will most frequently be visualized using the tools in quadrant 1, the declarative, conceptual quadrant.

EXHIBIT 4-2

The Four Chart Types

Source: S. Berinato, *Good Charts: The HBR Guide to Making Smarter, More Persuasive Data Visualizations* (Boston: Harvard Business Review Press, 2016).

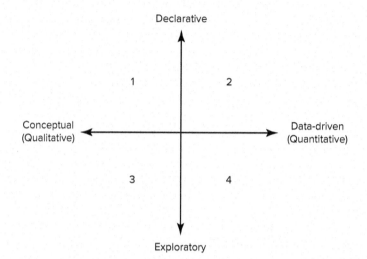

Once you know the answers to the two key questions and have determined which quadrant you're working in, you can determine the best tool for the job. Is a written report with a simple chart sufficient? If so, Word or Excel will suffice. Will an interactive dashboard and repeatable report be required? If so, Tableau may be a better tool. Later in the chapter, we will discuss these two tools in more depth, along with when each should be used.

Quadrants 1 and 3 versus Quadrants 2 and 4: Qualitative versus Quantitative

Qualitative data are categorical data. All you can do with these data is count them and group them, and in some cases, you can rank them. Qualitative data can be further defined in two ways, nominal data and ordinal data. **Nominal data** are the simplest form of data. Examples of nominal data are hair color, gender, and ethnic groups. If you have a set of data on people with different hair color, you can count the number of individuals who fit into the same hair color category, but you cannot rank it (brown hair isn't better than red hair), nor can you take an average or do any other further calculations beyond counting (you can't take an average of "blonde"). Increasing in complexity, but still categorized as qualitative data, are ordinal data. **Ordinal data** can also be counted and categorized like nominal data but can go a step further—the categories can also be ranked. Examples of ordinal data include gold, silver, and bronze medals, 1–5 rating scales on teacher evaluations, and letter grades. If you have a set of data of students and the letter grades they have earned in a given course, you can count the number of instances of A, B, C, and so on, and you can categorize them, just like with nominal data. You can also sort the data meaningfully—an A is better than a B, which is better than a C, and so on. But that's as far as you can take your calculations—as long as the grades remain as letters (and aren't transformed into the corresponding numerical grade for each individual), you cannot calculate an average, standard deviation, or any other more complex calculation.

Beyond counting and possibly sorting (if you have ordinal data), the primary statistic used with qualitative data is **proportion**. The proportion is calculated by counting the number of items in a particular category, then dividing that number by the total number of observations. For example, if you had a dataset of 150 people and had each individual's corresponding hair color with 25 people in your dataset having red hair, you could calculate the proportion of red-haired people in your dataset by dividing 25 (the number of people with red hair) by 150 (the total number of observations in your dataset). The proportion of red-haired people, then, would be 16.7 percent.

Qualitative data (both nominal and ordinal) can also be referred to as "conceptual" data because such data are text-driven and represent concepts instead of numbers.

Quantitative data are more complex than qualitative data because not only can they be counted and grouped just like qualitative data, but the differences between each data point are meaningful—when you subtract 4 from 5, the difference is a numerical measure that can be compared to subtracting 3 from 5. Quantitative data are made up of observations that are numerical and can be counted and ranked, just like ordinal qualitative data, but that can also be averaged. A standard deviation can be calculated, and datasets can be easily compared when standardized (if applicable).

Similar to qualitative data, quantitative data can be categorized into two different types: interval and ratio. However, there is some dispute among the analytics community on whether the difference between the two datasets is meaningful, and for the sake of the analytics and calculations you will be performing throughout this textbook, the difference is not pertinent. The simplest way to express the difference between interval and ratio data is that **ratio data** have a meaningful 0 and interval data do not. In other words, for ratio data, when a dataset approaches 0, 0 means "the absence of." Consider money as ratio data—we can have 5 dollars, 72 dollars, or 8,967 dollars, but as soon as we reach 0, we have "the absence of" money.

Interval data do not have a meaningful 0; in other words, in interval data, 0 does not mean "the absence of" but is simply another number. An example of interval data is the Fahrenheit scale of temperature measurement, where 90 degrees is hotter than 70 degrees, which is hotter than 0 degrees, but 0 degrees does not represent "the absence of" temperature—it's just another number on the scale.

Due to the "meaningful 0" difference between interval and ratio data, ratio data are considered the most sophisticated form of data. This is because the meaningful zero allows us to calculate fractions, proportions, and percentages—ratios reflecting the relationship between values. However, we can perform all other arithmetic functions on both interval and ratio data. In Chapter 3, you learned more about statistical tests such as hypothesis testing, regression, and correlation. We can run all of these tests and calculate the mean, median, and standard deviation on interval and ratio data.

Quantitative data can be further categorized as either discrete or continuous data. **Discrete data** are data that are represented by whole numbers. An example of discrete data is points in a basketball game—you can earn 2 points, 3 points, or 157 points, but you cannot earn 3.5 points. On the other hand, **continuous data** are data that can take on any value within a range. An example of continuous data is height: you can be 4.7 feet, 5 feet, or 6.27345 feet. The difference between discrete and continuous data can be blurry sometimes because you can express a discrete variable as continuous—for example, the number of children a person can have is discrete (a woman can't have 2.7 children, but she could have 2 or 3), but if you are researching the average number of children that women aged 25–40 have in the United States, the average would be a continuous variable. Whether your data are discrete or continuous can also help you determine the type of chart you create because continuous data lend themselves more to a line chart than do discrete data.

A Special Case of Quantitative Data: The Normal Distribution

Chapter 3 mentions the concept of the **normal distribution** in the context of profiling in continuous auditing. The normal distribution is a phenomenon that many naturally occurring datasets in our world follow, such as SAT scores and heights and weights of newborn babies. For a distribution of data to be considered normal, the data should have equal median, mean, and mode, with half of the observations falling below the mean and the other half falling above the mean. If you are comparing two datasets that follow the normal distribution, even if the two datasets have very different means, you can still compare them by **standardizing** the distributions with Z-scores. By using a formula, you can transform every normal distribution into a special case of the normal distribution called the **standard normal distribution**, which has 0 for its mean (and thus, for its mode and median, as well) and 1 for its standard deviation. The benefit of standardizing your data during a comparison of two datasets is to no longer have to compare wildly different numbers and attempt to eyeball how one observation differs from the other—if you standardize both datasets, you can place both distributions on the same chart and more swiftly generate insights.

Quadrants 1 and 2 versus Quadrants 3 and 4: Declarative versus Exploratory

In the context of the labs and tools we're providing through this textbook, the majority of your data visualizations created in step C of the IMPACT model will be created with a declarative purpose. **Declarative visualizations** are the product of wanting to "declare" or present your findings to an audience. The data analysis projects begin with a question, proceed through analysis, and end with communicating those findings. This means that while the visualization may prompt conversation and debate, the information provided in the charts should be solid. Even if your analysis in the previous steps of the IMPACT model had been exploratory, by the time you have arrived to communicate your results, you are declaring what you have found.

On the other hand, you will sometimes use data visualizations to satisfy an **exploratory visualization** purpose. When this is done, the lines between steps **P** (perform test plan), **A** (address and refine results), and **C** (communicate results) are not as clearly divided. Exploratory data visualization will align with performing the test plan within visualization software—for example, Tableau—and gaining insights while you are interacting with the data. Often the presenting of exploratory data will be done in an interactive setting, and the answers to the questions from step **I** (identify the questions) won't have already been answered before working with the data in the visualization software.

Exhibit 4-3 is similar to the first four chart types presented to you in Exhibit 4-2, but Exhibit 4-3 has more detail to help you determine what to do once you've answered the first two questions. Remember that the quadrant represents two main questions:

1. Are you explaining the results of the previously done analysis, or are you exploring the data through the visualization? (Is your purpose declarative or exploratory?)

EXHIBIT 4-3
The Four Chart Types
Quadrant with Detail

Source: S. Berinato, Good
Charts: *The HBR Guide
to Making Smarter, More
Persuasive Data Visualizations*
(Boston: Harvard Business
Review Press, 2016).

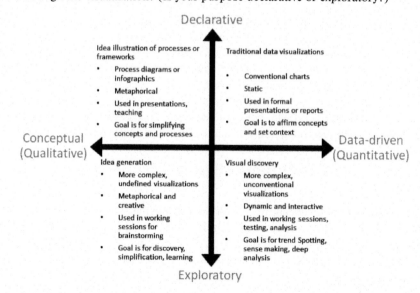

2. What type of information is being visualized (conceptual, qualitative information or data-driven, quantitative information)?

Once you have determined the answers to the first two questions, you are ready to begin determining which type of visualization will be the most appropriate for your purpose and dataset.

⊘ PROGRESS CHECK

1. What are two ways that complicated concepts were explained to you via categorization and data visualization as you were growing up?

2. Using the Internet or other resources (other textbooks, a newspaper, or a magazine), identify an example of a data visualization for each possible quadrant.

3. Identify which type of data scale the following variables are measured on (qualitative nominal, qualitative ordinal, or quantitative):

   a. Instructor evaluations in which students select excellent, good, average, or poor.

   b. Weekly closing price of gold throughout a year.

   c. Names of companies listed on the Dow Jones Industrial Average.

   d. Fahrenheit scale for measuring temperature.

CHOOSING THE RIGHT CHART

LO 4-2

Choose the best chart for your dataset.

Once you have determined the type of data you're working with and the purpose of your data visualization, the next questions have to do with the design of the visualization—color, font, graphics—and most importantly, type of chart/graph. The visual should speak for itself as much as necessary, without needing too much explanation for what's being represented. Aim for simplicity over bells and whistles that "look cool," but end up being distracting.

Charts Appropriate for Qualitative Data

Because qualitative and quantitative data have such different levels of complexity and sophistication, there are some charts that are not appropriate for qualitative data that do work for quantitative data.

When it comes to visually representing qualitative data, the charts most frequently considered are:

- Bar charts.
- Pie charts.
- Stacked bar chart.

The pie chart is probably the most famous (some would say infamous) data visualization for qualitative data. It shows the parts of the whole; in other words, it represents the proportion of each category as it corresponds to the whole dataset.

Similarly, a bar chart also shows the proportions of each category as compared to each of the others.

In most cases, a bar chart is more easily interpreted than a pie chart because our eyes are more skilled at comparing the height of columns (or the lengths of horizontal bars, depending on the orientation of your chart) than they are at comparing sizes of pie, especially if the proportions are relatively similar.

Consider the two different charts from the Sláinte dataset in Exhibit 4-4. Each compares the proportion of each beer type sold by the brewery.

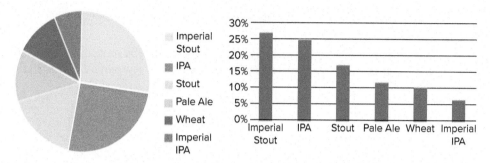

The magnitude of the difference between the Imperial Stout and the IPA is almost impossible to see in the pie chart. This difference is easier to digest in the bar chart.

Of course, we could improve the pie chart by adding in the percentages associated with each proportion, but it is much quicker for us to see the difference in proportions by glancing at the order and length of the bars in a bar chart (Exhibit 4-5).

EXHIBIT 4-5
Pie Chart Showing
Proportion

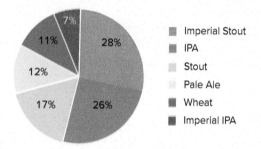

The same set of data could also be represented in a stacked bar chart or a 100 percent stacked bar chart (Exhibit 4-6). This chart is not a default option in Excel, but it does work in another data visualization tool that we introduce later in this chapter, Tableau. The first figure in Exhibit 4-6 is a stacked bar chart, which shows the proportion of each type of beer sold expressed in the number of beers sold for each product, while the latter shows the proportion expressed in terms of percentage of the whole in a 100 percent stacked bar chart.

While bar charts and pie charts are among the most common charts used for qualitative data, there are several other charts that function well for showing proportions:

- *Tree maps and heat maps.* These are similar types of visualizations, and they both use size and color to show proportional size of values. While tree maps show proportions using physical space, heat maps use color to highlight the scale of the values. However, both are heavily visual, so they are imperfect for situations where precision of the numbers or proportions represented is necessary.
- *Symbol maps.* Symbol maps are geographic maps, so they should be used when expressing qualitative data proportions across geographic areas such as states or countries.
- *Word clouds.* If you are working with text data instead of categorical data, you can represent them in a word cloud. Word clouds are formed by counting the frequency of each word mentioned in a dataset; the higher the frequency (proportion) of a given word, the larger and bolder the font will be for that word in the word cloud. Consider analyzing the results of an open-ended response question on a survey; a word cloud would be a great way to quickly spot the most commonly used words to tell if there is a positive or negative feeling toward what's being surveyed. There are also settings that you can put into place when creating the word cloud to leave out the most commonly used English words—such as *the, an,* and *a*—in order to not skew the data. Exhibit 4-7 is an example of a word cloud for the text of Chapter 2 from this textbook.

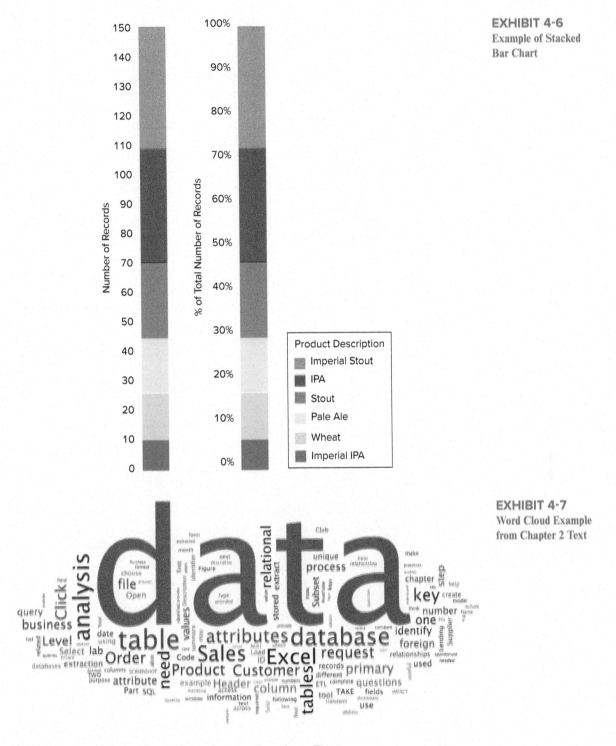

EXHIBIT 4-6
Example of Stacked
Bar Chart

EXHIBIT 4-7
Word Cloud Example
from Chapter 2 Text

Charts Appropriate for Quantitative Data

The data visualization and chart possibilities for charting quantitative data not only include those available for qualitative data (you can group and count it), but they have even more sophistication. You can use pie charts (with the same varying level of success) and bar charts with quantitative data, but you can also use a lot more.

There are many different methods for visualizing quantitative data. With the exception of the word cloud, all of the methods mentioned in the previous section for qualitative data can work for depicting quantitative data, but the following charts can depict more complex data:

- *Line charts.* Show similar information to what a bar chart shows, but line charts are good for showing data changes or trend lines over time. Line charts are useful for continuous data, while bar charts are often used for discrete data. For that reason, line charts are not recommended for qualitative data, which by nature of being categorical, can never be continuous.
- *Box and whisker plots.* Useful for when quartiles, median, and outliers are required for analysis and insights.
- *Scatter plots.* Useful for identifying the correlation between two variables or for identifying a trend line or line of best fit.
- *Filled geographic maps.* As opposed to symbol maps, a filled geographic map is used to illustrate data ranges for quantitative data across different geographic areas such as states or countries.

A summary of the chart types just described appears in Exhibit 4-8. Each chart option works equally well for exploratory and declarative data visualizations. The chart types are categorized based on when they will be best used (e.g., when comparing qualitative variables, a bar chart is an optimal choice), but this figure shouldn't be used to stifle creativity—bar charts can also be used to show comparisons among quantitative variables, just as many of the charts in the listed categories can work well with other datatypes and purposes than their primary categorization below.

EXHIBIT 4-8
Summary of Chart Types

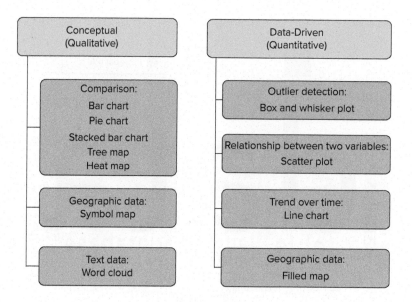

As with selecting and refining your analytical model, communicating results is more art than science. Once you are familiar with the tools that are available, your goal should always be to share critical information with stakeholders in a clear, concise manner. While visualizations can be incredibly impactful, they can become a distraction if you're not careful. For example, bar charts can be manipulated to show a bias and, while novel, 3D graphs are incredibly deceptive because they may distort the scale even if the numbers are fine.

Tools to Help When Picking a Visual

There are many tools available for data visualization and exploratory data analysis. Gartner annually assesses a collection of these tools and creates the "magic quadrant" for business intelligence, depicted in Exhibit 4-9. The magic quadrant can provide insight into which tools you should consider using.

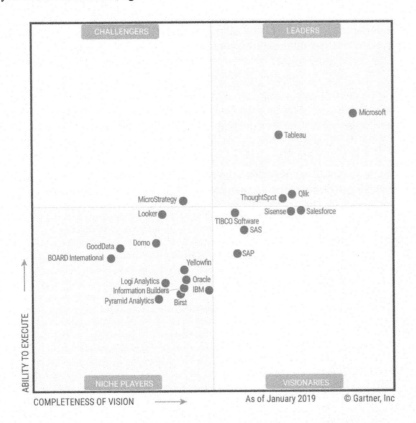

EXHIBIT 4-9
Gartner Magic Quadrant for Business Intelligence and Analytics Platforms

Source: Sallam, R. L., C. Howson, C. J. Idoine, T. W. Oestreich, J. L. Richardson, and J. Tapadinhas, "Magic Quadrant for Business Intelligence and Analytics Platforms," Gartner RAS Core Research Notes, Gartner, Stamford, CT (2019).

Based on Gartner's quadrant, it is easy to see that Tableau and Microsoft are two of the best and most popular options available. While other tools are used in industry, such as Qlik and TIBCO, we focus on Tableau and Microsoft because of their position as leaders in the data analytics space. The Microsoft tool that Gartner analyzed and compared with the other products is not just Excel, it includes the entire Microsoft BI suite, of which Excel is only a part. We will focus on Excel as the main driver of the Microsoft toolkit in this text.

In previous years, Tableau was ranked slightly higher than Microsoft on its ability to execute; in 2019, however, Gartner shifted Microsoft above Tableau in not only completeness of vision, but also ability to execute. Gartner assesses the tools in this quadrant not only on their ability to visualize data, but on each tool's ability to work with data throughout the entire analytics process—data extraction, transformation, data analysis and testing, and data visualization. Microsoft's tools slightly outperform Tableau in their execution of the entire analytics process. Tableau is a newer product and has placed the majority of its focus on data visualization, while Microsoft Excel has a much more robust platform for data analysis. Excel's biggest advantage over Tableau (and over any other data visualization software in the market) is its ubiquity. Excel has been on the market longer than any of its competitors, and it is rare to find a business or university that doesn't have a version of Excel on every computer. *If your data analysis project is more declarative than exploratory, it is more likely that you will perform your data visualization to communicate results in Excel,* simply because it is likely that you performed steps 2 through 4 in Excel, and it is convenient to create your charts in the same tool that you performed your analysis.

Tableau earns high praise for being intuitive and easy to use, which makes it ideal for exploratory data analysis. You may even find that you would prefer to immediately load your data from Excel or your relational database (or wherever else your data are stored) into Tableau during the second step of the IMPACT model and work on your analysis inside the tool, instead of waiting for step 5 to just communicate your results through Tableau. If your question isn't fully defined or specific, exploring your dataset in Tableau and changing your visualization type to discover different insights is as much a part of performing data analysis as crafting your communication. One of the biggest disadvantages to Tableau is its cost, but fortunately, Tableau is a tremendous supporter of education, and as a student, you can download a free academic license to use Tableau on your PC or Mac. The link to download your free license of Tableau is: https://www.tableau.com/academic/students. Once you have downloaded your license, we recommend opening the Superstore sample workbook provided. You will find it at the bottom of the start screen under "Sample workbooks" (Exhibit 4-10).

Once you open the workbook, you will see a variety of tabs at the bottom of the workbook that you can page through and see different ways that the same dataset can be analyzed and visualized. When you perform exploratory analysis in Tableau, or even if you have already performed

EXHIBIT 4-10

Source: ©Tableau Software, Inc. All rights reserved.

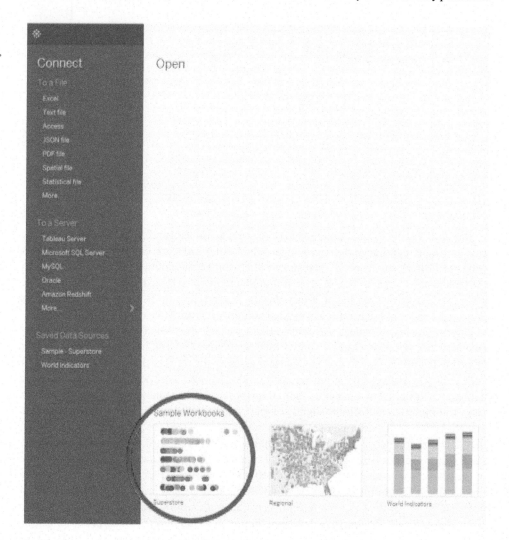

your analysis and you have uploaded the dataset into Tableau to communicate insights, we recommend trying several different types of charts to see which one makes your insights stand out the most effectively. In the top right corner of the Tableau workbook, you will see the Show Me window, which provides different options for visualizing your dataset (Exhibit 4-11).

EXHIBIT 4-11

Source: ©Tableau Software, Inc. All rights reserved.

In the Show Me tab, only the visualizations that will work for your particular dataset will appear in full color.

For more information on using Tableau, see Appendix G.

Learning to Create a Good Chart by (Bad) Example

Other than getting practice by looking at good visualizations and modifying the way you visualize your dataset in Tableau to see how different insights are showcased, one of the best ways to learn how to create a good visualization is to look at some problematic visualizations.

In the chart depicted in Exhibit 4-12, the Daily Mail, a UK-based newspaper, tried to emphasize an upgrade in the estimated growth of British economy. The estimate from the Office of National Statistics indicated that Q4 growth would be 0.7 percent instead of 0.6 percent (a relatively small increase of about 15 percent). Yet the visualization makes it appear as if this is a 200 percent increase because of the scale the newspaper chose. Another issue is that some time has passed between the estimates, and we don't see that disclosed here (Exhibit 4-12).

EXHIBIT 4-12

Bar Chart Distorting Data Comparison by Using Inappropriate Scale

Source: http://www.dailymail.co.uk/news/article-4248690/Economy-grew-0-7-final-three-months-2016.html.

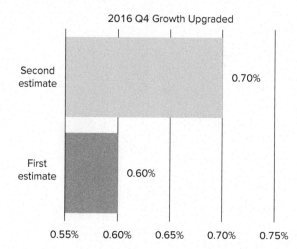

If we reworked the data points to show the correct scale (starting at 0 instead of 0.55) and the change over time (plotting the data along the horizontal axis), we'd see something like Exhibit 4-13. If we wanted to emphasize growth, we might choose a chart like Exhibit 4-14. Notice that both new graphs show an increase that is less dramatic and confusing.

EXHIBIT 4-13

Bar Chart Using Appropriate Scale for Less Biased Comparison

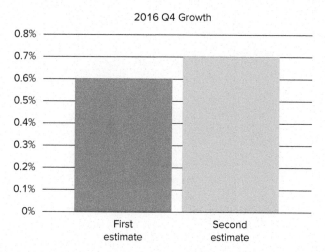

Our next example of a problematic method of data visualization is in Exhibit 4-15. The data represented come from a study assessing cyber-security attacks, and this chart in particular attempted to describe the number of cyber-security attacks employees fell victim to, as well as what their role was in their organization.

Assess the chart provided in Exhibit 4-15. Is a pie chart really the best way to present these data?

There are simply too many slices of pie, and the key referencing the job role of each user is unclear. There are a few ways we could improve this chart.

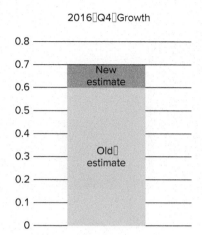

EXHIBIT 4-14
**Alternative Stacked Bar
Chart Showing Growth**

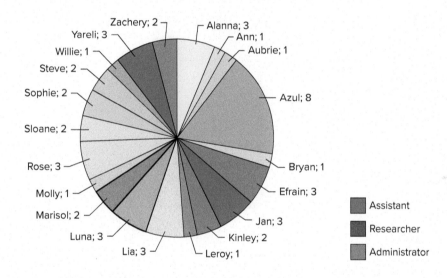

EXHIBIT 4-15
**Difficult to Interpret
Pie Chart**

Source: http://viz.wtf/
post/155727224217/the-
authors-explain-furthermore-
we-present-the.

If you want to emphasize users, consider a rank-ordered bar chart like Exhibit 4-16. To emphasize the category, a comparison like that in Exhibit 4-17 may be helpful. Or to show proportion, maybe a stacked bar (Exhibit 4-18).

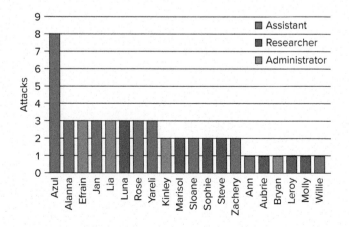

EXHIBIT 4-16
**More Clear
Rank-Ordered Bar
Chart**

EXHIBIT 4-17
Bar Chart Emphasizing
Attacks by Job
Function

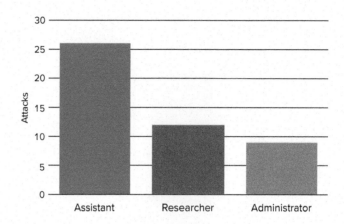

EXHIBIT 4-18
Stacked Bar Chart
Emphasizing
Proportion of Attacks
by Job Function

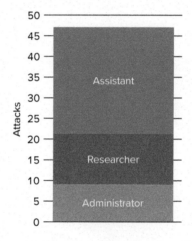

(✓) **PROGRESS CHECK**

4. The following two charts represent the exact same data—the quantity of beer
sold on each day in the Sláinte Sales Subset dataset. Which chart is more appropriate for working with dates, the column chart or the line chart? Which do you
prefer? Why?

a.

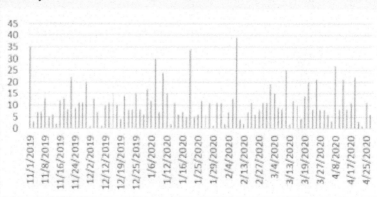

Source: Microsoft Excel 2016

b.

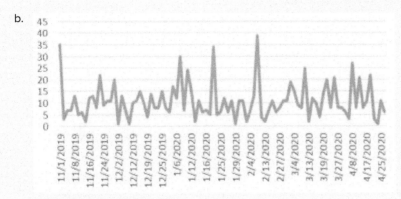

Source: Microsoft Excel 2016

5. The same dataset was consolidated into quarters. This chart was made with the chart wizard feature in Excel, which made the creation of it easy, but something went wrong. Can you identify what went wrong with this chart?

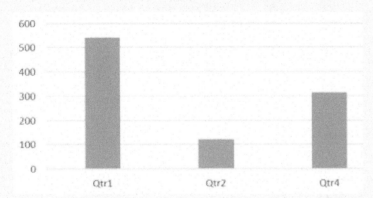

Source: Microsoft Excel 2016

6. The following four charts represent the exact same data quantity of each beer sold. Which do you prefer, the line chart or the column chart? Whichever you chose, line or column, which of the pair do you think is the easiest to digest?

a.

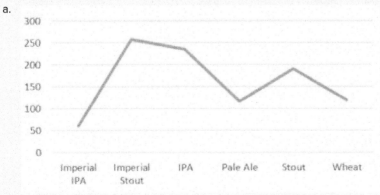

Source: Microsoft Excel 2016

b.

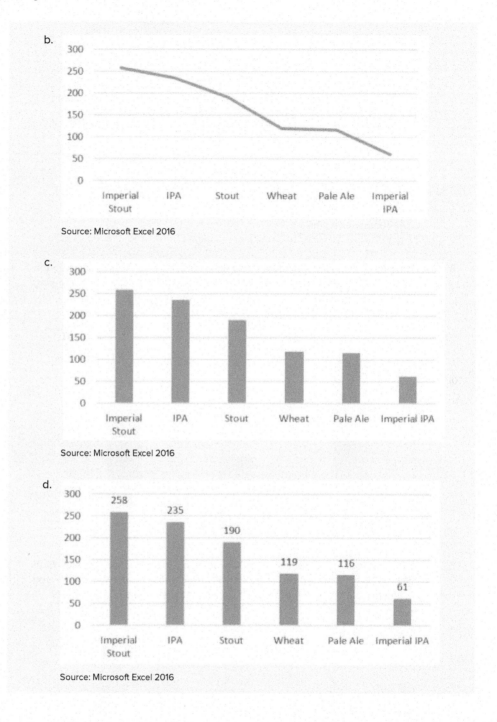

Source: Microsoft Excel 2016

c.

Source: Microsoft Excel 2016

d.

Source: Microsoft Excel 2016

LO 4-3

Refine your chart to communicate efficiently and effectively.

FURTHER REFINING YOUR CHART TO COMMUNICATE BETTER

After identifying the purpose of your visualization and which type of visual will be most effective in communicating your results, you will need to further refine your chart to pick the right data scale, color, and format.

Data Scale and Increments

As tools such as Excel and Tableau become more intuitive and more powerful, considering your data scale and increments is less of a concern because both tools will generally come up with scales and increments that make sense for your dataset. With that being said, there are still four main questions to consider when creating your data scale and increments:

1. How much data do you need to share in the visual to avoid being misleading, yet also avoid being distracting? (For example, do you need to display the past four years, or will the past two quarters suffice?) When you consider leaving out some data, is it to show only the insights that are meaningful, or is it an attempt to skew the data or to hide poor performance? Be careful to not hide data that are meaningful just because they don't align with your expectations.
2. If your data contain outliers, should they be displayed, or will they distort your scale to the extent that you can leave them out? If the purpose of your chart is to call attention to the outliers, then they need to remain (and you need to ensure that they are not errors, but this should have been done in step 2 of the IMPACT model when you mastered the data). If the purpose of your chart is to display the middle pack of the data, the outliers may not be relevant to the insights, and they could be left out.
3. Other than determining how much data you need to share, what scale should you place those data on? Typically, charts should begin with a baseline of 0, but if 0 is meaningless to your dataset, you could find a different baseline that makes sense. Be careful to not overexaggerate the height or the baseline so that your trendline or bar chart is over- or underemphasized; your trendline should take up two-thirds of the chart. Once you decide on a data scale, the increments for your data scale should be "natural" such as 1s, 2s, 5s, 100s, etc. (e.g., not 3s or 0.02s).
4. Do you need to provide context or reference points to make the scale meaningful? For example, if you were provided with a stock price of $100, would you immediately be able to tell if that is a high number or a low number? Not necessarily; without context of the company's stock price over time, the company's industry and its competitors' stock prices, or some other piece of context, certain numbers are not altogether useful.

Color

Similar to how Excel and Tableau have become stronger tools at picking appropriate data scales and increments, both Excel and Tableau will have default color themes when you begin creating your data visualizations. You may choose to customize the theme. However, if you do, here are a few points to consider:

- When should you use multiple colors? Using multiple colors to differentiate types of data is effective. Using a different color to highlight a focal point is also effective. However, don't use multiple colors to represent the same type of data. Be careful to not use color to make the chart look pretty—the point of the visualization is to showcase insights from your data, not to make art.
- We are trained to understand the differences among red, yellow, and green, with red meaning something negative that we would want to "stop" and green being something positive that we would want to "continue," just like with traffic lights. For that reason, use red and green only for those purposes. Using red to show something positive or green to show something negative is counterintuitive and will make your chart harder to understand. You may also want to consider a color-blind audience. If you are concerned that someone reading your visuals may be color blind, avoid a red/green scale and

consider using orange/blue. Tableau has begun defaulting to orange/blue color scales instead of red/green for this reason.

- Once your chart has been created, convert it to grayscale to ensure that the contrast still exists—this is both to ensure your color-blind audience can interpret your visuals and also to ensure that the contrast, in general, is stark enough with the color palette you have chosen.

 PROGRESS CHECK

7. Often, external consultants will use a firm's color scheme for a data visualization or will use a firm's logo for points on a scatter plot. While this might be a great approach to support a corporate culture, it is often not the most effective way to create a chart. Why would these methods harm a chart's effectiveness?

LO 4-4
Communicate your results in a written report.

COMMUNICATION: MORE THAN VISUALS—USING WORDS TO PROVIDE INSIGHTS

As a student, the majority of the writing you do is for your professors. You likely write emails to your professors, which should carry a respectful tone, or essays for your Comp 1 or literature professors, where you may have been encouraged to use descriptive language and an elevated tone; you might even have had the opportunity to write a business brief or report for your business professors. All the while, though, you were still aware that you were writing for a professor. When you enter the professional world, your writing will need to take on a different tone. If you are accustomed to writing with an academic tone, transitioning to writing for your colleagues in a business setting requires some practice. As Justin Zobel says in *Writing for Computer Science,* "good style for science is ultimately, nothing more than writing that is easy to understand. [It should be] clear, unambiguous, correct, interesting, and direct."[2] As an author team, we have tremendous respect for literature and the different styles of writing to be found, but for communicating your results of a data analysis project, you need to write directly to your audience, with only the necessary points included, and as little descriptive style as possible. The point is, get to the point.

Content and Organization

Each step of the IMPACT model should be communicated in your write-up, as noted here:

I: Explain what was being researched. Even if your audience is the people who requested the research, you should still restate the purpose of the project. Include any relevant history as well. If your project is part of a larger program or if it's a continued effort to explain an issue or help a decision come to fruition, then include the background.

M: Depending on your audience, you may not cover too much of what your process was in the "master the data" step of the IMPACT model, but an overview of the data source and which pieces of data are included in the analysis should be present. If your audience is technical and interested, you may go into detail on your ETL process, but it is more likely that you will leave out that piece.

P and A: Similar to how you write about mastering the data, you may not need to include a thorough description of your test plan or your process for refining your

---

[2]Source: Zobel, Justin. *Writing for Computer Science* (Singapore: Springer-Verlag, 1997).

results depending on what your audience is interested in and what they need to know, but including an overview of the type of analysis performed and any limitations that you encountered will be important to include.

C: If you are including a data visualization with your write-up, you need to explain how to use the visual. If there are certain aspects that you expect to stand out from the analysis and the accompanying visual, you should describe what those components are—the visual should speak for itself, but the write-up can provide confirmation that the important pieces are gleaned.

T: Discuss what's next in your analysis. Will the visual or the report result in a weekly or quarterly report? What trends or outliers should be paid attention to over time?

Audience and Tone

Carefully considering your audience is critical to ensuring your communication is effective. If you have three messages to write—one letting your mom know that you are coming home this weekend and you'll need to do laundry, one to your professor letting her know that you will miss class on Friday, and one to your best friend asking if he wants to join you for Chipotle—efficiency would suggest that you type it all into one email and click send. That would definitely be the quickest way to get out the message. But is it a good idea? Certainly not. Your mom does not need to know that you're not going to class on Friday, and you probably don't want your professor to show up at Chipotle to have lunch with you and your friend. Instead of sending the same message to all three people, you tailor the delivery—that is, you consider the audience. You include all of the information that they need to know and nothing else.

You should do the same thing when crafting your communication regarding your data analysis. If you have several different people to communicate results to, you may consider crafting several different versions: one that contains all of the extraction, transformation, and loading (ETL) details for the programmers and database administrators, one that is light on ETL but heavy on interpretation of the visual and results for your managers, and so on. Consider the knowledge and skill of your audience—don't talk down to them, but don't overwhelm a nontechnical crowd with technical jargon. Explain the basics when you should, and don't when you shouldn't.

An additional piece of communication to consider is the vehicle for communication. We have a myriad of options available to us for communicating: email, phone calls, Skype, instant messaging, printed reports, even face-to-face conversations that can be either informal or formal presentations in meetings. When crafting your communication, consider the best way to provide the information to your intended audience.

Is the concept difficult to understand? A written report will probably not suffice; plan to supplement your written material with a sit-down conversation or a phone call to explain the details and answer questions.

Is the topic an answer to a question and fairly simple to understand? An emailed response summarizing the visualization and results will likely suffice.

How does the person you are sending the report to communicate? Consider the professional culture of your organization. It may be commonplace to communicate casually using abbreviations and jargon in your workplace, but if that's not the way your workplace operates or even if it's not the way that the recipient of your message communicates, take the time to refine your message and mirror the norms of the organization and the recipients.

Is the report going to be updated and sent out at regular intervals (daily, weekly, monthly)? If so, keep a consistent template so that it is easy for the recipients to identify the information they seek on a regular basis.

There are, of course, many more concepts to consider that will be unique to each message that you craft. Take the time to always consider your audience, their communication style, and what they need from the communication—and provide it, via the right message, the right tone, and the right vehicle.

Revising

Just as you addressed and refined your results in the fourth step of the IMPACT model, you should refine your writing. Until you get plenty of practice (and even once you consider yourself an expert), you should ask other people to read through your writing to make sure that you are communicating clearly. Justin Zobel suggests that revising your writing requires you to "be egoless—ready to dislike anything you have previously written. . . . If someone dislikes something you have written, remember that it is the readers you need to please, not yourself."[3] Always placing your audience as the focus of your writing will help you maintain an appropriate tone, provide the right content, and avoid too much detail.

 PROGRESS CHECK

Progress Checks 5 and 6 display different charts depicting the quantity of beer sold on each day in the Sláinte Sales Subset dataset. If you had created those visuals, starting with the data request form and the ETL process all the way through data analysis, how would you tailor the written report for the following two roles?

  8. For the CEO of the brewery who is interested in how well the different products are performing.

  9. For the programmers who will be in charge of creating a report that contains the same information that needs to be sent to the CEO on a monthly basis.

[3]Source: Justin Zobel

Summary

- This chapter focused on the fifth step of the IMPACT model, or the "C," on how to communicate the results of your data analysis projects. Communication can be done through a variety of data visualizations and written reports, depending on your audience and the data you are exhibiting.
- In order to select the right chart, you must first determine the purpose of your data visualization. This can be done by answering two key questions:
  ○ Are you explaining the results of a previously done analysis, or are you exploring the data through the visualization? (Is your purpose declarative or exploratory?)
  ○ What type of data are being visualized (conceptual qualitative data or data-driven quantitative data)?
- The differences between each type of data (declarative and exploratory, qualitative and quantitative) are explained, as well as how each datatype affects both the tool you're likely to use (generally either Excel or Tableau) and the chart you should create.
- After selecting the right chart based on your purpose and datatype, your chart will need to be further refined. Selecting the appropriate data scale, scale increments, and color for your visualization is explained through the answers to the following questions:
  ○ How much data do you need to share in the visual to avoid being misleading, yet also avoid being distracting?

- If your data contain outliers, should they be displayed, or will they distort your scale to the extent that you can leave them out?
- Other than how much data you need to share, what scale should you place those data on?
- Do you need to provide context or reference points to make the scale meaningful?
- When should you use multiple colors?
- Finally, this chapter discusses how to provide a written report to describe your data analysis project. Each step of the IMPACT model should be communicated in your write-up, and the report should be tailored to the specific audience to whom it is being delivered.

Key Words

continuous data (*143*)   One way to categorize quantitative data, as opposed to discrete data. Continuous data can take on any value within a range. An example of continuous data is height.

declarative visualizations (*144*)   Made when the aim of your project is to "declare" or present your findings to an audience. Charts that are declarative are typically made after the data analysis has been completed and are meant to exhibit what was found in the analysis steps.

discrete data (*143*)   One way to categorize quantitative data, as opposed to continuous data. Discrete data are represented by whole numbers. An example of discrete data is points in a basketball game.

exploratory visualizations (*144*)   Made when the lines between steps **P** (perform test plan), **A** (address and refine results), and **C** (communicate results) are not as clearly divided as they are in a declarative visualization project. Often when you are exploring the data with visualizations, you are performing the test plan directly in visualization software such as Tableau instead of creating the chart after the analysis has been done.

interval data (*143*)   The third most sophisticated type of data on the scale of nominal, ordinal, interval, and ratio; a type of quantitative data. Interval data can be counted and grouped like qualitative data, and the differences between each data point are meaningful. However, interval data do not have a meaningful 0. In interval data, 0 does not mean "the absence of" but is simply another number. An example of interval data is the Fahrenheit scale of temperature measurement.

nominal data (*142*)   The least sophisticated type of data on the scale of nominal, ordinal, interval, and ratio; a type of qualitative data. The only thing you can do with nominal data is count, group, and take a proportion. Examples of nominal data are hair color, gender, and ethnic groups.

normal distribution (*143*)   A type of distribution in which the median, mean, and mode are all equal, so half of all the observations fall below the mean and the other half fall above the mean. This phenomenon is naturally occurring in many datasets in our world, such as SAT scores and heights and weights of newborn babies. When datasets follow a normal distribution, they can be standardized and compared for easier analysis.

ordinal data (*142*)   The second most sophisticated type of data on the scale of nominal, ordinal, interval, and ratio; a type of qualitative data. Ordinal can be counted and categorized like nominal data and the categories can also be ranked. Examples of ordinal data include gold, silver, and bronze medals.

proportion (*142*)   The primary statistic used with qualitative data. Proportion is calculated by counting the number of items in a particular category, then dividing that number by the total number of observations.

qualitative data (*142*)   Categorical data. All you can do with these data are count and group, and in some cases, you can rank the data. Qualitative data can be further defined in two ways: nominal data and ordinal data. There are not as many options for charting qualitative data because they are not as sophisticated as quantitative data.

quantitative data (*143*)   More complex than qualitative data. Quantitative data can be further defined in two ways: interval and ratio. In all quantitative data, the intervals between data points are meaningful, allowing the data to be not just counted, grouped, and ranked, but also to have more complex operations performed on them such as mean, median, and standard deviation.

ratio data (*143*)   The most sophisticated type of data on the scale of nominal, ordinal, interval, and ratio; a type of quantitative data. They can be counted and grouped just like qualitative data, and the differences between each data point are meaningful like with interval data. Additionally, ratio data have a meaningful 0. In other words, once a dataset approaches 0, 0 means "the absence of." An example of ratio data is currency.

standard normal distribution (*144*)   A special case of the normal distribution used for standardizing data. The standard normal distribution has 0 for its mean (and thus, for its mode and median, as well), and 1 for its standard deviation.

standardization (*144*)   The method used for comparing two datasets that follow the normal distribution. By using a formula, every normal distribution can be transformed into the standard normal distribution. If you standardize both datasets, you can place both distributions on the same chart and more swiftly generate your insights.

✓ ANSWERS TO PROGRESS CHECKS

1. Certainly, answers will vary given our own individual experiences. But we can note that complex topics can be explained and understood by linking them to categorizations or pictures, such as the food pyramid.

2. Answers will vary.

3. a. Qualitative ordinal

   b. Quantitative (ratio data)

   c. Qualitative nominal

   d. Quantitative (interval data)

4. While this question does ask for your preference, it is likely that you prefer image b because time series data are continuous and can be well represented with a line chart instead of bars.

5. Notice that the quarters are out of order (1, 2, then 4); this looks like quarter 3 has been skipped, but quarter 4 is actually the last quarter of 2019 instead of the last quarter of 2020, while quarters 1 and 2 are in 2020. Excel defaulted to simply ordering the quarters numerically instead of recognizing the order of the years in the underlying data. You want to be careful to avoid this sort of issue by paying careful attention to the charts, ordering, and scales that are automatically created through Excel (and other tools) wizards.

6. Answers will vary. Possible answers include the following: Quantity of beer sold is a discrete value, so it is likely better modeled with a bar chart than a line chart. Between the two line charts, the second one is easier to interpret because it is in order of highest sales to lowest. Between the two bar charts, it depends on what is important to convey to your audience— are the numbers critical? If so, the second chart is better. Is it most important to simply show which beers are performing better than others? If so, the first chart is better. There is no reason to provide more data than necessary because they will just clutter up the visual.

7. Color in a chart should be used purposefully; it is possible that a firm's color scheme may be counterproductive to interpreting the chart. The icons as points in a scatter plot might be distracting, which could make it take longer for a reader to gain insights from the chart.

8. Answers will vary. Possible answers include the following: Explain to the CEO how to read the visual, call out the important insights in the chart, tell the range of data that is included (is it one quarter, one year, all time?).

9. Answers will vary. Possible answers include the following: Explain the ETL process, exactly what data are extracted to create the visual, which tool the data were loaded into, and how the data were analyzed. Explain the mechanics of the visual. The particular insights of this visual are not pertinent to the programmer because the insights will potentially change over time. The mechanics of creating the report are most important.

Multiple Choice Questions

1. Gold, silver, and bronze medals would be examples of:
   a. nominal data.
   b. ordinal data.
   c. structured data.
   d. test data.

2. In the late 1960s, Ed Altman developed a model to predict if a company was at severe risk of going bankrupt. He called his statistic Altman's Z-score, now a widely used score in finance. Based on the name of the statistic, which statistical distribution would you guess this came from?
   a. Normal distribution
   b. Poisson distribution
   c. Standardized normal distribution
   d. Uniform distribution

3. Justin Zobel suggests that revising your writing requires you to "be egoless—ready to dislike anything you have previously written," suggesting that it is _____ you need to please:
   a. yourself
   b. the reader
   c. the customer
   d. your boss

4. Which of the following is *not* a typical example of nominal data?
   a. Gender
   b. SAT scores
   c. Hair color
   d. Ethnic group

5. The Fahrenheit scale of temperature measurement would best be described as an example of:
   a. interval data.
   b. discrete data.
   c. nominal data.
   d. continuous data.

6. _____ data would be considered the least sophisticated type of data.
   a. Ratio
   b. Interval
   c. Ordinal
   d. Nominal

7. _____ data would be considered the most sophisticated type of data.
   a. Ratio
   b. Interval
   c. Ordinal
   d. Nominal

8. Line charts are not recommended for what type of data?
   a. Normalized data
   b. Qualitative data

    c. Continuous data

    d. Trend lines

9. Exhibit 4-8 gives chart suggestions for what data you'd like to portray. Those options include all of the following *except:*

    a. relationship between variables

    b. geographic data

    c. outlier detection

    d. normal distribution curves

10. What is the most appropriate chart when showing a relationship between two variables (according to Exhibit 4-8)?

    a. Scatter chart

    b. Bar chart

    c. Pie graph

    d. Histogram

Discussion Questions

1. Explain Exhibit 4-2 and why these four dimensions are helpful in describing information to be communicated. Exhibit 4-2 lists conceptual and data-driven as being on two ends of the continuum. Does that make sense, or can you think of a better way to organize and differentiate the different chart types?

2. According to Exhibit 4-8, which is the best chart for showing a distribution of a single variable, like height? How about hair color? Major in college?

3. Box and whisker plots (or box plots) are particularly adept at showing extreme observations and outliers. In what situations would it be important to communicate these data to a reader? Any particular accounts on the balance sheet or income statement?

4. Based on the data from datavizcatalogue.com, a line graph is best at showing comparisons, relationships, compositions, or distributions? Name the best two.

5. Based on the data from datavizcatalogue.com, what are some major flaws of using word clouds to communicate the frequency of words in a document?

6. Based on the data from datavizcatalogue.com, how does a box and whisker plot show if the data are symmetrical?

7. What would be the best chart to use to illustrate earnings per share for one company over the past five years?

8. The text mentions, *"If your data analysis project is more declarative than exploratory, it is more likely that you will perform your data visualization to communicate results in Excel."* In your opinion, why is this true?

9. According to the text and your own experience, why is Tableau ideal for exploratory data analysis?

Problems

1. Why was the heat map associated with the opening vignette regarding the 1854 cholera epidemic effective? Now that we have more sophisticated tools and methods for visualizing data, what else could have been used to communicate this, and would it have been more or less effective in your opinion?

2. Evaluate the use of color in the graphic associated with the opening vignette regarding drug overdose deaths across America. Would you consider its use effective or ineffective? Why? How is this more or less effective than communicating the same data in a bar chart?

3. According to Exhibit 4-8, which is the best chart for comparisons of earnings per share over many periods? How about for only a few periods?

4. According to Exhibit 4-8, which is the best chart for static composition of a data item of the Accounts Receivable balance at the end of the year? Which is best for showing a change in composition of Accounts Receivable over two or more periods?

5. The Big 4 accounting firms (Deloitte, EY, KPMG, and PwC) dominate the audit and tax market in the United States. What chart would you use to show which accounting firm dominates in each state in terms of audit revenues? Any there other interesting ways you could use to find opportunities within the audit market?

6. Datavizcatalogue.com lists seven types of maps in its listing of charts. Which one would you use to assess geographic customer concentration by number? How could you show if some customers buy more than other customers on such a map? Would you use the same chart or a different one?

7. In your opinion, is the primary reason that analysts use inappropriate scales for their charts due to an error related to naiveté (or ineffective training), or are the inappropriate scales used so the analyst can sway the audience one way or the other?

Lab 4-1 Use PivotCharts to Visualize Declarative Data

This lab builds upon the steps completed in Lab 2-2 concerning the Sláinte brewery and the PivotTable report you prepared showing the total number of each item sold each month between January and April 2020.

When working with a data analysis project that is declarative in nature, the analysis will likely be done in Excel, and the data visualization will be done after the analysis has been completed as a means to communicate results.

Company summary

Sláinte is a fictional brewery that has recently gone through big change. Sláinte sells six different products. The brewery has only recently expanded its business to distributing from one state to distributing to nine states, and now the business has begun stabilizing after the expansion. With that stability comes a need for better analysis. One of Sláinte's first priorities is to identify its areas of success, as well as areas of potential improvement.

Data

- Sláinte dataset

Technique

- Some experience with spreadsheets and PivotTables is useful for this lab.

Software needed

- Excel
- Screen capture tool (Windows: Snipping Tool; Mac: Cmd + Shift + 4)

Parts 1–4 of the IMPACT Model

These steps were performed in Lab 2-2. You can either use the already prepared data in the file Lab_4_1_SlaintePivot.xlsx, or you can use the file that you saved after completing Lab 2-2, which should have been saved to your computer as Slainte_Pivot.xlsx.

Part 5: Communicate Your Findings

We demonstrate two alternate ways of communicating findings. Please work through both alternatives.

Alternative 1: Create a PivotChart

1. Ensuring that the active cell in your workbook is somewhere in the PivotTable, navigate to the **Analyze** tab in the ribbon.
2. If you are working with a PC, you should see a button for **PivotChart.** If you are working with a Mac, you can insert a regular chart from the **Insert** tab on the ribbon. Some of the functionality of this lab will be limited on a Mac, so you may opt to use a virtual PC lab environment to complete this lab.
3. Once you click into **PivotChart,** a window for **Insert Chart** appears, along with a list of options for how you can visualize your PivotTable. It defaults to column chart. Another good option is the bar chart, which displays your data in horizontal bars instead of columns. Create either a bar chart or a column chart by selecting the chart you prefer and clicking **OK.**
4. Take a screenshot that shows the PivotTable and the PivotChart (label it 4-1A).

5. The advantage of working with PivotCharts over regular charts is that you can slice and filter your data in the PivotTable and the PivotChart at the same time. If you are presenting your findings to a live audience and you anticipate questions about specific months or specific products, using Excel's slicer tool is a great way to filter your data in a way that is interactive and transparent. On the **Analyze** tab on the ribbon, you can select **Insert Slicer.**

6. In the window that pops up, select **Product Description.** This will create an interactive filter so that you can drill down into different product descriptions as they perform over the months.

7. Create a second slicer for **Sales_Order_Month** and click **OK.**

8. Take a screenshot that includes your PivotChart, PivotTable, and both slicers (label it 4-1B).

> Q1. Spend a few minutes filtering the data with the slicers. Name three important insights that were easy to identify through this visualization.
>
> Q2. What does the data visualization and the interactivity of the slicer provide your audience that the original PivotTable does not?

Alternative 2: Visualize the PivotTable with Conditional Formatting and Sparklines

Conditional formatting and sparklines are quick ways to visualize and compare data and trends when a full-fledged chart isn't necessary.

9. To quickly visualize how each product's total quantity sold over time compares across all six of Sláinte's projects, we can apply conditional formatting to the **Grand Total** column. Select the data in the **Grand Total** column of your PivotTable, and navigate to the **Home** tab on the ribbon.

Sum of Sales_Order_Quantity_Sold	Column Labels				
Row Labels	April	February	January	March	Grand Total
Imperial IPA	17		23	2	42
Imperial Stout	36	27	61	42	166
IPA	34	35	36	66	171
Pale Ale	18	4	27	32	81
Stout	16	33	65	4	118
Wheat		11	21	54	86
Grand Total	121	110	233	200	664

LAB EXHIBIT 4-1A

Source: Microsoft Excel 2016

10. From the **Home** tab, select the **Conditional Formatting** button, and a menu with the different types of formatting available will appear.

11. Select **Data Bars** and pick the first option for blue gradient fill bars.

12. This conditional formatting is helpful because it allows us to compare grand totals of each product. However, if we would like to see how each product's month-over-month sales compare to one another, we can display mini line charts next to each row with a sparkline. To do so, select all of the "meat" of your PivotTable—that is, don't select any of the product labels (such as Imperial IPA), month labels, or grand totals.

13. Navigate to the **Insert** tab on the ribbon, and select **Line** in the **Sparklines** category.

14. A window will appear specifying the data range you just selected and awaiting input for the **Location Range.** We'd like to see the trend lines to the immediate right of our PivotTable, so you can select the cells in the first empty column after your Grand Totals.

Sum of Sales_Order_Quantity_Sold	Column Labels �T				
Row Labels ▼	April	February	January	March	Grand Total
Imperial IPA	17		23	2	42
Imperial Stout	36	27	61	42	166
IPA	34	35	36	66	171
Pale Ale	18	4	27	32	81
Stout	16	33	65	4	118
Wheat		11	21	54	86
Grand Total	121	110	233	200	664

Sum of Sales_Order_Quantity_Sold	Column Labels �T					
Row Labels ▼	April	February	January	March	Grand Total	
Imperial IPA	17		23	2	42	
Imperial Stout	36	27	61	42	166	
IPA	34	35	36	66	171	
Pale Ale	18	4	27	32	81	
Stout	16	33	65	4	118	
Wheat		11	21	54	86	
Grand Total	121	110	233	200	664	

15. Click **OK,** and your sparklines will be created.
16. You will notice that there are gaps in the lines, though. If you'd rather see a continuous line to represent zero values for the blank cells, you can change this option. Ensure that one of the cells with the sparkline in it is active, and navigate to the **Sparkline Tools** tab on the ribbon.
17. Click the bottom half of the **Edit Data** button to make a menu appear.
18. From the menu, select **Hidden & Empty Cells. . .**
19. Select the option to **show empty cells as zero,** and click **OK.**
20. Take a screenshot to show the conditional formatting and the sparklines (label it 4-1C).

Q3. When do you think a sparkline and/or conditional formatting would be preferable over creating a PivotChart?

Q4. What other visualizations would be useful to interpret these data? If you were to create a report to be run monthly, what are two visualizations that should be included?

Q5. Provide a written report discussing the data analysis project and the insights that should be gained from this visualization.

End of Lab

Lab 4-2   Use Tableau to Perform Exploratory Analysis and Create Dashboards

When working with a data analysis project that is exploratory in nature, the analysis can be done in Tableau. You will likely enter the data analysis project with an overarching question in mind, but as you answer that question, your exploratory analysis will lead to ongoing questions. The data visualization will help explore the data, as well as ultimately be used as a means to communicate results.

Company summary

Sláinte is a fictional brewery that has recently gone through big change. Sláinte sells six different products. The brewery has only recently expanded its business to distributing from one state to distributing to nine states, and now the business has begun stabilizing after the expansion. With that stability comes a need for better analysis. One of Sláinte's first priorities is to identify its areas of success, as well as areas of potential improvement.

Data

- Sláinte dataset

Software needed

- Tableau. Visit with your instructor for instructions or follow this link to download Tableau, https://www.tableau.com/academic/students, and click **Get Tableau for Free** to register for a free student license. Your student license will last one year.
- Screen capture tool (Windows: Snipping Tool; Mac: Cmd + Shift + 4)

In this lab, you will:

Part 1: Identify appropriate questions.

Part 2: Complete the ETL process to load the data in Tableau for analysis.

Part 3: Analyze the data you receive with data visualization.

Part 4: Communicate the data you receive with a digital dashboard.

Part 1: Identify the Questions

If you completed Lab 2-1 or 2-2, you became familiar with the Sláinte dataset and identified questions regarding Sláinte.

In particular, we worked with this scenario: Sláinte has brought you in to help determine potential areas for sales growth in the next year. Additionally, the company has noticed that its margins aren't as high as it had budgeted and would like you to help identify some areas where it could improve its pricing, marketing, or strategy. Specifically, Sláinte would like to know how many of each product was sold.

We'll start with the same question—identifying the amount of each product sold, overall.

The Sláinte data include the following tables and fields, presented in a UML diagram:

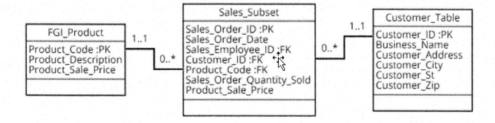

LAB EXHIBIT 4-2A

Q1. Using the UML diagram, identify which table(s) and attributes you will need to answer your initial question regarding amount of products sold.

Part 2: Master the Data

To complete the ETL process, we will need to extract the data from Access and transform and load it into Tableau.

1. Open Tableau.
2. Select **Microsoft Access** from the **Connect To a File** options.

Source: ©Tableau Software, Inc.
All rights reserved.

3. Browse to the Slainte_Subset.accdb file and click **Open.** This will extract the data.

Source: ©Tableau Software, Inc. All rights reserved.

4. The **Data Source** tab will open, with three tables for you to select from. We can begin by just exploring the Sales data. Double-click on the **Sales_Subset** table to load it into Tableau.

Source: ©Tableau Software, Inc. All rights reserved.

5. The data should load into Tableau without any problems. However, it is always a good idea to check the datatypes that each attribute loaded in as. Notice the **Abc** above **Sales Order ID,** and the **calendar** icon above **Sales Order Date.** These indicate that **Sales Order ID** data imported as text, while the **Sales Order Date** imported as calendar data. The number signs above **Sales Order Quantity** and **Product Sale Price** indicate that those attributes were imported as numerical data. This is all set up exactly as we'd like, so there's no need to transform the data.

Abc	🗓	Abc	Abc	Abc	#	#
Sales_Subset	Sales_Subset	Sales_Subset	Sales_Subset	Sales_Subset	Sales_Subset	Sales_Subset
Sales Order ID	Sales Order Date	Sales Employee ID	Customer ID	Product Code	Sales Order Quant...	Product Sale Price

Source: ©Tableau Software, Inc. All rights reserved.

Q2. If the Sales Order Date datatype had imported as number, how might that cause a problem with our analysis if we wanted to dig into the data by month, for example?

Q3. Why did your Sales Order ID attribute import as text when it looks like each field has numerical data in it? Would there be any benefit in Sales Order ID being stored as a number? Why will it not present a problem in our analysis to maintain these data as text?

Part 3: Perform Exploratory Analysis

Click into **Sheet 1** in the bottom left of the Tableau tool to begin working with the data. The Tableau screen can be compared to the way Excel's PivotTable Fields list is laid out. The attributes from the **Sales_Subset** table are categorized into **dimensions** and **measures.**

- **Dimensions** are descriptive attributes—these are the fields that we typically slice or group our data by in a PivotTable.
- **Measures** are numerical—these are the fields that you would typically drag into the VALUES area in the PivotTable to calculate a count, sum, or average of your data.

6. To view the number of products sold, begin by double-clicking on the measure **Sales Order Quantity Sold.**

Notice that Tableau doesn't default to showing you one number, but instead displays one bar of a bar chart. This is a clear indication of how Tableau treats data differently than Excel. Excel defaults to numerical data, while Tableau defaults to visualization.

7. To group the total amount of products sold by the products themselves, double-click on the dimension **Product Code.**
8. Take a screenshot (label it 4-2A).

The visualization you just created summarizes the answer to our initial question (how many of each product has sold), but this visual can be improved.

Q4. Identify two ways to improve this visual to make it more easily understandable.

9. Sort the bars: Across the top of the Tableau screen are a variety of icons. Toward the middle of that menu are two icons for sorting data. Click the icon to sort your data descending.

Source: ©Tableau Software, Inc. All rights reserved.

10. Add labels to the bars: To the left of your data viz, there is the **Marks** card. It has a variety of ways that you can enhance the way you're viewing the data. Click **Label,** then place a check mark in the box next to **Show mark labels.**

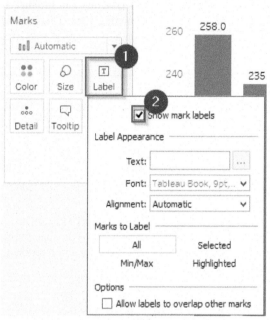

Source: ©Tableau Software, Inc. All rights reserved.

11. Instead of showing **Product Code,** show the **Product Description;** this will require you to join in another table. Click back into the **Data Source** tab in the bottom left.
12. Double-click on the **FGI_Product** table to load the product data into Tableau. You will see the **FGI_Product** data populate, as well as a Venn diagram joining the two datasets. Click on the Venn diagram to ensure the data are joined properly. You want to ensure that the primary key of **FGI_Product** is matched with the corresponding foreign key in the **Sales_Subset** data (the same way the two tables are joined in the UML diagram).

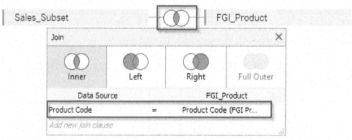

Source: ©Tableau Software, Inc. All rights reserved.

13. Return to **Sheet 1** to work with the new data.
14. Double-click on the dimension **Product Description** to add this detail to your data visualization.
15. Now that you have added the description to the visualization, you can remove the **Product Code** dimension. Remove **Product Code** from the data visualization by dragging and dropping the **Product Code** pill out of the **Columns** shelf. After removing the **Product Code** pill, you will need to sort your data again by using the same sort **descending** icon that you clicked in step 9.

16. Take a screenshot (label it 4-2B).

17. Sometimes when you're performing exploratory data analysis, you'll want to save the visualization you just made, while also giving yourself the opportunity to drill down into the data. We'll name this sheet after the analysis you just did, then duplicate the data to work with it further. Right-click **Sheet 1** and select **Rename Sheet.** Type **Total Products Sold** as the sheet's name.

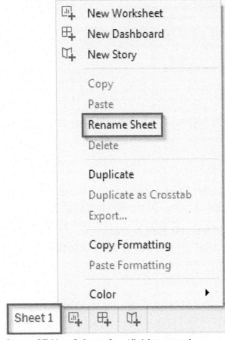

Source: ©Tableau Software, Inc. All rights reserved.

18. Right-click the sheet tab that you just renamed and select **Duplicate Sheet.**

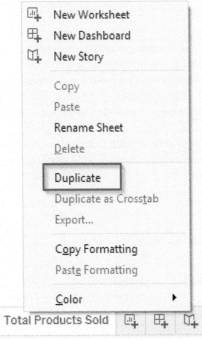

Source: ©Tableau Software, Inc. All rights reserved.

19. Let's dig into how these products have performed year over year. Drag and drop the dimension **Sales Order Date** to the **Columns** shelf, and place it to the left of **Product Description.**

Source: ©Tableau Software, Inc. All rights reserved.

Notice that the pill doesn't just say the name of the attribute, but it says **YEAR** and it has a button to expand the pill.

20. Take a screenshot (label it 4-2C).

If you expand the **Sales Order Date** function once, it will split the data among quarters. If you expand again, it will further drill down into months.

21. Rename this sheet **Total Products Sold by Year.**
22. Navigate to the **Data Source** tab and add in the **Customer** table.

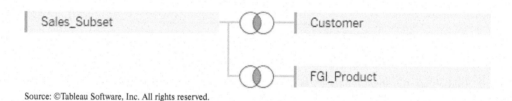

Source: ©Tableau Software, Inc. All rights reserved.

23. Ensure that the join is built on the appropriate primary key/foreign key relationship between **Sales_Subset** and **Customer** according to the UML diagram.
24. For each of the previous tables that we loaded into Tableau, **Sales_Subset** and **FGI_Product,** we didn't need to transform the data. This time, we will want to work with geographic data. Looking at the datatypes for each attribute that loaded in, you can see that Customer City and Customer Zip have **globe** icons for their datatypes, indicating that Tableau was able to intuit that these attributes are geographic. But the **Customer St** attribute has an **Abc** next to it, indicating that Tableau loaded it as only text (not geographic data). Click on the Abc icon above **Customer St** to change its datatype.

Source: ©Tableau Software, Inc. All rights reserved.

25. Select **Geographic Role,** and then select **State/Province.**

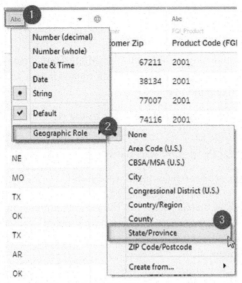

Source: ©Tableau Software, Inc. All rights reserved.

26. Create a new sheet (do not duplicate any of the previous sheets) by clicking the first icon to the right of the **Total Products Sold by Year** tab.

Source: ©Tableau Software, Inc. All rights reserved.

27. This time, we will create a report that shows total products sold by state. Double-click the measure **Customer St.** Tableau automatically populates a map with a dot in each state that's listed in the **Customer** table.
28. Double-click on the measure **Sales Order Quantity Sold.** The dots have changed to vary in size, which is proportional to the amount of sales in each state.
29. We can make the results easier to interpret by changing the visualization type. If the **Show Me** window isn't showing in the upper right corner, click **Show Me,** then select the **Filled Map.**

Source: ©Tableau Software, Inc. All rights reserved.

30. Rename this sheet **Total Products Sold by State.**
31. Take a screenshot (label it 4-2D).

Part 4: Communicate Results

Now that you have created three simple, but meaningful data visualizations, you can create a dashboard to communicate the results. Tableau makes it easy to place all of these visualizations on one interactive pane.

32. Select the icon for **New Dashboard,** which is to the right of the **New Worksheet** icon.

Source: ©Tableau Software, Inc. All rights reserved.

33. In the **Dashboard** view, instead of seeing the various dimensions and measures to drag and drop, you see the three sheets that you have created. You can drag and drop them into the area that says **Drop Sheets Here,** and you can arrange them any way you wish. Replicate this arrangement:

Total Products Sold by State

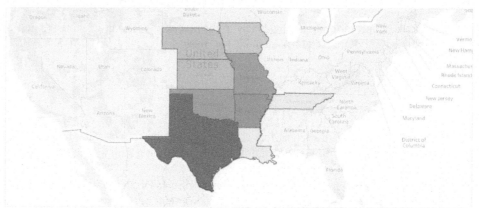

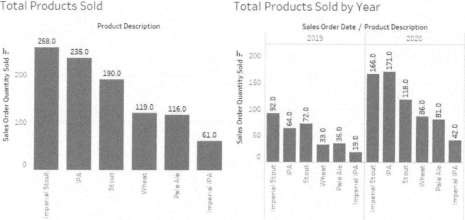

Source: ©Tableau Software, Inc. All rights reserved.

34. You can also use each sheet as a filter. Click the **Total Products Sold** section of your dashboard. There are three small icons in the top right of the sheet when the sheet is active. Clicking the middle one (which looks like a funnel) will allow you to use the bars as filters for the entire dashboard. Click to do so.

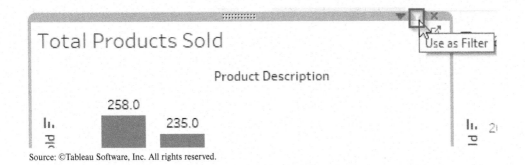

Total Products Sold

Product Description

258.0

235.0

Source: ©Tableau Software, Inc. All rights reserved.

35. Follow the same process to make the states work as filters for the dashboard by clicking **Use as Filter** in the **Total Products Sold by State** sheet.

Now, you can click any of the bars in the **Total Products Sold** chart or any of the states in the **Total Products Sold by State,** and the data in each of the three sheets will shift to focus on just those products and/or states.

36. Filter by either a state or a product, and take a screenshot (label it 4-2E).

    Q5. After creating these sheets and the dashboard, what additional data would you recommend that Sláinte analyze? What is another data visualization that would be helpful for Sláinte's decision making?

End of Lab

Lab 4-3 Comprehensive Case: Dillard's Store Data: Create Geographic Data Visualizations in Tableau and in Power BI

Company summary

Dillard's is a department store with approximately 330 stores in 29 states. Its headquarters is in Little Rock, Arkansas. You can learn more about Dillard's by looking at finance.yahoo.com (Ticker symbol = DDS) and the Wikipedia site for DDS. You'll quickly note that William T. Dillard II is an accounting grad of the University of Arkansas and the Walton College of Business, which may be why he shared transaction data with us to make available for this lab and labs throughout this text.

Data

The data for this lab and all other Dillard's labs must be accessed through the University of Arkansas Remote Desktop. Directions for accessing the Remote Desktop can be found at www.mhhe.com/richardsondaa2e. See your instructor for login credentials.

Software needed

- Microsoft SQL Server Management Studio and Microsoft Excel (available on the Remote Desktop at the University of Arkansas)
- Tableau (available on the Remote Desktop at the University of Arkansas)

In this lab, you will:

- Learn how to prepare data visualization in Tableau.

Part 1: Identify the Questions

Question 2 of Lab 3-4 was as follows: Do customers in the state with the highest transaction balances have a significantly higher transaction balance during the period September 1, 2016, to September 15, 2016, than all other states?

In this lab, we will work to visualize these transaction data in a way that helps users grasp the information needed to make decisions.

Q1. How would this information, average transaction balance by state, help a manager make decisions?

Q2. How would you think managers would like to visualize transaction balance by state? What would be the most (and less) effective ways to visualize these transactions?

Part 2: Master the Data

Load the data into Tableau.

1. Log on to **Remote Desktop** at the University of Arkansas. Open a new Tableau workbook and connect to Microsoft SQL Server.

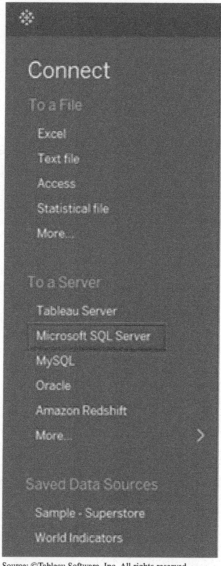

Source: ©Tableau Software, Inc. All rights reserved.

2. Input the **Server** and **Database** information that you received from your instructor for the Dillard's data, and then click **Sign In.**

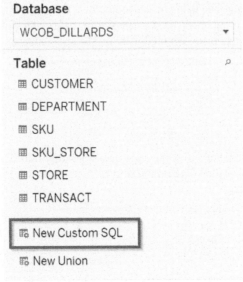

Source: ©Tableau Software, Inc. All rights reserved.

3. Wait for the connection to process, and then you have two options: If you are certain that you will only want to visualize one specific set of query results, you can input a query from the Connections page. Alternatively, you can connect to entire tables if you want the option to drill down into the data and answer more than one question.

Inputting a Custom Query into the Tableau Connections Page

4. Double-click **New Custom SQL.**

Database

WCOB_DILLARDS ▼

Table

- ⊞ CUSTOMER
- ⊞ DEPARTMENT
- ⊞ SKU
- ⊞ SKU_STORE
- ⊞ STORE
- ⊞ TRANSACT

- ⬚ New Custom SQL

- ⬚ New Union

Source: ©Tableau Software, Inc. All rights reserved.

5. Input your SQL query into the **Edit Custom SQL** window, and then click **OK**.

```
SELECT state, avg(tran_amt) AS Average
FROM transact
INNER JOIN store
ON transact.store = store.store
GROUP BY state
```

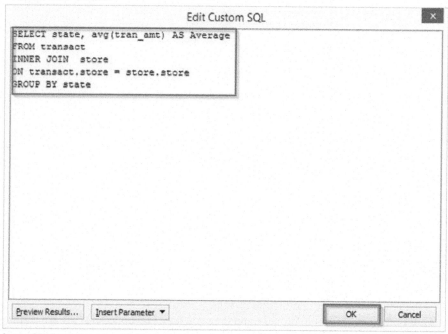

Source: ©Tableau Software, Inc. All rights reserved.

6. It may take a couple minutes for the results to populate. Once they do, we'll preview the data.

The data should load without a problem, but because Tableau is automatically interpreting the data, it is a good idea to look through the data to ensure that we don't need to transform them in any way. In Tableau, you should always check which datatype has been assigned to each attribute. The datatype is denoted by a little icon that is an **Abc** for a string of text, a **number sign** for numerical data, a **calendar** for dates, or a **globe** for geographic data.

The two attributes of state are denoted with an **Abc** and a **number sign**:

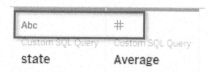

Source: ©Tableau Software, Inc. All rights reserved.

7. Of particular concern is the way the state data were imported. The **Abc** above the state column indicates that they were imported into Tableau as plain text instead of as a geographic attribute.

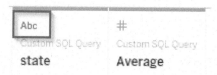

Source: ©Tableau Software, Inc. All rights reserved.

8. For us to view these data more meaningfully, we'll want to change the type of data that state is designated as. Click the **Abc,** then **Geographic Role,** and select **State/Province.**

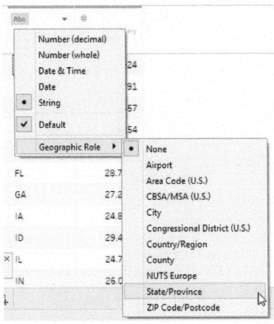

Source: ©Tableau Software, Inc. All rights reserved.

9. Once Tableau has processed the change, click **Sheet 1** on the bottom of the Tableau window to begin working with the data.

Source: ©Tableau Software, Inc. All rights reserved.

10. Double-click on **state** in **Dimensions**.

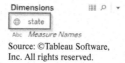

Source: ©Tableau Software,
Inc. All rights reserved.

You will see that Tableau immediately populates a map with a blue dot in each state that has a **Dillard's** store.

11. To make these data even more meaningful, we'll add average to this view. Double-click **Average** in **Measures**.

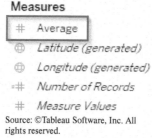

Source: ©Tableau Software, Inc. All
rights reserved.

12. Tableau might have defaulted to a symbol map. The difference in averages is easier to interpret with a filled map. Click **Show Me** in the top right corner of Tableau if your **Show Me** window isn't already available, then click **Filled Map.**

Source: ©Tableau Software, Inc. All rights reserved.

End of this process

Joining Tables into the Tableau Connections Page

This option will produce the same visualization that the steps above just created, but it will also provide more flexibility for digging into the data because more data will be loaded into Tableau.

Open up a new instance of Tableau and repeat steps 1 through 3 to connect to the Dillard's data.

13. Instead of creating a new customer query, drag the **Transact** table to the **Drag tables here** portion of the Tableau window.
14. Drag the **Store** table to the **Drag tables here** portion of the Tableau window.
15. Tableau will likely default to joining the tables on the appropriate attributes, but double-check that it did by clicking the visual representation of the join (it looks like a Venn diagram).

⊖ TRANSACT+ (WCOB_DILLARDS)

Source: ©Tableau Software, Inc. All rights reserved.

16. The join should indicate that it is an inner join based on the **transact.store** and **store. store** attributes. If it says something different, modify the join.

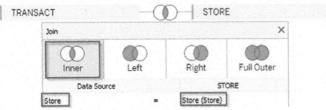

Source: ©Tableau Software, Inc. All rights reserved.

17. Check that the attributes pulled in as the appropriate datatypes. For example, **City** and **Zip Code** pulled in as geographic datatypes, but state did not. Click the **Abc** above the **State** attribute to change the datatype.

#	Abc	⊕	Abc	⊕	Abc
STORE	STORE	STORE	STORE	STORE	STORE
Store (Store)	Division	City	State	Zip Code	Zip Secseg

Source: ©Tableau Software, Inc. All rights reserved.

18. Click **Geographic Role,** then **State/Province.**

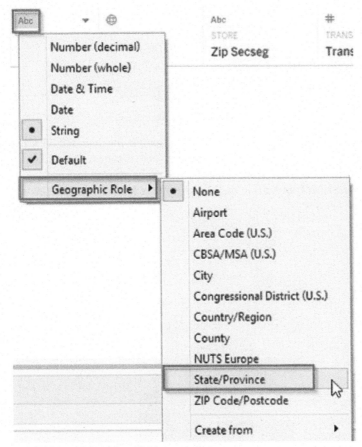

Source: ©Tableau Software, Inc. All rights reserved.

19. Click **Sheet 1** in the bottom left corner of the Tableau screen to begin working with the data.

20. Double-click **State** from **Dimensions.**

Source: ©Tableau Software, Inc. All rights reserved.

Tableau immediately populates a map with a blue dot in each state that has a **Dillard's** store.

21. To make these data even more meaningful, we'll add average transaction amount to this view. Start by double-clicking on **Tran Amt** from the **Measures.**

Source: ©Tableau Software, Inc. All rights reserved.

22. It may take a couple minutes for Tableau to populate the data, but the size of the blue dots will adjust to show how the amounts vary across states. The default value for this measure is SUM, though, so we need to edit it to be average.

23. Hover over **SUM(Tran Amt)** in the **Marks** window to make available an arrow for a drop-down window.

Source: ©Tableau Software, Inc. All rights reserved.

24. Click the drop-down, then click **Measure (Sum)** to change the measure to **Average.**

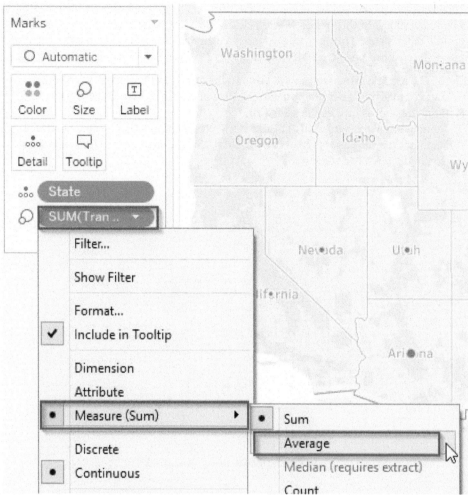

Source: ©Tableau Software, Inc. All rights reserved.

25. Tableau might have defaulted to a symbol map. The difference in averages is easier to interpret with a filled map. Click **Show Me** in the top right corner of Tableau if your **Show Me** window isn't already available, then click **Filled Map.**

26. Take a screenshot of your results (label it 4-3A).

Source: ©Tableau Software, Inc. All rights reserved.

End of this process

Part 3: Perform an Analysis of the Data

Visualizing data often makes it easier to see the answers to your questions, which then leads to more questions. In this case, Arkansas clearly has a higher average transaction amount than the other states. This may lead you to want to drill down into the data to see if the performance is the same across all of the stores in Arkansas, or if there is a stand-out store.

27. If you click **Arkansas,** Tableau will give you the option to filter out all of the other states so that you can drill down into this data point. Click **Keep Only.**
28. From the dimensions, double-click **City.**
29. Tableau doesn't recognize city lines, so it will change from a filled map to a symbol map. This may be easier to read as a bar chart, though, so click the **Horizontal Bars** icon in the **Show Me** window.

Source: ©Tableau Software, Inc. All rights reserved.

Q3. Which city has the highest average transaction amount? (It can be easier to answer this question if you sort the data. Clicking the "sort" button will re-order the bars so that the city with the highest average transaction amount will be the first bar listed.)

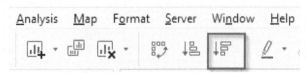

Source: ©Tableau Software, Inc. All rights reserved.

Q4. How would you think managers would like to see transaction balance by state?

Q5. What are further questions that would be meaningful to drill down into with this same dataset, given what you have seen so far?

To dig deeper into the data, we can drill down into which types of items are being sold the most in Maumelle. To do so, we need to join in two more tables. Joining in the SKU table will provide description of the items being sold, and joining in the DEPARTMENT table will provide categorical information for each individual item.

30. Click **Data Source** in the bottom left corner of the Tableau application.

Source: ©Tableau Software, Inc. All rights reserved.

31. Join in the **SKU** and **DEPARTMENT** tables.

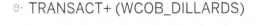

Source: ©Tableau Software, Inc. All rights reserved.

32. Return to your Tableau sheet with the horizontal bar chart, and click **Keep Only** for **Maumelle.**

The **DEPARTMENT** and **SKU** data are hierarchical, with an item belonging to a department, which groups into a **deptdec (decade)** through a **deptcent (century).**

33. Begin by viewing the Maumelle store data by the highest level of the hierarchy, the department century. The description attribute will be the most useful to interpret, so double-click on the **Deptcent Desc** attribute from the **DEPARTMENT** dimensions.

34. To drill down further into the data, add the department decade data to the chart. Double-click on **Deptdec Desc** to add another level of detail.

35. You can also add drill-down capabilities by creating the hierarchy in Tableau. Drag and drop **Deptdec Desc** on top of **Deptcent Cent** in the Dimensions window:

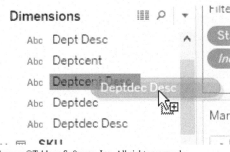

Source: ©Tableau Software, Inc. All rights reserved.

36. Click **OK** on the window to create the hierarchy.

Create Hierarchy ✕

Name: Deptcent Desc, Deptdec Desc

OK   Cancel

Source: ©Tableau Software, Inc. All rights reserved.

37. Notice that the **Deptcent Desc** pill in the **Rows** shelf changed to include a minus sign—this indicates that the hierarchy has been expanded. Click the minus sign to collapse the hierarchy.

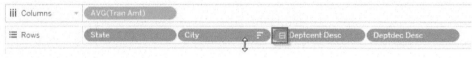

Source: ©Tableau Software, Inc. All rights reserved.

38. Take a screenshot of your results (label it 4-3B).

Part 4: Address and Refine Results

With this much data loaded into Tableau, there is a tremendous amount of analysis and visualization that you can do.

Q6.   Based on what you have seen of the average transaction amounts for different departments and products in the Maumelle store, what would you recommend to the Maumelle store manager who is trying to maximize profits? Advertise certain products more? Advertise certain products less? Open an additional store nearby? Close this store, etc.?

We can re-create the process that you completed in steps 13–38 in Power BI to get a feel for how that tool interacts with data differently than Tableau. You may wish to visit Appendix I for a general introduction to Power BI if you have not used the tool before. Keep in mind that Power BI has regular updates, so some screens and requirements may change from what's described in this text.

Two of the most significant differences from how we worked with this data in Tableau and how we will work with it in Power BI are the following:

- **Sheet view versus Dashboard view:**

  Tableau defaults to creating your visualizations one sheet at a time and displays them on a large scale while you are developing them. Creating a Dashboard is an additional step, and you can drag and drop the sheets that you have already created onto a dashboard.

  Power BI defaults to a dashboard view. Your visualizations are created in smaller tiles that you can immediately re-size and re-arrange around the canvas.

  Because of this difference, instead of manipulating the same sheet throughout this analysis, we will create copies of tiles and manipulate the copies as we work through the steps in Power BI.

- **Filtering:**

  Tableau offers two main methods for filtering: dragging a measure or dimension into the Filters shelf to create a Filter and using the "Keep Only" button on a portion of a visualization.

  Power BI does not have a "Keep Only" function, but it defaults to providing filters for every dimension or measures that you are interacting with throughout the dashboard.

  Because of this difference, we will use the Filter fields instead of using "Keep Only" as we drill down through our data in Power BI.

1. Open the **Power BI Desktop** application.
2. Click **Get Data** to connect to the database.
3. Select **SQL Server database,** then click **Connect.**

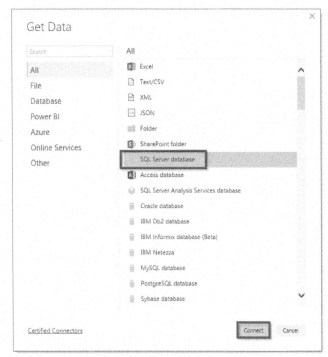

Source: Microsoft SQL Server Management Studio

The next steps are similar to how you connect to the database using Excel's PowerQuery tools.

4. Enter the server name (provided to you by your instructor and the database name (WCOB_DILLARDS) in the fields for Server and Database.
5. Select **DirectQuery** for the Data Connectivity mode. This option is not available in the PowerQuery tool in Excel, but it is similar to the "Live" connection option in Tableau. Both Power BI's DirectQuery and Tableau's Live options allow you to connect to the data without importing all of the rows into the report. This often helps you start working with the data faster because you do not have to wait for large datasets to load.

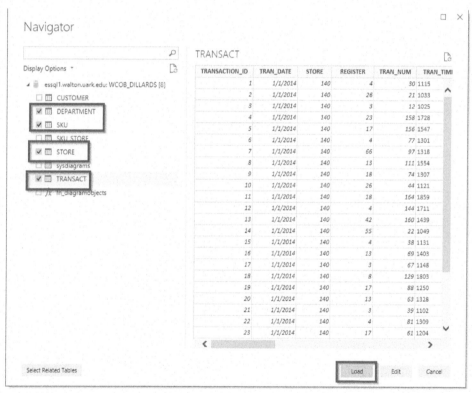

Source: Microsoft SQL Server Management Studio

6. Select the **Department, SKU, Store,** and **Transact** tables, then click **Load.**

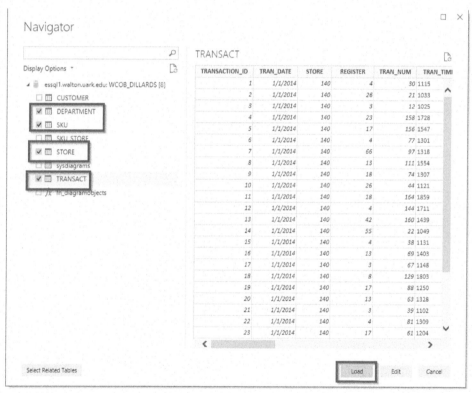

Source: Microsoft SQL Server Management Studio

It may take some time for the data to load. Once it does, you will see the tables populated in the Fields list.

7. Expand the **Store** table to see its attributes and select **State.**

Source: Microsoft SQL Server Management Studio

Power BI will create a symbol map showing each state that is listed in the Store table.

8. To compare the average Transaction Amount across each state, expand the **Transact** table and select **Tran_Amt.**

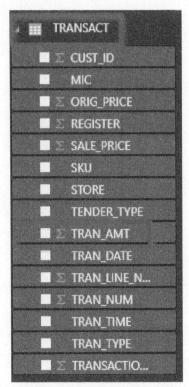

Source: Microsoft SQL Server Management
Studio

As the data loads, we can take a moment to look at the visualizations pane. The **State** field that you placed a checkmark in appears in the Location portion of the visualizations pane, and the **Tran_Amt** field appears in the Size portion. Both fields also appear in the Filters section of the visualization pane. By immediately creating filters for each field that you have selected for your visual, you can easily slice and drill-down your data. We'll work with these filters throughout the rest of this lab.

If you don't see any fields in Location, Size, or Filters, you just need to click on the visual tile that you have created first. If you click outside of the tile, you won't see the fields listed because you can add tiles to the report.

Source: Microsoft SQL Server Management Studio

9. Similar to what Tableau does with Measures and what Excel PivotTables does with Values, Power BI typically will default to summing data if you add numerical data to a visualization. For this report, we would rather work with average transaction amounts instead of the sum.

  To change it, click the **drop-down** on the **Tran_Amt** field in the Size section of the Visualizations Pane and select **Average.**

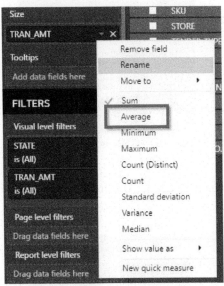

Source: Microsoft SQL Server Management Studio

Your tile should now show a visualization with a map that includes symbols that vary in size based on the average transaction amount across states.

Take a screenshot and label it 4-3C.

10. To drill down into the average transaction amount in the cities of Arkansas, we will start by duplicating the existing visual. Right click the map visual and select Copy (you can also select the visual and use the keyboard shortcut Ctrl + C to copy).

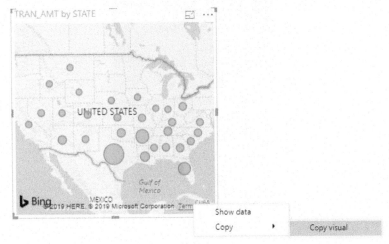

Source: Microsoft SQL Server Management Studio

11. Use the keyboard shortcut Ctrl + V to paste the visual (or Command + V on a Mac), then drag the copy beneath the original visual.
12. Change the visual type to a Bar Chart.

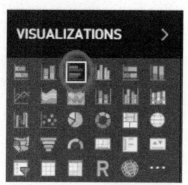

Source: Microsoft SQL Server Management Studio

13. Add a filter for Arkansas by clicking the drop-down next to **State** in the Filters field and selecting **AR**.

Source: Microsoft SQL Server Management Studio

14. The single bar representing Arkansas in this chart isn't very meaningful – from here we want to drill down to see the cities within Arkansas that have the highest average transaction amounts. Place a checkmark next to the City field (in the Store table) to add City to the Bar Chart to see which city in Arkansas has the highest returns.

Source: Microsoft SQL Server Management Studio

Just like it did in Tableau, the resulting bar chart shows that Maumelle had the highest average transaction amount across all Arkansas cities.

You might want to re-size the bar chart to make it easier to read.

Take a screenshot and label it 4-3D.

We'll dig into which products are sold most frequently in Maumelle next to learn more about why their average transaction amount is so high.

15. To work with just Maumelle's data, first copy and paste the Arkansas City Bar Chart. Place it to the right of the Arkansas City bar chart.

16. First, narrow this visual down to just view Maumelle. Place a check-mark in the box next to Maumelle in the city filter.

17. Next, we need to create a product description hierarchy in Power BI similar to how we did in Tableau. Expand the Department table field list and drag and drop **DEPTDEC_DESC** on top of **DEPTCENT_DESC.**

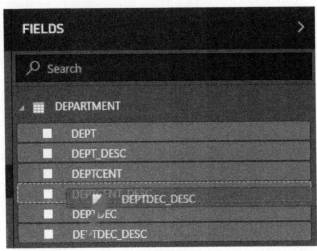

Source: Microsoft SQL Server Management Studio

18. Place a check mark next to the **DEPTCENT_DESC Hierarchy** to add it to your new tile to add details to the Maumelle bar chart.
19. To view the Department Centuries, right-click the bar and select **Drill Down.**

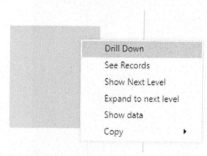

Source: Microsoft SQL Server Management Studio

20. To view Department Decades, repeat the same step by right-clicking on any of the Century bars in the chart to drill down again. This will show the decades beneath the specific century that you selected.
21. You can expand all centuries at once by clicking the Drill Down button in the top right of the tile.

Source: Microsoft SQL Server Management Studio

Take a screenshot and label it 4-3E.

Q7. After working through these steps in Tableau and in Power BI, what do you think are the pros and cons of creating data visualizations and exploring data each of the tools?

Lab 4-4   Comprehensive Case: Dillard's Store Data: Visualizing Regression in Tableau

Company summary

Dillard's is a department store with approximately 330 stores in 29 states. Its headquarters is in Little Rock, Arkansas. You can learn more about **Dillard's** by looking at finance.yahoo. com (Ticker symbol = DDS) and the Wikipedia site for DDS. You'll quickly note that William T. Dillard II is an accounting grad of the University of Arkansas and the Walton College of Business, which may be why he shared transaction data with us to make available for this lab and labs throughout this text.

Data

You will use an Excel file with data transformed and ready for regression analysis, Lab 4-4 Dummy.xlsx.

Software needed

- Tableau

In this lab, you will:

- Learn how to visualize regressions in Tableau.

Part 1: Identify the Questions

In Chapter 3, you ran a variety of regression and other analyses addressing the following questions:

- Do customers in the state with the largest total transaction amount have a significantly higher transaction balance during September 2016 than all other states?
- Are online transaction amounts statistically greater than or lesser than non-online transactions during the period September 1, 2016, to September 15, 2016?
- Do customers who charge their purchases to a **Dillard's** credit card spend more on each transaction during the time period September 1, 2016, to September 15, 2016?

In this lab, we will work to visualize these data in a way that helps users grasp the information needed to make decisions.

Part 2: Master the Data

To complete the ETL process, we will need to extract the data from the Excel spreadsheet that you saved in the Chapter 3 comprehensive labs and transform and load it into Tableau.

1. Open a new Tableau workbook and connect to Microsoft Excel.

Source: ©Tableau Software, Inc. All rights reserved.

2. Browse to Lab 4-4 Dummy.xlsx (or you can use the Excel output you created with the dummy variables from Lab 3-5) and click **Open.** This will extract the data.

3. When running a regression in Tableau, you will want to place your explanatory variables on the columns and your dependent variables on the rows. To do so, drag and drop the **Arkansas-dummy** measure to the **Columns** shelf and the **Tran Amt Measure** to the **Rows** shelf.

Source: ©Tableau Software, Inc. All rights reserved.

4. Tableau defaults to aggregating the measures, but we are interested in each individual observation. To disaggregate the variables, navigate to the **Analysis** tab and click **Aggregate Measures** to disaggregate the values.

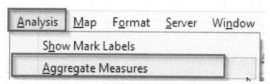

Source: ©Tableau Software, Inc. All rights reserved.

5. It may take some time for the data to disaggregate. Once they do, navigate back to the **Analysis** tab and click **Lines,** and then select **Show All Trend Lines.**

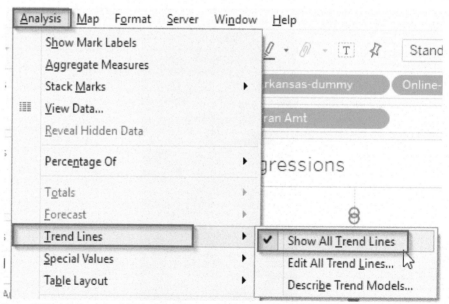

Source: ©Tableau Software, Inc. All rights reserved.

Part 3: Perform an Analysis of the Data

6. Hover over the **trend line** to see the regression formula and the *p*-value.

7. Each variable can be meaningful in explaining the total spent on each transaction (or Tran Amt), but when working with data visualization, it can be even more meaningful to compare models. Compare models by adding the **Online-dummy** and **DLRD-dummy**

variables (where DLRD represents the use of a **Dillard's** credit card in the transaction) to the columns. Note these are univariate analyses in that they compare only Arkansas, online, and the use of a **Dillard's** credit card one-by-one and not altogether.

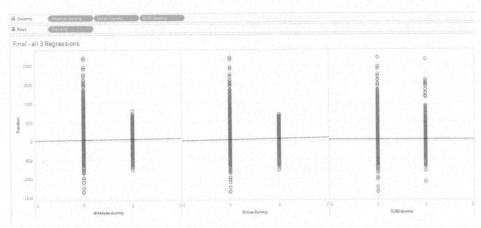

Source: ©Tableau Software, Inc. All rights reserved.

Part 4: Address and Refine Results

Q1.   Which of these three variables has a noticeable trend as compared to the others, suggesting greater explanatory power?

Q2.   Which of these three variables best explains the average transaction amount? (*Hint:* Consider the *r*-squared in each or the *p*-values among the three models.)

Q3.   The coefficient on the DLRD-dummy is negative here. What does that suggest? Is that consistent with the results of Lab 3-5?

Q4.   In the trend line looking at the Arkansas-dummy, what is the base level of Transaction Amount (the *y*-intercept) before considering the Arkansas-dummy?

Q5.   Let's suppose we could capture the net worth of each **Dillard's** customer. Would you expect net worth to have higher explanatory variables than either of the transaction took place in Arkansas, was an online purchase, or was paid for using a **Dillard's** credit card? Why or why not?

Chapter 5

The Modern Accounting Environment

A Look at This Chapter

Most of the focus of Data Analytics in accounting is focused on auditing, managerial accounting, financial statement analysis, and tax. This is partly due to the demand for high-quality data and the need for enhancing trust in the assurance process, informing management for decisions, and aiding investors as they select their portfolios. In this chapter, we look at how both auditors and managers are using technology in general to improve the decisions being made. We also introduce how Data Analytics helps facilitate continuous auditing and reporting.

A Look Back

Chapter 4 completed our discussion of the IMPACT model by explaining how to communicate your results through data visualization and through written reports. We discussed how to choose the best chart for your dataset and your purpose. We also helped you learn how to refine your chart so that it communicates as efficiently and effectively as possible. The chapter wrapped up by describing how to provide a written report tailored to specific audiences who will be interested in the results of your data analysis project.

A Look Ahead

In Chapter 6, you will learn how to use audit software to perform substantive audit tests, including when and how to select samples and how to confirm account balances. Specifically, we discuss the use of different types of descriptive, diagnostic, predictive, and prescriptive analytics as they are used to generate computer-assisted auditing techniques.

The large public accounting firms offer a variety of analytical tools to their customers. Take **PwC's** Halo, for example. This tool allows auditors to interrogate a client's data and identify patterns and relationships within the data in a user-friendly dashboard. By mapping the data, auditors and managers can identify inefficiencies in business processes, discover areas of risk exposure, and correct data quality issues by drilling down into the individual users, dates and times, and amounts of the entries. Tools like Halo allow auditors to develop their audit plan by narrowing their focus and audit scope to unusual and infrequent issues that represent high audit risk.

Source: http://halo.pwc.com

fizkes/Shutterstock

OBJECTIVES

After reading this chapter, you should be able to:

LO 5-1   Understand how automation has created a data-rich environment.

LO 5-2   Understand different approaches to organizing enterprise data and common data models.

LO 5-3   Describe the appropriate tasks and approaches to automating procedures.

LO 5-4   Evaluate continuous monitoring techniques and alarms.

LO 5-5   Understand cloud-based collaboration platforms.

LO 5-1

Understand how automation has created a data-rich environment.

THE MODERN DATA ENVIRONMENT

As businesses have embraced automation over the past several decades, more information about financial transactions is captured in large databases. In addition to details of transaction data, these systems capture metadata (e.g., timestamps, user details, and contents of unstructured data) that provide insight into the workings of the company. Sensors provide details on movement through a building to identify optimal location of resources, track the health of employees to help control health insurance costs, and allow detailed analysis of the volume of everyday events to help managers manage robotic scripts and tasks. Even traditional data-entry tasks are now performed by specialized software that recognizes text from documents and maps it into database fields. Once you have an understanding of the IMPACT model, understanding the needs and structure of the business will help your perform meaningful analyses.

Automation can include routine tasks, such as combining data from different sources for analysis, and more complex actions, such as responding to natural language queries. In the past, analytics and automation were performed by hobbyists and consultants within a firm. In a modern environment, companies form centers of expertise where they concentrate specialists in a single geographic location and use information and communication technologies to work in remote teams. Because the data are network-accessible, multiple users interact with the data and complete workflows of tasks with the assistance of remote team members and bots, or automated robotic scripts commonly called *robotics process automation.* The specialists manage the bots like they would normal employees, continuously evaluating their performance and contribution to the company.

You'll recall from your auditing course that assurance services are crucial to building and maintaining trust within the capital markets. In response to increasing regulation in the United States, the European Union, and other jurisdictions, both internal and external auditors have been tasked with providing enhanced assurance while also attempting to reduce (or at least maintain) the audit fees. This has spurred demand for more audit automation along with an increased reliance on auditors to use their judgment and decision-making skills to effectively interpret and support their audit findings with managers, shareholders, and other stakeholders.

Auditors have been applying simple Data Analytics for decades in evaluating risk within companies. Think about how an evaluation of inventory turnover can spur a discussion on inventory obsolescence or how working capital ratios are used to identify significant issues with a firm's liquidity. From an internal audit perspective, evaluating cost variances can help identify operational inefficiencies or unfavorable contracts with suppliers.

The audit concepts of professional skepticism and reasonable assurance are as much a part of the modern audit as in the past. There has been a shift, however, of simply providing reasonable assurance on the processes to the additional assurance of the robots that are performing a lot of the menial audit work. Where, before, an auditor may have looked at samples and gathered evidence to make inferences to the population, now that same auditor must understand the controls and parameters that have been programmed into the robot. In other words, as these automated bots do more of the routine analytics, auditors will be free to exercise more judgment to interpret the alarms and data while refocusing their effort on testing the parameters used by the robots.

Auditors use Data Analytics to improve audit quality by more accurately assessing risk and selecting better substantive procedures and tests of controls. While the exercises the auditors conduct are fairly routine, the models can be complex and require auditor judgment and interpretation. For example, if an auditor receives 1,000 notifications of a control violation during the day, does that mean there is a control weakness or that the settings on the automated control are too precise? Are all those notifications actual control violations that require immediate attention, or are most of them false positives—transactions that are flagged as exceptions but are normal and acceptable?

The auditors' role is to make sure that the appropriate analytics are used and that the output of those analytics—whether a dashboard, notifications of exceptions, or accuracy of predictive models—correspond to management's expectations and assertions.

The Increasing Importance of the Internal Audit

If you look at the assurance market, there are many trends that are affecting the profession. First, the major applications of Data Analytics in auditing are not solely focused on the financial statements as evaluated by public accounting firms. Rather, these tend to focus on data quality, internal controls, and the complex information systems that support the business process—areas typically reserved for the internal audit department at a firm. Second, the risk and advisory practices of the public accounting firms are experiencing greater growth, in large part due to firms' outsourcing or co-sourcing of the internal audit function. Third, external auditors are permitted to rely on the work of internal auditors to provide support for their opinion of financial statements.

For these reasons, most of the innovations in Data Analytics have originated in internal audit departments, where there is constant pressure to enhance business value while minimizing costs. In the recent past, many companies' experience with Data Analytics in the internal audit department have come from internal auditors who have investigated Data Analytics on their own. These individuals then find a champion with management and are encouraged to continue their work. Under the guidance of the chief audit executive (CAE) or another manager, these individuals build teams to develop and implement analytical techniques to aid the following audits:

1. Process efficiency and effectiveness.
2. Governance, risk, and compliance, including internal controls effectiveness.
3. Information technology and information systems audits.
4. Forensic audits in the case of fraud.
5. Support for the financial statement audit.

Internal auditors are also more likely to have working knowledge of the different types of systems implemented at their companies. They are familiar with how the general journals from a product like **Oracle's** JD Edwards actually reconcile to the general ledger in SAP to generate financial reports and drill down into the data. Because implementation of these systems varies across organizations (and even within organizations), internal auditors can understand how analytics are not simply a one-size-fits-all type of strategy.

 PROGRES CHECK

1. What types of sensors do businesses use to track activity?
2. Make the case for why an internal audit is increasingly important in the modern audit. Why is it also important for external auditors and the scope of their work?

ENTERPRISE DATA

> **LO 5-2**
>
> Understand different approaches to organizing enterprise data and common data models.

While organizations have become more data-centric as they have adopted enterprise systems (ES) over the past few decades, these systems can vary greatly among organizations. Some companies will take a **homogeneous systems approach** for their data structure by ensuring that all of its divisions and subsidiaries use a uniform installation of a common ES system, such as SAP. Homogenous systems enable management to consolidate the information from various locations and roll them up management reports, audit support, and financial statements with minimal additional effort. Other companies that grow through acquisition, take a **heterogeneous systems approach**, where they attempt to integrate the existing systems (such as SAP, Oracle, PeopleSoft, JD Edwards, and others) of the companies they acquire and use a series of translators to convert the output of those systems into usable financial information. **Systems translator software** attempts to map the various tables and fields from these varied enterprise systems into a **data warehouse**, where all of the data can be analyzed centrally, as shown in Exhibit 5-1. The data warehouse is updated periodically, typically on a daily basis, to reflect recent firm activity.

EXHIBIT 5-1
Homogeneous Systems, Heterogeneous Systems, and Software Translators

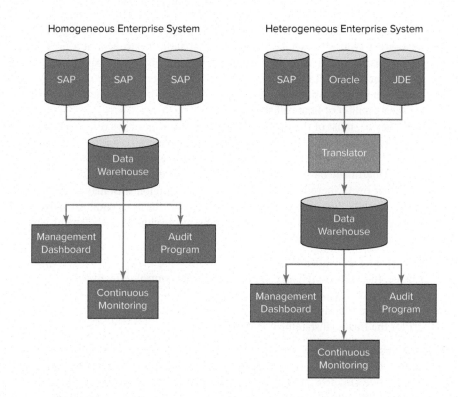

One of the primary obstacles that managers and auditors face is access to appropriate data. As noted in Chapter 2, managers and auditors may request **flat files** or extracts from an IT manager. Frequently, these files may be incomplete, unrelated, limited in scope, or delayed when they are not considered a priority by IT managers. Increasingly, managers and auditors request read-only access to the data warehouse so they can evaluate transaction data, such as purchases and sales, and the related master data, such as employees and vendors, in a timely manner. By avoiding a data broker, they get more relevant data for their analyses and analyze multiple relationships and explore other patterns in a more meaningful way. In either case, the managers and auditors work with duplicated data, rather than querying the **production or live systems** directly.

Common Data Models

As automation of data analytics procedures becomes more common, working within different data environments can present challenges, especially for auditors. To minimize some of the effort required to interact with data, analysts adopt a **common data model**, which is a tool used to map existing database tables and fields from various systems to a standardized set of tables and fields for use with analytics. When the underlying systems change, the model is updated to pull data from the new tables and fields. Similar to the translation software mentioned previously, a common data model makes it easier to perform and automate routine analytical procedures even when the underlying systems change.

The AICPA's **Audit Data Standards (ADS)** provide one example of a common data model with tables and fields that are needed by auditors to perform routine audit tasks. The AICPA recommends that ES vendors standardize the output of data that auditors are likely to use. The goal of the standards is to reduce the data loading and transformation effort required by the auditor, so they can focus on the analytics more quickly as well as define real-time or continuous analytics via the data warehouse. These standards are voluntary, and actual implementation is currently limited, but they provide a good basis for data needed to audit specific company functions.

The current set of audit data standards defines the following standards:

- *Base:* defines the formats for files and fields as well as master data requirements for users, business units, segments, and tax tables.
- *General Ledger:* defines the chart of accounts, source listings, trial balance, and general ledger or journal entry detail.
- *Order to Cash Subledger:* defines sales orders and line items, shipments and line items, invoices and line items, open accounts receivable and adjustments, cash receipts, and customer master data, shown in Exhibit 5-2.
- *Procure to Pay Subledger:* defines purchase orders and line items, goods received and line items, invoices received and line items, open accounts payable and adjustments, payments, and supplier master data.

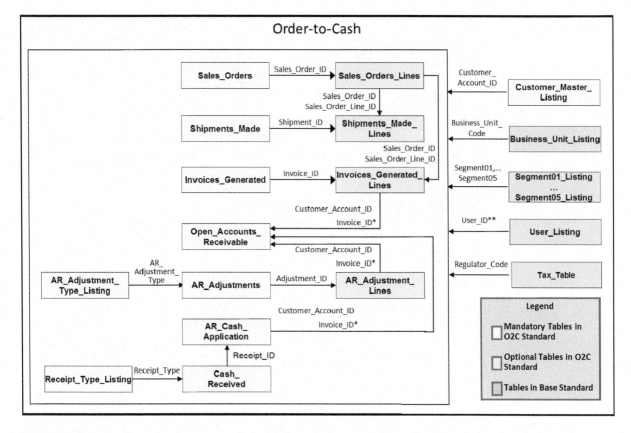

EXHIBIT 5-2 Audit Data Standards
The audit data standards define common elements needed to audit the order-to-cash or sales process.

Source: https://www.aicpa.org/InterestAreas/FRC/AssuranceAdvisoryServices/DownloadableDocuments/AuditDataStandards/AuditDataStandards.O2C.July2015.pdf
*if receivable balances are tracked by customer only (not by invoice), then Customer_Account_ID is used as a key to join tables to the Open_Accounts_Receivable table instead of both Customer_Account_ID and Invoice_ID
**The Uer_Listing table can be joined to three fields, all of which contain a user ID—Entered_by, Approved_By, Last_Modified_By

- *Inventory Subledger:* defines inventory location master data, product master data, inventory on hand data, and inventory movement transactions as well as physical inventory and material cost.
- *Fixed Asset Subledger:* defines fixed asset master data, additions, removal, and depreciation calculations.

With standard data elements in place, not only will internal auditors streamline their access to data, but they also will be able to build analytical tools that they can share with others within their company or professional organizations. This can foster greater collaboration among auditors and increased use of Data Analytics across organizations. These data elements will be useful when performing substantive testing in Chapter 6.

Even if the standard is never adopted by data suppliers, auditors can still take advantage of the audit data standards as a common data model. For example, Exhibit 5-3 shows the mapping of a set of Purchase Card data to the Procure to Pay Subledger Standard. Once the mapping algorithm has been generating using SQL or other tool, any new data can be analyzed quickly and easily.

EXHIBIT 5-3

Mapping Purchase Card Data to the Procure to Pay Subledger Audit Data Standard

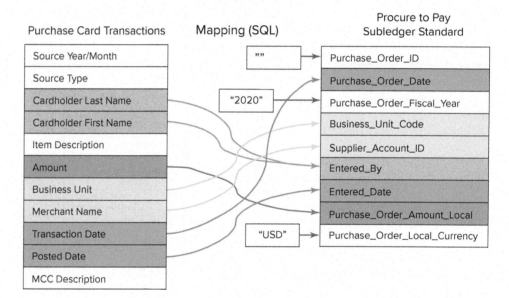

PROGRESS CHECK

3. What are the advantages of the use of homogeneous systems? Would a merger target be more attractive if it used a similar financial reporting system as the potential parent company?

4. How does the use of audit data standards facilitate data transfer between auditors and companies? How does it save time for both parties?

LO 5-3

Describe the appropriate tasks and approaches to automating procedures.

AUTOMATING DATA ANALYTICS

Most of the effort in Data Analytics is preparing the analysis for the first time. This involves identifying the data, mapping the tables and fields through ETL, and developing the visualization if needed. Once that task is complete, automation of the procedure involves identifying the timing or schedule of how often the procedure should run, any parameters that might change, and what should happen if a new observation appears as an outlier.

The steps you follow to perform the analysis are part of the algorithm, and they can be recorded using a scripting language, such as Python or R, or using off-the-shelf monitoring software. That process is outside the scope of this textbook, but there are many resources online to help you with this next step.

The main impact of automation and Data Analytics on the accounting profession comes through optimization of the management dashboard and audit plan. When beginning an engagement—whether to audit the financial statements, certify the enterprise system, or make a recommendation to improve a business process—auditors generally follow a standardized audit plan. The benefit of a standardized audit plan is that newer members of the audit team can jump into an audit and contribute. Audit plans also identify the priorities of the audit.

An audit plan consists of the one or more of the following elements:

- A *methodology* that directs that audit work.
- The *scope of the audit,* defining the time period, level of materiality, accounts and subsidiaries being audited and expected completion time for the audit.
- *Potential risk* within the area being audited.
- *Procedures and specific tasks* that the audit team will execute to collect and analyze evidence. These typically include tests of controls and substantive tests of transaction details.
- *Formal evaluation* by the auditor and supervisors.

Because audit plans are formalized and standardized, they lend themselves to the use of Data Analytics and, consequently, automation. For example,

- The methodology may be framed by specific standards, such as the Public Company Accounting Oversight Board's (PCAOB) auditing standards, the Committee of Sponsoring Organizations's (COSO) Enterprise Risk Management framework, or the Information Systems Audit and Control Association's (ISACA) Control Objectives for Information and Related Technologies (COBIT) framework. Data Analytics may be used to analyze the standards and determine which requirements apply to the organization being audited.
- The scope of the audit defines parameters that will be used to filter the records or transactions being evaluated.
- Simple to complex Data Analytics can be applied to a client's data during the planning stage of the audit to identify which areas the auditor should focus on. This may include outlier detection or other substantive tests of suspicious or risky transactions.
- Audit procedures themselves typically identify data, locations, and attributes that the auditors will evaluate. These are the variables that will provide the input for many of the substantive analytical procedures discussed in Chapter 6.
- The evaluation of audit data may be distilled into a risk score. This may be a function of the volume of exceptional records or level of exposure for the functional area. If the judgment and decision making can be easily defined, a rule-based analytic could automatically assign a score for the auditor to review. For more complex judgments, the increasing prevalence of artificial intelligence and machine learning discussed in Chapter 3 may be of assistance. Historical observations of the scores auditors assign to specific cases and outcomes, may assist the creation of an automated scoring model.

Typically, internal audit organizations that have adopted Data Analytics to enhance their audit have done so when an individual on the team has begun tinkering with Data Analytics. They convince their managers that there is value in using the data to direct the audit and the manager may become a champion in the process. Once they show the value proposition of Data Analytics, they are given more resources to build the program and adapt the existing audit program to include more data-centric evaluation where appropriate.

Because of the potential disruption to the organization, it is more likely that an internal auditor will adapt an existing audit plan than develop a new system from scratch.

Automating the audit plan and incorporating data analytics involve the following steps, which are similar to the IMPACT model:

1. *Identify* the questions or requirements in the existing audit plan.
2. *Master* the data by identifying attributes and elements that are automatable.
3. *Perform* the test plan, in this case by developing analytics (in the form of rules or models) for those attributes identified in step 2.
4. *Address* and refine results. List expected exceptions to these analytics and expected remedial action by the auditor, if any.
5. *Communicate* insight by testing the rules and comparing the output of the analytics to manual audit procedures.
6. *Track* outcomes by following up on alarms and refining the models as needed.

Let's assume that an internal auditor has been tasked with implementing data analytics to automate the evaluation of a segregation of duties control within SAP. The auditor evaluates the audit plan and identifies a procedure for testing this control. The audit plan identifies which tables and fields contain relevant data, such as an authorization matrix, and the specific roles or permissions that would be incompatible. The auditor would use that information to build a model that would search for users with incompatible roles and notify the auditors.

CONTINUOUS MONITORING TECHNIQUES

LO 5-4

Evaluate continuous monitoring techniques and alarms.

Data Analytics and automation allow management and internal auditors to continuously monitor and audit the systems and processes within their companies. Whereas a traditional audit may have the internal auditors perform a routine audit plan once every 12 to 36 months or so, the continuous audit evaluates data in a form that matches the pulse of the business. For example, purchase orders can be monitored for unauthorized activity in real time, while month-end adjusting entries would be evaluated once a month. When exceptions occur—for example, a purchase order is created with a customer whose address matches an employee's—the auditors are alerted immediately and given the option to respond right away to resolve the issue.

Continuous auditing is a process that provides real-time assurance over business processes and systems. It involves the application of rules or analytics that perform a **continuous monitoring** function that constantly evaluates internal controls and transactions and is the chief responsibility of management. It also generates **continuous reporting** on the status of the system so that an auditor can know at any given time whether the system is operating within the parameters set by management or not. In the future, continuous reporting may also enable firms to publish real-time financial accounting data for public analysis, but in practical use this may cause more problems for firms if they are unable to validate or provide assurance on the data being reported.

Implementing continuous auditing procedures is similar to automating an audit plan with the additional step of scheduling the automated procedures to match the timing and frequency of the data being evaluated and notifying the auditor when exceptions occur.

Alarms and Exceptions

Whenever an automated or continuous auditing rule is violated, an *exception* occurs. The record is flagged and systems generate an *exception report* that typically identifies the record and the date of the exception.

Alarms are essentially a classification problem. A data value is sent through a simple decision tree based on a series of rules and classified as a positive event (alarm) or a negative event (no alarm). Remember we talked about accuracy of models in Chapter 3: These alarms will not always be correct.

Once the notification of the alarm or exception arrives, auditors follow a set of procedures to resolve the issue. First, they must determine whether the alarm represents a *true positive,* a transaction that is problematic, such as an error or fraud, or a *false positive,* where a normal transaction is classified as problematic. When too many alarms are false positive, auditors face *information overload,* where there are too many incorrect alarms that distract them from adequately evaluating the system. Because auditors are mostly concerned with true positives, they should attempt to train or refine the models to minimize the potential *flood of alarms* that occurs when too many alarms are false positives. This is summarized in Table 5-1.

	Normal Event	Abnormal Event
Alarm	False positive	True positive
No Alarm	True negative	False negative

TABLE 5-1
Four Types of Alarms That an Auditor Must Evaluate

WORKING PAPERS AND AUDIT WORKFLOW

LO 5-5

Understand cloud-based collaboration platforms.

As audit procedures become increasingly technical, documentation continues to be an essential way for internal and external auditors to increase their reliance on automated controls and procedures. The idea of a black-box audit is no longer sufficient; rather, auditors must have a better understanding of the tools they use and the output of those tools. This is where working papers come into play.

Working papers are essential to audit planning, performance, and evaluation. They provide the documentation for the procedures the auditors follow, evidence they collect, and communication with the audit client. As they relate to Data Analytics, working papers should contain the following items:

- Work programs used to document the audit procedures to collect, manipulate, model, and evaluate data.
- IT-related documentation, including flowchart and process maps that provide system understanding.
- Database maps (such as UML diagrams) and data dictionaries that define the location and types of data auditors will analyze.
- Documentation about existing automated controls, including parameters and variables used for analysis.
- Evidence, including data extracts, transformed data, and model output, that provides support for the functioning controls and management assertions.

Policies and procedures that help provide consistent quality work are essential to maintaining a complete and consistent audit. The audit firm or chief audit executive is responsible for providing guidance and standardization so that different auditors and audit teams produce clear results. These standardizations include consistent use of symbols or tick marks and a uniform mechanism for cross-referencing output to source documents or data.

Electronic Working Papers and Remote Audit Work

As audit teams embrace a variety of information and communication technologies to enable collaboration from different locations, audit firms have done so, as well. Increasingly, internal and external audit teams consist of more specialized onsite auditors who interact with a team of experts and data scientists remotely at locations around the world. Many of the routine tasks are offloaded to the remote or seasonal workers, freeing up onsite auditors to use more professional judgment and expertise during the engagement. This results in cost savings for the firm through increased efficiency at the firm level. The glue that holds the audit team together is the electronic workpaper platform as well as other collaboration tools, such as Microsoft Teams or Slack. The electronic workpaper platforms, such as TeamMate or Xero, automate the workflow of evidence collection, evaluation, and opinion generation on the part of the audit teams. The large accounting firms have proprietary systems that accomplish a similar purpose. For example, PwC uses three systems to automate its audit process. Aura is used to direct the audit by identifying which evidence to collect and analyze, Halo performs Data Analytics on the collected evidence, and Connect provides the workflow process that allows managers and partners to review and sign off on the work. Most of these platforms are hosted in the cloud, so members of the audit team can participate in the various functions from any location. Smaller audit shops can build ad hoc workpaper repositories using OneDrive with Office 365, though there are fewer controls over the documents.

 PROGRESS CHECK

5. Continuous audit uses alarms to identify exceptions that might indicate an audit issue and require additional investigation. If there are too many alarms and exceptions based on the parameters of the continuous audit system, will continuous auditing actually help or hurt the overall audit effectiveness?

6. PwC uses three systems to automate its audit process. Aura is used to direct the audit by identifying which evidence to collect and analyze, Halo performs Data Analytics on the collected evidence, and Connect provides the workflow process that allows managers and partners to review and sign off on the work. How does that line up with the steps of the IMPACT model we've discussed throughout the text?

Summary

As accounting has evolved over the past few decades, automation has driven many of the changes in turn enabling additional Data Analytics. Enterprise data appears in many forms and the adoption of a common data model makes it easier to analyze data from a variety of systems with ease. Data Analytics has improved management's and auditors' ability to understand their business, assess risk, inform their opinions, and improve assurance over the processes and controls in their organizations.

Key Words

audit data standards (ADS) (*205*)   A set of standards developed by the AICPA that defines common tables and fields that are needed by auditors to perform common audit tasks.

common data model (*204*)   A tool used to map existing database tables and fields from various systems to a standardized set of tables and fields for use with analytics.

continuous auditing (*208*)   A process that provides real-time assurance over business processes and systems.

continuous monitoring (*208*)   A process that constantly evaluates internal controls and transactions and is the chief responsibility of management.

continuous reporting (*208*)   A process that provides real-time access to the system status and accounting information.

data warehouse (*204*)   A repository of data accumulated from internal and external data sources, including financial data, to help management decision making.

flat file (*204*)   A single table of data with user-defined attributes that is stored separately from any application.

homogeneous systems approach (*203*)   Homogeneous systems represent one single installation or instance of a system. It would be considered the opposite of a heterogeneous system.

heterogeneous systems approach (*204*)   Heterogeneous systems represent multiple installations or instances of a system. It would be considered the opposite of a homogeneous system.

production or live systems (*204*)   Active enterprise systems that collect and report and are directly affected by current transactions.

systems translator software (*204*)   Software used to map the various tables and fields from varied enterprise systems into a consistent format.

ANSWERS TO PROGRESS CHECKS

1. Sensors can include door sensors to track movement in a building, health sensors to track employee health, and metadata to track transaction activity to name a few.

2. There are many reasons for this trend, with perhaps the most important being that external auditors are permitted to rely on the work of internal auditors to provide support for their opinion of financial statements.

3. A homogeneous system allows effortless transmission of accounting and auditing data across company units and international borders. It also allows company executives (including the chief executive officer, chief financial officer, and chief information officer), accounting staff, and the internal audit team to intimately know the system. In the case of a merger, integration of the two systems will require less effort than if they were heterogeneous.

4. The use of audit data standards allows an efficient data transfer of data in a standardized format that auditors can use in their audit testing programs. It can also save the company time and effort in providing its transaction data in a usable fashion to auditors.

5. If there are too many alarms and exceptions, particularly with false negatives and false positives, continuous auditing becomes more of a burden than a blessing. Work must be done to ensure more true positives and negatives to be valuable to the auditor.

6. PwC's Aura system would help identify the questions and master the data, the first two steps of the IMPACT model. PwC's Halo system would help perform the test plan and address and refine results, the middle two steps of the IMPACT model. Finally, PwC's Connect system would help communicate insights and track outcomes, the final two steps of the IMPACT model.

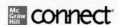

Multiple Choice Questions

1. Under the guidance of the chief audit executive (CAE) or another manager, internal auditors build teams to develop and implement analytical techniques to aid all of the following audits *except:*

   a. process efficiency and effectiveness.

   b. governance, risk, and compliance, including internal controls effectiveness.

   c. tax compliance.

   d. support for the financial statement audit.

2. Which audit data standards ledger defines product master data, location data, inventory on hand data, and inventory movement?

   a. Order to Cash Subledger

   b. Procure to Pay Subledger

   c. Inventory Subledger

   d. Base Subledger

3. Which audit data standards ledger identifies data needed for purchase orders, goods received, invoices, payments, and adjustments to accounts?

   a. Order to Cash Subledger

   b. Procure to Pay Subledger

   c. Inventory Subledger

   d. Base Subledger

4. A company has two divisions, one in the United States and the other in China. One uses Oracle and the other uses SAP for its basic accounting system. What would we call this?

   a. Homogeneous systems

   b. Heterogeneous systems

   c. Dual data warehouse systems

   d. Dual lingo accounting systems

5. Which of the following defines the time period, the level of materiality, and the expected time for an audit?

   a. Audit scope

   b. Potential risk

   c. Methodology

   d. Procedures and specific tasks

6. All of the following may serve as standards for the audit methodology *except:*

   a. PCAOB's auditing standards

   b. COSO's ERM framework

   c. ISACA's COBIT framework

   d. FASB's accounting standards

7. When there is an alarm in a continuous audit, but it is associated with a normal event, we would call that a:

   a. false negative.

   b. true negative.

   c. true positive.

   d. false positive.

8. When there is no alarm in a continuous audit, but there is an abnormal event, we would call that a:

   a. false negative.

   b. true negative.

   c. true positive.

   d. false positive.

9. If purchase orders are monitored for unauthorized activity in real time while month-end adjusting entries are evaluated once a month, those transactions monitored in real time would be an example of a:

   a. traditional audit.

   b. periodic test of internal controls.

   c. continuous audit.

   d. continuous monitoring.

10. Who is most likely to have a working knowledge of the various enterprise systems that are in use in the company?

    a. Chief executive officer

    b. External auditor

    c. Internal auditor

    d. IT staff

Discussion Questions

1. Why has most innovation in Data Analytics originated more in an internal audit than an external audit? Or if not, why not?

2. Is it possible for a firm to have general journals from a product like JD Edwards actually reconcile to the general ledger in SAP to generate financial reports or drill-down to see underlying transactions? Why or why not?

3. Is it possible for multinational firms to have many different financial reporting systems and enterprise systems packages all in use at the same time?

4. How does the systems translator software work? How does it store the merged data into a data warehouse?

5. Why is it better to extract data from a data warehouse than a production or live system directly?

6. Would an auditor view heterogeneous systems as an audit risk? Why or why not?

7. Why would audit firms prefer to use proprietary workpapers rather than just storing working papers on the cloud?

Problems

1. What are the advantages of the use of homogeneous systems? Would a merger target be more attractive if it used a similar financial reporting system as the potential parent company?

2. Consider Exhibit 5-2. Looking at the audit data standards order-to-cash process, what function is there for the AR_Adjustments transaction table—that is, adjustments to the Accounts Receivable? Why is this an audit data standard, and why is it important for an auditor to see?

3. Who developed the audit data standards? In your opinion, why is it the right group to develop and maintain them rather than, say, the Big 4 firms or a small practitioner?

4. Simple to complex Data Analytics can be applied to a client's data during the planning stage of the audit to identify which areas the auditor should focus on. Which types of techniques or tests might be used in this stage?

5. What approach should a company make if its continuous audit system has too many alarms that are false positives? How would that approach change if there are too many missed abnormal events (such as false negatives)?

6. Implementing continuous auditing procedures is similar to automating an audit plan with the additional step of scheduling the automated procedures to match the timing and frequency of the data being evaluated and the notification to the auditor when exceptions occur. In your opinion, will the traditional audit be replaced by continuous auditing?

Company summary

The State of Oklahoma captures purchase card transaction information for each of the state agencies to determine where resources are used. The comptroller has asked you to prepare the purchase card transactions using a common data model based on the audit data standards so they can be analyzed. The Fiscal Year runs from July 1 to June 30. FY2018 data includes 420,595 purchase transactions totaling $166,285,071.06.

Technique

- Use SQL to transform purchase card data into a common data model

Software needed

- DB Browser for SQLite

In this lab, you will:

Part 1: Import and validate the data.
Part 2: Write a SQL query to transform the data.

Part 1: Import and Validate the Data

In most cases, you will be able to begin working with the data in the form it is given to you. However, when you are preparing an analysis that you will use across multiple data sets and periods, there is some benefit to doing an additional transformation step to map the data to a common data model before you load it into the tool. For example, if you build analyses based on the AICPA's Audit Data Standard, you can simply map any new data table to the common fields without having to rewrite your analysis. This illustrates the Master the Data portion of the IMPACT model.

Note: If you're interested in getting more hands-on with the programming a data mapping model, search the Internet for object-relational mapping (ORM) as a method for querying and transforming data using more advanced programming tools.

This file uses PCARD_FY2018_SQL data from Connect.

1. Open DB Browser for SQLite.
2. Click the New Database button, name your file "PCARD_FY2018.db", and click **Save.** When the Edit table definition window appears, click **Cancel.**
3. Go to **File > Import > Table from CSV file. . .**
4. Browse to the PCARD_FY2018_SQL on your computer and click **Open.**
5. Name the table PCARD_FY2018 and click **OK.** Wait for it to import.
6. Click the **Browse Data** tab to review the data and verify that it imported properly.
7. Click the **Execute SQL** tab and run the following two queries one at a time to check the data integrity by comparing the numbers with those at the beginning of the lab:

```
SELECT COUNT(Amount)
FROM PCARD_FY2018;
SELECT SUM(Amount)
FROM PCARD_FY2018;
```

8. Take a screenshot of either query (label it 5-1A).
9. Save your database by going to **File > Write changes.**

Q1.   What was the purpose of executing the two queries?

Part 2: Write a SQL Query to Transform Your Data

Before we transform the data, we need to match the original attributes to the ADS attributes. In the table below, the attributes from PCard match up with the ADS with the exception of four attributes listed in *italics*. We may want to keep the attributes as an extension of the ADS so we don't lose some potentially useful data.

PCard (Source)	ADS Purchase_Order (Destination)
""	Purchase_Order_ID
TransactionDate	Purchase_Order_Date
"2018"	Purchase_Order_Fiscal_Year
BusinessUnit	Business_Unit_Code
MerchantName	Supplier_Account_ID
CardholderFirstInitial + CardholderLastName	Entered_By
PostedDate	Entered_Date
Amount	Purchase_Order_Amount_Local
"USD"	Purchase_Order_Local_Currency
SourceYearMonth	*SourceDate*
SourceType	*SourceType*
ItemDescription	*ItemDescription*
MCCDescription	*MerchantCategory*

10. Open your PCARD_FY2018 database from Part 1 in DB Browser for SQLite.
11. Click the **Execute SQL** tab.
12. Use the SQL code below as a template to remap the common elements. As you write the SQL code, replace [Table] with the name of your table and add a line for each mapping from the table above where [Field/Value] elements with either the fields or values from your source data table. These may include:

    a. The name of the field/attribute you're referencing (e.g., [TransactionDate]);
    b. Double quotes ("" or '' depending on the version of SQL) to leave the field blank;
    c. A specific value in quotes (e.g., "2020" AS Purchase_Order_Fiscal_Year to add the value 2020 for the fiscal year or "USD" to add a local currency); or
    d. An expression to combine values (e.g., [First_Name]&" "&[Last_Name] AS Entered_By or [First_Name] ||' '|| [Last_Name]AS Entered_By

    ```
    SELECT
    [Field/Value] AS Purchase_Order_ID,
    [Field/Value] AS Purchase_Order_Date,
    [Field/Value] AS Purchase_Order_Fiscal_Year,
    . . .
    FROM[TABLE];
    ```

13. Run the query by clicking the Play icon. Correct any errors in your SQL code if it didn't run correctly.
14. Take a screenshot (label it 5-1B).

15. Click the **Save Results** button and choose **Save as view.**

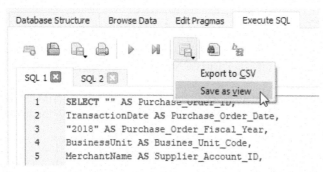

Source: Microsoft Excel 2016

16. Name it PCARD_FY2018_ADS and click **OK.**
17. Save your database by going to **File > Write changes.**
18. Click the **Save Results** button and choose **Export to CSV** followed by **Save.**
19. Name your CSV file PCARD_FY2018_ADS and click **OK.**
20. Close DB Browser for SQLite.

Q2. How does mapping the data to a common data model make it easier to perform analysis in the future?

End of Lab

Lab 5-2   Create a Dashboard Based on a Common Data Model

Company summary

The State of Oklahoma captures purchase card transaction information for each of the state agencies to determine where resources are used. The comptroller has asked you to prepare the purchase card transactions using a common data model based on the audit data standards so they can be analyzed. The Fiscal Year runs from July 1 to June 30. FY2018 data includes 420,595 purchase transactions totaling $166,285,071.06.

Technique

- Use Tableau visualize purchase card data based on the Audit Data Standard

Software needed

- Tableau

In this lab, you will:

Part 1: Import and validate the data.

Part 2: Create four visualizations.

Part 3: Combine the visualizations into a dashboard.

Part 1: Import and Validate the Data

Start by mastering the data and loading into Tableau:

1. Open Tableau.
2. Click **Connect to a File** and choose **Text file.**
3. Navigate to your PCARD_FY2018_ADS.csv from Lab 5-1 or Connect and click **Open.**
4. On the **Data Source** tab, click **Update Now** to preview your data and verify that it loaded correctly.
5. *Important!* Adjust your data types so they will be correctly interpreted by Tableau. Click the #, calendar, or Abc icon above each field and choose the following:

    1. Dates: Purchase Order Date, Entered Date, Source Date
    2. Number (decimal): Purchase Order Amount Local
    3. String: everything else.

6. Take a screenshot (label it 5-2A).
7. Save your workbook as PCARD_FY2018

    Q1.   What do you think would happen if you didn't update the data types in Tableau before you perform your analysis?

Part 2: Create Four Visualizations

Next, perform the test plan, address results, and communicate your findings:

8. Starting on Sheet 1, create the following visualizations (each on a separate sheet):

    a. Show a distribution of *total purchase amount by cardholder* showing the business unit as a color, sorted in descending order by purchase amount:
        I. Columns: SUM(Purchase Order Amount Local)
        II. Rows: Entered By
        III. Marks: Business Unit Code (color)
    b. Show a bar chart with the *total purchases for each month* showing the category as a color:
        I. Columns: YEAR(Purchase Order Date) MONTH(Purchase Order Date)
        II. Rows: SUM(Purchase Order Amount Local)
        III. Marks: Merchant Category (color)
    c. Show a tree map of total purchases by business unit:
        I. Marks: SUM(Purchase Order Amount Local) (size); SUM(Purchase Order Amount Local) (color); Business Unit Code (label)
    d. Show a distribution of *total purchase amount by supplier* showing the month of purchase as a color, sorted in descending order by purchase amount:
        I. Columns: SUM(Purchase Order Amount Local)
        II. Rows: Supplier Account ID
        III. Marks: MONTH(Purchase Order Date) (color)
9. Take a screenshot of any one of the four visualizations (label it Lab 5-2B).

Part 3: Combine the Visualizations into a Dashboard

10. In your Tableau workbook, create a Dashboard tab and drag each of the four visualizations into it from the pane on the left.
11. Take a screenshot (label it Lab 5-2C).

Q2. Which five suppliers receive the most purchases?

Q3. Which month has the highest total purchase amount? The lowest?

Q4. What would happen if you change the data source in Tableau to another file that is formatted following the ADS for purchase orders?

End of Lab

Lab 5-3   Set Up a Cloud Folder

Auditors collect evidence in electronic workpapers that include a permanent file with information about policies and procedures and a temporary file with evidence related to the current audit. These files could be stored locally on a laptop, but the increased use of remote communication makes collaboration through the cloud more necessary. There are a number of commercial workpaper applications, but we can simulate some of those features with consumer cloud platforms, like Microsoft OneDrive.

Company summary

You have rotated into the internal audit department at a mid-sized manufacturing company. Your team is still using company email to send evidence back and forth, usually in the form of documents and spreadsheets. There is a lot of duplication of these files, and no one is quite sure which version is the latest. You see an opportunity to streamline this process using OneDrive.

Technique

- Gather documents, explore document history and revisions

Software needed

- A modern web browser

In this lab, you will:

Part 1: Create a shared folder.
Part 2: Upload files.

Part 1: Create a Shared Folder

Note: These instructions are specific to the free consumer version of Microsoft OneDrive. The approach is similar for competing products, such as Box, Dropbox, Google Drive, or other commercial products.

1. Go to OneDrive.com.
2. Click **Sign in** in the top right corner.
3. Sign in with your Microsoft account. (If your organization subscribes to Office 365, use your school or work account here.)
4. On the main OneDrive screen, click **New > Folder.**
5. Name your folder **DA Audit Working Papers** and click **Create.**
6. Open your new folder and click **Share** from the bar at the top of the screen.

7. Add the email address of one of your classmates or your instructor, as directed. Choose **Anyone with a link can edit** from the sharing options, then click **Send.**
8. Take a screenshot (label it 5-3A).

> Q1. What advantage is there to sharing files in one location rather than emailing copies back and forth?

Part 2: Upload Files

Now that you have a folder, you can upload some documents that will be useful for labs in this chapter and the next.

9. From Connect, download the **Audit Analytics Lab Files,** as directed by your instructor.
10. Unzip the file you downloaded to your computer. You should see two folders: **Master Audit File** and **Current Audit File.**
11. Return to your OneDrive **DA Audit Working Papers** folder, and upload the two folders:
    a. Click **Upload > Folder** in OneDrive and navigate to the folder where you unzipped the lab files.
    b. Or drag and drop the two folders from your desktop to the OneDrive window in your browser.
12. You should see two new folders in your OneDrive. Because you added them to a shared folder, the people you shared the folder with can now see these as well.
13. Take a screenshot (label it 5-3B).

> Q2. Explore the two folders you just uploaded. What kinds of documents and files do you see?

> Q3. How do you think these files can be used for data analysis?

End of Lab

Lab 5-4   Review Changes to Working Papers

See Lab 5-3 for background information on this lab. The goal of a shared folder is that other members of the audit team can contribute and edit the documents. Commercial software provides an approval workflow and additional internal controls over the documents to reduce manipulation of audit evidence, for example. For consumer cloud platforms, one control appears in the versioning of documents. As revisions are made, old copies of the documents are kept so that they can be reverted to, if needed. Note: You must complete Lab 5-3 before beginning this lab.

In this lab, you will:

Part 1: Upload revised documents.
Part 2: Review document revision history.

Part 1: Upload Revised Documents

Let's start by making changes to files in your **DA Working Papers.**

1. From Connect, download **Audit Analytics Lab Files Revised,** as directed by your instructor.
2. Unzip the file you downloaded to your computer. You should see two files: **Audit Plan** and **User_Listing.**

3. Return to your OneDrive **DA Audit Working Papers** folder, and upload the **Audit Plan** into your **Master Audit File** and the **User_Listing** into your **Current Audit File.** You will be prompted to **Replace** or **Keep Both** files. Click **Replace** for each.
4. Take a screenshot (label it 5-4A).

Part 2: Review Document Revision History

Now let's look at the history of the document.

5. Right-click on one of the newly uploaded files, and choose **Version history** from the menu that appears. The document will open with a version pane appearing on the left.
6. Click the older version of the file from the **Versions** pane. Newer versions are at the top.
7. Take a screenshot (label it 5-4B).
8. Move between the old version of the file and the current version by clicking the time stamp in the panel on the left.

Q1.   What has changed between these two versions?

End of Lab

Lab 5-5   Identify Audit Data Requirements

As the new member of the internal audit team, you have introduced your team to the shared folder and are in the process of modernizing the internal audit at your firm. The chief audit executive is interested in using Data Analytics to make the audit more efficient. Your internal audit manager agrees and has tasked you with reviewing the audit plan. She has provided three "audit action sheets" with procedures that they have been using for the past three years to evaluate the procure-to-pay (purchasing) process and is interested in your thoughts for modernizing them. Note: You should complete Lab 5-3 before beginning this lab.

Technique
- Review the audit plan, look for procedures involving data, and identify the locations of the data.

Software needed
- A modern web browser

In this lab, you will:

Part 1: Look for audit procedures that evaluate data.
Part 2: Identify the location of the data.

Part 1: Look for Audit Procedures That Evaluate Data

1. Open your **DA Audit Working Papers** folder on OneDrive or download the Audit Action Sheets document from Connect.
2. Look inside the **Master Audit File** for the document titled **Audit Action Sheets** and open it to edit it.

3. Use the **Yellow highlighter** to identify any master or transaction tables, such as "Vendors" or "Purchase Orders."
4. Use the **Green highlighter** to identify any fields or attributes, such as "Name" or "Date."
5. Use the **Blue highlighter** to identify any specific values or rules, such as "TRUE," "January 1st," "Greater than . . ."
6. Create a new spreadsheet called **Audit Automation Summary** in your **Master Audit File** and summarize your highlighted data elements from the three audit action sheets. Use the following headers:

AAS#	Table	Attributes	Values/Rules	Step(s)	Notes

7. Take a screenshot (label it 5-5A).

Q1. Read the first audit action sheet. What other data elements that are not listed in the procedures do you think would be useful in analyzing this account?

Part 2: Identify the Location of the Data

Now that you have analyzed the action sheets, look through the systems documentation to see where those elements exist.

8. In the **Master Audit File,** open the **UML System Diagram** and **Data Dictionary** files.
9. Using the data elements you identified in your **Audit Automation Summary** file, locate the actual names of tables and attributes and acceptable data values. Add them in three new columns in your summary:

Database Table	Database Attribute	Acceptable Values

10. Take a screenshot (label it 5-5B).

Q2. Which attributes were difficult to locate or in unexpected places in the database?

11. Save and close your file.

End of Lab

Lab 5-6   Prepare Audit Plan

With the data elements identified, you can formalize your internal audit plan. In the past, your internal audit department performed each of the three action sheets once every 24 months. You have shared how increasing the frequency of some of the tests would provide a better control for the process and allow the auditor to respond quickly to the exceptions. Your internal audit manager has asked you to propose a new schedule for the three audit action sheets. Note: You should complete Lab 5-5 before beginning this lab.

Technique

- Review the audit plan, identify procedures that must be completed manually, and identify those that can be automated and scheduled.
- Also determine when the procedures should occur.

Software needed

• A modern web browser

In this lab, you will:

• Evaluate the timing and scheduling of audit procedures.

Set the Frequency of Your Audit Procedures

1. Open your **Audit Automation Summary** created in Lab 5-5.
2. Add two new columns:

Auto/Manual	Frequency

3. For each element and rule, determine whether it requires manual review or can be per-formed automatically and alert auditors when exceptions occur. Add either "Auto" or "Manual" to that column.
4. Finally, determine how frequently the data should be evaluated. Indicate "Daily," "Weekly," "Monthly," "Annually," or "During Audit." Think about when the data are being generated. For example, transactions occur every day, but new employees are added every few months.
5. Take a screenshot (label it 5-6A).
6. Save and close your file.

End of Lab

Chapter 6
Audit Data Analytics

A Look at This Chapter

In this chapter, we focus on substantive testing within the audit setting. We identify when to use descriptive analytics to understand the business environment, diagnostic analytics to compare expectation with reality, including Benford's analysis, and how predictive and prescriptive analytics are used to address future audit concerns.

A Look Back

In Chapter 5, we introduced Data Analytics in auditing by considering how both internal and external auditors are using technology in general, and audit analytics specifically, to evaluate firm data and generate support for management assertions. We emphasized audit planning, audit data standards, continuous auditing, and audit working papers.

A Look Ahead

Chapter 7 explains how to apply Data Analytics to measure performance for management accountants. By measuring past performance and comparing it to targeted goals, we are able to assess how well a company is working toward a goal and recommend actions to correct unexpected patterns.

ra2studio/Shutterstock

Internal auditors at **Hewlett-Packard Co. (HP)** understand how Data Analytics can improve processes and controls. Management identified abnormal behavior with manual journal entries, and the internal audit department responded by working with various governance and compliance teams to develop dashboards that would allow them to monitor accounting activity. The dashboard made it easier for management and the auditors to follow trends, identify spikes in activity, and drill down to identify the individuals posting entries. Leveraging accounting data allows the internal audit function to focus on the risks facing **HP** and act on data in real time by implementing better controls. Audit data analytics provides an enhanced level of control that is missing from a traditional periodic audit.

OBJECTIVES

After reading this chapter, you should be able to:

LO 6-1   Understand different types of analysis for auditing and when to use them.

LO 6-2   Understand basic descriptive audit analyses.

LO 6-3   Understand more complex statistical analyses, including Benford's law.

LO 6-4   Understand advanced predictive and prescriptive analytics.

LO 6-1

Understand different types of analysis for auditing and when to use them.

WHEN TO USE AUDIT DATA ANALYTICS

As discussed in Chapter 5, Data Analytics can be applied to the auditing function to increase coverage of the audit, while reducing the time the auditor dedicates to the audit tasks. Think about the nature, extent, and timing of audit procedures.

- *Nature* represents *why* auditors perform audit procedures. In other words, nature helps determine the objectives of the audit and the outputs generated by the business processes.
- *Extent* indicates *how much* auditors can test. The prevalence of data has expanded the extent of audit testing.
- *Timing* tells us *how often* the procedure should be run. Automation allows auditors to run analytics on a schedule and receive real-time alerts when exceptions occur.

All three of these elements help auditors identify when to apply Data Analytics to the audit process. Auditors should evaluate current capabilities within their department and identify the goal of Data Analytics. Does it add value? Does it enhance the process? Does it help the auditor be more efficient and effective? Applying Data Analytics, in theory, should add value. In reality, it is easy to overpromise on the expected benefits of Data Analytics and underdeliver with the results. Without clear objectives and expected outcomes, audit departments will fail with their use of Data Analytics. Here we refer once again to the IMPACT model.

Identify the Problem

What is the audit department trying to achieve using data analytics? Do auditors need to analyze the segregation of duties to test whether internal controls are operating effectively? Are auditors looking for operational inefficiencies, such as duplicate payments of invoices? Are auditors trying to identify phantom employees or vendors? Are auditors trying to collect evidence that the company is complying with specific regulations? Are auditors trying to test account balances to tie them to the financial statements?

These activities support the functional areas of compliance, fraud detection and investigation, operational performance, and internal controls for internal audit departments as well as the financial reporting and risk assessment functions of external audit.

Master the Data

In theory, auditors should have read-only access to enterprise data through a nonproduction data warehouse. In practice, they make multiple requests for flat files or data extractions from the IT manager that they then analyze with a software tool, such as Excel or Tableau. Most audit data are provided in structured or tabular form, such as a spreadsheet file.

Regardless of the source or type, the audit data standards provide a general overview of the basic data that auditors will evaluate. For example, consider the Sales_Orders table from the standards shown in Table 6-1. An auditor interested in user activity would want to focus on the Sales_Order_ID, Sales_Order_Date, Entered_By, Entered_Date, Entered_Time, Approved_By, Approved_Date, Approved_Time, and Sales_Order_Amount_Local attributes. These may give insight into transactions on unusual dates, such as weekends, or unusually high volume by specific users.

There are also many pieces of data that have traditionally evaded scrutiny, including handwritten logs, manuals and handbooks, and other paper or text-heavy documentation. Essentially, manual tasks including observation and inspection are generally areas where Data Analytics may not apply. While there have been significant advancements in artificial intelligence, there is still a need for auditors to exercise their judgment, and data cannot always supersede the auditor's reading of human behavior or a sense that something may not be quite right even when the data say it is. At least not yet.

Field Name	Description
Sales_Order_ID	Unique identifier for each sales order. This ID may need to be created by concatenating fields (e.g., document number, document type, and year) to uniquely identify each sales order.
Sales_Order_Document_ID	Identification number or code on the sales order.
Sales_Order_Date	The date of the sales order, regardless of the date the order is entered.
Sales_Order_Fiscal_Year	Fiscal year in which the Sales_Order_Date occurs: YYYY for delimited, CCYYMMDD fiscal year-end (ISO 8601) for XBRL-GL.
Sales_Order_Period	Fiscal period in which the Sales_Order_Date occurs. Examples include W1–W53 for weekly periods, M1–M12 for monthly periods, and Q1–Q4 for quarterly periods.
Business_Unit_Code	Used to identify the business unit, region, branch, and so on at the level that financial statements are being audited. Must match a Business_Unit_Code in the Business_Unit_Listing file.
Customer_Account_ID	Identifier of the customer from whom payment is expected or to whom unused credits have been applied. Must match a Customer_Account_ID in the Customer_Master_Listing_YYYYMMDD file.
Entered_By	User_ID (from User_Listing file) for person who created the record.
Entered_Date	Date the order was entered into the system. This is sometimes referred to as the creation date. This should be a system-generated date (rather than user-entered date), when possible. This date does not necessarily correspond with the date of the transaction itself.
Entered_Time	The time this transaction was entered into the system. ISO 8601 representing time in 24-hour time (hhmm) (e.g., 1:00 p.m. = 1300).
Approved_By	User ID (from User_Listing file) for person who approved customer master additions or changes.
Approved_Date	Date the entry was approved.
Approved_Time	The time the entry was approved. ISO 8601 representing time in 24-hour time (hhmm) (e.g., 1:00 p.m. = 1300).
Last_Modified_By	User_ID (from User_Listing file) for the last person modifying this entry.
Last_Modified_Date	The date the entry was last modified.
Last_Modified_Time	The time the entry was last modified. ISO 8601 representing time in 24-hour time (hhmm) (e.g., 1:00 p.m. = 1300).
Sales_Order_Amount_Local	Sales monetary amount recorded in the local currency.
Sales_Order_Local_Currency	The currency for local reporting requirements. See ISO 4217 coding.
Segment01	Reserved segment field that can be used for profit center, division, fund, program, branch, project, and so on.
Segment02	See above.
Segment03	See above.
Segment04	See above.
Segment05	See above.

TABLE 6-1

Elements in the Sales_ Order Table from the Audit Data Standards

Source: Adapted from https://www.aicpa.org/content/dam/aicpa/interestareas/frc/assuranceadvisoryservices/downloadabledocuments/ auditdatastandards/auditdatastandards.o2c.july2015.pdf, accessed January 1, 2018

Data may also be found in unlikely places. An auditor may be tasked with determining whether the steps of a process are being followed. Traditional evaluation would involve the auditor observing or interviewing the employee performing the work. Now that most processes are handled through online systems, an auditor can perform Data Analytics on the time stamps of the tasks and determine the sequence of approvals in a workflow along with the amount of time spent on each task. This form of process mining enables insight into areas where greater efficiency can be applied. Likewise, data stored in paper documents, such as invoices received from vendors, can be scanned and converted to tabular data using specialized software. These new pieces of data can be joined to other transactional data to enable new, thoughtful analytics.

There is an increasing opportunity to work with unstructured Big Data to provide additional insight into the economic events being evaluated by the auditors, such as surveillance video or text from e-mail, but those are still outside the scope of current Data Analytics that an auditor would develop.

Perform the Test Plan

While there are many different tests or models that auditors can incorporate into their audit procedures, Data Analytics procedures in auditing traditionally are found in **computer-assisted audit techniques (CAATs)**. CAATs are automated scripts that can be used to validate data, test controls, and enable substantive testing of transaction details or account balances and generate supporting evidence for the audit. They are especially useful for re-performing calculations, identifying high-risk samples, and performing other analytical reviews to identify unusual patterns of behavior or unusual items.

Most CAATs are designed to summarize and describe the data being evaluated based on a predetermined expected outcome. For example, an auditor evaluating an incentive plan that gives employees bonuses for opening new accounts would evaluate the number of new accounts by employee and the amount of bonus paid to see if they were aligned. The auditor could look for a count of new accounts by account type, count the number of customers, evaluate the opening date, and sort the data by employee to show the top-performing employees. These **descriptive analytics** summarize activity or master data elements based on certain attributes. The auditor may select a *sample* of the accounts to verify that they were opened and the documentation exists.

Once an auditor has a basic understanding of the data, he or she can then perform **diagnostic analytics**, which look for correlations or patterns of interest in the data. For example, the auditor may look for commonalities between the customers' demographic data and the employees' data to see if employees are creating new accounts for fake customers to inflate their performance numbers. They may also focus on customers who have common attributes like location or account age. Outliers may warrant further investigation by the auditor as they represent increased risk and/or exposure.

An auditor then performs **predictive analytics**, where he or she attempts to find hidden patterns or variables that are linked to abnormal behavior. The auditor uses the variables to build models that can be used to predict a likely value or classification. In our example, the predictive model might flag an employee or customer with similar characteristics to other high-risk employees or customers whenever a new account is opened.

Finally, the auditor may generate **prescriptive analytics** that identify a course of action for him or her to take based on the actions taken in similar situations in the past. These analytics can assist future auditors who encounter similar behavior. Using artificial intelligence and machine learning, these analytics become decision support tools for auditors who may lack experience to find potential audit issues. For example, when a new account is created for a customer who has been inactive for more than 12 months, a prescriptive analytic would allow an auditor to ask questions about the transaction to learn whether this new account is potentially fake, whether the employee is likely to create other fake accounts, and whether the account and/or employee should be suspended or not. The auditor would take the output, apply judgment, and proceed with what he or she felt was the appropriate action.

Most auditors will perform descriptive and diagnostic analytics as part of their audit plan. On rare occasions, they may experiment with predictive and prescriptive analytics directly. More likely, they may identify opportunities for the latter analytics and work with data scientists to build those for future use.

Some examples of CAATs and audit procedures related to the descriptive, diagnostic, predictive, and prescriptive analytics can be found in Table 6-2.

Analytic Type	Example CAATs	Example Audit Procedures
Descriptive—summarizes activity or master data based on certain attributes	*Age analysis*—groups balances by date *Sorting*—identifies largest or smallest values and helps identify patterns *Summary statistics*—mean, median, min, max, count, sum *Sampling*—random and monetary unit	Analysis of new accounts opened and employee bonuses by employee and location. Count the number/dollar amount of transactions that occur outside normal business hours or at the end/beginning of the period.
Diagnostic—detects correlations and patterns of interest and compares them to a benchmark	*Z-score*—outlier detection *Benford's law*—identifies transactions or users with non-typical activity based on the distribution of digits *Drill-down*—explores the details behind the values *Exact and* **fuzzy matching**—joins tables and identifies plausible relationships *Sequence check*—detects gaps in records and duplicates entries *Stratification*—groups data by categories *Clustering*—groups records by non-obvious similarities	Analysis of new accounts reveals that an agent has an unusual number of new accounts opened for customers who have been inactive for more than 12 months. An auditor assigns an expected Benford's value to purchase transactions, then averages them by employee to identify employees with unusually large purchases. An auditor filters out transactions that are below a materiality threshold.
Predictive—identifies common attributes or patterns that may be used to identify similar activity	*Regression*—predicts specific dependent values based on independent variable inputs *Classification*—predicts a category for a record *Probability*—uses a rank score to evaluate the strength of classification *Sentiment analysis*—evaluates text for positive or negative sentiment to predict positive or negative outcomes	Analysis of new accounts opened for customers who have been inactive for more than 12 months collects data that are common to new account opening, such as account type, demographics, and employee incentives.
Prescriptive—recommends action based on previously observed actions	*What-if analysis*—decision support systems *Applied statistics*—predicts a specific outcome or class *Artificial intelligence*—uses observations of past actions to predict future actions for similar events	Analysis determines procedures to follow when new accounts are opened for inactive customers, such as requiring approval.

TABLE 6-2
Examples of Audit Data Analytics

While many of these analyses can be performed using Excel, most CAATs are built on generalized audit software (GAS), such as IDEA, ACL, or TeamMate Analytics. The GAS software has two main advantages over traditional spreadsheet software. First, it enables analysis of very large datasets. Second, it automates several common analytical routines, so an auditor can click a few buttons to get to the results rather than writing a complex set of formulas. GAS is also scriptable and enables auditors to record or program common analyses that may be reused on future engagements.

Address and Refine Results

The models selected by the auditors will generate various results. A sample selection may give auditors a list of high-risk transactions to evaluate. A segregation of duties analysis may spit out a list of users with too much access. In every case, the auditors should develop procedures in the audit plan for handling these lists, exceptions, and anomalies. The process may be to evaluate documentation related to the sample, review employees engaging in risky activity, or simply notify the audit committee of irregular behavior.

Communicate Insights

Many analytics can be adapted to create an audit dashboard for measuring risk in transactions or exceptions to control rules, particularly if the firm has adopted continuous auditing. The primary output of CAATs is evidence that may be used to test management assertions about the processes, controls, and data quality. This evidence is included in the audit workpapers.

Track Outcomes

The detection and resolution of audit exceptions may be a valuable measure of the efficiency and effectiveness of the internal audit function itself. Additional analytics may track the number of exceptions over time and the time taken to report and resolve the issues. For the CAATs involved, a periodic validation process should occur to ensure that they continue to function as expected.

 PROGRESS CHECK

1. Using Table 6-2 as a guide, compare and contrast descriptive and diagnostic analytics. How might these be used in an audit?
2. In a continuous audit, how would a dashboard help to communicate audit findings and spur a response?

DESCRIPTIVE ANALYTICS

Now that you've been given an overview of the types of CAATs and analytics that are commonly used in an audit, we'll dive a little deeper into how these analytics work and what they generate. Remember that descriptive analytics are useful for sorting and summarizing data to create a baseline for more advanced analytics. These analytics enable auditors to set a baseline or point of reference for their evaluation. For example, if an auditor can identify the median value of a series of transactions, he or she can make a judgment as to how much higher the larger transactions are and whether they represent outliers or exceptions.

In this and the next few sections, we'll present some examples of procedures that auditors commonly use to evaluate enterprise data. In these examples, we show the basic process for Excel, including formulas, and IDEA. Note that in the Excel formulas, we identify data elements in [brackets]. To use these formulas, replace the bracketed [data element] with a value or range of values as appropriate. For example, [Aging date] would be replaced with C3 if the data are in column C, row 3.

Age Analysis

Aging of accounts receivable and accounts payable helps determine the likelihood that a balance will be paid. This substantive test of account balances evaluates the date of an order and groups it into buckets based on how old it is, typically in 0–30, 31–60, 61–90, and >90 days, or similar. See Table 6-3 for an example. Extremely old accounts that haven't been resolved or written off should be flagged for follow-up by the auditor. It could mean that (1) the data are bad, (2) a process is broken, (3) there's a reason someone is holding that account open, or (4) it was simply never resolved.

	0–30	31–60	61–90	>90
Total	154,322	74,539	42,220	16,900

TABLE 6-3
Aging of Accounts Receivable

There are many ways to calculate aging in Excel, including using pivot tables. If you have a simple list of accounts and balances, you can calculate a simple age of accounts in Excel using the following procedure.

Data

- Customer/vendor name
- Unpaid order number
- Order date
- Amount

In Excel

1. Open your worksheet.
2. Add a cell with the **aging date**.
3. Add a calculated column for the **days outstanding**: =[Aging date]-[Order date].
4. Add four new calculated columns for the buckets:
   a. **0–30 days**: =IF([Aging date]-[Order date]<=30,[Amount],0).
   b. **31–60 days**: =IF(AND([Aging date]-[Order date]<=60, [Aging date]-[Order date]>30),[Amount],0).
   c. **61–90 days**: =IF(AND([Aging date]-[Order date]<=90, [Aging date]-[Order date]>60),[Amount],0).
   d. **>90 days**: =IF([Aging date]-[Order date]>90),[Amount],0).
5. Copy the formulas for all records.
6. Add a **total** to the bottom of each bucket: =SUM([bucket column]).

In IDEA

1. Open your worksheet.
2. Go to **Analysis > Categorize > Aging**.

Source: IDCaseWare IDEA

3. Select **aging date**, **transaction date** for the Aging field to use, and **amount** for the Amount field to total field.
4. Click **OK**.

Sorting

Sometimes, simply viewing the largest or smallest values can provide meaningful insight. Sorting in ascending order shows the smallest number values first. Sorting in descending order shows the largest values first.

Data

- Any numerical, date, or text data of interest

In Excel

1. Open your worksheet.
2. Select the data you wish to sort.
3. Go to **Home > Styles > Format as Table**.
4. Click the **drop-down arrow** next to the header or the column you want to sort.
5. Click **Sort A to Z** for ascending order or **Sort Z to A** for descending order.

In IDEA

1. Open your data table.
2. Go to **Data > Order > Sort**.
3. Choose your desired field(s) and direction, **Ascending** or **Descending**.
4. Click **OK**.

Summary Statistics

Summary statistics provide insight into the relative size of a number compared with the population. The mean indicates the average value, while the median produces the middle value when all the transactions lined up in a row. The min shows the smallest value, while the max shows the largest. Finally, a count tells how many records exist, where the sum adds up the values to find a total. Once summary statistics are calculated, you have a reference point for an individual record. Is the amount above or below average? What percentage of the total does a group of transactions make up?

Data

- Any numerical data, such as a dollar amount or quantity

In Excel

1. Open your workbook.
2. Add the following calculated values:
    - Mean: =AVERAGE([range]).
    - Median: =MEDIAN([range]).
    - Minimum: =MIN([range]).
    - Maximum: =MAX([range]).
    - Count: =COUNT([range]).
    - Sum: =SUM([range]).
3. Alternatively, format your data as a table and show the total row at the bottom:
    a. Select your data.
    b. Go to **Home > Styles > Format as Table**.
    c. Select a table style and click **OK**.
    d. Go to **Table Tools > Design > Table Style Options** and click the **Total Row** box.
    e. Go to the bottom of the table and click the **drop-down arrow** next to the column total value that appears. Choose an appropriate statistic.

In IDEA

1. Open your worksheet.
2. In the **Properties** pane on the right, click **Field Statistics**.
3. Allow IDEA to create statistics for fields without statistics, if prompted.
4. In the output screen, you can click any blue number to locate those transactions.

Sampling

Sampling is useful when you have manual audit procedures, such as testing transaction details or evaluating source documents. The idea is that if the sample is an appropriate size, the features of the sample can be confidently generalized to the population. So, if the sample has no errors (misstatement), then the population is unlikely to have errors as well. Of course, sampling has its limitations. The confidence level is not a guarantee that you won't miss something critical like fraud. But it does limit the scope of the work the auditor must perform.

There are three determinants for sample size: confidence level, tolerable misstatement, and estimated misstatement.

Data

- Any list of transactions or master data

In Excel

1. Enable **Analysis ToolPak**:
   a. Go to **File > Options > Add-ins > Excel Add-ins > Go**.
   b. Select **Analysis ToolPak**, and click **OK**.
2. Go to **Data > Analysis > Data Analysis**.
3. Click **Sampling**, then **OK**.
   a. Select your **input range**, usually the transaction number.
   b. Choose **Random**, and input the number of items you want to appear in your sample.
   c. Click **OK**.
4. A new worksheet will appear with a list of your randomly selected transactions.

In IDEA

1. Open your worksheet.
2. Go to **Analysis > Sample > Random**.
   a. Input **number of records** to select for your sample size.
   b. Change other values as needed.
   c. Click **OK**.
3. A new worksheet will be created with your random sample.

Monetary unit sampling (MUS) allows auditors to evaluate account balances. MUS is more likely to pull accounts with large balances (higher risk and exposure) because it focuses on dollars, not account numbers.

Data

- The book value of the financial accounts you're evaluating
- The sample size

In Excel

1. Find the sampling interval. Divide the book value by sample size. In this example, 1,000,000 is the total rounded book value of a GL account and 132 is the desired sample size.
   a. $1,000,000/132 = \mathbf{7,575}$
2. Choose one of the following options to sort the line items or individual accounts. Then add a column to calculate the cumulative balance.
   a. Alphabetically by name.
   b. Numerically by number.
   c. By date.
3. Pick a random number between 1 and your sampling interval.
   a. This will be the starting value. For example, **1,243**.
4. Go down the list of cumulative balances until you pass your random number.
   a. For example, test the first account that passes **1,243**.
5. Continue down the list of cumulative balances until you pass the next sampling interval.
   a. For example, test the second account that passes $1,243 + 7,575 = \mathbf{8,818}$.
6. Repeat step 5 until you run out of accounts.
   a. $8,818 + 7,575 = \mathbf{16,393}$; $16,393 + 7,575 = \mathbf{23,968}\ldots$

In IDEA

1. Open your data table.
2. Go to **Analysis > Sample > Monetary Unit > Plan**.
   a. Choose your **monetary value field**.
   b. Set your **confidence level**, **tolerable error**, and **expected error**.
   c. Click **Estimate** to calculate your sample size.
   d. Adjust other values as needed, then click **Accept**.
   e. Click **OK**.
3. A new worksheet will appear with your sample transactions.

 PROGRESS CHECK

3. What type of descriptive analytics would you use to find negative numbers that were entered in error?

4. How does monetary unit sampling help you isolate the items of greatest potential significance to an auditor in evaluating materiality?

DIAGNOSTIC ANALYTICS AND BENFORD'S LAW

LO 6-3

Understand more complex statistical analyses, including Benford's law.

Diagnostic analytics provide more details into not just the records, but also records or groups of records that have some standout features. They may be significantly larger than other values, may not match a pattern within the population, or may be a little too similar to other records for an auditor's liking. Here we'll identify some common diagnostic analytics and how to use them.

Z-Score

A standard score or Z-score is a concept from statistics that assigns a value to a number based on how many standard deviations it stands from the mean, shown in Exhibit 6-1. By setting the mean to 0, you can see how far a point of interest is above or below it. For example, a point with a Z-score of 2.5 is two-and-a-half standard deviations above the mean. Because most values that come from a large population tend to be normally distributed (frequently skewed toward smaller values in the case of financial transactions), nearly all (98 percent) of the values should be within plus-or-minus three standard deviations. If a value has a Z-score of 3.9, it is very likely an outlier that warrants scrutiny.

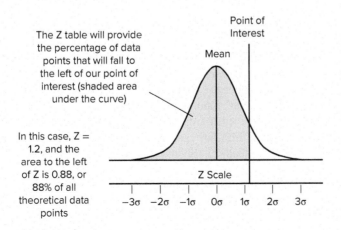

The Z table will provide the percentage of data points that will fall to the left of our point of interest (shaded area under the curve)

In this case, Z = 1.2, and the area to the left of Z is 0.88, or 88% of all theoretical data points

Point of Interest

Mean

Z Scale

−3σ −2σ −1σ 0σ 1σ 2σ 3σ

EXHIBIT 6-1
Z-Scores
The Z-score shows the relative position of a point of interest to the population.

Source: http://www.dmaictools.com/wp-content/uploads/2012/02/z-definition.jpg

In Excel

1. Calculate the average: =AVERAGE([range]).
2. Calculate the standard deviation: =STDEVPA([range]).
3. Add a new column called "Z-score" next to your number range.
4. Calculate the Z-score: =STANDARDIZE([value],[mean],[standard deviation]).
   a. Alternatively: =([value]–[mean])/[standard deviation].
5. Sort your values by Z-score in descending order.

In IDEA

• Z-score calculation is not a default feature of IDEA.

Benford's Law

Benford's law states that when you have a large set of naturally occurring numbers, the leading digit(s) are more likely to be small. The economic intuition behind it is that people are more likely to make $10, $100, or $1,000 purchases than $90, $900, or $9,000 purchases. This law has been shown in many settings, such as the amount of electricity bills, street addresses, and GDP figures from around the world (as shown in Exhibit 6-2).

EXHIBIT 6-2
Benford's Law
Benford's law predicts the distribution of first digits.

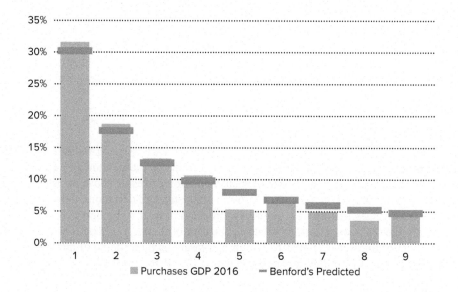

In auditing, we can use Benford's law to identify transactions or users with nontypical activity based on the distribution of the first digits of the number. For example, assume that purchases over $500 require manager approval. A cunning employee might try to make large purchases that are just under the approval limit to avoid suspicion. She will even be clever and make the numbers look random: $495, $463, $488, etc. What she doesn't realize is that the frequency of the leading digit 4 is going to be much higher than it should be, shown in Exhibit 6-3. Benford's law can also detect random computer-generated numbers because those will have equally distributed first digits. Adding additional leading digits refines the analysis.

We show an illustration of how to evaluate data and their frequency with respect to Benford's law in both Excel and IDEA.

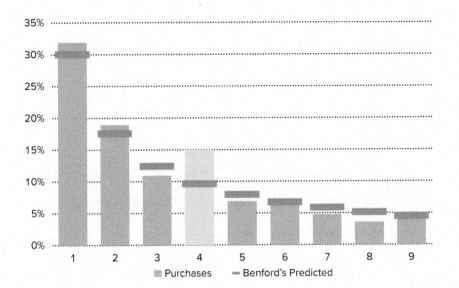

EXHIBIT 6-3
Using Benford's Law
Structured purchases
may look normal,
but they alter the
distribution under
Benford's law.

Data

• Large set of numerical data, such as monetary amounts or quantities

In Excel

1. Open your spreadsheet.
2. Add a new column **and extract the leading digit**: =LEFT([Amount],1).
3. Create a **frequency distribution**:
   a. Create a list on your sheet and copy the **Digit, Actual Count, Actual** %, and **Expected** % columns with their corresponding values and formulas, shown in Table 6-4.

Digit	Actual Count	Actual %	Expected %
1	=COUNTIF([Range],[Digit])	(=[Actual Count]/SUM[Actual Count])	30.1%
2	...	...	17.6%
3	...	...	12.5%
4	...	...	9.6%
5	...	...	7.9%
6	...	...	6.7%
7	...	...	5.8%
8	...	...	5.1%
9	...	...	4.6%
	=SUM([Actual Count])	=SUM([Actual %])	=SUM([Expected %])

TABLE 6-4
Illustration of Benford's
Law

4. Create a **combo chart** to plot your actual and expected percentages:
   a. Highlight the **Actual** % and **Expected** % columns.
   b. Go to **Insert > Charts > Recommended Charts**.
   c. Click the **All Charts** tab.
   d. Choose **Combo** from the list on the left.
   e. Click **Custom Combination**.

    f. For the **Actual %**, choose **Clustered Column**.

    g. For the **Expected %**, choose **Scatter**.

    h. Click **OK**.

    i. Adjust and format your chart as needed.

In IDEA

1. Open your worksheet.
2. Go to **Analysis > Explore > Benford's Law**.
   a. Choose the **numerical field** to analyze.
   b. Only check **First digit**. Uncheck everything else.
   c. Click **OK**.
3. A graph will appear with the Benford's expected amount and the actual frequency of the dataset.
4. Click any digits that are significantly above the bounds and choose **Extract Records**.

Bonus: Use the average expected Benford's law value to identify specific employees with abnormally large transactions. In this case, a user with lots of transactions should have an average expected Benford's law percentage of 11.1 percent or above. Employees whose average purchases are closer to 8 or 5 percent have a lot of 7, 8, and 9 values that are skewing their average.

In Excel

1. Open your spreadsheet with financial data that contain an employee name and transaction amount.
2. Add a new column and extract the **leading digit**. *Note:* the LEFT() function in Excel creates a text value. Use VALUE() to convert it to a number.
   =VALUE(LEFT([Amount],1))
3. Add the **expected Benford's law percentages** to your sheet similar to Table 6-5.

TABLE 6-5
Expected Benford's
Law Percentages

Digit	Benford Expected %
1	30.1%
2	17.6%
3	12.5%
4	9.6%
5	7.9%
6	6.7%
7	5.8%
8	5.1%
9	4.6%

4. Add a new column next to your data to **look up the expected Benford's law percentage** for your value: =INDEX([Benford Expected %], MATCH([Amount],[Digit],0)).
5. Create a PivotTable to see the **average % by user**:
   a. Select your data.
   b. Go to **Insert > Tables > PivotTable**.
   c. Click **OK** to add the **PivotTable** to a new sheet.
   d. Drag **[Employee Name]** to Rows.
   e. Drag **[Benford Expected]** to Values.

   f. Click **Sum of [Benford Expected]** and choose **Value Field Settings**.

   g. Change the summarize value field by to **Average**, and click **OK**.

   h. Select the **[Average of Benford Expected]** column in your PivotTable, and sort it in ascending order: Go to **Data > Sort & Filter > Sort Smallest to Largest**.

In IDEA

- This is not possible using the built-in tool.

Drill-Down

The most modern Data Analytics software allows auditors to drill down into specific values by simply double-clicking a value. This lets you see the underlying transactions that gave you the summary amount. For example, you might click the total sales amount in an income statement to see the sales general ledger summarizing the daily totals. Click a daily amount to see the individual transactions from that day.

Exact and Fuzzy Matching

Matching in CAAT is used to link records, join tables, and find potential issues. Auditors use *exact matching* to join database tables with a foreign key from one table to the primary key of another. In cases where the data are inconsistent or contain user-generated information, such as addresses, exact matches may not be sufficient. For example, "234 Second Avenue" and "234 Second Ave" are not the same value. To join tables on these values auditors will use a *fuzzy match* based on the similarity of the values. The auditor defines a threshold, such as 50 percent, and if the values share enough common characters, they will be matched. The threshold can be higher to reduce the number of potential matches or lower to increase the likelihood of a match.

   Note that not all matches are the same. Using queries and other database management tools, auditors may want only certain records, such as those that match or those that don't match. These matches require the use of certain join types. **Inner Join** will show only the records from both tables that match and exclude everything that doesn't match. **Left Join** will show all records from the first table and only records from the second table that match. **Right Join** will show all records from the second table and records from the first table that match. **Outer Join** will show all nonmatching ones. **Full Outer Join** will show all records, including matching and nonmatching ones. Fuzzy matching finds matches that may be less than 100 percent matching by finding correspondences between portions of the text or other entries.

Data needed

- Two tables/sheets with a common attribute, such as a primary key/foreign key, name, or address

In Excel

1. Search the Internet for **Fuzzy Lookup Add-In for Excel**, then download and install it to your computer.
2. Open your spreadsheet with two sheets you'd like to join using a fuzzy match. For example, employees and vendors. If your data is not already formatted as tables in Excel, select your data and choose **Home > Styles > Format as Table**. You can name the table in the Table Design tab.
3. Go to **Fuzzy Lookup > Fuzzy Lookup** (Go to **File > Options > Add-ins > COM Add-ins > Go**. . . and check **Fuzzy Lookup Add-in for Excel** if you don't see the bar).

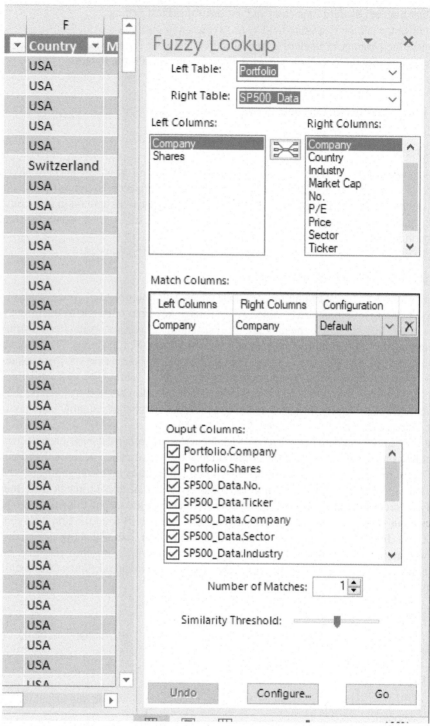

Source: Microsoft Excel 2016.

    a. Select the sheet you want for the **Left Table** and a sheet that has similar values for the **Right Table**.

    b. Choose the columns that you expect to find matching values in the **Left** and **Right Columns** pane. *Note:* For addresses, choose Address AND Zip Code for more likely matches.

    c. Select your **output columns**, if needed.

    d. Adjust the **similarity threshold**, if needed.

    e. Open a new **worksheet**.

    f. Click **Go**.

4. Evaluate the similarity.

In IDEA

To do a fuzzy address match, you must first join the two tables on numbers in the address, then compare the similarity in addresses.

1. Open your workbook with two data files you'd like to join.
2. Open the first table and double click any piece of data to show the **Field Manipulation** box.
3. Click **Append** and add a new field called "Table1 address numbers."
4. Click the empty box in the **Parameter** column to open the equation editor.
5. Use the IDEA function @JustNumbers([ADDRESS]+[ZIP]).
6. Click the green check mark. Click **OK**, then click **Yes**.
7. Repeat steps 2–6 for the second table.
8. Click on **Table 1**. Go to **Analysis > Visual Connector** to create a relationship.
9. Add the two tables and drag new "Table1 Address Numbers" field to the "Table2 Address Numbers" field to create a join.
10. Click **OK**, select Matches only, and name your dataset.
11. Click **OK** to show your matching data between the two tables. This only shows exact matches based on the numbers from the addresses.
12. Double-click the data to show the **Field Manipulation** box.
13. Click **Append** and add a new field called "Distance."
14. Set the **Dec** to 6, and click the **Parameter** box to open the equation editor.
15. Use the IDEA function @SimilarPhrase([ADDRESS1],[ADDRESS2]).
16. Click the green check mark. Click **OK**, then click **Yes**.
17. Sort the "Distance" column in descending order. The higher the percentage, the more similar they match.
18. Save your table.

Sequence Check

Another substantive procedure is the sequence check. This is used to validate data integrity and test the completeness assertion, making sure that all relevant transactions are accounted for. Simply put, sequence checks are useful for finding gaps, such as a missing check in the cash disbursements journal, or duplicate transactions, such as duplicate payments to vendors. This is a fairly simple procedure that can be deployed quickly and easily with great success. Begin by sorting your data by identification number.

In Excel

$$=IF([Second\ Value]-[First\ Value]=1,"","Missing")$$

Stratification and Clustering

There are several approaches to grouping transactions or individuals. In most cases, the items can be grouped by similar characteristics or strata. With stratification, the auditor identifies specific groups, such as geographic location or functional area, that can be used to simplify their analysis. When similarities are less obvious, such as personal preference or expressed behavior, clustering may be used to infer these groupings. Both stratification and clustering are generally used for data exploration, rather than substantive testing. The identification of these groupings, whether obvious or not, help narrow the scope of the audit and focus on risk. Clustering is discussed in depth in Chapter 3.

 PROGRESS CHECK

5. A sequence check will help us to see if there is a duplicate payment to vendors. Why is that important for the auditor to find?

6. Let's say a company has nine divisions, and each division has a different check number based on its division—so one starts with "1," another with "2," etc. Would Benford's law work in this situation?

LO 6-4

Understand advanced predictive and prescriptive analytics.

CREATING ADVANCED PREDICTIVE AND PRESCRIPTIVE ANALYTICS

Predictive and prescriptive analytics provide less deterministic output than the previous analytics. This is because we're moving away from deterministic values to more probabilistic models, judging things like *likelihood* and *possibility*. Here we'll briefly discuss some applications of these different concepts, but we refer you back to Chapter 3 for background information.

Regression

Regression allows an auditor to predict a specific dependent value based on independent variable inputs. In other words, what would we expect behavior to be given some inputs and does that match reality? In auditing, we could evaluate overtime booked for workers against productivity or the value of inventory shrinkage given environmental factors.

Classification

Classification in auditing is going to be mainly focused on risk assessment. The predicted classes may be *low risk* or *high risk*, where an individual transaction is classified in either group. In the case of known fraud, auditors would classify those cases or transactions as *fraud/not fraud* and develop a classification model that could predict whether similar transactions might also be potentially fraudulent.

There is a longstanding classification method used to predict whether a company is expected to go bankrupt or not. Altman's Z is a calculated score that helps predict bankruptcy and might be useful for auditors to evaluate a company's ability to continue as a going concern.

When using classification models, it is important to remember that large training sets are needed to generate relatively accurate models. Initially, this requires significant manual classification by the auditors or business process owner so that the model can be useful for the audit.

Probability

When talking about classification, the strength of the class can be important to the auditor, especially when trying to limit the scope (e.g., evaluate only the 10 riskiest transactions). Classifiers that use a rank score can identify the strength of classification by measuring the distance from the mean. That rank order focuses the auditor's efforts on the items of potentially greatest significance.

Sentiment Analysis

Evaluate text (e.g., 10-K or annual report) for positive or negative sentiment to predict positive or negative outcomes or to look for potential bias on management's part. There is more discussion on sentiment analysis in Chapter 8.

Applied Statistics

Additional mixed distributions and nontraditional statistics may also provide insight to the auditor. For example, an audit of inventory may reveal errors in the amount recorded in the system. The difference between the error amounts and the actual amounts may provide some valuable insight into how significant or material the problem may be. Auditors can plot the frequency distribution of errors and use Z-scores to hone in on the cause of the most significant or outlier errors.

Artificial Intelligence

As the audit team generates more data and takes specific action, the action itself can be modeled in a way that allows an algorithm to predict expected behavior. Artificial intelligence is designed around the idea that computers can learn about action or behavior from the past and predict the course of action for the future. Assume that an experienced auditor questions management about the estimate of allowance for doubtful accounts. The human auditor evaluates a number of inputs, such as the estimate calculation, market factors, and the possibility of income smoothing by management. Given these inputs, the auditor decides to challenge management's estimate. If the auditor consistently takes this action and it is recorded by the computer, the computer learns from this action and makes a recommendation when a new inexperienced auditor faces a similar situation.

Decision support systems that accountants have relied upon for years (e.g., TurboTax) are based on a formal set of rules and then updated based on what the user decides given several choices. Artificial intelligence can be used as a helpful assistant to auditors and may potentially be called upon to make judgment decisions itself.

Additional Analyses

The list of Data Analytics presented in this chapter is not exhaustive by any means. There are many other approaches to identifying interesting patterns and anomalies in enterprise data. Many ingenious auditors have developed automated scripts that can simplify several of the audit tasks presented here. Excel add-ins like TeamMate Analytics provide many different techniques that apply specifically to the audit of fixed assets, inventory, sales and purchase transactions, etc. Auditors will combine these tools with other techniques, such as periodically testing the effectiveness of automated tools by adding erroneous or fraudulent transactions, to enhance their audit process.

✓ PROGRESS CHECK

7. Why would a bankruptcy prediction be considered classification? And why would it be useful to auditors?
8. If sentiment analysis is used on a product advertisement, would you guess the overall sentiment would be positive or negative?

Summary

This chapter discusses a number of analytical techniques that auditors use to gather insight about controls and transaction data. These include descriptive analytics that are used to summarize and gain insight into the data, diagnostic analytics that identify patterns in the data that may not be immediately obvious, predictive analytics that look for common attributes of problematic data to help identify similar events in the future, and prescriptive analytics that provide decision support to auditors as they work to resolve issues with the processes and controls.

Key Words

computer-assisted audit techniques (CAATs) (*228*)   Automated scripts that can be used to validate data, test controls, and enable substantive testing of transaction details or account balances and generate supporting evidence for the audit.

descriptive analytics (*228*)   Procedures that summarize existing data to determine what has happened in the past. Some examples include summary statistics (e.g. Count, Min, Max, Average, Median), distributions, and proportions.

diagnostic analytics (*228*)   Procedures that explore the current data to determine why something has happened the way it has, typically comparing the data to a benchmark. As an example, these allow users to see how values compare those from a budget, a competitor, or trend.

fuzzy matching (*229*)   Process that finds matches that may be less than 100 percent matching by finding correspondences between portions of the text or other entries.

monetary unit sampling (MUS) (*234*)   Allows auditors to evaluate account balances. MUS is more likely to pull accounts with large balances (higher risk and exposure) because it focuses on dollars, not account numbers.

predictive analytics (*228*)   Procedures used to generate a model that can be used to determine what is likely to happen in the future. Examples include regression analysis, forecasting, classification, and other predictive modeling.

prescriptive analytics (*228*)   Procedures that model data to enable recommendations for what should be done in the future. These typically include developing more advanced machine learning and artificial intelligence models to recommend a course of action based on a current problem.

⊘ ANSWERS TO PROGRESS CHECKS

1. Descriptive activity summarizes activity by computing basic descriptive statistics like means, medians, minimums, maximums, and standard deviations. Diagnostic analytics compares variables or data items to each other and tries to find co-occurrence or correlation to find patterns of interest. Both of these approaches look at historic data. An auditor might use descriptive analytics to understand what they are auditing and diagnostic analytics to determine whether there is risk of misstatement based on the expected value or why the numbers are they way they are.

2. Use of a dashboard to highlight and communicate findings will help identify alarms for issues that are occurring on a real-time basis. This will allow issues to be addressed immediately.

3. By computing minimum values or by sorting, you can find the lowest reported value and, thus, potential negative numbers that might have been entered erroneously into the system and require further investigation.

4. Monetary unit sampling is more likely to pull accounts with large balances (higher risk and exposure) because it focuses on the amount of the transaction rather than giving each transaction an equal chance. The larger dollar value of the transaction, the more likely it is to affect materiality thresholds.

5. Duplicate payments to vendors suggest that there is a gap in the internal controls around payments. After the first payment was made, why did the accounting system allow a second payment? Were both transactions authorized? Who signed the checks or authorized payments? How can we prevent this from happening in the future?

6. Benford's law works best on naturally occurring numbers. If the company dictates the first number of its check sequence, Benford's law will not work the same way and thus would not be effective in finding potential issues with the check numbers.

7. Bankruptcy prediction predicts two conditions for a company: bankrupt or not bankrupt. Thus, it would be considered a classification activity. Auditors are required to assess a client's ability to continue as a going concern and the bankruptcy prediction helps with that.

8. Most product advertisements are very positive in nature and would have positive sentiment.

Mc Graw Hill connect®

Multiple Choice Questions

1. Which items would be currently out of scope for Data Analytics?
   a. Direct observation of processes
   b. Evaluation of time stamps to evaluate workflow
   c. Evaluation of phantom vendors
   d. Duplicate payment of invoices

2. What would be the sampling interval if we are using a manual approach to monetary unit sampling for a book value of $2,000,000 and a sample size of 200?
   a. 10,000
   b. 1,000
   c. 100,000
   d. Cannot be determined

3. Monetary unit sampling is more likely to:
   a. sample accounts with smaller balances.
   b. sample accounts with less risk.
   c. sample accounts with larger balances.
   d. sample accounts with more risk.

4. The determinants for sample size include all of the following *except:*
   a. confidence level.
   b. tolerable misstatement.
   c. potential risk of account.
   d. estimated misstatement.

5. CAATs are automated scripts that can be used to validate data, test controls, and enable substantive testing of transaction details or account balances and generate supporting evidence for the audit. What does CAAT stand for?
   a. Computer-aided audit techniques
   b. Computer-assisted audit techniques
   c. Computerized audit and accounting techniques
   d. Computerized audit aids and tests

6. Which type of audit analytics might be used to find hidden patterns or variables linked to abnormal behavior?

    a. Prescriptive analytics

    b. Predictive analytics

    c. Diagnostic analytics

    d. Descriptive analytics

7. What describes finding correspondences between at least two types of text or entries that may not match perfectly?

    a. Incomplete linkages

    b. Algorithmic matching

    c. Fuzzy matching

    d. Incomplete matching

8. Which testing approach would be used to predict whether certain cases should be evaluated as having fraud or no fraud?

    a. Classification

    b. Probability

    c. Sentiment analysis

    d. Artificial intelligence

9. Which testing approach would be useful in assessing the value of inventory shrinkage given multiple environmental factors?

    a. Probability

    b. Sentiment analysis

    c. Regression

    d. Applied statistics

10. What type of analysis would help auditors find missing checks?

    a. Sequence check

    b. Benford's law analysis

    c. Fuzzy matching

    d. Decision support systems

Discussion Questions

1. How do nature, extent, and timing of audit procedures help us identify when to apply Data Analytics to the audit process?

2. When do you believe that Data Analytics will add value to the audit process? How can it most help?

3. Using Table 6-2 as a guide, compare and contrast predictive and prescriptive analytics. How might these be used in an audit? Or a continuous audit?

4. Prescriptive analytics rely on models based on past actions to suggest recommended actions for new, similar situations. For example, auditors might review managers' approval of new credit applications for inactive customers. If auditors know the variables and values that were common among past approvals and denials, they could compare the action recommended by the model with the response of the manager. How else might this prescriptive analytics help auditors assess risk or test audit issues?

5. One type of descriptive analytics is simply sorting data. Why is seeing extreme values helpful (minimums, maximums, counts, etc.) in evaluating accuracy and completeness and in potentially finding errors and fraud and the like?

Problems

1. One type of descriptive analytics is age analysis. Why are auditors particularly interested in the aging of accounts receivable and accounts payable? How does this analysis help evaluate management judgment on collectability of receivables and potential payment of payables? Would a dashboard item reflecting this aging be useful in a continuous audit?

2. One of the benefits of Data Analytics is the ability to see and test the full population. In that case, why is sampling (even monetary sampling) still used, and how is it useful?

3. What does a Z-score greater than 3.0 (or −3.0) suggest? How is that useful in finding extreme values? What type of analysis should we do when we find extreme or outlier values?

4. What are some patterns that could be found using diagnostic analysis? Between which types of variables?

5. In a certain company, one accountant records most of the adjusting journal entries at the end of the month. What type of analysis could be used to identify that this happens and the cumulative size of the transactions that the one accountant records? Is this a problem or if not, when would it be?

6. Which distributions would you recommend be tested using Benford's law? What would a Benford's law evaluation of sales transaction amounts potentially show? What would a test of vendor numbers or employee numbers show? Anything different from a test of invoice or check numbers? Any cases where Benford's law wouldn't work?

7. How could artificial intelligence be used to help with the evaluation of the estimate for the allowance for doubtful accounts? Could past allowances be tested for their predictive ability that might be able to help set allowances in the current period?

8. How do you think sentiment analysis of the 10-K might assess the level of bias (positive or negative) of the annual reports? If management is too positive about the results of the company, can that be viewed as being neutral or impartial?

You're starting to make a name for yourself in the internal audit department. Your manager liked your analysis of the audit plan and now would like you to see what other ways data analytics could be applied beyond the existing audit action sheets.

As you've been reading about risk and fraud, you learned that one common risk is that employees may be tempted to create fictitious suppliers that they use to embezzle money. The premise is simple enough. An employee with access to create master data adds a supplier record for a spouse. She then submits an invoice for "cleaning services" that were never performed and is promptly paid, assuming there isn't good follow-up from the accounts payable department. The employee is smart enough to know that an exact address would raise red flags, so she alters it slightly to avoid detection. Other suspicious addresses may include PO Box addresses because they can obscure the identity of a fictitious supplier.

You know that one way to detect this issue is to look for fuzzy matches, and you're eager to show your manager what you know. Refer to Lab 3-2 for another example. This lab assumes you have completed Lab 5-1.

Techniques

- Data preparation
- Filtering
- Fuzzy matching

Software needed

- Excel

In this lab, you will:

Part 1: Identify the questions.

Part 2: Master the employee and vendor data.

Part 3: Perform the analysis.

Part 4: Address the results.

Part 1: Identify the Questions

Q1. Given what you know about vendor addresses, what types of addresses would be the most suspicious?

Q2. How could a vendor be added to an enterprise system with a suspicious address?

Part 2: Master the Employee and Vendor Data

In Excel

1. Open OneDrive and navigate to your **Current Audit File** folder.
2. Create a new **Excel workbook** and call it **User-Supplier Match**.
3. Rename the **Sheet1** to **Users** and add a new sheet called **Suppliers**.
4. Return to your OneDrive tab and open the **User_Listing** and **Supplier_Listing** files.
5. Copy the data from the **User_Listing** file to the **Users** sheet in your new spreadsheet.
6. Copy the data from the **Supplier_Listing** file to the **Suppliers** sheet in your new spreadsheet.
7. From your **User-Supplier Match** spreadsheet, click **Open in Desktop App**.
8. Take a screenshot (label it 6-1A).

In IDEA

1. Download the **P2P IDEA Audit Data** from Connect, as directed.
2. Unzip the file on your computer.

3. Open IDEA and go to **Home > Projects > Select**.
4. Click the **External Projects** tab, then navigate to your downloaded **P2P IDEA Audit Data** project folder.
5. Click **OK**.
6. Click the **+** to expand the project folder
7. Take a screenshot (label it 6-1B).

Part 3: Perform the Analysis

In Excel

There are a couple ways to look for suspicious addresses. You could look for specific values or use tools to help you link records.

1. Begin by narrowing down addresses with the word "box." This should include "PO Box," "P.O. Box," and "Box."
   a. Select the data in the Supplier sheet, and format it as a table of your choosing (**Home > Styles > Format as Table**).
   b. Click the drop-down arrow next to the **Supplier_Physical_Street_Address1** field to show the sort and filter menu.
   c. Choose **Text Filters > Contains. . .**
   d. Enter **box** and click **OK**.
2. Take a screenshot (label it 6-1C).

In IDEA

1. Open your **Supplier_Listing** table.
2. Go to **Data > Search > Search**.
   a. Text to find: **box**
   b. Fields to look in: **SUPPLIER_PHYSICAL_STREET_ADDRESS1**
   c. Click **OK**.
3. Take a screenshot (label it 6-1D).

Q3. How many PO Box addresses appear?

Q4. Why should you follow up on PO Box addresses?

Now let's look for fuzzy matches.

In Excel

1. Click the drop-down arrow next to the Address field, and choose **Clear Filter From "Supplier_Physical_Street_Address1"**.
2. Perform a fuzzy match on the **Supplier_Physical_Street_Address1,** and **Supplier_Physical_ZipPostalCode** from the **Suppliers** sheet and the **User_Physical_Street_Address1** and **User_Physical_Street_ZipPostalCode** from the **Users** sheet. Refer to the example in Chapter 6 or Lab 3-2 for specific step-by-step instructions.
3. Take a screenshot (label it 6-1E).

In IDEA

IDEA doesn't support fuzzy matching directly, but this works with a few steps by merging the supplier and user tables and then looking for fuzzy duplicate records. The resulting table will show duplicate records that will match despite not being exact.

1. Open the **Supplier_Listing** table.
2. Click **Data > Fields > Append**.
   a. Field name: **TYPE**
   b. Field type: **Virtual Character**
   c. Length: **20**

d. Parameter: **"Supplier"**

e. Click **OK**.

3. Open the **User_Listing** table.

4. Click **Data > Fields > Append**.

   a. Field name: **TYPE**

   b. Field type: **Virtual Character**

   c. Length: **20**

   d. Parameter: **"Employee"**

   e. Click **OK**.

5. Go to **Analysis > Relate > Append**.

   a. Click the + to expand the project folder.

   b. Double-click **SUPPLIER_LISTING**.

   c. Click **OK**.

6. Go to **Data > Fields > Append**.

   a. Field name: **COMBO_ADDRESS**

   b. Field type: **Virtual Character**

   c. Length: **100**

   d. Parameter: = **SUPPLIER_PHYSICAL_STREET_ADDRESS1 + USER_PHYSICAL_STREET_ADDRESS1**

   e. Click **OK**.

7. In your new **Append Databases** table, click **Analysis > Explore > Duplicate Key > Fuzzy**.

   a. Output: **Fuzzy matches**

   b. Similarity degree (%): **Adjust as needed**

   c. Key: **COMBO_ADDRESS**

   d. Click **OK**.

8. Take a screenshot (label it 6-1F).

   Q5. How many fuzzy matches appeared?

   Q6. Which of the matches are suspicious?

   Q7. Which of the matches are normal?

Part 4: Address the Results

   Q8. Are there any limitations to the way you just evaluated addresses?

   Q9. What other data values would indicate that there may be fictitious suppliers in the system?

End of Lab

Lab 6-2   Perform Substantive Tests of Account Balances

Account balances do not exist in databases. Rather, they are the combination of data elements that are added together to come up with a total through queries and formulas. The balance for accounts receivable, for example, is the combination of sales orders, cash receipts, and credit memos.

As an internal auditor, you have been tasked with validating the balance in accounts receivable. Your audit manager has given you a list of receivables for comparison. Additionally, company policy states that accounts receivables should be collected within 60 days of the sale. To test this policy, you have been asked to perform an aging of outstanding accounts.

Techniques

• Use Excel tools to calculate account balances and to group accounts by age

Software

• Excel

In this lab, you will:

Part 1: Identify the questions.

Part 2: Master the sales order and receipt data.

Part 3: Perform the analysis.

Part 1: Identify the Questions

Q1. What data do you need to calculate the account balances?

Q2. What is the formula needed to compute the balance in accounts receivable?

Q3. How would you compute and group the age of each receivable?

Part 2: Master the Data

1. To address the question of the data needed, we will compute the accounts receivable for each customer. That is, as of 9/30/2019, how many customers have yet to pay the amount they owe?

2. Open the File SlainteAging-Sept.xlsx.

3. Create a PivotTable using the Sales_Order data. Ensure that the PivotTable will use the Internal Data Model so that you can retrieve fields from both of the tables in the spreadsheet by placing a check mark next to **Add this data to the Data Model** in the Create PivotTable window. If you need a refresher on working with PivotTables in Excel, refer to Appendix C of the textbook.

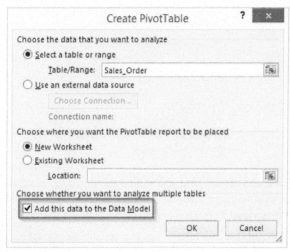

Source: Microsoft Excel 2016.

4. In the PivotTable Fields window, click **All** to view both tables in the workbook.

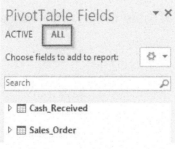

Source: Microsoft Excel 2016.

5. Create a PivotTable that shows the Sales_Order_Total and the Receipt_Amount for each Sales_Order_ID.

Source: Microsoft Excel 2016.

6. The data will look odd at first, and you will be prompted to create relationships. You can allow Excel to auto-detect the relationships, and it will identify the relationship between the Primary and Foreign Keys that exist between the two tables.

Q4. What is the primary and foreign key that relates the two tables in this workbook?

7. After creating the relationships, the top few records of your PivotTable output should look like the following:

Row Labels ▼	Sum of Sales_Order_Total	Sum of Receipt_Amount
20001	319.43	319.43
20002	2425.5	2425.5
20003	848.58	848.58
20004	2024.02	2024.02
20005	4217.51	4217.51
20006	2309.93	2309.93

Source: Microsoft Excel 2016.

8. Copy the data in the PivotTable to a **new spreadsheet** to convert the PivotTable data to a range. Doing so will allow us to be able to identify which of the invoices have yet to be paid in full yet. You can ensure that you're copying only the range by selecting and copying **all of the data** in the PivotTable, **except** for the last row containing the Grand Total.

9. Add a **column** to your new range, and calculate the **difference** between the Sales_Order_Total and the Receipt_Amount.

10. Add a **filter** to the **Difference** column, and filter out all values that appear as **0s**. This will allow you to view all of the invoices that haven't been paid in full yet.

Row Labe ▼	Sum of Sales_Order_Tot ▼	Sum of Receipt_Amou ▼	Differe ▼
20001			
20002			
20003			
20004			
20005			
20006			
20007			
20008			
20009			
20010			
20011			
20012			
20013			
20014			
20015			
20016			
20017			
20018			
20019			
20020			

Filter dropdown menu:
- Sort Smallest to Largest
- Sort Largest to Smallest
- Sort by Color ▸
- Clear Filter From "Difference"
- Filter by Color ▸
- Number Filters ▸
- Search
  - ☑ (Select All)
  - ☐ 0
  - ☑ 202.524
  - ☑ 268.05
  - ☑ 276.99
  - ☑ 284.046
  - ☑ 288.774
  - ☑ 304.514
  - ☑ 309.896
  - ☑ 340.459
- OK Cancel

Source: Microsoft Excel 2016.

11. This data can be made more interesting by identifying how late the payments are. Return to the **Cash_Received** spreadsheet in your workbook.

12. Add a new **column** to the Cash_Received table called **Sales_Order_Date**. This will allow you to easily compare the date of the original Sales Order to the date of the payment.

13. Use a False VLookup formula to look up the date that corresponds with the Sales_Order_ID that each cash receipt corresponds to. Hint: Your lookup value is the Sales_Order_ID (FK), your table_array is the Sales_Order table, and you want the data in column 2 (the Sales_Order_Date) to return.

	A	B	C	D	E	F	M	N	O	P
1	Receipt_I ▼	Customer_I ▼	Sales_Order_ID (FK ▼	Cash_Receipt_Dat ▼	Receipt_Amoun ▼	Sales_Order_Date ▼				
2	10001	2024	20001	1/10/2019	63.886	=VLOOKUP([@[Sales_Order_ID (FK)]],Sales_Order,2,FALSE)				

Source: Microsoft Excel 2016.

14. Now that you have the Sales_Order_Date easily accessible, you can create another column to calculate the difference between the dates. Create a new **column** labeled **Age**, and subtract the **Cash_Receipt_Date** from the **Sales_Order_Date**.

15. Your next step is to create a True VLookup formula to assign each cash receipt to an aging bucket. Create an **aging table** with the following information somewhere on your spreadsheet:

0	0–30
30	31–60
60	61–90
90	90+

16. Add another new **column** to the Cash_Received table labeled Bucket, and create a True VLookup formula to identify the bucket for each invoice.

F	G	H	I	J	K
Sales_Order_Date ▾	Age ▾	bucket ▾			
1/1/2019	9	=VLOOKUP([@Age],$J$4:$K$7,2,TRUE)			
1/1/2019	11				
1/3/2019	10			0	0-30
1/1/2019	18			30	31-60
1/1/2019	19			60	61-90
1/1/2019	21			90	90+
1/2/2019	21				

Source: Microsoft Excel 2016.

17. We can quickly create a summary of how many invoices fall into each bucket using Excel's COUNTIF function. In the column to the right of your aging table, create a **column** labeled **Count**.

18. In the cell to the right of your 0–30 bucket, type the COUNTIF function. COUNTIF requires two arguments, **range** and **criteria**. The range in this case is the bucket column. The criteria is 0–30. COUNTIF will count every instance of 0–30 in the bucket column.

G	H	I	J	K	L	M	N	O
Age ▾	bucket ▾							
9	0-30							
11	0-30				Count			
10	0-30			0 0-30	=countif(Cash_Received[bucket],K4)			
18	0-30			30 31-60				
19	0-30			60 61-90				
21	0-30			90 90+				
21	0-30							

Source: Microsoft Excel 2016.

19. Repeat the steps for the remaining three buckets. The top two records in the Count column should return the following data:

		Count
0	0-30	350
30	31-60	285

Source: Microsoft Excel 2016.

20. Return to your PivotTable, and refresh the data so that you can pull in your new fields for further analysis. You can refresh your data by clicking the **Refresh** button in the **Analyze** tab from the ribbon.

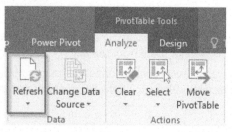

Source: Microsoft Excel 2016.

21. You should now be able to add the **bucket** field to the PivotTable. Do so. Remove Sales_Order_Total from the PivotTable as well.

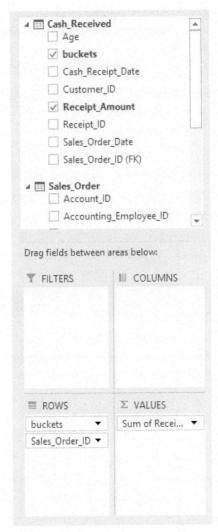

Source: Microsoft Excel 2016.

22. Collapse the fields so that you do not see the detail of each invoice within the buckets, but only the totals. The top two records of the PivotTable will appear as the following:

Row Labels	Sum of Receipt_Amount
⊞ 0-30	333198.629
⊞ 31-60	405447.962

Source: Microsoft Excel 2016.

23. Save your file.

    Q5.   Of the not yet collected balances in each of the four buckets, which bucket is least likely to be collected? Which bucket is most likely to be collected? How would this help us come up with an allowance for doubtful accounts?

24. Now, let's assume that three more months have passed. Open up the spreadsheet **SlainteAging-Dec.xlsx.**

    Q6.   Based on what you have viewed with the September data, what do you expect to find as far as outstanding balances now that the year has finished at the end of December?

25. Repeat the same steps as you did above in the new dataset.
   a. Create a PivotTable that shows the Sales_Order_Total and Receipt_Amount for each Sales_Order_ID.
      i. Remember to use the Internal Data Model and to build relationships so that the data in your PivotTable is accurate.
   b. Create a range from your PivotTable data and calculate the difference between the Sales_Order_Total and the Receipt_Amount. Filter the Difference column to show only the invoices that haven't been paid in full yet.
   c. Return to the Cash_Received table and create the additional columns so that you can identify the aging bucket for each invoice.
   d. Create a PivotTable to identify which invoices fall into each bucket.

26. Save your file as Lab6-2December.xslx, ensuring that the PivotTable with buckets is included in your final spreadsheet.

End of Lab

Lab 6-3   Finding Duplicate Payments

Companies occasionally make duplicate payments to suppliers due to lack of internal controls, errors, or fraud. In this lab you will analyze payment transactions to collect evidence about whether duplicate payments have been made to suppliers.

Technique

- Search for duplicates

Software needed

- Excel or IDEA

In this lab, you will:

    Part 1: Identify the questions.
    Part 2: Master the purchase order and payment data.
    Part 3: Perform the analysis.

Part 1: Identify the Questions

    Q1.   Before computerization or Data Analytics, how would companies find that they had made duplicate payments?

Part 2: Master the Data

    Q2.   What data items do you need to be able to find duplicate payments? Would the date of the duplicate payments usually be the same or different?

Part 3: Perform the Analysis

In Excel

1. Open OneDrive and go to the **Current Audit Data** folder.
2. Open the **Payments_Made** spreadsheet.
3. Click **Open in Desktop App** to load it in the desktop version of Excel.
4. Select the **Invoice_Reference** column and choose **Home > Styles > Conditional Formatting > Highlight Cell Rules > Duplicate Values. . .**, and click **OK**.

5. Select all of the data, choose **Home > Styles > Format as Table**, and pick a light, non-banded theme.
6. Click the drop-down next to **Invoice_Reference**, choose **Filter by color. . .**, and select the highlight color used in step 4.
7. Take a screenshot (label it 6-3A).
8. Remove the filter on **Invoice_Reference** and repeat steps 4–6 on the **Payment_Amount** column.

In IDEA

1. Open the **P2P IDEA Audit Data** project in IDEA.
2. Open the **Payments_Made** table.
3. Go to **Analysis > Explore > Duplicate Key > Detection**.
   a. Click **Output duplicate records**
   b. Click **Key**, then choose **INVOICE_REFERENCE** from the drop-down list and click **OK**.
   c. Click **OK**.
4. Take a screenshot (label it 6-3B).

5. Repeat steps 2-3 on the **Payment_Amount** column.

   Q3. How many duplicate records did you locate?

   Q4. What course of action would you recommend?

End of Lab

Lab 6-4   Comprehensive Case: Dillard's Store Data: Hypothesis Testing (Part I)

Company summary

Dillard's is a department store with approximately 330 stores in 29 states. Its headquarters is in Little Rock, Arkansas. You can learn more about Dillard's by looking at finance.yahoo.com (Ticker symbol = DDS) and the Wikipedia site for DDS. You'll quickly note that William T. Dillard II is an accounting grad of the University of Arkansas and the Walton College of Business, which may be why he shared transaction data with us to make available for this lab and labs throughout this text.

Data

The data for this lab and all other Dillard's labs must be accessed through the University of Arkansas Remote Desktop. Directions for accessing the Remote Desktop can be found at www.mhhe.com/richardsondaa2e. See your instructor for login credentials. The 2016 Dillard's data covers all transactions over the period 1/1/2014 to 10/17/2016.

Software needed

- Microsoft SQL Server Management Studio (available on the Remote Desktop at the University of Arkansas)
- Excel 2016 (available on the Remote Desktop at the University of Arkansas)
- PowerPivot add-in for Excel (available on the Remote Desktop at the University of Arkansas). If you do not see the PowerPivot tab on the Excel ribbon, you will need to enable the add-in.

In this lab, you will:

- Test a hypothesis in Excel. Specifically, we will see if the returns in January are greater than the rest of the year.

Part 1: Identify the Questions

January returns are associated with Christmas. Most retail establishments have fairly generous return policies in case a gift received was the wrong size or just not the desired item. Do retail companies have the same generous policies throughout the year, and do customers take advantage of them throughout the year?

Therefore, our specific question that we hope to test is whether there a significant difference in the amount of returns in January compared to the rest of the year.

Part 2: Master the Data

1. Extract data from SQL Server into Excel using Excel's **Get & Transform** functionality using the following query. If you need a refresher on how to do so, refer to Appendix F of the textbook. In this case, we will Edit the data when you see a preview of it.

```
Select Tran_Date, Tran_Type, SUM(Tran_Amt) AS Amount
From Transact
Group By Tran_Date, Tran_Type
Order By Tran_Date
```

This query will load all of the transactional history for both sales and refunds, grouped by day, as well as transactional type. The way the data are organized, all of the dollar amounts for sales and for refunds are in the same attribute, Tran_Amt, and the transaction type (i.e., Sale or Return) is differentiated with the attribute Tran_Type. In order to create a measure based on sales and refunds as separate values, we need to split the Tran_Amt data into two columns, one dedicated to sales, and one for the refund amounts. To do so, we will use the Query Editor to transform the data by "pivoting" the Tran_Type column.

2. From the **Query Editor** tool, select the **Tran_Type** column and click **Pivot Column** from the **Transform** tab.

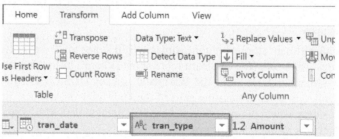

Source: Microsoft Excel 2016.

3. Change the **Values Column** drop-down to **Amount** in the **Pivot Column** window, then click **OK**.

Source: Microsoft Excel 2016.

4. Now that the data have been transformed, you can load them into Excel. Click **Close & Load** from the **Home** tab. It will take a moment for all of the data (1,014 rows) to load into Excel.

5. Create a PivotTable by clicking PivotTable from the **Insert** tab on the Excel ribbon.
6. Even though you have loaded the data into Excel, you have not added it to Excel's Internal Data Model. To do so, place a check mark in the box next to **Add this data to the Data Model** in the **Create PivotTable** window.

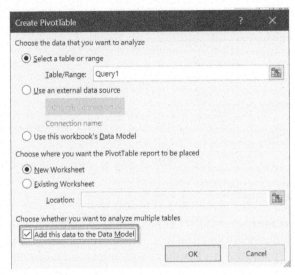

Source: Microsoft Excel 2016.

7. To create a measure for **Refunds over Purchases,** select **Measures > New Measure. . .** from the **PowerPivot** tab in the Excel ribbon. If the PowerPivot tab is not available, you can add it from Excel **Options > Add-ins > COM Add-ins**, then place a check mark next to Microsoft Power Pivot for Excel.

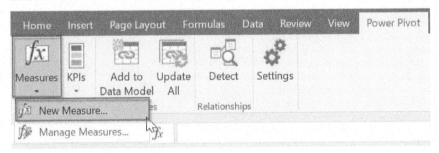

Source: Microsoft Excel 2016.

8. The new measure's name defaults to **measure 1**, which isn't very descriptive. Because we'll be measuring average Transaction amount, we'll change the name to R/P. Type **R/P** over the default text.

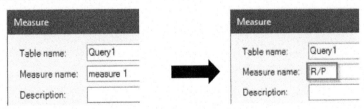

Source: Microsoft Excel 2016.

9. The formula will auto-populate as you type; begin typing SUM, then fill in the remainder of the measure to divide the purchasing transactions by the refund transactions: =sum(Query1[R])/SUM(Query1[P]).
10. At the bottom of the **Measure** window is an option to select a category. The Category has no bearing on how the measure or the KPI will work. For this measure, we'll leave it on the default of General. Click **OK** to create the measure.

Source: Microsoft Excel 2016.

11. Now that the measure is created, it has been added to the **PivotTable Fields** window. Create a PivotTable to view only the January dates (place **Tran_Date(Month)** in the filter) and days along the rows. Use the new measure you created, **R/P**, as the value.

Source: Microsoft Excel 2016.

Parsing out month and day will require placing **Tran_Date** in the rows column first, then removing the **Year** and **Quarter** attributes that automatically populate. Drag and Drop **Tran_Date(month)** to the filter, and keep the **Tran_Date** attribute in the rows.

12. Since we want to work with data from only January, we need to filter the PivotTable. Click the drop-down next to the Tran_Date (Month) filter, select **All** to expand the options, and select **Jan**. Click **OK** to save the filter.

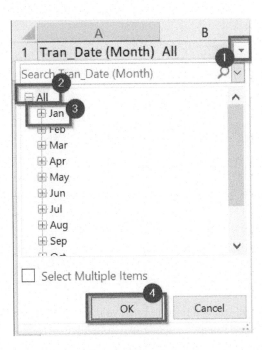

This PivotTable will provide the data we need for one part of our hypothesis test—the values from all January dates in the database. Now we need to separate the values from all non-January dates in the database. We'll do this by copying the PivotTable you just created, and modifying the filter.

13. Select the entire PivotTable (including the Filter cells), and copy the selection.

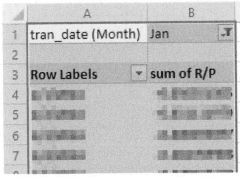

Source: Microsoft Excel 2016.

14. Place your cursor in cell **D1**, and paste the PivotTable there.
15. Now you can modify the filter. Place a check mark in the box next to **Select Multiple Items,** then scroll to the top of the filter options to select **All**. Finally, scroll down to take the check mark out of the box next to **January**. This will provide the data for all transactions, except for the items that are from January.

16. Take a screenshot of your results (label it 6-4A).
17. To clarify the difference between the two PivotTables, you can rename the labels that say sum of R/P in each table. Place your cursor inside the cell with the **sum of R/P** label, and type in **January** and **Rest of the Year** in its place:

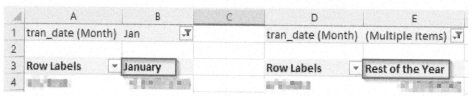

Source: Microsoft Excel 2016.

Part 3: Perform an Analysis of the Data

To run a hypothesis test in Excel, you need to first enable the **Data Analysis ToolPak** add-in. To do so, follow this menu path: **File > Options > Add-ins**. From this window, select the **Go...** button, and then place a check mark in the box next to **Analysis ToolPak**. Once you click **OK** you will be able to access the ToolPak from the **Data** tab on the Excel ribbon.

18. Click the **Data Analysis** button from the Excel ribbon and select **t-Test: Two-Sample Assuming Unequal Variances.** This will allow us to run a hypothesis test to see if there are significant differences between the January transactions and the rest of the year.
19. In the **t-Test** window, you will need to input your variable ranges. For **Variable 1 Range,** select all of the values except for the Grand Total that correspond with the January PivotTable (just the values—you do not need to select the corresponding dates).

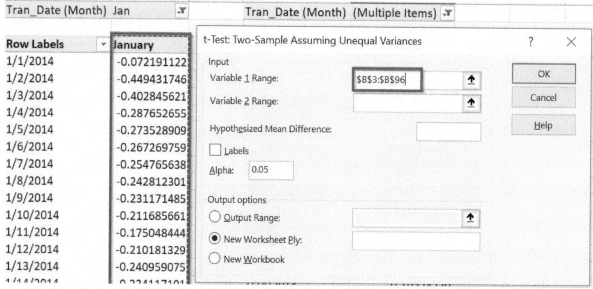

Source: Microsoft Excel 2016.

20. Follow the same pattern for Variable 2 by selecting all of the data that correspond with the second PivotTable's values, except for the Grand Total.

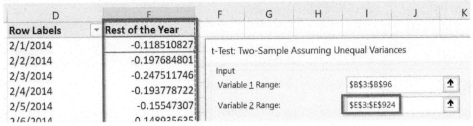

Source: Microsoft Excel 2016.

21. Place a check mark in the box next to **Labels** to ensure that the labels for the data (**January** and **Rest of the Year**) show up in the resulting output, and click **OK**.

Source: Microsoft Excel 2016.

Part 4: Address and Refine the Results

Q1. Using the *p*-values (or the t-statistic and critical values), are the returns as a percentage of sales in January greater than, less than, or the same as the returns as a percentage of sales for the rest of the year?

Q2. What can we conclude about returns?

Q3. Do you think most Christmas sales are returned in January, or do they also occur in early January? How would you modify your tests to take this into account?

Part 5: Communicate Insights and Track Outcomes

In Chapter 7, we'll learn more about dashboards and ways to communicate these results to management.

Q4. Do you think knowing the level of returns is important to management?

Q5. Assuming management want returns information, do you think they need this information on a daily, weekly, or monthly basis? Due to information overload, they can't track everything on a daily basis, but some information is important to disclose frequently.

End of Lab

Company summary

Dillard's is a department store with approximately 330 stores in 29 states. Its headquarters is in Little Rock, Arkansas. You can learn more about Dillard's by looking at finance.yahoo.com (Ticker symbol = DDS) and the Wikipedia site for DDS. You'll quickly note that William T. Dillard II is an accounting grad of the University of Arkansas and the Walton College of Business, which may be why he shared transaction data with us to make available for this lab and labs throughout this text.

Data

The data for this lab and all other Dillard's labs must be accessed through the University of Arkansas Remote Desktop. Directions for accessing the Remote Desktop can be found at www.mhhe.com/richardsondaa2e. See your instructor for login credentials. The 2016 Dillard's data covers all transactions over the period 1/1/2014 to 10/17/2016.

Software needed

- Microsoft SQL Server Management Studio (available on the Remote Desktop at the University of Arkansas)
- Excel 2016 (available on the Remote Desktop at the University of Arkansas)
- Tableau (available on the Remote Desktop at the University of Arkansas)

In this lab, you will:

- Develop a dashboard to display returns percentages across months and across states.

Prerequisite

- **Lab 6-4.** This lab requires some of the skills covered in Lab 6-4 for steps 1–4. If you haven't completed Lab 6-4, then you can still read through the steps in that lab to see the screenshots of the ETL process in Excel.
- **Lab 4-2.** Some Tableau skills from Lab 4-2 are also expected. If you haven't completed Lab 4-2, you can still read through the steps in that lab to learn the basics of how to build a map and a dashboard in Tableau.

Part 1: Identify the Questions

After performing a hypothesis test to determine that there is a significant difference between January's returns percentage and the rest of the months in a given year, you would like to dig further into the data to visualize that difference across months, and also across stores and in comparison to sales data.

Part 2: Master the Data

1. Loading the data into Tableau from the original SQL Server database first requires some transformation in Excel. Extract and load the transactional and store data into Excel's Query Editor using the following query:

```
Select Tran_Date, Tran_Type, State, Store.Store, SUM(Tran_amt) AS Amount
From Transact
Inner Join Store
```

```
On Transact.Store = Store.Store
Group By Tran_Date, Tran_Type, State, Store.Store
Order by Tran_Date
```

2. Pivot the **Tran_Type** column on the **Amount** values in the **Query Editor** window.
3. Close and load the data into Excel.
4. Once the data have loaded (298,527 rows), save the spreadsheet as Lab 6-6.xlsx.
5. Open Tableau, and connect to an Excel Data source. Browse and open the file you just saved. Now that the data are loaded into their final destination for analysis, Tableau, you have one more step to prepare the data. You need to create the Returns Percentage measure, just like it had to be created in Lab 6-4 in Excel.
6. On **Sheet 1**, create a **Calculated Field**. Right-click in the **Measures Area**, and select **Create Calculated Field**.

Source: Microsoft Excel 2016.

7. Name your new field **R/P**, and create the calculation SUM([R])/SUM([P]), then click **OK**.

Source: Microsoft Excel 2016.

Part 3: Perform the Analysis

8. We will create three data visualizations to display on a returns dashboard. First, we will create a map displaying the sales dollars per state.
9. Drag and drop the **state** dimension into the middle of the Tableau drawing to start your map.
10. Double-click the **P** measure to display customer purchases. Tableau will default to a symbol map, so change this to a filled map using the **Show Me** window.

11. Name the sheet **Sales by State** and take a screenshot (label it 6-5A).
12. Right-click your new **Sales by State** sheet, and click **Duplicate** to start a new sheet with this map as a base.
13. In the new sheet, drag the **P** measure out of the **Marks** card, and replace it with the calculated measure that you created, **R/P**. Drag **R/P** onto color in the **Marks** card so that the map has the correct shading.
14. Name the sheet **Returns Percentage by State** and take a screenshot (label it 6-5B).
15. Open a new sheet. Drag **Tran_Date** to the rows. It will default to **Years**. but you can expand the pill twice to see **Quarters**, then **Months**. Remove the **Years** and **Quarters** pills so that only the **Months** remains.
16. Double-click **R/P** so that it appears in the **Marks** card.
17. In the **Show Me** tab, replace the tabular data that Tableau defaults to with a highlight table. This may have caused Tableau to change your **Months** pill from the **Rows** to the **Columns**. You can just drag the **Months** pill back down to **Rows**.
18. Create a new dashboard. Arrange the three visualizations in whichever way you find most visually pleasing and easiest to read and take a screenshot (label it 6-5C).
19. Using the small filter button in the top right of the **Returns Percentage by State** visual on the dashboard, designate that visual as a filter for the entire dashboard. Now, you can click any of the states on that map to focus on that state in the sales map, as well as to see how the **Returns Percentages** differ monthly for that particular state.
20. Take a screenshot (label it 6-5D).

Part 4: Address and Refine the Results

Q1. What does getting the detail data (or drilled-down data) allow you to test and see? Which of these detail data would be most useful for management?

Q2. Why would it be useful to get return data by product code or product category? Would that cause the company to change its return policy for certain items?

Q3. What other data visualizations would be meaningful to drill down into these data?

End of Lab

Chapter 7

Managerial Analytics

A Look at This Chapter

This chapter explains how to apply Data Analytics to measure performance and answer managerial accounting questions. By measuring past performance and comparing it to targeted goals, we are able to assess how well a company is working toward a goal. Also, we can determine required adjustments to how decisions are made or how business processes are run, if any.

A Look Back

In Chapter 6, we focused on substantive testing within the audit setting. We highlighted discussion of the audit plan, and account balances were checked. We also highlighted the use of statistical analysis to find errors or fraud in the audit setting. In addition, we discussed the use of clustering to detect outliers and the use of Benford's analysis.

A Look Ahead

In Chapter 8, we will focus on how to access and analyze financial statement data. Through analysis of ratios and trends we identify how companies appear to stakeholders. We also discuss how to analyze financial performance, and how visualizations help find insight into the data. Finally, we discuss the use of text mining to analyze the sentiment in financial reporting data.

For years, **Kenya Red Cross** had attempted to refine its strategy and align its daily activities with its overall strategic goals. It had annual strategic planning meetings with external consultants that always resulted in the consultants presenting a new strategy to the organization that the **Red Cross** didn't have a particularly strong buy-in to, and the **Red Cross** never felt confident in what was developed or what it would mean for its future. When **Kenya Red Cross** went through a Data Analytics–backed Balanced Scorecard planning process for the first time, though, it immediately felt like its organization's mission and vision was involved in the strategic planning and that "strategy" was no longer so vague. The Balanced Scorecard approach helped the **Kenya Red Cross** align its goals into measurable metrics. The organization prided itself on being "first in and last out" but hadn't actively measured its success in that goal, nor had the organization fully analyzed how being the first in and last out of disaster scenarios affected other goals and areas of its organization. Using Data Analytics to refine its strategy and assign measurable performance metrics to its goals, **Kenya Red Cross** felt confident that its everyday activities were linked to measurable goals that would help the organization reach its goals and maintain a strong positive reputation and impact through its service. Exhibit 7-1 gives an illustration of the Balanced Scorecard at the **Kenya Red Cross**.

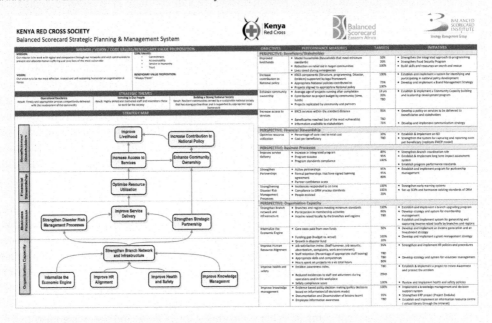

EXHIBIT 7-1   **The Kenya Red Cross Balanced Scorecard**

Source: Reprinted with permission from Balanced Scorecard Institute, a Strategy Management Group company. Copyright 2008–2017.

OBJECTIVES

After reading this chapter, you should be able to:

LO 7-1   Understand management accounting questions.

LO 7-2   Evaluate management requirements and identify useful KPIs.

LO 7-3   Evaluate underlying management data quality.

LO 7-4   Understand how to drill-down and follow up with results.

LO 7-1

Understand
management
accounting
questions.

IDENTIFYING MANAGEMENT ACCOUNTING QUESTIONS

In the past six chapters, you learned how to apply the IMPACT model to data analysis projects in general and, specifically, to internal and external auditing and financial statement analysis. The same accounting information used in internal and external auditing and financial statement analysis can also be used to determine how closely an organization is meeting its strategic objectives. Together with operational and performance measurement data, we can better determine the gaps in actual company performance and targeted strategic objectives, data should be condensed into easily digestible and useful digital dashboards, providing precisely the information needed to help make operational decisions that support a company's strategic direction.

This chapter brings us to how to apply Data Analytics to measure performance. More specifically, we measure past performance and compare it to targeted goals to assess how well a company is working toward a goal. In addition, we can determine required adjustments to how decisions are made or how business processes are run, if any.

Management accounting is one of the primary areas where Data Analytics helps the decision-making process. From assigning costs to jobs, processes, and activities; to understanding cost behavior and relevant costs in decisions; and to forecasting and performance evaluation, managers rely on real-time data to evaluate the effectiveness of their strategies. These data help with the planning, management, and controlling of firm resources.

Managers rely on a combination of descriptive analytics to compute the results of an initiative, diagnostic analytics to compare those results to a benchmark (such as a budget), predictive analytics to plan for future periods, and prescriptive analytics to guide the controlling process.

Relevant Costs

Most other management decisions rely on the interpretation of cost classification and which costs are relevant or not. Aggregating the total costs of, say, the cost to produce and item versus the cost to purchase them in a make-or-buy or outsourcing decision may be an appropriate use of descriptive analytics, as would determining capacity to accept special orders or processing further.

Relevant costs relates to relevant data, similar to the scope of and audit. Managers understand that companies are collecting a lot of data, and there is a push to find patterns in the data that help identify opportunities to connect with customers and better evaluate performance. However, not all data are relevant to the decision-making process. The more relevant data that are available to inform the decision and include in the relevant costs, the more confident management can be of the answer. Of course, there is always a trade-off between the cost of collecting that information and the incremental value of the analysis. Be careful not to include the sunk cost of data that has already been collected while considering the opportunity cost of not utilizing data to make profitable business decisions.

Key Performance Indicators and Variance Analysis

Because data are increasingly available and affordable for companies to access and store, and because the growth in technology has created robust and affordable business intelligence tools, data and information are becoming the key components for decision making, replacing limited analysis and complementing management's intuition. Specifically, various measures and metrics are defined, compiled from the data, and used for decision making. **Performance metrics** are, rather simply, any number used to measure performance at a company. The amount of inventory on hand is a metric, and that metric gains meaning when compared to a baseline (e.g., how much inventory was on hand yesterday?). A specific type of performance metric is a **key performance indicator (KPI)**. Just like any performance metric, a KPI should help managers keep track of performance and strategic objectives, but the KPIs are performance metrics that stand out as the most important—that is, "key" metrics that influence decision making and strategy. Nearly every organization can use data to create the same performance metrics (although, of course, with different results), but it is dependent upon each organization's particular strategy which performance metrics that organization would deem to be a KPI.

Variance analysis allows managers to evaluate the KPIs and how far they vary from the expected outcome. For example, managers compare actual results to budgeted results to determine whether a variance is favorable or unfavorable, similar to that shown in Exhibit 7-2. The ability to use these types of bullet charts to not only identify the benchmark, but also to see the relative distance from the goal helps managers identify root causes of the variance (e.g., the price we pay for a raw material or the increased volume of sales) and drill-down to determine the good performance to replicate and the poor performance to eliminate.

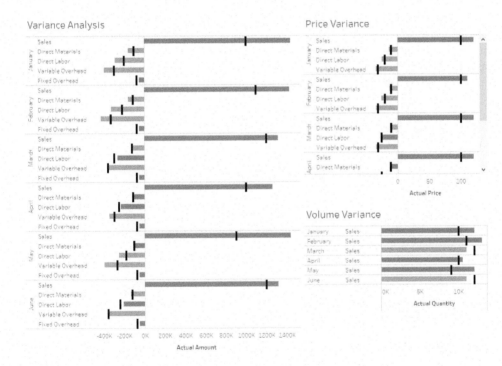

EXHIBIT 7-2
Variance Analysis Identifies Favorable and Unfavorable Variances

Cost Behavior

Managers must also understand what is driving the costs and profits to plan for the future and apply to budgets or use as input for lean accounting processes. For example, they must evaluate mixed costs to predict the portion of fixed and variable costs for a given period. Predictive analytics, such as regression analysis, might evaluate actual production volume and total costs to estimate the mixed cost line equation, such as the one shown in Exhibit 7-3.

This example was calculated using a scatter plot chart over a 12-month period in Excel. The mixed costs can be interpreted as consisting of fixed costs of approximately $181,480 per month (the intercept) and variable costs of approximately $13.30 per unit produced. The R^2 value of 0.84 tells us that this line fits the data pretty well and will predict the correct value 84 percent of the time.

EXHIBIT 7-3
Regression Analysis of
Mixed Costs

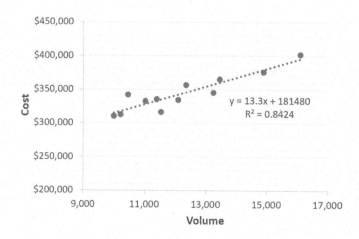

Regression and other predictive techniques help managers identify outliers, anomalies, and poor performers so they can act accordingly. They also rely on more observations so the prediction is much more accurate than other rudimentary accounting calculations, such as the High-Low method. These same trend analyses inform the master budget from sales to cash and can be combined with sensitivity or what-if analyses to predict a range of values.

✓ **PROGRESS CHECK**

1. If a manager is trying to decide whether to discontinue a product or division, he or she would look at the contribution margin of that object. What are some examples of relevant data that would be useful in this calculation? Irrelevant data?
2. A bullet chart (as shown in Exhibit 7-2) uses a reference line to show actual performance relative to a benchmark. What advantages does a bullet graph have over a gauge, such as a fan with red, yellow, and green zones and a needle pointing to the current value?

LO 7-2

Evaluate management requirements and identify useful KPIs.

BALANCED SCORECARD AND KEY PERFORMANCE INDICATORS

As you will recall from Chapter 4, the most effective way to communicate the results of any data analysis project is through data visualization. A project in which you are determining the right KPIs and communicating them to the appropriate stakeholders is no different. One of the most common ways to communicate a variety of KPIs is through a digital dashboard. A **digital dashboard** is an interactive report showing the most important metrics to help users understand how a company or an organization is performing. There are many public digital dashboards available; for example, the **Walton College of Business** at the University of Arkansas has an interactive dashboard to showcase enrollment, where students are from, where students study abroad, student retention and graduation rates, and where alumni work after graduation (**https://walton.uark.edu/osie/reports/data-dashboard. php**). The public dashboard detailing student diversity at the Walton College can be used by prospective students to learn more about the university and by the university itself to assess how it is doing in meeting goals. If the university has a goal of increasing gender balance in enrollment, for example, then monitoring the "Diverse Walton" metrics, pictured in Exhibit 7-4, can help the university understand how it is doing at reaching that goal.

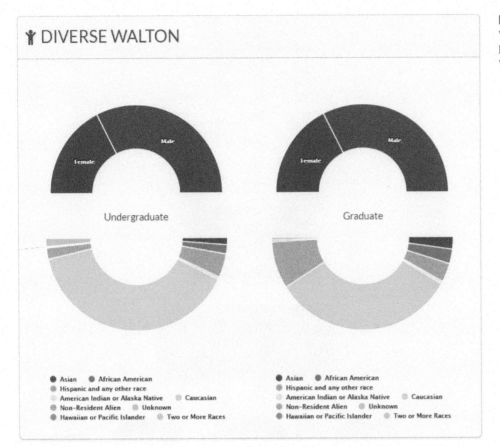

EXHIBIT 7-4
Walton College Digital
Dashboard—Diverse
Walton

Digital dashboards provide interesting information, but their value is maximized when the metrics provided on the dashboard are used to affect decision making and action. One iteration of a digital dashboard is the Balanced Scorecard. The **Balanced Scorecard** was created by Robert S. Kaplan and David P. Norton in 1996 to help companies turn their strategic goals into action by identifying the most important metrics to measure, as well as identifying target goals to compare metrics against.

The Balanced Scorecard is comprised of four components: financial (or stewardship), customer (or stakeholder), internal process, and organizational capacity (or learning and growth). As depicted in Exhibit 7-5, the measures in each category affect other categories, and all four should be directly related to the strategic objectives of an organization.

For each of the four components, objectives, measures, targets, and initiatives are identified. *Objectives* should be aligned with strategic goals of the organization, *measures* are the KPIs that show how well the organization is doing at meeting its objective, and *targets* should be achievable goals toward which to move the metric. *Initiatives* should be the actions that an organization can take to move its specified metrics in the direction of their stated target goal. Exhibit 7-6 is an example of different objectives that an organization might identify for each component. You can see how certain objectives relate to other objectives—for example, if the organization increases process efficiency (in the internal process component row), that should help with the objective of lowering cost in the financial component row.

Understanding how the four components interact to answer different types of questions and meet different strategic goals is critical when it comes to identifying the right measures to include in the dashboard, as well as using those measures to help with decision making.

EXHIBIT 7-5
Components of the
Balanced Scorecard

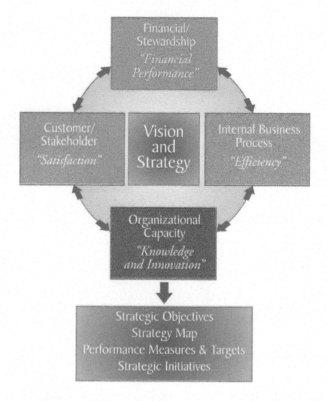

EXHIBIT 7-6
An Example of a
Balanced Scorecard
Reprinted with
permission from
Balanced Scorecard
Institute, a Strategy
Management Group
Company. Copyright
2008–2017.

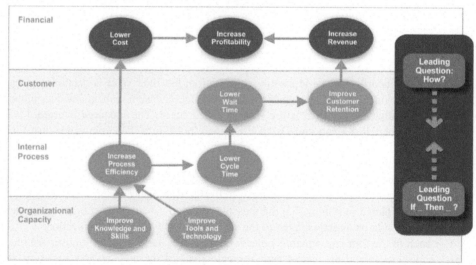

Creating a Balanced Scorecard or any type of digital dashboard to present KPIs for decision making follows the IMPACT model.

Bernard Marr identified 75 KPIs to measure performance in the different components that he considers the most important for decision makers to know, and these 75 KPIs are compiled in Exhibit 7-7. In a Balanced Scorecard, each component should focus on 3 or 4 KPIs. Including all 75 of these metrics in a given dashboard would be overwhelming and difficult to manage, but depending on the strategy of the company and the initiatives that are chosen as focal points, any of the KPIs in Exhibit 7-7 may be optimal for measuring (and ultimately improving) performance.

Financial Performance KPIs	Operational KPIs
1. Net Profit	38. Six Sigma Level
2. Net Profit Margin	39. Capacity Utilization Rate (CUR)
3. Gross Profit Margin	40. Process Waste Level
4. Operating Profit Margin	41. Order Fulfillment Cycle Time
5. EBITDA	42. Delivery in Full, on Time (DIFOT) Rate
6. Revenue Growth Rate	43. Inventory Shrinkage Rate (ISR)
7. Total Shareholder Return (TSR)	44. Project Schedule Variance (PSV)
8. Economic Value Added (EVA)	45. Project Cost Variance (PCV)
9. Return on Investment (ROI)	46. Earned Value (EV) Metric
10. Return on Capital Employed (ROCE)	47. Innovation Pipeline Strength (IPS)
11. Return on Assets (ROA)	48. Return on Innovation Investment (ROI2)
12. Return on Equity (ROE)	49. Time to Market
13. Debt-to-Equity (D/E) Ratio	50. First-Pass Yield (FPY)
14. Cash Conversion Cycle (CCC)	51. Rework Level
15. Working Capital Ratio	52. Quality Index
16. Operating Expense Ratio (OER)	53. Overall Equipment Effectiveness (OEE)
17. CAPEX to Sales Ratio	54. Process or Machine Downtime Level
18. Price-to-Earnings Ratio (P/E Ratio)	55. First Contact Resolution (FCR)

Customer KPIs	Employee Performance KPIs
19. Net Promoter Score (NPS)	56. Human Capital Value Added (HCVA)
20. Customer Retention Rate	57. Revenue per Employee
21. Customer Satisfaction Index	58. Employee Satisfaction Index
22. Customer Profitability Score	59. Employee Engagement Level
23. Customer Lifetime Value	60. Staff Advocacy Score
24. Customer Turnover Rate	61. Employee Churn Rate
25. Customer Engagement	62. Average Employee Tenure
26. Customer Complaints	63. Absenteeism Bradford Factor
	64. 360-Degree Feedback Score
	65. Salary Competitiveness Ratio (SCR)
	66. Time to Hire
	67. Training Return on Investment

Marketing KPIs	Environmental and Social Sustainability KPIs
27. Market Growth Rate	68. Carbon Footprint
28. Market Share	69. Water Footprint
29. Brand Equity	70. Energy Consumption
30. Cost per Lead	71. Saving Levels Due to Conservation and Improvement Efforts
31. Conversion Rate	72. Supply Chain Miles
32. Search Engine Rankings (by keyword) and Click-Through Rate	73. Waste Reduction Rate
33. Page Views and Bounce Rate	74. Waste Recycling Rate
34. Customer Online Engagement Level	75. Product Recycling Rate
35. Online Share of Voice (OSOV)	
36. Social Networking Footprint	
37. Klout Score	

EXHIBIT 7-7
Suggested KPIs That Every Manager Needs to Know[1]

Source: https://www.linkedin.com/pulse/20130905053105-64875646-the-75-kpis-every-manager-needs-to-know

The Balanced Scorecard is based around a company's strategy. A well-defined mission, vision, and set of values are integral in creating and maintaining a successful culture. In many cases, when tradition appears to stifle an organization, the two concepts of culture and tradition must be separated. An established sense of purpose and a robust tradition of service can serve as a catalyst to facilitate successful organizational changes. A proper strategy for growth considers what a firm does well and how it achieves it. With a proper strategy, an organization is less likely to be hamstrung by a "this is how we've always done it" mentality.

If a strategy is already developed, or after the strategy has been fully defined, it needs to be broken down into goals that can be measured. Identifying the pieces of the strategy that can be measured is critical. Without tracking performance and measuring results, the strategy is only symbolic. The adage "what gets measured, gets done" shows the motivation behind aligning strategy statements with KPIs—people are more inclined to focus their work and their projects on initiatives that are being paid attention to and measured. Of course, simply measuring something doesn't imply that anything will be done to improve the measure—the attainable initiative attached to a metric indicating how it can be improved is a key piece to ensuring that people will work to improve the measure.

 PROGRESS CHECK

3. To illustrate what KPIs emphasize in "what gets measured, gets done," **Walmart** has a goal of a "zero waste future."[2] How does reporting Walmart's waste recycling rate help the organization figure out if it is getting closer to its goal? Do you believe it helps the organization accomplish its goals?

4. How can management identify useful KPIs? How could Data Analytics help with that?

LO 7-3

Evaluate underlying management data quality.

MASTER THE DATA AND PERFORM THE TEST PLAN

Once the measures have been determined, the data that are necessary to showcase those measures need to be identified. You were first introduced to how to identify and obtain necessary data in Chapter 2 through the ETL (extract, transform, and load) process. In addition to working through the same data request process that is detailed in Chapter 2, there are two other questions to consider when obtaining data and evaluating their quality:

1. How often do the data get updated in the system? This will help you be aware of how up-to-date your metrics are so that you interpret the changes over time appropriately.
2. Additionally, how often do you need to see updated data? If the data in the system are updated on a near-real-time basis, it may not be necessary for you to have new updates pushed to your scorecard as frequently. For example, if your team will assess their progress only in a once-a-week meeting, there is no need to have a constantly updating scorecard.

[2]http://corporate.walmart.com/2016grr/enhancing-sustainability/moving-toward-a-zero-waste-future (accessed August 2017).

While the data for calculating KPIs are likely stored in the company's enterprise system or accounting information system, the digital dashboard containing the KPIs for data analysis should be created in a data visualization tool, such as Excel or Tableau. Loading the data into these tools should be done with precision and should be validated to ensure the data imported were complete and accurate.

Designing data visualizations and selecting the right way to express data (as whole numbers, percentages, or absolute values, etc.) was discussed in Chapter 4. Specifically for digital dashboards, the format of your dashboard can follow the pattern of a Balanced Scorecard with a strategy map, or it can take on a different format. Exhibit 7-8 shows a template for building out the objectives, measures, targets, and initiatives into a Balanced Scorecard format.

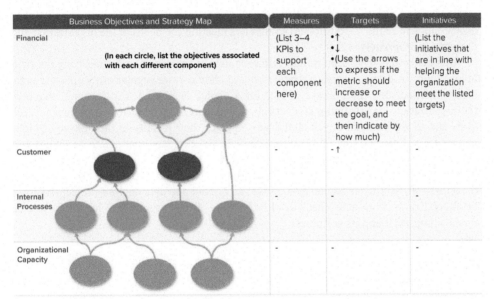

Business Objectives and Strategy Map	Measures	Targets	Initiatives
Financial (In each circle, list the objectives associated with each different component)	(List 3–4 KPIs to support each component here)	• ↑ • ↓ • (Use the arrows to express if the metric should increase or decrease to meet the goal, and then indicate by how much)	(List the initiatives that are in line with helping the organization meet the listed targets)
Customer	-	- ↑	-
Internal Processes	-	-	-
Organizational Capacity	-	-	-

EXHIBIT 7-8
Balanced Scorecard Strategy Map Template with Measures, Targets, and Initiatives

If the dashboard is not following the strategy map template, the most important KPIs should be placed in the top left corner, as our eyes are most naturally drawn to that part of any page that we are reading.

 PROGRESS CHECK

5. How often would you need to see the KPI of Waste Recycling Rate to know if you are making progress? Any different for the KPI of ROA?

6. Why do you think that the most important KPIs should be shown in the top left corner of a digital dashboard?

ADDRESS AND REFINE RESULTS

LO 7-4

Understand how to drill-down and follow up with results.

Once the dashboard is in use, an active communication plan should be implemented to ensure that the dashboard's metrics are meeting the needs of the business and the users. If there are multiple audiences who use dashboards, then either different dashboards should be created, or the dashboard should provide different views and ways to filter the information so users can customize their experience and see exactly the metrics they need for decision making and monitoring. Because dashboards tend to be monitored on a daily (or even more frequent) basis, communication with all of the users is imperative to ensure that the identified metrics are appropriate and useful.

Some questions that would be helpful in determining how the dashboard could be refined are the following:

1. Which metric are you using most frequently to help you make decisions?
2. Are you downloading the data to do any additional analysis after working with the dashboard, and if so, can the dashboard be improved to save those extra steps?
3. Are there any metrics that you do not use? If so, why aren't they helpful?
4. Are there any metrics that should be available on the dashboard to help you with decision making?

Checking in with the users will help to address any potential issues of missing or unnecessary data and refine the dashboard so that it is meeting the needs of the organization and the users appropriately.

After the results have been refined and each user of the dashboard is receiving the right information for decision making, the dashboard should enter regular use across the organization. Recall that the purpose of creating a digital dashboard is to communicate how the organization is performing so decision makers can improve their judgment and decisions and so workers can understand where to place their priority in their day-to-day jobs and projects. Ensuring that all of the appropriate stakeholders continue to be involved in using the dashboard and continually improving it is key to the success of the dashboard. The creation of a Balanced Scorecard or any type of digital dashboard is iterative—just as the entire IMPACT cycle should be iterative throughout any data analysis project—so it will be imperative to continually check in with the users of the dashboard to learn how to continually improve it and its usefulness.

 PROGRESS CHECK

7. Why are digital dashboards for KPIs an effective way to address and refine results, as well as communicate insights and track outcomes?
8. Consider the opening vignette of the **Kenya Red Cross**. How do KPIs help the organization prepare and carry out its goal of being the "first in and last out"?

Summary

- Management accountants must use descriptive analytics to understand and direct activity, diagnostic analytics to compare with a benchmark and control costs, predictive analytics to plan for the future, and prescriptive analytics to guide their decision process.
- Relevant costs and data help inform decisions, variance analysis and bullet graphs help determine where the company is, and regression helps managers understand and predict costs.
- Because data are increasingly available and affordable for companies to access and store, and because the growth in technology has created robust and affordable business

intelligence tools, data and information are becoming the key components for decision making, replacing gut response.

- Performance metrics are defined, compiled from the data, and used for decision making. A specific type of performance metrics, key performance indicators—or "key" metrics that influence decision making and strategy—are the most important.
- One of the most common ways to communicate a variety of KPIs is through a digital dashboard. A digital dashboard is an interactive report showing the most important metrics to help users understand how a company or an organization is performing. Their value is maximized when the metrics provided on the dashboard are used to affect decision making and action.
- One iteration of a digital dashboard is the Balanced Scorecard, which is used to help companies turn their strategic goals into action by identifying the most important metrics to measure, as well as identifying target goals to compare metrics against. The Balanced Scorecard is comprised of four components: financial (or stewardship), customer (or stakeholder), internal process, and organizational capacity (or learning and growth).
- For each of the four components, objectives, measures, targets, and initiatives are identified. Objectives should be aligned with strategic goals of the organization, measures are the KPIs that show how well the organization is doing at meeting its objective, and targets should be achievable goals toward which to move the metric. Initiatives should be the actions that an organization can take to move its specified metrics in the direction of its stated target goal.
- Regardless of whether you are creating a Balanced Scorecard or another type of digital dashboard to showcase performance metrics and KPIs, the IMPACT model should be used to complete the project.

Key Words

Balanced Scorecard (*273*)   A particular type of digital dashboard that is made up of strategic objectives, as well as KPIs, target measures, and initiatives, to help the organization reach its target measures in line with strategic goals.

digital dashboard (*272*)   An interactive report showing the most important metrics to help users understand how a company or an organization is performing. Often created using Excel or Tableau.

key performance indicator (KPI) (*271*)   A particular type of performance metric that an organization deems the most important and influential on decision making.

performance metric (*270*)   Any number measuring how an organization is performing, particularly when that measure is compared to a baseline.

✓ ANSWERS TO PROGRESS CHECKS

1. The contribution margin includes the revenues and variable costs that are traceable to that division or product. That data would be relevant. Other relevant data may be the types of customers and sentiment toward the product, products that are sold in conjunction with that product, or market size. Shared or allocated costs would not be.

2. A bullet graph uses a small amount of space to evaluate a large number of metrics. Gauges are more visually engaging and easier to understand, but waste a lot of space.

3. If waste reduction is an important goal for Walmart, having a KPI and, potentially, a digital dashboard that reports how well the organization is doing will likely be useful in helping it accomplish its goal. Using a digital dashboard helps an organization to see if, indeed, it is making progress.

4. The KPIs that are the most helpful are those that are consistent with the company's strategy and measure how well the company is doing in meeting its goals. Data Analytics will help gather and report the necessary data to report on the KPIs. The Data Analytics IMPACT model introduced in Chapter 1—from identifying the question to tracking outcomes—will be helpful in getting the necessary data.

5. The frequency of updating KPIs is always a good question. One determinant will be how often the data get updated in the system, and the second determinant is how often the data will be considered by those looking at the data. Whichever of those two determinants takes longer is probably correct frequency for updating KPIs.

6. Because our eyes are most naturally drawn to that part of any page that we are reading, the most important KPIs should be placed in the top left corner.

7. By identifying the KPIs that are most important to corporate strategy and finding the necessary data to support them and then reporting on them in a digital dashboard, decision makers will have the necessary information to make effective decisions and track outcomes.

8. As noted in the opening vignette, using Data Analytics to refine its strategy and assign measurable performance metrics to its goals, **Kenya Red Cross** felt confident that its everyday activities were linked to measurable goals that would help the organization reach its goals and maintain a strong positive reputation and impact through its service.

McGraw Hill **connect**

Multiple Choice Questions

1. What would you consider to be financial performance KPIs?
   a. Total Shareholder Return
   b. Customer Profitability Score
   c. Market Growth Rate
   d. Klout Score

2. What would you consider to be an operational KPI?
   a. Inventory Shrinkage Rate
   b. Brand Equity
   c. CAPEX to Sales Ratio
   d. Revenue per Employee

3. What does *KPI* stand for?
   a. Key performance index
   b. Key performance indicator
   c. Key paired index
   d. Key paired indicator

4. The most important KPIs should be placed in the _____ corner of the page even if we are not following a strategy map template.
   a. bottom right
   b. bottom left
   c. top left
   d. top right

5. According to the text, which of these are *not* helpful in refining a dashboard?

    a. Which metric are you using most frequently to help you make decisions?

    b. Are you downloading the data to do any additional analysis after working with the dashboard, and if so, can the dashboard be improved to save those extra steps?

    c. Are there any metrics that you do not use? If so, why aren't they helpful?

    d. Which data are the easiest to access or least costly to collect?

6. On a Balanced Scorecard, which is *not* included as a component?

    a. Financial Performance

    b. Customer/Stakeholder

    c. Internal Process

    d. Employee Capacity

7. On a Balanced Scorecard, which is *not* included as a component?

    a. Financial Performance

    b. Customer/Stakeholder

    c. Order Process

    d. Organizational Capacity

8. What is defined as an interactive report showing the most important metrics to help users understand how a company or an organization is performing?

    a. KPI

    b. Performance metric

    c. Digital dashboard

    d. Balanced Scorecard

9. What is defined as any calculation measuring how an organization is performing, particularly when that measure is compared to a baseline?

    a. KPI

    b. Performance metric

    c. Digital dashboard

    d. Balanced Scorecard

10. What would you consider to be marketing KPIs?

    a. Conversion Rate

    b. Six Sigma Level

    c. Employee Churn Rate

    d. Time to Market

Discussion Questions

1. We know that a Balanced Scorecard is comprised of four components: financial (or stewardship), customer (or stakeholder), internal process, and organizational capacity (or learning and growth). What would you include in a dashboard for the financial and customer components?

2. We know that a Balanced Scorecard is comprised of four components: financial (or stewardship), customer (or stakeholder), internal process, and organizational capacity (or learning and growth). What would you include in a dashboard for the internal process and organizational capacity components? How do digital dashboards make KPIs easier to track?

3. **Amazon**, in the author's opinion, has cared less about profitability in the short run but has cared about gaining market share. Arguably Amazon gains market share by taking care of the customer. Given the "Suggested 75 KPIs That Every Manager Needs

to Know" from Exhibit 7-7, what would be a natural KPI for the customer aspect for **Amazon**?

4. For an accounting firm like **PwC**, how would the Balanced Scorecard help balance the desire to be profitable for its partners with keeping the focus on its customers?

5. For a company like **Walmart**, how would the Balanced Scorecard help balance the desire to be profitable for its shareholders with continuing to develop organizational capacity to compete with **Amazon** (and other online retailers)?

6. Why is Customer Retention Rate a great KPI for understanding your **Tesla** customers?

7. If the data underlying your digital dashboard are updated in real time, why would you want to update your digital dashboard in real time? Are there situations when you would not want to update your digital dashboard in real time? Why or why not?

8. In which of the four components of a Balanced Scorecard would you put the Walton College's diversity initiative? Why do you think this is important for a public institution of higher learning?

Problems

1. From Exhibit 7-7, choose five financial performance KPIs to answer the following three questions. This URL (https://www.linkedin.com/pulse/20130905053105-64875646-the-75-kpis-every-manager-needs-to-know) provides background information for each individual KPI that may be helpful in understanding the individual KPIs and answering the questions.

   a. Identify the equation/relationship/data needed to calculate the KPI. If you need data, how frequently would the data need to be incorporated to be most useful?

   b. Describe a simple visualization that would help a manager track the KPI.

   c. Identify a benchmark for the KPI from the Internet. Choose an industry and find the average, if possible. This is for context only.

2. From Exhibit 7-7, choose 10 employee performance KPIs to answer the following three questions. This URL (https://www.linkedin.com/pulse/20130905053105-64875646-the-75-kpis-every-manager-needs-to-know) provides background information for each individual KPI that may be helpful in understanding the individual KPIs and answering the questions.

   a. Identify the equation/relationship/data needed to calculate the KPI. How frequently would it need to be incorporated to be most useful?

   b. Describe a simple visualization that would help a manager track the KPI.

   c. Identify a benchmark for the KPI from the Internet. Choose an industry and find the average, if possible. This is for context only.

3. From Exhibit 7-5, choose 10 marketing KPIs to answer the following three questions. This URL (https://www.linkedin.com/pulse/20130905053105-64875646-the-75-kpis-every-manager-needs-to-know) provides background information for each individual KPI that may be helpful in understanding the individual KPIs and answering the questions.

   a. Identify the equation/relationship/data needed to calculate the KPI. How frequently would it need to be incorporated to be most useful?

   b. Describe a simple visualization that would help a manager track the KPI.

   c. Identify a benchmark for the KPI from the Internet. Choose an industry and find the average, if possible. This is for context only.

4. How does Data Analytics help facilitate the use of the Balanced Scorecard and tracking KPIs? Does it make the data more timely? Are you able to access more information easier or faster, or what capabilities does it give?

5. If ROA is considered a key KPI for a company, what would be an appropriate benchmark? The industry's ROA? The average ROA for the company for the past five years? The competitors' ROA?

    a. How will you know if the company is making progress?

    b. How might Data Analytics help with this?

    c. How often would you need a measure of ROA? Monthly? Quarterly? Annually?

6. If Time to Market is considered a key KPI for a company, what would be an appropriate benchmark? The industry's time to market? The average time to market for the company for the past five years? The competitors' time to market?

    a. How will you know if the company is making progress?

    b. How might Data Analytics help with this?

    c. How often would you need a measure of Time to Market? Monthly? Quarterly? Annually?

7. Why is Order Fulfillment Cycle Time an appropriate KPI for a company like **Wayfair** (which sells furniture online)? How long does Wayfair think customers will be ready to wait if Amazon Prime promises items delivered to its customers in two business days? Might this be an important basis for competition?

Key performance indicators help managers keep track of performance and strategic objectives.

In this lab, you will:

- Learn about many of the key performance indicators.
- Evaluate which KPIs best work for Tesla.
- Consider the data needed and the desired frequency to provide each of these KPIs.

> Q1. Imagine you work for Tesla. Choose 20 KPIs that you believe are most important to Tesla's management (include five from each category).

The 75 KPIs Every Manager Needs to Know (Bernard Marr)[3]

To measure financial performance:	
	1. Net Profit
	2. Net Profit Margin
	3. Gross Profit Margin
	4. Operating Profit Margin
	5. EBITDA
	6. Revenue Growth Rate
	7. Total Shareholder Return (TSR)
	8. Economic Value Added (EVA)
	9. Return on Investment (ROI)
	10. Return on Capital Employed (ROCE)
	11. Return on Assets (ROA)
	12. Return on Equity (ROE)
	13. Debt-to-Equity (D/E) Ratio
	14. Cash Conversion Cycle (CCC)
	15. Working Capital Ratio
	16. Operating Expense Ratio (OER)
	17. CAPEX to Sales Ratio
	18. Price-to-Earnings Ratio (P/E Ratio)
To understand your customers:	19. Net Promoter Score (NPS)
	20. Customer Retention Rate
	21. Customer Satisfaction Index
	22. Customer Profitability Score
	23. Customer Lifetime Value
	24. Customer Turnover Rate
	25. Customer Engagement
	26. Customer Complaints

[3] https://www.linkedin.com/pulse/20130905053105-64875646-the-75-kpis-every-manager-needs-to-know/ (accessed October 13, 2017).

To gauge your market and marketing efforts:	27. Market Growth Rate
	28. Market Share
	29. Brand Equity
	30. Cost per Lead
	31. Conversion Rate
	32. Search Engine Rankings (by keyword) and Click-Through Rate
	33. Page Views and Bounce Rate
	34. Customer Online Engagement Level
	35. Online Share of Voice (OSOV)
	36. Social Networking Footprint
	37. Klout Score
To measure your operational performance:	38. Six Sigma Level
	39. Capacity Utilisation Rate (CUR)
	40. Process Waste Level
	41. Order Fulfillment Cycle Time
	42. Delivery in Full, on Time (DIFOT) Rate
	43. Inventory Shrinkage Rate (ISR)
	44. Project Schedule Variance (PSV)
	45. Project Cost Variance (PCV)
	46. Earned Value (EV) Metric
	47. Innovation Pipeline Strength (IPS)
	48. Return on Innovation Investment (ROI2)
	49. Time to Market
	50. First-Pass Yield (FPY)
	51. Rework Level
	52. Quality Index
	53. Overall Equipment Effectiveness (OEE)
	54. Process or Machine Downtime Level
	55. First Contact Resolution (FCR)
To understand your employees and their performance:	56. Human Capital Value Added (HCVA)
	57. Revenue per Employee
	58. Employee Satisfaction Index
	59. Employee Engagement Level
	60. Staff Advocacy Score
	61. Employee Churn Rate
	62. Average Employee Tenure
	63. Absenteeism Bradford Factor
	64. 360-Degree Feedback Score
	65. Salary Competitiveness Ratio (SCR)
	66. Time to Hire
	67. Training Return on Investment
To measure your environmental and social sustainability performance:	68. Carbon Footprint
	69. Water Footprint
	70. Energy Consumption
	71. Saving Levels Due to Conservation and Improvement Efforts
	72. Supply Chain Miles
	73. Waste Reduction Rate
	74. Waste Recycling Rate
	75. Product Recycling Rate

Part 1: Identify the Questions

For each of these 20 KPIs:

Q2. Identify the specific equation/relationship/data needed to calculate the KPI. How frequently do you expect data for these KPIs to be updated (e.g., daily, monthly)?

Q3. Describe a simple visualization or dashboard that would help a manager track the KPI. Does it use red, yellow, and green indicators, or do you have something else in mind that would be better?

Part 2: Master the Data

Q4. Identify a benchmark for five of these KPIs for Tesla. Where would you find these benchmarks? Would you base it on averages for Tesla or on performance from the prior week, month or year? For the car industry or a different industry?

End of Lab

Lab 7-2   Create a Balanced Scorecard Dashboard in Tableau

Superstore has brought you in to help it develop some metrics to evaluate performance across different dimensions of its business, including finance, customers, process, and employee growth.

Company summary

Superstore is a large seller of retail and wholesale office supplies, furniture, and technology. It operates in the United States and has divided its sales regions into North, South, East, and West. Each region has a regional sales representative who interacts with the customers to take orders and deal with returns.

Data

Sales order data are available for a four-year period, including demographic data about the customers, as well as main categories and subcategories of products. *Note that depending on the version of Tableau you use, the screenshots may differ from the examples below.*

Technique

- In this lab, you will use Tableau to generate a dashboard to evaluate four key performance indicators.

Software needed

- Tableau

In this lab, you will:

- Generate some key performance indicators.
- Evaluate the data.
- Perform analyses and generate visualizations.

Part 1: Identify the Questions

Your understanding of key performance indicators has given you some insight into how management at Superstore might measure and evaluate performance across different aspects of the business. They depend on your expertise to do just that.

Assuming you'll have access to sales order and returns data, as well as the sales representatives involved, think about different ways you could measure performance.

Q1. What KPIs would you consider using to evaluate sales financial performance?

Q2. What KPIs would you consider using to evaluate customer relationships?

Q3. What KPIs would you consider using to evaluate process efficiency?

Q4. What KPIs would you consider using to evaluate employee growth?

Q5. For each KPI, identify a benchmark value or KPI goal that you think management might use.

Part 2: Generate a Request for Data

The following data are available:

LAB TABLE 7-2A

Orders	Returns	People
Row ID	Order ID	Person
Order ID		Region
Order Date		
Ship Date		
Ship Mode		
Customer ID		
Customer Name		
Segment		
Country City		
State		
Postal Code		
Region Product ID		
Category		
Subcategory		
Product Name		
Sales		
Quantity		
Discount		
Profit		

Q6. Using the available fields, identify some calculations or relationships that would support your KPIs from Q1 to Q4.

Q7. Are there any KPIs you selected that don't have supporting data fields?

Part 3: Perform an Analysis of the Data

Now you'll use Tableau to generate some analytics that will provide visualizations for management to quickly evaluate some of the KPIs. To simplify the process, here are four KPIs that management has identified as high priorities:

Finance: Which product categories provide the highest amount of profit? The goal is 13 percent return on sales. Use *Profit ratio = Total profit/Total sales.*

Process: How long does it take to ship our product to each state on average? Management would like to see four days or less. Use *Delivery time in days = Ship date − Order date.*

Customers: Which regions have the highest return rates? Management says only 10 percent of sales orders should be returned normally. *Return rate = Number of returned/Number of orders.*

Employees: Who are our top-performing employees by sales each month? *Rank the total number of sales by employee.*

Now it's your turn to build a Balanced Scorecard dashboard in Tableau for each of these metrics. First, you'll create four individual worksheets; then you'll combine them into a dashboard for quick review.

Note: To compare actual performance to management's goals, you'll need to set some parameters and create some additional calculated fields.

Create a new project in Tableau

1. Open Tableau, and create a new Tableau book.
2. Click **Data > New Data Source > Excel.**
3. Navigate to **Documents > My Tableau Repository > Datasources > XX.X > en_US-US > Sample – Superstore.xls** or choose **Sample – Superstore** from the saved data sources on the open data screen.
4. Click **Open.**
5. In **Data Source,** drag **Orders** and **People** to the top pane to left join them. Then drag **Returns** to the whitespace and create a left join.
6. Click **Sheet 1** to begin your creating your visualizations.

Source: Tableau Software, Inc. All rights reserved.

Add parameters for management's benchmark goals

To create parameters, in the left pane, click the down-arrow next to **Dimensions** and choose **Create Parameter. . .**

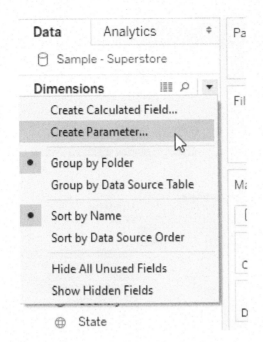

Tableau Software, Inc. All Rights Reserved

1. **Name:** KPI Target Return on Sales
   a. **Datatype:** Float
   b. **Display format:** Percentage, 0 decimals
   c. **Allowable values:** Range
   d. **Minimum:** 0.01
   e. **Maximum:** 1
   f. **Step size:** 0.01
   g. **Current value:** 0.13 <- *This is management's 13 percent return on sales goal.*
2. **Name:** KPI Target Delivery Days
   a. **Datatype:** Float
   b. **Display format:** Automatic
   c. **Allowable values:** Range
   d. **Minimum:** 1
   e. **Maximum:** 10
   f. **Step size:** 0.5
   g. **Current value:** 4 <- *This is management's four-day shipping goal.*
3. **Name:** KPI Target Return Rate
   a. **Datatype:** Float
   b. **Display format:** Percentage, 0 decimals
   c. **Allowable values:** Range
   d. **Minimum:** 0
   e. **Maximum:** 1
   f. **Step size:** 0.05
   g. **Current value:** 0.1 <- *This is management's 10 percent order return rate goal.*
4. **Name:** KPI Target Top Salespeople
   a. **Datatype:** Integer
   b. **Display format:** Number (standard)
   c. **Allowable values:** Range
   d. **Minimum:** 0
   e. **Maximum:** 3
   f. **Step size:** 1
   g. **Current value:** 1 <- *This shows the number of top employees management wants to recognize.*

Create the four worksheets

For simplicity, full instructions are provided for the first sheet. For subsequent sheets, drag the attributes to the appropriate places.

1. Create a new worksheet called **Finance.** In the end, it will look similar to this:

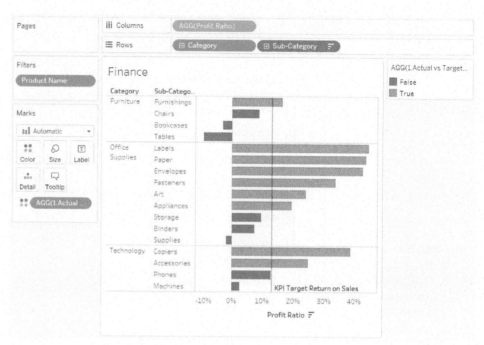

Source: Tableau Software, Inc. All rights reserved.

    a. Create calculated fields—click the down-arrow next to Dimensions in the left pane and choose **Create Calculated Field.** Enter the name of the new field, then type the expression in the box below.

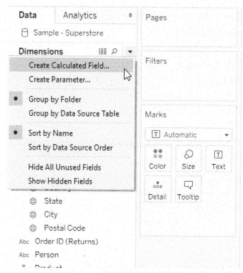

Tableau Software, Inc. All Rights Reserved

i. **Profit Ratio:** <- *if you get an error that this already exists, skip this step.*
     a. **Name:** Profit Ratio
     b. **Equation:** SUM([Profit])/SUM([Sales])
  ii. **Actual vs Target**
     a. Name: Actual vs Target Return on Sales
     b. Equation: [Profit Ratio] > [KPI Target Return on Sales]
b. Drag the following measure to the Columns shelf: **Profit Ratio** *This will become AGG(Profit Ratio).*
c. Drag the following dimensions to the Rows shelf: **Category, Sub-Category.**
d. Drag the following dimension to the Filters shelf: **Product Name.** Click the value and select **Custom Value List** in the window that appears. Then click **OK.**
e. Drag the following measure to the Marks pane: **Actual vs Target Return on Sales** becomes AGG (Actual vs Target – Return on Sales). Click the icon next to it and select **Color** from the list.
f. Click the **Analytics** tab in the left pane. In the **Custom** section, drag **Reference Line** onto the Finance table. In the window that appears, choose the following options:
   1. **Table**
   2. **Value:** KPI Target Return on Sales
g. Click **OK**
h. Hover over the top of the bar chart and click the sort icon that appears to place the values in descending order by profit ratio.
i. Save your project.
j. Take a screenshot (label it 7-2A).

2. Create a new worksheet called **Process.** In the end, the visualization will look similar to this.

Source: Tableau Software, Inc. All rights reserved.

a. **Create calculated fields:**
   i. **Delivery Time Days:** ROUND(FLOAT(DATEDIFF('day', [Order Date], [Ship Date])),2)
   ii. **Actual vs Target Delivery:** AVG([Delivery Time Days]) < [KPI Target Delivery Days]

b. **Columns:** Longitude (generated)
c. **Rows:** Latitude (generated)
d. **Type:** Filled Map
e. Marks:
  i. **Delivery Time Days** > Use the drop-down menu on the attribute to change from Sum to Average > Change the mark to Color
  ii. **Country** > Detail
  iii. **State** > Detail
f. Double-click **AVG(Delivery Time Days)** color scale on the left:

  i. Red-Green Diverging
  ii. Reversed
  iii. Advanced: Center: 4
g. Take a screenshot (label it 7-2B).
3. Create a new worksheet called **Customer.** In the end, the visualization will look similar to this.

Source: Tableau Software, Inc. All rights reserved.

a. Create calculated fields:
  i. **Return Rate:** COUNT([Returned])/COUNT([Order ID])
  ii. **Actual vs Target Return Rate:**[Return Rate] < [KPI Target Return Rate]

    ii. **Columns:** YEAR(Order Date)
   iii. **Rows:** AGG(Return Rate)
    iv. **Type: Line**
     v. **Marks:**
         i. **AGG(Actual vs Target - Return Rate) > Color**
        ii. **Region > Label**
    vi. **Analytics > Reference Line > Entire Table > KPI Target Return Rate**
   vii. Take a screenshot (label it 7-2C).
4. Create a new worksheet called **Growth.** In the end, the visualization will look similar to this.

Source: Tableau Software, Inc. All rights reserved.

   a. Create calculated fields:
       i. **Rank:** Index( )
      ii. **Actual vs Target Seller:** [Rank] < = [KPI Target Top Salespeople]
   b. **Columns:** SUM(Sales)
   c. **Rows:** Person
   d. **Type:** Horizontal Bar
   e. **Marks:**
       i. **Actual vs Target Seller > Color**
      ii. **SUM(Sales) > Label**
   f. **Pages:** YEAR(Order Date) <- *This will allow you to select a year to see the top-performing seller for that year.*
   g. Rows > Person > Sort > Descending
   h. Take a screenshot (label it 7-2D).

5. Finally, create a new dashboard sheet called **Balanced Scorecard.** In the end, the visualization will look similar to this.

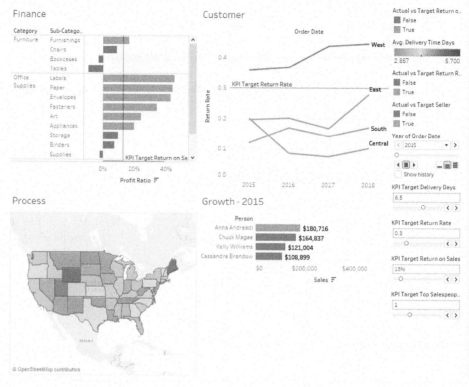

Source: Tableau Software, Inc. All rights reserved.

a. Drag **Finance, Customer, Process,** and **Growth** to main body of your dashboard.
b. To enable management to adjust its goals (and corresponding reference lines), add the parameters to the dashboard along the side.
c. From the menu, click **Analysis** > Parameters, and add each of the four parameters to the dashboard.
d. Take a screenshot (label it 7-2E).

Part 4: Address and Refine Results

Now that you've created the dashboard, take a moment to interpret the results.

Q8. Which product categories have fallen below the profit goal of 13 percent?

Q9. Which states are taking significantly more than four days to ship to?

Q10. Which region(s) has (have) experienced a higher than 10 percent return rate from customers?

Q11. Which sales representative is leading the rest for the most recent month?

End of Lab

Company summary

Dillard's is a department store with approximately 330 stores in 29 states. Its headquarters is in Little Rock, Arkansas. You can learn more about Dillard's by looking at finance.yahoo. com (Ticker symbol = DDS) and the Wikipedia site for DDS. You'll quickly note that William T. Dillard II is an accounting grad of the University of Arkansas and the Walton College of Business, which may be why he shared transaction data with us to make available for this lab and labs throughout this text.

Data

To begin mastering the data, you will need to connect to SQL Server data through Excel using **Data > Get & Transform**. If you need a refresher on how to do so, refer to Appendix F. Once you connect to the SQL Server dataset WCOB_DILLARDS in Excel and expand the options to input a query, input the following SQL query to extract the data needed for our analysis.

```
Select Transact.*, Store.STATE
From Transact
Inner Join Store
On Transact.Store = Store.STORE
Where TRAN_DATE BETWEEN '20160901' and '20160915'
Order By Tran_Date
```

Software needed

- Microsoft SQL Server Management Studio (available on the Remote Desktop at the University of Arkansas)
- Excel 2016 (available on the Remote Desktop at the University of Arkansas)
- Power Pivot Excel add-in. To create a date table, we'll extract and load the data through Power Pivot instead of through the Get & Transform tab. If you don't see Power Pivot as a tab in the Excel ribbon, you will need to activate the add-in.

In this lab, you will:

- Learn to build a KPI. In this case, we are trying to assess whether sales have improved the same date a year earlier.
- Specifically, create a baseline measure in Excel and set a target value. These two measures will be used to create a KPI to compare sales data across two different periods.

1. From the Remote Desktop, open Excel. From the **File** tab on the ribbon, open **Options.**

Source: Microsoft Excel 2016

2. Select **Add-ins** from the left side of the **Excel Options** window.

Source: Microsoft Excel 2016

3. From the drop-down window at the bottom of the **Add-ins** screen, select **COM add-ins,** then click **Go. . .**

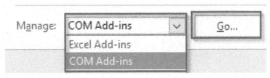

Source: Microsoft Excel 2016.

4. Place a check mark in the box next to **Microsoft Power Pivot for Excel,** then click **OK.**

COM Add-Ins	? ✕
Add-Ins available:	
☐ Dropbox for Office	OK
☐ Inquire	Cancel
☐ Microsoft Power Map for Excel	
☑ Microsoft Power Pivot for Excel	Add...
☐ Microsoft Power View for Excel	Remove

Source: Microsoft Excel 2016

Part 1: Identify the Questions

Our question for this lab is whether sales from September 1 to September 15, 2016, are different (better, worse, approximately the same) than the average sales from the same time period in 2015.

Q1. Why would comparing current year sales to prior year sales be useful?

Part 2: Mastering the Data and Performing the Analysis

While you loaded the data into the spreadsheet originally with a query from an external data source, that didn't automatically load it into Excel's Internal Data Model. Excel has a way to super-charge its conditional formatting by creating KPIs in Power Pivot. Power Pivot is a plug-in to Excel 2013 and 2010 and compares pre-prepared as an add-in to Excel 2016. Because you'll be using Excel in Walton College's virtual lab, you'll have access to Excel 2016. To create KPIs in Excel, the data must be added to the Internal Data Model.

- Identify a base performance metric, and create a **measure.** Measures can be implicit or explicit.
  - ○ Implicit measures are measures created in a PivotTable—any time you drag and drop a field into the values section of the PivotTable, it becomes an implicit measure. Implicit measures are restricted to the value field settings' standard aggregations (SUM, COUNT, MIN, MAX, DISTINCTCOUNT, or AVG). These implicit measures cannot be used to create KPIs.
  - ○ Explicit measures can be created in the Power Pivot Data Model window or in the Excel main window Form the Measure dialog box in the Power Pivot tab on the Excel ribbon.
- Identify a **target value** to compare the measure to the baseline.
- Create a **KPI** to signal performance of the measure in comparison to the baseline.

5. From the **Insert** tab on the ribbon, click **PivotTable.**

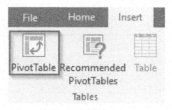

Source: Microsoft Excel 2016

6. In the **Create PivotTable** window, make sure to place a check mark in the box next to **Add this data to the Data Model.** Then click **OK.**

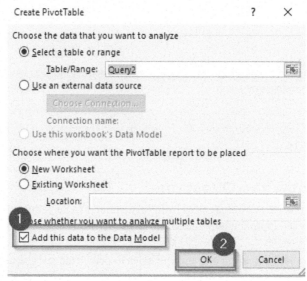

Source: Microsoft Excel 2016

7. Once the PivotTable has been created (this may take a few moments as the data are loaded into the data model), you can create a measure and a KPI. Navigate to the **Power Pivot** tab in the ribbon.
   Click **Measures,** then select **New Measure. . .**

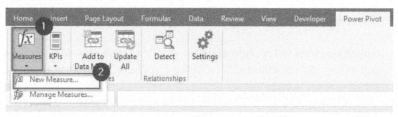

Source: Microsoft Excel 2016

8. The new measure's name defaults to **Measure 1,** which isn't very descriptive. Because we'll be measuring average Transaction amount, we'll change the name to **AVG(Tran_ Amt).** Type AVG(Tran_Amt) over the default text.

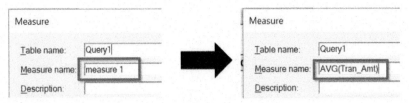

Source: Microsoft Excel 2016

9. The formula will auto-populate as you type. Begin typing average, and then begin typing the field Tran_Amt to fill in the formula.

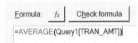

Source: Microsoft Excel 2016

10. The category has no bearing on how the measure or the KPI will work. For this measure, we'll leave it on the default of **General.** Click **OK** to create the measure.

Source: Microsoft Excel 2016

11. If you scroll down on the **PivotTable Fields** window, you will see that the explicit measure has been added to the bottom of the field list.

Source: Microsoft Excel 2016

12. Now we will create the KPI. In the Power Pivot tab of the ribbon, click **KPIs** and select **New KPI...**

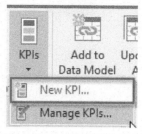

Source: Microsoft Excel 2016

13. Because you have only one measure added to this spreadsheet for now, the base field defaults to your newly created measure. If you had more than one measure, you would use the drop-down to select the measure you wanted to use for your base field. The target value can be defined by another measure or by an absolute value. For this first KPI, we'll define it by an Absolute Value. Let's assume that **Dillard's** has a goal of averaging at least $23 per Transaction.

   Input **23** as the **Absolute value** for the target value.
   Leave the default for the **status thresholds.**

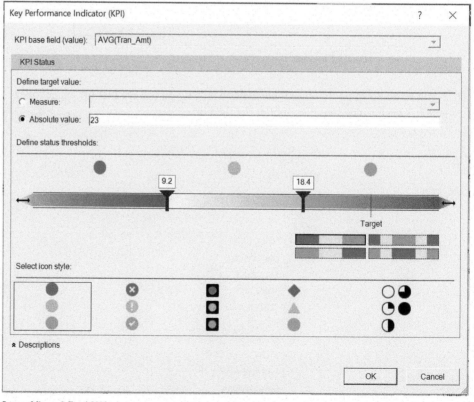

Source: Microsoft Excel 2016

Q2. Why might you want to edit the status thresholds? Does 18.4 seem low for the upper limit?

14. Now that you have your KPI created, you can see each of them in the PivotTable Fields list.

    If you expand the KPI fields, you see three options:

    - The Value (2016 Sales) will show the actual sale totals associated with the year 2016 (or sliced by month or day, depending on the other values you drill into in the PivotTable).
    - The Goal will show 2015 sales totals—this is the measure that you are using to compare 2016 sales against. The Goal is for the sales to be at least 2 percent higher than the previous year's sales.
    - The Status will show stoplight icons indicating red, yellow, or green circles based on the thresholds you selected when setting the KPI. *Note:* When the KPI fields are added to the PivotTable, they are designed to show up as stoplights (red, yellow, or green circles, depending on the status). It is likely, however, that the KPI status was automatically added to your PivotTable and that the stoplight signals show as -1, 0, and 1 instead of stoplights. If you remove the AVG(Tran_Amt) Status from the PivotTable (you can do so by unchecking the KPI Status in the PivotTable field list) and then place it back into the PivotTable by replacing the check mark, it should correct the issue and the stoplight icons will show in the PivotTable.

15. Create a PivotTable that shows the KPI status for average Transaction by each of the 15 days in your data range. Place TRAN_DATE in the Rows and AVG(Tran_Amt) and AVG (Tran_Amt) Status in the Values, as shown in the image below.

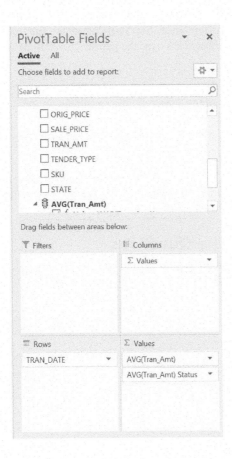

16. Take a screenshot (label 7-3A).

> Q3. How did **Dillard's** perform in September 2016 compared to September 2015? Do you think the target is set too high or too low? Which day(s) performed the worst, compared to the same date(s) in the previous period? Why do you think that is?

End of Lab

Lab 7-4 Comprehensive Case: Dillard's Store Data: Creating KPIs in Excel (Part II)

Company summary

Dillard's is a department store with approximately 330 stores in 29 states. Its headquarters is in Little Rock, Arkansas. You can learn more about Dillard's by looking at finance.yahoo.com (Ticker symbol = DDS) and the Wikipedia site for DDS. You'll quickly note that William T. Dillard II is an accounting grad of the University of Arkansas and the Walton College of Business, which may be why he shared transaction data with us to make available for this lab and labs throughout this text.

Data

The data for this lab and all other Dillard's labs must be accessed through the University of Arkansas Remote Desktop. Directions for accessing the Remote Desktop can be found at www.mhhe.com/richardsondaa2e. See your instructor for login credentials. The 2016 Dillard's data cover all transactions over the period 1/1/2014 to 10/17/2016.

Software needed

- Microsoft SQL Server Management Studio (available on the Remote Desktop at the University of Arkansas)
- Excel 2016 (available on the Remote Desktop at the University of Arkansas)

In this lab, you will:

- Compare total sales across all Dillard's stores year over year, month over month, and day over day and develop it as a KPI.

Part 1: Identify the Questions

Compare 2014, 2015, and 2016 sales data in parallel periods.

Part 2: Master the Data

1. Before we can create measures and KPIs to analyze the data, we need to extract the data from SQL Server and load them into Excel. To begin mastering the data, you will need to connect to SQL Server data through Excel using **Data > Get & Transform**. If you need a refresher on how to do so, refer to Appendix F. Once you connect to the SQL Server dataset WCOB_DILLARDS in Excel and expand the options to input a query, input the following SQL query to extract the data needed for our analysis.

```
Select year(Tran_Date) as year, month(Tran_Date) as month, day(Tran_Date)
as day, sum(Tran_Amt) as amount
From TRANSACT
Where TRAN_TYPE = 'P'
Group By year(Tran_Date), month(Tran_Date), day(Tran_Date)
Order By year(Tran_Date), month(Tran_Date), day(Tran_Date)
```

2. Once you have input the query and the preview of your data is presented, click **Edit** to transform the data in the **Query Editor**.

essql1.walton.uark.edu: wcob_dillards

year	month	day	amount
2014	1	1	20634886.6
2014	1	2	1930514.63
2014	1	3	2134284.81
2014	1	4	2648740.79
2014	1	5	1213884.05
2014	1	6	1210416.59
2014	1	7	1308792.36
2014	1	8	1452412.62
2014	1	9	1538225.01
2014	1	10	1867837.14
2014	1	11	2792623.79
2014	1	12	1431630.26

Load   Edit   Cancel

Source: Microsoft Excel 2016

The data have been fully extracted from SQL Server into Excel's Internal Data Model, but they need to be transformed so that we can more easily compare daily sales amounts year over year. Instead of seeing a separate record for each day, beginning with January 1, 2014, and ending with October 17, 2016, we would prefer to see only 365 records—one record for each day in a calendar year, but with separate columns for each year (2014, 2015, and 2016), each with the transaction amount associated with that year's month and day.

3. Select the **year** column.

4. Select **Pivot Column** from the **Transform** tab on the **Query Editor** ribbon.

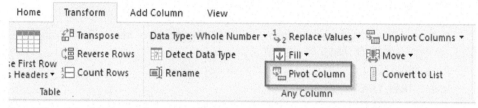

Source: Microsoft Excel 2016

5. Select **Amount** from the drop-down for the **Values** column and click **OK.**

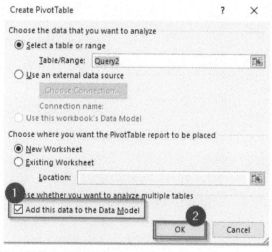

Source: Microsoft Excel 2016

6. Now that the data have been transformed, we're ready to load them into Excel. From the **Home** button on the **Query Editor**'s ribbon, click **Close and Load.**

7. Insert a PivotTable from your new data. In the **Create PivotTable** window, make sure to place a check mark in the box next to **Add this data to the Data Model.** Then click **OK.**

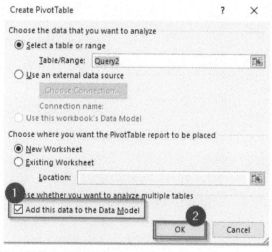

Source: Microsoft Excel 2016

Once the PivotTable has been created (this may take a few moments as the data are loaded into the data model), you can create a measure and a KPI using Excel's Power Pivot capabilities. Excel has a way to super-charge its conditional formatting by creating KPIs in Power Pivot. If you do not have this add-in added to Excel yet, see instructions in Lab 7-3 steps 1-4. KPIs require three decisions:

- Identify a base performance metric, and create a measure. Measures can be implicit or explicit.
    - Implicit measures are measures created in a PivotTable—any time you drag and drop a field into the values section of the PivotTable, it becomes an implicit measure. Implicit measures are restricted to the value field settings' standard aggregations (SUM, COUNT, MIN, MAX, DISTINCTCOUNT, or AVG). These implicit measures cannot be used to create KPIs.
    - Explicit measures can be created in the Power Pivot Data Model window or in the Excel main window from the Measure dialog box in the Power Pivot tab on the Excel ribbon.
- Identify a target value to compare the measure to.
- Create a KPI to signal performance of the measure in comparison to the baseline, and determine the range of values that indicate poor performance, good performance, and great performance.

We will need to create three measures, the sums of each of the year's sales Transactions.

8. Navigate to the **Power Pivot** tab in the ribbon. Click **Measures,** then Select **New Measure. . .**

Source: Microsoft Excel 2016

9. The new measure's name defaults to **Measure 1,** which isn't very descriptive. Because we'll be measuring average transaction amount, we'll change the first KPI's name to **2014 Sales.** Type 2014 Sales over the default text.

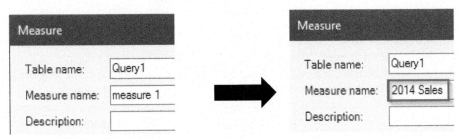

Source: Microsoft Excel 2016

10. The formula will auto-populate as you type, begin typing SUM, then fill in the parentheses with the column name **2014.**
11. At the bottom of the Measure window is an option to select a category. The Category has no bearing on how the measure or the KPI will work. For this measure, we'll leave it on the default of **General.** Click **OK** to create the measure.

Measure

Table name:	Query1
Measure name:	2014 Sales
Description:	

Formula: *fx*   Check formula

```
=SUM([2014])
```

Formatting Options

Category:

```
General
Number
Currency
```

OK   Cancel

Source: Microsoft Excel 2016

12. Repeat the same steps used to create the measure for 2014 sales to create measures for 2015 sales and 2016 sales.

13. Now we will create the KPIs to compare 2015 sales to 2014, and 2016 sales to 2015. In the Power Pivot tab of the ribbon, click **KPIs** and select **New KPI. . .**

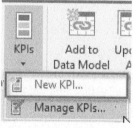

KPIs   Add to   Upd
       Data Model A

New KPI...

Manage KPIs...

Source: Microsoft Excel 2016

14. The first KPI we will create is comparing 2016 sales to the previous year's sales. Use the drop-down to select 2016 Sales for your base field. The target value can be defined by another measure or by an absolute value. We have already defined the measure to compare 2016 sales to, so select 2015 Sales for the target value Measure.

We will define excellent performance as a 2 percent improvement over last year's sales, so move the upper range of the target slider to 102%. Poor performance will be defined as a 2 percent decline from last year's sales. Move the lower range of the target slider to 98%.

Q1. Do you think +/− 2 percent is the right benchmark to set? Would you propose a different percentage change to track here?

Once all of your settings are correct, click **OK** to create the KPI.

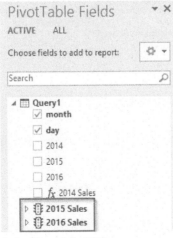

Key Performance Indicator (KPI) | ? | X

1

KPI base field (value): 2016 Sales

KPI Status

Define target value:

● Measure: 2015 Sales 2

2014 Sales
2015 Sales

○ Absolute value:

Define status thresholds: 3

98 102 %

Target

Select icon style:

Descriptions

4

OK | Cancel

Source: Microsoft Excel 2016

15. Create the KPI comparing 2015 sales to 2014 sales using the same thresholds for measuring performance.
16. Now that you have your two KPIs created, you can see each of them in the PivotTable Fields list.

PivotTable Fields ▾ ✕

ACTIVE   ALL

Choose fields to add to report: ⚙ ▾

Search 🔍

▲ ▦ Query1
  ☑ month
  ☑ day
  ☐ 2014
  ☐ 2015
  ☐ 2016
  ☐ *fx* 2014 Sales
  ▷ 🚦 2015 Sales
  ▷ 🚦 2016 Sales

Source: Microsoft Excel 2016

Occasionally, if the KPI status is automatically added to your PivotTable, the stoplight signals show as -1, 0, and 1. If you uncheck and recheck the status field from the fields list, this will correct the issue and the stoplight icons will show.

If you expand the KPI fields, you see three options:

Source: Microsoft Excel 2016

- The Value (2016 Sales) will show the actual sale totals associated with the year 2016 (or sliced by month or day, depending on the other values you drill into in the PivotTable).
- The Goal will show 2015 sales totals—this is the measure that you are using to compare 2016 sales against. The Goal is for the sales to be at least 2 percent higher than the previous year's sales.
- The Status will show stoplight icons indicating red, yellow, or green circles based on the thresholds you selected when setting the KPI.

17. Create a PivotTable that shows the KPI status of 2015 and 2016 sales by month. To do so, drag and drop **Months** into the **Rows** and Status for both KPIs into the **Values.**

Source: Microsoft Excel 2016

If you just place a check mark in the box next to the month field, you will notice that the PivotTable defaults to reading Month values as numerical data instead of calendar data, so it places it as a value and sums the month numbers. You just need to drag and drop month outside of Values and into Rows.

18. Take a Screenshot (label it 7-4A).

19. To provide some drill-down capabilities, add the **Day** field to the **Rows** (beneath **Month**).

   Q2. Do you notice a pattern with how frequently the "bad" (red icon) days appear in 2016 in relation to 2015?

   Q3. What do you think is the potential problem with comparing days (e.g., comparing September 1, 2016 to September 1, 2015)? How could this be improved?

End of Lab

Lab 7-5 Comprehensive Case: Dillard's Store Data: Creating KPIs in Excel (Part III)

Company summary

Dillard's is a department store with approximately 330 stores in 29 states. Its headquarters is in Little Rock, Arkansas. You can learn more about Dillard's by looking at finance.yahoo. com (Ticker symbol = DDS) and the Wikipedia site for DDS. You'll quickly note that William T. Dillard II is an accounting grad of the University of Arkansas and the Walton College of Business, which may be why he shared transaction data with us to make available for this lab and labs throughout this text.

Data

The data for this lab and all other Dillard's labs must be accessed through the University of Arkansas Remote Desktop. Directions for accessing the Remote Desktop can be found at www.mhhe.com/richardsondaa2e. See your instructor for login credentials. The 2016 Dillard's data cover all transactions over the period 1/1/2014 to 10/17/2016.

Software needed

- Microsoft SQL Server Management Studio (available on the Remote Desktop at the University of Arkansas)
- Excel 2016 (available on the Remote Desktop at the University of Arkansas)
- Power Pivot Excel add-in. To create a date table, we'll extract and load the data through Power Pivot instead of through the Get & Transform tab. If you don't see Power Pivot as a tab in the Excel ribbon, you will need to activate the add-in.

Part 1: Identify the Questions

How do we line up sales periods to be in parallel periods, by day of week in one period with day of week with previous period?

Part 2: Master the Data

1. In this lab, we will connect to the database through PowerPivot instead of through "Get and Transform" that we have used in previous labs. In order to do so, you need to have the PowerPivot add-in added into Excel. If you have not added it in before, you can follow steps 1-4 in Lab 7-3." To extract and load the data into Power Pivot, click **Manage** on the **Power Pivot** tab in the Excel ribbon.

Source: Microsoft Excel 2016

2. In the **Power Pivot for Excel** window, click **Get External Data** from the **Home** tab, then navigate through **From Database** and **From SQL Server.**

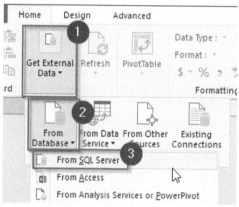

Source: Microsoft Excel 2016

3. The **Table Import Wizard** window will open. Input the SQL Server name and the Database name that you received from your instructor, then click **Next.**

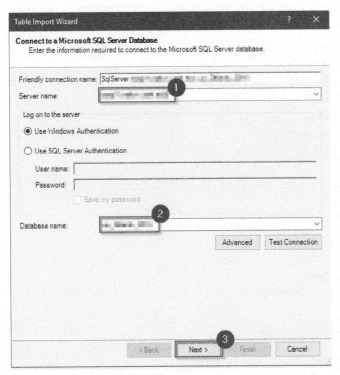

Source: Microsoft Excel 2016

4. We will import the data with a query, so select the radio button next to Write a query that will specify the data to import.

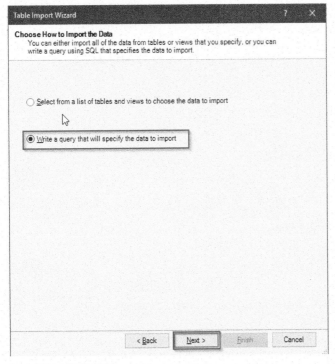

Source: Microsoft Excel 2016

5. We need to bring in only two attributes. In Lab 7-3, we had to parse out the different date parts in order to group our data by month and year, instead of just by day. In this lab, we will use Excel's Power Pivot tool to create a **Date** table. The tool will be able to parse out the date parts for us, instead of us having to do so with our query. This will also allow us to view more interesting date parts, such as the day of the week (not just the date).

Input the following query into the **Table Import Wizard** window to extract the total amount of Transactions for each day in the database:

Select Tran_Date, SUM(Tran_Amt) AS Sales

From Transact

Group By Tran_Date

After entering the SQL text, click Validate to ensure the query will run, and then click Finish.

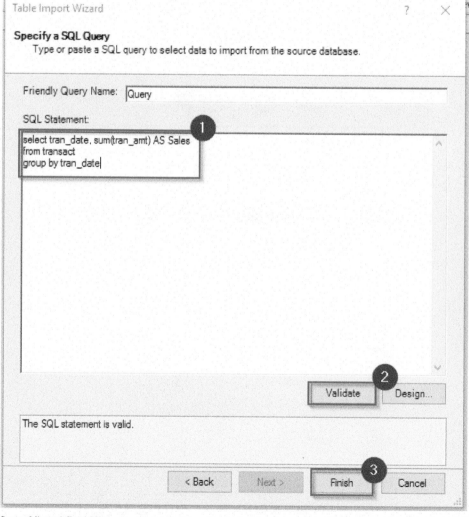

Source: Microsoft Excel 2016

The table will import. This may take a few moments.

6. Once the data are loaded, you can close the **Table Import Wizard** window. Click **Close.**

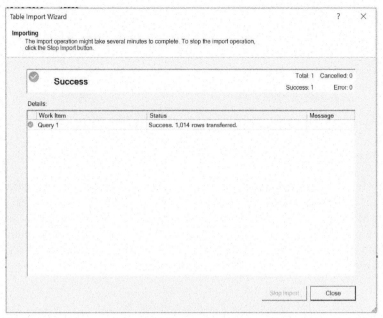

Source: Microsoft Excel 2016

7. After closing the **Table Import Wizard,** you will see your data loaded into Power Pivot. This does not mean the data have been loaded into Excel yet, so you can transform the data within the Power Pivot tool first. Creating the date table takes three steps: Select the **Tran_Date** column, click **Date** Table from the **Design** tab on the ribbon, then click **New.**

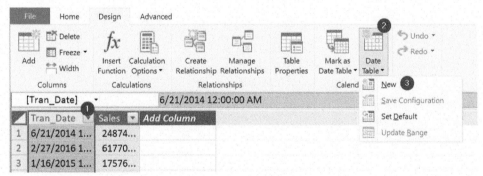

Source: Microsoft Excel 2016

You have created a **Date** table. Now it's time to load the transformed data into Excel.

8. Return to the **Home** tab on the **Power Pivot** ribbon, and select **PivotTable.**

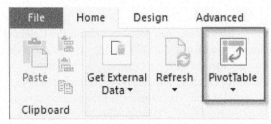

Source: Microsoft Excel 2016

9. Select **OK** to create the PivotTable in a New Worksheet.

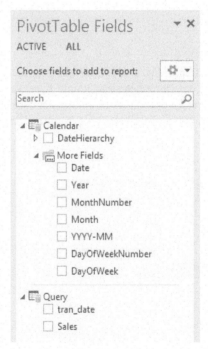

Source: Microsoft Excel 2016

The PivotTable Fields list contains two tables, **Calendar** and **Query.** The **Calendar** table contains the **Date Hierarchy** for drilling down, but it also contains attributes beneath the **More Fields** title. These contain the same attributes in the hierarchy, as well as different ways of viewing the data, such as **Day of Week.** The **Query** table contains the data that you extracted with your SQL query. The valuable field from the query table is **Sales,** which you will use as a value (or an implicit measure).

Source: Microsoft Excel 2016

Part 3: Perform an Analysis of the Data

10. Create a PivotTable to compare sales performance on different weekdays of each month, year over year. To do so, drag and drop year (from the **Calendar > More fields** drop-down) into **Columns, Month** and **DayofWeek** into **Rows,** and **Sales** into **Values**). The Sales data will be transformed into a measure, Sum of Sales, automatically. *Note:* If a relationship wasn't created automatically, you may see a warning in the PivotTable field list that states that "Relationships between tables may need to be created." You can select auto-detect for the relationship between the Query table and the new Date table to be created.

11. Take a screenshot (label it 7-5A).

Q1. Something should seem a bit off with your numbers. There are some big disparities month over month for some weekdays. Look back over our query and the ER Diagram (and if you completed Lab 7-4, compare the query you executed in this lab to the query from that lab). What did we leave out of this query? How could it cause us to make poor decisions?

Part 4: Analyze and Refine the Results

The query can be improved by not simply importing all of the transaction amount data, but by bringing in only the sales data. The way the data are organized, all of the dollar amounts for sales and for refunds are in the same attribute, Tran_Amt, and the transaction type is differentiated with the attribute Tran_Type. If we filter out any record that holds return data, we can load only the data that hold sales transactions into Excel.

12. To edit our original query, click **Manage** in the **Power Pivot** tab in the Excel ribbon.
13. In the **Power Pivot** tool, click **Table Properties** from the **Design** tab.

Note: If **Table Properties** is grayed out, switch the table in view in the Power Pivot window to **Query** in the bottom left corner (instead of **Calendar**).

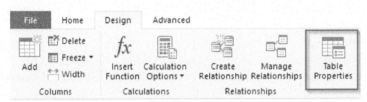

Source: Microsoft Excel 2016

14. Add in a WHERE clause to the query, validate the new query, and save it.

```
Select Tran_Date, SUM(Tran_Amt) AS Sales
From Transact
Where Tran_Type = 'p'
Group By Tran_Date
```

Source: Microsoft Excel 2016

315

15. The data will be automatically refreshed in the **Power Pivot** tool and in the Excel worksheet with the PivotTable. Close the **Power Pivot** tool.

Part 5: Communicate Results

The refreshed data in the PivotTable is better for making decisions with, but it still isn't easy to read at a glance. Adding some data visualization or conditional formatting can make these data more meaningful and easier to interpret.

Q2.   What would be the best way to visualize these data to ease decision making and insight?

End of Lab

Lab 7-6   Comprehensive Case: Dillard's Store Data: Creating KPIs in Excel (Part IV—Putting It All Together)

Company summary

Dillard's is a department store with approximately 330 stores in 29 states. Its headquarters is in Little Rock, Arkansas. You can learn more about Dillard's by looking at finance.yahoo. com (Ticker symbol = DDS) and the Wikipedia site for DDS. You'll quickly note that William T. Dillard II is an accounting grad of the University of Arkansas and the Walton College of Business, which may be why he shared Transaction data with us to make available for this lab and labs throughout this text.

Data

The data for this lab and all other Dillard's labs must be accessed through the University of Arkansas Remote Desktop. Directions for accessing the Remote Desktop can be found at www.mhhe.com/richardsondaa2e. See your instructor for login credentials. The 2016 Dillard's data cover all transactions over the period 1/1/2014 to 10/17/2016.

Software needed

- Microsoft SQL Server Management Studio (available on the Remote Desktop at the University of Arkansas)
- Excel 2016 (available on the Remote Desktop at the University of Arkansas)
- Power Pivot Excel add-in. To create a date table, we'll extract and load the data through Power Pivot instead of through the Get & Transform tab. If you don't see Power Pivot as a tab in the Excel ribbon, you will need to activate the add-in.

In this lab, you will:

- Develop a dashboard to display a variety of KPIs that you can drill into for state and store details.

Prerequisite

- **Labs 7-4 and 7-5.** If you haven't completed these labs, then you can still read through the steps in Labs 7-4 and 7-5 to see the screenshots of the ETL process in Excel (Lab 7-5) and the KPI creation process (Lab 7-4) to be ready for this lab.

Part 1: Identify the Questions

In Lab 7-4, you created KPIs for comparing 2015 sales to 2014 sales, but the date was parsed out from the original Tran_Date attribute. In Lab 7-5, you created a date table so that the date fields were more descriptive in the Excel report, but you didn't create any KPIs. In this lab, we will combine those two skills to create a descriptive report with KPIs. We will also expand the reports capabilities by extracting and loading state and store data in addition to date and transaction data.

Part 2: Master the Data

1. Loading the data into Excel from the original SQL Server database requires some transformation in Excel's Power Pivot tool. Extract and load **Dillard's** transactional and store data into Power Pivot using the following query:

```
Select Tran_Date, State, Store.Store, SUM(Tran_Amt) AS Amount
From Transact
Inner Join Store
On Transact.Store = Store.Store
Where Tran_Type = 'p'
Group By Tran_Date, State, Store.Store
Order By Tran_Date
```

2. It will take a few minutes for these data to load. Once they do (298,516 rows), close the **Table Import Wizard** window. Locate the **Tran_Date** attribute and use it to create a **Date Table.** (*Hint:* Look in the **Design** tab.)
3. Now that you have two tables in your data model, return to the **Home** tab to create a **PivotTable**, and close the **Power Pivot** tool.
4. In the **Power Pivot** tab in the Excel ribbon, create a new measure for Sum(amount). You can call this measure **Current Year.** This measure will be used as a base measure to compare to previous year's sales data. Leave the default category as "General."
5. Open the window to create a new measure to calculate the previous year's sales. To create this measure, you will use Microsoft's Data Analysis Expressions language (DAX), which is a formula language for creating custom calculations and measures. The function you will use is the = CALCULATE function, which allows you to not only create a calculation, but also filter it.

   Enter the following expression in the **formula box:**

   ```
   = CALCULATE(sum([Amount]), SAMEPERIODLASTYEAR ('Calendar'[Date]))
   ```

   You can name this measure **Last Year.**
6. Create a new KPI, setting Current Year as the Base Measure and Last Year as the Target Measure. Change the Status Thresholds to the following:
   ◦ Anything below 98 percent of last year's sales (the target) should be red.
   ◦ Anything between 98 percent and 102 percent of the target should be yellow.
   ◦ Anything above 102 percent of the target should be green.

7. This KPI will function only with the Date Hierarchy (not with the date parts). Create a PivotTable with the **Date Hierarchy** on the rows and the KPI Status as the values (if the KPI status is showing –1, 0, and 1 instead of the stoplight icons, remove the KPI status from the value fields and then place it back in).

Note: If a relationship wasn't created automatically, you may see a warning in the PivotTable field list that states that "Relationships between tables may need to be created." You can select auto-detect for the relationship between the Query table and the new Date table to be created.

Create another KPI, this time to compare any month with the month that precedes it (so instead of comparing September 2016 to September 2015, you will compare September 2016 to August 2016).

8. Even though the calculation for current month is technically the same as the calculation for current year (Sum(Amount)), we have to create a new measure to use as the KPI's base. Each base measure can only have one KPI assigned to it. Create a new measure called **Current Month** to calculate sales (this will be the exact same as how you created **Current Year** in step 4, but with a different Measure Name).

9. Create a new measure to use as the monthly target measure. The DAX expression for calculating last month's sales is:

```
= CALCULATE(SUM([Amount]), PREVIOUSMONTH('Calendar'[Date]))
```

You can name this measure **Previous Month.**

10. Create a new KPI comparing current sales (your base measure) to previous month as your target measure. Create the same status thresholds as the KPI comparing years (<98%, 98%–102%, >102%).

11. Add this KPI status to your PivotTable.

12. Take a screenshot (label it 7-6A).

Part 3: Address and Refine the Results

This report may be useful at a very high level, but for state-level and store-level analysis, the level is too high. Next, we will add in two slicers to help filter the data based on state and store.

13. From the **PivotTable Analyze** tab in the Excel ribbon, click **Slicer** to insert an interactive filter.

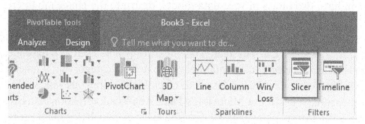

Source: Microsoft Excel 2016

14. Place a check mark in the boxes next to **State** and **Store** to create the slicers and click **OK.**

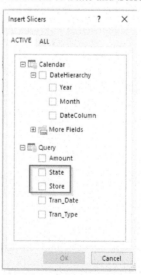

Source: Microsoft Excel 2016

15. Notice what happens as you select different states: Not only do the data change to reflect the KPI status for the state that you selected, but the stores that are associated with that state shift to the top of the store slicer, making it easier to drill down.

16. Take a screenshot (label it 7-6B).

We can ease drill-down capabilities even more by creating a hierarchy between state and store.

17. Open the **Power Pivot** tool by clicking **Manage** from the **Power Pivot** tab in the Excel ribbon.

18. From the **Power Pivot Home** tab, switch to **Diagram View.**

Source: Microsoft Excel 2016

19. Select both the **State** and the **Store** attributes from the **Query** table, then right-click one of the attributes to create a hierarchy.

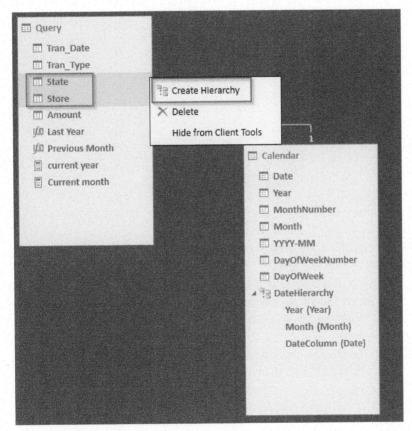

Source: Microsoft Excel 2016

20. You can change the name of the **Hierarchy** to **Store and State Hierarchy.**

21. Close the **Power Pivot** tool. The PivotTable will have refreshed automatically.

22. You will see that the hierarchy has been added to your PivotTable Fields list. Drag and drop the hierarchy to the Rows (above the Date hierarchy).

23. Take a screenshot (label it 7-6C).

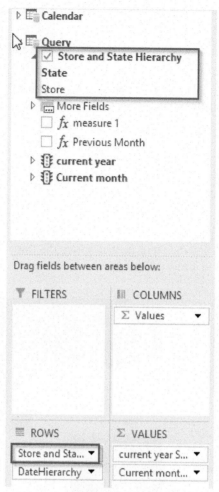

Source: Microsoft Excel 2016

Now you can drill down from **State** to **Store** directly in the PivotTable, or you can filter it via the slicer.

Q1. How does the ability to drill down into the state and store data give management critical information and help them to identify issues that are occurring or opportunities that might be available?

Q2. What would you get sales changes of certain products (SKUs) or product categories from one month to the next? Having this type of information will help you do what to help plan future promotions or future purchases?

End of Lab

Company summary

Dillard's is a department store with approximately 330 stores in 29 states. Its headquarters is in Little Rock, Arkansas. You can learn more about Dillard's by looking at finance.yahoo. com (Ticker symbol = DDS) and the Wikipedia site for DDS. You'll quickly note that William T. Dillard II is an accounting grad of the University of Arkansas and the Walton College of Business, which may be why he shared Transaction data with us to make available for this lab and labs throughout this text.

Data

The data for this lab and all other Dillard's labs must be accessed through the University of Arkansas Remote Desktop. Directions for accessing the Remote Desktop can be found at www.mhhe.com/richardsondaa2e. See your instructor for login credentials. The 2016 Dillard's data cover all transactions over the period 1/1/2014 to 10/17/2016.

Software needed

- Tableau (available on the Remote Desktop at the University of Arkansas)

In this lab, you will:

- Develop visualizations to display a variety of performance data for cluster analysis and store comparisons.

  We're now going to look at Dillard's Department store data to identify outliers and trends in different stores' transaction activity.

1. Create a new book in Tableau.
2. Go to Connect > To a Server > Microsoft SQL Server.
3. Enter the following and click **Sign In:**
   a. Server: **essql1.walton.uark.edu**
   b. Database: **WCOB_DILLARDS**
4. Double click the **Transact** table.
5. Double click the **Store** table.
6. Change the join to a **Right** outer join to include all stores and transactions they involve.

   Note: Tableau will try to query the server after each change you make and will take a up to a minute. After each change, click **Cancel** to stop the query until you're ready to prepare the final report.

Part 1: Cluster Analysis of High Volume Stores

In this analysis, we want to see which stores are doing well. In other words, stores with high volume of transactions and high average transaction price. Cluster analysis will group the stores that share similar performance.

1. Create a new worksheet called **Cluster Transactions.**
   a. Columns: **Transaction ID** > Measure > Count
   b. Rows: **Tran Amt** > Measure > Average
   c. Marks:
      i. **Store** > Color

d. Let the query run at this point.

e. You'll notice an outlier in top-right corner. In this case, it is the online division of **Dillard's**. Because we're evaluating brick-and-mortar stores, we want to exclude this one.

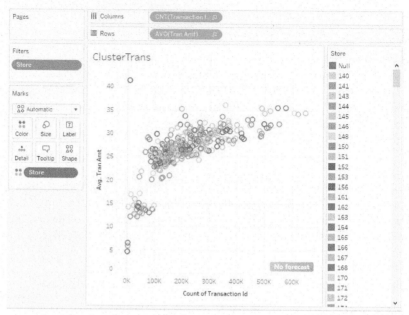

Source: Tableau Software, Inc. All rights reserved.

f. Right-click on the outlier (Store 698) and click **Exclude.**

g. To create clusters, click the **Analytics** tab and drag **Cluster** to the scatter plot.
   i. Number of clusters: **8**

h. Take a screenshot (label it 7-7A).

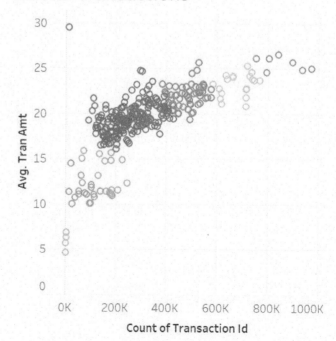

Source: Tableau Software, Inc. All rights reserved.

Q1. Write down the store numbers in Cluster 10 (three low performing stores) and Cluster 8 (seven high performing stores).

Part 2: Stacked Bar Chart of Monthly Store Performance

Now we should evaluate the low performing stores and determine how bad things are.

2. Create a new sheet called **Sales By Month.**
   a. Columns: **Tran Amt** > Measure > Sum
   b. Rows: **Store, Tran Date** > Year
   c. Marks:
      i. Type: **Bar**
      ii. **Tran Date** > Color
      A. Discrete
      B. Month <- There are two month options in the drop-down. Choose the top one without a year.
      C. Sort. . . > Descending
      iii. **Tran Date** > Year > Label
   d. Let the query run at this point.
   e. Now filter your results. Right-click outside the work area and click Filters > **Store.** Then right-click again and click Filters > **Year of Tran Date.**

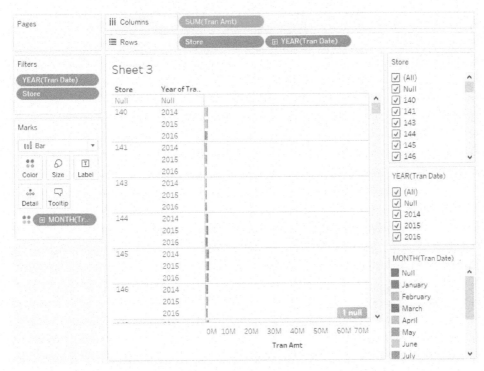

Source: Tableau Software, Inc. All rights reserved.

   f. Now let's narrow in on the high performing stores we identified in our cluster analysis.
      i. Uncheck **All** in the Store filter list.
      ii. Check the stores: 405, 716, 743, 760, 768, 775, 796.
   g. Finally let's make a year-over-year comparison on sales performance by filtering the years.
      i. Uncheck **All** in the Year(Tran Date)filter list.
      ii. Check **2014,** and **2015.**

Q2. What do you notice about sales for these stores from 2014 to 2015? Does anything stand out?

Q3. What do you notice about sales for these stores from 2015 to 2016?

3. Uncheck **2014** and check **2016.**

Q4. How would you expect November and December 2016 sales to be, given they haven't been recorded yet?

4. Take a screenshot (label it 7-7B).

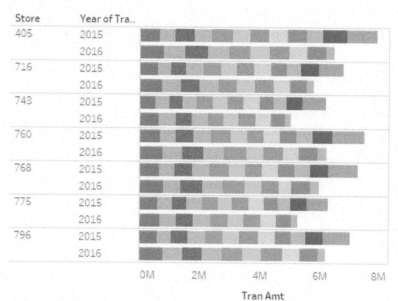

©Tableau Software, Inc. All rights reserved.

Part 3: Tree Map of Sales by Department

Now we'll look at sales by department. Because we want to see department names, we'll need to adjust our data model first.

5. Click **Data Source.**
6. Double-click **SKU and Department.**
7. Change the joins to a **Left Outer Join** so we include all transactions and only departments that sold things.
8. Create a new sheet called **Sales By Department.**
   a. No columns or rows
   b. Marks:
      i. **Tran Amt** > SUM > Size
      ii. **Tran Amt** > SUM > Color
      iii. **Deptcent Desc** > Label

c. Let the query run at this point. Once the query runs, the output should look like the following screenshot.

Sales By Department

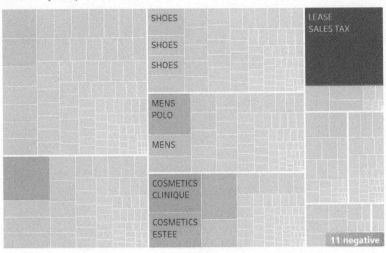

Tableau

d. Which department has the highest dollar amount of sales? Lowest?
9. To drill down to subcategories, we can create a hierarchy in Tableau.
   a. In the attributes list, drag **Dept Desc** onto **Deptcent Desc** to create a hierarchy and click **OK.**
   b. Now in the Marks list, click the **+** next to **Deptcent Desc** to show the brands in each department.
   Q5. Which is the best-selling brand of Shoes? The top three cosmetics brands?

10. Take a screenshot (label it 7-7C).

End of Lab

Chapter 8

Financial Statement Analytics

A Look at This Chapter

In this chapter, we focus on how to access and analyze financial statement data. We highlight the use of XBRL to quickly and efficiently gain computer access to financial statement data while addressing the data quality and consistency issues of XBRL data in the United States. Next, we discuss how ratios are used to analyze financial performance. We also discuss the use of sparklines and other visualization tools to help users identify trends and points of interest in the data. Finally, we discuss the use of text mining to analyze the sentiment in financial reporting data.

A Look Back

Chapter 7 focused on generating and evaluating key performance metrics that are used primarily in managerial accounting. By measuring past performance and comparing it to targeted goals, we are able to assess how well a company is working toward a goal. Also, we can determine required adjustments to how decisions are made or how business processes are run, if any.

A Look Ahead

In Chapter 9, we highlight the use of data analytics for the tax function. First, we consider how tax departments get the data they need from the financial reporting system. Second, we investigate how data analytics is used to help with tax compliance issues and tax planning.

Sometimes the future is now. The StockSnips app uses sentiment analysis, machine learning, and artificial intelligence to aggregate and analyze news related to publicly traded companies on **Nasdaq** and the **New York Stock Exchange** to "gain stock insights and track a company's financial and business operations." The use of Data Analytics helps classify the new to help predict revenue, earnings, and cash flows, which are in turn used to predict the stock performance. What will Data Analytics do next?

S Narayan/Dinodia Photo/AGE Fotostock

OBJECTIVES

After reading this chapter, you should be able to:

LO 8-1   Understand different types of financial statement analysis.

LO 8-2   Explain how to create and read visualizations of financial statement data.

LO 8-3   Describe the value of text mining and sentiment analysis of financial reporting.

LO 8-4   Describe how XBRL tags financial reporting data.

LO 8-1

Understand
different types of
financial statement
analysis.

FINANCIAL STATEMENT ANALYSIS

Financial statement analysis is used by investors, analysts, auditors, and other interested stakeholders to review and evaluate a company's financial statements and financial performance. Such analysis allows the stakeholder to gain an understanding of the financial health of the company to allow more insightful and effective decision making. Most financial statement users will perform descriptive and diagnostic analytics to understand the firm and identify trends and relationships among different accounts. Where there is sufficient data, predictive analytics provides insight into the future and helps identify companies that may have abnormal returns (and would be good investments).

Descriptive Financial Analytics

The primary objective of descriptive analytics for financial statements is to set a benchmark to compare against a company or portfolio of interest. We may want to calculate the mean rate of return or working capital within an industry or set of competitors. We may also use a series of ratio analyses to learn about the composition of certain accounts or to identify indicators of risk.

Ratio analysis is a tool used to evaluate relationships among different financial statement items to help understand a company's financial and operating performance. It tells us how much of one account we get for each dollar of another. For example, the gross profit ratio (gross profit/revenue) tells us how many cents we have from every dollar of sales that will cover operating expenses.

Financial ratio analysis is a key tool used by accounting, auditing, and finance professionals to assess the financial health of a business organization, to assess the reasonableness of reported financial results, and to predict future performance. Analytical procedures, including ratio analysis, are recognized as an essential component of both planning an audit and carrying out substantive testing. AS 2305 states:

A basic premise underlying the application of analytical procedures is that plausible relationships among data may reasonably be expected to exist and continue in the absence of known conditions to the contrary.[1]

Knowledge of financial statement analysis using ratios is a component of several professional certifications, including the CPA (certified public accountant), CMA (certified management accountant), and CFA (chartered financial analyst) certifications, so clearly critical for any accountant.

Vertical and Horizontal Analysis

One way that analysts calculate ratios between different accounts is by preparing a common size financial statement, like the one shown in Exhibit 8-1. A **common size financial statement** is a type of financial statement that contains only basic accounts that are common across companies. With this we can perform a **vertical analysis**, which is an analysis that shows the proportional value of accounts to a primary account, such as Revenue. In the

[1]Source: PCAOB, AS 2305, https://pcaobus.org/Standards/Auditing/Pages/AS2305.aspx.

Microsoft Corp

	2017	2018	Vertical
Revenue	$ 96,571	$ 110,360	100.00%
Cost of revenue	$ 34,261	$ 38,353	34.75%
Gross profit	$ 62,310	$ 72,007	65.25%
Total operating expenses	$ 32,979	$ 36,949	33.48%
Operating income	$ 29,025	$ 35,058	31.77%
Other expenses	$ 3,536	$ 18,487	16.75%
Net income	$ 25,489	$ 16,571	15.02%

EXHIBIT 8-1
Vertical Analysis of a
Common Size Financial
Statement

Apple Inc

	2017	2018	Vertical
Revenue	$ 229,234	$ 265,595	100.00%
Cost of revenue	$ 141,048	$ 163,756	61.66%
Gross profit	$ 88,186	$ 101,839	38.34%
Total operating expenses	$ 26,842	$ 30,941	11.65%
Operating income	$ 61,344	$ 70,898	26.69%
Other expenses	$ 12,993	$ 11,367	4.28%
Net income	$ 48,351	$ 59,531	22.41%

following example, we divide operating income by revenue to show that Apple earns about $0.27 for every dollar in sales. This is the operating income margin. On the balance sheet we would use vertical analysis to identify the proportion of assets or liabilities, for example dividing accounts receivable by total assets.

Other Classes of Ratios

For other indicators of financial health, there are four main types of ratios: liquidity, activity, solvency (or financing), and profitability. In practice, these ratios may vary slightly depending on which accounts the user decided to include or exclude.

Liquidity is the ability to satisfy the company's short-term obligations using assets that can be most readily converted into cash. Liquidity ratios help measure the liquidity of a company. Here are some common liquidity ratios:

Current ratio = Current assets/Current liabilities

Quick (acid test) ratio = (Current assets − Inventory)/Current liabilities

Working capital = Current assets − Current liabilities

Activity ratios are a computation of a firm's operating efficiency. Company activity is often measured by use of turnover ratios reflect the number of times assets flow into and out of the company during the period and serve as a gauge of the efficiency of putting assets to work. Receivables, inventory, and total asset turnover are all examples of activity ratios. Note that when you compare income statement (duration) accounts with balance sheet (point in time) accounts, you need to average the balance sheet accounts to match the period. Also for turnover ratios, analysts may use 365 days or round down to 360 days depending on preference.

Asset turnover ratio = Net sales/Average total assets

Receivable turnover ratio = Net sales/Average net accounts receivable

Average collection period ratio = 365/Receivables turnover

Inventory turnover ratio = Cost of goods sold/Average inventory

Average days in inventory ratio = 365/Inventory turnover

We use *solvency* (or sometimes called *financing*) ratios to help assess a company's ability to pay its debts and stay in business. In other words, we assess the company's financial risk—that is, the risk resulting from a company's choice of financing the business using debt or equity. Debt-to-equity, long-term debt-to-equity, and times interest earned ratios are also useful in assessing the level of solvency.

Debt-to-equity ratio = Total liabilities/Shareholders' equity

Times interest earned ratio = Income before interest and taxes/Interest expense

Profitability ratios are a common calculation when assessing a company. They are used to provide information on the profitability of a company and its prospects for the future.

Profit margin on sales ratio = Net income/Net sales

Return on assets ratio = Net income/Average total assets

Return on equity ratio = Net income/Average shareholders' equity

Asset turnover ratio = Net sales/Average total assets

Equity multiplier ratio = Average total assets/Average total equity

Profitability ratios are commonly associated with the **DuPont ratio**. The DuPont ratio was developed by the DuPont Corporation to measure performance as a decomposition of the return on equity ratio in this way.

Return on equity (ROE) = Profit margin x Asset turnover x Equity multiplier

It decomposes return on equity into three different types of ratios: profitability (profit margin), activity (operating leverage or asset turnover), and solvency (equity multiplier) ratios.

Diagnostic Financial Analytics

Is a debt-to-equity ratio value of 2.0 good or bad? Does an asset turnover ratio value of 60 days indicate a problem with obsolete inventory? Without a benchmark, these ratios give us nothing more than a data point. We need to compare these to other descriptive statistics to be able to make a judgment call. For example, if the industry average debt-to-equity ratio is 1.0 or the average company has $1 in debt to $1 in equity (a 50/50 split), the comparison would tell us that the company is quite a bit over leveraged and it is $2 in debt to every $1 in equity (a 66/33 split).

Benchmarks for financial statements can include direct competitors, industry averages, or a company's own past performance. If a competitor has an asset turnover ratio of 40 days, our 60 days means we're less efficient at getting our product out the door. But if last period we had an asset turnover of 65 days, our current period's 60 days reveals improvement in inventory management since the last period. Using these diagnostic analytics give a relative sense of place for firm performance. Refer to Exhibit 8-2 to see how Microsoft compares with Apple and Facebook in converting revenue into profit.

Auditors will use ratio analysis to pinpoint potential audit issues by considering how a company's financial statements depart from industry performance, a close competitor, or even the same company's prior-year performance. Competitors might use ratio analysis to understand the vulnerabilities of a competitor. Bond investors might use ratio analysis to see if a bond covenant is violated (e.g., some bond contracts require a borrower to maintain a current ratio above 1.0 to help ensure the loan can be paid off).

Predictive Financial Analytics

Predicting future performance of a company is the work of trading analysts, researchers, the finance department, and managers responsible for budgeting.

A **horizontal analysis** is an analysis that shows the change of a value from one period to the next. This is sometimes called a trend analysis. When you have two or more periods, you calculate the proportional change in value from one to the next similar to a ratio analysis. In Exhibit 8-3 below, we take Revenue in 2018 and divide it by Revenue in 2017 to show a 114.28 percent change or a 14.28 percent increase from one year to the next for Microsoft.

EXHIBIT 8-2
Comparison of Ratios among Three Companies

Microsoft Corp

	Return on equity (ROE)		Market Comparison		

2015	2016	2017	$ 25,489	Net income	MSFT	AAPL	FB
0.14	0.25	0.30	$ 85,401	Average shareholders' equity	0.30	0.37	0.72

				Profit margin on sales (PM)			
2015	2016	2017	$ 25,489	Net income	MSFT	AAPL	FB
0.13	0.23	0.26	$ 96,571	Net sales	0.26	0.21	0.21

				Asset turnover (AT)			
2015	2016	2017	$ 96,571	Net sales	MSFT	AAPL	FB
0.54	0.50	0.44	$ 221,890	Average total assets	0.44	0.66	3.07

				Equity multiplier (EM)			
2015	2016	2017	$ 221,890	Average total assets	MSFT	AAPL	FB
2.04	2.25	2.60	$ 85,401	Average total equity	2.60	2.66	1.12

	DuPont Framework	MSFT	AAPL	FB
	ROE = PM x AT x EM	0.30	0.37	0.72

EXHIBIT 8-3
Horizontal Analysis
of a Common Size
Financial Statement

Microsoft Corp

	2017	2018	$ Change	% Change
Revenue	$ 96,571	$ 110,360	$ 13,789	14.28%
Cost of revenue	$ 34,261	$ 38,353	$ 4,092	11.94%
Gross profit	$ 62,310	$ 72,007	$ 9,697	15.56%
Total operating expenses	$ 32,979	$ 36,949	$ 3,970	12.04%
Operating income	$ 29,025	$ 35,058	$ 6,033	20.79%
Other expenses	$ 3,536	$ 18,487	$ 14,951	422.82%
Net income	$ 25,489	$ 16,571	$ (8,918)	-34.99%

Apple Inc

	2017	2018	$ Change	% Change
Revenue	$ 229,234	$ 265,595	$ 36,361	15.86%
Cost of revenue	$ 141,048	$ 163,756	$ 22,708	16.10%
Gross profit	$ 88,186	$ 101,839	$ 13,653	15.48%
Total operating expenses	$ 26,842	$ 30,941	$ 4,099	15.27%
Operating income	$ 61,344	$ 70,898	$ 9,554	15.57%
Other expenses	$ 12,993	$ 11,367	$ (1,626)	-12.51%
Net income	$ 48,351	$ 59,531	$ 11,180	23.12%

Horizontal analysis can be used to calculate trends from one period to the next or over time.

Change amount = Current year amount – Base year amount

Change percent = (Current year amount – Base year amount)/Base year amount

When you calculate the trend over a large period of time relative to a single base year, you create an index. An **index** is a metric that shows how much any given subsequent year has changed relative to the base year. The formula is the same as above, but we lock the base year value when creating our formula, shown in Exhibit 8-4.

Using these trends and indices, we can better understand how a company performs over time, calculate the average amount of change and predict what the value is likely to be in the next period.

EXHIBIT 8-4
Index Showing Change
in Value Relative to
Base Year

	Base	Microsoft Corp		
	2015	2016	2017	2018
Revenue	$ 93,580	$ 91,154	$ 96,571	$ 110,360
$ Change	$ -	$ (2,426)	$ 2,991	$ 16,780
% Change	0.00%	-2.59%	3.20%	17.93%

⊘ PROGRESS CHECK

1. Which ratios would a financial institution be most interested in when determining whether to grant a loan to a business?
2. What would a horizontal trend tell you about a firm's performance?

VISUALIZING FINANCIAL DATA

> **LO 8-2**
>
> Explain how to create and read visualizations of financial statement data.

Visualizations help to highlight key figures present in the financial data. Whether to describe the data or show the relative value in diagnosing points of interest, color and graphs show many different dimensions.

Showing Trends

Sparklines and trendlines are used to help, financial statement users easily see the data visually and give meaning to the underlying financial data. A **sparkline** is a small visual trendline or bar chart that efficiently summarizes numbers or statistics in a single spreadsheet cell. Because it generally can fit in a single cell within a spreadsheet, it can easily add to the data without detracting from the tabular results.

For what types of reports or spreadsheets should sparklines be used? It usually depends on the type of reporting that is selected. For example, if used in a digital dashboard that already has many charts and dials, additional sparklines might clutter up the overall appearance. However, if used to show trends where it replaces or complements lots of numbers, it might be used as a very effective visualization. The nice thing about sparklines is they are generally small and just show simple trends rather than all the details regarding the horizontal and vertical axes that you would expect on a normal graph.

Exhibit 8-5 provides an example of the use of sparklines in a horizontal trend analysis for Microsoft. It shows the relative value of each line item and the overall trend.

Microsoft Corp

	2014	2015	2016	2017	2018	
Revenue	$ 86,833	$ 93,580	$ 91,154	$ 96,571	$ 110,360	
Cost of revenue	$ 27,078	$ 33,038	$ 32,780	$ 34,261	$ 38,353	
Gross profit	$ 59,755	$ 60,542	$ 58,374	$ 62,310	$ 72,007	
Total operating expenses	$ 31,869	$ 32,370	$ 31,186	$ 32,979	$ 36,949	
Operating income	$ 27,759	$ 18,161	$ 26,078	$ 29,025	$ 35,058	
Other expenses	$ 5,685	$ 5,968	$ 5,539	$ 3,536	$ 18,487	
Net income	$ 22,074	$ 12,193	$ 20,539	$ 25,489	$ 16,571	

EXHIBIT 8-5
Visualizing Financial Data with Heat Maps and Sparklines

Relative Size of Accounts

Another way to visualize financial data is to use heat maps (conditional formatting in Excel) and charts. A heat map shows the relative size of values by applying a color scale to the data. In Exhibit 8-5, the vertical composition of the accounts changes over the five-year period. Color helps highlight dramatic shifts in each year, such as the drop in income in 2015.

A balance sheet, on the other hand, has an inherent hierarchy of accounts that is a good candidate for a sunburst diagram. As shown in Exhibit 8-6, the center of the ring shows the main sections of the balance sheet and their proportional size. As you move out, you see the subgroups and individual accounts that make up the balance sheet.

EXHIBIT 8-6
Sunburst Diagram
Showing Composition
of a Balance Sheet

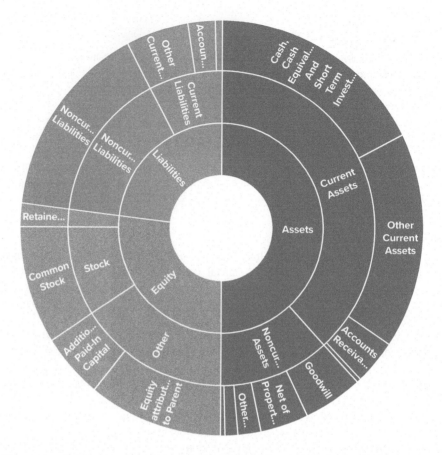

For some additional examples of visualizations that show financial data, including tree diagrams, geographic maps, chord diagrams, and heat maps for word frequency in management discussion and analysis, explore the following website: rankandfiled.com.

 PROGRESS CHECK

3. How might sparklines be used to enhance the DuPont analysis? Would you show the sparklines for each component of the DuPont ROE disaggregation, or would you propose it be shown only for the total?

LO 8-3

Describe the value of text mining and sentiment analysis of financial reporting.

TEXT MINING AND SENTIMENT ANALYSIS

Some data analysis is used to determine the sentiment included in text. For example, Uber might use text mining and sentiment analysis to read all of the words used in social media associated with its driving or the quality of its smartphone app and its services. The company can analyze the words for sentiment to see how the social media participants feel about its services and new innovations, as well as perform similar analysis on its competitors (like Lyft or traditional cab services).

Similar analysis might be done to learn more about financial reports, SEC submissions, analyst reports, and other related documents based on the words that are used. They might provide a gauge of the overall tone of the financial reports. This tone might help us understand management expectations of past or future performance that might complement the numbers and figures in the reports.

To provide an illustration of the use and predictive ability of text mining and sentiment analysis, Loughran and McDonald[2] use text mining and sentiment analysis to predict the stock market reaction to the issuance of a 10-K form by examining the proportion of negative words used in a 10-K report. Exhibit 8-7 comes from their research suggesting that the stock market reaction is related to the proportion of negative words (or inversely, the proportion of positive words). They call this method *overlap*. Thus, using this method to define the tone of the article, they indeed find a direct association, or relationship, between the proportion of negative words and the stock market reaction to the disclosure of 10-K reports.

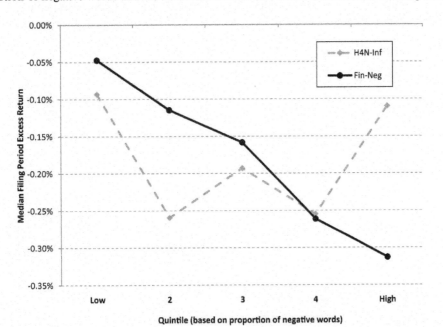

EXHIBIT 8-7
Stock Market Reaction (Excess Return) of Companies Sorted by Proportion of Negative Words
The lines represent the words from a financial dictionary (Fin-Neg) and a standard English dictionary (H4N-INF).

Source: Loughran, Tim, and Bill McDonald. (2011). "When Is a Liability Not a Liability? Textual Analysis, Dictionaries, and 10-Ks." *Journal of Finance* 66, no. 1, pp. 35–65.

They measure proportion first by developing a dictionary of 2,337 negative words in the financial context and then counting how many of those words are used as compared to the total words used (called Fin-Neg in Exhibit 8-7). One of their arguments is that a financial dictionary is better than a dictionary created from standard English usage. For that reason, they differentiate their financial dictionary (Fin-Neg) from the negative words used in normal English usage (as shown in Exhibit 8-7 as H4N-Inf). Whereas *cost, expense,* or *liability* might be viewed as negative in normal English, they are not considered to be negative words in the financial dictionary. The most frequent negative words in the financial dictionary include words like *loss, claims, impairment, adverse, restructuring,* and *litigation.*

✓ PROGRESS CHECK

4. Which would you predict would have more positive sentiment in a 10-K, the footnotes to the financial statements or the MD&A (management discussion and analysis) of the financial statements?

5. Why would you guess the results between the proportion of negative words and the stock market reaction to the 10-K issuance diverge the Fin-Neg and the H4N-Inf dictionary?

---

[2]Tim Loughran and Bill McDonald, "When Is a Liability Not a Liability? Textual Analysis, Dictionaries, and 10-Ks," *Journal of Finance* 66, no. 1 (2011), pp. 35–65.

LO 8-4

Describe how XBRL tags financial reporting data.

XBRL AND FINANCIAL DATA QUALITY

XBRL is a global standard for tagging and reporting financial information in a computer-readable format. XBRL stands for eXtensible Business Reporting Language and is a type of XML (extensible markup language) used for organizing and defining financial elements. In the United States and other jurisdictions, companies are required to tag each piece of financial data that appears in their financial statements so that it is machine readable. Once these instance documents are submitted and validated by the regulatory body, they are immediately available for public consumption by different types of financial statement users, including financial analysts, investors, or lenders. These users can then leverage data models to quickly analyze large amounts of data from the entire population of listed companies with minimal effort.

As of June 2011, the Securities and Exchange Commission requires all public company filers, including smaller reporting companies and foreign private issuers, to file an XBRL instance document, which contains the same information found the in the traditional financial statements but in computer-readable format. In addition to tagging financial values, such as account balances and lease amounts, companies must tag every date, fact, figure, percentage, and paragraph of text in management discussion and analysis and footnotes.

EXHIBIT 8-8
Creating an XBRL
Instance Document

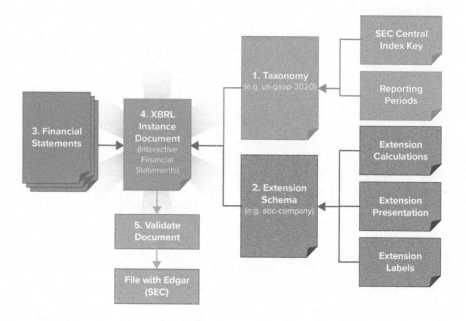

The preparer of an XBRL instance document must begin by identifying a correct taxonomy that defines and describes each key standardized data element (like cash or accounts payable), shown in Exhibit 8-8. The **XBRL taxonomy** also defines the relationships between each element—for example, buildings and improvements are a component of property, plant, and equipment, which is a component of noncurrent assets, which is a component of assets, which is in the statement of financial position (balance sheet), shown in Exhibit 8-9.

The current U.S. GAAP Financial Reporting Taxonomy can be explored interactively at xbrlview.fasb.org. It defines more than 19,000 elements with descriptions and links to the

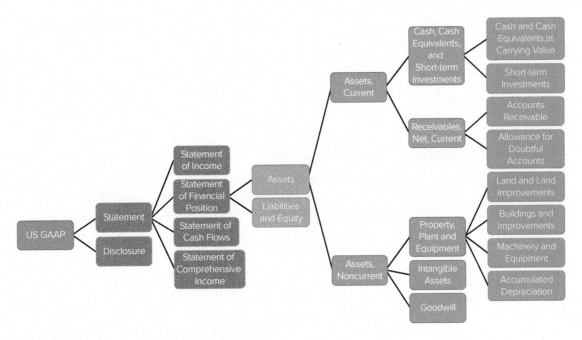

EXHIBIT 8-9 Organization of Accounts within the XBRL Taxonomy

FASB codification. For example, the XBRL tag for cash is labeled "Cash" and is defined as follows:

> Amount of currency on hand as well as demand deposits with banks or financial institutions. Includes other kinds of accounts that have the general characteristics of demand deposits. Excludes cash and cash equivalents within disposal group and discontinued operation.[3]

The XBRL tag for cash and cash equivalents footnote disclosure is labeled as "CashAndCashEquivalentsDisclosureTextBlock" and is defined as follows:

> The entire disclosure for cash and cash equivalent footnotes, which may include the types of deposits and money market instruments, applicable carrying amounts, restricted amounts and compensating balance arrangements. Cash and equivalents include: (1) currency on hand (2) demand deposits with banks or financial institutions (3) other kinds of accounts that have the general characteristics of demand deposits (4) short-term, highly liquid investments that are both readily convertible to known amounts of cash and so near their maturity that they present insignificant risk of changes in value because of changes in interest rates. Generally, only investments maturing within three months from the date of acquisition qualify.[4]

The use of tags allows data to be quickly transmitted and received, and the tags serve as an input for financial analysts valuing a company, an auditor finding areas where an error

[3]Source:https://xbrl.us/xbrl-taxonomy/2017-us-gaap/
[4]Source: https://xbrl.us/xbrl-taxonomy/2017-us-gaap/

might occur, or regulators seeing if firms are in compliance with various regulations and laws (like the SEC or IRS).

Preparers of the XBRL instance document compare the financial statement figures with the tags in the taxonomy. When a tag does not exist, the preparer can extend the taxonomy with their own custom tags. The taxonomy and extension schema are combined with the financial data to generate the XBRL instance document which is then validated for errors and submitted to the regulatory authority.

XBRL Data Quality

While XBRL enables data analytics models to quickly process and present interesting patterns in the data, the user must be careful not to trust all of the numbers at face value. Users may notice that data values may be missing or incorrect. The XBRL-US Center for Data Quality laments that:

> Investors and analysts have been reluctant to use the data because of concerns about its accuracy, consistency, and reliability. Inconsistent or incorrect data tagging, including the use of custom tags in lieu of standard tags and input mistakes, causes translation errors, which make automated analysis of the data unduly difficult.[5]

Part of the problem is that most companies outsource the preparation of XBRL financial statements to other companies, such as Fujitsu and R.R. Donnelley, and don't validate the data themselves. Another problem is that ambiguity in the taxonomy leads companies to select incorrect tags or use extension tags where a standard tag exists. Because these statements are not audited, there is little incentive to improve data quality unless stricter validation measures are put in place.

Improved data quality for analysts comes at a cost. As analysts wait for improved data quality in XBRL data, they will turn to expensive commercial datasets, such as Compustat, that have been automatically and manually transformed to improve data quality.

Despite these issues, there is still some value in analyzing XBRL data for illustrative purposes and some providers have additional solutions to make XBRL data comparable. Sometimes outside data vendors create **standardized metrics** to make the company reported XBRL data more comparable. For example, Calcbench, a data vendor that eases financial analysis for XBRL uses, makes standardized metrics, noting:

> IBM labels revenue as "Total revenue" and uses the tag "Revenues", whereas Apple, labels their revenue as "Net sales" and uses the tag "SalesRevenueNet". This is a relatively simple case, because both companies used tags from the FASB taxonomy.
>
> Users are typically not interested in the subtle differences of how companies tag or label information. In the previous example, most users would want Apple and IBM's revenue, regardless of how it was tagged. To that end, we create standardized metrics.[6]

[5]Source: https://xbrl.us/data-quality/
[6]Source: Accessed August 2017. https://knowledge.calcbench.com/hc/en-us/articles/230017408-What-is-a-standardized-metric.

Different data vendors such as **XBRLAnalyst** and **Calcbench** both provide a trace function that allows you to trace the standardized metric back to the original source to see which XBRL tags are referenced or used to make up the standardized metric.[7]

Exhibit 8-10 shows what a report using standardized metrics looks like for **Boeing**'s balance sheet. Note the standardized tags used for **Boeing** could be used for any of the SEC filers to gather their balance sheet and other financial statements.

Ticker	BA	Boeing Co	
Year	2015	2014	2013
Period	Y	Y	Y
Calcbench Normalized Point			
Assets			
Current Assets			
Cash	$11,302,000,000	$11,733,000,000	$9,088,000,000
AccountsReceivable	$8,713,000,000	$7,729,000,000	$6,546,000,000
Inventory	$47,257,000,000	$46,756,000,000	$42,912,000,000
PrepaidExpense	#N/A	#N/A	#N/A
CurrentAssets	$68,234,000,000	$67,767,000,000	$65,074,000,000
PPE	$12,076,000,000	$11,007,000,000	$10,224,000,000
Goodwill	$5,126,000,000	$5,119,000,000	$5,043,000,000
LongTermInvestments	$1,284,000,000	$1,154,000,000	$1,204,000,000
Assets	$94,408,000,000	$92,921,000,000	$92,663,000,000
Liabilities And Equity			
AccountsPayable	$10,800,000,000	$10,667,000,000	$9,498,000,000
AccruedLiabilities	$14,014,000,000	$13,462,000,000	$14,131,000,000
ShortTermDebt	$1,234,000,000	$929,000,000	$1,563,000,000
DeferredRevenue	$24,364,000,000	$23,175,000,000	$20,027,000,000
CurrentLiabilities	$50,412,000,000	$48,233,000,000	$51,486,000,000
NonCurrentLiabilities			
LongTermDebt	$8,730,000,000	$8,141,000,000	$8,072,000,000
NonCurrentTaxLiability	$2,392,000,000	#N/A	#N/A
PensionAndOtherPostretirementDe	$17,783,000,000	$17,182,000,000	$10,474,000,000
Liabilities	$88,011,000,000	$84,131,000,000	$77,666,000,000
Equity			
RetainedEarnings	$38,756,000,000	$36,180,000,000	$32,964,000,000
TreasuryStockValue	$29,568,000,000	$23,298,000,000	$17,671,000,000
StockHoldersEquity	$6,397,000,000	$8,790,000,000	$14,997,000,000

EXHIBIT 8-10
Balance Sheet from XBRL Data
Note the XBRL tag names in the far left column.

Source: https://www.calcbench.com/xbrl_to_excel

[7] https://knowledge.calcbench.com/hc/en-us/articles/230017408-What-is-a-standardized-metric.

XBRL, XBRL-GL, and Real-Time Financial Reporting

The desire for machine-readable data doesn't stop at the financial statements. Many financial reporting systems within enterprise systems such as Oracle and SAP have a general ledger that is consistent with XBRL, called **XBRL-GL** (XBRL-Global Ledger). That means once the numbers are input into a financial system, they are already tagged and able to be transmitted in real time to interested users in a continuous reporting function.

Of course, there are a number of reasons this information is not transmitted in real time. For example, the accounting information has not yet been audited, and it may contain errors. Other information such as goodwill or long-term debt will likely not change on a minute-by-minute basis, so there would be no use for it on a real-time basis. But as systems advance and continuous, real-time auditing becomes more prevalent, and with our understanding of how and exactly what type of real-time information might be used, there may be a chance of providing real-time accounting information in the relative short term by use of XBRL-GL.

Examples of Financial Statement Analytics Using XBRL

We illustrate the DuPont Ratios in Exhibit 8-11 by considering a calculation from some standard XBRL data.

You'll note for the Quarter 2 analysis in 2009, for **DuPont** (Ticker Symbol = DD), if you take its profit margin, 0.294, multiplied by asset turnover of 20.1 percent multiplied by the financial leverage of 471.7 percent, you get a return on equity of 27.8 percent.

EXHIBIT 8-11
DuPont Ratios Using XBRL Data

Source: https://www.calcbench.com/xbrl_to_excel.

ticker	year	period	revenue	cost of revenue	profit margin	assets	operating leverage	equity	financial leverage	return on equity
DD	2009	Q2	$7,088,000,000	$5,007,000,000	29.4%	$35,258,000,000	20.1%	$7,474,000,000	471.7%	27.8%
DD	2009	Q3	$6,156,000,000	$4,560,000,000	25.9%	$36,168,000,000	17.0%	$8,083,000,000	447.5%	19.7%
DD	2009	Y	$27,328,000,000	$19,708,000,000	27.9%	$38,185,000,000	71.6%	$7,651,000,000	499.1%	99.6%
DD	2010	Q1	$8,844,000,000	$5,796,000,000	34.5%	$37,986,000,000	23.3%	$8,429,000,000	451.0%	36.2%
DD	2010	Q2	$9,080,000,000	$5,984,000,000	34.1%	$37,712,000,000	24.1%	$9,276,000,000	406.6%	33.4%
DD	2010	Q3	$7,067,000,000	$5,443,000,000	23.0%	$39,918,000,000	17.7%	$9,651,000,000	413.6%	16.8%
DD	2010	Y	$28,899,000,000	$20,574,000,000	28.8%	$40,410,000,000	71.5%	$9,800,000,000	412.3%	84.9%
DD	2011	Q1	$10,059,000,000	$6,831,000,000	32.1%	$42,600,000,000	23.6%	$11,279,000,000	377.7%	28.6%
DD	2011	Q2	$10,493,000,000	$7,191,000,000	31.5%	$47,736,000,000	22.0%	$12,502,000,000	381.8%	26.4%
DD	2011	Q3	$8,303,000,000	$6,345,000,000	23.6%	$47,794,000,000	17.4%	$12,024,000,000	397.5%	16.3%
DD	2011	Y	$34,429,000,000	$21,264,000,000	38.2%	$48,643,000,000	70.8%	$9,208,000,000	528.3%	142.9%
DD	2012	Q1	$10,194,000,000	$6,816,000,000	33.1%	$50,223,000,000	20.3%	$10,427,000,000	481.7%	32.4%
DD	2012	Q2	$10,208,000,000	$5,844,000,000	42.8%	$50,051,000,000	20.4%	$10,645,000,000	470.0%	41.0%
DD	2012	Q3	$7,336,000,000	$4,779,000,000	34.9%	$50,607,000,000	14.5%	$10,711,000,000	472.5%	23.9%
DD	2012	Y	$35,310,000,000	$21,538,000,000	39.0%	$49,859,000,000	70.8%	$10,299,000,000	484.1%	133.7%
DD	2013	Q1	$10,500,000,000	$7,105,000,000	32.3%	$50,564,000,000	20.8%	$12,315,000,000	410.6%	27.6%
DD	2013	Q2	$10,003,000,000	$6,057,000,000	39.4%	$51,349,000,000	19.5%	$13,355,000,000	384.5%	29.5%
DD	2013	Q3	$7,805,000,000	$5,165,000,000	33.8%	$51,990,000,000	15.0%	$13,900,000,000	374.0%	19.0%
DD	2014	Q1	$10,145,000,000	$6,000,000,000	40.9%	$47,800,000,000	21.2%	$16,442,000,000	290.7%	25.2%

✓ PROGRESS CHECK

6. How does XBRL facilitate Data Analytics by analysts?
7. How might standardized XBRL metrics be useful in comparing the financial statements of **General Motors**, **Alphabet**, and **Alibaba**?
8. Assuming XBRL-GL is able to disseminate real-time financial reports, which real-time financial elements (account names) might be most useful to decision makers? And which information might not be useful?
9. Using Exhibit 8-11 as the source of data and using the raw accounts, show the components of profit margin, operating leverage and financial leverage and how they are combined to equal ROE for Q2 2009 for **DuPont** (Ticker = DD).

Summary

Data Analytics extends to the financial accounting and financial reporting space.

- Financial statement analytics includes descriptive analytics, such as financial ratios and vertical analysis; diagnostic analytics, where we compare those to benchmarks from prior periods or competitors; and predictive analytics, including horizontal trend analysis.
- Sparklines and trendlines are efficient and effective tools to visualize firm performance, and sunburst diagrams and heat maps help highlight values of interest.
- Sentiment analysis could be used with financial statements, other financial reports, and other financially related information to gauge positive and negative meaning from otherwise text-heavy notes.
- The XBRL taxonomy provides tags for 19,000 financial elements and allows for the use of company-defined tags when the normal XBRL tags are not suitable.
- By tagging financial elements in a computer readable manner, XBRL facilitates the accurate and timely transmission of financial reporting to all interested stakeholders.
- XBRL and Data Analytics allow timely analysis of the financial statements and the computation of financial ratios. We illustrated its usage by showing the DuPont ratio framework.

Key Words

common size financial statements (*328*) A type of financial statement that contains only basic accounts that are common across companies.

DuPont ratio analysis (*330*) Developed by the DuPont Corporation to decompose performance (particularly return on equity [ROE]) into its component parts.

financial statement analysis (*328*) Used by investors, analysts, auditors, and other interested stakeholders to review and evaluate a company's financial statements and financial performance.

horizontal analysis (*331*) An analysis that shows the change of a value from one period to the next.

index (*332*) A metric that shows how much any given subsequent year has changed relative to the base year.

ratio analysis (*328*) A tool used to evaluate relationships among different financial statement items to help understand a company's financial and operating performance.

sparkline (*333*) A small visual trendline or bar chart that efficiently summarizes numbers or statistics in a single spreadsheet cell.

standardized metrics (*338*) Metrics used by data vendors to allow easier comparison of company reported XBRL data.

vertical analysis (*328*) An analysis that shows the proportional value of accounts to a primary account, such as Revenue

XBRL (*336*) XBRL stands for extensible Business Reporting Language and is a type of XML (extensible markup language) used for organizing and defining financial elements.

XBRL-GL (*340*) Stands for XBRL-General Ledger; relates to the ability of enterprise system to tag financial elements within the firm's financial reporting system.

XBRL taxonomy (*336*) Defines and describes each key data element (like cash or accounts payable). The taxonomy also defines the relationships between each element (like inventory is a component of current assets and current assets is a component of total assets).

✓ ANSWERS TO PROGRESS CHECKS

1. Liquidity ratios (e.g., current ratio or quick ratio) would tell the bank whether the business could make payments. Solvency ratios (e.g., debt-to-equity ratio) would indicate how leveraged the company was and the likelihood of paying us back. It may also determine the interest rate we charge.

2. The horizontal analysis shows the trend over time. We could see if revenues are going up and costs are going down as the result of good management or the opposite in the case of inefficiencies or decline.

3. Answers may vary on how to visualize the data. It might depend on the type of reporting that is selected. For example, is it solely a digital dashboard, or is it a report with many facts and figures where more sparklines might clutter up the overall appearance? The nice thing about sparklines is they are generally small and just show simple trends rather than details about the horizontal and vertical axes.

4. The MD&A section of the 10-K has management reporting on what happened in the most recent period and what they expect will happen in the coming year. They are usually upbeat and generally optimistic about the future. The footnotes are generally background looking and would be much more factual-based, careful, and conservative. We would expect the MD&A section to be much more optimistic than the footnotes.

5. Accounting has its own lingo. Words that might seem negative for the English language are not necessarily negative for financial reports. For this reason, the results diverge based on whether the standard English usage dictionary (H4N-inf) or the financial dictionary (Fin-Neg) is used. The relationship between the excess stock market return and the financial dictionary is what we would expect.

6. By each company providing tags for each piece of its financial data as computer readable, XBRL allows immediate access to each type of financial statement user, be they financial analysts, investors, lenders, for their own specific use.

7. When journal entries and transactions are made in an XBRL-GL system, there is the possibility of real-time financial reporting. In the author's opinion, income statement information (including sales, cost of goods sold, and SG&A expenditures) would be useful to financial users on a real-time basis. Any information that does not change frequently would not be as useful. Examples include real-time financial elements, including goodwill; long-term debt; and property, plant, and equipment.

8. Standardized metrics are useful for comparing companies because they allow for similar accounts to have the same title regardless of the account names used by the various companies. They allow for ease of comparison across multiple companies.

9. Profit margin = (Revenues − Cost of revenue)/Revenues = ($7.088B − $5.007B)/$7.088B = 29.4%

   Operating leverage = Sales/Assets = ($7.088B / $35.258B) = 20.1%

   Financial leverage = Assets/Equity = $35.258B / $7.474B = 471.7%

   ROE = Profit margin × Operating leverage (or Asset turnover) × Financial leverage = 0.294 × 0.201 × 4.717 = 0.278

Multiple Choice Questions

1. The DuPont analysis of return on equity (ROE) includes all of the following component ratios *except:*
   a. asset turnover.
   b. inventory turnover.
   c. financial leverage.
   d. profit margin.

2. XBRL stands for:
   a. Extensible Business Reporting Language.
   b. Extensive Business Reporting Language.
   c. XML Business Reporting Language.
   d. Excel Business Reporting Language.

3. Which term defines and describes each XBRL financial element?
   a. Data dictionary
   b. Descriptive statistics
   c. XBRL-GL
   d. Taxonomy

4. Which stage of the IMPACT model (introduced in Chapter 1) would the use of sparklines fit?
   a. Track outcomes
   b. Communicate insights
   c. Address and refine results
   d. Perform test plan

5. What is the name of the output from data vendors to help compare companies using different XBRL tags for revenue?
   a. XBRL taxonomy
   b. Data assimilation
   c. Consonant tagging
   d. Standardized metrics

6. What is the term used to describe the process of assigning XBRL tags internally within a financial reporting/enterprise system?
   a. XBRL tagging
   b. XBRL taxonomy
   c. XBRL-GL
   d. XBRL dictionary

7. What computerized technique would be used to perform sentiment analysis on an annual accounting report?
   a. Text mining
   b. Sentiment mining
   c. Textual analysis
   d. Decision trees

8. What type of ratios measure a firm's operating efficiency?

    a. DuPont ratios

    b. Liquidity ratios

    c. Activity ratios

    d. Solvency ratios

9. What type of ratios measure a firm's ability to pay its debts and stay in business?

    a. DuPont ratios

    b. Liquidity ratios

    c. Activity ratios

    d. Solvency ratios

10. What is considered an essential component of planning an audit and carrying out substantive testing that involves ratio analysis?

    a. Environmental analysis

    b. Competitive analysis

    c. Management integrity analysis

    d. Analytical procedures

Discussion Questions

1. Which would you predict would have more positive sentiment in a 10-K, the financial statements or the MD&A (management discussion and analysis) of the financial statements? More positive sentiment in the footnotes or MD&A? Why?

2. Would you recommend the Securities and Exchange Commission require the use of sparklines on the face of the financial statements? Why or why not?

3. Why do audit firms perform analytical procedures to identify risk? Which type of ratios (liquidity, solvency, activity, and profitability ratios) would you use to evaluate the company's ability to continue as a going concern?

4. Go to https://xbrl.us/data-rule/dqc_0015-lepr/ and find the XBRL element name for Interest expense and Sales, General, and Administrative expense.

5. Go to https://xbrl.us/data-rule/dqc_0015-lepr/ and find the XBRL element name for Other NonOperating Income and indicate whether XBRL says that should normally be a debit or credit entry.

6. Go to finance.yahoo.com and type in the ticker symbol for **Apple** (AAPL) and click on the statistics tab. Which of those variables would be useful in assessing profitability?

7. Can you think of any other settings, besides financial reports, where tagged data might be useful for fast, accurate analysis generally completed by computers? How could it be used in a hospital setting? Or at your university?

8. Can you think of how sentiment analysis might be used in a marketing setting? How could it be used in a hospital setting? Or at your university? When would it be especially good to measure the sentiment?

Problems

1. Can you think of situations where sentiment analysis might be helpful to analyze press releases or earnings announcements? What additional information might it provide that is not directly in the overall announcement? Would it be useful to have sentiment analysis automated to just get a basic sentiment measure versus the base level of sentiment expected in a press announcement or earnings announcement?

2. We noted in the text that negative words in the financial dictionary include words like *loss, claims, impairment, adverse, restructuring,* and *litigation.* What are other negative words might you add to that list? What are your thoughts on positive words that would be included in the financial dictionary, particularly those that might be different than standard English dictionary usage?

3. You're asked to figure out how the stock market responded to **Amazon**'s announcement on June 16, 2017, that it would purchase **Whole Foods**—arguably a transformational change for **Amazon, Walmart**, and the whole retail industry.

   Required:

   a. Go to finance.yahoo.com, type in the ticker symbol for **Amazon** (AMZN), click on historical data, and input the dates around June 16, 2017. Specifically, see how much the stock price changed on June 16.

   b. Do the same analysis for **Walmart** (WMT) over the same dates, which was arguably most directly affected, and see what happened to its stock price.

4. The preceding question asked you to figure out how the stock market responded to **Amazon**'s announcement that it would purchase **Whole Foods**. The question now is if the stock market for **Amazon** had higher trade volume on that day than the average of the month before.

   Required:

   a. Go to finance.yahoo.com, type in the ticker symbol for **Amazon** (AMZN), click on historical data, and input the dates from May 15, 2017, to June 16, 2017. Download the data, calculate the average volume for the month prior to June 16, and compare it to the trading volume on June 16. Any effect on trading volume of the **Whole Foods** announcement by **Amazon**?

   b. Do the same analysis for **Walmart** (WMT) over the same dates and see what happened to its trading volume. Any effect on trading volume of the **Whole Foods** announcement by **Amazon**?

5. Go to Loughran and McDonald's sentiment word lists at https://sraf.nd.edu/textual-analysis/resources/ and download the Master Dictionary. These lists are what they've used to assess sentiment in financial statements and related financial reports. Give five words that are considered to be "negative" and five words that are considered to be "constraining." How would you use this in your analysis of sentiment of an accounting report?

6. Go to Loughran and McDonald's sentiment word lists at https://sraf.nd.edu/textual-analysis/resources/ and download the Master Dictionary. These lists are what they've used to assess sentiment in financial statements and related financial reports. Give five words that are considered to be "litigious" and five words that are considered to be "positive."

Company summary

This lab will pull in XBRL data from *Fortune* 100 companies listed with the SEC. You have the option to analyze a pair of companies of your choice based on your own interest level. This lab will have you compare other companies as well.

Data

The data used in this analysis are XBRL-tagged data from *Fortune* 100 companies. The data are pulled from FinDynamics, which in turn pulls the data from the SEC.

Technique

- You will use a combination of spreadsheet formulas and live XBRL data to generate a spreadsheet that is adaptable and dynamic. In other words, you will create a template that can be used to answer several financial statement analysis questions.

Software needed

- Google Sheets (sheets.google.com)
- iXBRLAnalyst script (https://findynamics.com/gsheets/ixbrlanalyst.gs)

In this lab, you will:

Part 1: Identify questions related to the income statement.

Part 2: Master the data.

Part 3: Perform an analysis of the financial data.

Part 4: Address and refine your results.

Part 1: Identify the Questions

Financial statement analysis frequently involves identifying relationships between specific pieces of data. We may want to see how financial data have changed over time or how the composition has changed.

Q1.   Select a *Fortune* 100 company, such as **Apple** (AAPL) or **Nike** (NKE), and identify three questions you might want to know about that company's financial performance over the past three years. For example, "What is the trend of operating costs?"

Q2.   Form a hypothesis for each of your questions. For example, "I expect **Nike**'s operating costs have gone up."

Part 2: Master the Data

To create a dynamic spreadsheet, you must first connect your sheet to a data source on the Internet. In this case, you will use Google Sheets because it is hosted online and then add the iXBRLAnalyst script to connect it to FinDynamics so you can use formulas to query financial statement elements.

1. Log into Google Sheets (sheets.google.com), and create a new, blank sheet called **XBRL Common.**
2. Click **Tools > Script Editor** from the menu.
3. In a new window (i.e., tab), go to findynamics.com/gsheets/ixbrlanalyst.gs.
4. Copy and paste the entire script from the FinDynamics page into the **Script Editor** window, replacing any existing text.

5. Click **Save** and name the project **XBRL**. Click **OK**.
6. Close the **Script Editor** window and return to your Google Sheet.
7. Reload/refresh the page. If you see a new **iXBRLAnalyst** menu appear, you are now connected to the XBRL data.
8. Test your connection by typing in the following formula anywhere on your sheet: =XBRLFact("AAPL","AssetsCurrent","2017"). If your connection is good, it should return the value 128645000000 for Apple Inc.'s 2017 balance in current assets.
9. Delete the formula and continue to the next step.

Note: Once you've added the iXBRLAnalyst script to a Google Sheet, you can simply open that sheet, then go to **File > Make a copy . . . ,** and the script will automatically be copied to the new sheet.

The basic formulas available with the iXBRLAnalyst script are:

=FinValue(company, tag, year, period, member, scale)
=XBRLFact(company, tag, year, period, member, scale, true)
=SharePriceStats(company, date, duration, request)

where:

company = ticker symbol (e.g., "AAPL" for Apple Inc.)
tag = XBRL tag or normalized tag (e.g., "NetIncomeLoss" or "[Net Income]")
year = reporting year (e.g., "2017")
period = fiscal period (e.g., "Q1" for 1st Quarter or "Y" for year)
scale = rounding (e.g., "k," "thousands," or "1000" for thousands) [*Note:* There is an error with rounding, so it is suggested to simply divide the formula by the scale instead, e.g. =XBRLFact(c,t,y,p)/scale.]

Because companies frequently use different tags to represents similar concepts (such as the tags ProfitLoss or NetIncomeLoss to identify Net Income), it is important to make sure you're using the correct values. FinDynamics attempts to coordinate the diversity of tags by using normalized tags that use formulas and relationships instead of direct tags. Normalized tags must be contained within brackets []. Some examples are given in Lab Table 8-1A.

If you're looking for specific XBRL tags, you can explore the current XBRL taxonomy at xbrlview.fasb.org.

Balance Sheet	Income Statement	Statement of Cash Flows
[Cash, Cash Equivalents and Short-Term Investments]	[Revenue]	[Cash From Operations (CFO)]
[Short-Term Investments]	[Cost of Revenue]	[Changes in Working Capital]
[Accounts Receivable, Current]	[Gross Profit]	[Changes in Accounts Receivables]
[Inventory]	[Selling, General & Administrative Expense]	[Changes in Liabilities]
[Other Current Assets]	[Research & Development Expense]	[Changes in Inventories]
[Current Assets]	[Depreciation (&Amortization), IS]	[Adjustments of Non-Cash Items, CF]
[Net of Property, Plant & Equipment]	[Non-Interest Expense]	[Provision For Doubtful Accounts]
[Long-Term Investments]	[Other Operating Expenses]	[Depreciation (&Amortization), CF]
[Intangible Assets, Net]	[Operating Expenses]	[Stock-Based Compensation]
[Goodwill]	[Operating Income]	[Pension and Other Retirement Benefits]
[Other Noncurrent Assets]	[Other Operating Income]	[Interest Paid]
[Noncurrent Assets]	[Non-Operating Income (Expense)]	[Other CFO]
[Assets]	[Interest Expense]	[Cash from Investing (CFI)]
[Accounts Payable and Accrued Liabilities, Current]	[Costs and Expenses]	[Capital Expenditures]
[Short-Term Borrowing]	[Earnings Before Taxes]	[Payments to Acquire Investments]
[Long-Term Debt, Current]	[Income Taxes]	[Proceeds from Investments]
[Other Current Liabilities]	[Income from Continuing Operations]	[Other CFI]
		[Cash From Financing (CFF)]
		[Payment of Dividends]

LAB TABLE 8-1A Normalized Accounts Created by FinDynamics for XBRLAnalyst

Balance Sheet	Income Statement	Statement of Cash Flows
[Current Liabilities] [Other Noncurrent Liabilities] [Noncurrent Liabilities] [Liabilities] [Preferred Stock] [Common Stock] [Additional Paid-in Capital] [Retained Earnings (Accumulated Deficit)] [Equity Attributable to Parent] [Equity Attributable to Noncontrolling Interest] [Stockholders' Equity] [Liabilities & Equity]	[Income from Discontinued Operations, Net of Taxes] [Extraordinary Items, Gain (Loss)] [Net Income] [Net Income Attributable to Parent] [Net Income Attributable to Noncontrolling Interest] [Preferred Stock Dividends and Other Adjustments] [Comprehensive Income (Loss)] [Other Comprehensive Income (Loss)] [Comprehensive Income (Loss) Attributable to Parent] [Comprehensive Income (Loss) Attributable to Noncontrolling Interest]	[Proceeds from Sale of Equity] [Repurchase of Equity] [Net Borrowing] [Other CFF] [Effect of Exchange Rate Changes] [Total Cash, Change] [Net Cash, Continuing Operations] [Net CFO, Continuing Operations] [Net CFI, Continuing Operations] [Net CFF, Continuing Operations] [Net Cash, DO] [Net CFO, DO] [Net CFI, DO] [Net CFF, DO]

LAB TABLE 8-1A *(Continued)*

Part 3: Perform an Analysis of the Data

We will begin by creating a common size income statement for one company over a three-year period.

10. In your Google Sheet, begin by entering the values for the tags, as shown:

LAB EXHIBIT 8-1A

	A	B
1	Company	AAPL
2	Year	2016
3	Period	Y
4	Scale	1000000

11. Then set up your financial statement using the following normalized tags and periods. *Note:* Because we already identified the most current year in A2, we'll use a formula to find the three most recent years.

LAB EXHIBIT 8-1B

	A	B	C	D
6		=$B2	=B6-1	=C6-1
7	[Revenue]			
8	[Cost of Revenue]			
9	[Gross Profit]			
10	[Selling, General & Administrative Expense]			
11	[Research & Development Expense]			
12	[Other Operating Expenses]			
13	*[Operating Expenses]*			
14	[Operating Income]			
15	[Depreciation (&Amortization), CF]			
16	[Interest Income]			
17	[Earnings before Taxes]			

	A	B	C	D
18	[Income Taxes]			
19	[Net Income]			

12. Now enter the =XBRLFact() formula to pull in the correct values, using relative or absolute references (e.g., $A7, $B$1, etc.) as necessary. For example, the formula in B7 should be =XBRLFact($B$1,$A7,B$6,$B$3)/$B$4.

13. If you've used relative references correctly, you can either drag the formula down and across columns B, C, and D, or copy and paste the cell (not the formula itself) into the rest of the table.

14. Use the formatting tools to clean up your spreadsheet, then take a screenshot (label it 8-1A).

Next, you can begin editing your dynamic data and expanding your analysis, identifying trends and ratios.

15. In your Google Sheet, use a sparkline to show the change in income statement accounts:
    a. In cell E7, type: =SPARKLINE(B7:D7). Next, copy the sparkline down the column.
    b. Note: The line is trending toward the left.

16. Now perform a vertical analysis in the columns to the right showing each value as a percentage of revenue:
    a. Copy cells B6:D6 into F6:H6.
    b. In F7, type =B7/B$7.
    c. Drag the formula to fill in F7:H19.
    d. Format the numbers as a percentage.
    e. Add a sparkline in Column I.

17. Take a screenshot (label it 8-1B).

Part 4: Address and Refine Results

Now that you have a common-size income statement, replace the company ticker in cell B1 with your selected company's ticker and press Enter. The data on the spreadsheet will update.

Q3. Look at the trends and composition of the income statement, then answer your three questions from Q1.

Q4. How did the actual results compare with your hypothesis?

Q5. Replace the company ticker with a competitor of your company (e.g., MSFT vs. AAPL). How do their trends compare with your initial company?

Q6. How could you expand this spreadsheet to include multiple competitors' data on the same sheet for quick analysis?

End of Lab

Lab 8-2 Create Dynamic Common Size Financial Statements

XBRLAnalyst allows us to easily create common size financial statements. Using the skills learned in Lab 8-1, now extend the analysis to identify some companies based on their financial performance. The *Fortune* 100 companies listed in Lab Exhibit 8-2A operate in a variety of industries. Their FY2016 revenue and assets appear below:

Company	Revenue (millions) FY2016	Assets (millions) FY2016
BANK OF AMERICA (BAC), through its subsidiaries, provides various banking and financial products and services for individual consumers, small- and middle-market businesses, institutional investors, corporations, and governments in the United States and internationally.	$80,104	$2,187,702
WALMART (WMT) operates retail stores in various formats worldwide. The company operates in three segments: Walmart U.S., Walmart International, and Sam's Club.	$482,130	$199,581
CISCO (CSCO) designs, manufactures, and sells Internet protocol (IP)–based networking and other products related to the communications and information technology industries worldwide.	$49,247	$121,652
COCA-COLA (KO) is a beverage company engaging in the manufacture, marketing, and sale of nonalcoholic beverages worldwide.	$41,863	$87,270
BOEING (BA) engages in the design, development, manufacture, sale, and support of commercial jetliners, military aircraft, satellites, missile defense, human space flight, and launch systems and services worldwide.	$94,571	$89,997
EBAY (EBAY) provides online platforms, tools, and services to help individuals and merchants in online and mobile commerce and payments in the United States and internationally.	$8,979	$23,847
AMAZON (AMZN) operates as an online retailer in North America and internationally.	$135,987	$83,402
MERCK (MRK) provides various health solutions through its prescription medicines, vaccines, biologic therapies, animal health, and consumer care products worldwide.	$39,807	$95,377
WALT DISNEY COMPANY (DIS) is an entertainment company that operates television and movie studios as well as theme parks.	$55,632	$92,033
MONDELEZ (MDLZ) produces consumer food products, such as Oreo cookies.	$25,923	$61,538

In Lab Exhibit 8-2B, you'll find the common size ratios for each Lab Exhibit 8-2A company's income statement (as a percentage of revenue) and balance sheet (as a percentage of assets).

	A	B	C	D	E	F	G	H	I	J
As a Percentage of Sales	**100.0**	**100.0**	**100.0**	**100.0**	**100.0**	**100.0**	**100.0**	**100.0**	**100.0**	**100.0**
Revenue	100.0	100.0	100.0	100.0	100.0	100.0	100.0	100.0	100.0	100.0
Cost of Goods Sold	64.9	37.1	74.9	22.4	9.6	34.9	60.9	4.5	39.3	85.4
Gross Profit	35.1	62.9	25.1	77.6	90.4	65.1	39.1	95.5	60.7	14.6
Research and Development	0.0	12.8	0.0	12.4	0.0	25.4	0.0	0.0	0.0	4.9
Selling, General, and Administrative Expenses	7.1	23.2	20.1	36.4	15.7	24.5	25.2	53.8	36.5	3.8
Other Operating Expenses	89.8	0.5	0.0	3.0	-4.3	1.6	3.3	0.0	0.0	0.0
Total Operating Expenses	96.9	37.2	20.1	51.8	16.0	51.6	29.2	54.7	36.5	8.7
Operating Income/Loss	3.1	25.7	5.0	25.9	84.0	13.5	9.9	47.7	20.6	6.2

LAB EXHIBIT 8-2B Mystery Ratios

	A	B	C	D	E	F	G	H	I	J
As a Percentage of Sales	**100.0**	**100.0**	**100.0**	**100.0**	**100.0**	**100.0**	**100.0**	**100.0**	**100.0**	**100.0**
Total Other Income/Expenses Net	-0.2	0.5	0.0	0.0	0.0	-1.8	-4.3	0.6	-1.4	0.0
Interest Expense	0.4	1.4	0.5	0.0	-0.5	0.0	0.0	12.4	1.8	0.3
Income before Tax	2.8	26.2	4.5	40.7	26.7	11.7	5.6	31.4	19.4	5.9
Income Tax Expense	1.0	4.4	1.4	-40.5	9.1	1.8	0.5	9.0	3.8	0.7
Minority Interest	0.0	0.0	0.1	0.0	0.7	0.1	0.0	0.0	0.1	0.0
Net Income	1.7	21.8	3.1	80.9	17.6	9.9	6.4	22.4	15.6	5.2
As a Percentage of Assets	**100.0**	**100.0**	**100.0**	**100.0**	**100.0**	**100.0**	**100.0**	**100.0**	**100.0**	**100.0**
Current Assets	54.9	64.7	30.2	37.2	18.4	32.1	13.8	0.0	39.0	69.4
Cash	23.2	6.3	4.4	7.6	5.0	6.8	0.0	6.8	9.8	9.8
Investments	8.0	47.8	0.0	22.4	0.0	8.2	0.0	8.2	15.6	1.4
Receivables	10.0	4.8	2.8	2.5	9.8	7.4	4.2	40.9	4.4	9.8
Inventory	13.7	1.0	22.3	0.0	1.5	5.1	4.0	0.0	3.1	48.0
Other Current Assets	8.0	52.6	4.9	27.1	6.9	12.8	2.7	0.0	21.7	11.5
Total Current Assets	54.9	64.7	30.2	37.2	18.4	32.1	13.8	0.0	39.0	69.4
Long-Term Investments	0.0	3.4	0.0	16.6	4.7	12.0	9.1	13.4	18.6	1.5
Property, Plant and Equipment	34.9	2.9	55.2	6.4	29.7	12.6	13.4	0.4	12.2	14.2
Goodwill	4.5	21.9	8.4	18.9	30.2	19.0	32.9	3.2	12.2	5.9
Intangible Assets	0.0	2.1	0.0	0.4	7.6	18.1	29.4	0.1	11.2	2.8
Amortization	0.0	0.0	0.0	0.0	0.0	0.0	0.0	0.0	0.0	0.0
Other Assets	5.7	5.0	6.3	20.5	9.4	6.1	1.4	0.0	6.8	6.1
Long-Term Assets	45.1	35.3	69.8	62.8	81.6	67.9	86.2	85.0	61.0	30.6
Total Assets	100.0	100.0	100.0	100.0	100.0	100.0	100.0	100.0	100.0	100.0
Liabilities	76.9	47.7	58.1	55.8	48.6	57.7	59.0	87.8	73.4	99.0
Current Liabilities	52.5	20.5	32.4	16.1	18.3	18.0	23.4	0.0	30.4	55.7
Accounts Payable	30.3	3.7	29.4	1.6	9.9	6.7	12.7	0.0	10.9	28.8
Current Portion of Long-Term Debt	0.0	0.0	1.7	0.0	4.0	0.0	2.4	7.8	4.0	0.0
Other Current Liabilities	22.2	13.3	0.0	8.4	4.4	10.8	4.3	57.6	15.5	26.5
Long-Term Debt	9.2	20.1	19.1	31.5	17.9	25.5	0.0	0.0	34.0	0.0
Other Liabilities	15.1	6.4	2.9	8.2	12.4	14.2	14.1	0.0	9.0	32.7
Minority Interest	0.0	0.0	1.5	0.0	4.4	0.2	0.1	0.0	0.2	0.1
Total Liabilities	76.9	47.7	58.1	55.8	48.6	57.7	59.0	87.8	73.4	99.0
Total Stockholders' Equity	23.1	52.3	41.9	44.2	51.4	42.3	41.0	12.2	26.6	1.0
Total Liabilities and Stockholders' Equity	100.0	100.0	100.0	100.0	100.0	100.0	100.0	100.0	100.0	100.0

LAB EXHIBIT 8-2B (*Continued*)

1. Use a Google Sheet with the iXBRLAnalyst script as well as the normalized accounts in Lab Exhibit 8.2B (or search for XBRL tags in the FASB taxonomy if normalized accounts aren't available) to recreate the ratios above.
2. Take a screenshot (label it 8-2A) of your completed worksheet.

   Q1. Using the skills learned from your prior financial accounting classes, your ability to extract information from XBRL, and your knowledge of common-size financial statements, match the company names in Lab Exhibit 8-2A with their corresponding ratios in each column of Lab Exhibit 8-2B.

- Column A = _____ which company?
- Column B = _____
- Column C = _____
- Column D = _____
- Column E = _____
- Column F = _____
- Column G = _____
- Column H = _____
- Column I = _____
- Column J = _____

End of Lab

Lab 8-3   Analyze Financial Statement Ratios

Financial analysts, investors, lenders, auditors, and many others perform ratio analysis to help review and evaluate a company's financial statements and financial performance. This analysis allows the stakeholder to gain an understanding of the financial health of the company and gives insights to allow more insightful and, hopefully, more effective decision making.

In this lab, you will access XBRL data to complete data analysis and generate financial ratios to compare the financial performance of several companies. Financial ratios can more easily be calculated using spreadsheets and XBRL. You will (1) select an industry to analyze, (2) create a copy of a spreadsheet template, (3) input ticker symbols from three U.S. public companies, and (4) calculate financial ratios and make observations about the state of the companies using these financial ratios.

Data

- Financial Elements from XBRL from SEC Filings

Software needed

- Google Account
- Google Sheets
- Browser connected to Internet

Specifically, you will:

Part 1: Identify the questions.

Part 2: Master the data and prepare for analysis.

Part 3: Input ticker symbols into the template.

Part 4: Analyze the financial ratios.

Part 1: Identify the Questions

Interested stakeholders of the firm need access to real-time, accurate financial data. Since 2011, stakeholders have used XBRL data to meet this need.

Q1. How does XBRL fulfill the need for real-time, accurate financial data?

Q2. Why is it useful to compare multiple companies at once?

Part 2: Master the Data and Prepare for Analysis

To master the data and prepare for analysis, we need to pick which industry and which companies to analyze.

1. Below is a list of 15 *Fortune* 100 companies in five different industries. Each of these companies has attributes and strategies that are similar to and different from its competitors. Choose one industry to analyze.

   Retail: Walmart (WMT), Target (TGT), Costco (Cost)

   Technology: Microsoft (MSFT), Apple (AAPL), Facebook (FB)

   Pharmaceutical: Johnson & Johnson (JNJ), Merck (MRK), Bristol-Myers Squibb (BMY)

   Finance: Citigroup (C), Wells-Fargo (WFC), JPMorgan Chase (JPM)

   Energy: ExxonMobil (XOM), Chevron (CVX), ConocoPhillips (COP)

   Create a copy of a spreadsheet template in the following way:

2. Open a web browser and go to drive.google.com.
3. If you haven't done so already, sign in to your Google account.
4. Go to http://tinyurl.com/xbrlratios. You will see a spreadsheet similar to Lab Exhibit 8-3A.
5. Click **File > Make a copy. . .** as shown in Lab Exhibit 8-3A.
6. Rename your spreadsheet if desired and click **OK** to save a copy to your Drive. A new tab will open with your copy of the spreadsheet. You may now edit the values and formulas.

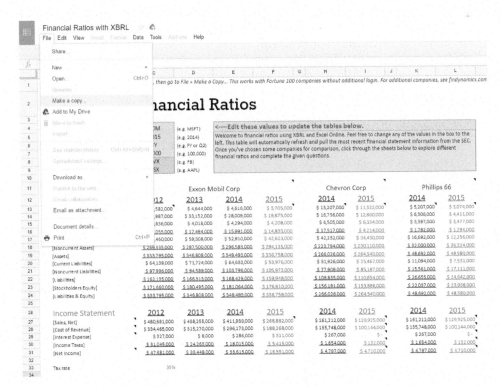

LAB EXHIBIT 8-3A
XBRL Financial Ratios in Google Sheets

Microsoft Excel 2016

Part 3: Input Ticker Symbols

Refer to Lab Exhibit 8-3B for your industry's ticker symbols.

LAB EXHIBIT 8-3B

Input Ticker Symbols

Retail	Technology	Pharmaceutical	Finance	Energy
WMT	MSFT	JNJ	C	XOM
TGT	AAPL	MRK	WFC	CVS
KR	FB	BMY	JPM	PSX

7. Referring to Lab Exhibit 8-3B for your industry's ticker symbols, in the **Main Company Ticker** field, input the ticker of the company you would like to focus your analysis on and press **Enter**. In a moment, the value on the spreadsheet will change to **Loading. . .** and then show your company's financial figures.

8. In the **Most Recent Year** field, enter the most recent reporting year. It may be the current year or the previous year.

9. In the **Period** field, enter either **FY** for a fiscal year or **Q1** for first quarter, etc.

10. In the **Round to** field, choose the rounding amount. 1,000 will round to thousands of dollars; 1,000,000 will round to millions of dollars.

11. In the **Comparable 1 Ticker** field, input the ticker of a second company you would like to compare with your first company.

12. In the **Comparable 2 Ticker** field, input the ticker of a third company you would like to compare with your first company.

13. Take a screenshot (label it 8-3A) of your figure with the financial statements of your chosen companies.

Part 4: Analyze the Financial Ratios

First, review the Facts sheet (or tab) to determine whether there are any values missing for the companies you are analyzing. Describe what impact (if any) the missing data have on the ratios. Once you have determined whether any data are missing, you have a chance to find some interesting trends and comparisons in the data. You will click through the sheets at the bottom to review the ratios. To aid in this analysis, the template also includes sparklines that provide a mini-graph to help you quickly visualize any significant values or trends.

Q3. Review the 14 financial ratios shown across the tabs and make some conclusions or judgments about the values, trends, or comparisons with the other companies. For example, if one company has a significantly higher debt-to-equity ratio than the other two, what might be driving this?

Q4. Has the company you are analyzing seen any major changes in its ratios in the past three years? Which of the three companies is most liquid in the most current year?

Q5. How has your company managed short-term liabilities over the last three years?

Q6. Analyze liquidity, profitability, financing (leverage), and activity for your company. Where is it strong?

Q7. Consider the DuPont framework to interpret the results and make sure you make a judgment about your company's financial position based upon the data.

End of Lab

Lab 8-4   Use PivotTables to Analyze Data from an XBRL Database

Company summary

As the chapter mentioned, there are 19,000 tags in the XBRL taxonomy, which doesn't even include the custom tags that organizations have created for themselves. The normalized tags XBRLAnalyst provides can be helpful, but sometimes you will need to find a more specific tag. One way that you can do this is by using SQL to query an XBRL database for all tags that are similar to the normalized tag you are working with.

Data

We have provided a subset of the XBRL database in two database files, an Access database and a SQLite database. This lab will specifically walk through connecting to the Access database, XBRL.accdb, and how to work with that data in Excel. If you prefer to work with the data in SQLite, you can answer the questions directly in the database with SQL queries.

We have used the Arelle open-source XBRL platform to build our subset, which in turn pulls the data from the SEC.

Technique

- You will use both the database tool of your choice (Microsoft Access or SQLite) and Microsoft Excel. You will use the database tool to view the data, then you will work with the data in Microsoft Excel by connecting to a database and using PivotTables.

Software needed

- Microsoft Access (or SQLite)
- Microsoft Excel

In this lab, you will:

Part 1: Identify questions related to XBRL tags and taxonomy.

Part 2: Analyze tags and then do more in-depth querying.

Part 1: Identify the Questions

One of the aspects that querying the XBRL database can be most helpful for is quickly viewing a list of tags that are similar or for quickly viewing a list of companies that have something in common over the years or even during a specific filing period.

Q1. Identify three questions that would be interesting regarding finding commonalities in XBRL tags or in filtering the data to view a subset based on similar criteria.

Q2. If you didn't know how to use SQL to query an XBRL database, how would you go about trying to answer the three questions you identified in Q1?

The questions we will answer are the following:

1. To see another way of working with the data, using a filter to only see companies that meet a certain type of criteria, what large accelerated filers filed?
2. To help us identify how many different iterations there are within one type of financial statement data element, we will create a query to show us all of the XBRL tags that contain "cash" in their description.

Part 2: Master the Data

The XBRL database in full is a very large database. Our subset is a bit easier to manage. Lab Exhibit 8-4A is a database schema of the tables, attributes, and relationships in the Access database that you will work with in this lab. The database schema in full can be found at this URL: http://arelle.org/wordpress/wp-content/uploads/2014/07/sql_diagram.png if you are interested.

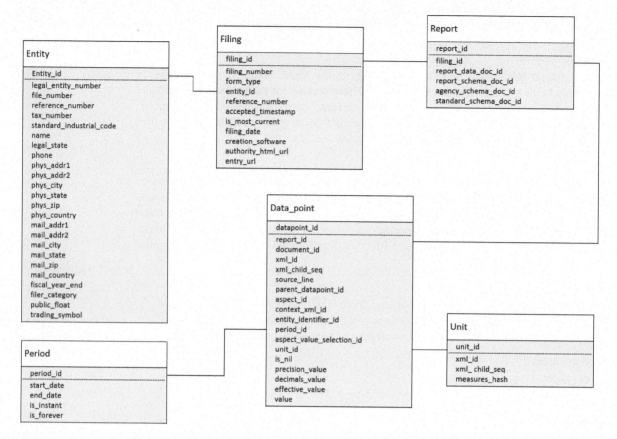

LAB EXHIBIT 8-4A   XBRL Database Schema–Subset

Lab Exhibit 8-4B describes the most common table functions.

LAB EXHIBIT 8-4B
Table Explanations

Table Name	Description
Entity	Information on the entity that submitted the filing
Filing	Information about individual filings
Report	Link from the information *about* the filing to the information *in* the filing
Period	Date information
Unit	To what degree any observation was recorded

Part 3: Perform an Analysis of the Data – Identify Large Accelerated Filers

To answer the first question (to identify the number of large, accelerated filers), we will first assess the data in the database, then we will connect the database to Excel to further analyze the data.

3. Begin by identifying which tables contain the data you will need to answer the problem. Look at the Table Explanations figure (Lab Exhibit 8-4B).

   Q3.   Which tables seem to have relevant data to (1) describe a filer to determine if it is categorized as large, accelerated filers and (2) determine the filing date?

4. In the database, double-click into the tables to get a glimpse of the data contained in each. Open the file Lab_8-4_XBRLsubset.accdb (or the SQLite database Lab_8-4_XBRLsubset_SQLite).

   Q4.   Which attributes are relevant?

5. You can write a query in Access to answer the question at this point, if you prefer, but in this lab we will connect the database to Excel to create a PivotTable to find the answer. **Open** a new, blank Excel file.

6. From the **Data** tab on the ribbon, click **Get External Data** and then click **From Access.**

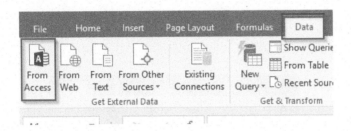

Source: Microsoft Excel 2016

7. **Browse** to the file location to select it.

8. Select **Enable selection of multiple tables,** and then select the check boxes next to **Entity** and **Filing,** then click **OK.** Click **OK** twice more.

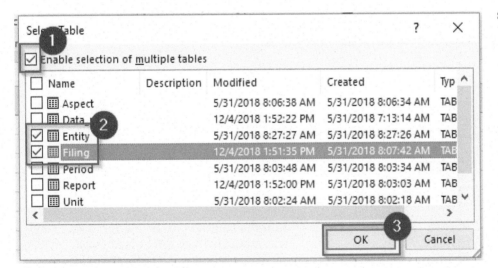

Source: Microsoft Excel 2016

9. It should default to a PivotTable Report, but if it doesn't, select that option and click **OK.**

10. It will take a little while for the data to load, but once it loads, place **Name** in the Rows, and create a **Slicer** for Filer_Category to filter for Large Accelerated Filers.
11. Take a screenshot that shows the results of your PivotTable (label it 8-4A).

For Question 2, identify how many different iterations there are within one type of financial statement data element, the Aspect table will be most useful. This table contains the basic building blocks of XBRL taxonomy, and specifically the **Name** column contains the different names of the XBRL elements that have been used in the sample.

12. Double-click this table in the Access Database **XBRLsubset.accdb** to get a glimpse of the different elements stored.
13. Return to Excel to import the Aspect table. From the **Data** tab on the ribbon, click **From Access.**

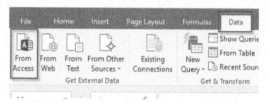

Source: Microsoft Excel 2016

14. **Browse** to the file location to select it.
15. Select the **Aspect** table, then click **OK.**

Source: Microsoft Excel 2016

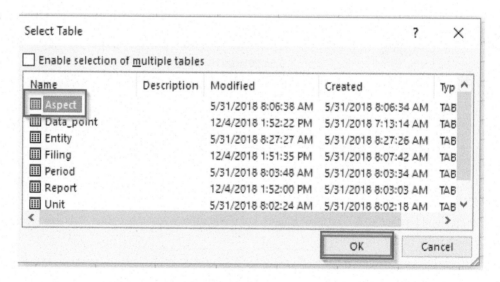

16. It should default to a PivotTable Report, but if it doesn't, select that option and click **OK.**

Source: Microsoft Excel 2016

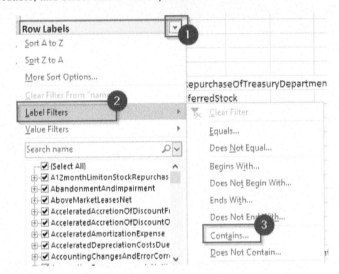

17. It will take a little while for the data to load, but once it loads, place **Name** in the Rows. This will create a distinct list of all the element names included in the Aspect table.
18. To filter for the names that contain Cash, click the **filter button** next to **Row Labels** on the PivotTable, and select **Label Values,** then select **Contains.**

Source: Microsoft Excel 2016

19. Type **Cash** in the Label Filter box, then click **OK.**
20. Take a screenshot of your PivotTable (label it 8-4B).

Part 4: Address and Refine Results

Based on the massive amount of tags that contain the word *cash* in them, we may decide to be more specific with the query.

21. This time, refine the query or your PivotTable filter to show only the tags that *begin* with the word *Cash*.
22. Take a screenshot of your refined results (label it 8-4C).

Q5. How would you further drill down into the first question about the large filers?

Q6. Do you think the number of outputs you got for the different types of tags with the word *Cash* is reasonable? What recommendation would you have regarding the numerous elements in the taxonomy?

End of Lab

Chapter 9

Tax Analytics

A Look at This Chapter

We highlight the use of data analytics for the tax function. First, we consider how tax departments could better control the data they receive from the financial reporting system. Second, we investigate how data analytics is used to help with tax compliance issues. Finally, we consider how data analysis might be used to assist in tax planning including what-if analysis for new legislation, the possibility of a merger with another company, a shift in product mix or a plan to set up operations in a new low-tax jurisdiction (and/or transfer pricing).

A Look Back

In Chapter 8, we focus on how to access and analyze financial statement data. We highlight the use of XBRL to quickly and efficiently gain computer access to financial statement data. Next, we discuss how ratios are used to analyze financial performance. We also discuss the use of Sparklines to help users visualize trends in the data. Finally, we discuss the use of text mining to analyze the sentiment in financial reporting data.

A Look Forward

In Chapter 10, we bring all of the accounting Data Analytics concepts together with a set of exercises that walk all the way through the IMPACT model. The chapter serves as a great way to bring together all of the elements learned in the course.

Knowing the tax liability for a move to a new jurisdiction is important for corporations and individuals alike. For example, a tax accountant might have advised LeBron James not to sign with the Los Angeles Lakers in summer 2018 because it is expected it will cost him $21 million more in extra state income taxes since California has higher taxes than Ohio. Tax data analytics for this type of "what-if scenario analysis" is important for tax planning purposes. It has wide applications when contemplating new legislation, a merger possibility, a shift in product mix, or a plan to set up operations in a new low-tax jurisdiction. Amazon recently used this when considering the tax incentives for property taxes, payroll taxes, and sales taxes for its second headquarters location (or its HQ2) which landed near Washington, DC.

Source: https://www.forbes.com/sites/seanpackard/2018/07/02/lebrons-move-could-cost-him-21-million-in-extra-state-taxes/#6517d3156280, accessed August 2, 2018; https://www.cnbc.com/2018/11/13/amazon-tax-incentives-in-new-york-city-virginia-and-nashville.html, accessed August 2, 2018.

Jim McIsaac/Getty images

OBJECTIVES

After reading this chapter, you should be able to:

LO 9-1   Describe how tax data has traditionally been managed and how it should be managed for data analysis purposes.

LO 9-2   Describe the use of Data Analytics in tax planning.

LO 9-3   Understand the use of tax analytics in visualizations.

LO 9-4   Understand the use of tax data for tax planning and perform what-if scenario analysis.

LO 9-1

Describe how tax data has traditionally been managed and how it should be managed for data analysis purposes.

INTRODUCTION TO TAX ANALYTICS

With more and more data available, just like other areas in accounting, there is an increased focus on tax analytics. New regulations are requiring greater detail, and tax regulators are getting more adept at the use of analytics. In addition to the regulator side, tax filers now have more data to support their tax calculations.

Here are a few ways increased access to data and tax analytics are used by regulators and by companies:

IRS and tax analytics. The IRS has a huge trove of data about each taxpayer. There are three main sources of information, including the following:

- Not only do they have data of the reportable financial transactions that occur during the year (including W-2s, Form 1099s, Schedule K-1s), but also the IRS has a repository of tax returns from prior years that they have stored in a data warehouse.
- The IRS mines and monitors personal data from social media (such as Facebook, Twitter, Instagram, etc.)[1] about taxpayers. For example, posts about a new car, new house, or fancy vacation could help the IRS capture the taxpayer dodging or misreporting income. Divorce lawyers certainly use the same tactics to learn the lifestyle and related income of a divorcing spouse!
- The IRS has personal financial data about each taxpayer, including Social Security numbers, bank accounts, and property holdings. While most of this is gathered from prior returns and transactions (see item 1), the IRS can also access your credit report during an audit or criminal investigation to determine if spending/credit looks proportional to income and if they are trying to collect an assessment.

Each of these sources of information can help the IRS to establish a profile (using the profiling test approach discussed in Chapter 3). The IRS has an algorithm called Discriminant Function that pulls historical data for average amount and type of deductions related to income level and predicts the likelihood of underreported income. When the amount self-reported by the taxpayer is significantly less than the amount estimated, additional investigation and a potential tax audit might be warranted if the potential tax revenue is greater than the expected cost of the investigation.

- *Documenting book-tax differences.* One way for tax regulators to assess if companies are paying sufficient tax is to look at the differences between the amount of income reported for financial reporting purposes (like form 10-Q or 10-K submitted to the SEC) and the amount reported to the IRS (or other tax authorities) for income tax purposes. Increasingly, tax software and analytics (such as Hyperion or Corptax) is used to help with the reconciliation to find both permanent and temporary differences between the two methods of computing income and also to provide needed support for IRS schedule M-3 (Form 1120).
- *R&D Tax Credit.* The R&D Tax Credit is a tax credit under Internal Revenue Code section 41 for companies that incur research and development (R&D) costs. To receive this credit, firms must document an appropriate level of detail before receiving R&D tax credit. For example, companies have to link an employee's time directly to a research activity or to a specific project to qualify for the tax credit. Let's suppose that a firm spent money on qualifying R&D expenditures but simply did not keep the sufficient detail needed as supporting evidence to receive the credit. Analytics could be used to consider to find the needed detail (timesheets, calendars, project timelines, document meetings between various employees, time needed for management review, etc.) to qualify for the R&D tax credit.

[1] https://washington.cbslocal.com/2014/04/16/report-irs-data-mining-facebook-twitter-instagram-and-other-social-media-sites/,accessed August 2018.

In terms of the IMPACT model, types of appropriate questions for the tax function in terms of data analytics might be as follows:

1. What can tax analytics do to reduce the overall current and future tax liability for an individual or for a company?
2. How might tax analytics reduce the cost of compliance and tax planning by companies?
3. If certain tax legislation passes, what level of exposure (additional tax) might the company face?

✓ PROGRESS CHECK

1. What are examples of tools the IRS has to monitor tax evasion?
2. How can tax analytics support and potentially increase the amount of R&D tax credit taken by a company?

MASTERING THE DATA THROUGH TAX DATA MANAGEMENT

> **LO 9-2**
>
> Describe the use of Data Analytics in tax planning.

The tax function typically uses data from the financial reporting system (or enterprise system). However, the financial reporting system is primarily designed and used for financial accounting purposes, where transactions that have an economic impact are recorded as an input for the financial statements and other financial reporting purposes. In addition, these financial reporting systems along with other data have also been used for management accounting purposes to allow management to calculate the cost of a product or to optimize a product mix that would maximize profits for the firm. There is generally not a completely separate information system solely collecting tax data needed for tax compliance and tax planning.

With little integration between the financial reporting system and the needs of the tax function, tax departments would manually collect and extract data from its financial reporting system and generalized **data warehouse**. After gathering data from these generalized data warehouses, tax departments would use Excel spreadsheets to capture and store the detail needed to support tax calculations. Such lack of integration hampered efforts of tax accountants to have the needed information to comply with tax law, to minimize current taxes and to allow for tax planning for future transactions.

With recent advances in technology, there are increasing opportunities for tax departments to have greater control of their data, which allows them to work more effectively and efficiently. Specifically, instead of use of a generalized data warehouse, enterprise systems increasingly use specific **data marts** for their tax function. Data marts are defined as being a subset of the data warehouse oriented toward a specific need. Such a **tax data mart** is used to extract past and real-time data from the financial reporting system that is most applicable to the tax function. Tax departments are able to specify what data might affect their tax calculations for their tax data mart and have a continuous feed of that data. Such a tax data mart allows tax departments to more completely own the data than from a more generalized data warehouse or generalized data mart. They can add to that tax data mart, other relevant information that might come from other sources.

They are also able to keep it as a centralized repository so that different users of the tax function can have access to the data. Exhibit 9-1 provides a good illustration of how data is accumulated and subsequently dedicated for the tax function. Consistent with the IMPACT model, tax data warehouses and tax data marts help tax departments to "master the data" to address tax questions and issues inside the company.

EXHIBIT 9-1
Tax Data in a Data
Warehouse

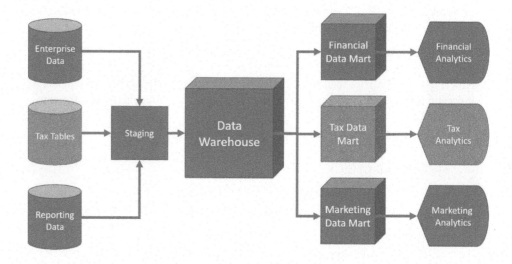

Accounting firms can also keep track of its clients using another type of data mart; for example, a tax data mart kept at an accounting firm that might have marketing implications. Let's suppose an accounting firm has a tax data mart that keeps track of clients and their unrealized capital gains. The **2018 Tax Cuts and Jobs Act Tax Reform** offers a major change to investors, allowing them to invest in opportunity zones (in low-income communities) to defer or completely eliminate taxes on realized capital gains if reinvested in opportunity zones. While only a fraction of the estimated total unrealized capital gains market of $6.1 trillion actually qualifies for opportunity zones,[2] there seems to be an almost endless set of investors that could reap tax savings via an opportunity zone. If a tax data mart allows accounting firms to know which investors have unrealized capital gains, they can effectively market tax assistance, education about opportunity zones, or market investments in opportunity funds to them directly.

 PROGRESS CHECK

3. Why do tax departments need to extract data for tax calculation from a financial reporting system?

4. How is a tax data mart specifically able to target the needs of the tax department?

LO 9-3

Understand the use of tax analytics in visualizations.

TAX DATA ANALYTICS VISUALIZATIONS

Tax Data Analytics Visualizations and Tax Compliance

Increasingly, tax regulators are using Data Analytics to evaluate tax compliance by those with potential tax liability. Tax regulators use Data Analytics to see if companies are close to actually paying what would be expected based on tax rates and expected income or sales. To date, companies have not engaged in the same level of Data Analytics. If for no other reason, companies might engage in Data Analytics to avoid a tax audit. In some sense, this allows companies to "see what the regulator is seeing." The European Union is way ahead of the United States on use of Data Analytics in a tax audit, both by the regulator and the company hoping to not be audited.

[2]https://www.forbes.com/sites/jenniferpryce/2018/08/14/theres-a-6-trillion-opportunity-in-opportunity-zones-heres-what-we-need-to-do-to-make-good-on-it/#527391d46ffc, accessed August 15, 2018.

Evaluating Sales Tax Liability

Evaluating sales tax liability can quickly be complicated by customer sales returns where sales taxes are returned to customers. That complexity is compounded by the differing tax rates in each city, county and state jurisdiction. In preparation for an audit, sales tax regulators could ask for gross sales or net sales (gross sales less returns) by store and compute the total taxes owed to see if it is close to the amount of sales taxes actually paid by the company. Companies can run the same type of analysis to see where they stand to avoid an audit or at least be prepared in the eventuality that a tax audit does occur.

With the recent Supreme Court *Wayfair* decision and the tidal wave of states passing legislation to copy the decision, collection of sales tax on every online purchase (based on where the customer lives) is a serious compliance issue. Companies need to get data collection processes in place to collect, summarize, and process this information so that they can have functional compliance with the new laws in states where they sell online.

A dashboard (similar to that introduced in Chapter 4) is a type of visualization that might be helpful for compliance with state sales tax. The comprehensive labs at the end of this chapter provide an example of how Data Analytics might be used with respect to state sales tax data. Companies pay sales tax regularly based on the amount of sales they collect.

Evaluating Income Tax Liability

Tax data analytics allows tax departments to view multiple years, periods, jurisdictions (state or federal or international, etc.) and differing scenarios of data typically through use of a dashboard . Dashboards allow tax departments to evaluate those jurisdictions where current state income tax liabilities have departed most from the liability of prior years. This allows tax departments to evaluate further why current year jurisdictional taxable income and tax liability have changed from the past and address if any issues or irregularities occur.

TAX DATA ANALYTICS VISUALIZATIONS ALLOWS A WAY TO MONITOR AND TRACK KPIs

As noted in this text, a key output of rich data from tax analytics is the ability to create visualizations. As noted in Chapter 7, tracking KPIs using visualizations is a good way to easily see how well the company is performing. Such KPIs might be used to monitor different aspects of the tax function.

In the article, "Defining Success: What KPIs Are Driving the Tax Function Today,"[3] PwC points out four general categories of tax-focused KPIs, including tax cost, tax risk, tax efficiency and effectiveness, and tax sustainability. Below we list some KPIs that might be used to measure performance in each of these areas:

Tax cost: The actual amount of tax paid. Example KPIs include:

- Effective tax rate (ETR).
- Cash taxes paid.
- Effect of loss carry-forwards.
- Expiration of tax credits.

---

[3]"Defining Success: What KPIs Are Driving the Tax Function Today" PwC, September 2017, https://www.pwc.com/gx/en/tax/publications/assets/pwc_tax_function_of_the_future_tax_function_KPI_sept17.pdf, accessed August 14, 2018.

- Tax adjustments in response to new tax legislation.
- Deferred taxes.

Tax risk(financial and reputational): With increased regulator and stakeholder scrutiny, firms bear the financial and reputation risk of the misreporting or tax provision adjustments. Example KPIs include:

- Frequency and magnitude of tax audit adjustments.
- Frequency of concerns pertaining to the organization's tax position.
- Levels of late filing or error penalties and fines.
- Number of resubmitted tax returns due to errors.

Tax efficiency and effectiveness: This includes the efficiency and effectiveness of technology, processes, and people in carrying out the tax function. Example KPIs include:

- Levels of technology/tax training.
- Amount of time spent on compliance versus strategic activities.
- Level of job satisfaction of the tax personnel.
- Employee turnover of the tax personnel.
- Improved operational efficiency.

Tax sustainability: Refers to the ability to sustain similar tax performance over time. Example KPIs include:

- Number of company tax audits closed and significance of assessment over time.
- The effective tax rate (ETR) over time.

Additionally, tax managers should track permanent differences between book and tax revenue and expenses to ensure compliance and dispute overpayments of taxes. These include:

- Penalties and fines (excluded from taxable income).
- Meals and entertainment (100 percent books, 50 percent tax).
- Interest on municipal bonds (non-taxed income).
- Life insurance proceeds (non-taxed income).
- Dividends received deduction (taxed based on percentage of ownership).
- Excess depreciation.

These tax-focused KPIs appear on dashboards or cockpits, consistent with the "C" (communicate insights) and the "T" (tracking outcomes) of the IMPACT model. Cockpits are similar to dashboards but are much narrower in scope and focus than a dashboard. This focus allows the tax function to highlight potential high impact or single areas of concern like reconciliation. We also note that the tax sustainability KPIs, in particular, measure performance over time and are consistent with the "T" (tracking outcomes) of the IMPACT model.

✓ PROGRESS CHECK

5. Why is ETR (effective tax rate) a good example of a tax cost KPI? Why is ETR over time considered to be a good tax sustainability KPI?
6. Why would a company want to track the levels of late filing or error penalties as a tax risk KPI?

TAX DATA ANALYTICS FOR TAX PLANNING

LO 9-4

Understand the use of tax data for tax planning and perform what-if scenario analysis.

Tax planning is the analysis of potential tax liability and formulation of a plan to reduce the amount of taxes paid. It involves forecasting corporate activity and calculating the anticipated tax liabilities or benefits from operations in various jurisdictions. Tax analytics helps organizations operate in a way that helps them be as tax efficient as possible by identifying opportunities to minimize the amount of current and future taxes paid as well as to recover tax overpayment. Tax accountants can utilize the abundance of detailed transaction and metadata (e.g., descriptions of data, such as categories) to filter and analyze the data, identify opportunities for tax savings, and plan. Tax savings and recovery are especially important because they represent value-adding functions of tax accountants since every tax dollar saved goes directly to the bottom line (e.g., net income after tax).

Changes in tax legislation, changes in ownership, expansion into new territories, and transfer pricing for intercompany sales affect future tax liability. Beyond calculating tax rates across multiple jurisdictions, tax planning involves identifying transactions and investments that are subject to deductions, credits, and other exclusions from income. Tax planning may involve the following questions:

- What will be the impact of a new tax rate on our tax liability?
- Are we minimizing our tax burden by tracking all eligible deductible expenses and transactions that qualify for tax credits?
- What would be the impact of relocating our headquarters to a different city, state or country?
- What is the tax exposure for owners in the case of a potential merger or significant change in ownership?
- Do our transfer pricing contracts on certain products put us at higher risk of a tax audit because they have abnormal margins?
- What monthly trends can we identify to help us avoid surprises?
- Can we reduce the number of assumptions in our tax plan?
- How are we addressing tax complexities resulting from online sales due to new sales tax legislation?
- How would tax law changes affect our pension or profit-sharing plans and top employee compensation packages (including stock options)?
- How would the use of independent contractors affect our payroll tax liabilities?

The answers to these questions come from analysis of current transaction data and a collection of parameters that represent potential assumption changes. A combination of descriptive and predictive analytics with visualizations provide guidance for decision makers in each of these cases.

Descriptive tax analytics provide insight into the current processes, policies, and calculations related to determining tax liability. These analytics involve summarizing transactions by jurisdiction or category to more accurately calculate tax liability. Diagnostic tax analytics might help identify items of interest, such as high tax areas or excluded transactions. For example, creating a trend analysis for sales and use tax paid in different locations would help identify seasonal patterns or abnormal transaction volume that warrant further investigation.

Predictive tax analytics use historical data and new information to identify future tax liabilities. On the basic level, this includes regression and what-if analyses and requires a specific target, such as the value of a tax credit or deferred tax asset. The addition of ancillary data, including growth rates, trends, and other identified patterns, aids to the usefulness of these analyses. Additionally, tax analytics rely on tax calculation logic and tax determination, such as proportional deductions, to determine the potential tax liability.

What-If Scenarios

What-if scenario analysis tests the impact of various input data on an expected output. In tax, this means the manipulation of inputs—such as multiple tax rates, a series of transactions, and varying profit margins—to estimate the future outputs, including estimated book income, cash taxes paid, and effective tax rates. These analyses attempt to optimize the inputs to reach a desired goal, such as minimizing the effective tax rate or generating a portfolio of possible outputs given the inputs. In these cases, we need to estimate the possible inputs and outputs as well as determine the expected probabilities of those items.

For example, assume the Pennsylvania General Assembly is debating a reduction in the statutory corporate income tax rate from 10% to either 8% or 7% with a positive (+5%), neutral, or negative (−5%) change in corporate income. A company with expected earnings before tax of $1,000,000 might see potential tax savings shown in Table 9-1.

TABLE 9-1

Estimated Change in Tax Burden under Different Income Tax Proposals

Based on average earnings before tax of $1,000,000. Negative values represent tax savings.

Change in Taxable Income / Change in Tax Rate	10%	8%	7%
Positive change (+5%)	5,000	(16,000)	(26,500)
Neutral change (+0%)	0	(20,000)	(30,000)
Negative change (−5%)	(5,000)	(24,000)	(33,500)

By itself, this analysis may indicate the path to minimizing tax would be the lower tax rate with negative growth. An estimate of the joint probabilities of each of the nine scenarios determines the expected value of each, or the most likely impact of a change (as shown in Table 9-2) and the dollar impact of the expected change in value (in Table 9-3). For example, there is a 0.05 probability (as shown in Table 9-2) that there will be +5% change in taxable income but no change in tax rate. This would result in a $250 increase in taxes (as shown in Table 9-3). In this case, the total expected value of the proposed decrease in taxes is $15,575, which is the sum of the individual expected values as shown in Table 9-3.

TABLE 9-2

Joint Probabilities of Changes in Tax Rate and Change in Income

Change in Taxable Income / Change in Tax Rate	10%	8%	7%	Sum
Positive change (+5%)	0.05	0.10	0.10	**0.25**
Neutral change (+0%)	0.20	0.20	0.10	**0.50**
Negative change (−5%)	0.10	0.10	0.05	**0.25**
Sum	**0.35**	**0.40**	**0.25**	**1.00**

TABLE 9-3

Expected Value of Each of the Scenarios

Change in Taxable Income / Change in Tax Rate	10%	8%	7%
Positive change (+5%)	250	(1,600)	(2,650)
Neutral change (+0%)	0	(4,000)	(3,000)
Negative change (−5%)	(500)	(2,400)	(1,675)

The usefulness of the what-if analysis is that decision makers can see the possible impact of changes in tax rates across multiple scenarios. This model relies heavily on assumptions that drive each scenario, such as the initial earnings before tax, the expected change in earnings, and the possible tax rates. Data Analytics help confirm or refine the details guiding the scenarios so the decision maker doesn't have to rely on as many assumptions. The more analyzed data that are available to inform the assumptions of the model, the more accurate the estimates and expected values can be. Here, data analysis of before-tax income and other external factors can help determine more accurate probability estimates. Likewise, an analysis of the legislative proceedings may help determine the likelihood of a change.

What-If Scenarios for Potential Legislation, Deductions, and Credits

Changes in the tax code complicate tax estimates and payments. Potential changes in legislation are generally complex, involving identification of qualifying transactions, calculating partial transaction amounts, analyzing groups of transactions, and determining the impact of the change from current policy. Changes involve updating rules and decision aides, as well as capturing previously ignored metadata (such as categories).

Just like scenario analysis involving changes to corporate tax rates, we examine another scenario analysis with the use of R&D tax credits. For example, the United States allows companies to take a research credit of up to 20 percent of qualified research expenditures (QREs) used to develop new products exceeding a calculated base amount, limited by a ceiling. The use of tax analytics to determine adjustments to the research credits requires a correct determination of expenses related to qualifying research. If any part of the research credit were to change—such as the percentage, base amount, or ceiling—companies would need to anticipate the change and enact policies and reporting to calculate the new values.

Data Analytics helps refine the model by more accurately calculating current levels of activity and estimating trends for most likely changes in the future. To determine the level of research activity within a firm, the system designers would need to appropriately code transactions and individuals that qualify for the research credit. Some of these inputs and variables require compiled data that includes:

- Qualified research activities.
- Wages, bonuses, and stock options for employees engaged in, supporting, or supervising qualified research.
- Supplies used to conduct qualified research.
- Contract research expense paid for qualified research by a third party.
- Average gross receipts over a four-year period.
- Limits on research credit.
- Carry-forward credit balance.

If the metadata and tagging for qualified research activities is inaccurate or missing, additional data ETL would be required.

Scenarios involving changes to the research credit would most likely include the following variables:

- Fixed-base percentage.
- Ceiling for fixed-base percentage.
- Floor of current QREs.
- Credit percentage.
- Current and future levels of qualified research activity.

One current change to research and development expenses that provides an interesting opportunity for analysis is the recent change in U.S. tax code. While companies currently expense research and experimental (R&E) expenditures in the year they are incurred, as of December 31, 2021, the IRS will require companies to capitalize R&E expenditures and amortize them over 5 years. This will result in an increase in taxable income and corresponding tax liability. What-if scenario analysis of current research activity and expected activity through 2022 can provide insight into the amount of tax that is likely to be collected after the change goes into effect.

 PROGRESS CHECK

7. What are some data a tax manager would need in order to perform a what-if analysis of the potential effects of a stock buyback?
8. How does having more metadata help a tax accountant minimize taxes?

Summary

Recent advances in Data Analytics extend to the tax functions, allowing them to work more effectively, efficiently, and with greater control over the data.

- New regulations are requiring greater detail, and tax regulators are getting more adept in the use of analytics. In addition to the regulator side, tax filers now have more data to support their tax calculations.
- While the tax department has traditionally just used data from the financial reporting system, there are increasing opportunities to control and expand upon available tax data to help address the most important tax questions.
- Tax visualizations (dashboards, cockpits) can be helpful in monitoring how the tax function is doing in meeting its KPIs (key performance indicators).
- Tax data analytics can be especially powerful in doing tax planning and formulating what-if scenarios.

Key Words

2018 Tax Cuts and Jobs Act Tax Reform (*364*)   Tax legislation offering a major change to the existing tax code.

data mart (*363*)   A subset of the data warehouse focused on a specific function or department to assist and support its needed data requirements.

data warehouse (*363*)   A data warehouse is a repository of data accumulated from internal and external data sources, including financial data, to help management decision making.

tax data mart (*363*)   A subset of a company-owned data warehouse focused on the specific needs of the tax department.

tax planning (*367*)   Predictive analysis of potential tax liability and the formulation of a plan to reduce the amount of taxes paid.

what-if scenario analysis (*368*)   Evaluation of the impact of different tax scenarios/alternatives on various outcome measures including the amount of taxable income or tax paid.

✓ ANSWERS TO PROGRESS CHECKS

1. The IRS has all reportable financial (taxable) transactions at their disposal (including W-2s, Form 1099s, Schedule K-1s, etc.); access to social media feeds for taxpayers; and access to credit reports, bank accounts, etc., to help monitor the potential for tax evasion.

2. Analytics could be used to find the needed detail (timesheets, calendars, project time-lines, document meetings between various employees, time needed for management review, etc.) to qualify for the R&D Tax Credit.

3. Tax data marts are a repository of data from the financial reporting and other systems to get the data to support tax department needs.

4. Tax departments are able to specify what data might affect their tax calculations for their tax data mart and have a continuous feed of that data. This data mart is essentially one where the tax department can, in some sense, "own" the data because no other group has rights to modify it.

5. The ETR (effective tax rate) is generally used as a measure of the tax cost used by the tax department to understand how well they are keeping the tax cost at a minimum. The lower the effective tax rate, the more effective the tax department is at finding ways to structure transactions to minimize taxes and find applicable tax deductions and tax credits (like the R&D tax credit or other tax loopholes). Monitoring the level of the ETR over time helps us know if the tax department is persistent and consistent in reducing the taxes paid, or if this rate is highly variable. Generally, most tax professionals would consider the more stable the ETR over time, the better. Tracking ETR over time as part of the tax sustainability KPIs allows management and the tax department figure out if the ETR is persistent or if the rate bounces around each year in an unsustainable way.

6. The greater the number of levels of late filings or error penalties, the more vulnerable the company is to penalties, tax audits, and missed tax saving opportunities.

7. Data may include the possible price of the stock, the potential capital gains incurred by the stockholders, and number of shares.

8. The more metadata, the better the tax accountant can accurately calculate the amounts of taxable and nontaxable items. For example, they can more clearly identify expenses that qualify for the research and development credit or track meal and entertainment expenses that may trigger tax presence in other locations.

 connect

Multiple Choice Questions

1. Which stage of the IMPACT model (introduced in Chapter 1) would the use of tax cock-pits fit?
   a. Track outcomes
   b. Master the data
   c. Address and refine results
   d. Perform test plan

2. Tax departments interested in maintaining their own data are likely to have their own
   a. tax reporting system.
   b. tax data mart.
   c. tax dashboard.
   d. tax analytics.

3. According to the textbook, an example of a tax efficiency and effective KPI would be:
   a. number of audits closed.
   b. ETR (effective tax rate) over time.
   c. number of resubmitted tax returns due to errors.
   d. amount of time spent on compliance versus strategic activities.

4. According to the textbook, an example of a tax sustainability KPI would be:
   a. frequency of concerns pertaining to the organization's tax position.
   b. level of job satisfaction of the tax personnel.
   c. levels of technology/tax training.
   d. number of audits closed and significance of assessment over time.

5. According to the textbook, an example of a tax cost KPI would be:
   a. employee turnover of the tax personnel.
   b. levels of technology/tax training.
   c. ETR (effective tax rate).
   d. levels of late filing or error penalties.

6. The task of tax accountants and tax departments to minimize the amount of taxes paid in the future is called:
   a. tax planning.
   b. tax compliance.
   c. tax minimization.
   d. tax sustainability.

7. According to the textbook, an example of a tax risk KPI would be:
   a. employee turnover of the tax personnel.
   b. levels of technology/tax training.
   c. ETR (effective tax rate).
   d. levels of late filing or error penalties.

8. _____ allows tax departments to view multiple years, periods, jurisdictions (state or federal or international, etc.), and differing scenarios of data, typically through use of a dashboard.
   a. Tax data analytics
   b. Tax data warehouses
   c. Tax compliance data
   d. Tax planning

9. _____ is defined as predictive analysis of potential tax liability and the formulation of a plan to reduce the amount of taxes paid.
   a. Tax data analytics
   b. Tax data warehouses
   c. Tax compliance data
   d. Tax planning

10. _____ is defined as the evaluation of the impact of different tax scenarios/alternatives on various outcome measures including the amount of taxable income or tax paid.
   a. Tax planning
   b. What-if scenario analysis
   c. Tax compliance
   d. Data warehouse

Discussion Questions

1. Explain how the IRS might use social media data to profile taxpayers who might be underpaying taxes. What additional information would the IRS need to consider in addition to social media data to build a full taxpayer profile?

2. Why would a company be interested in documenting the book-tax differences to identify potential items of interest to the IRS?

3. Explain why the needs of the tax accountant are different than the needs of the financial accountants. Why does this lead to a tax data warehouse or tax data mart?

4. Why would tracking a client's unrealized capital gains be important to businesses trying to capitalize on the tax opportunities inherent in opportunity zones (a new investment opportunity available as a result of the Tax Cuts and Jobs Act of 2017)? How would accounting firms access this data regarding their clients?

5. Why would employee turnover of the tax personnel be a good KPI to track a company's overall tax efficiency and effectiveness? What does low employee turnover (as compared to high turnover) allow a tax department to do?

Problems

1. How do visualizations of tax compliance assist a company in its efforts to reduce tax risk and minimize the costs of tax preparation and compliance? In your opinion, what would be needed to consistently make visualizations a key part of the tax department evaluation of tax risk and tax cost minimization?

2. How does tax planning differ from tax compliance? Why might the company leadership be more excited about the value-creating efforts of tax planning versus that of tax compliance?

3. How do Data Analytics facilitate what-if scenario analysis? How does the presence of a tax data mart help with the needed data to support such analysis?

4. In your opinion, which of the four general categories of tax KPIs mentioned in the text would be most important to the CEO? Support your opinion.

5. Explain why tax sustainability would be of interest to the tax department. What does it allow them to do if they are able to gain tax sustainability versus what they are not able to do without tax sustainability?

6. Descriptive analytics help calculate tax liability more accurately. Give some examples of tax-related descriptive analytics.

7. Predictive analytics help identify future tax liabilities. What data would a tax accountant need in order to perform a predictive analysis?

8. Explain how probability helps refine a what-if analysis.

9. Assume that a company has the option of staying in a tax jurisdiction with an effective tax rate of 20 percent or moving to a different location where the effective tax rates are 11 percent and 4 percent. What other drivers besides the tax rate may affect the decision to stay or move?

10. If a company knows that the IRS will change a tax calculation in the future, such as the capitalization of research and experimental expense in 2021, what actions might management take today to reduce their tax liability when the new policy goes into effect?

11. Match the tax analytics definitions to their terms: data mart, data warehouse, tax planning, tax data mart, what-if scenario analysis.

Tax Analytics Definition	Tax Analytics Term
A subset of the data warehouse focused on a specific function or department to assist and support its needed data requirements	
A repository of data accumulated from internal and external sources, including financial data, to help management decision making	
Predictive analysis of potential tax liability and the formulation of a plan to reduce the amount of taxes paid	
A subset of a company-owned data warehouse focused on the specific needs of the tax department	
Evaluation of the impact of different tax scenarios/alternatives on various outcome measures including the amount of taxable income or tax paid	

Lab 9-1 State Sales Taxes and Create a Data Visualization

Lab Summary

Since taxes vary by state, this lab teaches how to gather the state sales tax data, and how to analyze and visualize it.

Data

- Ch 9 State_SalesTax.xlsx

Technique

- Some experience with spreadsheets and simple visualization in Tableau is useful for this lab.

Software needed

- Excel
- Screen capture tool (Windows: Snipping Tool; Mac: Cmd+Shift+4)
- Tableau

In this lab, you will:

Part 1: Look up state sales tax on the Internet.

Part 2: Create a spreadsheet with the sales tax data in Excel.

Part 3: Visualize and analyze sales tax data in Tableau.

Part 1: Identify the Questions

Q1. What advantage does a state have in charging a relatively high state sales tax? In contrast, what advantage does a state have in charging relatively low (or no) sales tax? If one state has a high sales tax and the state next door has a low sales tax, would that affect your answer to the first two questions?

Part 2: Master the Data: Prepare Data for Analysis Using Excel

1. Open the Excel spreadsheet, **Ch 9 State_SalesTax.xlsx**.
2. You are going to create a frequency distribution and histogram, and to do so you need to set up some bins. Input the following set of numbers somewhere in the Excel data file (Ch 9 State_SalesTax.xlsx) to use as the bins for your frequency distribution and histogram:

    0

    0.019

    0.038

    0.054

    0.073

Part 3: Perform an Analysis by Creating a Frequency Distribution and Histogram in Excel

3. Create a frequency distribution and histogram by accessing the Data Analysis ToolPak from the Excel ribbon.

Source: Microsoft Excel 2016

4. Select **Histogram** from the Data Analysis window and click **OK**.

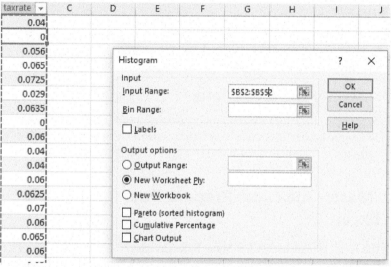

Source: Microsoft Excel 2016

5. Select the tax rate column for the Input Range.

Source: Microsoft Excel 2016

6. Select the bins that you entered for the Bin Range.

Source: Microsoft Excel 2016

7. Place a checkmark in the box next to **Chart Output**.

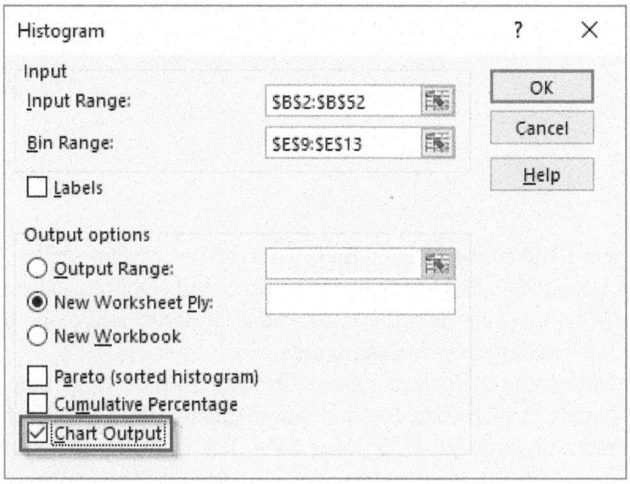

Source: Microsoft Excel 2016

8. Click **OK**.

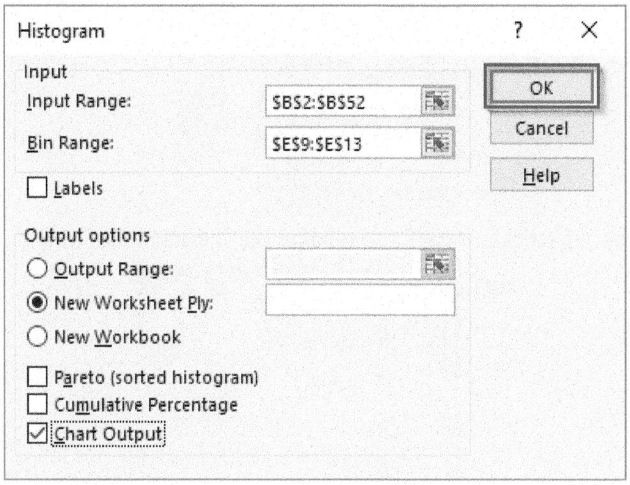

Source: Microsoft Excel 2016

9. Take a screenshot of your frequency distribution and the histogram. Label it "Lab 9-1 Histogram."

Analyze the Results

Q2. Based on the histogram of the distribution of tax rates, are you surprised by its shape where there are observations on both extremes but none in the middle? Why would some states have zero sales tax, but most states have higher sales taxes?

Part 3, continued: Perform an Analysis Using Tableau

10. Open Tableau and connect to the Ch 9 Lab 9-1 State_SalesTax.xlsx file.
11. Ensure that the fields imported into Tableau in the correct format—geographic string for State and number for State Tax Rate.

⊕	#
Sheet1	Sheet1
State	**State Tax Rate**
Alabama	0.0400000
Alaska	0.0000000
Arizona	0.0560000

Source: Microsoft Excel 2016

12. Click into Sheet 1 and double-click on **State** from the Dimensions section. Automatically, Latitude and Longitude pills will appear in the Rows and Columns shelves, and Tableau will default to a symbol map since the State field is formatted as a geographic string.
13. Double-click on **TaxRate** from Measures area.
14. In the **Show Me** section of Tableau, change the map from a symbol map to a **filled map**. If the shading in each state does not automatically adjust to reflect the different levels of tax rates, drag the pill SUM(State Sales Tax) to Color on the Marks shelf.

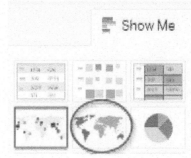

Source: Microsoft Excel 2016

15. Right-click on the label for Sheet 1 to rename the sheet as **Filled Map**.

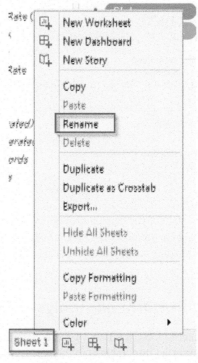

Source: Microsoft Excel 2016

16. Take a screenshot of the filled map and label it "Lab 9-1 Filled Map."
17. Right-click the label for Filled Map (previously labeled Sheet 1) to duplicate the sheet.
18. Using the different options available in the Show Me tab, create another visual that you find useful. Re-label the sheet appropriately. If your Show Me tab has disappeared, you can click Ctrl +1 on your keyboard for it to reappear.
19. Take a screenshot of your new visual and label it "Lab 9-1 Visual."

Q2.   Based on this visualization, which states paying 0 percent sales tax are next to states with really high sales tax rates?

End of Lab

Lab 9-2   Comprehensive Case 1: Dillard's Store Data: Calculate Sales Tax for Dillard's States

Company summary

Dillard's is a department store with approximately 330 stores in 29 states. Its headquarters is in Little Rock, Arkansas. You can learn more about Dillard's by looking at finance.yahoo .com (Ticker symbol = DDS) and the Wikipedia site on DDS. You'll quickly note that William T. Dillard II is an accounting grad of the University of Arkansas and the Walton College of Business, which may be why he shared transaction data with us to make available for this lab and labs throughout this text.

Data

The data for this lab and other Dillard's labs is available at http://walton.uark.edu/enterprise/. Your instructor will either give you specific instructions on how to access the data, or there will be information available in Connect. The 2016 Dillard's data covers all transactions over the period 1/1/2014 to 10/17/2016.
   Additionally, the data found in the Ch 9 State_SalesTax.xlsx is used.

Software needed

- Microsoft SQL Server Management Studio (available on the VMWare at the University of Arkansas)
- Microsoft Excel

In this lab, you will:

- Calculate total sales across all Dillard's stores year over year in order to compare sales tax paid across periods.

Part 1: Identify the Questions

What is an estimate of the amount of sales taxes we owe from Dillard's purchases? What is an estimate of the amount of sales taxes we owe from Dillard's *net* purchases?

Part 2: Master the Data

1. Before we can analyze the data and look up the sales tax owed in each state, we need to extract the sales data From SQL Server and load it into Excel. To do so, you will need to connect to SQL Server data through Excel using Excel's Get & Transform tool. If you need a refresher on how to use that tool, refer to the textbook's Appendix F.

2. Once you connect to the SQL Server dataset in Excel and expand the options to input a query, input the following SQL query to extract the data needed for our analysis.

```
SELECT State, SUM(Tran_Amt) AS Amount
FROM Store
INNER JOIN Transact
ON Store.Store = Transact.Store
WHERE Tran_Type = 'P' AND YEAR(Tran_Date) = 2015 AND State <> 'U'
GROUP BY State
```

3. Thirty rows (including the header) should load into your spreadsheet.
4. Add a column to your SQL Server data table titled **State Sales Tax Rate**.
5. Save your file as Ch_9_Comprehensive_Lab_1.xlsx.
6. Open the Ch 9 State_SalesTax.xlsx file and copy the Sales Tax table to columns E and F of the file you just created, Ch_9_Comprehensive_Lab_1.xlsx. You will use this table to calculate the sales tax **Dillard's** owed in each state. You can find this file in the "DAA 2e Data Files" folder on the remote desktop.
7. Use a VLookup to populate the new column that matches the state sales tax with the sales amount for each state.
   - The Lookup_Value is the state field.
   - The table_array is the entire Sales Tax table that you copied into this Excel file. Refer to this either as Table1 (if made into a table) or refer directly to the cells in columns E and F.
   - The col_index_number is 2.
   - The range_lookup value is FALSE.

	A	B	C	D	E	F
1	State	Amount	state Sales Tax Rate		state	taxrate
2	MO	24272901.66	=VLOOKUP([@State],Table2,2,FALSE)			0.04
3	IL	5650816.15			AK	0
4	OH		*This is the column you are adding to the table that you loaded with the query*		AZ	0.056
5	IA				AR	0.065
6	GA				CA	0.0725
7	ID			*This is the Sales Tax table that you copied in from the Ch 9 SalesTax.xlsx*		0.029
8	UT					0.0635
9	MS	15635410.23				0
10	TN	35852350.06			FL	0.06
11	AL	23691920.01			GA	0.04
12	NC	22295334.16			HI	0.04
13	AZ	40534125.79			ID	0.06
14	OK	36510372.2			IL	0.0625
15	SC	17214318.86			IN	0.07
16	NM	15015216.32			IA	0.06

Source: Microsoft Excel 2016

8. Add a column to your SQL Server data table titled **State Tax Owed** to calculate the sales tax owed in each state in 2016 using the formula shown in the image below.

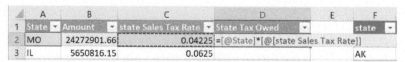

	A	B	C	D	E	F
1	State	Amount	state Sales Tax Rate	State Tax Owed		state
2	MO	24272901.66	0.04225	=[@State]*[@[state Sales Tax Rate]]		
3	IL	5650816.15	0.0625			AK

Source: Microsoft Excel 2016

Part 2, Continued: Refining the Query

The query you entered in the previous steps included a filter that only showed transactions that were marked with a "P" for their tran_type, indicating a customer purchase. However, if there were returns during the period, these should also be included in the calculation so that the dollar amounts associated with the returns are subtracted from the total.

Q1. Why is it important to subtract the return transaction amount when calculating sales tax owed?

Re-run the query with the following text (which omits the filter for only purchases), and then repeat the steps to add the two additional columns (State Sales Tax Rate and Tax Owed) to look up the total amount of sales tax owed for each state, but now deducting the returns.

```
SELECT State, SUM(Tran_Amt) AS Amount
FROM Store
INNER JOIN Transact
ON Store.Store = Transact.Store
WHERE YEAR(Tran_Date) = 2015 AND State <> 'U'
GROUP BY State
```

Q2. How vast is the difference in the amount of total state sales tax **Dillard's** would end up paying if you didn't correct the error by refining the query (and reducing it by the amount of returned items)?

Q3. Is it safe to assume that all of the returns made in 2015 are aligned with the fiscal period for which **Dillard's** owes sales tax? For example, would all returns in 2015 be from 2015 sales? What should **Dillard's** due to account for any potential misalignment?

End of Lab

Lab 9-3   Comprehensive Case 2: Dillard's Store Data: Calculate Sales Tax for Dillard's States Part 2—Compare Year over Year

Company Summary

Dillard's is a department store with approximately 330 stores in 29 states. Its headquarters is in Little Rock, Arkansas. You can learn more about **Dillard's** by looking at finance.yahoo.com (Ticker symbol = DDS) and the Wikipedia site on DDS. You'll quickly note that William T. Dillard II is an accounting grad of the University of Arkansas and the Walton College of Business, which may be why he shared transaction data with us to make available for this lab and labs throughout this text.

Data

The data for this lab and other **Dillard's** labs is available at http://walton.uark.edu/enterprise/. Your instructor will either give you specific instructions on how to access the data or there will be information available on Connect. The 2016 **Dillard's** data covers all transactions over the period 1/1/2014 to 10/17/2016.

Additionally, the data found in the Ch 9 State_SalesTax.xlsx is used.

Software needed

- Microsoft SQL Server Management Studio (available on the VMWare at the University of Arkansas)
- Microsoft Excel

In this lab, you will:

- Calculate total sales across all Dillard's stores year over year and month over month in order to compare sales tax paid across periods.

Part 1: Identify the Questions

Compare 2014, 2015, and 2016 sales tax data across states in parallel periods.

Part 2: Master the Data

1. Before we can analyze the data, we need to extract the data From SQL Server and load it into Excel. To do so, click New Query from the Data tab, and follow the path to select from Database and from SQL Server Database.

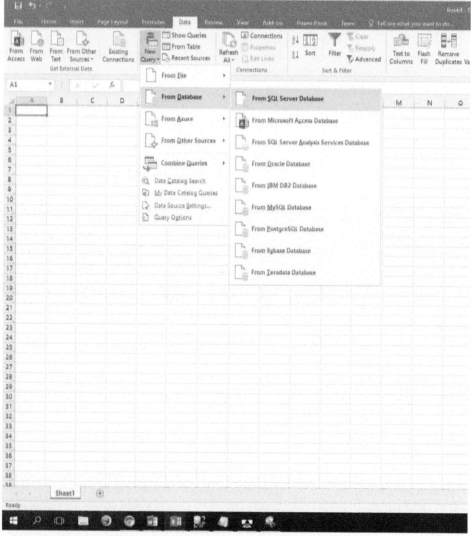

Source: Microsoft Excel 2016

2. To address this question, you will need to connect to SQL Server data through Excel using Excel's Get & Transform tool. If you need a refresher on how to use that tool, refer to the textbook's Appendix F.

```
Select year(Tran_Date) as year, datename(month,tran_date) as month, state,
sum(Tran_Amt) as SalesAmount
From TRANSACT
INNER JOIN STORE
ON TRANSACT.STORE = STORE.STORE
WHERE State <> 'U'
Group By year(Tran_Date), datename(month,tran_date), STATE
Order By year(Tran_Date), datename(month,tran_date), STATE
```

3. Once the query runs (it may take a few minutes), click **Load** the data into Excel; 986 rows should load.
4. Now, we need to add two columns to this table, a State Tax Rate column and a State Tax Owed column.
5. Use a VLookup and your state sales tax table to populate the tax_rate column (replicate the steps 4-7 from Lab 9-2 Comprehensive Lab 1).
6. Multiply the State Tax Rate by the SalesAmount to populate the State Tax Owed column.

Part 3: Perform the Analysis

7. From the insert tab on the ribbon, click PivotTable to insert a PivotTable.

Source: Microsoft Excel 2016

8. Ensure that the data from Query 1 is selected, and click **OK**.

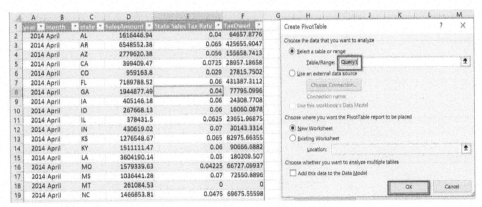

Source: Microsoft Excel 2016

To view how state sales tax owed changed in each state from 2014 to 2015, add the State field to the PivotTable Rows, the Year field to the PivotTable columns, and State Tax Owed to the PivotTable Values (ensure that Tax Owed is summarized by SUM).

Source: Microsoft Excel 2016

9. To limit the years viewed, click the drop-down next to Column Labels on the PivotTable, and unselect the checkmark next to 2016. Click **OK** to apply the filter.

Source: Microsoft Excel 2016

Part 4: Address, Refine, and Communicate the Results

The filtered data provides the information you need to see the states that **Dillard's** owed more (or less) state sales tax in from 2014 to 2015, but it would be easier to understand by cleaning up the data included and with a visualization.

10. The Grand Totals don't add important information for our analysis in this PivotTable, so they need to be removed. From the PivotTable Design tab on the ribbon, click **Grand Totals**, and turn them off for rows and columns:

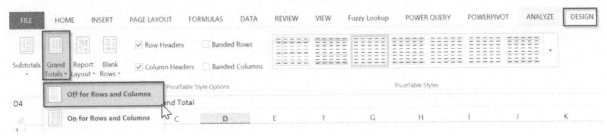

Source: Microsoft Excel 2016

11. To visualize the data, we'll add sparklines next to each state's numbers. Place your cursor in cell D5 next to the end of the data for Alabama (AL). From the Insert tab in the ribbon, click **Line** from the Sparklines section to add a Sparkline.

Source: Microsoft Excel 2016

12. In the Create Sparklines box, select Alabama's set of data for the Data Range and click **OK** (the Location Range should default to D5 because of where your cursor was when you began inserting the sparkline).

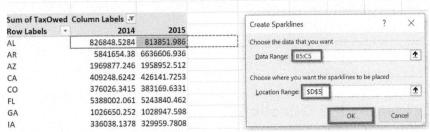

Source: Microsoft Excel 2016

13. Copy the sparkline all the way down your data so that you can see how the State Tax Owed changed year over year for each state.

Sum of TaxOwed	Column Labels		
Row Labels	2014	2015	
AL	826848.5284	813851.986	
AR	5841654.38	6636606.936	
AZ	1969877.246	1958952.512	
CA	409248.6242	426141.7253	
CO	376026.3415	383169.6331	
FL	5388002.061	5243840.462	

Source: Microsoft Excel 2016

385

Q1. Are total state sales taxes increasing or decreasing each year from 2014 to 2015 in the state of Missouri? The state of Ohio?

End of Lab

Lab 9-4 Comprehensive Case 3: Dillard's Store Data: Calculate Sales Tax for Dillard's States Part 3—Calculate City Tax and Compare Tax Owed Year over Year

Company Summary

Dillard's is a department store with approximately 330 stores in 29 states. Its headquarters is in Little Rock, Arkansas. You can learn more about Dillard's by looking at finance.yahoo .com (Ticker symbol = DDS) and the Wikipedia site on DDS. You'll quickly note that William T. Dillard II is an accounting grad of the University of Arkansas and the Walton College of Business, which may be why he shared transaction data with us to make available for this lab and labs throughout this text.

Data

The data for this lab and other Dillard's labs is available at http://walton.uark.edu/enterprise/. Your instructor will either give you specific instructions on how to access the data, or there will be information available on Connect.

Additionally, the data found in the Ch 9 State_SalesTax.xlsx is used.

Optionally, a data file for Arkansas' cities sales tax is included: Ch 9 Lab - Comprehensive Lab 3 Total Sales Tax in AR Cities.xlsx

Software needed

- Microsoft SQL Server Management Studio (available on the VMWare at the University of Arkansas)
- Microsoft Excel

In this lab, you will:

- Calculate total sales across all Dillard's stores in a particular state (the example given in this lab is for Arkansas) each January, year over year, in order to compare sales tax paid in each city across periods.

Part 1: Identify the Questions

Compare 2014, 2015, and 2016 sales tax data across cities.

Part 2: Master the Data

1. To address our question, you will need to connect to SQL Server data through Excel using Excel's Get & Transform tool. If you need a refresher on how to use that tool, refer to the textbook's Appendix F.

   Once you connect to the SQL Server dataset in Excel and expand the options to input a query, input the following SQL query to extract the data needed for our analysis.

   ```
   SELECT YEAR(Tran_Date) AS Year, State, City, SUM(Tran_Amt) AS Amount
   FROM Transact
   INNER JOIN Store
   ```

```
ON Transact.Store = Store.Store
WHERE DATENAME(MONTH,Tran_Date) = 'January' AND State = 'AR'
GROUP BY YEAR(Tran_Date), State, Store.City
ORDER BY YEAR(Tran_Date), State, Store.City
```

Notice that this query text has a filter for state = 'AR'. If you would prefer to look up city tax in a different state, simply change the criteria to any state's abbreviation you choose.

2. Using your web browser, search for the city tax in the state that you are filtering for. Typically, the tables for the popular cities in each state are fairly easy to find, and that will likely suffice. Alternatively, a clean version of City Sales tax data for the state of Arkansas is provided that you can use (File name: Ch 9 Lab - Comprehensive Lab 3 Total Sales Tax in AR Cities.xlsx).

3. Using your ETL skills that you learned in Chapter 2, clean the city tax data in Excel so that you can use a VLookup to calculate the city tax owed in each of the state's cities that have Dillard's stores.

4. Following the same steps that you learned in Lab 9-2, steps 6-8, calculate the city tax owed in each of the state's cities that have Dillard's stores.

Part 3: Perform the Analysis and Communicate Results

5. Using the skills you learned in Lab 9-3, steps 8-12, create a PivotTable to compare the city sales tax owed in each city across the three years of data. Then, create sparklines to visualize the change over the three years.

Q1. Are sales taxes increasing or decreasing each year from 2014 to 2016 in the city of Little Rock? Fayetteville?

End of Lab

Lab 9-5   Comprehensive Case 4: Dillard's Store Data: Does a State's Tax Rate Affect Dillard's Decision to Open Stores There?

Company Summary

Dillard's is a department store with approximately 330 stores in 29 states. Its headquarters is in Little Rock, Arkansas. You can learn more about Dillard's by looking at finance.yahoo .com (Ticker symbol = DDS) and the Wikipedia site on DDS. You'll quickly note that William T. Dillard II is an accounting grad of the University of Arkansas and the Walton College of Business, which may be why he shared transaction data with us to make available for this lab and labs throughout this text.

Data

The data for this lab and other Dillard's labs is available at http://walton.uark.edu/enterprise/. Your instructor will either give you specific instructions on how to access the data, or there will be information available on Connect.

Additionally, the data found in the Ch 9 State_SalesTax.xlsx is used.

Software needed

- Microsoft SQL Server Management Studio (available on the VMWare at the University of Arkansas)
- Microsoft Excel

In this lab, you will:

- Run a regression to test to see if a state's sales tax rate influenced their decision to place stores in that state.

Part 1: Identify the Questions

Does a state's sales tax rate have a significant impact on **Dillard's** decision to open stores there?

Part 2: Master the Data

1. To address our question, you will need to connect to SQL Server data through Excel using Excel's Get & Transform tool. If you need a refresher on how to use that tool, refer to the textbook's Appendix F.

   Once you connect to the SQL Server dataset in Excel and expand the options to input a query, input the following SQL query to extract the data needed for our analysis.

   ```
   SELECT State, COUNT(Store) as NumStores
   FROM Store
   WHERE State <> 'U'
   GROUP BY State
   ```

   After loading the data, you should see 30 rows (including a header).

2. Following the same steps that you learned in Lab 9-2, steps 6-8, add a column to include the sales tax rate for each state.

Part 3: Perform the Analysis

3. To run a regression to see if a state's sales tax rate helps to explain how many stores **Dillard's** would have placed in a given state, first click into the Data Analysis ToolPak in the Data Tab.

Source: Microsoft Excel 2016

4. In the Data Analysis window, Select **Regression** and click **OK**.
5. Select the NumStores column of data for your Y Range and the State sales tax rate column of data for your X Range.

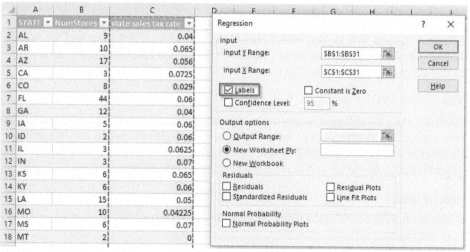

Source: Microsoft Excel 2016

Remember that when you select the labels in your Y and X ranges, place a check mark next to Labels, as shown in the visual.

6. Click **OK** to run the regression.

Part 4: Address and Refine the Results: Interpret R-Square and P-Value

Q1. The coefficient for state sales tax is positive but not significantly different from zero. What does that suggest? Is the coefficient different than what you would expect? Why or why not?

Q2. The adjusted R-squared tells us how much of the variance is explained by this model. The adjusted R-squared is less than zero, suggesting it doesn't do a very good job. What do you think would do a better job in predicting the number of stores in a state than sales tax rate?

End of Lab

Chapter 10

Project Chapter (Basic)

A Look at This Chapter

This chapter will take you through a series of problems to help you analyze and communicate answers to accounting questions that are asked every day. This will provide a review of the Data Analytics concepts we've discussed in the previous chapters and put them into perspective. For each analysis, we will look at the data from a managerial, auditing, and financial accounting perspective.

A Look Back

Chapter 9 discussed the application of Data Analytics to tax questions and looked at how data can drive strategy and help managers understand the underlying tax behavior.

A Look Forward

Chapter 11 will revisit the Dillard's sales and returns data to provide an advanced overview of different analytical tools and techniques to provide additional understanding of the data.

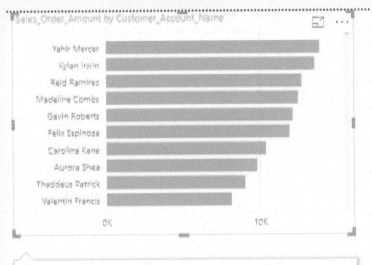

Sales_Order_Amount by Customer_Account_Name

What is the total sales order amount by customer account name?

Source: Microsoft PowerBI

Tools like Tableau and Power BI are popular because they enable quick analysis of simple descriptive and diagnostic analytics. By creating visual answers to data problems, accountants can tell stories that help inform management decisions, aid auditors, and provide insight into financial data.

Both Tableau and Power BI enable more simplified analysis by incorporating natural language processing into their cloud-based offerings. Instead of dragging dimensions and measures to build the analyses, you can simply ask a question in a natural sentence, and the tool will map your question to your existing data model.

OBJECTIVES

After reading this chapter, you should be able to:

LO 10-1 Analyze data in the order-to-cash process.

LO 10-2 Analyze data in the procure-to-pay process.

EVALUATING BUSINESS PROCESSES

As a manager, auditor, or financial accountant, your role is to understand how different business processes operate and ensure controls exist over those processes. Companies use Data Analytics to summarize data for reports, evaluate performance, and identify risk in these cycles.

In this basic project chapter, we will work through a series of questions that help you understand how data from different aspects of each business process can answer a variety of questions depending on the user's perspective.

There are two main question sets that explore the following:

1. Question Set 1 looks at the order-to-cash process or sales/revenue cycle within a company; you will summarize flows of sales order transactions, accounts receivables, and customer activity.
2. Question Set 2 moves into the procure-to-pay process or purchasing cycle to evaluate purchasing activity and potential savings when paying or interacting with vendors.

Each set walks you through the analysis using a prepared Tableau workbook. The data has already been cleaned and converted to mimic the audit data standard format. As you complete the steps, you will encounter several questions that ask you about your approach to the analysis, how to interpret the results, and how you would expand the analysis using a comprehensive data set.

LO 10-1
Analyze data in the order-to-cash process.

QUESTION SET 1: ORDER-TO-CASH

The order-to-cash (O2C) process or sales cycle involves three main processes:

1. Sales order processing.
2. Order fulfillment and shipping.
3. Billing and cash collections.

Managers are concerned with making the process as efficient as possible to ensure increased sales volume, sufficient profitability, and fast cash collection.

Auditors should test sales transaction and master data to ensure that only authorized users are processing orders, that sales prices match master data and aren't altered, and that customers aren't exceeding approval limits in addition to evaluating prompt payment by customers through the aging of accounts receivable.

Financial accountants are interested in determining the amount of sales revenue on the income statement and accounts receivable balance on the balance sheet as well as the calculation of bad debts expense.

To answer the following questions, use the Tableau Workbook O2C found on Connect. The O2C data, shown in Exhibit 10-1, has joined together the following tables into one file.

When you open the O2C Tableau Workbook, you will see the data pre-populated and ready for analysis, similar to Exhibit 10-2. You are now ready to complete the questions in this set.

Question 1.1: How Efficiently Are We Collecting Our Cash?

Before you begin, put yourself in a manager's shoes, and answer the following questions about the order-to-cash process. You might want to discuss these with a classmate, review Chapter 7, or search the Internet for some suggestions.

Q1-1   What risks are present if you take too long to collect our accounts receivable?

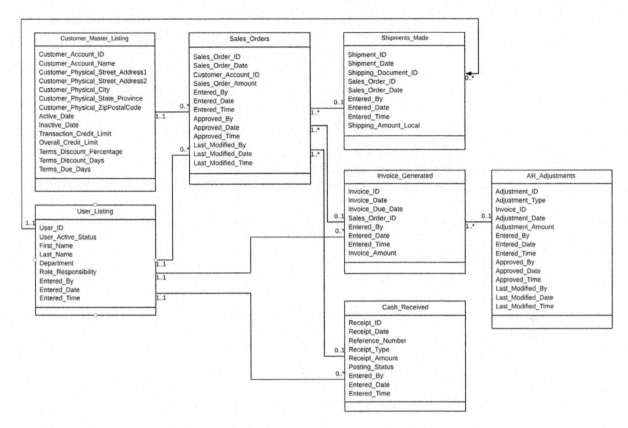

EXHIBIT 10-1   **Order-to-Cash Data**

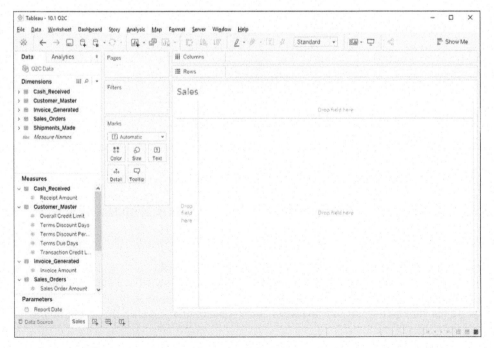

EXHIBIT 10-2

O2C Data Ready for Analysis in Tableau

Source: Tableau Software, Inc. All rights reserved.

Q1-2. What are some analyses you could perform that would provide insight into how efficiently your company is collecting cash from customers? Are there any KPIs that would be appropriate here?

Q1-3. In your opinion, what would be an appropriate benchmark for the average number of days sales outstanding (i.e., Accounts receivable/Sales × 365)? Would management want this number higher or lower?

Now let's go to Tableau to find some answers about sales:

1. Open the Tableau workbook called O2C.twbx.
2. Rename Sheet 1 to **Total Sales.**
3. On the Sales sheet, drag **Sales Order Amount** measure to the Text button in Marks pane.
4. Drag the **Sales Order Date** dimension to the Filters shelf. Choose Years, then click Next, check 2020, and click **OK.**

Source: Tableau Software, Inc. All rights reserved.

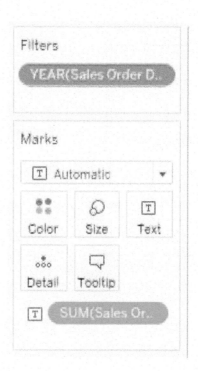

5. Drag the **Sales Order Date** dimension to the Rows pane.

Q1-4. What are the total sales for 2020?

6. Click the + next to **YEAR(Sales Order Date)** in the Rows pane to show the quarters.

Q1-5. Which quarter had the highest sales?

7. Create a new worksheet called **Sales by Customer.**
8. Drag the **Sales Order Amount** measure to the Columns shelf.
9. Drag the **Customer Account Name** dimension to the Rows shelf and click **Add All Members** if prompted.
10. In the bar chart, hover over the **Sales Order Amount** title and click the sort button to show sales by customer.

Q1-6. Which customer had the most sales? How much did we sell to that customer?

Source: Tableau Software, Inc. All rights reserved.

Now let's find some answers related to accounts receivable:

11. Create a new worksheet called **AR by Customer.**
12. We need to create some calculations and parameters to answer questions about receivables:

    a. Create a new parameter to set your reporting date. Click the down arrow next to Dimensions and choose **Create Parameter. . .** Name the parameter **Report Date,** set the data type to Date and the current value to 12/31/2020 (choose this date from the calendar pop up), and click **OK.**

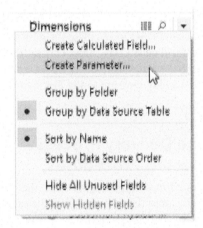

Source: Tableau Software, Inc. All rights reserved.

    b. Now add a calculated field to determine the age of accounts. Click the down arrow next to Dimensions and choose **Create Calculated Field. . .** Name the field **Age,** enter the equation [Report Date]-[Invoice Due Date], and then click **OK.**

Source: Tableau Software, Inc. All rights reserved.

    c. Create a new calculated field to determine the account balance. Name the field **Balance** and enter the equation [Invoice Amount]-IFNULL([Receipt Amount],0)-IFNULL([Adjustment Amount],0). The IFNULL will place a 0 value in for invoices without matching receipts. Click **OK.**

13. Now we're ready for the analysis. Drag the **Customer Account Name** (if prompted, choose Add All Members), **Invoice ID,** and **Invoice Due Date** dimensions to the Rows shelf. To show the actual date, right-click the **YEAR(Invoice Due Date)** and choose Measure > Maximum from the menu.
14. Drag the **Measure Names** dimension to the Columns shelf and the **Measure Values** measure to the Text button in the Marks card.
15. In the Measure Values pane, remove all of the measures e*xcept* **SUM(Adjustment Amount), SUM(Age), SUM(Balance), SUM(Invoice Amount),** and **SUM(Receipt Amount).** Drag and drop the items to reorder them as Invoice Amount, Receipt Amount, Adjustment Amount, Balance, and Age.
16. Drag the **Balance** measure to the Filters shelf. Click **Next,** then set the minimum value to 1 and click **OK.** Now you will see a list of all outstanding invoices.

> Q1-7. What is the value of the the first outstanding invoice? What is its age?
>
> Q1-8. Some of the accounts have a negative age. What does that mean?

Finally, let's determine how old the accounts receivable are on average.

17. Create a new worksheet called **DSO** to calculate the days sales outstanding KPI.
18. Create a new Calculated Field called **Days Sales Outstanding.** The equation should be SUM([Balance])/SUM([Sales Order Amount])*365. Click **OK.**
19. Drag the **Days Sales Outstanding** measure to the Text button in the Marks card.

> Q1-9. What is the current days sales outstanding KPI value? What does it mean?

Question 1.2: Is the Delivery Process Following the Expected Procedure?

As an auditor, you're interested in determining whether the delivery process follows the expected sequence. Specifically, does the delivery follow the sales order, and has each delivery been matched with an invoice? Before you continue with your analysis, answer the following questions about the delivery process.

> Q1-10. Under what circumstances might a delivery take place before a sales order? Should this happen?
>
> Q1-11. What types of controls would prevent the system from skipping a process or step?

20. Return to your O2C Tableau Workbook and create a new worksheet called **Exceptions.**
21. Create a new calculated field called **Order to Ship Days** with the equation [Shipment Date]-[Sales Order Date] and click **OK.**
22. Drag **Order to Ship Days** to the Label button in the Marks pane and **Sales Order ID** to the Rows shelf (if prompted, click Add All Members).
23. Click the Sort button next to the **Order to Ship Days** two times to sort by ascending order.

> Q1-12. Which orders were created after shipment? How do you know?

24. Now create a new worksheet called **No Invoice** to determine whether any orders have shipped but have not been invoiced yet.
25. Drag **Sales Order ID, Shipment Date, Shipment ID,** and **Invoice ID** to the Rows shelf (choose Add All Members if prompted).
26. Right-click **Shipment Date** and choose Measure > Maximum from the menu.

27. Drag **Invoice ID** to the Filters shelf. Choose Select from list, click **None,** then check Null, and click **OK.**

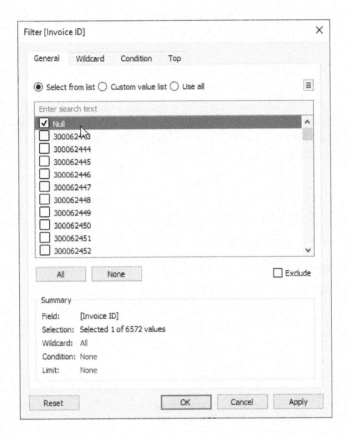

Source: Tableau Software, Inc. All rights reserved.

Q1-13.   Of the 12 orders listed, which one is the most problematic? Why?

Q1-14.   Why aren't the other orders suspicious?

Q1-15.   While you still have your auditor hat on, what are some additional analyses you could perform to understand whether the process or processes are being followed or controls are functioning properly?

Question 1.3: What Is the Total Revenue and Balance in Accounts Receivable?

Finally, imagine you are preparing financial statements and need to calculate the revenue and accounts receivable balances for the income statement and balance sheet, respectively.

Q1-16. How could analytics provide additional insight into financial information beyond calculating balances?

28. Return to your O2C Tableau Workbook and create a new worksheet called **Aging Report.** This sheet relies on the **Balance** calculated field you created previously.
29. Create buckets for the day categories. Right-click the **Age** measure and choose Create > Bins from the menu.

Source: Tableau Software, Inc. All rights reserved.

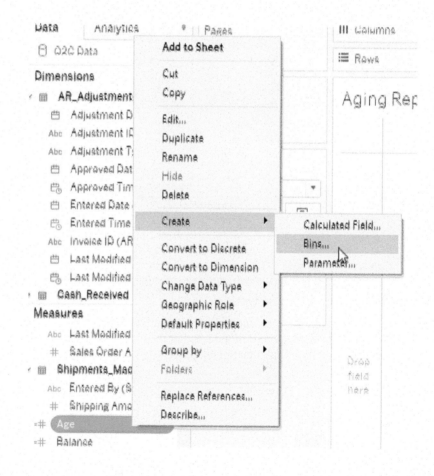

30. Leave the new field name, set the size of bins to 30, and click **OK.**
31. Drag the **Balance** measure to the Columns pane and the **Age (bin)** dimension to the Rows shelf.
32. Drag the **Balance** measure to the Label button in the Marks pane to show the value of each bucket alongside the bar chart.

> Q1-17. What is the value of open accounts that are between 60 and 90 days old? *Hint:* Look for the 60 bin.

> Q1-18. Should we be writing any of these accounts off, in your opinion?

33. Finally, let's evaluate write-offs. Create a new worksheet called **Bad Debts.**
34. Create a new Calculated Field called **Write-off Percent** with the equation SUM([Adjustment Amount])/SUM([Sales Order Amount]). This will show the percent of sales order dollars that were written off during the year.
35. Drag **Sales Order Date** dimension to the Columns shelf. Right-click the Sales Order Date and choose **Month** from the menu.
36. Drag **Sales Order Amount** and **Adjustment Amount** measures to the Rows shelf.
37. In the Marks card, under All, change the chart type from **Automatic** to **Bar.**
38. Right click the Adjustment Amount label in the graph and choose **Dual Axis** to combine the charts.

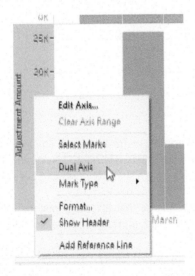

Source: Tableau Software, Inc. All rights reserved.

39. Right click the Adjustment Amount label again and choose **Synchronize Axis** to place the numbers on the same scale.
40. Finally, drag the **Write-off Percent** measure to the Label button in the Marks card to add the percentage value to the write-offs.
41. Right click the AGG(Write-off Percent) in the Marks card and click **Format** from the menu. In the formatting pane, change the default numbers from Automatic to Percentage.

> Q1-19. If management expects about 5 percent of the accounts receivables to be written off, which month(s) exceeded that estimate?

> Q1-20. Looking at the trend of write-offs for the end of the year, do you expect there to be no write-offs in November and December? Why or why not? How would you account for these?

Question 1.4: What Else Can You Determine about the O2C Process?

We've discussed a few different ways to analyze O2C data to understand the processes and controls. Now it's your chance to find answers to your own questions.

42. Identify five questions that you think management or auditors would want to know about the O2C process. If you need help, search for some common questions asked by accountants on the Internet.

43. Using the the data you have already loaded into Tableau, generate at least three analyses and visualizations that will help you find the answers to your five questions.

Q1-21.   Write your first question and provide an answer based on your analysis.

Q1-22.   Write your second question and provide an answer based on your analysis.

Q1-23.   Write your third question and provide an answer based on your analysis.

Q1-24.   Write your fourth question and provide an answer based on your analysis.

Q1-25.   Write your fifth question and provide an answer based on your analysis.

<table>
<tr><td>

LO 10-2

Analyze data in the procure-to-pay process.

</td></tr>
</table>

QUESTION SET 2: PROCURE-TO-PAY

The procure-to-pay process (P2P) or purchasing cycle for a retailer involves four main processes:

1. Create and submit a purchase order.
2. Receive inventory.
3. Receive an invoice.
4. Pay the invoice.

The procure-to-pay process has some additional challenges in that there are numerous opportunities to divert company funds. Therefore you should focus on the risk of unauthorized and fictitious payments (e.g., to shell vendors) and ensure that the process is appropriately controlled.

Managers would want to ensure that inventory matches what they (or their company) ordered, that invoices aren't paid more than once, and that the payments are sent to approved parties.

Auditors are interested in testing the internal controls that govern who can create orders, receive items, and approve payments. In addition to segregation of duties, they may be interested in matching each of the documents (i.e., purchase order, receiving report, and vendor invoice) in a three-way match.

To answer the following questions, use the Tableau workbook and Excel data files found on Connect. The P2P data, shown in Exhibit 10-3, has joined together the following tables into one file.

When you open the P2P Tableau Workbook, you will see the data pre-populated and ready for analysis, similar to Exhibit 10-4. You are now ready to complete the questions in this set.

Question 2.1: How Long Are We Taking to Pay Our Invoices?

Before you begin, put yourself in a manager's shoes, and answer the following questions about the procure-to-pay process. You might want to discuss these with a classmate, review Chapter 7, or search the Internet for some suggestions.

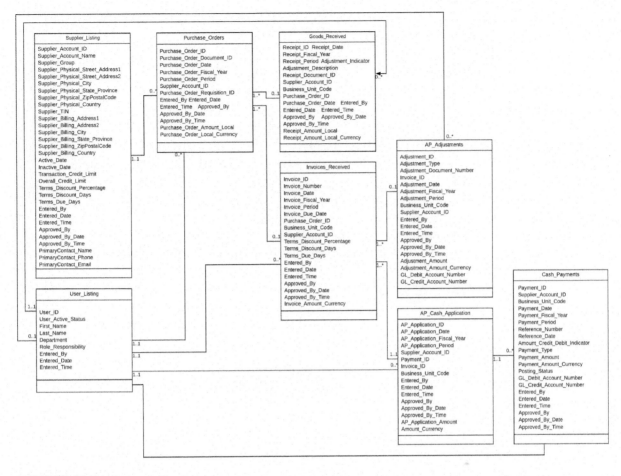

EXHIBIT 10-3   Procure-to-Pay Data

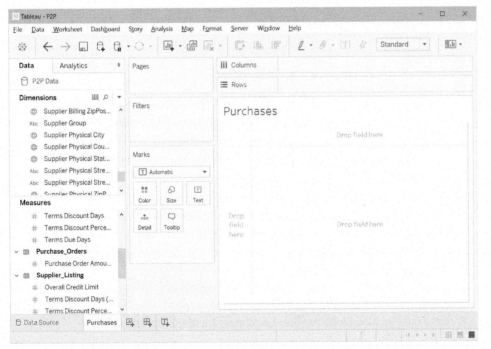

EXHIBIT 10-4
**P2P Data Ready for
Analysis in Tableau**

Source: Tableau Software,
Inc. All rights reserved.

Q2-1.   What risks are present if you take too long to pay our accounts payable?

Q2-2.   What are some analyses you could perform that would provide insight into how efficiently your company is processing payments to suppliers? Are there any KPIs that would be appropriate here?

Q2-3.   In your opinion, what would be an appropriate benchmark for the average number of discount dollars lost as a percentage of available discount dollars? How about erroneous payments as a percentage of total payments? Would management want these numbers to be higher or lower?

Now let's go to Tableau to find some answers about purchases and payments:

1. Open the Tableau workbook called P2P.twbx. If prompted for a data file, choose the P2P Data.xlsx file that you downloaded from Connect. Alternatively, choose the Purchase_Orders+ (P2P Data) option and click **OK**.
2. Rename Sheet 1 to **Total Purchases.**
3. On the Total Purchases sheet, drag the **Purchase Order Amount Local** measure to the Text button on the Marks card.
4. Drag the **Purchase Order Date** dimension to the Filters shelf. Choose **Years,** then click **Next,** check **2020,** and click **OK.**

Source: Tableau Software, Inc. All rights reserved.

5. Drag the **Purchase Order Date** dimension to the Rows shelf.

Q2-4.   What are the total purchases for 2020?

6. Click the + next to **YEAR(Purchase Order Date)** in the Rows shelf to show the quarters.

Q2-5.   Which quarter had the highest total purchases?

7. Create a new worksheet called **Purchases by Supplier.**
8. Drag the **Purchase Order Amount Local** measure to the Columns shelf.

9. Drag the **Supplier Account Name** dimension to the Rows shelf and click **Add All Members** if prompted.

10. In the bar chart, hover over the **Purchase Order Amount Local** title and click the sort button to show purchases by supplier.

> Q2-6.   Which supplier did we purchase the most from? How much did we purchase from that supplier?

Now let's find some answers related to accounts payable:

11. Create a new worksheet called **AP by Supplier.**

12. We need to create some calculations and parameters to answer these questions:

  a. Create a new parameter to set your reporting date. Click the down arrow next to Dimensions and choose **Create Parameter. . .** Name the parameter **Report Date,** set the data type to Date and the current value to 12/31/2020, and click **OK.**

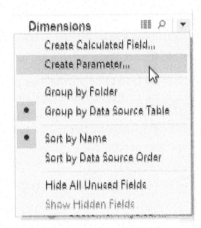

Source: Tableau Software, Inc. All rights reserved.

  b. Now add a calculated field to determine the age of accounts. Click the down arrow next to Dimensions and choose **Create Calculated Field. . .** Name the field **Age,** enter the equation [Report Date]-[Invoice Due Date], and then click **OK.**

Source: Tableau Software, Inc. All rights reserved.

  c. Create a new calculated field to determine the account balance. Name the field **Balance** and enter the equation [Invoice Amount]-IFNULL([Payment Amount],0). The IFNULL will place a 0 value in for invoices without matching payments. Click **OK.**

13. Now we're ready for the analysis. Drag the **Supplier Account Name, Invoice ID,** and **Invoice Due Date** dimensions to the Rows shelf. If prompted, add all members. To show the actual date, right-click the **YEAR(Invoice Due Date)** and choose Measure > Maximum from the menu.
14. Drag the **Measure Names** dimension to the Columns shelf and the **Measure Values** measure to the Text button in the Marks card.
15. In the Measure Values pane, remove all of the measures *except* **SUM(Age), SUM(Balance), SUM(Invoice Amount),** and **SUM(Payment Amount).** Reorder them to show the Invoice Amount, Payment Amount, Balance, and Age.
16. Drag the **Balance** measure to the Filters shelf. Click **Next,** then set the minimum value to 1 and click **OK.** Drag the **Payment Amount** measure to the Filters shelf. Click **Next,** then set the minimum and maximum values to 0 and check **Include Null Values** and click **OK.** Now you will see a list of all outstanding invoices.

> Q2-7. What is the invoice amount of the first outstanding invoice for Danbam? What is its age?

> Q2-8. Some of the accounts have a negative age. What does that mean?

Finally, let's determine how old the accounts payable are on average.

17. Create a new worksheet called **DPO** to calculate the days payable outstanding KPI.
18. Create a new Calculated Field called **Days Payable Outstanding.** The equation should be SUM([Balance])/SUM([Purchase Order Amount Local])*365. Click **OK.**
19. Drag the **Days Payable Outstanding** measure to the Text button in the Marks card.

> Q2-9. What is the current days payable outstanding KPI value? What does it mean?

Question 2.2: Are There Any Erroneous Payments?

Auditors would be interested in evaluating the origin of invoices and payables to make sure that they are paid correctly and aren't out of normal behavior. Before you continue your analysis, answer the following questions about the payment process.

> Q2-10. What statistical tools can we use to diagnose behavior that is outside of normal behavior?

> Q2-11. How might an outlier be used to focus the auditors on high-risk transactions?

Let's look at the data and use an average Z-score value to determine which suppliers are receiving an abnormally high amount of purchases.

20. Return to your P2P Tableau workbook and create a new worksheet called **Outliers.**
21. Create a new calculated field called **Average Purchases** with the equation WINDOW_AVG(SUM([Purchase Order Amount Local])).
22. Create another calculated field called **Std Dev Purchases** with the equation WINDOW_STDEVP(SUM([Purchase Order Amount Local])).
23. Finally create a calculated field called **Z-Score Purchases** with the equation (SUM([Purchase Order Amount Local])-[Average Purchases])/[Std Dev Purchases].
24. Drag **Z-Score Purchases** to the Columns shelf and **Supplier Account Name** to the Rows shelf.
25. Right-click **Z-Score Purchases** in the Columns shelf and choose **Compute Using > Supplier Account Name.**
26. Hover over the Z-Score Purchases label in the x-axis of the graph and click **Sort Descending.**

> Q2-12. Which supplier(s) had an abnormally high dollar amount of purchases? What do you consider "abnormally high"? Are these suspicious?

27. Now create a new worksheet called **No Order** to determine if any invoices have been received that don't match existing orders.

28. Drag **Invoice ID** and **Purchase Order ID (from Invoices Received)** to the Rows shelf. Click Add All Members if prompted.
29. Drag the **Purchase Order ID (from Invoices Received)** to the Filters shelf. Choose **Select** from the list, click **None,** then click **Null,** and click **OK.**

   Q2-13. Of the invoices received, which are the most problematic? Why?

   Q2-14. Why aren't the other purchases suspicious?

   Q2-15. While you still have your auditor hat on, what are some additional analyses you could perform to understand whether the purchase process is being followed or controls are functioning properly?

Question 2.3: Are We Missing Out on Discounts by Paying Late?

Finally, imagine you are being offered discounts on your payments. If you pay within the discount period, you may receive up to 5 percent off of the invoice amount.

   Q2-16. When might a large company prefer to forfeit discounts on its invoices?

   For this step to work properly, you'll need to adjust the data model to show only invoices that have been paid.

30. Return to your P2P Tableau workbook and save a copy of the workbook as P2P Paid. twbx. If Tableau asks, choose Save as Extract.
31. Click the **Data Source** tab. If Tableau prompts you for a data file, browse to the P2P Data.xlsx file you downloaded from Connect.
32. Click the join between Invoices_Received and AP_Cash_Application and change the join type from a Left Join to an Inner Join.

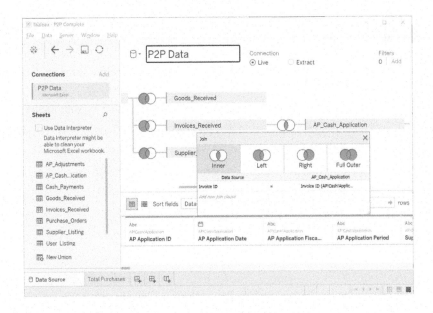

Source: Tableau Software, Inc. All rights reserved.

33. Now create a new worksheet called **Forfeited Discounts.**
34. Create a new calculated field called **Discounts Available** with the calculation SUM([Invoice Amount]*[Terms Discount Percentage (Invoices!Received)]).
35. Create a new calculated field called **Discounts Taken** with the calculation SUM([Invoice Amount]-IIF(ISNULL([Payment Amount]),[Invoice Amount], [Payment Amount])).

36. Create a new calculate field called **Discounts Forfeited** with the calculation [Discounts Available]-[Discounts Taken].
37. Create another calculated field called **Forfeited Ratio** with the calculation [Discounts Forfeited]/[Discounts Available].
38. Drag **Discounts Available** and **Discounts Taken** to the Columns shelf and **Discounts Forfeited** to the Detail button in the Marks card. They will become aggregate functions (AGG) to show the total amounts by supplier.
39. Drag the **Supplier Account Name** to the Rows shelf.
40. Drag **Forfeited Ratio** to the Detail button in the Marks card.
41. In the Marks card, under All, change the chart type from **Automatic** to **Bar.**
42. Right-click the **Discounts Taken** label in the graph and choose **Dual Axis** to combine the charts.
43. Right-click the **Discounts Taken** label again and choose **Synchronize Axis** to place the numbers on the same scale.
44. Sort by **Discount Available.**

> Q2-17. How much discount (in dollars) have we forfeited from our top three suppliers?
>
> Q2-18. Should we adjust our policy to pay them more quickly, in your opinion?
>
> Q2-19. What alternative options could we use to reduce our accounts payable, in your opinion?

Question 2.4: What Else Can You Determine about the P2P Process?

We've discussed a few different ways to analyze P2P data to understand the processes and controls. Now it's your chance to find answers to your own questions.

45. Identify five questions that you think management or auditors would want to know about the P2P process. If you need help, search for some common questions asked by accountants on the Internet.
46. Using the the data you have already loaded into Tableau, generate some analyses and visualizations that will help you find the answers to your questions.

> Q2-20. Write your first question and provide an answer based on your analysis.
>
> Q2-21. Write your second question and provide an answer based on your analysis.
>
> Q2-22. Write your third question and provide an answer based on your analysis.
>
> Q2-23. Write your fourth question and provide an answer based on your analysis.
>
> Q2-24. Write your fifth question and provide an answer based on your analysis.

Chapter 11

Project Chapter (Advanced): Analyzing Dillard's Data to Predict Sales Returns

A Look at This Chapter

Similar to the previous chapter, this chapter will take you through a series of problems to help you analyze and communicate answers to typical accounting questions related to predicting sales returns. To answer these questions, we will return to the Dillard's data set found on the University of Arkansas Remote Desktop to explore the data as it relates to understanding and predicting sales returns. After exploring the data, we will work through a series of questions to describe the state of sales returns, diagnose why the returns are the way they are, and predict future sales returns based on a selection of explanatory variables. This will provide a review of the Data Analytics concepts we've discussed in the previous chapters and put them into perspective.

A Look Back

Chapter 10 had a project chapter that emphasized basic data analytic skills related to the order to cash and purchase to pay processes.

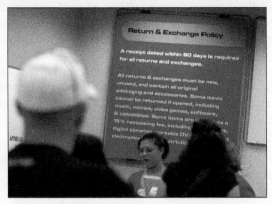

Chris Salata/ZUMA Press/Newscom.

Retail's Ticking Time Bomb: Sales (Particularly Online Sales) Returns

Americans returned $260 billion in merchandise to retailers in 2015. While the average rate of return at retailers is just 8 percent, it increases on average to 10 percent during the holiday sales returns. However, it increases dramatically for online sales—to 30 percent or higher with clothing returns from online sales hitting 40 percent. With a much higher return rate, as online retailers such as **Amazon** continue to increase their market share of total retail sales, it's only going to get worse.

What's more? Not only is product being returned in greater numbers, but the value of the unwanted and damaged returns is greatly diminished:

Unwanted and damaged goods either get tossed out or sent through a lengthy chain of liquidators and wholesalers, paying pennies on the dollar to the retailer before eventually selling them to bargain-hunting consumers.*

Because accountants are required to estimate sales returns (and the diminished value of returned items), and offset sales in the same period that the original sales are made, accountants need to establish a reasonable and hopefully reliable method to estimate such returns. This chapter establishes various descriptive, diagnostic, and predictive analytics that may be used to help evaluate the estimate of sales returns.

Source: https://www.cnbc.com/2016/12/16/a-260-billion-ticking-time-bomb-the-costly-business-of-retail-returns.html, accessed April 2019. https://www.forbes.com/sites/stevendennis/2018/02/14/the-ticking-time-bomb-of-e-commerce-returns/#46d599754c7f, accessed April 2019.

*Source: CNBC LLC

OBJECTIVES

After reading this chapter, you should be able to:

LO 11-1 Analyze returned sales to find explanatory (independent) variables using descriptive and exploratory analytics.

LO 11-2 Illustrate hypothesis testing using diagnostic analytics to compare and contrast sales returns around the holiday season, as well as comparing sales returns in Arkansas (where Dillard's is based) and the rest of the country.

LO 11-3 Predict returned sales in future periods using predictive analytics.

ESTIMATING SALES RETURNS

The recent revenue recognition standards[1] increased the emphasis on valid, reasonable estimates of sales returns matched to the same time period the original sale was made. Companies must assess whether their models and methods of estimating returns are appropriate.

In this chapter, we will work through a project to describe (Question Set 1), diagnose (Question Set 2), and predict sales returns for Dillard's (Question Set 3). Using these various analyses, we develop a potential model useful in predicting Dillard's sales returns and test it for reasonableness.

There are three main question sets:

1. Question Set 1 focuses on exploring the sum of returns and the percentage of returned sales by state, product, and month using Tableau data visualizations.
2. Question Set 2 continues the analysis with hypothesis tests to see if the percent of sales returned is significantly higher in Arkansas (where Dillard's is headquartered) versus other states, as well as to see if the percent of sales returned is significantly higher during the holiday season (December and January) than any other time of the year.
3. Question Set 3 focuses on exploring how historical data can help predict the future percentage of returned sales through PivotTables, PivotCharts, and regression testing in Excel.

Each question set has a set of instructions to guide you through mastering the data, performing the analysis, and communicating your results.

<table>
<tr><td>

LO 11-1

Analyze returned sales to find explanatory (independent) variables using descriptive and exploratory analytics.

</td></tr>
</table>

QUESTION SET 1: DESCRIPTIVE AND EXPLORATORY ANALYSIS

In this question set, we use analytics to find explanatory variables.

Question 1.1: Which Attributes Could Help Predict Percentage of Returned Sales?

To answer this question, we will analyze the Dillard's database ER-Diagram in Microsoft SQL Server and run some short queries to explore the data.

1. Look at the ER-Diagram for Dillard's Data in Appendix J WCOB_DILLARDS ER Diagram.

   Q1-1.   Which of the attributes listed seem like they might be interesting as explanatory variables to help Dillard's explain and plan for percentage of returned sales?

Dive into the Tables: Create Queries to See What Sort of Data Each Attribute Represents

To get a better idea of what data is represented by each of the attributes, we can run preview queries to see the top 10 rows of each table. If you previously completed Lab 2-7, you explored the data in a similar way. Getting a preview of just the top 10 rows in a table

---

[1]Accounting Standards Codification (ASC) 606, Revenue from Contracts with Customers, as amended, and created by Accounting Standards Update (ASU) 2014-09, Revenue from Contracts with Customers.

is helpful because the queries can run quickly (a benefit when the tables hold a massive amount of data—running a query to return all of the records would take quite a long time!).

2. Ensure that you are connected to the University of Arkansas Remote Desktop. Open Microsoft SQL Server Management Studio to access the WCOB_Dillards data and input the Server Name in the Connect to Server window that your instructor provided you. (Leave the default for authentication to Windows Authentication, and click **Connect**.)

Source: SQL

3. To write a new query, select **New Query** from the menu at the top of the SQL Server application. Ensure that the database selected is WCOB_DILLARDS.

Source: SQL

4. To view the top 10 rows in the TRANSACT table, type the following query into the query window:

```
SELECT TOP 10 *
FROM TRANSACT
```

5. To see the result of the query, click **Execute**. F5 also works to run queries as a PC shortcut.

Source: SQL

6. Explore the STORE, SKU, and DEPARTMENT tables with queries to preview the first 500 rows, to get a better feel for the data.

   Q1-2. What benefit can you gain from selecting only the top few rows of your data, particularly from a large dataset?

Q1-3.   After looking at the top 10 rows in the DEPARTMENT table, what do you think the attributes DEPTCENT_DESC, DEPTDEC_DESC, and DEPT_DESC represent? How are the three attributes different from one another?

Q1-4.   After executing these queries, which attributes do you think would be useful to help understand percentage of returned sales?

Question 1.2: How Can We Explore the Product Hierarchy Through Data Visualization?

The three attributes that you discovered in the DEPARTMENT table, DEPTCENT_DESC, DEPTDEC_DESC, and DEPT_DESC, represent "century," "decade," and "department," and it is the way **Dillard's** organizes its product hierarchy. Its product hierarchy contains Department Century (example: Children's), Department Decade (Example: Basics, girls, infants, seasonal, etc.), and Department (example: girls coats, girls swim, boys coats, etc.). The individual products are only identified by SKU and Item ID (not description).

We can use Tableau to explore which centuries, decades, and departments have the highest average percentage of returned sales in our sample period.

Explore and Visualize Data in Tableau

Analyze Returns by Product and State

7. While still in the UArk system, open **Tableau**.
8. Because the raw data is stored in SQL Server, click **Microsoft SQL Server**, then enter the Server and Database information associated with the **Dillard's** data.
9. We can work with data from several tables at once. Drag the following tables into the Data source window to work with them in Tableau:
   - TRANSACT
   - SKU
   - STORE
   - DEPARTMENT
10. Click **Sheet 1** to begin working with your data.

Source: ©Tableau Software, Inc. All rights reserved.

11. Double-click on the Measure **Sale Price** and the Dimension **Tran Type** to get a glimpse of the grand totals of returns and purchases in the dataset.

Tableau responded to your double-click with three defaults: it placed the measure (Sale Price) in the Rows and the dimension (Tran Type) in the Columns, it created a bar chart, and it defaulted the aggregate measure to SUM. All of these defaults are sufficient for the level of analysis we are doing at this stage.

Q1-5.   We can drill down into this grand total to make a more meaningful bar chart. Before we do so, make a prediction about which types of products get returned the most frequently to **Dillard's**.

12. To focus on only returns, we can add Tran Type to the **Filters** shelf. Remove the checkmark in the box next to P so that the only data we see are Returns data, and click **OK**.

Source: ©Tableau Software, Inc. All rights reserved.

13. Once this filter is created, you can apply it to every worksheet in this Tableau workbook. Right-click the Tran Type filter pill and select **Apply to Worksheets**. From the options provided, select **All Using Related Data Sources**.

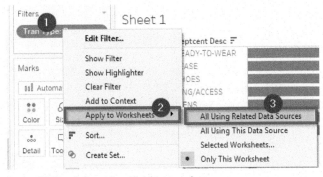

Source: ©Tableau Software, Inc. All rights reserved.

14. Double-click the **Deptcent Desc** dimension. This is the top of the product hierarchy; it contains the broadest categories. Deptcent Desc should be automatically added to the Columns after Tran Type.
15. We can make this easier to read by swapping the rows and columns and by sorting the data. These buttons are located near each other near the top of the Tableau window. Click each of them.

Source: ©Tableau Software, Inc. All rights reserved.

Q1-6. Which two Centuries have the highest sum of returned sales?

16. Right-click **Sheet 1** to rename this sheet. Name it **Returns by Century**.

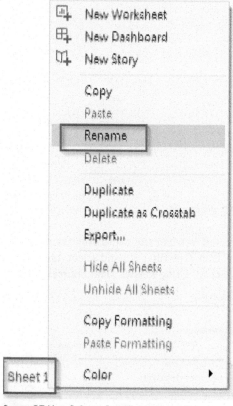

Source: ©Tableau Software, Inc. All rights reserved.

17. Right-click the tab (now named Returns by Century) again to duplicate it.

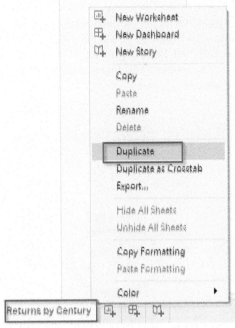

Source: ©Tableau Software, Inc. All rights reserved.

This will allow you to modify the same bar chart by adding more detail while still preserving the original chart.

18. Rename the new sheet (defaulted to being named **Returns by Century (2)**) **Sandbox** so that it is recognizable as a sheet for exploring.
19. Double-click the **Deptdec Desc** dimension to further drill down into the product details. Deptdec Desc will be added to the Rows shelf.
20. Continue working with the data in a variety of ways to explore it. Removing DeptCent Desc provides you a way to look at the returns by Decade without the hierarchy. Adding Dept Desc provides even more detail. You can also click the **Show Me** tab to change the way your data is visualized.

    Q1-7.   Write down three insights that you have gained from exploring the data in the Sandbox sheet.

21. Create a new sheet by clicking the icon to the right of the current sheet you are working on:

Source: ©Tableau Software, Inc. All rights reserved.

22. Double-click the dimension **State** to create a map. Tableau will default to a symbol map with a symbol in each state that **Dillard's** has had returns in during our sample period. If it does not default to a filled map, State may not have imported as a geographic datatype. Right-click on the Abc icon next to the State attribute to select Geographic Role, and then assign it as a State/Province datatype.
23. Double-click the measure **Sale Price** to provide more detail to the map.
24. This map will be easier to read as a filled map instead of a symbol map, so select **Filled Map** from the **Show Me** tab.

Source: ©Tableau Software, Inc. All rights reserved.

25. Rename this sheet **Returns by State**.

To explore the data in greater detail, we can create a Dashboard with both of our sheets (Returns by Century and Returns by State) and have them interact with one another.

26. Click the **New Dashboard** icon.

Source: ©Tableau Software, Inc. All rights reserved.

27. Drag and drop the two sheets, Returns by Century and Returns by State, into the dashboard and arrange them so that they are one on top of the other.

28. Click anywhere in Returns by Century to bring up interactive buttons to the right. Click the **Filter** button (it looks like a funnel) to use this sheet as a filter.

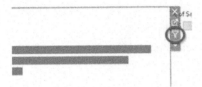

Source: ©Tableau Software, Inc. All rights reserved.

29. Do the same for Returns by State.

Using the sheets as filters in the dashboard allows you to click one century to see how the levels of percentage of sales returned changes in each state, and also allows you to click one state to see which centuries have higher percentage of sales returned in each state.

Explore the data in the dashboard and answer the next two questions:

Q1-8.   Which Century has the highest sum of returns in Utah?

Q1-9.   Which state has a higher sum of returns in the Cosmetics century than any other?

Analyze Returns by Month

It would also be interesting to see which months have the highest amount of returns.

Q1-10.   Make a guess about which months you think likely see the highest amount of returns.

30. Create a new worksheet and re-name it **Returns by Month**.
31. Double-click the **Sale Price** measure.
32. Double-click the **Tran Date** dimension. Tableau defaults to showing the change in returns over year in a line chart. Click the expand button on the **YEAR(Tran Date)** pill in the Columns shelf to see quarters, then click the expand button on the new QUARTER pill to see Months.

Source: ©Tableau Software, Inc. All rights reserved.

33. To make the distinction in months clearer, change the line charts to a bar chart on the **Show Me** tab.

Source: ©Tableau Software, Inc. All rights reserved.

34. Remove the Quarter pill from the Rows shelf–this will make it easier to focus on each month over the three years of data provided.

> Q1-11. Which month saw the highest amount of returns in 2016? 2015? 2014? Why do you think these months see such high amounts of returns?

After looking through total sums of returns across products, states, and months, it's time to turn our focus to a more precise measure of returns: the percentage of returned sales.

> Q1-12. Why can we draw more precise insights from analyzing percentage of returned sales than just analyzing sums of returns?

> Q1-13. Do you think the same two months that saw high sums of returns in 2014, 2015, and 2016 will also be the two months with the highest percentage of returned sales? Why or why not?

In order to explore percentage of returned sales, we first need to transform the data using Excel's Power Query tools, then we'll pull the transformed data into Excel to see how the percentage of returned sales differs from the sums of returns across states and across months.

Transform the Data to Prepare It for Analysis of Percentage of Returned Sales

Here is a summary of the Master the Data work that you need to do in Excel (remember that you need to connect to the WCOB_Dillards database in Excel on the University of Arkansas Remote Desktop):

35. Navigate to the **Data** tab on the Excel ribbon and click **New Query** > From Database > from SQL Server Database, then retrieve data using the following query (remember to click Advanced Options to input the query):

```
select year(tran_date) as year, month(tran_date) as month, state,
transact.store,
tran_type, sum(sale_price) as amount
from transact
inner join store
on transact.store = store.store
where year(tran_date) = 2014 or year(tran_date) = 2015
group by year(tran_date), month(tran_date), state, transact.store,
tran_type
order by year(tran_date), month(tran_date), state
```

This query returns only the specific attributes we will use to analyze the data. For the next several steps of analysis, we are going to focus solely on differences across months, states, and years. We are also limiting the dataset to two years so that we can work with this data in Excel (if we bring in all of the years' worth of data, there are too many records for Excel to hold).

36. If the Power Query Editor does not show up immediately, click **Edit** in the data preview window to open the Power Query Editor.

The first transformation we need to do is to create two separate columns: one column for returns and one column for purchases. This will allow us to look at the separate transaction types more easily (without having to add a filter), and it will also allow us to create a Percentage of Sales Returned column.

37. In the Power Query Editor, select **Transform** then Pivot Column to pivot the Tran_ Type column (select amount for the Value Column).

After this transformation is done, each Purchase transaction resulted in a "null" value in the new Returns column, and each Returns transaction resulted in a "null" value in the Purchases column. We need to replace each null value with 0.

38. Replace Values (Transform Tab) in both the new P and R columns; replace Null with 0.
39. From the **Add Column** tab, click **Custom Column** to create a % of Sales Returned column using the formula: (IF [P]=0 THEN 0 ELSE [R]/[P]).
40. From the **Home** tab on the ribbon, click **Close and Load** to load the data into Excel. You should have 7,139 rows (excluding the header) loaded.
41. Save your Excel file as Chapter11Dataset.xlsx. Ensure that you are saving the file on the University of Arkansas Remote Desktop so that you can access it again with Tableau from the remote desktop.

Load and Work with Data in Tableau

42. After mastering the data in Excel, open Tableau.
43. Since your data is stored in Excel, click **Microsoft Excel**, then browse to the file location to **Open** it.

The data will appear in the Data Source window. Notice that each of the attributes has a datatype that Tableau automatically selected.

Source: ©Tableau Software, Inc. All rights reserved.

44. Year and Month are not easy to filter when they're classified as a Number, so click the # sign on each variable and change them to String. This will have Tableau treat those variables as text, making them easier to filter.

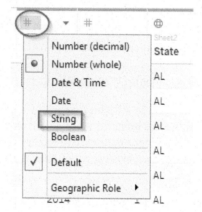

Source: ©Tableau Software, Inc. All rights reserved.

Analyze Percentage of Sales Returned by Month

Now that data is loaded, we can create a map to see how average percentage of returned sales compares across states.

45. Click **Sheet 1** to begin working with your data.
46. Rename this sheet **Sales Returned by Month**.

Source: ©Tableau Software, Inc. All rights reserved.

47. Double-click on the Measure **% of Sales Returned**.

Tableau defaulted the aggregate measure to **SUM**. It would be more meaningful to view the % of Sales Returned aggregated as an Average.

48. Right-click the **SUM(% of Sales Returned)** pill in the Rows shelf.
49. Select **Measure (Sum)** from the window that pops up.
50. Select **Average**.

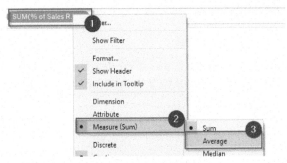

Source: ©Tableau Software, Inc. All rights reserved.

51. Double-click **Year** and **Month** dimensions to add them to the Columns shelf.

   Q1-14. Which month has the highest percentage of returned sales in 2014? 2015?

   Q1-15. Which month has the lowest percentage of returned sales in both years?

   Q1-16. Why do you think this difference occurs from analyzing sums of returns?

Analyze Percentage of Sales Returned by State

52. Create a new worksheet.
53. Double-click the dimension **State** to create a map. Tableau will default to a symbol map with a symbol in each state that Dillard's has had sales or returns during our sample period.
54. Double-click the measure **% of Sales Returned** to provide more detail to the map.
55. This map will be easier to read as a filled map instead of a symbol map, so select **Filled Map** from the **Show Me** tab.

Source: ©Tableau Software, Inc. All rights reserved.

56. The aggregate for % of Sales Returned defaulted to **Sum** again, so change it to an **Average**.

57. Re-name this sheet **Returns by State**.

To explore the data in greater detail, we can create a Dashboard with both of our sheets (Sales Returned by Month and Returns by State) and have them interact with one another.

58. Click the **New Dashboard** icon.

Source: Tableau Software, Inc.
All rights reserved.

59. Create a dashboard that contains both sheets. Set both sheets as filters for the dashboard so that you can explore the data.

> Q1-17. Which state had the highest amount of returns in 2014? 2015? (Remember to activate your visuals as filters for the dashboard. To filter for 2014 or 2015, select the labels of 2014 or 2015).
>
> Q1-18. What was the percentage of sales returned in California in January 2014?

LO 11-2

Illustrate hypothesis testing using diagnostic analytics to compare and contrast sales returns around the holiday season, as well as comparing sales returns in Arkansas (where Dillard's is based) and the rest of the country.

QUESTION SET 2: DIAGNOSTIC ANALYTICS—HYPOTHESIS TESTING

Question 2.1: Is the Percentage of Sales Returned Significantly Higher in January After the Holiday Season?

In the previous activity for this dataset, you found that January has the highest percentage of sales returned of all of the months. This is likely due to the holiday season. While it's helpful to see which month has the highest amount of returns, it would be more useful to find out if the difference is statistically significant. In order to do so, we can run a hypothesis test to determine if a significantly higher percentage of sales are returned during the month of January than the rest of the months.

To do so, we need to return to the Power Query Editor. Ensure you are in the University of Arkansas Remote Desktop. If you have closed the file you worked with in Question Set 1, re-open it.

If you have closed the file, you will need to access the Power Query window. To do so, return to the spreadsheet that contains the data that was extracted via the query originally and select a cell of the table to activate the Query tab in the Excel ribbon. From the Query tab, select **Edit** to open the Power Query editor. If prompted to do so, click **Edit Permissions** and **Run** the Native Database Query in the window that pops up. Then repeat a similar process by clicking Edit Credentials. The query data should show up in the Power Query Editor now.

In the Chapter11Dataset.xlsx Power Query Editor, do the following:

1. From the **Add Column** tab in the ribbon, select **Conditional Column**.

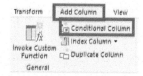

Source: Microsoft Excel 2016

2. In the Conditional Column window that pops up, fill in the condition (you can leave
   the column name as 'Custom,' we will pivot this column shortly, so the name is unim-
   portant). Indicate that anytime the month variable equals 1, then the column should
   display "Holiday," otherwise, it should display "Non-Holiday". Once you've input all of
   the information, click **OK**.

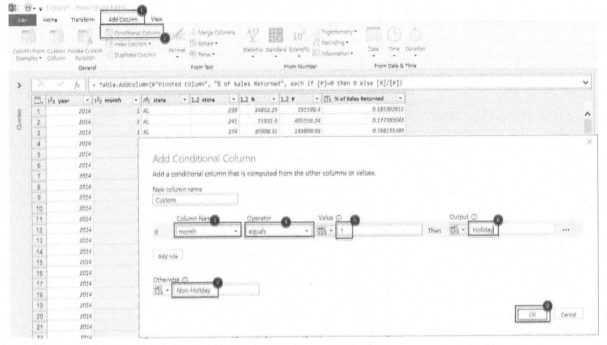

Source: Microsoft Excel 2016

At this point we need to be able to pivot the new Holiday/Non-Holiday dummy
variable column based on % of Sales Returned. This will allow you to have one column
devoted to the % of Sales Returned during the Holiday (January) month, and another
column for the % of Sales Returned during the non-holiday months. To do so, we need
to first duplicate the % of sales returned column, then we will pivot the Holiday/Non-
Holiday dummy variable column based on the % of Sales Returned duplicate column.

3. From the Power Query Editor ribbon, click **Add Column** if you are not already there.
4. We will add a duplicate column of the % **of Sales Returned** column. Select that column, then click **Duplicate column**.

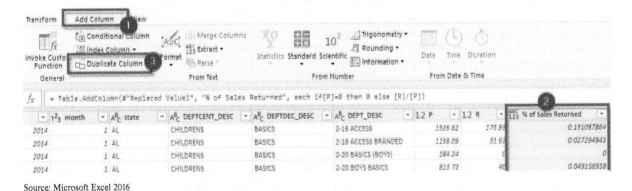

Source: Microsoft Excel 2016

5. Once the duplicate column is created, we can pivot the Holiday/Non-Holiday column. First you will need to click the **Transform** tab on the ribbon of the Power Query Editor window.

6. Select the Holiday/Non-Holiday custom column, then click **Pivot Column**. Use the column you just copied, **% of Sales Returned – Copy** as the values column. Click **OK**.

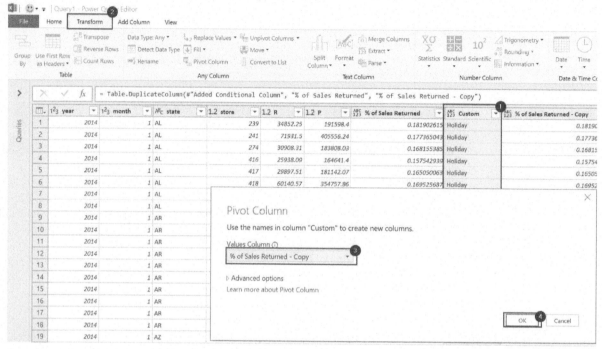

Source: Microsoft Excel 2016

We will use these two new Holiday and non-Holiday columns to run a t-test to see if the percentage of sales returned during the December and January holiday season is significantly higher than the rest of the year.

7. Load the transformed data into Excel by navigating to the **Home** tab on the ribbon and selecting **Close & Load**.

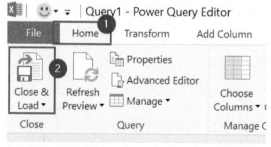

Source: Microsoft Excel 2016

It may take a couple minutes for the data to load.

8. Once the data has loaded, navigate to the Data Analysis Toolpak in the Data tab in the ribbon. If the Data Analysis Toolpak hasn't been added in, see Appendix B

for directions on how to add it. Click **Data Analysis** to open the Analysis Tools window.

Source: Microsoft Excel 2016

9. Scroll to find the **t-Test: Two Sample Assuming Unequal Variances** tool and click **OK**.

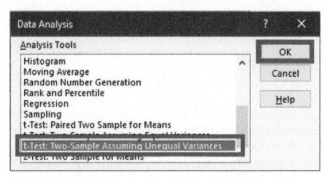

Source: Microsoft Excel 2016

10. In the t-Test window, you will need to input your variable ranges. For **Variable 1 Range**, select all of the values that correspond with the **Holiday** column.

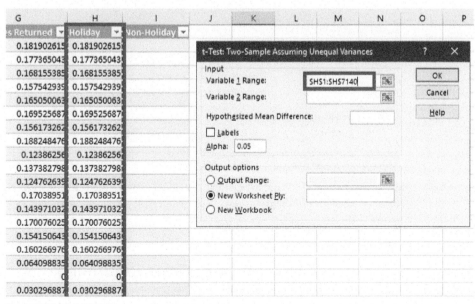

Source: Microsoft Excel 2016

11. Follow the same pattern for Variable 2 by selecting all of the data that correspond with the **Non-Holiday** column.

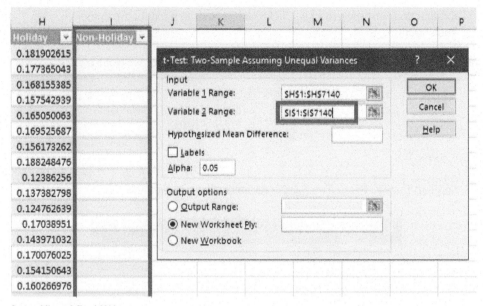

Source: Microsoft Excel 2016

12. If you selected labels (Holiday and Non-Holiday) in addition to just the data, place a check mark in the box next to **Labels**.
13. Click **OK** to run the hypothesis test. The output for the hypothesis test will appear on a new sheet in your Excel workbook.

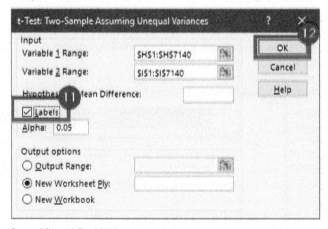

Source: Microsoft Excel 2016

Q2-1.   Based on the *p*-values (or the *t*-statistic and critical values), are the returns as a percentage of sales in January greater, less than, or the same as the returns as a percentage of sales for the rest of the year?

Q2-2.   What can we conclude about returns?

Question 2.2: Is the Percentage of Sales Returned Significantly Different in Arkansas Than the Rest of the Country?

Following similar steps that you completed in Question 2.1 above, determine if the percentage of sales returned is significantly different in Arkansas, where Dillard's is based, than the rest of the country.

First, you will need to create dummy variable columns for "AR" and "Non-AR"—follow the same steps that you did in steps 1-7 to create the Holiday and non-Holiday variables (Open the Power Query window by selecting Edit from the Query tab in the ribbon. From the Add Column tab, create a conditional column to separate AR from Non-AR states. Next, duplicate the % of Sales Returned column again. From the Transform tab, Pivot your new custom column for AR/Non-AR - use the copy of % of Sales Returned as the values).

Your next step will be to run a new t-test, similar to the steps you completed in steps 8-12.

Q2-3.   Using the *p*-values (or the *t*-statistic and critical values), are the returns as a percentage of sales in Arkansas and January greater, less than, or the same as the returns as a percentage of sales for the rest of the country?

Q2-4.   What can we conclude about returns?

QUESTION SET 3: PREDICTIVE ANALYTICS

LO 11-3

Predict returned sales in future periods using predictive analytics.

Question 3.1: By Looking at Line Charts for 2014 and 2015, Does the Average Percentage of Sales Returned in 2014 Seem to Be Predictive of Returns in 2015?

After assessing how different variables impact returns, we have a better idea of how to help Dillard's prepare for returns—both across states and for the holiday season. We can also get an idea of how much a previous year's percentage of returned sales can help predict the next year's. To answer this question, we will create a PivotTable, a PivotChart, and use slicers to see if we can improve our predictions by looking state-by-state.

Create a PivotTable and a PivotChart to Compare 2014 and 2015 Returns

1. Open the data you transformed and built into spreadsheet Chapter11Dataset.xlsx.
2. Create a PivotTable from the dataset.

To view a comparison of how the average percentage of sales returned changed each year, we want to view the years as columns, and see a row for each month's average percent of sales returned for either year.

3. Drag **Month** to the Rows.
4. Drag **Year** to columns.
5. Drag % **of Sales Returned** to Values.
6. Change the aggregate for % of Sales from **Sum** to **Average** using the Value Field Settings.
7. To view this data as a line chart, we need to insert a PivotChart. To do so, click the **Analyze** tab on the ribbon, underneath PivotTable tools (if you do not see this option, select one of the cells in your PivotTable to open the interactive ribbon).
8. Click **PivotChart** to see the different chart options.

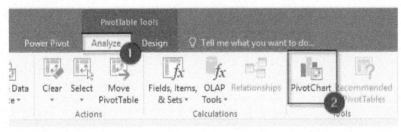

Source: Microsoft Excel 2016

9. Change the default to **Line** and then click **OK**.

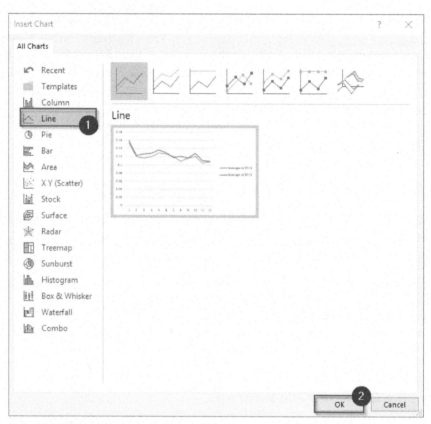

Source: Microsoft Excel 2016

Q3-1. Based on the line chart, does 2014 seem to be useful in predicting 2015's percentage of sales returned?

10. Now we can add a Slicer to interactively filter the PivotTable and PivotChart to see how the values changed by state each year. Click into the data of your PivotTable to make the options for adding slicers available.

11. In the **Insert** tab on the ribbon, select **Slicer**.

Source: Microsoft Excel 2016

12. Select **State** and then click **OK**.

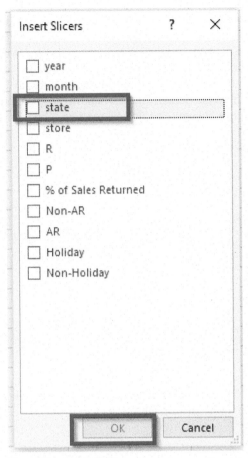

Source: Microsoft Excel 2016

13. Filter first for **AR** (Arkansas). Try again to filter for UT (Utah).

   Q3-2.   Based on these line charts, does it seem more beneficial to predict percentage
   of sales returned on a state-by-state basis or in aggregate form?

Question 3.2: Using Regression, What Can We Predict for Returns as a Percentage of Sales Based on Historical Transactions?

14. Because the line graphs seemed to suggest that the percentage of sales returned in
   2014 will help predict the percentage of sales returned in 2015, we can run a regression to build a model that will help stores predict the percentage of sales that will be
   returned each month. First, we will need to transform the data one more time. This
   transformation requires removing several columns, so you may choose to create a

duplicate file of your current chapter 11 spreadsheet if you need to save your progress from Question Set 2.

15. Return to the worksheet that contains the raw data. From this worksheet, you can access the Query tab in the ribbon and click Edit in order to open the Power Query tool.

16. We ultimately need to pivot the year column so that we have two separate columns for comparing 2014 and 2015, but before we can do that, we need to remove several columns. Select columns P, R, Holiday, Non-Holiday, Non-AR, and AR, and then select Remove Columns from the ribbon. You can remove each column individually, or you can select multiple columns at a time by pressing "Ctrl" on your keyboard as you select the columns.

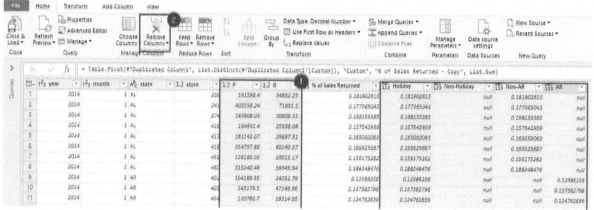

Source: Microsoft Excel 2016

17. Now you're ready to pivot the year column. Select the year column, and then click Pivot Column from the Transform tab.

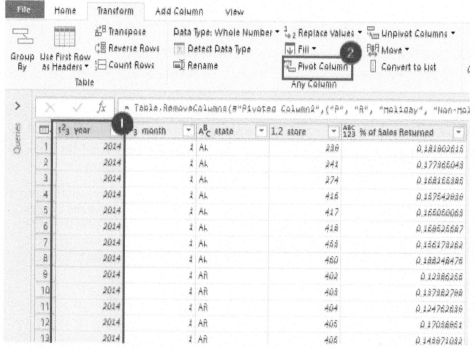

Source: Microsoft Excel 2016

18. Select % of Sales Returned as your Values, then click **OK**.

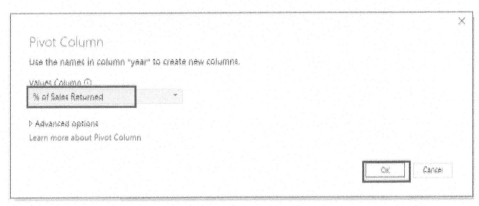

Source: Microsoft Excel 2016

19. The last step to prepare this data for analysis is to remove zeros and null values from your new 2014 and 2015 columns. Select the drop-down next to the column for 2014 and remove the checkmarks next to (null) and 0.

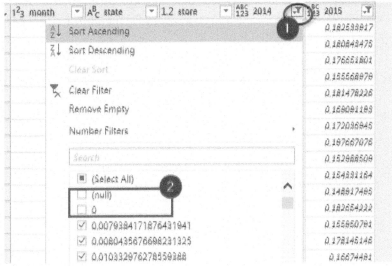

Source: Microsoft Excel 2016

20. Do the same for the 2015 column.
21. Now your data is ready for Analysis. Click **Close & Load** from the Home tab to return to Excel.
22. To run a Regression Analysis, you need to have the Data Analysis Toolpak added in to Excel (see Statistics Appendix B for information on how to do so).
23. Select **Data Analysis** from the **Data** tab in the ribbon.

Source: Microsoft Excel 2016

24. Scroll to find the **Regression** tool in the Analysis Tools window and click **OK**.

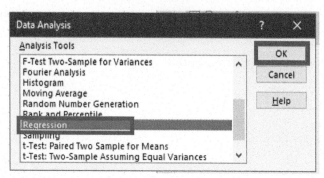

Source: Microsoft Excel 2016

25. Because you will be predicting 2015 values based on 2014's values, 2014's values are our (X) variables and 2015's values are our (Y) variables. Enter the following information in the Regression window (these input ranges should come from the original data worksheet, not the PivotTable):
    - **Input Y Range:** This is the column containing the 2015 data.
    - **Input X Range:** This is the column containing the 2014 data.
    - **Labels:** Place a checkmark in this box if you included the labels for 2014 and 2015 in your selections for the Y and X ranges.
    - Click **OK**.

    Q3-3.   Looking at your regression output, was the relationship between 2014 and 2015 percentage of sales returned significant? How can you tell?

    Q3-4.   Brainstorm at least four other data items (e.g., economy, type of customer, etc.) that would be helpful in predicting future the next year's percentage of sales returned.

    Q3-5.   Upon project completion of Question Sets 1, 2, and 3, what have you learned from completing this analysis?

Appendix A
Basic Statistics Tutorial

POPULATION VS. SAMPLE

Restaurant stores and retail stores are often faced with the decision of whether to stay open on Sunday. Like Chick-Fil-A, retail owners and restaurant owners sometimes like to close on Sunday to allow their employees to spend time with families or simply to take a break for the day.

What percentage of the restaurants and retail owners close on Sunday? We'd love to ask a survey question on SurveyMonkey or Qualtrics and get every retail/restaurant owner to respond. If we could get every response from every restaurant/retail owner, we'd call this the results of the population, defined as the total set of observations. Because it is virtually impossible to get every owner to respond to our survey, we often just get a sample (defined a subset of the data collected from the population) to reply and hope that the results we find from the sample are representative of what we would find had we been able to get the total population to respond.

As a side note, in the past, auditors were only able to view a sample of the accounting transactions that were made. But with new high-powered analytics tools as well as having accountants trained to use such tools, auditors are increasingly able to consider data from the full population instead of a small sample!

PARAMETERS VS. STATISTICS: WHAT IS THE DIFFERENCE?

Whereas a *parameter* comes from a population, a *statistic* comes from a sample. For example, the population average (or mean) would be the parameter we would call the greek letter mu (μ). For example, the population average of stores close on Sunday might be 24 percent. However, since we're only able to survey a sample, the result of surveying the sample would be sample statistic average x-bar, or $\bar{x}$. If we don't know the true population average, μ, we will use the sample average, or , to make inferences about the true population average.

DESCRIBING THE SAMPLE BY ITS CENTRAL TENDENCY, THE MIDDLE, OR MOST TYPICAL VALUE

To learn more about a sample, we often use measures of the central, the middle, or most typical value to describe the sample. The mean, median, and mode are three common measures used to assess central tendency.

The sample arithmetic mean is the sum of all the data points divided by the number of observations. The median is the midpoint of the data and is especially useful when there are skewed numbers one way or another. The mode is the observation that occurs most frequently.

DESCRIBING THE SPREAD (OR VARIABILITY) OF THE DATA

The next step after describing the central tendency of the data is to assess its spread, or variability. This might include considering the maximum and minimum values and the difference between those two values, which we define as the range.

The most common measures of spread or variability is standard deviation or variance, where each ith observation in the sample is x_i, and the total number of observations is N. The standard deviation, the greek letter sigma, σ, is computed as follows:

$$\sigma = \sqrt{\frac{1}{N} \sum_{i=1}^{N} (x_i - \mu)^2}$$

And relatedly, the variance, σ^2 is computed as follows:

$$\sigma^2 = \frac{1}{N} \sum_{i=1}^{N} (x_i - \bar{x})^2$$

The greater the sample standard deviation or variance, the greater the variability.

PROBABILITY DISTRIBUTIONS

There are three primary probability distributions used in statistics and data analytics, including normal distribution, the uniform distribution, and the poisson distribution.

Normal Distribution

A normal distribution is arguably the most important probability distribution because it fits so many naturally occurring phenomenon in and out of accounting—from the distribution of return on assets to the IQ of the human population.

The normal distribution is a bell-shaped probability distribution that is symmetric about its mean, with the data points closer to the mean more frequent than those data points further from its mean. As shown in Exhibit A-1, data within one standard deviation (+/− one standard deviation) includes 68 percent of the data points. Within two standard deviations, 95 percent of the data points; three standard deviations, 99.7 percent of the data points.

A z-score is computed to tell us how many standard deviations (σ), a data point (or observation), x_i, is from its population mean, μ, using the formula $z = (x_i - \mu)/\sigma$. A z-score of 1 suggests that the observation is one standard deviation above its mean. A *z*-score of –2 suggests that the observation is two standard deviations below its mean.

Many of the statistical tests employed in data analysis are based on the normal distribution and how many standard deviations a sample observation is from its mean.

EXHIBIT A-1
Normal Distribution and the Frequency of Observations around Its Mean (Using 1, 2, or 3 Standard Deviations)

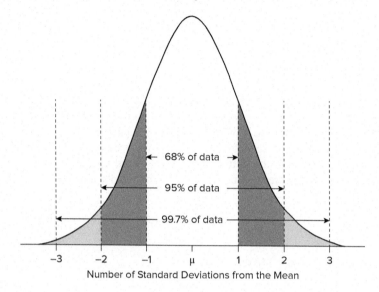

Uniform Distribution and Poisson Distribution

The uniform distribution is a probability distribution where all outcomes are equally likely. Like in a fair coin toss, the distribution of heads and tails are equally likely. A deck of cards has an equal distribution of hearts, clubs, diamonds, or spades. Likewise, a deck of cards has an equal distribution of "queen"s and "3"s. A poisson distribution is a distribution with a low mean and highly skewed to the right.

HYPOTHESIS TESTING

As we learn in Data Analytics, data by itself is not really that interesting. It is using data to answer, or at least address, questions posed by management that makes it interesting.

Management might pose a question in terms of a hypothesis, like their belief that sales at their stores are higher on Saturdays than on Sundays. Perhaps they want to know this answer to decide if they will need more staff to support sales (e.g., cashiers, shelf stockers, parking lot attendants, etc.) on Saturday as compared to Sunday. In other words, management holds an assumption that sales are higher on Saturday than on Sundays.

Usually hypotheses are paired in two's: the null hypothesis and the alternate hypothesis.

The first is the base case, often called the null hypothesis, and assumes the hypothesized relationship does not exist. In this case, the null hypothesis would be stated as follows:

Null hypothesis: H_0: Sales on Saturday are less than or equal to sales on Sunday.

The alternate hypothesis would be the case that management believes to be true.

Alternate hypothesis: H_A: Sales on Saturday are greater than sales on Sunday.

For the null hypothesis to hold, we would assume that Saturday sales are the same as (or less than) Sunday sales. Evidence for the alternate hypothesis occurs when null hypothesis does not hold and is rejected at some level of statistical significance. In other words, before we can reject or fail to reject the null hypothesis, we need to do a statistical test of the data with sales on Saturday and Sundays and then interpret the results of that statistical test.

STATISTICAL TESTING

There are two types of results from a statistical test of hypotheses that may occur or may be interpreted in different ways: the *p*-value and/or the critical values.

The *p*-Value

We describe a finding as statistically significant by interpreting the *p*-value.

A statistical test of hypothesis may return a *p*-value. The *p*-value is the result of a test that either rejects or fails to reject the null hypothesis. The *p*-value is compared to a threshold value, called the significance level (or alpha). A common value used for alpha is 5 percent or 0.05 (as is 1 percent or 0.01).

The *p*-value is compared to the alpha threshold. A result is statistically significant when the *p*-value is less than alpha. This signifies a change was detected: that the default hypothesis can be rejected.

If *p*-value > alpha: Fail to reject the null hypothesis (i.e., not significant result).

If *p*-value <= alpha: Reject the null hypothesis (i.e., significant result).

For example, if we were performing a test of whether Saturday sales were greater than Sunday sales and the test statistic was a *p*-value of .09, we would state something like, *"The test found that the Saturday sales are not different than Sunday sales, failing to reject the null hypothesis at a 5% level of significance."*

This statistical result should then be reported to management, reporting the results of the statistical test.

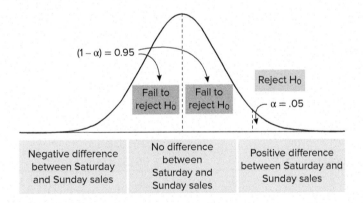

EXHIBIT A-2
Statistical Testing Using Alpha, *p*-Values, and Confidence Intervals

The Confidence Interval

The significance level can be computed by subtracting alpha from 1 to give a confidence level of the hypothesis given the statistical test of the data.

For example, if the confidence level is 95 percent, then alpha (α) is 5 percent. In Exhibit A-2, the 95 percent of the figure represents the confidence interval—we are 95 percent confident that the true population parameter of Saturday and Sunday sales falls somewhere in that area.

Therefore, statements such as the following can also be made:

With a *p*-value of 0.09, the test found that Saturday and Sunday sales are not different than Sunday sales, failing to reject the null hypothesis at a 95% confidence level.

This statistical result should then be reported to management, reporting the results of the statistical test.

INTERPRETING THE STATISTICAL OUTPUT FROM A SAMPLE *t*-TEST OF A DIFFERENCE OF MEANS OF TWO GROUPS

A sample *t*-test is a statistical test used to compare the means of two sets of data observations.

For example, it might be comparing means of two independent groups. For example, a *t*-test might be used to compare the mean return on asset (ROA) for companies in the retail industry to the mean ROA for companies in the entertainment industry to see if one is statistically higher than the other.

Or it could be a paired *t*-test of the same group of companies but at different times. Such a *t*-test might compare the mean return on assets (ROA) for companies in the retail industry in 2020 to the mean ROA same companies in the retail industry in 2021.

Let's suppose that a company is trying to understand if its rate of sales returns is higher around the end-of-year holidays than at other times (non-holidays) during the year. To assess whether the sales returns are different, a *t*-test is performed in Excel to see if there is a difference of daily mean sales returns (as a percentage of total sales that day) between the holidays and non-holiday periods. After performing the *t*-test, Excel returns the following statistical output:

t-Test: Two-Sample Assuming Unequal Variances		
	Holiday	*Non-Holiday*
Mean	0.130283127	0.118963739
Variance	0.002110326	0.001550751
Observations	1167	5839
Hypothesized Mean Difference	0	
df	1527	
t Stat	7.860081545	
P(T<=t) one-tail	3.59752E-15	
t Critical one-tail	1.64585212	
P(T<=t) two-tail	7.19505E-15	
t Critical two-tail	1.961518746	

The *t*-test output found that the mean holiday sales returns over 1,167 days is 0.13 (or 13 percent) of sales, and the mean non-holiday sales returns are 0.119 (or 11.9 percent) of sales. The question is if those two numbers are statistically different from each other. The *t* Stat of 7.86 and the *p*-value (shown as "P(T<=t) one tail") is 3.59E-15 (i.e., well below .01 percent), suggesting the two sample means are significantly different from each other.

The *t*-test output notes the difference in crucial *p*-values for a one-tailed *t*-test and a two-tailed *t*-test. A one-tailed *t*-test is used if we hypothesize that holiday returns are significantly greater (or significantly smaller) than non-holiday returns. A two-tailed *t*-test is used if we don't hypothesize holiday or non-holiday returns are greater or smaller than the other, only that we expect the two sample means will be different from each other.

INTERPRETING THE STATISTICAL OUTPUT FROM A REGRESSION

Regressions are used to help measure the relationship between one output variables and various inputs. We can think about this like an algebraic equation where y is the dependent variable and x is the independent variables, where $y = f(x)$. As an example, we hypothesize a model where y (or College Completion Rate) $= f($factors potentially predicting college completion rate) including the independent variable SAT score (SAT_AVG). In other words, we hypothesize that college completion rates depend on SAT scores.

Through regression analysis, we can assess if the college completion rate is statistically related to the SAT score.

As you recall from Lab 2-5 and Lab 3-2, we are considering the relationship between SAT scores and the college completion rate for first-time, full-time students at four-year institutions.

Here is the regression output from Lab 3-2:

SUMMARY OUTPUT

Regression Statistics	
Multiple R	0.801478347
R Square	0.642367541
Adjusted R Square	0.642085718
Standard Error	0.104863363
Observations	1271

ANOVA

	df	SS	MS	F	Significance F
Regression	1	25.06431511	25.06431511	2279.335635	1.2641E-285
Residual	1269	13.95433624	0.010996325		
Total	1270	39.01865135			

	Coefficients	Standard Error	t Stat	P-value	Lower 95%	Upper 95%	Lower 95.0%	Upper 95.0%
Intercept	-0.57417365	0.023762418	-24.1630984	2.0004E-106	-0.620791597	-0.527555703	-0.620791597	-0.527555703
SAT_AVG	0.001059838	2.21991E-05	47.74238825	1.2641E-285	0.001016287	0.001103389	0.001016287	0.001103389

There are many things to note about the regression results. The first is that the overall regression model did better than chance at predicting the college completion rate as shown by the "F"-score. We note that by seeing the p-score representing "Significance F" result is very small, almost zero, suggesting there virtually zero probability that the completion rate can be explained by no independent variables than a model that has independent variables. This is exactly the situation we want suggesting we should be able to identify a factor that explains completion rates.

There is another statistic used to measure how the overall regression model did at predicting the dependent variable of completion rates. The adjusted R-squared is a value between 0 and 1. An adjusted R-squared value of 0 represents no ability of the model to explain the dependent variable and an adjusted R-squared value of 1 represents perfect ability of the model to explain the dependent variable. In this case, the adjusted R-squared value is 0.642, which represents a reasonably high ability to explain the changes in the college completion rate.

The statistics also report that the SAT score (SAT_AVG) helps predict the completion rate. This is shown by the "t Stat" that is greater than 2 (or less than -2) for SAT_AVG (with t Stat of 47.74) and a p-value less than an alpha of 0.05 (as shown with the p-value of 1.564E-285). As expected, given the positive coefficient on SAT_AVG, the greater the SAT score, the greater the college completion rate.

Appendix B

Accessing the Excel Data Analysis Toolpak

Excel offers a toolpak that helps perform much of the data analysis, called the Excel Data Analysis Toolpak.

To run a correlation, form a histogram, run a regression, or perform other similar analysis using the Excel Data Analysis Toolpak, we need to make sure our Analysis Toolpak is loaded up, by looking at the ribbon of **Data > Analysis** and seeing if the Data Analysis Add-In has been installed.

Source: Microsoft Excel 2016

If it has not yet been added, go to **File> Options > Add-Ins,** select the **Analysis Toolpak,** and select **OK:**

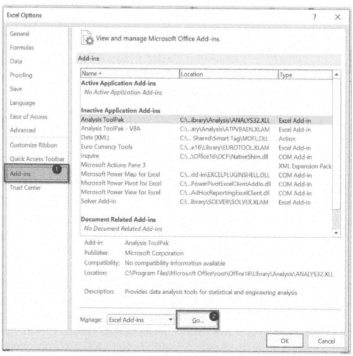

Source: Microsoft Excel 2016

In the Add-ins window that appears, place a check mark next to **Analysis ToolPak** and then click **OK**. This will add the Data Analysis ToolPak to the Data tab so you can perform additional data analysis.

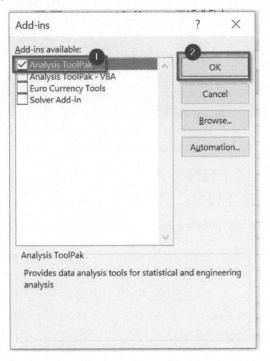

Step 2:

To perform the additional data analysis, please select **Data > Analysis > Data Analysis.** A dialog box will open.

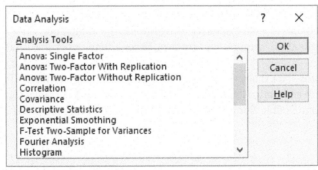

Source: Microsoft Excel 2016

In this text, we will highlight the use of the following analysis tools:

Correlation: To understand the if and the extent to which variables are related to each other.

Descriptive statistics: To understand the basic statistics, including the mean, standard deviation, minimums, and maximums of a data set.

Histogram: To understand the frequency of the data using a display of rectangles with area proportional to the underlying frequency of the data.

Regression: To understand the relation between specific dependent variable values and independent variable inputs.

T-tests: To understand the probability of a difference in means between either two independent samples or a paired sample through time.

Appendix C

Excel (Formatting, Sorting, Filtering, and PivotTables)

BASIC FORMATTING AN INCOME STATEMENT USING EXCEL FUNCTION SUM()

Suppose we want to put the following data into the appropriate income-statement format:

Revenues	**50000**
Expenses	
Cost of Goods Sold	20000
Research and Development Expenses	10000
Selling, General, and Administrative Expenses	10000
Interest Expense	3000

Required:

1. Add a comma as a 1000 separator for each number.
2. Insert the words "Total Expenses" below the list of expenses.
3. Calculate subtotal for Total Expenses using the **SUM()** command.
4. Insert a single bottom border under Interest Expense and under the Total Expenses subtotal.
5. Insert the words "Net Income," and calculate Net Income (Revenues – Total Expenses).
6. Format the top and bottom numbers of the column with a $ currency sign.
7. Insert a Bottom Double Border to underline the final Net Income total.

Solution:

1. Open Appendix C Data.xlsx and access the sheet named "Income Statement Formatting."

2. Add a comma as a 1000 separator for each number.

    Highlight the column with all of the numbers. Right click on Format Cells. . . to open this dialog box:

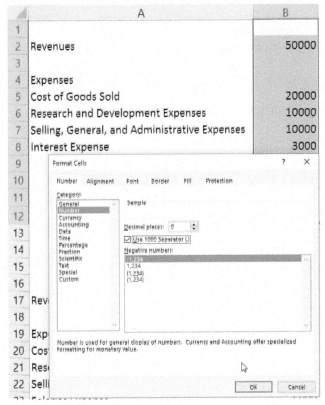

Microsoft Excel 2016

Click on Number and set Decimal places to zero. Click on **Use 1000 Separator (,)** and click **OK.**

3. Insert the words "Total Expenses" below the list of expenses.

    Type "Total Expenses" at the bottom of the list of expenses.

4. Calculate subtotal for Total Expenses using the **SUM()** command.

    Use the **SUM()** command to sum all of the expenses, as follows.

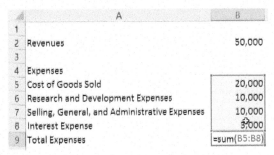

Microsoft Excel 2016

Here is the result:

Revenues	50,000
Expenses	
Cost of Goods Sold	20,000
Research and Development Expenses	10,000
Selling, General, and Administrative Expenses	10,000
Interest Expense	3,000
Total Expenses	43,000

5. Insert a single bottom border under Interest Expense and under the Total Expenses subtotal.

   Use the icon indicated to add the bottom border.

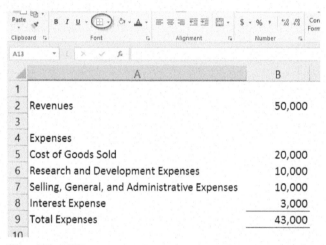

Microsoft Excel 2016

6. Insert the words "Net Income" and calculate Net Income (Revenues – Total Expenses).

   Type "Net Income" at the bottom of the spreadsheet. Calculate Net Income by inserting the correct formula in the cell (here, =B2-B9):

	A	B
1		
2	Revenues	50,000
3		
4	Expenses	
5	Cost of Goods Sold	20,000
6	Research and Development Expenses	10,000
7	Selling, General, and Administrative Expenses	10,000
8	Interest Expense	3,000
9	Total Expenses	43,000
10		
11	Net Income	=B2-B9

Microsoft Excel

7. Format the top and bottom numbers of the column with a $ currency sign.

   Right click on each number and Format Cells, select currency and no decimal points and click **OK**.

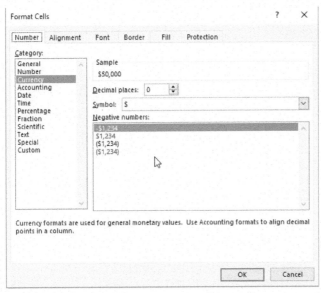

Microsoft Excel

8. Insert a Bottom Double Border to underline the final Net Income total.

   Place your cursor on the cell containing Net Income (7,000). Then select Bottom Double Border from the Font > Borders menu.

   This is the final product:

Revenues	$50,000
Expenses	
Cost of Goods Sold	20,000
Research and Development Expenses	10,000
Selling, General, and Administrative Expenses	10,000
Interest Expense	3,000
Total Expenses	43,000
Net Income	$7,000

Microsoft Excel

(Level 1) Basic Data Manipulation (Filters, Sorts, PivotTables)

9. Open Appendix C Data.xlsx and access the sheet named "Basic Data Manipulation."
10. Look at the data.

(Level 2) Sorting the Data

11. Let's sort the data. To do so, go to **Data > Sort & Filter > Sort**.

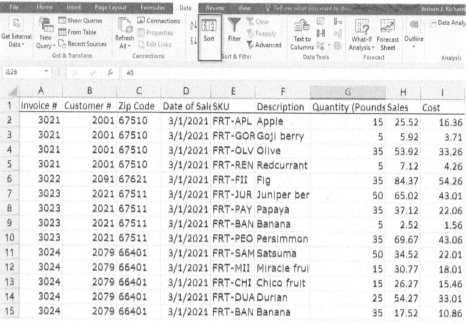

Microsoft Excel

12. Let's sort by sales price from largest to smallest. Input **Sales** into the Sort by, select Largest to Smallest in the dialog box, and select **OK**.

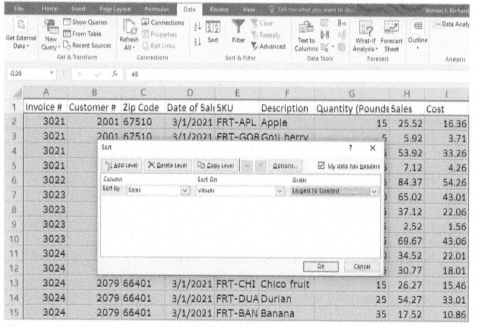

Microsoft Excel

The highest sales price appears to be Apricots at a cost of $140.

	A	B	C	D	E	F	G	H	I
1	Invoice #	Customer #	Zip Code	Date of Sale	SKU	Description	Quantity (Pounds	Sales	Cost
2	3069	2047	67838	3/4/2021	FRT-APO	Apricot	50	140	88.01
3	3026	2088	67004	3/1/2021	FRT-FII	Fig	50	120.5	77.51
4	3043	2087	67731	3/2/2021	FRT-TAN	Tamarind	50	109.5	69.01
5	3028	2086	67416	3/1/2021	FRT-COU	Coconut	45	108.5	69.31
6	3046	2064	67732	3/2/2021	FRT-SOO	Soursop	45	108	65.71
7	3039	2060	67518	3/2/2021	FRT-PLT	Plumcot (or	50	105	62.01
8	3067	2072	66736	3/4/2021	FRT-LYE	Lychee	50	100.5	62.51
9	3069	2047	67838	3/4/2021	FRT-BIT	Bilberry	50	100	58.51
10	3068	2046	67035	3/4/2021	FRT-LEO	Lemon	40	98.42	59.21
11	3048	2031	67626	3/2/2021	FRT-SOO	Soursop	40	96.02	58.41

Microsoft Excel

Looking down at the bottom of this list, we see that the lowest sales price appears to be bananas for $2.52.

(Level 3) Filtering the Data

Next, let's filter the data to only look at only the banana transactions.
13. Let's sort the data. To do so, go to **Data > Sort & Filter > Filter**.
14. An upside down triangle (or a chevron) will appear. Click the chevron in cell F1, click **Select All** to unselect all, and then select only the word "Banana".
15. The resulting data should appear as follows:

Invoice #	Customer #	Zip Code	Date of S	SKU	Description	Quantity (Poun	Sales	Cost
3041	2066	66408	3/2/2021	FRT-BAN	Banana	50	25.02	15.51
3025	2099	66710	3/1/2021	FRT-BAN	Banana	45	22.52	13.96
3055	2081	66014	3/3/2021	FRT-BAN	Banana	45	22.52	13.96
3028	2086	67416	3/1/2021	FRT-BAN	Banana	40	20.02	12.41
3054	2088	66842	3/2/2021	FRT-BAN	Banana	40	20.02	12.41
3069	2047	67838	3/4/2021	FRT-BAN	Banana	40	20.02	12.41
3024	2079	66401	3/1/2021	FRT-BAN	Banana	35	17.52	10.86
3048	2031	67626	3/2/2021	FRT-BAN	Banana	35	17.52	10.86
3049	2043	66840	3/2/2021	FRT-BAN	Banana	25	12.52	7.76
3048	2031	67626	3/2/2021	FRT-BAN	Banana	15	7.52	4.66
3050	2084	66936	3/2/2021	FRT-BAN	Banana	15	7.52	4.66
3061	2024	66937	3/3/2021	FRT-BAN	Banana	15	7.52	4.66
3023	2021	67511	3/1/2021	FRT-BAN	Banana	5	2.52	1.56

Microsoft Excel

16. Alternatively, we could filter based on date to get all transactions on 3/2/2021. We first need to clear the filter in cell F1, by clicking on the Filter symbol and selecting **Select All.**

17. Click the chevron in cell C1, click **Select All** to unselect all, and then select only the word "2021" then "March" then "2".

	A	B	C	D	E		F	G	H	I
1	Invoice #	Customer #	Zip Code	Date of Sa	SKU		Description	Quantity (Poun	Sales	Cost
4	3043	2087	67731	3/2/2021	FRT-TAN	Tamarind		50	109.5	69.01
6	3046	2064	67732	3/2/2021	FRT-SOO	Soursop		45	108	65.71
7	3039	2060	67518	3/2/2021	FRT-PLT	Plumcot (or		50	105	62.01
11	3048	2031	67626	3/2/2021	FRT-SOO	Soursop		40	96.02	58.41
12	3045	2100	66226	3/2/2021	FRT-PEA	Pear		50	91.52	53.51
14	3043	2087	67731	3/2/2021	FRT-CUE	Cucumber		50	91.02	54.51
15	3053	2032	66414	3/2/2021	FRT-JAU	Jambul		45	87.77	50.86
16	3043	2087	67731	3/2/2021	FRT-APL	Apple		50	85.02	54.51
26	3046	2064	67732	3/2/2021	FRT-FEO	Feijoa		40	79.22	52.01

Microsoft Excel

(Level 4) Pivot Tables

18. Let's compute the accumulated gross margin for bananas, apricots, and apples by taking the sales.
19. First, unclick the filter at **Data > Sort & Filter > Filter** by clicking on and unselecting **Filter.**
20. Next, let's compute the gross margin for each line item in the invoice. In cell J1, input the words "Gross Margin". Underline it with a bottom border. In cell J2, input "=H2-I2" and hit <Enter> in this way.

	A	B	C	D	E	F	G	H	I	J
1	Invoice #	Customer #	Zip Code	Date of Sal	SKU	Description	Quantity (Pounds	Sales	Cost	Gross Margin
2	3069	2047	67838	3/4/2021	FRT-APO	Apricot	50	140	88.01	=H2-I2
3	3026	2088	67004	3/1/2021	FRT-FII	Fig	50	120.5	77.51	
4	3043	2087	67731	3/2/2021	FRT-TAN	Tamarind	50	109.5	69.01	

Microsoft Excel

21. Copy the result from cell J2 to J3:J194.
22. Now it is time to use the pivot table. Recall that a pivot table summarizes selected columns in a spreadsheet, but doesn't change the spreadsheet itself. Recall we are trying to summarize the accumulated gross margin for bananas, apricots and apples.
23. Select **Insert > Tables > PivotTable.**

Analytics Tool: Excel PivotTables

PivotTables allow you to quickly summarize large amounts of data. In Excel, click **Insert > PivotTable**, *choose your data source, then click the checkmark next to or drag your fields to the appropriate boxes in the PivotTable Fields pane to identify filters, columns, rows, or values. You can easily move attributes from one pane to another to quickly "pivot" your data. Here is a brief description of each section:*

> *Rows:* Show the main item of interest. You usually want master data here, such as customers, products, or accounts.
>
> *Columns:* Slice the data into categories or buckets. Most commonly, columns are used for time (e.g., years, quarters, months, dates).
>
> *Values:* This area represents the meat of your data. Any measure that you would like to count, sum, average, or otherwise aggregate should be placed here. The aggregated values will combine all records that match a given row and column.
>
> *Filters:* Placing a field in the Filters area will allow you to filter the data based on that field, but it will not show that field in the data. For example, if you wanted to filter based on a date, but didn't care to view a particular date, you could use this area of the field list. With more recent versions of Excel, there are improved methods for filtering, but this legacy feature is still functional.

24. Make sure all data is selected as follows in Table/Range and select **OK.**

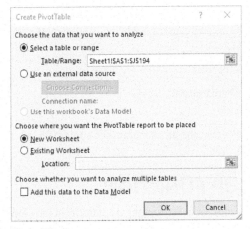

Microsoft Excel

25. The empty pivot table will open up in a new worksheet, ready for the pivot table analysis.

> Columns:
> Rows: [Description]
> ΣValues: [Gross Margin]

Inputs into PivotTable
Drag [Description from **FIELD NAME** into the **Rows** and [Gross Margin] from **FIELD NAME** into ΣValues fields in the pivot table. The ΣValues will default to "Sum of Gross Margin".

The resulting pivot table will look like this:

Source: Microsoft Excel 2016

26. The analysis suggests that the gross margin for apples is $140.39; for apricots, $78.02 and for bananas, $77.08.

THE VLOOKUP FUNCTION

One of Excel's most useful tools for looking up data from two separate tables and providing matching information based on related fields (often based on a primary key/foreign key relationship) is the VLookup function.

To demonstrate the VLookup function, we will work with sales transactions and tax rate data. Sometimes when you access or request sales transaction data, the tax rate may not be included. In order to calculate the amount of tax owed for each transaction, we need to match the state tax rate with the state the customer is from. This would be an arduous task to do manually, particularly in datasets that are large. We can use Excel's VLookup function to match the state the customers are from with the state tax rate.

Open Excel File Appendix C Data.xlsx and access the sheet named "VLookup."

The dataset contains information about sales transactions to different customers. This is similar to the dataset that you use in Lab 2-2 of chapter 2. There are 132 unique transactions, but 150 rows—this is because some of the transactions had multiple products on them.

1. The location of each store where the sales were made.
2. A second table with sales tax information for each state.

You may need to scroll to the right to see the sales tax table.

Data Dictionary:

Sales_Transactions table:

Sales_Order_ID: Unique identifier for each individual Sales Order

Sales_Order_Date: Date each sales order was placed

Sales_Order_Quantity_Sold: Quantity of each product sold on the transaction

product_description: Description of the product sold

Product_Sale_Price: Price of each product sold on the transaction

Store_Location: State in which the store is located

State Sales Tax table:

State: the state abbreviation

State Tax Rate: the tax rate for each state

There are two columns which match in these two tables: Store_Location (from the Sales_Transaction table) and State (from the State Sales Tax table). These two tables are placed next to one another to make the VLOOKUP function easier to manage.

Step 1: We will add a new column to the Sales_Transactions table to bring in the State_Sales_Tax associated with every Customer_St listed in the transactions table.

1. Add a new column to the right of the Store_Location named Sales_Tax (cell G1).

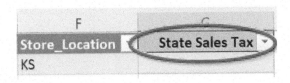

In cell G2, we will create a VLOOKUP Function. VLOOKUP Functions have four arguments:

- **Cell_reference**: the cell in the current table that has a match in the related table. In this case, it is a reference to the row's corresponding Store_Location. Excel will match that state with the corresponding state in the sales tax table.
- **Table_array**: an entire table reference to the table that contains the descriptive data that you wish to be returned. In this case, it is the entire State Sales Tax table.
- **Column_number**: the number of the column (not the letter!) that contains the descriptive data that you wish to be returned. In this case, State Sales Tax Rate is in the second column of the State Sales Tax table, so we would type 2.
- **True or False**: there are two types of VLOOKUP functions, true and false. TRUE is for looking up what Excel calls "approximate" data – this is useful for looking up tax rates based on income buckets or discount rates based on buckets corresponding with dates that the customer pays by. In our case, we'll use FALSE. A FALSE VLOOKUP will only return matches for when there is an exact match between the two tables (whenever your data is 'relational,' structured data, a perfect match should be easily discoverable).

Step 2: Because the ranges of data are not only formatted as tables, but also named properly, the VLOOKUP Function should be relatively easy to follow:

2. Type in the following function (using cell references will be easier than typing manually):

F	G	H	I	J	K
Store_Location ▾	**State Sales Tax** ▾			**state** ▾	**State Tax Rate** ▾
KS	=VLOOKUP(			AL	0.04
TN	[@[Store_Location]],			AK	0
TX	State_Sales_Tax,2,			AZ	0.056
OK	FALSE)			AR	0.065
TX				CA	0.0725

3. Once you click Enter, the formula should copy all the way down—once again exhibiting the benefits of working with Excel tables instead of ranges.

Appendix D
SQL Part 1

SQL can be used to create tables, delete records, or edit databases, but in Data Analytics, we primarily use SQL to extract data from the database—that is, not to edit or manipulate the data, but to create different views of the data to help us answer business questions. SQL extraction queries are also referred to as SELECT queries, because they each begin with the word SELECT.

Throughout this appendix, all the examples and the practice problems refer to Appendix D Data.accdb. This is a very small database to help you be able to immediately visualize what a query's results would look like.

INTRODUCTION TO SQL CLAUSES

Every SQL SELECT query must have two key SQL clauses, SELECT and FROM.

Introduction to SELECT

SELECT indicates which attributes you wish to view. For example, the Customers table contains a complete customer list with several descriptive attributes for each of the company's customers. If you would like to see a full customer list, but you just want to see FirstName, LastName, and State, you can just select those three attributes in the first line of your query:

```
SELECT FirstName, LastName, State
```

Introduction to FROM

FROM lets the database management system know which table(s) contains the attributes that you are selecting. For instance, in the query begun above, the three attributes in the SELECT clause come from the Customers table. So that query can be completed with the following FROM clause:

```
FROM Customers
```

Try putting that query all together to see the results:

```
SELECT FirstName, LastName, State
FROM Customers
```

This returns the result in Figure D-1:

FIGURE D-1

Source: Microsoft Excel 2016

FirstName	LastName	State
Paula	George	Oklahoma
Terry	Herman	Texas
Edna	Orgeron	Louisiana
Jeremy	Jones	Texas
Pamela	Subban	Tennessee
Gary	Decker	Arkansas
Jenna	Carter	Tennessee
Thomas	Green	Arkansas
Linda	Edwards	Missouri
Nick	Sadan	Alabama

If you wish to view the same three columns, but you want to see the LastName column as the first column, so that the results more closely resemble a phone book, you can change the order of the attributes listed in your SELECT statement:

```
SELECT LastName, FirstName, State
FROM Customers
```

Now the query returns the same number of records, but with a different order of attributes (columns), seen in Figure D-2:

FIGURE D-2

Source: Microsoft Excel, 2016

LastName	FirstName	State
George	Paula	Oklahoma
Herman	Terry	Texas
Orgeron	Edna	Louisiana
Jones	Jeremy	Texas
Subban	Pamela	Tennessee
Decker	Gary	Arkansas
Carter	Jenna	Tennessee
Green	Thomas	Arkansas
Edwards	Linda	Missouri
Sadan	Nick	Alabama

SELECT FROM Practice

1. Create a query that will return only the Inventory_Description and Price from the Inventory table.
2. Create a query that will show only the Order_date and CustomerID from the Sales_Order table.
3. Create a query that will show the City and State from the Customers table.

After you get the hang of creating simple SELECT FROM queries, you can begin to bring in some of the SQL clauses that can make our queries even more interesting. The next two SQL clauses we will cover are WHERE and ORDER BY. They follow FROM, to make a query in this order:

```
SELECT
FROM
WHERE
ORDER BY
```

One more bit of SELECT information—how to SELECT all of the attributes:

If you wish to view every attribute in the same order as they exist in the table, you can use a shortcut to select all:

```
SELECT *
FROM Inventory
```

A simple SELECT FROM query with SELECT * isn't very interesting on its own, but when we begin filtering records, SELECT * can be a quick way to view how many records fit a certain criteria. We filter records with the WHERE clause.

Introduction to WHERE

WHERE behaves like a filter in Excel. An example of using WHERE to modify the query in is the following:

```
SELECT LastName, FirstName, State
FROM Customers
WHERE State = "Arkansas"
```

That query would return only the customers who were from Arkansas, the result is shown in Figure D-3:

LastName ▾	FirstName ▾	State ▾
Decker	Gary	Arkansas
Green	Thomas	Arkansas

FIGURE D-3

Source: Microsoft Excel, 2016

The syntax of a simple WHERE clause is the following:

WHERE [*attribute_name*] = [*criteria*]

The attribute_name needs to spelled exactly the way it is in the database without any formatting (for example, do not place the attribute name in quotes).

Formatting criteria in a WHERE clause, or "So, what's the deal with the quotes around Arkansas?"

There are three main datatypes that you will work with in SQL: text, numbers, and dates. Every attribute in a database is stored as one of those datatypes. Let's look at the Inventory table in the Ch2_SQL_Tutorial database. It has three fields:

- InventoryID (example entries: I-1, I-2)
- Inventory_Description (example entries: Dalton Dress Boot, Ray-Ban Wayfarer)
- Price (example entries: 495, 1250)

Text Datatypes

Both InventoryID and Inventory_Description are **text** datatypes. Most text datatypes are descriptive or categorical elements in the database. When you filter for criteria from a text attribute, the criteria must be surrounded in quotes. Examples:

- WHERE State = "Arkansas"
- WHERE Inventory_Description = "Dalton Dress Boot"

A word of caution! Programs like Microsoft Word apply formatting to quotes by turning them into "curly quotes." Microsoft Access and other relational database systems cannot read the curly quotes. If you draft your queries in Word and then copy and paste them into a SQL editor, the quotes will need to be re-typed in the query editor for the database application to be able to read the criteria appropriately.

Number Datatypes

Price, on the other hand, is a **number** datatype. You could sum or average the contents of that attribute and arrive at a meaningful value. Another example of number datatypes are Quantity_Sold in the Sales_Order table. When you filter for criteria from a number attribute, there is no need to format the criteria at all. Examples:

- WHERE Price = 395
- WHERE Quantity = 2

Date Datatypes

For an example of the third datatype, date, look at the Sales_Order table to find the Order_Date attribute. When you filter for criteria from a date attribute, the date should be enclosed in # signs and follow the following format #mm/dd/yyyy# Examples:

- WHERE Order_Date = #01/02/2019#
- WHERE Order_Date = #12/31/2018#

Date formats in other database management systems: Date formatting in SQL is variable across relational database management systems.

- In SQLite, date format is 'yyyy-mm-dd' For example, '2019-01-02' or '2018-12-31'
- In SQL Server, date format is 'yyyymmdd' For example '20190102' or '20181231'

Other methods of filtering, or, do we always have to filter for an exact match?

Each of the WHERE examples we've seen so far have used the equals sign operator. But there are many other ways to filter other than for exact matches. For now, we'll just start with a few other operators, shown in Exhibit D-1:

EXHIBIT D-1

Operator	Description
> used with a number datatype	Returns all records that have numbers in that field greater than the criteria specified.
> used with a text datatype	Returns all records that follow the criteria alphabetically (a–z).
< used with a number datatype	Returns all records that have numbers in that field less than the criteria specified.
< used with a text datatype	Returns all records that precede the criteria alphabetically (a–z).
>= and <=	Similar to the above criteria, but will also include numbers or text that is an exact match to what is listed in the criteria.
<>	functions as the inverse as the exact match (=) filter, it will return all of the records except those that match the criteria listed in the WHERE clause.

More SELECT FROM WHERE Examples

To extract all of the records from the Inventory table that have prices greater than $1,000:

```
SELECT *
FROM Inventory
WHERE Price > 1000
```

That query returns the following records shown in Figure D-4:

InventoryID ▾	Inventory_Description ▾	Price ▾
I-3	David Yurman Bracelet	6750
I-4	Saint Laurent Leather Jacket	1250
I-6	Giorgio Armani Suit	2450
I-7	Jason Wu Blazer	1450

FIGURE D-4

Source: Microsoft Excel 2016

To extract all of the records from the Customers table that follow the last name "jones" alphabetically:

```
SELECT *
FROM Customers
WHERE LastName > "Jones"
```

That query returns the following records shown in Figure D-5:

CustomerID ▾	FirstName ▾	LastName ▾	City ▾	State ▾	Phone_Num ▾
3	Edna	Orgeron	Baton Rouge	Louisiana	225-578-2184
5	Pamela	Subban	Nashville	Tennessee	615-770-2000
10	Nick	Sadan	Tuscaloosa	Alabama	205-348-3697

FIGURE D-5

Source: Microsoft Excel 2016

If you wanted to include any employees with the last name of Jones in the list, you would change the operator from > to >= :

```
SELECT *
FROM Customers
WHERE LastName >= "Jones"
```

The revised output is shown in Figure D-6:

CustomerID ▾	FirstName ▾	LastName ▾	City ▾	State ▾	Phone_Num ▾
3	Edna	Orgeron	Baton Rouge	Louisiana	225-578-2184
4	Jeremy	Jones	Dallas	Texas	817-892-4000
5	Pamela	Subban	Nashville	Tennessee	615-770-2000
10	Nick	Sadan	Tuscaloosa	Alabama	205-348-3697

FIGURE D-6

Source: Microsoft Excel 2016

You can see that Jeremy Jones is included in this output.

SELECT FROM WHERE Practice

1. Write a query that will return all of the records from the Sales_Order table that have a quantity greater than 4.
2. Write a query that will return all of the records from the Sales_Order table that have a quantity less than or equal to 3.
3. Write a query that will return all of the records from the Sales_Order table that had exactly one item on it.
4. Write a query that will return all of the records from the Customers table of the customers from Texas.
5. Write a query that will return all of the records from the Customers table of the customers from Baton Rouge

Introduction to ORDER BY

In Figure D-6 above, when you added Jeremy Jones to the output, you might have been surprised that the order of the records didn't change. The default order of SQL queries is ascending based on the first column selected. When you SELECT *, the default will be in the order of the Primary Key, which is the order of the records in the original table.

If you would like to sort the records in a query output based on any other column, you can do so with the ORDER BY clause.

The syntax of an ORDER BY clause is the following:

To sort the records in ascending order (1 to infinity or A to Z): ORDER BY [*attribute_name*] ASC
To sort the records in descending order (infinity to 1 or Z to A): ORDER BY [*attribute name*] DESC

Similar to WHERE, the attribute_name needs to spelled exactly the way it is in the database without any formatting (for example, do not place the attribute name in quotes).

ORDER BY is always the last line in any query, no matter how complex the query is.

Example Queries with ORDER BY

To revise the first query in the appendix from Figure D-6, order the output by state, ascending:

```
SELECT LastName, FirstName, State
FROM Customers
ORDER BY State ASC
```

That query returns the following records shown in Figure D-7:

FIGURE D-7

Source: Microsoft Excel 2016

LastName ▾	FirstName ▾	State ▾
Sadan	Nick	Alabama
Green	Thomas	Arkansas
Decker	Gary	Arkansas
Orgeron	Edna	Louisiana
Edwards	Linda	Missouri
George	Paula	Oklahoma
Carter	Jenna	Tennessee
Subban	Pamela	Tennessee
Jones	Jeremy	Texas
Herman	Terry	Texas

Notice how the two figures have the same information, the same order of attributes, and the same number of records, but the ordering of the records has changed.

To revise the same query, but this time to order the results by both Last Name and First Name (ascending):

```
SELECT LastName, FirstName, State
FROM Customers
ORDER BY LastName ASC, FirstName ASC
```

That query returns the following records shown in Figure D-8:

LastName	FirstName	State
Carter	Jenna	Tennessee
Decker	Gary	Arkansas
Edwards	Linda	Missouri
George	Paula	Oklahoma
Green	Thomas	Arkansas
Herman	Terry	Texas
Jones	Jeremy	Texas
Orgeron	Edna	Louisiana
Sadan	Nick	Alabama
Subban	Pamela	Tennessee

FIGURE D-8

Source: Microsoft Excel 2016

EXPANDING THE USAGE OF SELECT

So far, you have learned the SQL keywords SELECT, FROM, WHERE, and ORDER BY. These words are useful for creating views of a limited amount of data from one table, but other than limiting the amount of rows and columns returned (with WHERE and SELECT, respectively) and changing the order in which they are returned, the table data that returns from these queries is still presented in the same format as it is stored in the database.

We can extend the usage of SELECT to manipulate the data that returns from a query with aggregates.

More Actions You Can Take in SELECT: Aggregates and Aliases

To aggregate means to form a group or a cluster. In SQL, aggregate data represents grand totals or subtotals of data. For example, if you did not want to simply view all of the individual orders in a Sales_Orders table, but you wanted instead to see a total count of how many orders were in a table, or you wanted to see the grand total quantity of products ever sold, you would want to aggregate the data.

The following functions are commonly used in the SELECT clause to aggregate data:

- SUM(attribute)
- COUNT(attribute)
- AVG(attribute)

The following query uses an aggregate function to create a query that would show the total count of orders in the Sales_Orders table:

```
SELECT COUNT(Sales_Order_ID)
FROM Sales_Orders
```

The output of that query would produce only one column and one row, shown in Figure D-9:

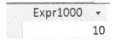

Expr1000
10

FIGURE D-9

Source: Microsoft Excel 2016

The problem with this output, of course, is the lack of description. The column is titled **Expr1000,** which is not very descriptive. This title is produced because there isn't a column named COUNT(Sales_Order_ID), so the database management system doesn't know what to title the column in the output.

To make this column more meaningful, we can use **aliases**. An **alias** simply re-names a column. It is written as AS. To re-name the column COUNT(Sales_Order_ID) to Count_Total_Orders, the query would look like the following:

```
SELECT COUNT(Sales_Order_ID) AS Count_Total_Orders
FROM Sales_Orders
```

The output is more meaningful with the alias added in, shown in Figure D-10:

FIGURE D-10

Source: Microsoft Excel 2016

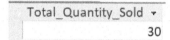

Total_Quantity_Sold ▾
30

To create a query that would show the grand total quantity of products ever sold (as stored in the Sales_Orders table) with a meaningful column name, we could run the following:

```
SELECT SUM(Quantity_Sold) AS Total_Quantity_Sold
FROM Sales_Orders
```

Which returns the following output, shown in Figure D-11:

FIGURE D-11

Source: Microsoft Excel 2016

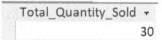

Total_Quantity_Sold ▾
30

Aggregates and Aliases Practice

1. Create a query that would show the average price of our inventory items (use the Inventory table). Re-name the column in the output Avg_Price.
2. Create a query that would show the total number of Customers we have stored in the Customers table. Re-name the column in the output Num_Customers.

EXTENDING THE QUERY WITH GROUP BY AND HAVING CLAUSES

Aggregates are extremely useful to return grand totals of the data that is stored in a database. But sometimes, we would prefer to view that data by subtotals, as well.

Introduction to GROUP BY

In the introduction to aggregates, we worked through an example that provided the grand total count of orders in the Sales Order table:

```
SELECT COUNT(Sales_Order_ID) AS Count_Total_Orders
FROM Sales_Orders
```

That query results in a grand total of 10, but what if we would like to see how that data splits up among customers who have ordered from us? This is where GROUP BY comes in. GROUP BY works as the "engine" that powers subtotaling the data. After the key word GROUP BY, you indicate the attribute by which you would like to slice the data. In this case, we want to slice the grand total by CustomerID.

```
SELECT COUNT(Sales_Order_ID) AS Count_Total_Orders
FROM Sales_Orders
GROUP BY CustomerID
```

The problem with this query, is that it does slice the data by customer, but it doesn't actually show us the CustomerID associated with each subtotal. The output is shown in Figure D-12:

Count_Total_Orders
1
1
1
1
1
1
1
2
1

FIGURE D-12

Source: Microsoft Excel 2016

If we want to actually view the CustomerID that is associated with each subtotal, we need to not only put the attribute in the GROUP BY field, but also add it to the SELECT field.

Remember from earlier in this tutorial, that the order in which you place the attributes in the SELECT clause indicates the order that those columns will display in the output. For this output, it would make the most sense to see CustomerID before Count_Total, because CustomerID is acting as a label for the totals. We can modify the query to include CustomerID in the following way:

```
SELECT CustomerID, COUNT(Sales_Order_ID) AS Count_Total_Orders
FROM Sales_Orders
GROUP BY CustomerID
```

This provides the following output, shown in Figure D-13:

CustomerID	Count_Total_Orders
1	1
2	1
4	1
5	1
6	1
7	1
8	1
9	2
10	1

FIGURE D-13

Source: Microsoft Excel 2016

Similarly, we can extend the second example provided in the Aggregates section that created a grand total of the quantity sold from the Sales_Order table. If we would prefer to not see the grand total quantity sold, but instead slice that total by InventoryID in order to see the subtotal of the quantity of each inventory item sold, we can create the following query:

```
SELECT InventoryID, SUM(Quantity_Sold) AS Total_Quantity_Sold
FROM Sales_Orders
GROUP BY InventoryID
```

Which produces the following query, shown in Figure D-14:

FIGURE D-14

Source: Microsoft Excel 2016

InventoryID	Total_Quantity_Sold
I-1	3
I-2	2
I-3	5
I-4	6
I-5	10
I-6	1
I-7	3

Notice that InventoryID needs to be added in two places: you must place it in the GROUP BY clause to provide the "engine" that subtotals a grandtotal (or slices it), and then you must also place InventoryID in the SELECT clause so that you can see the labels associated with each subtotal.

GROUP BY Practice

1. Create a query that would show the total quantity of items sold each day. Re-name the aggregate Total_Quantity_Sold.
2. Create a query that would show the total number of Customers we have stored in the Customers table, and group them by the State the customers are from. Re-name the aggregate column in the output Num_Customers.

Introduction to HAVING

Occasionally when running a query to gather subtotals (using a GROUP BY clause), you do not want to see all of the results, but instead would rather filter the results for certain subtotals. Unfortunately, SQL cannot filter aggregate measures in the WHERE clause, but fortunately, we have a different clause that can—HAVING.

Any time you wish to filter your query results based on aggregate values (e.g., SUM(Quantity_Sold), you can do so in the HAVING clause.

For example, in the previous section about GROUP BY, we created a query to see the total count of orders each customer had been on. The output showed that the vast majority of our customers had participated in only one order. But what if we wanted to only see the customer(s) who had participated in more than one order?

We can create the following query to add in this filter:

```
SELECT CustomerID, COUNT(Sales_Order_ID) AS Count_Total_Orders
FROM Sales_Orders
GROUP BY CustomerID
HAVING COUNT(Sales_Order_ID) > 1
```

As it turns out, there is only one customer who participated in more than one order, as we can see in the query output, shown in Figure D-15:

FIGURE D-15

Source: Microsoft Excel 2016

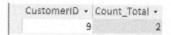

CustomerID	Count_Total
9	2

The format of the HAVING clause is similar to WHERE:

```
HAVING aggregate(attribute) = number
```

- The aggregate can be any of our aggregate values, SUM(), AVG(), or COUNT().
- The attribute is the field that you are aggregating, SUM(Quantity) or COUNT(CustomerID).
- The = can be replaced with any operator, =, <, >, =<, =>, <>.
- The number is the value that you are filtering your results on.

Let's work through another example. The second example in the GROUP BY section showed the quantity sold of each inventory item. If we want to view only those items that have sold less than 5 items, we can create the following query:

```
SELECT InventoryID, SUM(Quantity_Sold) AS Total_Quantity_Sold
FROM Sales_Orders
GROUP BY InventoryId
HAVING SUM(Quantity_Sold) < 5
```

This query produces the following output, shown in Figure D-16:

InventoryID ▾	Total_Quantity_Sold ▾
I-1	3
I-2	2
I-6	1
I-7	3

FIGURE D-16

Source: Microsoft Excel 2016

HAVING Practice

1. Create a query that would show the total quantity of items sold each day. Re-name the aggregate Total_Quantity_Sold. Show only the days on which more than 6 items were sold.
2. Create a query that would show the total number of Customers we have stored in the Customers table, and group them by the State the customers are from. Re-name the aggregate column in the output Num_Customers. Show only the states that more than one customer is from.

EXTENDING THE USE OF THE FROM CLAUSE: SELECTING DATA FROM MORE THAN ONE TABLE

Some of the real power of SQL extends beyond relatively simple SELECT FROM WHERE clauses. Since relational databases are focused on reducing redundancy, there are often important details that we would like to use for analysis stored across two or three different tables.

For example, in our sample database, we may be interested to know the phone number of the customer associated with each order. Each order is stored in the Sales_Order table, but the details about our customers (including their phone numbers) are stored in the Customers table. To retrieve data from both tables, we need to first make sure that the tables are related. We can do that by looking at the database design:

The call-out circle and boxes in the figure can help us find how these two tables are related. First, we can see the circle that indicates the relationship connecting the Customers and Sales_Orders table. This shows us that the two tables are indeed related. The next

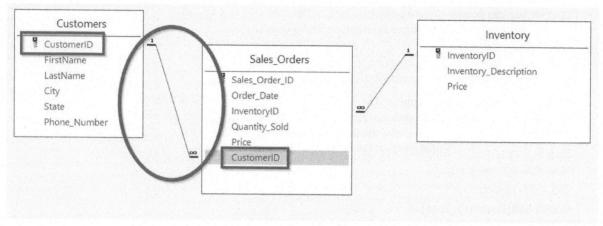

FIGURE D-17

step is to identify how they are related. The two red boxes in Figure D-17 indicate the related fields, CustomerID is the Primary Key in the Customers table, and CustomerID is the Foreign Key in the Sales_Order table. Since these two tables are related, we can retrieve them fairly easily with a JOIN clause.

In order to retrieve data from more than one table, we need to use SQL JOINs. There are three types of JOINs, but for much of our analysis, an INNER JOIN will suffice. JOINs are technically part of the FROM clause. They follow the following template:

```
FROM table1
INNER JOIN table2
ON table1.matching_key = table2.matching_key
```

The order of the tables does not matter, you could place the Customers table in either the FROM or the INNER JOIN clause, and the order of the tables does not matter in the ON clause. It just matters that you indicate both tables you want to retrieve data from, and that you indicate the two different tables with their matching keys in the ON clause.

To select all of the data from the Customers table and the Sales_Orders table, you can run the following query:

```
SELECT *
FROM Customers
INNER JOIN Sales_Orders
ON Customers.CustomerID = Sales_Orders.CustomerID
```

If you want to only select the Sales_Order_ID and the Order_Date from the Sales_Orders table, but also select the State attribute from the Customers table, you could run the following query:

```
SELECT Sales_Order_ID, Order_Date, State
FROM Customers
INNER JOIN Sales_Orders
ON Customers.CustomerID = Sales_Orders.CustomerID
```

INNER JOIN ON Practice

1. Create a query that will show the Customer's First and Last Names, as well as the Quantity_Sold and Price of each order the customer was on.
2. Create a query that will show the Order_Date and Quantity_Sold on each order, as well as the Inventory_Description of the items associated with each order.

Parentheses Are Key to Joining More Than One Table

Sometimes you will want to not only join two tables, but three or more. When you join more than two tables together, you need to nest the extra joins in parentheses.

In more detail, if you define the number of tables you're trying to join as "n," then the number of parentheses you need after the word FROM is n-2, and you need to have one right parentheses before the start of each new join clause.

For example, if you are joining three tables, you need a parentheses after the word FROM and after the first ON clause. Then you can proceed with the query as normal. To join all three tables in our example database, it would look like the following:

```
SELECT *
FROM (Customers
INNER JOIN Sales_Orders
ON Customers.CustomerID = Sales_Orders.CustomerID)
INNER JOIN Inventory
ON Sales_Orders.InventoryID = Inventory.InventoryID
```

Note: there are other types of joins! Beyond INNER JOINs, we can also create LEFT and RIGHT JOINs to get slightly different results, depending on our data and our needs. There is a deep dive to LEFT and RIGHT JOINs in Appendix H.

Putting It All Together

This tutorial has introduced you to the majority of the SQL keywords you will need to extract data for data analysis or even to answer simple data analysis questions directly in the database. If you were to use all of the SQL words that we have discovered in this tutorial in one query, the keywords must go in the following order:

```
SELECT
FROM
INNER JOIN
ON
WHERE
GROUP BY
HAVING
ORDER BY
```

I typically indent the INNER JOIN and ON clauses when drafting queries to help to remember that those clauses are technically part of the FROM clause, this helps with remembering the order of all of the clauses.

Appendix E

SQLite

SQLite is a free open source database browser that may be installed on any Windows or Mac computer, including labs, without administrative privileges. It is a simple, open-source alternative to Microsoft Access.

To get started, save the file Appendix E Data to a folder on your computer. This way you can access it through SQLite.

Windows:

1. Go to https://sqlitebrowser.org/dl/.
2. Choose the **DB Browser for SQLite - .zip (no installer) for 64-bit Windows** option.
3. In your Downloads folder, open the zip file and drag the **DB Browser for SQLite** folder to the desktop.
4. Open the folder on the desktop and open **DB Browser for SQLite.exe.**

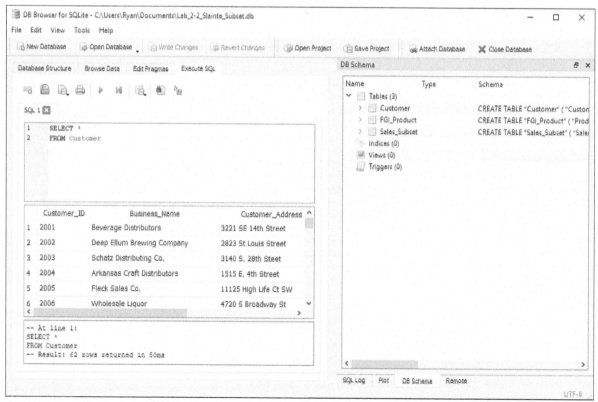

Source: SQL

Mac:

1. Go to https://sqlitebrowser.org/dl/
2. Choose the **DB Browser for SQLite** option under macOS.
3. In your Downloads folder, open the DMG and drag **DB Browser for SQLite** to your Applications or Desktop folder.
4. Open your Applications or Desktop folder and double-click **DB Browser for SQLite**. If you receive a message indicating that the app you are trying to install is not a Microsoft-verified app, select **Install Anyway**.

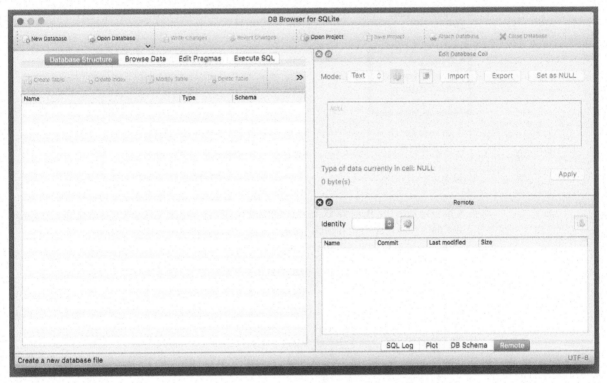

Source: SQL

NAVIGATING SQLITE AND EXECUTING SQL QUERIES

1. Once you have DB Browser for SQLite open, you can select **Open Database** to open an existing database file.

Source: SQL

2. Navigate to the Appendix E Data file to open it.
3. The first view will be of the Database Structure. You can expand the tables to get a glimpse of the attributes that are stored in each table and their datatypes.

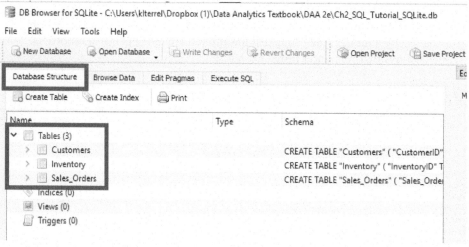

Source: SQL

4. Clicking into the **Browse Data** tab will allow you to switch views between tables to view the data that is stored in each table.

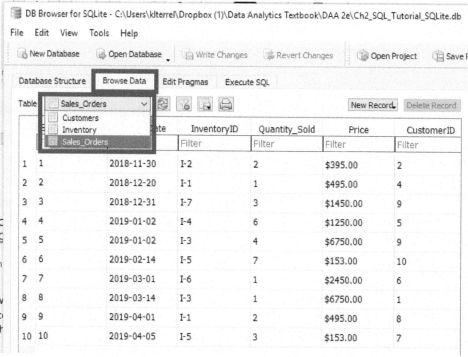

Source: SQL

5. To execute a SQL query, click the **Execute SQL** tab.

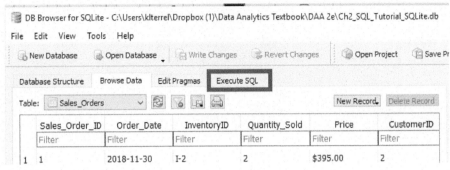

Source: SQL

6. Add the text of your query in the open box.
7. To execute your query, click the **blue arrow,** or you can click **F5** on your keyboard as a keyboard shortcut.
8. Once the query has executed, you will see the results, as well as a window describing that your query ran successfully. If there was an error in your query, the third window would indicate where the error was.

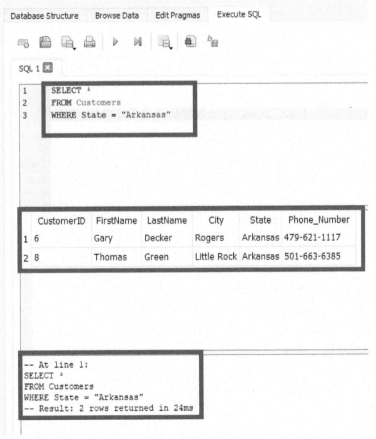

Source: SQL

Microsoft applications (such as Excel or Power BI) do not have a default mechanism for connecting to SQLite files, but if you just want to explore data using SQL, SQLite is a great tool for working with queries and exploring data.

Appendix F

Power Query

Excel's Get and Transform tools are a part of the Power BI suite that is integrated into Excel 2016. These tools allow you to connect directly to a dataset stored in a variety of locations, including other Excel files; .csv files; the web; and a multitude of relational databases, including Microsoft Access, SQL Server, Teradata, Oracle, PostGreSQL, and MySQL.

Throughout this text, the majority of the times we analyze the Dillard's dataset in the Comprehensive Labs, we will load the data from SQL Server into Excel using this Get and Transform tool.

When we extract the data, we may want to extract entire tables, or we may want to extract only a portion via a SQL query.

In this appendix, we will connect to the Dillard's data. The Dillard's data is stored on the University of Arkansas' remote desktop, so make sure to log in to the desktop in order to work through these steps. Ask your instructor for login information if you do not have it already.

CONNECT TO SQL SERVER THROUGH EXCEL'S GET AND TRANSFORM TOOL

1. Open Excel in the University of Arkansas remove desktop. From the **Data** tab on the ribbon, click **New Query.** Then select **From Database > From SQL Server Database.**

Source: Microsoft Excel 2016

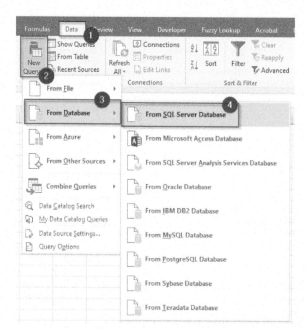

2. The following box will pop up, into which you should provide the name of the Server and the Database name that your instructor provides you. For the majority of the exercises, we use the Database name WCOB_DILLARDS. Labs 3-4, 3-5, and 4-4 use a different database, titled UA_DILLARDS_2016.

Source: SQL

   If prompted to input your credentials, select **Use my Current Credentials**. Once you have input the Server and Database name, you have two options:

3. Extract entire tables by clicking **OK. Continue to Step 5.**
4. Extract only a portion of data from one or more tables based on the criteria of a SQL query. To do so, click **Advanced Options. Skip to Step 7.**

To Extract Entire Tables

5. Click **OK.**

Source: SQL

6. Select the table(s) that you would like to load into Excel. If you would like to select more than one table, place a checkmark in the box next to **Select multiple items.**

Navigator

☐ Select multiple items

Display Options ▾

▲ 🗑 essql1.walton.uark.edu: wcob_dillards [8]

　　▦ CUSTOMER
　　▦ DEPARTMENT
　　▦ SKU
　　▦ SKU_STORE
　　▦ STORE
　　▦ sysdiagrams
　　▦ TRANSACT

　fx fn_diagramobjects

Source: SQL

To Extract a Portion of the Data

7. Click **Advanced Options** to input your SQL query. Input your query in the space provided and click **OK.**

Source: SQL

SQL Server database

Server ⓘ
essql1.walton.uark.edu

Database (optional)
WCOB_DILLARDS

▲ Advanced options ①

Command timeout in minutes (optional)

SQL statement (optional, requires database) ②

```
SELECT *
FROM STORE
INNER JOIN TRANSACT
ON STORE.STORE = TRANSACT.STORE
WHERE STATE = 'AR'
```

☑ Include relationship columns
☐ Navigate using full hierarchy
☐ Enable SQL Server Failover support

OK ③　Cancel

EDITING THE DATA IN POWER QUERY

Regardless of whether you extracted entire tables or extracted data based on a query, you can either Load the data directly into Excel, or you can Edit the data in Power Query first.

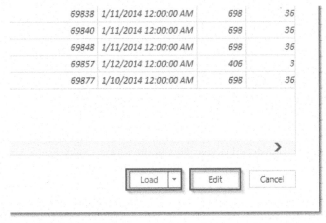

Source: Microsoft Excel 2016

- *Clicking **Load** will load the data directly into an Excel table.*
- *Clicking **Edit** will open the Power Query window for you to transform the data before it is loaded into Excel (add or delete columns, remove or transform null values, aggregate data, etc.)*

8. To Edit (Transform) the data, click **Edit.**
9. The Power Query ribbon has several tabs that provide useful ways to transform the data. A few of the buttons that we use throughout the text are called out for the Home tab and the Transform tab on the ribbon below.

Home tab on the ribbon:

Source: Microsoft Excel 2016

- *Click the **Close & Load** button when you are finished transforming the data to load it into Excel.*
- *The **Remove Rows** button provides options to remove rows with nulls in selected columns, with duplicates in selected columns, or based on other criteria*

Transform tab on the ribbon:

Source: Microsoft Excel 2016

- **Replace Values** functions the same way in Power Query as it does in Excel, except the transformation is stored and thus repeatable when created in Power Query.
- **Pivot Column** creates two new columns out of an existing category column (for example, we can pivot the Transaction_Type column by the transaction amount.
- The **Date** button will allow you to transform an existing date column into a date part (year, month, day, etc.) or change the date format. It is also useful to create duplicates of existing date columns, then transform the copies into the date parts.

AFTER LOADING THE DATA INTO EXCEL: HOW TO CONTINUE WORKING WITH YOUR DATA

Once you are finished transforming your data in the Power Query Editor and you click the Close & Load button, your data will begin to load into a worksheet.

What to Do if the Load to the Worksheet Fails

This process may take several minutes depending on how large of a datafile you are loading.

Sometimes, the query load will fail—this will often occur due to an attempt to load more than 1,048,576 records. If the load fails, you can hover over the error message to view what caused the error. In this case, the query result was too large, so we can select **Load to Data Model.**

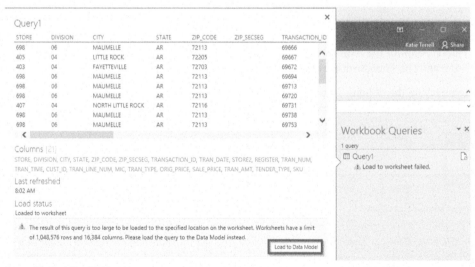

Source: Microsoft Excel 2016

Loading the data to the data model will allow us to work with a large dataset in a PivotTable, even though the dataset itself is too large for the worksheet.

How to Return to the Power Query Window after Closing It

If you wish to further transform your data using the Power Query window, you can do so by double-clicking on the Query label in the Workbook Queries window (if the Workbook Queries pane is not showing, you can click the Data tab on the ribbon, then click **Show Queries**).

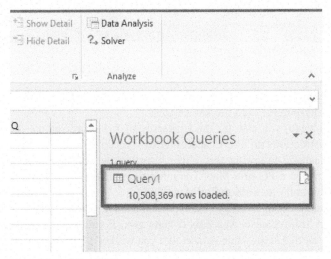

Source: Microsoft Excel 2016

Appendix G

Tableau

Before jumping into the labs, you may wish to introduce yourself to Tableau through this appendix if you have never used the Tableau tool.

To access Tableau, you can use the University of Arkansas' remote desktop (see your instructor for instructions on how to access it), or you can download a free academic usage license of Tableau by following this URL: https://www.tableau.com/academic/students. Tableau will work on a PC or a Mac. The images in this textbook will reflect Tableau for PC, but it is very similar to Tableau for Mac.

Tableau can connect to a variety of datatypes, including Excel, Access, and SQL Server. We will connect to the dataset **Appendix G Data.xlsx.** If you worked through Appendix C about PivotTables, this is the same dataset that you worked with previously.

1. Open **Tableau.**
2. Immediately upon opening Tableau, you will see a list of file types that you can connect to. We'll connect to an Excel file, so click Microsoft Excel.

©Tableau Software, Inc. All rights reserved.

3. Navigate to where your file is stored and click **Open.**

Tableau automatically detects the data types of the attributes you import. In this dataset, the attributes probably all imported as the data type you would expect. Notice that the first two, Invoice # and Customer # imported as number. Continue looking at the attributes, and you will notice the **globe** icon above **Zip Code.** This is Tableau showing you one of its best features, it shows that the **Zip Code** data was imported as geographic data. This will allow you to create maps.

Sheet1 Invoice #	Sheet1 Customer #	Sheet1 Zip Code	Sheet1 Date of Sale	Sheet1 SKU	Sheet1 Description	Sheet1 Quantity (P...	Sheet1 Sales	Sheet1 Cost	Sheet1 Gross Margin
3,069	2,047	67838	3/4/2021	FRT-APO	Apricot	50	140.020	88.0100	52.0100
3,026	2,088	67004	3/1/2021	FRT-FII	Fig	50	120.520	77.5100	43.0100
3,043	2,087	67731	3/2/2021	FRT-TAN	Tamarind	50	109.520	69.0100	40.5100

©Tableau Software, Inc. All rights reserved.

4. To begin working with the data, click **Sheet 1** in the bottom left.

©Tableau Software, Inc. All rights reserved.

Here is a quick introduction to pieces of the Tableau canvass:

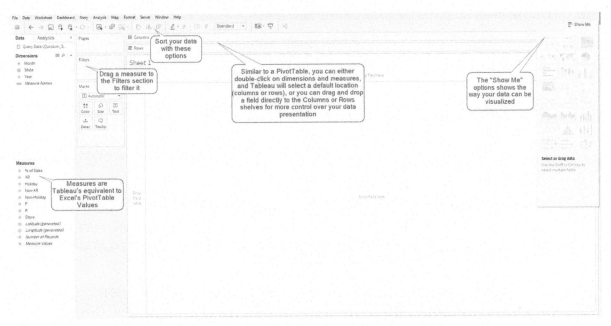

©Tableau Software, Inc. All rights reserved.

5. To begin working with the data, double-click on the measure **Gross Margin.**

©Tableau Software, Inc. All rights reserved.

Immediately you will see how Tableau interacts with data differently than Excel because it has defaulted to displaying a bar chart. This isn't a very meaningful chart as it is, but you can add meaning by adding a dimension.

6. Double-click **Description** from the dimensions.

Similar to the analysis found in Appendix C regarding PivotTables, you find the same numbers: Apples with a gross margin of 140.4, apricots with a gross margin of 78.0, and so on.

7. To make this data easier to interpret, you can sort it. Click the **Sort Descending** icon to sort the data.

©Tableau Software, Inc. All rights reserved.

You can continue adding pills to the columns or rows shelves and changing the method of visualization using the Show Me tab to further familiarize yourself with the tool.

Appendix H

SQL Part 2

In Appendix D, you learned about many key terms in SQL, including how to join tables. The purpose of joining tables is to enable you to retrieve data that is stored in more than one table all at once. The join type that you learned about in Appendix D is an INNER JOIN. There are two other popular join types, though, LEFT and RIGHT.

We will work with the same Access Database that you used in Appendix D. Although it contains the same data, you can access it through the Appendix H Data.accdb.

We'll start with bringing this data into Tableau.

1. Open Tableau.
2. Select **Microsoft Access** to connect to the file and navigate to where you have stored the file, then click **Open**.
3. In the Data Source view, drag both the Customers table and the Sales_Orders tables to the **Drag tables here** section.

EXPLANATION OF INNER JOINS

Notice the Venn diagram that appears connecting the two tables:

©Tableau Software, Inc. All rights reserved.

And if you click the Venn diagram, you can see the following details about how the tables are related:

©Tableau Software, Inc. All rights reserved.

Tableau has defaulted to joining these two tables with an INNER join, and it has accurately identified the two keys that are related between the two tables, Customer ID in the Customers table, and CustomerID in the Sales Order table.

This is very similar to how you would write a query to gather the same information directly in the Access database, where one of the tables is indicated in the FROM clause, the second table is indicated in the INNER JOIN clause, and the keys that are common between the two tables are indicated with an equal sign between them in the ON clause:

```
SELECT *
FROM Customers
INNER JOIN Sales_Orders
ON Customers.CustomerID = Sales_Orders.CustomerID
```

As the Venn diagram suggests, an INNER join will show all of the data for which there is a match between the two tables. However, it is important to notice what that means it leaves out – it will not return any of the data for which there is NOT a match between the two tables.

In this instance, there is actually one customer held in the Customers table that is not included in the Sales_Orders table (Customer 3, Edna Orgeron). Why would this happen? Perhaps this fictional company records data on potential customers, so even though someone may have not actually purchased anything yet, the company can still contact them. Whatever the reason might be—the fact that CustomerID 3 does not exist in both tables—CustomerID 3 will not be included in the results.

If the above SQL query were to be run, the following result would return:

Customers.C	FirstName	LastName	City	State	Phone_Num	Sales_Order	Order_Date	InventoryID	Quantity_Sol	Price	Sales_Order:
1 Paula	George	Oklahoma City	Oklahoma	405-208-4800	8	2019-03-14	I-3	1	$6,750.00	1
2 Terry	Herman	Austin	Texas	512-471-3333	1	2018-11-30	I-2	2	$395.00	2
4 Jeremy	Jones	Dallas	Texas	817-892-4000	2	2018-12-20	I-1	1	$495.00	4
5 Pamela	Subban	Nashville	Tennessee	615-770-2000	4	2019-01-02	I-4	6	$1,250.00	5
6 Gary	Decker	Rogers	Arkansas	479-621-1117	7	2019-03-01	I-6	1	$2,450.00	6
7 Jenna	Carter	Memphis	Tennessee	901-888-4667	10	2019-04-05	I-5	3	$153.00	7
8 Thomas	Green	Little Rock	Arkansas	501-663-6385	9	2019-04-01	I-1	2	$495.00	8
9 Linda	Edwards	Kansas City	Missouri	816-920-4237	3	2018-12-31	I-7	3	$1,450.00	9
9 Linda	Edwards	Kansas City	Missouri	816-920-4237	5	2019-01-02	I-3	4	$6,750.00	9
10 Nick	Sadan	Tuscaloosa	Alabama	205-348-3697	6	2019-02-14	I-5	7	$153.00	10
* (New)						(New)				

Source: SQL

Notice that the red box surrounding the records for customers 2 and 4 do not include anything for customer 3.

EXPLANATION OF LEFT JOINS

If we wanted to see all of the data from the Customers table, even if there isn't a match in the Sales_Order table, then we need to change our join type.

Back to the Tableau image—if we click into the Venn Diagram, we can change the join type to a LEFT join.

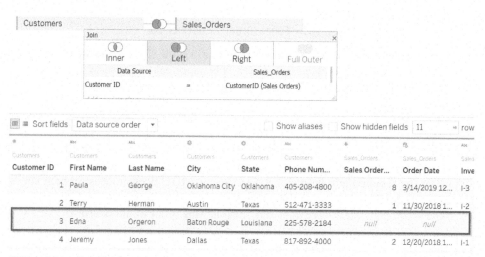

©Tableau Software, Inc. All rights reserved.

The red box indicates an important change that occurs as soon as you we made the change to a LEFT join—Customer 3 is included! But not only that, while we see Customer 3's name and contact information, we see *null* values for any attributes from the Sales_Order table. That is because there isn't any corresponding information for Customer 3 in the Sales_Order table.

To replicate this query in Access, the only change that needs to be made is swap the word INNER with LEFT:

```
SELECT *
FROM Customers
LEFT JOIN Sales_Orders
ON Customers.CustomerID = Sales_Orders.CustomerID
```

It is easier to visualize how joins are created in Tableau, but they work the same way in SQL. The table that you place in the FROM clause is the "left" table, and the table that you place in the JOIN clause is the "right table."

EXPLANATION OF RIGHT JOINS

Looking back to the Venn diagram, we can see that a RIGHT join would return the opposite result of a left join. In this specific instance, if there were any Sales_Orders that had a CustomerID on them that were not associated with a CustomerID in the Customers table, the only we would see them is if we created a RIGHT join.

We dive more deeply into this concept in the text when we discuss audit analytics, but perhaps you can already imagine how this type of join would be useful for detecting errors or fraud—we definitely would want to isolate any sales orders that had Customer information on them that didn't align with our verified customer listing!

Appendix I

Power BI

Power BI Desktop is a Microsoft tool that combines ETL tools with reporting tools. When we work with Power Query or PowerPivot in Excel, we're actually working with Power BI tools. If you will ultimately want to run statistical tests such as hypothesis testing or regression analysis, it's best to work within Excel directly and use the Power Query add-in. However, if you need to transform your data using Power Query prior to creating reports or dashboards or even if you just want to explore your data, Power BI Desktop can be a great alternative to other reporting and visualization tools such as Tableau.

When it comes to creating visualizations in Power BI, you can create extremely similar results to what you can create in Tableau, but the path to getting there is different. Power BI defaults to a report mode (similar to Tableau's Dashboard mode), so that as you create visuals, they appear as tiles that you can resize and rearrange around the canvas.

When you open Power BI Desktop, you will be greeted with a startup screen similar to the following:

Source: Powe BI Desktop

The tutorials and other training resources on the right of the startup screen are helpful for getting started with the tool.

The Get Data button on the left of the startup screen will bring you into Power BI's Power Query tool. It is set up exactly like the Power Query tool is set up in Excel, so you can use it to connect to a variety of sources (Excel, SQL Server, Access, etc.).

To familiarize yourself with Power BI, we will use the Appendix I data.xlsx. It is a modified version of the Slainte_Subset file that you might work with in Lab 2-2, Lab 4-2, or Lab 6-2. The data are a subset of the sales data related to a fictional brewery named Slainte.

1. Click **Get Data** on the startup screen.
2. Select **Excel** from the list of possible data sources, then click **Connect.**

Source: Microsoft Excel 2016

3. Browse to the file location for Power BI_Appendix.xlsx and **Open** the file.
4. Because there are three spreadsheets in the file, the Navigator provides you the option to select 1, 2, or all of the spreadsheets. Place checkmarks in each.
5. You are also given an option to either Load or Edit the data. If you click Edit, you will enter the Power Query window with the same ribbon and options to transform the data as you are familiar with from the Excel version of the tool (add columns, split columns, pivot data, etc.). This data does not need to be transformed, so we will click **Load.**

6. Once the data is loaded, you will see a blank canvas on which you can build a report. There are three key elements bordering the canvas:

   a. To the left of the blank canvas, you are presented with three options:

Source: Microsoft Excel 2016

Report Mode: The first option, represented with an icon that looks like a bar chart, is for Report mode. This is the default view and is where you can build your visualizations and explore your data.

Data Mode: The second option, represented with an icon that looks like a table or a spreadsheet, is for Data mode. If you click into this icon, you can view the raw data that you have imported into Power BI. You can also create new measures or new columns from this mode.

Model Mode: The third option, which looks like a database diagram, is for Model mode. If you click into this icon, you enter PowerPivot. From this mode, you can edit the table and attribute names or edit relationships between tables.

b. To the right of the blank canvas is your Fields list and your options for Visualizations.

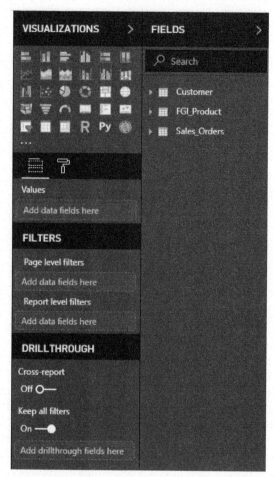

Source: Powe BI Desktop

Visualizations: You can drag any of these options over into the canvas to begin designing a visualization. Once you have tiles on your report, you can change the type of visualization being used to depict a set of fields by clicking the tile then selecting any of the visualization options to change the way the data is presented.
Fields: This section is similar to your PivotTable field list. You can expand the tables to see the attributes that are within each and placing a check mark in the fields will add them to an active tile.
Values, Filters, etc.: this section will vary based on the tile and the fields you are actively working with. Any time you add a field to a visualization, that field gets automatically added to the filters, which cuts out the need to manually add filters or slicers to your PivotTable.
c. Immediately above the canvas is the familiar ribbon that you can expect from Microsoft applications. The four tabs—Home, View, Modeling, and Help—stay consistent across the three different modes (report, data, and model), but the options that you can select will vary based on the mode in which you are working.

7. To begin working with the data, Expand the Customer table to place a checkmark in the
   State field.

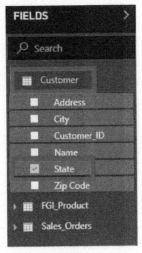

Source: Powe BI Desktop

8. Power BI will default to creating a tile with a map visualization. This is similar to how
   Tableau defaults to working with geographic data. To make the map more interesting,
   expand the Sales_Orders table to place a checkmark in the **Quantity Sold** field.

Source: Powe BI Desktop

This will make the tile more interesting by changing the size of the symbol associated with each state–the larger the symbol, the higher the quantity sold in that state.

9. You can also change the way the data is presented by selecting a different visualization type. Select the first option to view the data in a horizontal bar chart.

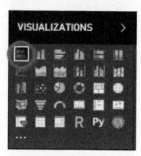

Source: Powe BI Desktop

10. One of the most exciting offerings from Power BI is its natural language processing for data exploration. From the Home tab in the ribbon, click **Buttons.** In the drop-down, select **Q&A.**

Source: Microsoft Excel 2016

11. The following icon will appear as a separate tile. If the placement defaults to being on top of the bar chart, you can click and drag it to somewhere else on the canvas:

Source: Powe BI Desktop

12. To activate the Q&A, **ctrl + click** the icon. The following window will pop-up, and you can select from the list of questions that Power BI has come up with, or you can type directly into the "Ask a question about your data" box.

Questions to get you started	
total sales order product sale price	
how many states are there	
what is the most recent sales order	
show FGI products and FGI product product sale prices	
top sales orders by quantity sold	
how many customers are there	
customers sorted by customer ID	
total sales order product sale price by quantity sold	
number of sales orders over time	
count sales orders over time	

Ask a question about your data

Ask a related question   Clear

Source: Microsoft Excel 2016

13. You can also add a question directly to the canvas by selecting **Ask a Question** from the Home tab on the ribbon. In the screenshot that follows, I typed "sum of quantity sold by state" to get a replicated visualization of the first visualization we made by manually selecting the fields State and Quantity Sold:

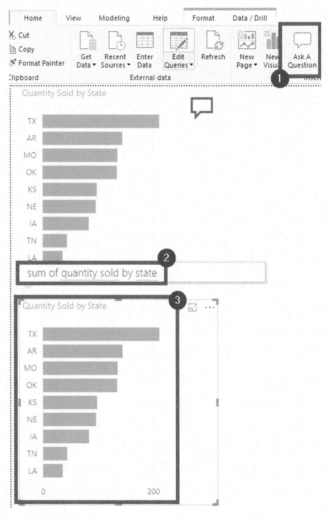

Source: Powe BI Desktop

There are many other exciting benefits that Power BI can do, but with this introduction you should have the confidence to jump in and explore more that Power BI has to offer. To get more step-by-step help with Power BI, you can work through the final portion of Lab 4-3, which replicates a Tableau lab in Power BI.

Dillard's ER Diagram

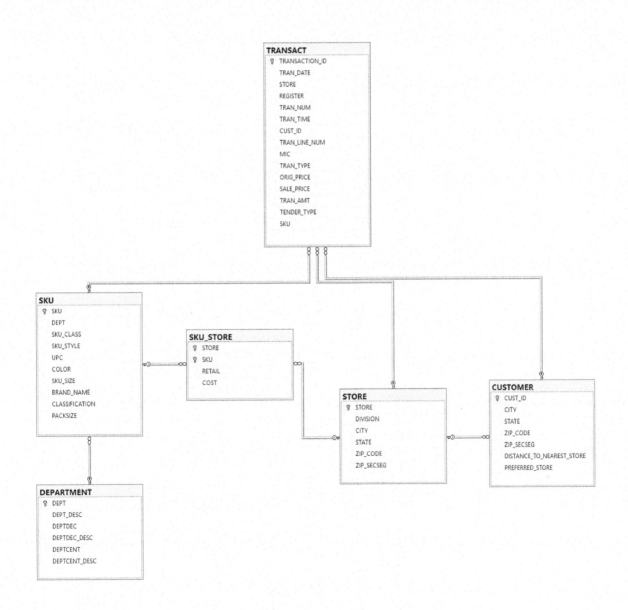

Appendix K
Data Dictionaries

This appendix contains the data dictionary and validation statistics for the datasets used in this textbook.
- CollegeScorecard
- Lending Club
- OK PCard

COLLEGESCORECARD

Attribute	Description
UNITID	A unique identifier for the institution
INSTNM	Institution name
CITY	City
STABBR	State postcode
CONTROL	1 = Public. 2 = Private nonprofit. 3 = Private for-profit
CCBASIC	Carnegie Classification, basic: −2 Not applicable 0 (Not classified) 1 Associate's Colleges: High Transfer-High Traditional 2 Associate's Colleges: High Transfer-Mixed Traditional/Nontraditional 3 Associate's Colleges: High Transfer-High Nontraditional 4 Associate's Colleges: Mixed Transfer/Vocational & Technical-High Traditional 5 Associate's Colleges: Mixed Transfer/Vocational & Technical-Mixed Traditional/Nontraditional 6 Associate's Colleges: Mixed Transfer/Vocational & Technical-High Nontraditional 7 Associate's Colleges: High Vocational & Technical-High Traditional 8 Associate's Colleges: High Vocational & Technical-Mixed Traditional/Nontraditional 9 Associate's Colleges: High Vocational & Technical-High Nontraditional 10 Special Focus Two-Year: Health Professions 11 Special Focus Two-Year: Technical Professions 12 Special Focus Two-Year: Arts & Design 13 Special Focus Two-Year: Other Fields 14 Baccalaureate/Associate's Colleges: Associate's Dominant 15 Doctoral Universities: Highest Research Activity

Attribute	Description
	16 Doctoral Universities: Higher Research Activity
	17 Doctoral Universities: Moderate Research Activity
	18 Master's Colleges & Universities: Larger Programs
	19 Master's Colleges & Universities: Medium Programs
	20 Master's Colleges & Universities: Small Programs
	21 Baccalaureate Colleges: Arts & Sciences Focus
	22 Baccalaureate Colleges: Diverse Fields
	23 Baccalaureate/Associate's Colleges: Mixed Baccalaureate/Associate's
	24 Special Focus Four-Year: Faith-Related Institutions
	25 Special Focus Four-Year: Medical Schools & Centers
	26 Special Focus Four-Year: Other Health Professions Schools
	27 Special Focus Four-Year: Engineering Schools
	28 Special Focus Four-Year: Other Technology-Related Schools
	29 Special Focus Four-Year: Business & Management Schools
	30 Special Focus Four-Year: Arts, Music & Design Schools
	31 Special Focus Four-Year: Law Schools
	32 Special Focus Four-Year: Other Special Focus Institutions
	33 Tribal Colleges
ADM_RATE	Admission rate
SAT_AVG	Average equivalent SAT of students admitted
UGDS	Enrollment of undergraduate certificate/degree-seeking students
UGDS_WHITE	Total share of enrollment of undergraduates who are White
UGDS_BLACK	Total share of enrollment of undergraduates who are Black
UGDS_HISP	Total share of enrollment of undergraduates who are Hispanic
UGDS_ASIAN	Total share of enrollment of undergraduates who are Asian
UGDS_AIAN	Total share of enrollment of undergraduates who are American Indian/Alaska Native
UGDS_NHPI	Total share of enrollment of undergraduates who are Native Hawaiian/Pacific Islander
UGDS_2MOR	Total share of enrollment of undergraduates who are two or more races
UGDS_NRA	Total share of enrollment of undergraduates who are nonresident aliens
UGDS_UNKN	Total share of enrollment of undergraduates whose race is unknown
PPTUG_EF	Share of undergraduate degree/certificate-seeking students who are part-time
NPT4_PUB	Average net price for Title IV institutions (public)
NPT4_PRIV	Average net price for Title IV institutions (private for-profit and nonprofit)
COSTT4_A	Average cost of attendance
TUITFTE	Net tuition revenue per full-time equivalent student
INEXPFTE	Instructional expenditures per full-time equivalent student
PFTFAC	Proportion of faculty that is full-time
PCTPELL	Percentage of undergraduates who receive a Pell Grant
C150_4	Completion rate for first-time, full-time students at four-year institutions (six-year)
PFTFTUG1_EF	Share of undergraduate students who are first-time, full-time, degree seeking undergraduates
RET_FT4	First-time, full-time student retention rate at four-year institutions
PCTFLOAN	Percent of all federal undergraduates receiving a federal student loan

LENDING CLUB

LoanStats

LoanStatNew	Description
acc_now_delinq	The number of accounts on which the borrower is now delinquent
acc_open_past_24mths	Number of trades opened in past 24 months
addr_state	The state provided by the borrower in the loan application
all_util	Balance to credit limit on all trades
annual_inc	The self-reported annual income provided by the borrower during registration
annual_inc_joint	The combined self-reported annual income provided by the co-borrowers during registration
application_type	Indicates whether the loan is an individual application or a joint application with two co-borrowers
avg_cur_bal	Average current balance of all accounts
bc_open_to_buy	Total open to buy on revolving bankcards
bc_util	Ratio of total current balance to high credit/credit limit for all bankcard accounts.
chargeoff_within_12_mths	Number of charge-offs within 12 months
collection_recovery_fee	post charge off collection fee
collections_12_mths_ex_med	Number of collections in 12 months excluding medical collections
delinq_2yrs	The number of 30+ days past-due incidences of delinquency in the borrower's credit file for the past 2 years
delinq_amnt	The past-due amount owed for the accounts on which the borrower is now delinquent.
desc	Loan description provided by the borrower
dti	A ratio calculated using the borrower's total monthly debt payments on the total debt obligations, excluding mortgage and the requested LC loan, divided by the borrower's self-reported monthly income
dti_joint	A ratio calculated using the co-borrowers' total monthly payments on the total debt obligations, excluding mortgages and the requested LC loan, divided by the co-borrowers' combined self-reported monthly income
earliest_cr_line	The month the borrower's earliest reported credit line was opened
emp_length	Employment length in years. Possible values are between 0 and 10 where 0 means less than one year and 10 means 10 or more years.
emp_title	The job title supplied by the borrower when applying for the loan.*
fico_range_high	The upper boundary range the borrower's FICO at loan origination belongs to
fico_range_low	The lower boundary range the borrower's FICO at loan origination belongs to
funded_amnt	The total amount committed to that loan at that point in time

LoanStatNew	Description
funded_amnt_inv	The total amount committed by investors for that loan at that point in time
grade	LC assigned loan grade
home_ownership	The home ownership status provided by the borrower during registration or obtained from the credit report; our values are RENT, OWN, MORTGAGE, OTHER
id	A unique LC assigned ID for the loan listing
il_util	Ratio of total current balance to high credit/credit limit on all install accounts
initial_list_status	The initial listing status of the loan; possible values are W, F
inq_fi	Number of personal finance inquiries
inq_last_12m	Number of credit inquiries in past 12 months
inq_last_6mths	The number of inquiries in past 6 months (excluding auto and mortgage inquiries)
installment	The monthly payment owed by the borrower if the loan originates
int_rate	Interest rate on the loan
issue_d	The month in which the loan was funded
last_credit_pull_d	The most recent month LC pulled credit for this loan
last_fico_range_high	The upper boundary range the borrower's last FICO pulled belongs to
last_fico_range_low	The lower boundary range the borrower's last FICO pulled belongs to
last_pymnt_amnt	Last total payment amount received
last_pymnt_d	Last month payment was received
loan_amnt	The listed amount of the loan applied for by the borrower. If at some point in time, the credit department reduces the loan amount, then it will be reflected in this value.
loan_status	Current status of the loan
max_bal_bc	Maximum current balance owed on all revolving accounts
member_id	A unique LC assigned Id for the borrower member
mo_sin_old_il_acct	Months since oldest bank installment account opened
mo_sin_old_rev_tl_op	Months since oldest revolving account opened
mo_sin_rcnt_rev_tl_op	Months since most recent revolving account opened
mo_sin_rcnt_tl	Months since most recent account opened
mort_acc	Number of mortgage accounts
mths_since_last_delinq	The number of months since the borrower's last delinquency
mths_since_last_major_derog	Months since most recent 90-day or worse rating
mths_since_last_record	The number of months since the last public record.
mths_since_rcnt_il	Months since most recent installment accounts opened
mths_since_recent_bc	Months since most recent bankcard account opened.
mths_since_recent_bc_dlq	Months since most recent bankcard delinquency
mths_since_recent_inq	Months since most recent inquiry.
mths_since_recent_revol_delinq	Months since most recent revolving delinquency.
next_pymnt_d	Next scheduled payment date

(Continued)

LoanStatNew	Description
num_accts_ever_120_pd	Number of accounts ever 120 or more days past due
num_actv_bc_tl	Number of currently active bankcard accounts
num_actv_rev_tl	Number of currently active revolving trades
num_bc_sats	Number of satisfactory bankcard accounts
num_bc_tl	Number of bankcard accounts
num_il_tl	Number of installment accounts
num_op_rev_tl	Number of open revolving accounts
num_rev_accts	Number of revolving accounts
num_rev_tl_bal_gt_0	Number of revolving trades with balance >0
num_sats	Number of satisfactory accounts
num_tl_120dpd_2m	Number of accounts currently 120 days past due (updated in past 2 months)
num_tl_30dpd	Number of accounts currently 30 days past due (updated in past 2 months)
num_tl_90g_dpd_24m	Number of accounts 90 or more days past due in last 24 months
num_tl_op_past_12m	Number of accounts opened in past 12 months
open_acc	The number of open credit lines in the borrower's credit file
open_acc_6m	Number of open trades in last 6 months
open_il_12m	Number of installment accounts opened in past 12 months
open_il_24m	Number of installment accounts opened in past 24 months
open_act_il	Number of currently active installment trades
open_rv_12m	Number of revolving trades opened in past 12 months
open_rv_24m	Number of revolving trades opened in past 24 months
out_prncp	Remaining outstanding principal for total amount funded
out_prncp_inv	Remaining outstanding principal for portion of total amount funded by investors
pct_tl_nvr_dlq	Percent of trades never delinquent
percent_bc_gt_75	Percentage of all bankcard accounts > 75% of limit
policy_code	Publicly available policy_code=1;new products not publicly available policy_code=2
pub_rec	Number of derogatory public records
pub_rec_bankruptcies	Number of public record bankruptcies
purpose	A category provided by the borrower for the loan request.
pymnt_plan	Indicates if a payment plan has been put in place for the loan
recoveries	Post charge-off gross recovery
revol_bal	Total credit revolving balance
revol_util	Revolving line utilization rate, or the amount of credit the borrower is using relative to all available revolving credit.
sub_grade	LC assigned loan subgrade
tax_liens	Number of tax liens
term	The number of payments on the loan; values are in months and can be either 36 or 60
title	The loan title provided by the borrower
tot_coll_amt	Total collection amounts ever owed

LoanStatNew	Description
tot_cur_bal	Total current balance of all accounts
tot_hi_cred_lim	Total high credit/credit limit
total_acc	The total number of credit lines currently in the borrower's credit file
total_bal_ex_mort	Total credit balance excluding mortgage
total_bal_il	Total current balance of all installment accounts
total_bc_limit	Total bankcard high credit/credit limit
total_cu_tl	Number of finance trades
total_il_high_credit_limit	Total installment high credit/credit limit
total_pymnt	Payments received to date for total amount funded
total_pymnt_inv	Payments received to date for portion of total amount funded by investors
total_rec_int	Interest received to date
total_rec_late_fee	Late fees received to date
total_rec_prncp	Principal received to date
total_rev_hi_lim	Total revolving high credit/credit limit
url	URL for the LC page with listing data
verification_status	Indicates if income was verified by LC, not verified, or if the income source was verified
verified_status_joint	Indicates if the co-borrowers' joint income was verified by LC, not verified, or if the income source was verified
zip_code	The first 3 numbers of the zip code provided by the borrower in the loan application.
revol_bal_joint	Sum of revolving credit balance of the co-borrowers, net of duplicate balances
sec_app_fico_range_low	FICO range (high) for the secondary applicant
sec_app_fico_range_high	FICO range (low) for the secondary applicant
sec_app_earliest_cr_line	Earliest credit line at time of application for the secondary applicant
sec_app_inq_last_6mths	Credit inquiries in the last 6 months at time of application for the secondary applicant
sec_app_mort_acc	Number of mortgage accounts at time of application for the secondary applicant
sec_app_open_acc	Number of open trades at time of application for the secondary applicant
sec_app_revol_util	Ratio of total current balance to high credit/credit limit for all revolving accounts
sec_app_open_act_il	Number of currently active installment trades at time of application for the secondary applicant
sec_app_num_rev_accts	Number of revolving accounts at time of application for the secondary applicant
sec_app_chargeoff_within_12_mths	Number of charge-offs within last 12 months at time of application for the secondary applicant
sec_app_collections_12_mths_ex_med	Number of collections within last 12 months excluding medical collections at time of application for the secondary applicant
sec_app_mths_since_last_major_derog	Months since most recent 90-day or worse rating at time of application for the secondary applicant

(Continued)

LoanStatNew	Description
hardship_flag	Flags whether or not the borrower is on a hardship plan
hardship_type	Describes the hardship plan offering
hardship_reason	Describes the reason the hardship plan was offered
hardship_status	Describes if the hardship plan is active, pending, canceled, completed, or broken
deferral_term	Amount of months that the borrower is expected to pay less than the contractual monthly payment amount due to a hardship plan
hardship_amount	The interest payment that the borrower has committed to make each month while they are on a hardship plan
hardship_start_date	The start date of the hardship plan period
hardship_end_date	The end date of the hardship plan period
payment_plan_start_date	The day the first hardship plan payment is due—for example, if a borrower has a hardship plan period of 3 months, the start date is the start of the three-month period in which the borrower is allowed to make interest-only payments
hardship_length	The number of months the borrower will make smaller payments than normally obligated due to a hardship plan
hardship_dpd	Account days past due as of the hardship plan start date
hardship_loan_status	Loan status as of the hardship plan start date
orig_projected_additional_accrued_interest	The original projected additional interest amount that will accrue for the given hardship payment plan as of the Hardship Start Date; this field will be null if the borrower has broken his/her hardship payment plan
hardship_payoff_balance_amount	The payoff balance amount as of the hardship plan start date
hardship_last_payment_amount	The last payment amount as of the hardship plan start date
disbursement_method	The method by which the borrower receives his/her loan; possible values are CASH, DIRECT_PAY
debt_settlement_flag	Flags whether or not the borrower, who has charged-off, is working with a debt-settlement company.
debt_settlement_flag_date	The most recent date that the Debt_Settlement_Flag has been set
settlement_status	The status of the borrower's settlement plan; possible values are COMPLETE, ACTIVE, BROKEN, CANCELLED, DENIED, DRAFT
settlement_date	The date that the borrower agrees to the settlement plan
settlement_amount	The loan amount that the borrower has agreed to settle for
settlement_percentage	The settlement amount as a percentage of the payoff balance amount on the loan
settlement_term	The number of months that the borrower will be on the settlement plan

RejectStats

RejectStats File	Description
Amount Requested	The total amount requested by the borrower
Application Date	The date which the borrower applied
Loan Title	The loan title provided by the borrower
Risk_Score	For applications prior to November 5, 2013, the risk score is the borrower's FICO score; for applications after November 5, 2013, the risk score is the borrower's Vantage score
Debt-To-Income Ratio	A ratio calculated using the borrower's total monthly debt payments on the total debt obligations, excluding mortgage and the requested LC loan, divided by the borrower's self-reported monthly income
Zip Code	The first 3 numbers of the zip code provided by the borrower in the loan application
State	The state provided by the borrower in the loan application
Employment Length	Employment length in years; possible values are between 0 and 10, where 0 means less than one year and 10 means 10 or more years.
Policy Code	publicly available policy_code=1;new products not publicly available policy_code=2

OK PCARD

Attribute	Description
SourceYearMonth	Year and month of the transaction
SourceType	Data source, e.g. Bank
CardholderLastName	Cardholder's last name
CardholderFirstInitial	Cardholder's first initial
ItemDescription	Description of item purchased
Amount	Purchase amount in U.S. dollars
BusinessUnit	Identifier for business unite
MerchantName	Supplier's name, provided by the issuing bank
TransactionDate	Date of purchase
PostedDate	Date of transaction posting to account
MCCDescription	Merchant Category Code, provided by the issuing bank

Glossary

2018 Tax Cuts and Jobs Act Tax Reform *(366)* Tax legislation offering a major change to the existing tax code.

A

audit data standards (ADS) *(205)* The audit data standards define common tables and fields that are needed by auditors to perform common audit tasks. The AICPA developed these standards.

B

Balanced Scorecard *(271)* A particular type of digital dashboard that is made up of strategic objectives, as well as KPIs, target measures, and initiatives, to help the organization reach its target measures in line with strategic goals.

Benford's law *(103)* An observation about the frequency of leading digits in many real-life sets of numerical data. The law states that in many naturally occurring collections of numbers, the significant lending digit is likely to be small.

Big Data *(4)* Datasets that are too large and complex for businesses' existing systems to handle utilizing their traditional capabilities to capture, store, manage, and analyze these datasets.

C

causal modeling *(106)* A data approach similar to regression, but used when the relationship between independent and dependent variables where it is hypothesized that the independent variables cause or are associated with the dependent variable.

classification *(9, 106)* A data approach that attempts to assign each unit in a population into a few categories potentially to help with predictions.

clustering *(10, 106)* A data approach that attempts to divide individuals (like customers) into groups (or clusters) in a useful or meaningful way.

co-occurrence grouping *(10)* A data approach that attempts to discover associations between individuals based on transactions involving them.

common data model *(10, 103)* A tool used to map existing database tables and fields from various systems to a standardized set of tables and fields for use with analytics.

common size financial statement *(328)* A type of financial statement that contains only basic accounts that are common across companies.

composite primary key *(43)* A special case of a primary key that exists in linking tables. The composite primary key is made up of the two primary keys in the table that it is linking.

computer-assisted audit techniques (CAATs) *(228)* Automated scripts that can be used to validate data, test controls, and enable substantive testing of transaction details or account balances and generate supporting evidence for the audit.

continuous auditing *(208)* A process that provides real-time assurance over business processes and systems.

continuous data *(143)* One way to categorize quantitative data, as opposed to discrete data. Continuous data can take on any value within a range. An example of continuous data is height.

continuous monitoring *(208)* A process that constantly evaluates internal controls and transactions and is the chief responsibility of management.

continuous reporting *(208)* A process that provides real-time access to the system status and accounting information.

D

Data Analytics *(4)* The process of evaluating data with the purpose of drawing conclusions to address business questions. Indeed, effective Data Analytics provides a way to search through large structured and unstructured data to identify unknown patterns or relationships.

data dictionary *(14, 44)* Centralized repository of descriptions for all of the data attributes of the dataset.

data mart *(365)* A subset of the data warehouse focused on a specific function or department to assist and support its needed data requirements.

data reduction *(10, 98)* A data approach that attempts to reduce the amount of information that needs to be considered to focus on the most critical items (i.e., highest cost, highest risk, largest impact, etc.).

data request form *(47)* A method for obtaining data if you do not have access to obtain the data directly yourself.

data warehouse *(204, 365)* A data warehouse is a repository of data accumulated from internal and external data sources, including financial data, to help management decision making.

decision boundaries *(109)*   Technique used to mark the split between one class and another.

Decision support system *(112)*   An information system that supports decision-making activity within a business by combining data and expertise to solve problems and perform calculations.

decision tree *(109)*   Tool used to divide data into smaller groups.

declarative visualizations *(144)*   Made when the aim of your project is to "declare" or present your findings to an audience. Charts that are declarative are typically made after the data analysis has been completed and are meant to exhibit what was found in the analysis steps.

descriptive analytics *(94, 228)*   Procedures that summarize existing data to determine what has happened in the past. Some examples include summary statistics (e.g. Count, Min, Max, Average, Median), distributions, and proportions.

descriptive attributes *(43)*   Attributes that exist in relational databases that are neither primary nor foreign keys. These attributes provide business information, but are not required to build a database. An example would be "Company Name" or "Employee Address."

diagnostic analytics *(94, 228)*   Procedures that explore the current data to determine why something has happened the way it has, typically comparing the data to a benchmark. As an example, these allow users to drill-down in the data and see how it compares to a budget, a competitor, or trend.

digital dashboard *(270)*   An interactive report showing the most important metrics to help users understand how a company or an organization is performing. Often created using Excel or Tableau.

discrete data *(143)*   One way to categorize quantitative data, as opposed to continuous data. Discrete data are represented by whole numbers. An example of discrete data is points in a basketball game.

DuPont ratio *(330)*   Ratios developed by the DuPont Corporation to decompose return on equity (ROE) into its component ratios: Profit margin x Asset turnover x Equity multiplier.

E

ETL *(45)*   The extract, transform, and load process that is integral to mastering the data.

exploratory visualizations *(144)*   Made when the lines between steps **P** (perform test plan), **A** (address and refine results), and **C** (communicate results) are not as clearly divided as they are in a declarative visualization project. Often when you are exploring the data with visualizations, you are performing the test plan directly in visualization software such as Tableau instead of creating the chart after the analysis has been done.

F

financial statement analysis *(328)*   Used by investors, analysts, auditors, and other interested stakeholders to review and evaluate a company's financial statements and financial performance.

flat file *(41, 204)*   A means of storing data in one place, such as in an Excel spreadsheet, as opposed to storing the data in multiple tables, such as in a relational database.

foreign key *(43)*   An attribute that exists in relational databases in order to carry out the relationship between two tables. This does not serve as the "unique identifier" for each record in a table. These must be identified when mastering the data from a relational database in order to extract the data correctly from more than one table.

fuzzy match *(124)*   A computer-assisted technique of finding matches that are less than 100 percent perfect by finding correspondencies between portions of the text of each potential match.

fuzzy matching *(229)*   Process that finds matches that may be less than 100 percent matching by finding correspondences between portions of the text or other entries.

H

heterogeneous systems approach *(204)*   Heterogeneous systems represent multiple installations or instances of a system. It would be considered the opposite of a homogeneous system.

homogeneous systems approach *(203)*   Homogeneous systems represent one single installation or instance of a system. It would be considered the opposite of a heterogeneous system.

horizontal analysis *(331)*   An analysis that shows the change of a value from one period to the next.

I

index *(332)*   A metric that shows how much any given subsequent year has changed relative to the base year.

interval data *(143)*   The third most sophisticated type of data on the scale of nominal, ordinal, interval, and ratio; a type of quantitative data. Interval data can be counted and grouped like qualitative data, and the differences between each data point are meaningful. However, interval data do not have a meaningful 0. In interval data, 0 does not mean "the absence of" but is simply another number. An example of interval data is the Fahrenheit scale of temperature measurement.

K

key performance indicator (KPI) *(269)*   A particular type of performance metric that an organization deems the most important and influential on decision making.

L

link prediction *(10, 106)*   A data approach that attempts to predict a relationship between two data items.

M

mastering the data *(40)*   The second step in the IMPACT cycle; it involves identifying and obtaining the data needed for solving the data analysis problem, as well as cleaning and preparing the data for analysis.

monetary unit sampling (MUS) *(234)*   Allows auditors to evaluate account balances. MUS is more likely to pull accounts with large balances (higher risk and exposure) because it focuses on dollars, not account numbers.

N

nominal data *(142)*   The least sophisticated type of data on the scale of nominal, ordinal, interval, and ratio; a type of qualitative data. The only thing you can do with nominal data is count, group, and take a proportion. Examples of nominal data are hair color, gender, and ethnic groups.

normal distribution *(143)*   A type of distribution in which the median, mean, and mode are all equal, so half of all the observations fall below the mean and the other half fall above the mean. This phenomenon is naturally occurring in many datasets in our world, such as SAT scores and heights and weights of newborn babies. When datasets follow a normal distribution, they can be standardized and compared for easier analysis.

O

ordinal data *(142)*   The second most sophisticated type of data on the scale of nominal, ordinal, interval, and ratio; a type of qualitative data. Ordinal can be counted and categorized like nominal data and the categories can also be ranked. Examples of ordinal data include gold, silver, and bronze medals.

P

performance metric *(268)*   Any calculation measuring how an organization is performing, particularly when that measure is compared to a baseline.

predictive analytics *(94, 228)*   Procedures used to generate a model that can be used to determine what is likely to happen in the future. Examples include regression analysis, forecasting, classification, and other predictive modeling.

predictor (or independent or explanatory) variable *(9)*   A variable that predicts or explains another variable, typically called a predictor or independent variable.

prescriptive analytics *(95, 228)*   Procedures that model data to enable recommendations for what should be done in the future. These typically include developing more advanced machine learning and artificial intelligence models to recommend a course of action based on a current problem.

primary key *(42)*   An attribute that is required to exist in each table of a relational database and serves as the "unique identifier" for each record in a table.

production or live systems *(204)*   Production (or live systems) are those active systems that collect and report and are directly affected by current transactions.

profiling *(10, 100)*   A data approach that attempts to characterize the "typical" behavior of an individual, group, or population by generating summary statistics about the data (including mean, standard deviations, etc.).

proportion *(142)*   The primary statistic used with quantitative data. Proportion is calculated by counting the number of items in a particular category, then dividing that number by the total number of observations.

Q

qualitative data *(142)*   Categorical data. All you can do with these data are count and group, and in some cases, you can rank the data. Qualitative data can be further defined in two ways: nominal data and ordinal data. There are not as many options for charting qualitative data because they are not as sophisticated as quantitative data.

quantitative data *(143)*   More complex than qualitative data. Quantitative data can be further defined in two ways: interval and ratio. In all quantitative data, the intervals between data points are meaningful, allowing the data to be not just counted, grouped, and ranked, but also to have more complex operations performed on them such as mean, median, and standard deviation.

R

ratio analysis *(328)*   A tool that attempts to evaluate relationships among different financial statement items to help understand a company's financial and operating performance.

ratio data *(143)*   The most sophisticated type of data on the scale of nominal, ordinal, interval, and ratio; a type of quantitative data. They can be counted and grouped just like qualitative data, and the differences between each data point are meaningful like with interval data. Additionally, ratio data have a meaningful 0. In other words, once a dataset approaches 0, 0 means "the absence of." An example of ratio data is currency.

regression *(9, 106)*   A data approach that attempts to estimate or predict, for each unit, the numerical value of some variable using some type of statistical model.

relational database *(41)*   A means of storing data in order to ensure that the data are complete, not redundant, and to help enforce business rules. Relational databases also aid in communication and integration of business processes across an organization.

response (or dependent) variable *(9)*   A variable that responds to, or is dependent on, another.

S

similarity matching *(10, 106)*   A data approach that attempts to identify similar individuals based on data known about them.

sparkline *(333)*   A small visual trendline or bar chart that efficiently summarizes numbers or statistics in a single spreadsheet cell.

standard normal distribution *(144)*   A special case of the normal distribution used for standardizing data. The standard normal distribution has 0 for its mean (and thus, for its mode and median, as well), and 1 for its standard deviation.

standardization *(144)*   The method used for comparing two datasets that follow the normal distribution. By using a formula, every normal distribution can be transformed into the standard normal distribution. If you standardize both datasets, you can place both distributions on the same chart and more swiftly come to your insights.

standardized metrics *(338)*   Metrics used by data vendors to allow easier comparison of company reported XBRL data.

structured data *(100)*   Data that are organized and reside in a fixed field with a record or a file. Such data are generally contained in a relational database or spreadsheet and are readily searchable by search algorithms.

summary statistics *(97)*   Describe the location, spread, shape, and dependence of a set of observations. These commonly include the count, sum, minimum, maximum, mean or average, standard deviation, median, quartiles,correlation covariance, and frequency that describe a specific measurable value.

supervised approach/method *(103)*   Approach used to learn more about the basic relationships between independent and dependent variables that are hypothesized to exist.

support vector machines *(110)*   A discriminating classifier that is defined by a separating hyperplane that works first to find the widest margin (or biggest pipe).

systems translator software *(204)*   Systems translator software maps the various tables and fields from varied ERP systems into a consistent format.

T

tax data mart *(365)*   A subset of a company-owned data warehouse focused on the specific needs of the tax department.

tax planning *(369)*   Predictive analysis of potential tax liability and the formulation of a plan to reduce the amount of taxes paid.

test data *(109)*   A set of data used to assess the degree and strength of a predicted relationship established by the analysis of training data.

training data *(109)*   Existing data that have been manually evaluated and assigned a class, which assists in classifying the test data.

U

unsupervised approach/method *(103)*   Approach used for data exploration looking for potential patterns of interest.

V

Vendor address - Warehouse address   Software such as Tableau can calculate distances, but it requires a little more work. See http://www.vizwiz.com/2012/01/tableau-tip-calculating-distance.html to learn how.

vertical analysis *(328)*   An analysis that shows the proportional value of accounts to a primary account, such as Revenue

W

what-if scenario analysis *(370)*   Evaluation of the impact of different tax scenarios/alternatives on various outcome measures including the amount of taxable income or tax paid.

X

XBRL *(99, 336)*   XBRL stands for eXtensible Business Reporting Language and is a type of XML (extensible markup language) used for organizing and defining financial elements.

XBRL (eXtensible Business Reporting Language) *(99)*   A global standard for exchanging financial reporting information that uses XML.

XBRL taxonomy *(336)*   Defines and describes each key data element (like cash or accounts payable). The taxonomy also defines the relationships between each element (like inventory is a component of current assets and current assets is a component of total assets).

XBRL-GL *(340)*   Stands for XBRL-General Ledger; relates to the ability of enterprise system to tag financial elements within the firm's financial reporting system.

Index

A

Access. *See* Microsoft Access
Accountants, skills for analytic, 12
Accounting
    analytic models for, 94–97
    auditing and, 5–6
    Data Analytics and, 5–7
    data reduction and, 98–100
    decision support systems and, 112–113
    regression approach, 108–109
    profiling example in management, 102
    summary statistics, 97–98
Accounting data, using/storing, 40–41
Account organization, XBRL
    taxonomy, 337
Accounts receivable
    Question 1.1: How Effectively Are We
        Collecting Our Cash?, 392–396
    Question 1.3: What Is the Total Revenue
        and Balance in Accounts
        Receivable, 398–399
ACL software, 230
Activity ratios, 329–330
Address and Refine Results
    audit data analytics and, 230
    Lab 2-2: Use PivotTables to Denormalize
        and Analyze the Data, 67
    Lab 2-6: Comprehensive Case: Dillard's
        Store Data: How to Create an
        Entity-Relationship Diagram, 78
    Lab 2-7: Comprehensive Case: Dillard's
        Store Data: How to Preview Data
        from Tables In a Query, 80
    Lab 2-8: Comprehensive Case: Dillard's
        Store Data: Connecting Excel to
        a SQL Database, 89–90
    Lab 3-3: Classification, 130
    Lab 3-4: Comprehensive Case: Dillard's
        Store Data: Data Abstract (SQL)
        and Regression (Part 1), 135
    Lab 3-5: Comprehensive Case: Dillard's
        Store Data: Data Abstract (SQL)
        and Regression (Part II), 137
    Lab 4-1: Use PivotCharts to Visualize
        Declarative Data, 166
    Lab 4-3: Comprehensive Case: Dillard's
        Store Data: Create Geographic
        Data Visualizations in Tableau
        and in Power BI, 188–196
    Lab 4-4: Comprehensive Case: Dillard's
        Store Data: Visualizing
        Regression in Tableau, 199
    Lab 6-1: Evaluate the Master Data for
        Interesting Addresses, 250

    Lab 6-4: Comprehensive Case: Dillard's
        Store Data: Hypothesis Testing
        (Part I), 263
    Lab 6-5: Comprehensive Case: Dillard's
        Store Data: Hypothesis Testing
        (Part II—Data Visualization), 265
    Lab 7-2: Create a Balanced Scorecard
        Dashboard in Tableau, 292
    Lab 7-6: Comprehensive Case: Dillard's
        Store Data: Creating KPIs in
        Excel (Part IV—Putting It All
        Together), 317–319
    Lab 8-1: Create a Horizontal and Vertical
        Analysis Using XBRL Data, 349
    Lab 8-4: Use SQL to Query an XBRL
        Database, 360
    Lab 9-3: Comprehensive Case 2: Dillard's
        Store Data: Calculate Sales Tax for
        Dillard's States Part 2—Compare
        Year over Year, 385–386
    Lab 9-5: Comprehensive Case 4: Dillard's
        Store Data: Does a State's Tax
        Rate Affect Dillard's Decision to
        Open Stores There?, 389
    LendingClub, 17–19
    management accounting, 275–276
Advanced Environmental Recycling
    Technologies (AERT), 102
Age analysis, descriptive analytics, 229,
    231–232
Aggregates/aliases, expand SELECT SQL,
    459–460
Ahmed, A. S., 108n3
Alarms, continuous monitoring, 208–209
Alibaba, 3, 10, 96, 340
Alphabet, 340
Alternative stacked bar chart, 153
Amazon, 3, 10, 96, 114, 279–280, 345, 409
Amazon (AMZN), 345
Amazon Prime, 281
Amazon RDS, 41
American Institute of Certified Public
    Accountants (AICPA), 47, 205
Analytics mindset, 12
Analyze and Refine Results, 314–315 (lab)
Analyze the Financial Ratios, 354 (lab)
Apple, Inc. (AAPL), 29, 329, 331, 332, 344,
    346, 347, 353
Applied statistics, predictive analytics and,
    229, 243
Arelle.org, 356
Artificial intelligence (AI), prescriptive ana-
    lytics and, 96, 113–114, 228, 229, 243
Asset turnover ratio, 330

Audience, effective communication and,
    159–160
Audit Data Analytics
    Address and Refine Results, 230. *See
        also* Address and Refine Results
    Benford's law, 236–239
    communicate insights, 230
    descriptive analytics and, 230–235,
        239–242
    diagnostic analytics, 235–236
    examples of, 229
    identify the problem, 226
    Lab 6-1: Evaluate the Master Data for
        Interesting Addresses, 248–250
    Lab 6-2: Perform Substantive Tests of
        Account Balances, 250–256
    Lab 6-3: Finding Duplicate Payments,
        256–257
    Lab 6-4: Comprehensive Case: Dillard's
        Store Data: Hypothesis Testing
        (Part I), 257–263
    nature/extent/timing of, 226
    perform the test plan, 226–228
    predictive analytics and, 242–243
    sentiment analysis, 243
    track outcomes, 230
    See also Auditing
Audit Data Standards (ADS), 47, 205, 210
Auditing
    automated systems for, 210
    clustering approach in, 105–106
    Data Analytics and, 5–6
    data reduction and, 98–100
    Lab 1-3: Data Analytics in Auditing, 33–34
    Lab 5-5: Identify Audit Data
        Requirements, 221–222
    predictive analytics, regression and, 108
    profiling in, 103
    remote, 209–210
    tax compliance and, 364
    workflow, working papers, 209–210
    See also Audit Data Analytics
Auditing standards (PCAOB), 207
Auditors
    Data Analytics and, 5–6
    Question Set 1: Order-To-Cash (O2C),
        392–400
    Question Set 2: Procure-to-Pay (P2P),
        400–406
Audit plan
    automating, steps for, 208
    characteristics of, 207
    Lab 5-6: Prepare Audit Plan, 222–223
    methodology/standards, 207

Aura, PwC tool, 210, 211
Automating data analytics
Automating data analytics, computer-assisted
    audit techniques (CAATs), 228–230
Automation, 202
    audit plan, 207–208
    scripts, 228–230
Average collection period ratio, 330
Average days in inventory ratio, 330

B

Background information, select *Fortune* 100
    companies, 350 (lab)
Balanced Scorecard
    components of, 271–272
    defined, 271, 277
    example, 267, 272
    key performance indicators, 270–274
    Lab 7-2: Create a Balanced
        Scorecard Dashboard in
        Tableau, 284–292
    strategy map template, 275
    See also Scorecard
Balance sheet composition
    sunburst diagram, visualize, 334
    XBRL data, 339
Bar charts, 145, 154
Bay Area Rapid Transit (BART), 93
Benchmarks, financial statements and, 331
Benford's law, 103–104, 115
    diagnostic analytics and, 229
    predicting distribution, 236–239
Berinato, Scott, 141
Big Data, 4, 20
Bjerrekaer, J. D., 39
Boeing Co., 339
Boundaries, support vector machine, 111
Box, cloud computing, 219
Box and whisker plots, 148
Box Chart, 152
Bristol-Myers Squibb (BMY), 353
Bullet graph, 270
Business, Data Analytics effects on, 4–5
Business process
    defining, 392
    Order-To-Cash (O2C) sales cycle,
        392–400
    Procure-To-Pay (P2P), 400–406

C

Calcbench data vendor, 338, 339, 342
Cash, accounts receivable and, 392–396
Cash tag, XBRL and, 337
Categorical data, 142–143
Causal modeling, 106, 115
Central tendency, describing sample by,
    434–435
Certified management accountant
    (CMA), 328

Certified public accountant (CPA), 328
Change amount, 332
Change in value relative to base year, 332
Change percent, 332
Charting data
    create good, study bad, 151–154
    qualitative, 145–147
    quantitative, 147–148
    refining charts, 156–158
    types of charts, summary of, 148
    See also Data visualization
Chevron (CVX), 353
Chick-Fil-A, 434
Chief audit executive (CAE), 203
Citigroup (C), 353
Class, 106
Classification
    defined, 9, 115
    evaluating, 111
    goals of, predictive analytics and, 109
    Lab 3-3: Classification, 127–130
    lease, flowchart, 113
    model, trade-off, complexity v., 112
    overfitting, 111–112
    predictive analytics and, 96, 229, 242
    steps of, 109
    terminology of, 109–111
Classification analysis, setup/conduct,
    119–120
Classification model, 106
Clean data, 50
Cloud folder, 219–220 (lab)
Cluster analysis
    auditing and, 105–106
    high volume stores, 320–322 (lab)
    unsupervised approach, 103
Clustering
    defined, 10, 115
    diagnostic analytics and, 96, 229, 242
COLLEGESCORECARD data, 492–493
College Scorecard data, 57, 125–126 (lab)
Color
    charts and, 157–158
    visualizing financial data, 333–334
    See also Data visualization
Column charts, 146
Columns, tables and, 42–43
Combine Visualizations into a Dashboard,
    218 (lab)
Committee of Sponsoring Organization
    (COSO), 207
Common data model
    defined, 210
    Lab 5-1: Create a Common Data Model,
        215–217
    Lab 5-2: Create a Dashboard Based on a
        Common Data Model, 217–219
    AICPA and, 204–206
Common size financial statement, 328–329,
    332, 341, 349–352 (lab)

Common table functions, 356 (lab)
Communicate Findings/Results
    audit data analytics and, 230
    charting data, 156–158
    content/organization, 158–159
    Lab 2-2: Use PivotTables to Denormalize
        and Analyze the Data, 67
    Lab 4-1: Use PivotCharts to Visualize
        Declarative Data, 166–168
    Lab 4-2: Use Tableau to Perform
        Exploratory Analysis and Create
        Dashboards, 176–177
    Lab 6-4: Comprehensive Case: Dillard's
        Store Data: Hypothesis Testing
        (Part I), 263
    Lab 7-5: Comprehensive Case: Dillard's
        Store Data: Creating KPIs in
        Excel (Part III), 315
    revising message, 160
    See also Charting data; Data visualization
Communicate Insights
    LendingClub, 19
    tracking outcomes and, 1, 11–12
Complexity of model, classification of *v.*, 112
Composite primary key, 43, 53
Comprehensive Case
    Lab 1-4: Dillard's Store Data, 34–37
    Lab 2-6: Dillard's Store Data: How to
        Create an Entity-Relationship
        Diagram, 75–78
    Lab 2-7: Dillard's Store Data: How to
        Preview Data from Tables In a
        Query, 78–80
    Lab 2-8: Dillard's Store Data:
        Connecting Excel to a SQL
        Database, 80–90
    Lab 2-9: Dillard's Store Data: Joining
        tables, 90–91
    Lab 3-4: Dillard's Store Data: Data
        Abstract (SQL) and Regression
        (Part 1), 130–135
    Lab 3-5: Dillard's Store Data: Data
        Abstract (SQL) and Regression
        (Part II), 135–137
    Lab 4-3: Dillard's Store Data: Create
        Geographic Data Visualizations
        in Tableau and in Power BI,
        177–196
    Lab 4-4: Dillard's Store Data: Visualizing
        Regression in Tableau, 196–199
    Lab 6-4: Dillard's Store Data: Hypothesis
        Testing (Part I), 257–263
    Lab 6-5: Dillard's Store Data:
        Hypothesis Testing (Part II—Data
        Visualization), 263
    Lab 7-3: Dillard's Store Data: Creating
        KPIs in Excel (Part I), 293–299
    Lab 7-4: Dillard's Store Data:
        Creating KPIs in Excel (Part II),
        299–307

Comprehensive Case—*Cont.*
  Lab 7-5: Dillard's Store Data: Creating
      KPIs in Excel (Part III), 307–315
  Lab 9-2: Case 1: Dillard's Store Data:
      Calculate Sales Tax for Dillard's
      States, 379–381
  Lab 9-3: Case 2: Dillard's Store Data:
      Calculate Sales Tax for Dillard's
      States Part 2—Compare Year over
      Year, 381–386
  Lab 9-4: Case 3: Dillard's Store Data:
      Calculate Sales Tax for Dillard's
      States Part 3—Calculate City Tax
      and Compare Tax Owed Year
      over Year, 386–397
  Lab 9-5: Dillard's Store Data: Does a
      State's Tax Rate Affect Dillard's
      Decision to Open Stores There?,
      387–389
Computer-assisted audit techniques
      (CAATs), 228–230, 229, 244
Conceptual chart, 142
Conceptual data, 143
Confidence interval, 437
Confidence level, 234
Connect, PwC tool, 210, 211
ConocoPhillips (COP), 353
Content, data visualization and, 158–159
Continuous auditing, 103, 208, 211
Continuous data, 143, 161
Continuous monitoring, 208
  alarms/exceptions, 208–209
  defined, 211
Continuous reporting, 208, 211
Co-occurrence grouping, 10, 21
  cluster analysis and, 103
  defined, 115
  diagnostic analytics and, 96
Corptax, 362
Cost behavior, 269–270
Costco (Cost), 353
Coughlin, Tom, 103
Create Four Visualizations, 218 (lab)
Current ratio, 329

D

Daily Mail, 152
Dashboards, 101, 141
  balanced scorecard dashboard, 275
  digital, 270, 277
  Lab 4-2: Use Tableau to Perform
      Exploratory Analysis and Create
      Dashboards, 168–177
  Lab 5-2: Create a Dashboard Based on a
      Common Data Model, 218–219
  Lab 6-5: Comprehensive Case: Dillard's
      Store Data: Hypothesis Testing
      (Part II—Data Visualization),
      263–265
  Lab 7-2: Create a Balanced Scorecard
      Dashboard in Tableau, 284–292

Data
  Big, 4, 20
  cleaning, 50
  ethics breach and, 39
  gather/review, 8–9
  quality, 50–52
  relationships, relational databases and,
      42–43
  storing, 48–49
  validate, 49–50
  variability/spread, describing, 435
Data Analysis ToolPak, Excel add-in
  accessing, 440–441
  Lab 6-4: Comprehensive Case: Dillard's
      Store Data: Hypothesis Testing
      (Part I), 258–261
  tutorial, 440–441
Data Analytics
  auditing and, 5–6
  automating. *See* Automating data
      analytics, 206–208
  business and, 4–5
  defined, 4, 21
  financial reporting and, 6–7
  four categories of, 94–97
  IMPACT cycle, 8
  Lab 1-1: Data Analytics in Financial
      Accounting, 28–31
  Lab 1-2: Data Analytics in Managerial
      Accounting, 31–33
  Lab 2-1: Create a Request for Data
      Extraction, 59–60
  taxes and, 7
Database maps, 209
Databases
  computer languages for, 48–49
  data dictionary, 44–45
  ETL process, 45–49
  management, software, 41
  relationships, relational, 42–43
  table attributes, 42–43
  types of, 29
Database Schema, 41
Data dictionary, 14, 21
  COLLEGESCORECARD, 492–493
  defined, 53
  LendingClub, 44–45, 494–498
  LoadStats, 494–498
  OK PCARD, 499
  RejectStats, 499
Data-driven chart, 142
Data environment, modern, 202–203
Data management, taxes and, 363–364
Data marts, 363, 370
Data profiling. *See* Profiling data
Data quality, XBRL and, 338–339
Data reduction, 10–11, 21
  cluster analysis and, 103
  defined, 98, 115
  descriptive analytics and, 95–96,
      98–100

Lab 3-1: Data Reduction Using Fuzzy
      Matching, 122–125
Data request, 46–47, 59 (lab)
Data request form, 47, 53
Data scale, charting data, 157
Datasets
  ethics and, 39
  See also Data dictionary; Dillard's Stores
      Inc.; LendingClub; Sláinte
Data types, 142–143
Data visualization, 12
  audience/tone, effective communication,
      159–160
  bar charts, 154
  box charts, 152
  categorical data, choosing, 142–143
  chart types, 142
  color, charts and, 157–158
  content/organization and, 158–159
  create good charts, study bad, 151–154
  data scale/increments and, 157
  declarative, explanatory *v.,* 144–145
  designing, 275
  heat map, 139
  Lab 4-1: Use PivotCharts to Visualize
      Declarative Data, 166–168
  Lab 5-2: Create a Dashboard Based
      on a Common Data Model,
      218–219
  Lab 7-7: Comprehensive Case: Dillard's
      Store Data: Advanced Models in
      Tableau, 320–324
  Lab 9-1: State Sales Taxes and Create a
      Data Visualization, 375–379
  normal distribution, 143–144
  pie chart, stacked bar chart *v.,* 153
  purpose of, determine, 141–142
  qualitative data, charts for, 145–147
  quantitative data, charts for, 147–148
  Question 1.2: How Can We Explore the
      Product Hierarchy Through Data
      Visualization?, 412–422
  Question 3.1: By Looking at Line Charts
      for 2014 and 2015, Does the
      Average Percentage of Sales
      Returned in 2014 Seem to Be
      Predictive of Returns in 2015,
      427–429
  Question Set 1: Descriptive and
      Exploratory Analysis, 410–422
  rank-ordered bar chart, 153
  refining charts, 156–158
  relative size of accounts, 333–334
  revising message, 160
  sparklines/heat maps, 333
  stacked bar chart, 154
  tracking KPS, tax data and, 365–366
  trends, sparkline/trendlines, 333
  USA Drug Overdose, 140
  visuals, tools for choosing, 149–151
  See also Charting data

Data warehouse, 204, 211, 363, 364
Date datatypes, SQL WHERE clause, 456
Dates, data quality and, 50–51
DB Browser, SQLite, 215 (lab). *See also* Web browser
Debt-to-equity ratio, 330
Debt-to-income ratio, 15, 16, 19
Decision boundaries, classification, 109, 110, 115
Decision support systems, prescriptive analytics and, 96, 112–113, 115
Decision trees, classification, 109, 110, 115
Declarative chart, 142
Declarative visualization, 144–145, 161
Deductions, tax planning what-if scenarios and, 369–370
Delivery process, 396–398
Dependent variables, 9, 21
Descriptive analytics
    age analysis, 231–232
    defined, 94, 115, 228, 244
    example, 229
    financial, 328
    Question Set 1: Descriptive and Exploratory Analysis, 410–422
    sampling, 233–235
    sorting, 232–233
    summary of approaches, 95–96
    summary statistics, 97–98, 233
Descriptive attributes, 43, 53
Diagnostic analytics
    Benford's law and, 236–239
    cluster analysis, 103–106
    defined, 94, 100, 115, 228, 244
    drill down, 239
    exact and fuzzy matching, 239–241
    example, 229
    financial, 331
    profiling data and, 100–103
    Question 2.1: Is the Percentage of Sales Returned Significantly Higher in January After the Holiday Season?, 422–426
    Question 2.2: Is the Percentage of Sales Returned Significantly Different in Arkansas Than the Rest of the Country?, 426–427
    sequence check, 241
    stratification/clustering, 242
    summary of, 95–96
    z-score, 235–236
Digital dashboard, 270, 277
Dillard's Stores Inc.
    ER Diagram, 491
    estimating sales returns, question sets for, 410–432. *See also* Estimating sales returns, question sets for
    Lab 1-4: Comprehensive Case: Dillard's Store Data, 35
    Lab 1-4: Dillard's Store Data, 34–37

Lab 2-6: Comprehensive Case: Dillard's Store Data: How to Create an Entity-Relationship Diagram, 75–78
Lab 2-7: Dillard's Store Data: How to Preview Data from Tables In a Query, 78–80
Lab 2-8: Dillard's Store Data: Connecting Excel to a SQL Database, 80–90
Lab 6-4: Comprehensive Case: Dillard's Store Data: Hypothesis Testing (Part I), 257–263
Lab 6-5: Comprehensive Case: Dillard's Store Data: Hypothesis Testing (Part II–Data Visualization), 263–265
Lab 7-3: Comprehensive Case: Dillard's Store Data: Creating KPIs in Excel (Part I), 293–299
Lab 7-4: Comprehensive Case: Dillard's Store Data: Creating KPIs in Excel (Part II), 299–307
Lab 7-5: Comprehensive Case: Dillard's Store Data: Creating KPIs in Excel (Part III), 307–315
Lab 7-6: Comprehensive Case: Dillard's Store Data: Creating KPIs in Excel (Part IV–Putting It All Together), 315–319
Lab 7-7: Comprehensive Case: Dillard's Store Data: Advanced Models in Tableau, 320–324
Lab 9-2: Comprehensive Case 1: Dillard's Store Data: Calculate Sales Tax for Dillard's States, 379–381
Lab 9-3: Comprehensive Case 2: Dillard's Store Data: Calculate Sales Tax for Dillard's States Part 2–Compare Year over Year, 381–386
Lab 9-4: Comprehensive Case 3: Dillard's Store Data: Calculate Sales Tax for Dillard's States Part 3–Calculate City Tax and Compare Tax Owed Year over Year, 386–397
Lab 9-5: Comprehensive Case 4: Dillard's Store Data: Does a State's Tax Rate Affect Dillard's Decision to Open Stores There?, 387–389
Discrete data, 143, 161
Distribution
    predicting, Benford's law and, 236–239
    probability, 435–436
Documents
    create using OneDrive (lab), 27–28
    See also Electronic working papers
Drill-down, diagnostic analytics and, 229, 239
Dropbox, 219
DuPont ratio, 330, 340, 341

E

eBay, 3
EDGAR database (SEC), 29
Effective tax rate (ETR), 365–366
Electronic working papers, 209–210
    Lab 5-3: Set up a Cloud Folder, 219–220
    platforms for, 210
ELT process, loading data, 52
Encoding, data quality and, 51
English dictionary (H4N-INF), 335
Enterprise data
    common data model, 204–206
    systems approaches to, 203–204
Enterprise Risk Management (COSO), 207
Entity-relationship diagram (ERD), 75–78 (lab)
Equifax, 21
Equity multiplier ratio, 330
ER Diagram, Dillard's Stores Inc., 491
Errors, data quality and, 52
Estimated misstatement, 234
Estimating sales returns, question sets for
    Q. 1.1: Which Attributes Could Help Predict Percentage of Returned Sales?, 410–412
    Q. 1.2: How Can We Explore the Product Hierarchy Through Data Visualization?, 412–422
    Q. 2.1: Is the Percentage of Sales Returned Significantly Higher in January After the Holiday Season?, 422–426
    Q. 2.2: Is the Percentage of Sales Returned Significantly Different in Arkansas Than the Rest of the Country?, 426–427
    Q. 3.1: By Looking at Line Charts for 2014 and 2015, Does the Average Percentage of Sales Returned in 2014 Seem to Be Predictive of Returns in 2015, 427–429
    Q. 3.2: Using Regression, What Can We Predict for Returns as a Percentage of Sales Based on Historical Transactions?, 429–432
Ethics, breach of, datasets and, 39
ETL process
    automating data analytics and, 206–207
    defined, 53
    extract, 46–47
    Lab 2-1: Create a Request for Data Extraction, 58–60
    Lab 2-2: Use PivotTables to Denormalize and Analyze the Data, 61
    Lab 2-5: College Scorecard Extraction and Data Preparation, 73–75
    Lab 4-2: Use Tableau to Perform Exploratory Analysis and Create Dashboards, 169–171
    Lab 4-4: Comprehensive Case: Dillard's Store Data: Visualizing Regression in Tableau, 197–198

ETL process—*Cont.*
    Lab 5-1: Create a Common Data Model,
        216–217
    Lab 6-5: Comprehensive Case: Dillard's
        Store Data: Hypothesis Testing
        (Part II—Data Visualization),
        263–265
    load data, 52
    transform, 49–50
European Union, 364
Evaluate data, 221–222 (lab)
Exact matching, diagnostic analytics and,
    229, 239
Excel. *See* Microsoft Excel *entries*
Exception report, 208–209
Exceptions, generate/follow up, 101
Experian, 21
Explanatory variables, 9, 21
Exploratory analysis
    Lab 4-2: Use Tableau to Perform
        Exploratory Analysis and Create
        Dashboards, 168–177
    Question 1.2: How Can We Explore the
        Product Hierarchy Through Data
        Visualization?, 412–422
    Question Set 1: Descriptive and
        Exploratory Analysis, 410–422
Exploratory chart, 142
Exploratory visualization, 144–145, 161
eXtensible Business Reporting Language
    (XBRL), 29, 99–100, 116
    cash tag, 337
    data quality, 338–339
    defined, uses of, 336–338, 341
    financial ratios on Google Sheets, 353
    financial statement analytics using, 340
    instance document, 336–338
    Lab 8-1: Create a Horizontal and Vertical
        Analysis Using XBRL Data,
        346–349
    Lab 8-2: Create Dynamic Common Size
        Financial Statements, 349–352
    Lab 8-3: Analyze Financial Statement
        Ratios, 352–353
    Lab 8-4: Use SQL to Query an XBRL
        Database, 355–360
    standardized metrics, 338
    standardized tags, 339
    taxonomy, 336
    XBRL-Global Ledger, real-time financial
        reporting, 340
Extensible markup language (XML), 336
External auditing, data reduction and, 98–99
Extracting data. *See* ETL process
ExxonMobile (XOM), 353

F

Facebook, 7, 11, 21
Facebook (FB), 21, 353
False positive, 209

FASB taxonomy, 338
Favorable variances, 269
Fawcett, T., 9n
Filled geographic maps, 148
Financial accounting, data analytics in,
    28–31 (lab)
Financial Accounting Standards Board
    (FASB), 29
Financial analysis, text mining/sentiment
    analysis, 334–335
Financial dictionary (Fin-Neg), 335
Financial reporting
    Data Analytics and, 6–7
    real-time, XBRL/XBRL-GL, 340
Financial Statement Analysis
    common size financial statement,
        328–329, 331–332
    defined, 341
    descriptive, 328
    diagnostic financial analytics, 331
    EXBRL examples, 340
    index showing change in value relative to
        base year, 332
    Lab 8-1: Create a Horizontal and Vertical
        Analysis Using XBRL Data,
        346–349
    Lab 8-2: Create Dynamic Common Size
        Financial Statements, 349–352
    Lab 8-3: Analyze Financial Statement
        Ratios, 352–354
    predictive financial analytics, 331–332
    ratios, comparison among three
        companies, 331
    ratio types, 329–330
    vertical/horizontal analysis, 328–329,
        331–332
Financing ratio, 330
Findings. *See* Address and Refine Results;
    Communicate Findings/Results
FinDynamics, 346, 347
Flat file, 41, 53, 204, 211
Forbes.com, 361
Forbes Insights/KPMG report, 5–6
Foreign keys, 43, 53
Fortune 100, 346, 350
Frequency distribution, 375–377 (lab)
FROM, SQL clause, 453–454, 463–464
Fujitsu, 338
Fuzzy Lookup add-in, 121 (lab), 239–241
Fuzzy match, 98, 99
    defined, 244
    diagnostic analytics and, 229, 239–241
    Lab 3-1: Data Reduction Using Fuzzy
        Matching, 122–125
    Lab 6-1: Evaluate the Master Data for
        Interesting Addresses, 249–250

G

Gartner Magic Quadrant for Business
    Intelligence and Analytics Platform, 149

Generalized audit software (GAS), 230
General Motors (GM), 340
Generate a Request for Data, 285 (lab)
Good classification, 109
Google, 7, 114
Google Account, 352–354 (lab)
Google Drive, 219
Google Sheets
    Lab 8-1: Create a Horizontal and
        Vertical Analysis Using XBRL
        Data, 346
    Lab 8-3: Analyze Financial Statement
        Ratios, 352–354
GROUP BY, SQL clause, 460–462

H

Halo, PwC tool, 201, 210, 211
Harriott, J. S., 8n, 40n
Harvard Business Review, 141
HAVING, SQL clause, 462–463
Heat map, data visualization, 139, 146, 333
Heterogeneous systems approach, data struc-
    ture, 204, 211
Hewlett-Packard Co. (HP), 225
Histogram, data visualization, 375–377 (lab)
Homogeneous systems approach, data struc-
    ture, 203–204, 211
Horizontal financial statement analysis, 328–
    329, 331–332, 341, 346–349 (lab)
Hyperion, 362
Hypothesis testing
    Lab 6-4: Comprehensive Case: Dillard's
        Store Data: Hypothesis Testing
        (Part I), 257–263
    Q. 2.1: Is the Percentage of Sales
        Returned Significantly Higher
        in January After the Holiday
        Season?, 422–426
    Q. 2.2: Is the Percentage of Sales
        Returned Significantly Different
        in Arkansas Than the Rest of the
        Country?, 426–427
    statistics and, 436–437

I

IBM, 338
IBM DB2, 41
IDEA software, 230
    age analysis, 231–232
    Benford's law, 238
    fuzzy address match, 241
    Lab 6-1: Evaluate the Master Data
        for Interesting Addresses,
        248–250
    monetary unit sample (MUS), 235
    sample size, 234
    sorting, 233
    summary statistics, 233

Identify Questions
Lab 1-1: Data Analytics in Financial Accounting, 28–29
Lab 1-2: Data Analytics in Managerial Accounting, 31–32
Lab 1-3: Data Analytics in Auditing, 33–34
Lab 1-4: Dillard's Store Data (comprehensive case), 35–36
Lab 2-1: Create a Request for Data Extraction, 58–59
Lab 2-2: Use PivotTables to Denormalize and Analyze the Data, 61
Lab 2-3: Resolve Common Data Problems in Excel and Access, 68
Lab 2-5: College Scorecard Extraction and Data Preparation, 74
Lab 2-6: Comprehensive Case: Dillard's Store Data: How to Create an Entity-Relationship Diagram, 76
Lab 2-7: Comprehensive Case: Dillard's Store Data: How to Preview Data from Tables In a Query, 78–79
Lab 2-9: Comprehensive Case: Dillard's Store Data: Joining tables, 90
Lab 3-2: Regression in Excel, 125
Lab 3-3: Classification, 127
Lab 3-4: Comprehensive Case: Dillard's Store Data: Data Abstract (SQL) and Regression (Part 1), 131
Lab 3-5: Comprehensive Case: Dillard's Store Data: Data Abstract (SQL) and Regression (Part II), 135
Lab 4-1: Use PivotCharts to Visualize Declarative Data, 166
Lab 4-2: Use Tableau to Perform Exploratory Analysis and Create Dashboards, 169
Lab 4-3: Comprehensive Case: Dillard's Store Data: Create Geographic Data Visualizations in Tableau and in Power BI, 178
Lab 4-4: Comprehensive Case: Dillard's Store Data: Visualizing Regression in Tableau, 197
Lab 6-1: Evaluate the Master Data for Interesting Addresses, 248
Lab 6-2: Perform Substantive Tests of Account Balances, 251
Lab 6-3: Finding Duplicate Payments, 256
Lab 6-4: Comprehensive Case: Dillard's Store Data: Hypothesis Testing (Part I), 258
Lab 6-5: Comprehensive Case: Dillard's Store Data: Hypothesis Testing (Part II—Data Visualization), 264
Lab 7-1: Evaluate Management Requirement and Identify Useful KPIs from a List, 284

Lab 7-2: Create a Balanced Scorecard Dashboard in Tableau, 284–285
Lab 7-3: Comprehensive Case: Dillard's Store Data: Creating KPIs in Excel (Part I), 295
Lab 7-4: Comprehensive Case: Dillard's Store Data: Creating KPIs in Excel (Part II), 300
Lab 7-5: Comprehensive Case: Dillard's Store Data: Creating KPIs in Excel (Part III), 309
Lab 7-6: Comprehensive Case: Dillard's Store Data: Creating KPIs in Excel (Part IV—Putting It All Together), 316
Lab 8-1: Create a Horizontal and Vertical Analysis Using XBRL Data, 346
Lab 8-3: Analyze Financial Statement Ratios, 352–353
Lab 8-4: Use SQL to Query an XBRL Database, 355
Lab 9-1: State Sales Taxes and Create a Data Visualization, 375
Lab 9-2: Comprehensive Case 1: Dillard's Store Data: Calculate Sales Tax for Dillard's States, 379
Lab 9-3: Comprehensive Case 2: Dillard's Store Data: Calculate Sales Tax for Dillard's States Part 2—Compare Year over Year, 382
Lab 9-4: Comprehensive Case 3: Dillard's Store Data: Calculate Sales Tax for Dillard's States Part 3—Calculate City Tax and Compare Tax Owed Year over Year, 386
Lab 9-5: Comprehensive Case 4: Dillard's Store Data: Does a State's Tax Rate Affect Dillard's Decision to Open Stores There?, 388
management accounting, 268–270
Identify the Location of the Data, 222 (lab)
Identify the Problem
auditing data analytics, 226
Lab 3-1: Data Reduction Using Fuzzy Matching, 121
IMPACT cycle
data, gather/review, 8–9
data visualization, 141
outcomes, track, 11–12
questions, identify, 8
results, address/refine, 11
test plan, perform, 9–11, 94–97
IMPACT model
audit data analytics and, 226–230
hands-on, Lendingclub example. *See* LendingClub *entries*
KPIs for decision-making and, 272, 366
mastering the data, 40
tax data and, 363

Import and Validate the Data
Lab 5-1: Create a Common Data Model, 215
Lab 5-2: Create a Dashboard Based on a Common Data Model, 218
Income tax liability, 365
Increments, charting data, 157
Independent variables, 9, 21
Index, 332, 341
INNER join, 480–481
Inner join, 239
INNER JOIN ON, SQL clause, 464–465
Input Ticker Symbols, 354 (lab)
Instagram, 7, 21
Instance document, XBRL and, 336
Internal auditing
data reduction and, 98–99
importance of, 203
profiling and, 103
International characters, data quality and, 51
Interval data, 143, 161
Inventory turnover ratio, 330
Invoices, paying, Question Set 2: Procure-To-Pay (P2P), 400–406
IRS and tax analytics, 362
Isson, J. P., 8n, 40n
iXBRLAnalyist script, 346 (lab)

J
James, LeBron, 361
JD Edwards, 203, 213
Johnson & Johnson (JNJ), 353
JPMorgan Chase (JPM), 353

K
Kaplan, Robert S., 271
Kenya Red Cross, 267
Key performance indicators (KPIs), 141, 268–269
balanced scorecard and, 270–274
defined, 277
financial performance/operational, 273
Lab 7-1: Evaluate Management Requirement and Identify Useful KPIs from a List, 282–283
Lab 7-3: Comprehensive Case: Dillard's Store Data: Creating KPIs in Excel (Part I), 293–299
Lab 7-4: Comprehensive Case: Dillard's Store Data: Creating KPIs in Excel (Part II), 299–307
Lab 7-5: Comprehensive Case: Dillard's Store Data: Creating KPIs in Excel (Part III), 307–315
Lab 7-6: Comprehensive Case: Dillard's Store Data: Creating KPIs in Excel (Part IV—Putting It All Together), 315–319
monitor/track, tax data analytics, 365–366

Kirkegaard, E., 39
KPIs. *See* Key performance indicators
  (KPIs)

L

Labs
  1-0: How to Complete Labs in This Text,
    27-28
  1-1: Data Analytics in Financial
    Accounting, 28-31
  1-1: Data Analytics in Financial
    Accounting, 28-31
  1-2: Data Analytics in Managerial
    Accounting, 31-33
  1-3: Data Analytics in Auditing, 33-34
  1-4: Dillard's Store Data (comprehensive
    case), 35-37
  2-1: Create a Request for Data
    Extraction, 58-60
  2-2: Use PivotTables to Denormalize and
    Analyze the Data, 60-67
  2-3: Resolve Common Data Problems in
    Excel and Access, 67-71
  2-4: Generate Summary Statistics in
    Excel, 71-73
  2-5: College Scorecard Extraction and
    Data Preparation, 73-75
  2-6: Comprehensive Case: Dillard's
    Store Data: How to Create an
    Entity-Relationship Diagram,
    75-78
  2-8: Comprehensive Case: Dillard's Store
    Data: Connecting Excel to a SQL
    Database, 80-90
  2-9: Comprehensive Case: Dillard's Store
    Data: Joining tables, 90-91
  3-1: Data Reduction Using Fuzzy
    Matching, 121-125
  3-2: Regression in Excel, 125-126
  3-3: Classification, 127-130
  3-4: Comprehensive Case: Dillard's Store
    Data: Data Abstract (SQL) and
    Regression (Part 1), 130-135
  3-5: Comprehensive Case: Dillard's Store
    Data: Data Abstract (SQL) and
    Regression (Part II), 135-137
  4-1: Use PivotCharts to Visualize
    Declarative Data, 166-168
  4-2: Use Tableau to Perform Exploratory
    Analysis and Create Dashboards,
    168-177
  4-3: Comprehensive Case: Dillard's Store
    Data: Create Geographic Data
    Visualizations in Tableau and in
    Power BI, 177-196
  4-4: Comprehensive Case: Dillard's Store
    Data: Visualizing Regression in
    Tableau, 196-199
  5-1: Create a Common Data Model,
    215-217

  5-2: Create a Dashboard Based on a
    Common Data Model, 217-219
  5-3: Set up a Cloud Folder, 219-220
  5-4: Review Changes to Working Papers,
    220-221
  5-5: Identify Audit Data Requirements,
    221-222
  5-6: Prepare Audit Plan, 222-223
  6-1: Evaluate the Master Data for
    Interesting Addresses, 248-250
  6-2: Perform Substantive Tests of
    Account Balances, 250-256
  6-3: Finding Duplicate Payments,
    256-257
  6-5: Comprehensive Case: Dillard's Store
    Data: Hypothesis Testing (Part
    II—Data Visualization), 263-265
  7-1: Evaluate Management Requirement
    and Identify Useful KPIs from a
    List, 282-283
  7-2: Create a Balanced Scorecard
    Dashboard in Tableau, 284-292
  7-3: Comprehensive Case: Dillard's Store
    Data: Creating KPIs in Excel
    (Part I), 293-299
  7-4: Comprehensive Case: Dillard's Store
    Data: Creating KPIs in Excel
    (Part II), 299-307
  7-5: Comprehensive Case: Dillard's Store
    Data: Creating KPIs in Excel
    (Part III), 307-315
  7-6: Comprehensive Case: Dillard's Store
    Data: Creating KPIs in Excel
    (Part IV—Putting It All Together),
    315-319
  7-7: Comprehensive Case: Dillard's
    Store Data: Advanced Models in
    Tableau, 320-324
  8-1: Create a Horizontal and Vertical
    Analysis Using XBRL Data,
    346-349
  8-2: Create Dynamic Common Size
    Financial Statements, 349-352
  8-3: Analyze Financial Statement Ratios,
    352-354
  8-4: Use SQL to Query an XBRL
    Database, 355-360
  9-1: State Sales Taxes and Create a Data
    Visualization, 375-379
  9-2: Comprehensive Case 1: Dillard's
    Store Data: Calculate Sales Tax
    for Dillard's States, 379-381
  9-3: Comprehensive Case 2: Dillard's
    Store Data: Calculate Sales
    Tax for Dillard's States Part
    2—Compare Year over Year,
    381-386
  9-4: Comprehensive Case 3: Dillard's
    Store Data: Calculate Sales
    Tax for Dillard's States Part 3—
    Calculate City Tax and Compare

    Tax Owed Year over Year,
    386-397
  9-5: Comprehensive Case 4: Dillard's
    Store Data: Does a State's Tax
    Rate Affect Dillard's Decision to
    Open Stores There?, 387-389
  Question Set 1: Descriptive and
    Exploratory Analysis, 410-422
  Question Set 2: Procure-To-Pay (P2P),
    392-400
  Question Set 3: Predictive Analytics,
    427-432
  Question set 1 Order-To-Cash (O2C),
    392-400
Languages
  data quality and, 51
  SQL, 48
  text mining, sentiment analysis and, 335
  XML, EBRL and, 336
Left join, 239
LEFT join, SQL clause, 482
Legislation, tax planning what-if scenarios
  and, 369-370
LendingClub
  Credit Risk Scores, customer, 17, 19
  credit score data, 116
  data, 494-498
  data, gather/review, 13-15
  data dictionary, 44-45
  datasets/data dictionary, website, 14
  debt-to-income ratio, declined loan
    applications by, 16, 19
  debt-to-income ratio, loans declined by,
    19
  declined loan data, 14
  employment length, declined loan
    applications by, 16
  insights, communicate, 19
  Lab 1-2: Data Analytics in Managerial
    Accounting, 31-33
  Lab 1-3: Data Analytics in Auditing,
    33-34
  Lab 2-3: Resolve Common Data
    Problems in Excel and Access,
    67-71
  Lab 2-4: Generate Summary Statistics in
    Excel, 71-73
  Lab 3-3: Classification, 127-128
  loan rejection, predicting, 112
  loans issued, 13
  outcomes, tracking, 19
  pivot tables, 16, 18, 19
  questions, identify, 13
  regression, predictive analytics and,
    108-109
  RejectStatsA dataset, 15
  reported loan purpose, 13
  results, address/refine, 17-19
  test plan, 15-19
Linear classifiers, 110
Line charts, 148, 427-429

Link prediction
   defined, 10, 21, 115
   example, 11
   predictive analytics and, 96, 106
Liquidity ratio, 329
Load data. *See* ETL process, 52
Look for Audit Procedures that Evaluate
   Data, 221–222 (lab)
Loughran, Tim, 335, 345
Lyft, 334

M

Machine learning, prescriptive analytics and,
   96, 113–114, 228, 243
Magic quadrant, 149
Management accounting
   balanced scorecard/KPIs, 270
   cost behavior, 269–270
   data visualization, 275
   drill-down/refine results, 275–276
   evaluate data quality, 274–275
   identify questions, 268–270
   key performance indicators (KPIs)/
      variance analysis and, 268–269
   KPIs for, 273
   Lab 7-1: Evaluate Management
      Requirement and Identify Useful
      KPIs from a List, 282–283
   Lab 7-2: Create a Balanced Scorecard
      Dashboard in Tableau, 284–292
   Lab 7-3: Comprehensive Case: Dillard's
      Store Data: Creating KPIs in
      Excel (Part I), 293–299
   Lab 7-4: Comprehensive Case: Dillard's
      Store Data: Creating KPIs in
      Excel (Part II), 299–307
   Lab 7-6: Comprehensive Case: Dillard's
      Store Data: Creating KPIs in
      Excel (Part IV–Putting It All
      Together), 315–319
   Lab 7-7: Comprehensive Case: Dillard's
      Store Data: Advanced Models in
      Tableau, 320–324
   predictive analytics, regression and, 108
   profiling in, 102
   relevant costs, 268
Management discussion, word frequency,
   334
Managerial accounting, data analytics in,
   32–33 (lab)
Managers
   Question Set 1: Order-To-Cash (O2C),
      392–400
   Question Set 2: Procure-To-Pay (P2P),
      400–406
Manipulating data, 12
Mapping data, 215–217 (lab)
Marr, Bernard, 282
Mastering the Data and Performing the
   Analysis

Lab 7-3: Comprehensive Case: Dillard's
   Store Data: Creating KPIs in
   Excel (Part I), 295–299
Master the Data and Prepare for Analysis
   Lab 8-3: Analyze Financial Statement
      Ratios, 353
Master the Data and Prepare for Analysis
   Using Excel
   Lab 9-1: State Sales Taxes and Create a
      Data Visualization, 375
Master the Data
   6-5: Comprehensive Case: Dillard's Store
      Data: Hypothesis Testing (Part
      II–Data Visualization), 264–265
   audit data analytics and, 226–228
   defining, 40, 53
   extract, 45–49
   Lab 1-1: Data Analytics in Financial
      Accounting, 29–30
   Lab 1-2: Data Analytics in Managerial
      Accounting, 32–33
   Lab 1-3: Data Analytics in Auditing,
      33–34
   Lab 1-4: Dillard's Store Data
      (comprehensive case), 36–37
   Lab 2-1: Create a Request for Data
      Extraction
   Lab 2-2: Use PivotTables to Denormalize
      and Analyze the Data, 61–66
   Lab 2-3: Resolve Common Data
      Problems in Excel and Access,
      68–71
   Lab 2-5: College Scorecard Extraction
      and Data Preparation, 74–75
   Lab 2-6: Comprehensive Case: Dillard's
      Store Data: How to Create an
      Entity-Relationship Diagram,
      76–78
   Lab 2-7: Comprehensive Case: Dillard's
      Store Data: How to Preview Data
      from Tables In a Query, 79–80
   Lab 2-8: Comprehensive Case: Dillard's
      Store Data: Connecting Excel to
      a SQL Database, 81–88
   Lab 2-9: Comprehensive Case: Dillard's
      Store Data: Joining tables, 90–91
   Lab 3-1: Data Reduction Using Fuzzy
      Matching, 121–122
   Lab 3-2: Regression in Excel, 126
   Lab 3-3: Classification, 127–128
   Lab 3-4: Comprehensive Case: Dillard's
      Store Data: Data Abstract (SQL)
      and Regression (Part 1), 131
   Lab 3-5: Comprehensive Case: Dillard's
      Store Data: Data Abstract (SQL)
      and Regression (Part II), 135
   Lab 4-1: Use PivotCharts to Visualize
      Declarative Data, 166
   Lab 4-2: Use Tableau to Perform
      Exploratory Analysis and Create
      Dashboards, 169–171

Lab 4-3: Comprehensive Case: Dillard's
   Store Data: Create Geographic
   Data Visualizations in Tableau
   and in Power BI, 178–185
Lab 4-4: Comprehensive Case: Dillard's
   Store Data: Visualizing
   Regression in Tableau, 197–198
Lab 5-1: Create a Common Data Model,
   215
Lab 6-2: Perform Substantive Tests of
   Account Balances, 251–256
   THERE APPEARS TO BE A
   STAGE MISSING
Lab 6-3: Finding Duplicate Payments,
   256
Lab 6-4: Comprehensive Case: Dillard's
   Store Data: Hypothesis Testing
   (Part I), 258–261
Lab 7-1: Evaluate Management
   Requirement and Identify Useful
   KPIs from a List, 284
Lab 7-4: Comprehensive Case: Dillard's
   Store Data: Creating KPIs in
   Excel (Part II), 300–307
Lab 7-5: Comprehensive Case: Dillard's
   Store Data: Creating KPIs in
   Excel (Part III), 309–313
Lab 7-6: Comprehensive Case: Dillard's
   Store Data: Creating KPIs in
   Excel (Part IV–Putting It All
   Together), 316–317
Lab 8-1: Create a Horizontal and Vertical
   Analysis Using XBRL Data,
   346–348
Lab 8-4: Use SQL to Query an XBRL
   Database, 355–356
Lab 9-2: Comprehensive Case 1:
   Dillard's Store Data: Calculate
   Sales Tax for Dillard's States,
   379–380
Lab 9-3: Comprehensive Case 2:
   Dillard's Store Data: Calculate
   Sales Tax for Dillard's States
   Part 2–Compare Year over Year,
   382–383
Lab 9-4: Comprehensive Case 3:
   Dillard's Store Data: Calculate
   Sales Tax for Dillard's States
   Part 3–Calculate City Tax and
   Compare Tax Owed Year over
   Year, 386–387
Lab 9-5: Comprehensive Case 4:
   Dillard's Store Data: Does a
   State's Tax Rate Affect Dillard's
   Decision to Open Stores
   There?, 388
load the data, 52
management accounting, 274–275
Question Set 1: Descriptive and
   Exploratory Analysis, 419
transform, 49–50

Master the Employee and Vendor Data
Lab 6-1: Evaluate the Master Data for
Interesting Addresses, 248–249
McDonald, Bill, 335, 345
McKinsey Global Institute, 5
Measures, data quality and, 51
Merck (MRK), 353
Merge data, 63–65 (lab)
Metadata, Lab 1-4: Dillard's Store Data
(comprehensive case), 37
Microsoft Access
defined, 41
Lab 2-2: Use PivotTables to Denormalize
and Analyze the Data, 60
Lab 2-3: Resolve Common Data
Problems in Excel and Access,
67–71
Lab 6-2: Perform Substantive Tests of
Account Balances, 251
Lab 8-4: Use SQL to Query an XBRL
Database, 355–360
Microsoft BI suite, 149
Microsoft Corp. (MSFT), 114, 329, 331, 332,
333, 353
Microsoft Excel
add-ins, 308–309
age analysis, 231
Benford's law, predicting distribution,
237–238
Benford's law percentages, 238–239
formatting, income statement using
SUM(), 442–450
Fuzzy Lookup add-in, 239–241
Get and Transform tool, 470–472
Lab 6-1: Evaluate the Master Data for
Interesting Addresses, 248, 249
Lab 6-3: Finding Duplicate Payments,
256–257
Lab 7-4: Comprehensive Case: Dillard's
Store Data: Creating KPIs in
Excel (Part II), 299–307
Lab 9-1: State Sales Taxes and Create a
Data Visualization, 375–379
Lab 9-2: Comprehensive Case 1: Dillard's
Store Data: Calculate Sales Tax
for Dillard's States, 379–381
Lab 9-3: Comprehensive Case 2:
Dillard's Store Data: Calculate
Sales Tax for Dillard's States
Part 2—Compare Year over Year,
382–386
Lab 9-4: Comprehensive Case 3:
Dillard's Store Data: Calculate
Sales Tax for Dillard's States
Part 3—Calculate City Tax and
Compare Tax Owed Year over
Year, 386–387
Lab 9-5: Comprehensive Case 4: Dillard's
Store Data: Does a State's Tax
Rate Affect Dillard's Decision to
Open Stores There?, 387–389

monetary unit sample (MUS), 234
PivotTables, 448–449. *See also* Microsoft
Excel PivotTable
Question Set 1: Descriptive and
Exploratory Analysis, 410–422
sample size, 234
sorting, 232
spreadsheets, tax data and, 363
summary statistics, 233
Tableau and, 476–478
tutorial, 442–452
VLookup function, 450–452
z-score calculation, 236
Microsoft Excel 2016
Data Analysis Toolpak tutorial, 440–441
Lab 3-5: Comprehensive Case: Dillard's
Store Data: Data Abstract
(SQL) and Regression (Part
II), 136
Lab 6-4: Comprehensive Case: Dillard's
Store Data: Hypothesis Testing
(Part I), 257–263
Lab 6-5: Comprehensive Case: Dillard's
Store Data: Hypothesis Testing
(Part II—Data Visualization),
263–265
Lab 7-3: Comprehensive Case: Dillard's
Store Data: Creating KPIs in
Excel (Part I), 293–299
Lab 7-5: Comprehensive Case: Dillard's
Store Data: Creating KPIs in
Excel (Part III), 307–315
Lab 7-6: Comprehensive Case: Dillard's
Store Data: Creating KPIs in
Excel (Part IV—Putting It All
Together), 315–319
Question Set 3: Predictive Analytics,
427–432
Microsoft Excel Data Analysis Toolpak
accessing, 440–441
Lab 6-4: Comprehensive Case: Dillard's
Store Data: Hypothesis Testing
(Part I), 258–261
tutorial, 440–441
Microsoft Excel database
Lab 1-3: Data Analytics in Auditing, 33
Lab 2-2: Use PivotTables to Denormalize
and Analyze the Data, 60, 61–66
Lab 2-3: Resolve Common Data
Problems in Excel and Access,
67–71
Lab 2-4: Generate Summary Statistics in
Excel, 71–73
Lab 2-5: College Scorecard Extraction
and Data Preparation, 74
Lab 2-8: Comprehensive Case: Dillard's
Store Data: Connecting Excel to
a SQL Database, 80–90
Lab 3-1: Data Reduction Using Fuzzy
Matching, 121
Lab 3-2: Regression in Excel, 125–126

Lab 3-4: Comprehensive Case: Dillard's
Store Data: Data Abstract (SQL)
and Regression (Part 1), 130
Lab 4-1: Use PivotCharts to Visualize
Declarative Data, 166
storing data, 48–49
summary statistics in, 72–73
VLookup function, 48–49
Microsoft Excel Internal Data Model, 62–63
(lab)
Microsoft Excel PivotTable
Lab 2-2: Use PivotTables to Denormalize
and Analyze the Data, 60–67
Lab 4-1: Use PivotCharts to Visualize
Declarative Data, 166–168
Lab 6-2: Perform Substantive Tests of
Account Balances, 251–256
Lab 6-4: Comprehensive Case: Dillard's
Store Data: Hypothesis Testing
(Part I), 258–261
Lab 8-4: Use SQL to Query an XBRL
Database, 356–360
Lab 9-3: Comprehensive Case 2:
Dillard's Store Data: Calculate
Sales Tax for Dillard's States
Part 2—Compare Year over Year,
383–384
LendingClub, 15, 16, 18, 19
Question 3.2: Using Regression, What
Can We Predict for Returns
as a Percentage of Sales Based
on Historical Transactions?,
429–432
Question Set 3: Predictive Analytics,
427–432
tools for, 448–449
Microsoft Excel PowerPivot add-in
Lab 6-4: Comprehensive Case: Dillard's
Store Data: Hypothesis Testing
(Part I), 257–263
Lab 7-3: Comprehensive Case: Dillard's
Store Data: Creating KPIs in
Excel (Part I), 293
Lab 7-5: Comprehensive Case: Dillard's
Store Data: Creating KPIs in
Excel (Part III), 309–314
Lab 7-6: Comprehensive Case: Dillard's
Store Data: Creating KPIs in
Excel (Part IV—Putting It All
Together), 315–319
Microsoft Excel Query Editor, 63–65 (lab)
Microsoft OneDrive
Lab 1-0: How to Complete Labs in This
Text, 27–28
Lab 5-3: Set up a Cloud Folder,
219–220
Lab 5-6: Prepare Audit Plan, 223
Microsoft SQL Server Management Studio
connect, Excel's Get and Transform
Tool, 470–472
defined, 41

Lab 2-6: Comprehensive Case: Dillard's Store Data: How to Create an Entity-Relationship Diagram, 75-78

Lab 2-7: Comprehensive Case: Dillard's Store Data: How to Preview Data from Tables In a Query, 78-80

Lab 2-8: Comprehensive Case: Dillard's Store Data: Connecting Excel to a SQL Database, 80-90

Lab 2-9: Comprehensive Case: Dillard's Store Data: Joining tables, 90-91

Lab 3-4: Comprehensive Case: Dillard's Store Data: Data Abstract (SQL) and Regression (Part 1), 130

Lab 3-5: Comprehensive Case: Dillard's Store Data: Data Abstract (SQL) and Regression (Part II) 135-137

Lab 4-3: Comprehensive Case: Dillard's Store Data: Create Geographic Data Visualizations in Tableau and in Power BI, 177

Lab 6-4: Comprehensive Case: Dillard's Store Data: Hypothesis Testing (Part I), 257-263

Lab 6-5: Comprehensive Case: Dillard's Store Data: Hypothesis Testing (Part II—Data Visualization), 263-265

Lab 7-3: Comprehensive Case: Dillard's Store Data: Creating KPIs in Excel (Part I), 293

Lab 7-4: Comprehensive Case: Dillard's Store Data: Creating KPIs in Excel (Part II), 299

Lab 7-5: Comprehensive Case: Dillard's Store Data: Creating KPIs in Excel (Part III), 307

Lab 7-6: Comprehensive Case: Dillard's Store Data: Creating KPIs in Excel (Part IV—Putting It All Together), 315

Lab 9-2: Comprehensive Case 1: Dillard's Store Data: Calculate Sales Tax for Dillard's States, 379-381

Lab 9-3: Comprehensive Case 2: Dillard's Store Data: Calculate Sales Tax for Dillard's States Part 2—Compare Year over Year, 382-386

Lab 9-4: Comprehensive Case 3: Dillard's Store Data: Calculate Sales Tax for Dillard's States Part 3—Calculate City Tax and Compare Tax Owed Year over Year, 386-387

Question 1.1: Which Attributes Could Help Predict Percentage of Returned Sales?, 410-412

Middle value, describing sample by, 434-435

Monetary unit sample (MUS), 234-235, 244

Mystery ratios, 350 (lab)

N

NASDAQ, 327

New York Stock Exchange, 327

Nike (NKE), 346

Nominal data, 142, 161

Normal distribution, 143-144, 161, 435-436

Norton, David P., 271

Number datatypes, SQL WHERE clause, 456

Numbers, data quality and, 51

O

Object-relational mapping (ORM), 215

Obtain data

data request, 46-47

personally, 48

Office 363, 210

Office.com, 27-28, 27-28 (lab)

Office of National Statistics, 152

OkCupid, 39

OK PCARD data, 498, 499

Online sales, analyzing, 409

Open Science Framework, 39

Oracle, 41, 340

ORDER BY, SQL clause, 458-459

Order-To-Cash (O2C), 392-400. *See also* Question Set 1: Order-To-Cash (O2C)

Ordinal data, 142, 161

Organization, data visualization and, 158-159

Outcomes. *See* Track Outcomes

Outer join, 239

Overfitting, classification, 111-112

Overlap method, text mining and, 335

P

Parameters, statistics *v.*, 434

Payments, Procure-to-Pay (P2P), 400-406 (lab)

Perform an Analysis of the Data

Lab 4-3: Comprehensive Case: Dillard's Store Data: Create Geographic Data Visualizations in Tableau and in Power BI, 185-188

Lab 4-4: Comprehensive Case: Dillard's Store Data: Visualizing Regression in Tableau, 198-199

Lab 6-4: Comprehensive Case: Dillard's Store Data: Hypothesis Testing (Part I), 261-262

Lab 7-2: Create a Balanced Scorecard Dashboard in Tableau, 285-292

Lab 7-5: Comprehensive Case: Dillard's Store Data: Creating KPIs in Excel (Part III), 314

Lab 8-1: Create a Horizontal and Vertical Analysis Using XBRL Data, 348-349

Lab 8-4: Use SQL to Query an XBRL Database, 356-360

Lab 9-1: State Sales Taxes and Create a Data Visualization, 375-379

Performance metrics, 268-269

balanced scorecard/KPIs and, 270-274

defined, 277

Perform the Analysis

Lab 1-1: Data Analytics in Financial Accounting, 30-31

Lab 2-2: Use PivotTables to Denormalize and Analyze the Data, 66-67

Lab 2-6: Comprehensive Case: Dillard's Store Data: How to Create an Entity-Relationship Diagram, 76-78

Lab 2-7: Comprehensive Case: Dillard's Store Data: How to Preview Data from Tables In a Query, 79-80

Lab 2-8: Comprehensive Case: Dillard's Store Data: Connecting Excel to a SQL Database, 81-88

Lab 2-9: Comprehensive Case: Dillard's Store Data: Joining tables, 90-91

Lab 3-2: Regression in Excel, 126

Lab 3-3: Classification, 129-130

Lab 3-4: Comprehensive Case: Dillard's Store Data: Data Abstract (SQL) and Regression (Part 1), 131-135

Lab 3-5: Comprehensive Case: Dillard's Store Data: Data Abstract (SQL) and Regression (Part II), 135-137

Lab 4-1: Use PivotCharts to Visualize Declarative Data, 166

Lab 4-2: Use Tableau to Perform Exploratory Analysis and Create Dashboards, 171-176

Lab 6-1: Evaluate the Master Data for Interesting Addresses, 249-250

Lab 6-3: Finding Duplicate Payments, 256-257

Lab 6-5: Comprehensive Case: Dillard's Store Data: Hypothesis Testing (Part II—Data Visualization), 265

Lab 9-3: Comprehensive Case 2: Dillard's Store Data: Calculate Sales Tax for Dillard's States Part 2—Compare Year over Year, 383-384

Lab 9-4: Comprehensive Case 3: Dillard's Store Data: Calculate Sales Tax for Dillard's States Part 3— Calculate City Tax and Compare Tax Owed Year over Year, 387

Lab 9-5: Comprehensive Case 4: Dillard's Store Data: Does a State's Tax Rate Affect Dillard's Decision to Open Stores There?, 388-389

Perform the Test Plan

audit data analytics and, 228-230

management accounting, 274-275

Pie charts, 145, 146, 153
PivotTable. *See* Excel PivotTable
Poisson distribution, probability, 436
Population, sample *v.,* 434
PostGreSQL, 41
Post-pruning, decision tree, 109
Power BI
    analytics tool, 391
    ask a question, 490
    Lab 4-3: Comprehensive Case: Dillard's
        Store Data: Create Geographic
        Data Visualizations in Tableau
        and in Power BI, 177–196
    load data, 485
    mode, choose, 485
    opening, startup screen, 483–484
    tutorial, 483–490
    visualizations/fields/values, 486–489
PowerPivot. *See* Excel PowerPivot add-in
Power Query
    editing data in, 473–474
    load data into Excel, 474
    return to window after closing, 475
    SQL server, Excel Get and Transform,
        470–472
    tutorial, 470–475
    worksheet failure, workaround, 474
Power Query Editor, 426–427
Predictive analytics
    applied statistics and, 229, 243
    approaches to, 106
    auditing and, 108
    classification and, 109–111, 242
    defined, 94, 115, 228, 244
    examples, 229
    financial, 331–332
    managerial accounting, regression and,
        108
    overfitting data, 111–112
    probability and, 229, 242–243
    Question 1.1: Which Attributes Could
        Help Predict Percentage of
        Returned Sales?, 410–412
    Question 3.1: By Looking at Line Charts for
        2014 and 2015, Does the Average
        Percentage of Sales Returned in
        2014 Seem to Be Predictive of
        Returns in 2015, 427–429
    Question 3.2: Using Regression, What
        Can We Predict for Returns as
        a Percentage of Sales Based on
        Historical Transactions?, 429–432
    regression and, 107–108, 242
    sentiment analysis, 243
    summary of, 95, 96
Predictor variables, 9, 21
Prepare for Analysis, 121–122 (lab)
Pre-pruning, decision tree, 109
Prescriptive analytics
    decision support systems, 112–113
    defined, 95, 115, 228, 244

    examples, 229
    machine learning/artificial intelligence,
        113–114, 228, 229, 243
    summary of, 95, 96
    uses of, 112
Primary keys, 42–43, 53
Probability
    auditing and, 242–243
    predictive analytics and, 229
Probability distributions
    normal, 435–436
    uniform/Poisson, 436
Procure-To-Pay (P2P), 400–406. *See also*
        Question Set 2: Procure-To-Pay (P2P)
Production or live systems, 204, 211
Profiling, 21
    defined, 10
    IRS and, 362
Profiling data, 21
    cluster analysis and, 103
    defined, 10, 115
    diagnostic analytics and, 96
    internal audit, 103
    steps of, 101
    structured data and, 100
Profitability ratio, 330
Profit margin on sales ratio, 330
Proportion, quantitative data and, 142, 161
Provost, F., 9*n*
Pruning, decision tree, 109, 110
Public Company Accounting Oversight
    Board (PCAOB), 207
Purchasing cycle processes, 400–406. *See
    also* Question Set 2: Procure-To-Pay
    (P2P)
P-value
    Lab 9-5: Comprehensive Case 4: Dillard's
        Store Data: Does a State's Tax
        Rate Affect Dillard's Decision to
        Open Stores There?, 389
    statistical testing, 437
PwC, 4–5, 201, 210, 211, 280
Python, 70 (lab), 206

Q

Qualified research expenditures (QREs), 369
Qualitative chart, 142
Qualitative data
    charts for, 145–147
    defined, 161
Qualtrics, 434
Quantitative chart, 142
Quantitative data
    charts for, 147–148
    defined, 161
    normal distribution, 143–144
Query, preview data from tables in, 78–80
    (lab)
Questions, identify problems. *See* Identify
    Questions

Question Set 1: Descriptive and Exploratory
    Analysis
    1.1: Which Attributes Could Help Predict
        Percentage of Returned Sales?,
        410–412
    1.2: How Can We Explore the Product
        Hierarchy Through Data
        Visualization?, 412–422
Question Set 1: Order-To-Cash (O2C)
    1.1: How Effectively Are We Collecting
        Our Cash?, 392–396
    1.2: Is the Delivery Process Following the
        Expected Procedure?, 396–398
    1.3: What Is the Total Revenue and
        Balance in Accounts Receivable,
        398–399
    1.4: What Else Can You Determine about
        the O2C Process?, 400
    processes, 392
Question Set 2: Diagnostic Analytics–
    Hypothesis Testing
    2.1: Is the Percentage of Sales Returned
        Significantly Higher in January
        After the Holiday Season?,
        422–426
    2.2: Is the Percentage of Sales Returned
        Significantly Different in
        Arkansas Than the Rest of the
        Country?, 426–427
Question Set 2: Procure-To-Pay (P2P)
    2.1: How Long Are We Taking to Pay
        Our Invoices?, 400–404
    2.2: Are There Any Erroneous
        Payments?, 404–405
    2.3: Are We Missing Out on Discounts
        by Paying Late?, 405–406
    2.4: What Else Can You Determine
        about the P2P Process?, 406
    purchasing cycle processes, 400
Question Set 3: Predictive Analytics
    3.1: By Looking at Line Charts for 2014
        and 2015, Does the Average
        Percentage of Sales Returned in
        2014 Seem to Be Predictive of
        Returns in 2015, 427–429
    3.2: Using Regression, What Can
        We Predict for Returns as a
        Percentage of Sales Based
        on Historical Transactions?,
        429–432
Quick (acid test) ratio, 329

R

R, 206
R. R. Donnelley, 338
Rankandfiled.com, 334
Rank-ordered bar chart, 153
Ratio analysis, 328, 341, 352–354 (lab)
Ratio data, 143, 161–162
Ratio types, 329–330

R&D Tax Credit, 362, 369–370
Real-time financial reporting, XBRL/
    EBRL-GL and, 340
Red Cross, 267
Refine the Query, 381 (lab)
Regression, 21
    accounting/auditing, predictive analytics
        and, 108–109
    defined, 9, 115
    Lab 3-2: Regression in Excel, 125–126
    Lab 3-5: Comprehensive Case: Dillard's
        Store Data: Data Abstract (SQL)
        and Regression (Part II), 135–137
    predictive analytics and, 96, 106–108,
        229, 242
    Question 3.2: Using Regression, What
        Can We Predict for Returns as
        a Percentage of Sales Based on
        Historical Transactions?, 429–432
    statistical output from, interpreting, 439
Regression analysis
    cost behavior, 270
    mixed costs, 270
RejectStats, data, 498, 499
Relational database
    defined, 42, 53
    Lab 2-2: Use PivotTables to Denormalize
        and Analyze the Data, 65–66
    Lab 2-6: Comprehensive Case: Dillard's
        Store Data: How to Create an
        Entity-Relationship Diagram, 75–78
Relational Database Management Systems
    (RDBMS), 41
Relationships, relational databases and, 42–43
Relevant costs, 268
Remote audit work, 209–210
Research, transparency and, 39
Resource planning systems (RPS), 203
Response variables, 9, 21
Results, communicate. See Address and
    Refine Results; Communicate
    Findings/Results
Return on assets ratio, 330
Return on equity ratio, 330
Return on equity ratio (ROE), 330
Returns, estimating sales, 410–432
Reviewable turnover ratio, 330
Review Document Revision History, 221 (lab)
Revising message, 160
Right join, 239
RIGHT join, SQL clause, 482
Risk, accounts receivable and, 392–396
Risk scores, 17, 19
Robotics process automation, 202
R-Square, interpret, 389 (lab)

S

Sales, analyzing, 409
Sales returns, estimating. See Estimating
    sales returns, question sets for

Sales returns, predicting percentage, 410–412
Sales tax liability, evaluate, 365
    Lab 9-1: State Sales Taxes and Create a
        Data Visualization, 375–379
    Lab 9-2: Comprehensive Case 1: Dillard's
        Store Data: Calculate Sales Tax
        for Dillard's States, 379–381
    Lab 9-3: Comprehensive Case 2:
        Dillard's Store Data: Calculate
        Sales Tax for Dillard's States
        Part 2—Compare Year over Year,
        381–386
    Lab 9-5: Comprehensive Case 4:
        Dillard's Store Data: Does a
        State's Tax Rate Affect Dillard's
        Decision to Open Stores There?,
        387–389
Sample
    describing, 434–435
    population v., 434
Sampling, descriptive analytics and, 229,
    233–235
Samsung, 21
SAP, 340
Scale, charting data, 157
Scatter plots, 148, 269–270
Scorecard, 267. See also Balanced Scorecard
Screen capture tool
    Lab: 1-0: How to Complete Labs in This
        Text, 27–28
    Lab 1-1: Data Analytics in Financial
        Accounting, 28
    Lab 1-3: Data Analytics in Auditing, 33
    Lab 1-4: Dillard's Store Data
        (comprehensive case), 35
    Lab 2-2: Use PivotTables to Denormalize
        and Analyze the Data, 60
    Lab 2-3: Resolve Common Data
        Problems in Excel and Access, 68
    Lab 2-4: Generate Summary Statistics in
        Excel, 71
    Lab 2-5: College Scorecard Extraction
        and Data Preparation, 74
    Lab 3-2: Regression in Excel, 125–126
    Lab 4-1: Use PivotCharts to Visualize
        Declarative Data, 166
    Lab 4-2: Use Tableau to Perform
        Exploratory Analysis and Create
        Dashboards, 169
    Lab 5-1: Create a Common Data Model,
        215, 216
    Lab 5-2: Create a Dashboard Based on a
        Common Data Model, 218
    Lab 5-2:: Create a Dashboard Based on a
        Common Data Model, 218
    Lab 5-3: Set up a Cloud Folder, 220
    Lab 5-4: Review Changes to Working
        Papers, 221
    Lab 5-5: Identify Audit Data
        Requirements, 222
    Lab 5-6: Prepare Audit Plan, 223

Lab 6-1: Evaluate the Master Data for
    Interesting Addresses, 248–250
Lab 6-3: Finding Duplicate Payments,
    257
Lab 6-4: Comprehensive Case: Dillard's
    Store Data: Hypothesis Testing
    (Part I), 261
Lab 6-5: Comprehensive Case: Dillard's
    Store Data: Hypothesis Testing
    (Part II–Data Visualization), 265
Lab 7-2: Create a Balanced Scorecard
    Dashboard in Tableau, 289, 290,
    291, 292
Lab 7-3: Comprehensive Case: Dillard's
    Store Data: Creating KPIs in
    Excel (Part I), 299
Lab 7-4: Comprehensive Case: Dillard's
    Store Data: Creating KPIs in
    Excel (Part II), 307
Lab 7-5: Comprehensive Case: Dillard's
    Store Data: Creating KPIs in
    Excel (Part III), 314
Lab 7-6: Comprehensive Case: Dillard's
    Store Data: Creating KPIs in
    Excel (Part IV—Putting It All
    Together), 317, 318, 319
Lab 7-7: Comprehensive Case: Dillard's
    Store Data: Advanced Models in
    Tableau, 321, 323, 324
Lab 8-1: Create a Horizontal and Vertical
    Analysis Using XBRL Data, 349
Lab 8-2: Create Dynamic Common Size
    Financial Statements, 351
Lab 8-3: Analyze Financial Statement
    Ratios, 354
Lab 8-4: Use SQL to Query an XBRL
    Database, 358, 360
Lab 9-1: State Sales Taxes and Create a
    Data Visualization, 377, 379
Scripting language, 206
Scrubbing data, 12
Security and Exchange Commission (SEC),
    29, 99
SELECT, SQL clause, 453, 459–460
SELECT FROM practice, SQL clause,
    454–455
SELECT FROM WHERE practice, SQL
    clause, 456–457
Sentiment analysis, 243
    predictive analytics and, 229, 243
    text mining and, 334–335
Sequence check, 229, 241
Shared folder, create, 219–220 (lab)
Similarity matching, 10, 21
    defined, 115
    diagnostic analytics and, 96
    predictive analysis, 106
Simsion, G. C., 42n
Singleton, T., 46n
Sláinte Sales Subset, 160
Snapchat, 21

Snow, John, 139
Software
    age analysis, 231–232
    auditing and, 230
    See also IDEA software; Microsoft
        Access; Microsoft Excel *entries;*
        Tableau
Software needs
    database, 41
    exact and fuzzy matching, 239–241
    Lab 1-0: How to Complete Labs in This
        Text, 27
    Lab 1-1: Data Analytics in Financial
        Accounting, 28
    Lab 1-2: Data Analytics in Managerial
        Accounting, 31
    Lab 1-3: Data Analytics in Auditing, 33
    Lab 2-2: Use PivotTables to Denormalize
        and Analyze the Data, 60
    Lab 2-3: Resolve Common Data
        Problems in Excel and Access, 68
    Lab 2-4: Generate Summary Statistics in
        Excel, 71
    Lab 2-5: College Scorecard Extraction
        and Data Preparation, 74
    Lab 2-6: Comprehensive Case: Dillard's
        Store Data: How to Create an
        Entity-Relationship Diagram, 76
    Lab 2-7: Comprehensive Case: Dillard's
        Store Data: How to Preview Data
        from Tables In a Query, 78
    Lab 2-9: Comprehensive Case: Dillard's
        Store Data: Joining tables, 90
    Lab 3-4: Comprehensive Case: Dillard's
        Store Data: Data Abstract
        (SQL) and Regression
        (Part 1), 130
    Lab 3-5: Comprehensive Case: Dillard's
        Store Data: Data Abstract (SQL)
        and Regression (Part II), 135
    Lab 4-1: Use PivotCharts to Visualize
        Declarative Data, 166
    Lab 4-2: Use Tableau to Perform
        Exploratory Analysis and Create
        Dashboards, 169
    Lab 4-3: Comprehensive Case: Dillard's
        Store Data: Create Geographic
        Data Visualizations in Tableau
        and in Power BI, 177
    Lab 5-1: Create a Common Data
        Model, 215
    Lab 5-2: Create a Dashboard Based on a
        Common Data Model, 217
    Lab 5-3: Set up a Cloud Folder, 219
    Lab 5-5: Identify Audit Data
        Requirements, 221
    Lab 5-6: Prepare Audit Plan, 223
    Lab 6-1: Evaluate the Master Data for
        Interesting Addresses, 248
    Lab 6-3: Finding Duplicate
        Payments, 256

Lab 6-4: Comprehensive Case: Dillard's
    Store Data: Hypothesis Testing
    (Part I), 257
Lab 7-4: Comprehensive Case: Dillard's
    Store Data: Creating KPIs in
    Excel (Part II), 299
Lab 7-5: Comprehensive Case: Dillard's
    Store Data: Creating KPIs in
    Excel (Part III), 307
Lab 7-6: Comprehensive Case: Dillard's
    Store Data: Creating KPIs in
    Excel (Part IV—Putting It All
    Together), 315
Lab 7-7: Comprehensive Case: Dillard's
    Store Data: Advanced Models in
    Tableau, 320
Lab 8-1: Create a Horizontal and Vertical
    Analysis Using XBRL Data, 346
Lab 9-1: State Sales Taxes and Create a
    Data Visualization, 375
Lab 9-3: Comprehensive Case 2: Dillard's
    Store Data: Calculate Sales
    Tax for Dillard's States Part 2—
    Compare Year over Year, 382
Lab 9-4: Comprehensive Case 3: Dillard's
    Store Data: Calculate Sales
    Tax for Dillard's States Part 3—
    Calculate City Tax and Compare
    Tax Owed Year over Year, 386
Lab 9-5: Comprehensive Case 4: Dillard's
    Store Data: Does a State's Tax
    Rate Affect Dillard's Decision to
    Open Stores There?, 387
Lab 7-2 Create a Balanced Scorecard
    Dashboard in Tableau, 284
sampling, 234–235
sorting, 232–233
storing data, 48–49
summary statistics, 233
visualization tools, 149
Software translators, 204
Solvency ratio, 330
Sorting, descriptive analytics, 229, 232–233
Sparkline, visualizing trends, 333, 341
SQL clauses
    FROM, 453–454
    aggregates/aliases, expand SELECT,
        459–460
    example queries, ORDER BY, 458–459
    FROM, select data from more than one
        table, 463–464
    GROUP BY, 460–462
    HAVING, 462–463
    INNER join, 480–481
    INNER JOIN ON practice, 464–465
    LEFT join, 482
    ORDER BY, 458
    parenthesis, joining tables, 465
    RIGHT join, 482
    SELECT, 453
    SELECT FROM practice, 454–455

SELECT FROM WHERE, 456–457
SELECT FROM WHERE practice, 457
tutorials, 453–465, 480–482
WHERE, 455–456
SQLite
    defined, 41
    download/install, 466–467
    execute/navigate in, 467–469
    Lab 2-2: Use PivotTables to Denormalize
        and Analyze the Data, 60
    Lab 5-1: Create a Common Data
        Model, 215
    tutorial, 466–469
SQL queries
    Lab 2-2: Use PivotTables to Denormalize
        and Analyze the Data, 65–66
    Lab 8-4: Use SQL to Query an XBRL
        Database, 355–356
SQL (Structured Query Language), 48.
    See also Microsoft SQL Server
        Management Studio
Stacked bar chart, data visualization, 145,
    147, 153, 154
Stacked Bar Chart of Monthly Store
    Performance, 322–323 (lab)
Standardization, 144, 162
Standardized metrics, 338–339, 341
Standardized tags, XBRL and, 339
Standardizing distributions,
    Z-scores, 144
Standard normal distribution, 144, 162
Statistical testing
    confidence interval, 437
    p-value, 437
Statistics
    describing sample, 434–435
    hypothesis testing and, 436–437
    output from sample *t*-test difference
        of means of two groups,
        interpreting, 438
    parameters *v.*, 434
    population, sample *v.*, 434
    probability distribution
        and, 435–436
    regression, interpreting statistical output
        from, 439
    statistical testing, 437
    tutorial, 434–439
StockSnips (app), 327
Storing data, 48–49
Strategy Management Group Company, 272
Stratification, diagnostic analytics,
    229, 242
Structured data, 98, 101, 115
Structured Query Language (SQL), 48.
    See also Microsoft SQL Server
        Management Studio; SQL *entries*
Summary statistics
    defined, 115
    descriptive analytics and, 95, 97–98
    diagnostic analytics and, 229

Lab 2-8: Comprehensive Case: Dillard's Store Data: Connecting Excel to a SQL Database, 88–89
view in excel, 72
Sunburst diagram, balance sheet composition, 334
Supervised approach, predictive analysis, 106, 115
Support vector machine, classification, 110, 111, 115
SurveyMonkey, 434
Sweet spot, 112
Symbol maps, 146
Systems translator software, 204, 211

T

Table attributes, databases and, 42–43
Tableau software, 149–151
    accessing, connect to Excel, 476–478
    analytics tool, 391
    data storage, 48–49
    data visualizations, 410–422
    joins in, 480–482
    Lab 4-2: Use Tableau to Perform Exploratory Analysis and Create Dashboards, 168–177
    Lab 4-3: Comprehensive Case: Dillard's Store Data: Create Geographic Data Visualizations in Tableau and in Power BI, 177–196
    Lab 4-4: Comprehensive Case: Dillard's Store Data: Visualizing Regression in Tableau, 196–199
    Lab 5-2: Create a Dashboard Based on a Common Data Model, 217–219
    Lab 6-5: Comprehensive Case: Dillard's Store Data: Hypothesis Testing (Part II—Data Visualization), 264–265
    Lab 7-2: Create a Balanced Scorecard Dashboard in Tableau, 284–292
    Lab 7-7: Comprehensive Case: Dillard's Store Data: Advanced Models in Tableau, 320–324
    Lab 9-1: State Sales Taxes and Create a Data Visualization, 375–379
    Question Set 1: Descriptive and Exploratory Analysis, 410–422
    tutorial, 476–479
Tableau Workbook
    Question Set 1: Order-To-Cash (O2C), 392–400
    Question Set 2: Procure-To-Pay (P2P), 400–406
Table Import Wizard, 312
Tables
    Lab 2-7: Comprehensive Case: Dillard's Store Data: How to Preview Data from Tables In a Query, 78–80

Lab 2-9: Comprehensive Case: Dillard's Store Data: Joining tables, 90
Lab 8-4: Use SQL to Query an XBRL Database, 356
Takeda, C., 108n3
Target, 106
Target (TGT), 353
Tax analytics
    compliance and liability, 364
    data for planning and, 367–370. *See also* Tax planning, data analytics
    data management and, 363–364
    income tax liability, 365
    IRS and, 362
    Lab 9-1: State Sales Taxes and Create a Data Visualization, 375–379
    Lab 9-2: Comprehensive Case 1: Dillard's Store Data: Calculate Sales Tax for Dillard's States, 379–381
    Lab 9-3: Comprehensive Case 2: Dillard's Store Data: Calculate Sales Tax for Dillard's States Part 2—Compare Year over Year, 381–386
    Lab 9-4: Comprehensive Case 3: Dillard's Store Data: Calculate Sales Tax for Dillard's States Part 3—Calculate City Tax and Compare Tax Owed Year over Year, 386–387
    Lab 9-5: Comprehensive Case 4: Dillard's Store Data: Does a State's Tax Rate Affect Dillard's Decision to Open Stores There?, 387–389
    sales tax liability, 365
    uses for, 362–363
    visualizations, monitor/track KPIs, 365–366
Tax cost, 365–366
Tax credits, tax planning what-if scenarios and, 369–370
Tax Cuts and Jobs Act Reform of 2018, 364, 370
Tax data mart, 363, 370
Tax efficiency/effectiveness, 366
Taxes, Data Analytics and, 7
Tax planning
    defined/uses for, 367, 370
    legislation, deductions, credits, What-if scenarios for, 369–370
    what-if scenario analysis, 368–369
Tax risk, 366
Tax sustainability, 366
TeamMate, 210
TeamMate Analytics, 230, 243
Teradata, 41
Tesla, 280, 282
Test data, classification, 109, 116
Testing data, classification, 112
Test plan
    LendingClub, 15–19
    performing, 9–11, 94–97, 226–228

Text datatypes, SQL WHERE clause, 455–456
Text editor, 74 (lab)
Text mining, sentiment analysis and, 334–335
Thomas, S., 108n3
Times interest earned ratio, 330
Tolerable misstatement, 234
Tone, effective communication and, 159–160
Total revenue, 398–399
Track Outcomes
    audit data analytics and, 230
    Lab 6-4: Comprehensive Case: Dillard's Store Data: Hypothesis Testing (Part I), 263
    LendingClub, 19
    tracking insights and, 11–12
Trade-off, 112
Training data, classification, 109, 112, 116
Transform data
    Question 3.2: Using Regression, What Can We Predict for Returns as a Percentage of Sales Based on Historical Transactions?, 429–432
    Question Set 1: Descriptive and Exploratory Analysis, 419
    See also ETL process, 49–50
TransUnion, 21
Tree maps, 146, 332–324 (lab)
Trendlines, visualizing, 333
T-test, interpreting output from sample, 438
Turnover ratio, 330
Twitter, 7
Typical value, describing sample by, 434–435

U

Uber, 334
UML diagram, 169
Underfitting data, 111
Unfavorable variances, 269
UNICODE, 51
Unified Modeling Language (UML), 41
Uniform distribution, probability, 436
Unique identifier, 42
Unsupervised approach, clustering, 103, 116
Upload files
    Lab 5-3: Set up a Cloud Folder, 220
    Lab 5-4: Review Changes to Working Papers, 220–221
U.S. GAAP Financial Reporting Taxonomy, 336–337
U.S. Supreme Court, 365

V

Validate data, 49–50
Value, describing sample by middle or typical, 434–435
Variability of data, describing, 435
Variables, types of, 9

Variance analysis, data profiling, 102
Variance analysis, KPIs and, 268–269
Vertical analysis, 341
Vertical financial statement analysis, 328–329
Vertical financial statement analysis, XBRL Data, 346–349 (lab)
Visualizing data. *See* Data visualization
VLookup function, Excel, 48–49, 450–452

W

Walmart (WMT), 103–106, 116, 274, 345, 353
Washington.cbslocal.com, 362
Wayfair, 281
Wayfair decision, SCOTUS, 365
Web browser
    Lab 1-0: How to Complete Labs in This Text, 27
    Lab 1-1: Data Analytics in Financial Accounting, 28
    Lab 1-3: Data Analytics in Auditing, 33
    Lab 1-4: Dillard's Store Data (comprehensive case), 35
    Lab 5-3: Set up a Cloud Folder, 219–220
    Lab 5-5: Identify Audit Data Requirements, 221–222
    Lab 5-6: Prepare Audit Plan, 223
    Lab 8-3: Analyze Financial Statement Ratios, 352–354
    See also DB Browser, SQLite

Weka software, 33 (lab)
Wells-Fargo (WFC), 353
What-if analysis
    prescriptive analytics and, 229
    scenario, 368–370
WHERE, SQL clause
    date datatypes, 456
    number datatypes, 456
    text datatypes, 455–456
Whole Foods, 345
Wikipedia, 130, 135, 196
Witt, G. C., 42n
Word Cloud, 146
Word frequency, text mining and, 334–335
Word processor
    Lab 1-0: How to Complete Labs in This Text, 27
    Lab 1-1: Data Analytics in Financial Accounting, 28
    Lab 1-2: Data Analytics in Managerial Accounting, 31
    Lab 1-3: Data Analytics in Auditing, 33
    Lab 1-4: Dillard's Store Data (comprehensive case), 35
    Lab 2-1: Create a Request for Data Extraction, 58
Workflow, audit, 209–210
Working capital ratio, 329
Working papers
    audit workflow and, 209
    Lab 5-4: Review Changes to Working Papers, 220–221

remote audit work, 209–210
    See also Electronic working papers
Workpapers. *See* Working papers
Write a SQL Query to Transform Your Data, 216–217 (lab)
Write-off classification, 109

X

XBRL. *See* eXtensible Business Reporting Language (XBRL), 29
XBRLAnalyst, 339, 342
XBRL-GL (global ledger), 340, 341
XBRL instance document, 336–338
XBRL taxonomy, 336, 341
XBRL-US Center for Data Quality, 338
Xbrlview.fasb.org, 336–337
Xero, 210

Y

Young, Steve, 435

Z

Zobel, J., 158n2
Zobel, Justin, 160
Z-score, 100–101, 103
    diagnostic analytics, 235–236
    outlier detection, 229
    standardizing distributions with, 144